Praise for *The Fall of the Ottomans*

"The book is not only exact and readable but also has the elements of a thriller and thus is all the more remarkable in view of its thoroughness in covering a linguistically and historically difficult subject." —*Wall Street Journal*

"Rogan offers an intricately worked but very readable account of a theocracy's demise." —*New York Times Book Review* Editors' Choice

"This engrossing history unfolds in the Middle Eastern theatre of the First World War, capturing the complex array of battles, brutalities, and alliances that brought down the six-hundred-year-old Ottoman Empire. . . . Rogan argues that the empire's ultimate demise was the result not of losing the war but of a clumsily negotiated peace. His balanced narrative unearths many seeds of current conflicts." —*New Yorker*

"How a multinational Muslim empire was destroyed by the first world war, by a historian of the 20th century who is director of the Middle East Centre at Oxford University." —*Economist*, One of the Best Books of the Year

"[A] masterly history of the Ottoman empire in its final years. . . . Eugene Rogan has written a meticulously researched, panoramic and engrossing history. The book is essential reading for understanding the evolution of the modern Middle East and the root causes of nearly all the conflicts that now plague the area. *The Fall of the Ottomans* is an altogether splendid work of historical writing." —*Spectator* (UK)

"Admirable and thoroughly researched. . . . A comprehensive history of World War I in the Middle East." —*New York Review of Books*

"[A] comprehensive, lucid and revealing history. . . . This book will surely become the definitive history of the war." —*The Times* (UK)

"Compared to the western front, the Middle East was a sideshow for all but those who called it home. Rogan has rightly put these Turks, Armenians and Arabs at the centre of his account." —*Guardian* (UK)

"*The Fall of the Ottomans* is a remarkably lucid and accessible work of history. . . . [Rogan] seems equally at home explaining the parameters of Ottoman grand strategy and the tensions of the British-Arab Alliance as he is at conjuring up the unique challenges of maneuver warfare in the Sinai and Palestine, or the brutal stalemate in the Gallipoli trenches. Telling quotations from diplomats, field commanders, and ordinary soldiers of all the combatants lend the narrative a powerful sense of immediacy." —*Daily Beast*

"[A] timely and capacious history which leaves the over-trodden Flanders mud and football truces in favor of the various campaigns—at best imperfectly understood, at worst woefully unfamiliar—which the Allies waged in the Middle East. It's in the former Ottoman lands, traumatised by war, sectarianism and repression, that the legacies of the Great War continue to be grievously felt. . . . Here's a book whose instructive geopolitical relevance should be immediately apparent. . . . [A] compelling and brilliant book." —*Sunday Telegraph* (UK)

"[A] fresh and meticulous portrait of the Ottoman Empire: modern and modernizing, then declining, and eventually kaput." —*Washington Independent Review of Books*

"Fiercely readable. . . . In a series of fast-moving and very skillfully-written chapters, Rogan describes in great detail the politics and personalities of the Ottoman side of WWI." —*Open Letters Monthly*

"Personal stories drawn from diaries and memoirs enliven Eugene Rogan's satisfyingly straightforward narrative." —*Independent* (UK)

"Readers of his previous work, *The Arabs,* will know how comfortably [Eugene Rogan] handles multiple themes, ambitious narratives and a crowd of characters. . . . Even the familiar has resonance, such as General Maude's insistence to the battered people of Baghdad that his soldiers were 'liberators.' . . . That resonance adds relevance to this thorough and absorbing book, because it reminds us that the postwar Middle East settlements were as flawed as the conditions imposed on Germany, and that in turn explains why the land they fought over then is still being contested today." —*Observer*

"[Rogan's] account is geopolitical and military writing at its best—taut, anecdotal and extraordinarily researched. A tangled story, to be sure, one that both commands and rewards the reader's attention." —*Washington Times*

"[A] landmark study. . . . This is a formidable narrative history, written with great verve and empathy. Through its meticulous scholarship and its deft weaving together of the social, economic, diplomatic and military history of this neglected front, *The Fall of the Ottomans* provides an engrossing picture of a deadly conflict that proved catastrophic for the peoples of the region." — *The National* (Dubai)

"This is narrative history at its very best: disciplined, well-paced, judicious and spiked with detail, character and incident."   —*Prospect Magazine* (UK)

"Rogan handles the tricky subjects of jihad, secularism, Arab nationalism and Turkish paranoia about a possible Armenian fifth column with historical precision and a keen awareness of their implications for the modern world."
                                                    — *Shelf Awareness for Readers*

"[A] well-researched and well-written book. . . . A much-needed addition to World War I scholarship that is recommended for anyone interested in that conflict and the history of the Middle East or Turkey."   —*Library Journal*

"[A] sweeping and nuanced work. . . . Rogan's multifaceted analysis touches on everything from the use of Islamist discourse in political movements to the treatment of minorities in the modern Middle East."   —*Publishers Weekly*

"[A] well-researched, evenhanded treatment of the Ottomans' role in World War I. . . . An illuminating work that offers new understanding to the troubled history of this key geopolitical region."—*Kirkus*

"This is a gripping, masterful account of World War One in the Middle East from the vantage point of the Ottoman Empire. It uses the full panoply of primary sources in Turkish, Arabic, and European languages to brilliantly illuminating effect. Combining magisterial scholarship with a keen sense of drama and lively narrative style, it tells a grim story but a fascinating one. There is a great deal of new material here which not only brings events alive but also leads to fresh assessments of all the participants in the Great War but especially Arabs and Turks. If you want to understand the underlying causes of conflict and violence in the Middle East in the last century, you will not find a better book."
          —AVI SHLAIM, author of *The Iron Wall: Israel and the Arab World*

"This book opens up a window on vital chapters in the shaping of the Middle East as well as the history of the Great War, bringing together vivid personal details with a broad historical panorama of human suffering and heroism, the incompetence and folly of the general staffs, and the scheming of the great powers."
          —RASHID KHALIDI, author of *Resurrecting Empire:*
          Western Footprints and America's Perilous Path in the Middle East

"Thoroughly researched and elegantly written by one of the leading experts on the region, *The Fall of the Ottomans* reminds us that the 1914–18 conflict was truly a world war with huge and continuing consequences. No one is better equipped than Eugene Rogan to handle the course and impact of the war in the Middle East, and he does a superb job, telling a complex and multifaceted story with great clarity, understanding, and compassion. This timely and important work restores the Middle East to its rightful place in the history of the Great War."

—MARGARET MACMILLAN, author of
The War That Ended Peace: The Road to 1914

"Eugene Rogan has given us an absorbing history of the war's principal military and political battles in the Middle East through the eyes of those who fought them. Weaving together accounts of the horrors of life in the trenches with those on the home front, he exposes the deadly dynamic emerging between the two, from the disastrous Ottoman attempt to invade Russia to the calamity of the Armenian deportations, from the British invasion to the Arab revolt and the Ottoman Empire's final defeat and partition."

—MUSTAFA AKSAKAL, chair of Modern Turkish Studies
and associate professor of history at Georgetown University

"A fantastic, readable, and much needed study of the most chronically neglected of all of the Great War's participants: the Ottoman Empire. Informative and enlightening."

—ALEXANDER WATSON, author of *Ring of Steel:
Germany and Austria-Hungary in World War I*

"Eugene Rogan has written a meticulously researched, panoramic, and engrossing history of the final years of the Ottoman Empire. This book is essential reading for understanding the evolution of the modern Middle East and the root causes of nearly all the conflicts that now plague the area. An altogether splendid work of historical writing."

—ALI ALLAWI, author of *The Occupation of Iraq:
Winning the War, Losing the Peace*

"Thrilling, superb, and colorful, Eugene Rogan's *Fall of the Ottomans* is brilliant storytelling. Filled with flamboyant characters, impeccable scholarship that illuminates the neglected Near Eastern theater of WWI—showing how the Ottomans managed to perform unexpectedly well against the Allies—and revelatory analysis that explains the modern Mideast, *The Fall of the Ottomans* is truly essential but also truly exciting reading."

—SIMON SEBAG MONTEFIORE, author of *Jerusalem: The Biography*

"A vivid account of the fighting that led to the fall of one of the world's great empires."

—ROGER OWEN, professor emeritus of
Middle East history, Harvard University

THE FALL
of the
OTTOMANS

THE GREAT WAR IN THE MIDDLE EAST

Eugene Rogan

BASIC BOOKS
New York

Copyright © 2015 by Eugene Rogan

Hardcover first published in 2015 in the United States by Basic Books,
an imprint of Perseus Books, a division of PBG Publishing, LLC,
a subsidiary of Hachette Book Group, Inc.

Paperback first published in 2016 in the United States by Basic Books

All rights reserved. Printed in the United States of America. No part
of this book may be reproduced in any manner whatsoever without
written permission except in the case of brief quotations embodied
in critical articles and reviews. For information, address Basic Books,
250 West 57th Street, New York, NY 10107.

Books published by Basic Books are available at special discounts for
bulk purchases in the United States by corporations, institutions, and
other organizations. For more information, please contact the Special
Markets Department at the Perseus Books Group, 2300 Chestnut Street,
Suite 200, Philadelphia, PA 19103, or call (800) 810-4145, ext. 5000,
or e-mail special.markets@perseusbooks.com.

A CIP catalog record for this book is available from the Library
of Congress.

ISBN 978-0-465-02307-3 (hardcover)
ISBN 978-0-465-09742-5 (paperback)
ISBN 978-0-465-05669-9 (e-book)

10 9 8 7 6 5 4 3 2 1

Contents

This book is dedicated to
Isabelle Tui Woods Rogan

List of Maps

A Note on Nomenclature

IT WAS STANDARD PRACTICE BY THE EARLY TWENTIETH CENTURY TO refer to the Ottoman Empire as Turkey. This usage neglected the ethnic and religious diversity of the Ottoman Empire, where Arabs, Kurds, Greeks, and Armenians had as much claim to an Ottoman identity as Turks did. Yet, to avoid the tedious repetition of the word "Ottoman" throughout the following pages, I have adopted this usage and frequently use "Ottoman" and "Turkish" interchangeably, particularly with reference to the army. Whenever I wish to distinguish a specific ethnic or religious community from the Turkish majority, I write of "Ottoman Arabs" or "Ottoman Armenians".

I have tended to refer to cities by their modern Turkish names rather than the classical European forms that were in common use in the early twentieth century. Thus, I refer to "Istanbul" rather than "Constantinople", "Izmir" rather than "Smyrna", and "Trabzon" rather than "Trebizond", in the hope that readers will find it easier to locate these cities on modern maps. I have used standard Western spellings for Arab cities—thus, Beirut, Damascus, Mecca, and Medina rather than Bayrut, Dimashq, Makka, and Madina—for the same reason.

Preface

Lance Corporal John McDonald died at Gallipoli on 28 June 1915. He was nineteen years old, and though he wasn't to know it, he was my great-uncle.

Nothing in his life would have prepared John McDonald for death in faraway lands. He was born in a small Scottish village near Perth and attended the Dollar Academy, where he met his best friend, Charles Beveridge. They left school together at fourteen to look for work. The two friends moved to Glasgow, where they found jobs with the North British Locomotive Company. When war broke out in Europe in the summer of 1914, Beveridge and McDonald enlisted together with the Scottish Rifles (also known as the Cameronians). The impatient recruits of the 8th Scottish Rifles spent the autumn months in training, envious of other battalions that preceded them to battle in France. Only in April 1915 was the 1/8th Battalion called into service—not in France but in Ottoman Turkey.

McDonald and Beveridge said their final farewells to friends and family on 17 May 1915, when their battalion set off for war. They sailed to the Greek island of Lemnos, which served as the staging post for British and Allied forces before deployment to Gallipoli. As they drew into the island's port of Moudros on 29 May—one month after the initial Gallipoli landings—they passed a vast armada of warships and transports lying at anchor. The young recruits would have been awestruck by the dreadnoughts and super-dreadnoughts—some of the greatest ships afloat. Many bore the marks of heavy fighting in the Dardanelles, their hulls and funnels holed by Turkish artillery and ground batteries.

The Scots had two weeks to acclimatize to the eastern Mediterranean summer before going into battle. In mid-June, they sailed out of Moudros Harbour, cheered by soldiers and sailors from the decks of the ships at anchor. Only those who had been to Gallipoli and knew what lay before the fresh-faced young recruits refrained from cheering. "To a shipload of Australian sick and wounded," one Cameronian recalled, "some of our fellows yelled out the stock phrase at that time: 'Are we downhearted? No!' and when some Australian wag shouted back: 'Well, you damned soon will be', our chaps, though taken aback, were incredulous."[1]

On 14 June, the entire battalion was safely ashore. Four days later the 8th Scottish Rifles moved up Gully Ravine to the front line. Under the relentless machine-gun and artillery fire for which Gallipoli was already notorious, the Cameronians suffered their first casualties in the trenches. By the time the Scottish Rifles were given their orders to attack Turkish positions, the men had lost their boyish enthusiasm. As one officer reflected, "Whether it was premonition or merely the strain of newly acquired responsibility, I could not feel the buoyancy of success" among the soldiers.[2]

The British attack on 28 June was preceded by two hours of bombardment from the sea. Eyewitnesses dismissed the shelling as ineffectual—far too little to drive the determined Ottoman soldiers from their defensive positions. The British assault began on schedule at 1100 hours. As on the western front, the men climbed out of their trenches to the shrill signal of whistles. When the Cameronians went "over the top", they faced the full fire of Ottoman soldiers who held their positions, undeterred by the bombardment from British ships. Within five minutes, the 1/8th Scottish Rifles were practically wiped out. John McDonald died of his wounds in a camp hospital and was buried in the Lancaster Landing Cemetery. Charles Beveridge fell beyond the reach of stretcher-bearers. His remains were only recovered after the 1918 armistice, when his bones were indistinguishable from those of the men who had fallen around him. He lies in a mass grave, his name engraved on the great monument at Cape Helles.

The fate of the Cameronians brought shock and grief to their friends and families in Scotland. The Dollar Academy published obituaries for John McDonald and Charles Beveridge in the autumn issue of the school quarterly. The magazine described the two young men as the best of friends: "They worked together, lived together in rooms, enlisted together, and 'in their death they were not divided.' Both were young men of sterling character," the obituary concluded, "well worthy of the positions they held." The magazine expressed sympathy for the two boys' bereaved parents.

In fact, the grief proved more than my great-grandparents could bear. One year after the death of their only son, the McDonalds took the extraordinary step of leaving wartime Scotland to emigrate to the United States. In July 1916, during a pause in German U-boat attacks on Atlantic shipping, they boarded the poignantly named SS *Cameronia* with two of their daughters, headed for New York City. They never returned. The family ultimately settled in Oregon, where my maternal grandmother later married and gave birth to my mother and uncle. They and all of their descendants owe their lives to John McDonald's premature death.

My personal connection to the First World War is hardly unique. A 2013 poll conducted in the United Kingdom by the YouGov agency found that 46 percent of Britons knew of a family or community member who had served in the Great War. Such personal connections explain the enduring fascination the First World War holds over so many of us a century after its outbreak. The sheer scale of the mobilisation and the carnage left few families untouched in those countries caught up in the conflict.[3]

I came to learn my great-uncle's history while preparing for a trip to Gallipoli in 2005. My mother, Margaret, my son, Richard, and I, representatives of three generations, went to pay our respects, his first family visitors in over nine decades. As we made our way down the twisted lanes of the Gallipoli Peninsula towards the Lancashire Landing Cemetery, we took a wrong turn and chanced on the Nuri Yamut Monument, a memorial to the Turkish war dead of 28 June—the same battle in which John McDonald and Charles Beveridge had died.

The monument to the Turkish war dead of what they called the Battle of Zığındere, or Gully Ravine, came as a total revelation to me. While my great-uncle's unit had suffered 1,400 casualties—half its total strength—and British losses overall reached 3,800, as many as 14,000 Ottomans fell dead and wounded at Gully Ravine. The Nuri Yamut Monument is the mass grave of those Ottoman soldiers, interred under a common marble tombstone inscribed, simply, "Şehidlik (Martyrdom) 1915". All the books I had read on the Cameronians treated the terrible waste of British life on the day my great-uncle had died. None of the English sources had mentioned the thousands of Turkish war dead. It was sobering to realize that the number of bereaved Turkish families would have so surpassed the number of those grieving in Scotland.

I came away from Gallipoli struck by how little we in the West know about the Turkish and Arab experiences of the Great War. The scores of books published in English on the different Middle Eastern fronts reflect British or Allied experiences. Gallipoli was "Churchill's debacle"; Kut al-Amara was "Townshend's surrender"; the Arab Revolt was led by "Lawrence of Arabia"; it was "Maude's entry" to Baghdad and "Allenby's conquest" of Jerusalem. Social historians, keen to break with the official history's top-down approach, probed the experiences of the common soldier by reading the diaries and letters held in private paper archives in London's Imperial War Museum, Canberra's Australian War Memorial, and Wellington's Alexander Turnbull Library. After a century of research, we have a comprehensive view of the Allied side of the trenches. But we are only just beginning to come to terms with the other side—the experiences of Ottoman soldiers caught up in a desperate struggle for survival against powerful invaders.

It is actually quite difficult to approach the Ottoman front from the Turkish side of the trenches. While there are dozens of diaries and memoirs published in Turkey and the Arab world, few Western historians have the language skills to read them, and only a fraction of published primary sources are available in translation. Archival materials are even harder to access. The Turkish Military and Strategic Studies Archive in Ankara (Askeri Tarih ve Stratejic Etüt Başkanlığı Arşivi, or ATASE) holds the largest collection of primary materials on the First World War in the Middle East. Yet access to ATASE is strictly controlled, with researchers required to pass a security clearance that can take months—and is often denied. Large parts of the collection are closed to researchers, who face restrictions on copying materials. However, a number of Turkish and Western scholars have gained access to this collection and are beginning to publish important studies on the Ottoman experience of the Great War. Elsewhere in the Middle East, national archives, where they exist, were established well after the conflict and do not place particular emphasis on the Great War.[4]

Neglect of the First World War in Arab archives is reflected in Arab society at large. Unlike in Turkey, where the Gallipoli battlefield is punctuated with Turkish monuments and memorial celebrations are held each year, there are no war memorials in the towns and cities of the Arab world. Though nearly every modern Arab state was drawn into the Great War in one way or another, the conflict is remembered as someone else's war—a time of suffering inflicted on the Arab people by the failing Ottoman Empire and its rash Young Turk leadership. In the Arab world, the Great War left martyrs (especially Arab activists hanged in central squares of Beirut and Damascus that were subsequently renamed "Martyrs' Square" in both cities) but no heroes.

It is time to restore the Ottoman front to its rightful place in the history of both the Great War and the modern Middle East. For, more than any other event, the Ottoman entry into the war turned Europe's conflict into a world war. As opposed to the minor skirmishes in the Far East and East Africa, major battles were fought over the full four years of the war in the Middle East. Moreover, the Middle Eastern battlefields were often the most international of the war. Australians and New Zealanders, every ethnicity in South Asia, North Africans, Senegalese, and Sudanese made common cause with French, English, Welsh, Scottish, and Irish soldiers against the Turkish, Arab, Kurdish, Armenian, and Circassian combatants in the Ottoman army and their German and Austrian allies. The Ottoman front was a veritable tower of Babel, an unprecedented conflict between international armies.

Most Entente war planners dismissed the fighting in the Ottoman Empire as a sideshow to the main theatres of the war on the western and eastern fronts. Influential Britons like Horatio Herbert Kitchener and Winston Churchill only lobbied to take the war to the Turks in the mistaken belief this would provide the Allies with a quick victory against the Central Powers that would hasten the end of the war. Having underestimated their opponents, the Allies found themselves embroiled in major campaigns—in the Caucasus, the Dardanelles, Mesopotamia, and Palestine—that diverted hundreds of thousands of troops from the western front and served to lengthen the Great War.

Allied failures on the Ottoman front provoked grave political crises at home. The foundering Dardanelles campaign forced British Liberal prime minister H. H. Asquith into a coalition government with the Conservatives in May 1915 and contributed to Asquith's downfall the following year. British wartime defeats in Gallipoli and Mesopotamia led to two separate parliamentary commissions of enquiry whose reports were equally damning of political and military decision-makers.

If the Ottomans turned Europe's conflict into a world war, it is equally true that the Great War transformed the modern Middle East. Virtually no part of the region was spared its ravages. Men were recruited from across Turkey and the Arab provinces of the Ottoman Empire and from every colonial state in North Africa. Civilians too suffered from the economic hardship and epidemics unleashed by the war. Battles were fought in territory of the modern states of Egypt, Yemen, Saudi Arabia, Jordan, Israel and the Palestinian territories, Syria, Lebanon, Iraq, Turkey, and Iran. The majority of those countries emerged into statehood as a direct consequence of the fall of the Ottoman Empire following the end of the First World War.

The fall of the Ottomans was an epochal event. For over six centuries, theirs stood as the greatest Islamic empire in the world. Founded at the end of the thirteenth century by tribesmen from Central Asia, the Ottoman sultanate emerged as a dynasty to challenge the Byzantine Empire in both Asia Minor and the Balkans. Following Sultan Mehmed II's conquest of the Byzantine capital, Constantinople, in 1453, the Ottomans emerged as the greatest power in the Mediterranean world.

With Constantinople (subsequently renamed Istanbul) as their capital, the Ottomans rapidly extended their conquests. In 1516, Selim I defeated the Cairo-based Mamluk Empire and added Syria, Egypt, and the Red Sea province of the Hijaz to Ottoman domains. In 1529, Sultan Suleyman the Magnificent was at the gates of Vienna, spreading fear across Europe. The Ottomans continued to expand until their final attempt on Vienna in 1683, by which time the empire spanned three continents, comprising the Balkans, Asia Minor (known to the Turks as Anatolia), the Black Sea, and most of the Arab lands from Iraq to the borders of Morocco.

Over the next two centuries, the Ottomans were overtaken by the dynamism of Europe. They began to lose wars to their neighbours—to the Russian Empire of Catherine the Great and to the Habsburg emperors whose capital, Vienna, they previously had menaced. Starting in 1699, Ottoman frontiers retreated in the face of external challenges. By the early nineteenth century, the Ottomans began to lose territory to new nationalist movements emerging within their Balkan provinces. Greece was the first to make a bid for independence, after an eight-year war against Istanbul's rule (1821–1829). Romania, Serbia, and Montenegro secured their independence in 1878, with Bosnia, Herzegovina, and Bulgaria gaining autonomy at the same time.

The Great Powers continued to seize Ottoman territory, with Britain claiming Cyprus and Egypt between 1878 and 1882, France occupying

Tunisia in 1881, and Russia annexing three provinces in the Ottoman Caucasus in 1878. As it struggled against internal and external threats to its territory, by the early twentieth century, political analysts predicted the imminent demise of the Ottoman Empire. A group of patriotic young officers, calling themselves the Young Turks, held out the hope that the empire could be revived through constitutional reform. In 1908, they rose in rebellion against the autocratic reign of Sultan Abdülhamid II (r. 1876–1909) in a desperate bid to save their state. With the rise of the Young Turks to power, the Ottomans entered a period of unprecedented turbulence that would ultimately draw the empire into its last and greatest war.

THE MEDITERRANEAN WORLD IN 1914

St Petersburg

Moscow

RUSSIAN EMPIRE

AUSTRO-HUNGARIAN EMPIRE

Budapest

ROMANIA

Belgrade

Bucharest

arajevo

SERBIA

Sofia

Sevastopol

Black Sea

NTENEGRO

BULGARIA

Caspian Sea

Tirana

Edirne

Bosphorus

Baku

BANIA

Gallipoli

Istanbul

Salonica

Sea of Marmara

Ankara

Trabzon

Limnos

GREECE

Mytilene

Izmir

OTTOMAN EMPIRE

Athens

Chios

Aegean Sea

Adana

Alexandretta

Mosul

Rhodes

Aleppo

Crete

Cyprus

Mediterranean Sea

Beirut

Baghdad

Damascus

PERSIA

Benghazi

Alexandria

Port Said

Jerusalem

Basrah

Cairo

Suez Canal

Kuwait

Gulf of Suez

Gulf of Aqaba

BAHRAIN

Persian Gulf

LIBYA

EGYPT

CENTRAL ARABIA

OMAN

Medina

Red

FRENCH QUATORIAL AFRICA

SUDAN

Sea

Jeddah

Mecca

ERITREA

Sana'a

YEMEN

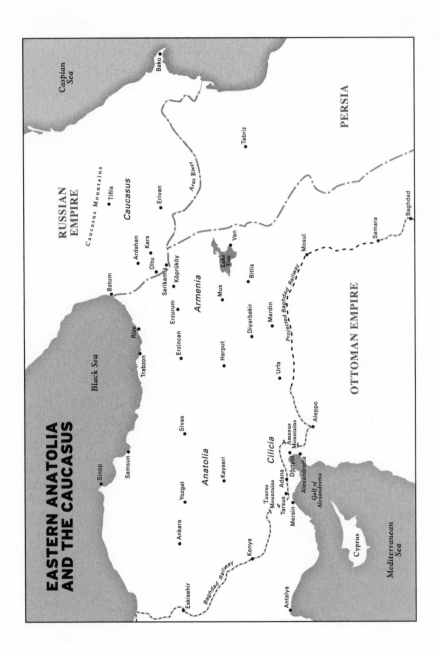

EASTERN ANATOLIA
AND THE CAUCASUS

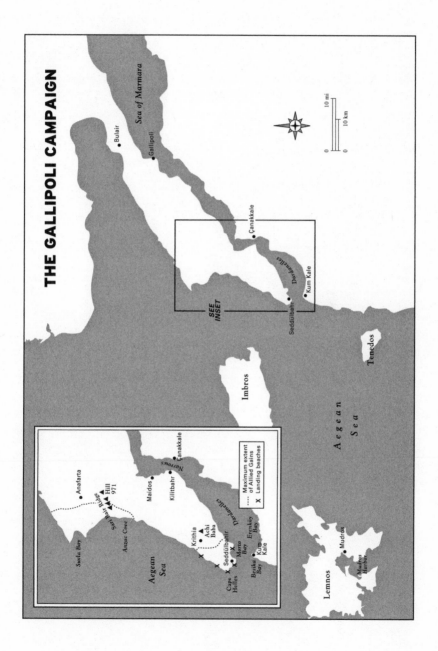

THE GALLIPOLI CAMPAIGN

Sea of Marmara

Bulair

Gallipoli

Çanakkale

Dardanelles

Kum Kale

Seddülbahr

SEE INSET

Imbros

Tenedos

Aegean Sea

10 mi

10 km

Anafarta

Hill 971

Maidos

Kilitbahr

Çanakkale

Narrows

Suvla Bay

Sari Bair Ridge

Anzac Cove

Krithia

Achi Baba

Dardanelles

Eren Köy Bay

Cape Helles

Seddülbahr

Morto Bay

Kum Kale

Besika Bay

Aegean Sea

Maximum extent of Allied Gains

X Landing beaches

Lemnos

Mudros

Mudros Harbor

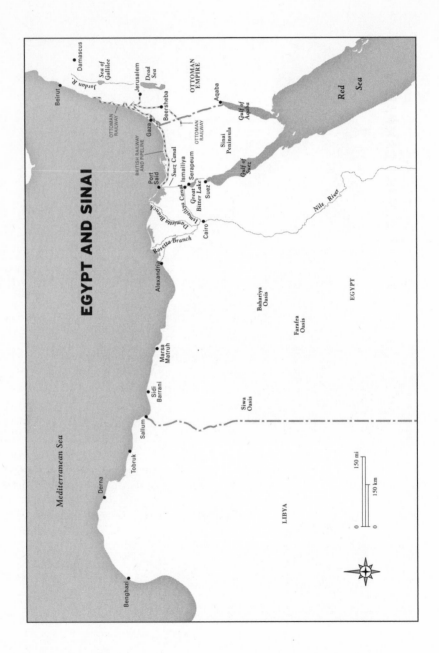

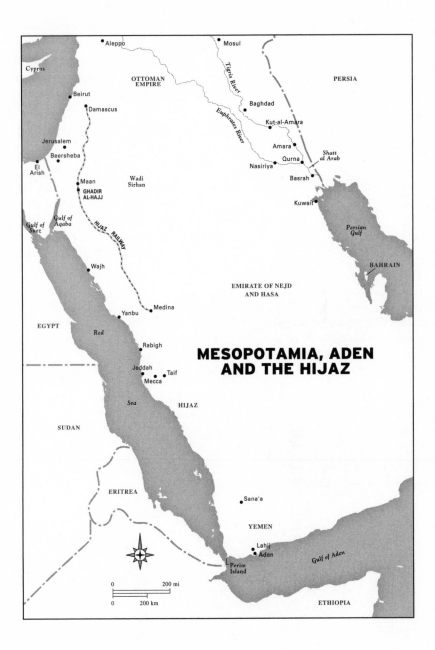

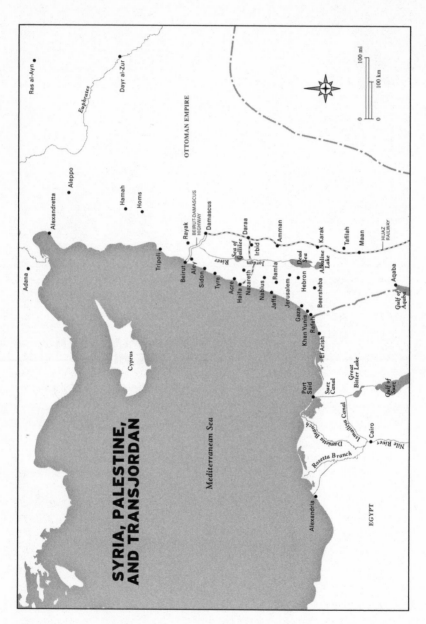

SYRIA, PALESTINE, AND TRANSJORDAN

Ras al-Ayn

Dayr al-Zur

Euphrates

OTTOMAN EMPIRE

Aleppo

Alexandretta

Hamah

Homs

Adana

Tripoli

Rayak

BEIRUT-DAMASCUS HIGHWAY

Damascus

Beirut

Aley

Sidon

Daraa

Sea of Galilee

Irbid

Amman

Tyre

Jordan River

Karak

Acre

Haifa

Nazareth

Dead Sea

Tafilah

Maan

HIJAZ RAILWAY

Nablus

Ramla

Alkaline Lake

Jaffa

Jerusalem

Hebron

Beersheba

Gaza

Khan Yunis

Aqaba

Rafah

Gulf of Aqaba

El Arish

Mediterranean Sea

Cyprus

Great Bitter Lake

Port Said

Suez Canal

Ismailiyya Canal

Gulf of Suez

Damietta Branch

Cairo

Nile River

Rosetta Branch

Alexandria

EGYPT

100 mi

100 km

0

0

ONE

A Revolution and Three Wars, 1908–1913

BETWEEN 1908 AND 1913, THE OTTOMAN EMPIRE FACED GRAVE internal and external threats. Starting with the Young Turk Revolution in 1908, the political institutions of the centuries-old empire came under unprecedented strain. Domestic reformers sought to bring the empire into the twentieth century. European imperial powers and the newly emergent Balkan states went to war with the Turks in pursuit of Ottoman territory. Armenian and Arab activists sought greater autonomy from the weakened Turkish state. These issues, which dominated the Ottoman government's agenda in the years leading up to 1914, laid the foundations for the Ottoman Great War.

THE AGING SULTAN ABDÜLHAMID II CONVENED HIS CABINET IN A CRISIS session on 23 July 1908. The autocratic monarch faced the greatest domestic threat to his rule in over three decades on the throne. The Ottoman army in Macedonia—that volatile Balkan region straddling the modern states of Greece, Bulgaria, and Macedonia—had risen in rebellion, demanding the restoration of the 1876 constitution and a return to parliamentary rule. The sultan knew the contents of the constitution better than his opponents. One of his first measures on ascending the Ottoman throne in 1876 had been to promulgate the constitution as the culmination of four decades of government-led reforms known as the Tanzimat. In those days he was seen as an enlightened reformer. But the experience of ruling the Ottoman Empire had hardened Abdülhamid from reformer into absolutist.

The roots of Abdülhamid's absolutism can be traced to a series of crises the young sultan faced at the very start of his reign. The empire he inherited from his predecessors was in disarray. The Ottoman treasury had declared bankruptcy in 1875, and its European creditors were quick to impose economic sanctions on the sultan's government. The Ottomans faced growing hostility from European public opinion in 1876 for the violent suppression of Bulgarian separatists branded the "Bulgarian horrors" by the Western press. The Liberal leader William Gladstone led British condemnation of Turkey, and war was brewing with Russia. The pressure took its toll on the rulers of the empire. A powerful group of reformist officers deposed Sultan Abdülaziz (r. 1861–1876), who, less than a week later, was found dead in his apartments, the veins of his wrist slashed, an apparent suicide. His successor, Murat V, collapsed in a nervous breakdown after only three months on the throne. Against this inauspicious background, the thirty-three-year-old Abdülhamid II ascended to power on 31 August 1876.

Powerful cabinet ministers pressed the new sultan to introduce a liberal constitution and an elected parliament with Muslim, Christian, and Jewish members as a means to prevent further European intervention in domestic Ottoman affairs. Abdülhamid conceded to the demands of the reformists in his government, more out of a sense of pragmatism than conviction. On 23 December 1876, he promulgated the Ottoman constitution, and on 19 March 1877, he opened the first session of the elected Ottoman parliament. Yet, no sooner had the parliament met than the empire was embroiled in a devastating war with Russia.

The Russian Empire saw itself as the successor to Byzantium and the spiritual head of the Eastern Orthodox Church. Russia also had expansionist aims. It coveted the Ottoman capital, Istanbul, which until 1453 had been the centre of Orthodox Christianity and the Byzantine capital, Constantinople. These were more than just cultural ambitions. Once in possession of Istanbul, the Russians would control the geostrategic straits of the Bosporus and the Dardanelles linking Russia's Black Sea ports to the Mediterranean. Throughout the nineteenth century, however, it suited Russia's European neighbours to confine the tsar's fleet to the Black Sea by preserving the territorial integrity of the Ottoman Empire. Frustrated in their aspirations to occupy Istanbul and the straits, the Russians exploited Balkan nationalist independence movements to interfere with Ottoman affairs while advancing their territorial aims through periodic wars with the Ottomans. By the end of 1876, troubles in Serbia and Bulgaria provided Russia the opportunity for another expansionist war. After securing Austrian neutrality and Romania's permission for Russian forces to march through its territory, Russia declared war on the Ottomans in April 1877.

The tsar's forces made rapid gains into Ottoman territory in the Balkans and, attacking through the Caucasus, into eastern Anatolia, massacring Turkish and Muslim peasants as they swept forward in their two-front assault. The Russian attack provoked public outrage in Ottoman domains. Sultan Abdülhamid II played on his Islamic credentials to secure popular support in the war against Russia. He took the banner of the Prophet Muhammad, which had been in Ottoman keeping since the empire occupied the Arab lands in the sixteenth century, and declared jihad, or holy war, against the Russians. The Ottoman public rallied to their warrior-sultan, volunteering for military service and contributing money to the war effort—and the armed forces managed to bring the Russian advances into Ottoman territory to a halt.

While Abdülhamid was gaining popular support for the war effort, members of parliament (MPs) were growing increasingly critical of the government's handling of the conflict. Despite the sultan's jihad, the Russians had resumed their forward progress by the end of 1877 and reached the outskirts of Istanbul in late January 1878. In February, the sultan convened a meeting with parliamentarians to consult on the conduct of the war. One MP, who was the head of the bakers' guild, chided the sultan: "You have asked for our opinions too late; you should have consulted us when it was still possible to avert disaster. The Chamber declines all responsibility for a situation for which it had nothing to do." The baker's intervention seems to have convinced the sultan that the parliament was more of a hindrance than a help to the national cause. The very next day, Abdülhamid suspended the constitution, dissolved parliament, and placed some of the most critical MPs under house arrest. Abdülhamid then began to exercise direct control over the affairs of state. By that point, however, the military situation was beyond salvation, and the young sultan had to accept an armistice in January 1878 with Russian forces at the gates of his capital.[1]

In the aftermath of defeat to Russia in 1878, the Ottomans suffered tremendous territorial losses in the peace treaty concluded in the Congress of

Berlin (June–July 1878). Hosted by Germany and attended by the European powers (Britain, France, Austria-Hungary, and Italy), the congress sought to resolve not just the Russo-Turkish War but the many conflicts in the Balkans as well. By the terms of the Treaty of Berlin, the Ottomans lost two-fifths of the empire's territory and one-fifth of its population in the Balkans and eastern Anatolia. Among the territories surrendered were three provinces in the Caucasus region of eastern Anatolia—Kars, Ardahan, and Batum—that, as Turkish Muslim heartlands they could not be reconciled to losing, would come to be the Ottomans' Alsace-Lorraine.

The Ottomans lost further territories to the European powers in addition to those surrendered in the Treaty of Berlin. Britain secured Cyprus as a colony in 1878, France occupied Tunisia in 1881, and after intervening in Egypt's 1882 crisis, Britain placed that autonomous Ottoman province under British colonial rule. These losses seemed to convince Sultan Abdülhamid II that he needed to rule the Ottoman Empire with a strong hand in order to protect it from further dismemberment by ambitious European powers. To his credit, between 1882 and 1908 Abdülhamid protected Ottoman domains from further dismemberment. Yet the territorial integrity of the state was preserved at the expense of its citizens' political rights.

Abdülhamid's autocratic style of rule eventually gave rise to an increasingly organized opposition movement. The Young Turks were a disparate coalition of parties bound by the common goals of constraining Abdülhamid's absolutism, restoring constitutional rule, and returning to parliamentary democracy. Among the most prominent parties under the Young Turk umbrella was the Committee of Union and Progress (CUP), a secret society of civilians and military men founded in the early 1900s. Though the CUP had branches in all parts of the Ottoman Empire—the Arab lands, the Turkish provinces, and the Balkans—the movement had faced most repression in the Turkish and Arab provinces. By 1908, the CUP's centre of operations lay in the surviving Ottoman possessions in the Balkans—in Albania, Macedonia, and Thrace.[2]

In June 1908, spies working for the sultan uncovered a CUP cell in the Ottoman Third Army in Macedonia. Faced with imminent court-martial, the military men decided to take action. On 3 July 1908, a CUP cell leader named Adjutant Major Ahmed Niyazi led two hundred well-armed soldiers and their civilian supporters in a revolt, demanding that the sultan restore the 1876 constitution. They all fully expected to die in the attempt. However, the rebels captured the public's mood and their movement gained momentum as it drew increasing support from the population at large. Whole cities in Macedonia rose in rebellion and declared their adherence to the constitution. A Young Turk officer named Major Ismail Enver—who later rose to fame as just Enver—proclaimed the constitution in the Macedonian towns of Köprülü and Tikveş to popular acclaim. The Ottoman Third Army threatened to march on Istanbul to impose the constitution in the empire's capital.

Three weeks on, the revolutionary movement had grown so big that the sultan could no longer count on the loyalty of his military to contain the uprising in Macedonia. This was the emergency that drove the sultan to convene his cabinet on 23 July. They met in Yildiz Palace, perched on a hill overlooking the Bosporus Straits on the European side of Istanbul. Intimidated by the sixty-five-year-old sultan, the ministers avoided raising the crucial question of the restoration of constitutional rule. They spent hours deliberating about whom to blame rather than addressing the necessary solution to the crisis.

After a day spent listening to the tergiversations of his ministers, Abdülhamid brought the discussion to a close. "I will follow the current," he announced to the cabinet. "The constitution was first promulgated under my reign. I am the one who established it. For reasons of necessity, it was suspended. I now wish for the ministers to prepare a proclamation" restoring the constitution. The relieved ministers acted immediately on the sultan's instructions and dispatched telegrams to all of the provinces of the empire to announce the dawn of the second constitutional era. For their success in forcing the sultan to restore the constitution, the Young Turks were credited with having waged a revolution.[3]

It took a moment for the significance of the events to sink in. The newspapers ran the story without banner headlines and with no commentary: "Parliament has been reconvened in conformity with the terms of the constitution, by order of His Imperial Majesty." Perhaps it was a reflection of how few people bothered to read the heavily censored Ottoman press that it took a full twenty-four hours before the public reacted to the news. On 24 July, crowds gathered in the public spaces of Istanbul and provincial towns and cities across the empire to celebrate the return to constitutional life. Major Enver rode the train to Salonica (in modern Greece), the centre of the Young Turk movement, where the jubilant crowds greeted him as a "champion of freedom". On the platform to greet Enver were his colleagues Major Ahmet Cemal, military inspector of the Ottoman railways, and Mehmed Talat, a postal clerk. Both had risen through the hierarchy of the CUP and, like

Enver, came to be known by their middle names, Cemal and Talat. "Enver," they cheered, "you are now Napoleon!"[4]

Over the following days, red-and-white banners emblazoned with the revolutionary slogan "Justice, Equality, and Fraternity" festooned city streets. Photographs of Niyazi, Enver, and the military's other "Freedom Heroes" were posted in town squares across the empire. Political activists gave public orations about the blessings of the constitution, sharing their hopes and aspirations with the general public.

The hopes raised by the constitutional revolution drew together all parts of the diverse Ottoman population in a moment of shared patriotism. Ottoman society comprised a wide range of ethnic groups, including Turks, Albanians, Arabs, and Kurds, as well as many different faith communities—the Sunni majority and Shiite Muslims, over a dozen different Christian denominations, and sizeable Jewish communities. Past attempts by the government to foster an Ottoman national identity had foundered on this diversity, until the constitutional revolution. As one political activist wrote, the Arabs "embraced the Turks wholeheartedly, in the belief that there were no longer Arabs or Turks or Armenians or Kurds in the state, but that everyone had become an Ottoman with equal rights and responsibilities".[5]

The joyful celebrations of newfound freedoms were marred by acts of retaliation against those suspected of taking part in Abdülhamid's repressive apparatus. The Ottoman Empire under the sultan had degenerated into a police state. Political activists were imprisoned and exiled, newspapers and magazines were heavily censored, and citizens looked over their shoulders before speaking, fearful of the ubiquitous spies working for the government. Muhammad Izzat Darwaza, a native of the Palestinian hill town of Nablus, described the "explosion of resentments in the first days of the Revolution against those government officials great and small known to be a spy or corrupt or oppressive".[6]

Yet, for most people, the Young Turk Revolution inspired a newfound sense of hope and freedom that was nothing short of intoxicating. The joys of the moment were captured in verse, as poets from across the Arab and Turkish lands composed odes to celebrate the Young Turks and their revolution.

> Today we rejoice in liberty thanks to you
> We go forth in the morning and return in the evening without
>   concern or strain
> The free man has been set loose from prison where he was demeaned

And the beloved exile has returned to the homeland
For there are no spies whose slanders he need fear
And no newspapers we need fear to touch
We sleep at night with no dreams that cause us anxiety
And we rise in the morning without dread or terror[7]

YET THE REVOLUTION THAT RAISED SO MANY HOPES LED ONLY TO disillusionment.

Those who had hoped for political transformation were disappointed when the revolution produced no major changes in the government of the Ottoman Empire. The CUP decided to leave Sultan Abdülhamid II on the throne. He had managed to take some credit for the restoration of the constitution and was revered by the Ottoman masses as both their sultan and the caliph, or spiritual head, of the Muslim world. Deposing Abdülhamid might have generated more problems than benefits for the Young Turks in 1908. Moreover, the CUP's leaders were indeed young Turks. Mostly junior officers and low-ranking bureaucrats in their late twenties and thirties, they lacked the confidence to take power into their own hands. Instead, they left the exercise of government to the grand vizier (prime minister), Said Pasha, and his cabinet and took on the role of oversight committee to ensure the sultan and his government upheld the constitution.

If Ottoman citizens believed the constitution would solve their economic problems, they were soon to be disappointed. The political instability provoked by the revolution undermined confidence in Turkish currency. Inflation soared to 20 percent in August and September 1908, putting the working classes under intense pressure. Ottoman workers organized demonstrations seeking better pay and work conditions, but the treasury was in no position to meet the workers' legitimate demands. Labour activists mounted over one hundred strikes in the first six months after the revolution, leading to severe laws and a government crackdown on workers.[8]

Crucially, those who believed the return to parliamentary democracy would gain Europe's support and respect for the territorial integrity of the Ottoman Empire were to be humiliated. Turkey's European neighbours seized on the instability created by the Young Turk Revolution to annex yet more Ottoman territory. On 5 October 1908, the former Ottoman province of Bulgaria declared its independence. The following day, the Austro-Hungarian Habsburg Empire announced the annexation of the autonomous Ottoman provinces of Bosnia and Herzegovina. Also on 6 October, Crete announced its union with Greece. Turkey's democratic turn had not won it more support from the European powers and instead rendered the empire more vulnerable.

The Young Turks sought to regain control over the revolution through the Ottoman parliament. The CUP was one of only two parties to contest the election, held in late November and early December 1908, and the Unionists (as members of the CUP were called) won an overwhelming majority in the lower house, co-opting many independents into CUP ranks. On 17 December, the sultan opened the first session of parliament with a speech that asserted his commitment to the constitution. The leaders of both the elected lower chamber and the appointed upper chamber replied to the sultan's speech, praising Abdülhamid for the wisdom he showed in restoring constitutional government. The exchange created the illusion of harmony between the sultan and the CUP. Yet absolute monarchs do not change overnight, and Abdülhamid, unreconciled to constitutional constraints on his powers or parliamentary scrutiny, bided his time for the first opportunity to dispense with the Young Turks.

Once the enthusiasm for revolution had abated, the CUP came to face serious opposition within Ottoman political circles and from influential elements of civil society. The religion of state was Islam, and the religious establishment condemned what they saw as the secular culture of the Young Turks. Within the military, there were clear splits between the officers, who were graduates of the military academies and had liberal reformist leanings, and the ordinary soldiers, who placed a higher premium on the loyalty they had pledged to the sultan. Within the parliament, members of the liberal faction suspected the CUP of authoritarian tendencies and used their access to the press and to European officials—particularly in the British embassy—to undermine the CUP's position in the lower chamber. From his palace, Abdülhamid II quietly encouraged all elements that challenged the CUP.

On the night of 12–13 April 1909, the enemies of the CUP mounted a counter-revolution. Soldiers of the First Army Corps loyal to Sultan Abdülhamid II mutinied against their officers and made common cause with religious scholars from the capital's theological colleges. Together they marched on the parliament in a noisy demonstration that drew growing numbers of Islamic scholars and mutinous soldiers overnight. They demanded a new cabinet, banishment of a number of Unionist politicians, and restoration of Islamic law—even though the country had in fact been under a mixed set of legal codes for decades. The Unionist deputies fled the capital, fearing for their lives. The cabinet tendered its resignation. And the sultan opportunistically conceded to the demands of the mob, reasserting his control over the politics of the Ottoman Empire.

Abdülhamid's restoration proved short-lived. The Ottoman Third Army in Macedonia saw the counter-revolution in Istanbul as an assault on the constitution they believed essential for the empire's political future. Young Turk loyalists in Macedonia mobilized a campaign force called "the Action Army" to march on Istanbul under the command of Major Ahmed Niyazi, a hero of the Young Turk Revolution. This relief force set out from Salonica for the imperial capital on 17 April. In the early morning hours of 24 April, the Action Army occupied Istanbul, suppressed the revolt with little opposition, and imposed martial law. The two chambers of the Ottoman parliament reconvened as the General National Assembly and on 27 April voted to depose Sultan Abdülhamid II and to install his younger brother Mehmed Reşad as Sultan Mehmed V. With the return of the CUP to power, the counter-revolution was decisively defeated—all within two weeks.

THE COUNTER-REVOLUTION EXPOSED DEEP DIVISIONS WITHIN OTTOMAN society—none more dangerous than the Turkish-Armenian antagonism. Immediately after the Action Army restored the CUP to power in Istanbul, Muslim crowds massacred thousands of Armenians in the south-eastern city of Adana. The roots of the pogrom dated back to the 1870s. In the course of the First World War, that hostility would metastasize into the first genocide of the twentieth century.

In 1909, many Ottoman Turks suspected the Armenians of being a minority community with a nationalist agenda, intent on seceding from the empire. Comprising a distinct ethnic group with its own language and Christian liturgy and centuries of communal organization under the Ottomans as a distinct *millet*, or faith community, the Armenians had all of the prerequisites for a nineteenth-century nationalist movement bar one: they were not concentrated in one geographic area. As a people they were dispersed between the Russian and Ottoman empires and within Ottoman domains across eastern Anatolia, the Mediterranean coastal regions, and the main trading cities of the empire. The largest concentration of Armenians resided in the capital city, Istanbul. Without a critical mass in one geographical location, the

Armenians could never hope to achieve statehood—unless, of course, they could secure the support of a Great Power for their cause.

The Armenians made their first territorial claim at the 1878 Congress of Berlin. As part of the settlement of the Russo-Turkish War, the Ottomans were forced to cede three provinces with sizeable Armenian populations to Russia: Kars, Ardahan, and Batum. The transfer of hundreds of thousands of Armenians to Russian rule provided the context for Armenian demands for greater autonomy within Ottoman domains. The Armenian delegation set out their ambitions, claiming the Ottoman provinces of Erzurum, Bitlis, and Van as the "provinces inhabited by the Armenians". The delegation sought an autonomous region under a Christian governor on the model of Mount Lebanon, with its volatile mix of Christian and Muslim communities. The European powers responded by including an article in the Treaty of Berlin requiring the Ottoman government to implement immediately such "improvements and reforms demanded by local requirements in the provinces inhabited by the Armenians" and to provide them with security from attack by the Muslim majority. The treaty required Istanbul to report periodically to the European powers on the measures it was taking on behalf of its Armenian citizens.[9]

European support for Christian nationalist movements in the Balkans had made the Ottomans understandably wary of foreign intentions in other strategic Ottoman domains. The new status accorded by the Treaty of Berlin to Armenian communal aspirations in the Turkish heartlands of Anatolia posed a distinct threat to the Ottoman Empire. Having just surrendered the three provinces of Kars, Ardahan, and Batum to Russia as a war indemnity, the Ottomans could not contemplate ceding further territory in eastern Anatolia. Consequently, Abdülhamid II's government did all it could to suppress the nascent Armenian movement and its ties to Britain and Russia. When, in the late 1880s, Armenian activists began to form political organizations to pursue their national aspirations, the Ottoman government treated them like any other domestic opposition group and responded with the full range of repressive action—surveillance, arrest, imprisonment, and exile.

Two distinct Armenian nationalist societies emerged at the end of the nineteenth century. A group of Armenian students in Switzerland and France created the Hunchak (Armenian for "bell") Society in Geneva in 1887. In 1890, a group of activists inside the Russian Empire launched the Armenian Revolutionary Federation, better known as the Dashnak (short for *dashnaksutiun*, or "federation" in Armenian). They were very different movements, with divergent ideologies and methods. The Hunchaks debated the relative merits of socialism and national liberation, while the Dashnaks promoted self-defence among Armenian communities in both Russia and the Ottoman Empire. Both societies espoused the use of violence to achieve Armenian political aims. They saw themselves as freedom fighters, but the Ottomans branded them terrorists. Activities by the Hunchaks and Dashnaks exacerbated tensions between Muslims and Christians in eastern Anatolia, which the Armenian activists hoped might provoke European intervention and the Ottomans exploited to try to quell what they saw as a nascent nationalist movement. The volatile situation inevitably led to bloodshed.[10]

Between 1894 and 1896, Ottoman Armenians were the target of a series of terrible massacres. The violence began in the Sasun region of southeastern Anatolia in the summer of 1894, when Kurdish nomads attacked Armenian villagers for refusing to make the traditional protection payments on top of their tax payments to Ottoman officials. Armenian activists took up the cause of the overtaxed Armenian peasants and encouraged their revolt. British traveller and businessman H. F. B. Lynch, who journeyed through the Sasun region on the eve of the massacres, described the Armenian agitators: "The object of these men is to keep the Armenian cause alive by lighting a flame here and there and calling: Fire! The cry is taken up in the European press; and when people run to look there are sure to be some Turkish officials drawn into the trap and committing abominations." The Ottoman government dispatched the Fourth Army, reinforced by a Kurdish cavalry regiment, in a bid to restore order. Thousands of Armenians were killed as a result, provoking the European calls for intervention that the Hunchaks actively sought and the Ottomans most wanted to avoid.[11]

In September 1895, the Hunchaks organized a march in Istanbul to petition for reforms in the eastern Anatolian provinces that Europeans increasingly referred to as Turkish Armenia. They gave both the Ottoman government and all foreign embassies forty-eight-hours' advance notice and set out their demands, including the appointment of a Christian governor general to oversee reforms in eastern Anatolia and the right of Armenian villagers to bear arms to protect themselves against their well-armed Kurdish neighbours. The Ottomans surrounded the Sublime Porte, the walled compound housing the offices of the Ottoman prime minister and his cabinet (the term is also used to refer to the Ottoman government, in the same way that Whitehall is used for the British government), with a police cordon to drive back the crowd of Armenian protestors. A policeman was killed in the melee, setting off a riot in which a hostile Muslim crowd turned on the Armenians. Sixty protesters were killed outside the Porte alone. The European powers protested the killing of peaceful demonstrators. Faced with mounting international pressure, Sultan Abdülhamid issued a decree on 17 October promising reforms in the six provinces of eastern Anatolia with Armenian populations: Erzurum, Van, Bitlis, Diyarbakır, Harput, and Sivas.

The sultan's reform decree served only to heighten the fears of Ottoman Muslims in the six provinces. They saw the measure as a prelude to Armenian independence in eastern Anatolia, which would force the Muslim majority either to live under a Christian authority or to abandon their homes and villages to resettle in Muslim lands—as thousands of Muslims from Crimea, the Caucasus, and the Balkans had already been forced to do when the Ottomans had relinquished those lands to Christian rule. Ottoman officials did little to dispel these fears, and within days of the sultan's decree, a new and far more lethal wave of massacres swept the towns and villages of central and eastern Anatolia. By February 1896, American missionaries estimated that no fewer than 37,000 Armenians had been killed and 300,000 left homeless. Other estimates put the casualty figures between 100,000 and 300,000 Armenian dead and wounded. Given the isolated nature of the region, we are unlikely to obtain a more precise figure for the casualties of the 1895 massacres. Yet the level of violence against the Armenians was clearly unprecedented in Ottoman history.[12]

A terrorist attack in Istanbul marked the third and final episode in the Armenian atrocities of 1894 to 1896. A group of twenty-six Dashnak activists, disguised as porters, carried weapons and explosives hidden in money bags into the headquarters of the Ottoman Bank in Istanbul on 26 August 1896. They killed two guards and took hostage 150 bank workers and clients, threatening to blow up the building and everyone in it unless their demands—the appointment of a European high commissioner to impose reforms in eastern Anatolia and a general amnesty for all Armenian political exiles—were met. Despite its name, the Ottoman Bank was a foreign-owned institution, with nearly all its shares held by British and French concerns. The bid to force the European powers to intervene in Ottoman-Armenian affairs backfired entirely. The terrorists were forced to abandon their occupation of the bank with their demands unmet, taking refuge on a French ship to escape Ottoman domains. Not only were the Dashnaks' actions condemned by the European powers, but the attack on the bank set off pogroms against Armenians in Istanbul in which as many as 8,000 were killed. The European powers, divided in their policies on the Armenian question, forced no changes on the Ottoman Empire. For the Armenian movement, the bloody events of 1894 to 1896 proved nothing short of a catastrophe.

Over the following years, the Armenian movement changed tactics and worked with the liberal parties seeking the reform of the Ottoman Empire. The Dashnaks attended the Second Congress of Ottoman Opposition Parties in Paris in 1907, alongside the Committee of Union and Progress. They were enthusiastic supporters of the Young Turk Revolution of 1908 and emerged from it as a legally recognized group for the first time. The Armenian community fielded a number of candidates for the Ottoman parliament later that year, and fourteen were elected to the lower chamber. Many hoped that Armenian political objectives could be realized within the context of the Ottoman constitution, the citizenship rights it promised, and the prospect of administrative decentralization. Those hopes were dashed in the aftermath of the 1909 counter-revolution when, between 25 and 28 April 1909, some 20,000 Armenians were killed in a frenzy of bloodletting.[13]

Minaret from which Turks fired on Christians. In April 1909, Muslim mobs destroyed Christian homes and shops in Adana and its environs and killed some 20,000 Armenians. Bain News Service, an American photo agency, captured the ruins of the Christian quarters in the aftermath of the Adana massacre.

Zabel Essayan, one of the most prominent Armenian literary figures at the start of the twentieth century, travelled to Adana shortly after the massacres to assist in the relief efforts. She found a city in ruins, inhabited by widows, orphans, and elderly men and women traumatized by what they had witnessed. "One cannot take in the abominable reality in one sweep: it remains well beyond the limits of human imagination," she recounted of the horror. "Even those who lived the experience are incapable of giving the whole picture. They stutter, sigh, cry, and in the end can only tell you about isolated events." Influential public figures like Essayan drew international attention to the massacres and condemnation of the Ottoman Empire.[14]

The Young Turks moved quickly and dispatched Cemal Pasha to restore peace in Adana after the violence had run its course. The Unionists needed to regain the confidence of the Dashnaks, to prevent them seeking European intervention on behalf of Armenian aspirations. The Dashnaks agreed to preserve cooperation with the CUP on condition that the government arrest and punish all those responsible for the Adana massacres, restore property to Armenian survivors, relieve their tax burdens, and provide funds for the destitute. In his memoirs, Cemal claimed to have rebuilt every damaged house in Adana within four months and to have executed "not less than thirty Mohammedans" in Adana and seventeen in nearby Erzine, "members of the oldest and highest families" among them. These measures were taken as much to reassure the Armenians as to forestall European interventions, and for the moment they bought the Young Turks time on the Armenian question.[15]

WHILE THE OTTOMANS STRUGGLED TO PRESERVE THEIR TERRITORIAL integrity in eastern Anatolia, they faced a fresh crisis in the Mediterranean. The provinces of Benghazi and Tripoli in the modern state of Libya were the Ottomans' last possessions in North Africa, after the French occupation of Algeria (1830) and Tunisia (1881) and the British occupation of Egypt in 1882. Italy was a new state—its unification into a single kingdom was only completed in 1871—and aspired to an empire in Africa. The government of King Victor Emmanuel III turned to Libya to satisfy its imperial ambitions.

The Ottomans had done nothing to provoke war with Italy in 1911. Yet with British and French neutrality assured in advance, Rome knew that nothing stood in the way of its pursuing its imperial ambitions in North

Africa by military means. Seizing on the pretext of an Ottoman arms shipment to its garrisons in Libya as a threat to the safety of Italian citizens living in Tripoli and Benghazi, Rome declared war on 29 September and launched a full-scale invasion of the Libyan coastal cities.[16]

The Ottoman position in Libya was completely untenable. Some 4,200 Turkish soldiers were posted in garrisons with virtually no naval support to protect them from the invading Italian army of more than 34,000 men. The Ottoman minister of war admitted freely to his own officers that Libya could not be defended. In the first weeks of October 1911, the coastal towns of the Ottoman provinces of Tripoli (Western Libya) and Benghazi (Eastern Libya, also known as Cyrenaica) fell to the triumphant Italian army.[17]

The Ottoman government and the Young Turks took radically different positions on the invasion. The grand vizier and his government did not believe they could save Libya and so preferred to write off the marginal North African territory rather than embroil their armed forces in a fight they could not win. The ultranationalist Young Turks could not accept the loss of Ottoman territory without a fight.

In early October 1911, Major Enver travelled to Salonica to address the Central Committee of the CUP. In a five-hour meeting, he persuaded his colleagues to raise a guerrilla war against the Italians in Libya. He outlined the plan in a letter to his childhood friend and foster brother, German naval attaché Hans Humann: "We will gather our forces in the [Libyan] interior. Mounted bands of Arabs, citizens of the country, commanded by young [Ottoman] officers, will stay close to the Italians and harass them night and day. Each [Italian] soldier or small detachment will be surprised and annihilated. When the enemy is too strong, the bands will withdraw into the open country and continue to harry the enemy at every occasion."[18]

On securing CUP approval for his plan, Enver set off for Istanbul, where he boarded ship incognito for Alexandria. Dozens of patriotic young officers followed in his wake, using Egypt as the launching pad for their guerrilla war against Italy—among them a young adjutant major named Mustafa Kemal, the future Atatürk. Others entered through Tunisia. Officially, these young officers were disowned by their government as "adventurers acting against the wishes of the Ottoman government" (though in fact the Ottoman treasury made monthly payments to their commanders serving in Libya). They called themselves *fedaî* officers, fighters willing to sacrifice their lives for their cause.[19]

From the moment he entered the country at the end of October, Enver threw himself into the Libyan conflict with passion and commitment. He donned Arab robes and rode on camelback into the Libyan interior. He revelled in the austerity and hardships of desert life and admired the courage of the Bedouin, with whom he had to communicate through a translator as he spoke no Arabic. The tribesmen, for their part, showed Enver great respect. Enver's fiancée was the niece of Sultan Mehmed V, Princess Emine Naciye Sultan. Though she was only thirteen at the time (they married in 1914, when she was seventeen), the connection to the imperial household greatly enhanced Enver's standing among the Libyans. "Here I am the son-in-law of the Sultan, the envoy of the Caliph who is giving orders," he wrote, "and it is this tie alone that helps me."[20]

Enver confined his movements to the eastern province of Benghazi. Italian troops were concentrated in the three port cities of Cyrenaica— Benghazi, Derna, and Tobruk. Stubborn resistance by Libyan tribesmen had prevented the Italian troops from moving beyond the coastal plain into the Libyan interior. After surveying Italian positions, Enver made his camp on the plateau overlooking the port of Derna. The 10,000 inhabitants of Derna were unwilling hosts to an invasion army of some 15,000 Italian infantry, who became the primary target of Enver's war. He rallied the demoralized Ottoman soldiers who had escaped capture, he recruited tribesmen and members of the powerful Sanussi brotherhood (a mystical religious confraternity whose network of lodges extended across urban and rural Libya), and he received other Young Turk *fedaî* officers at his base camp in Ayn al-Mansur. Through his work in Libya—recruiting local fighters under Ottoman officers, deploying Islamic hostility to foreign rule to subvert European enemies, and creating an effective intelligence network—Enver laid the foundations for a new secret service that would prove highly influential in the Ottoman Great War: the Teşkilât-i Mahsusa (Special Organization).

Judging by Enver's accounts, many of the Arab tribes of Libya rallied to the Ottoman volunteers. They appreciated the way the Young Turks threw themselves into the Libyan people's cause and risked their lives for the tribesmen's freedom from foreign rule. Though they did not share a common language, the bond of Islam proved very strong between the Turkish-speaking Young Turks and the Arabic-speaking Libyan tribesmen. Enver described the Arab fighters in Libya as "fanatical Muslims who see death before the enemy as a gift from God". This was particularly true of the powerful Sanussi Sufi order whose devotion to the Ottoman sultan was linked to his role as the caliph of Islam. Nor did Enver, the secular Young Turk, disavow this devotion to Islam. Rather, he saw religion as a strong mobilizing force to rally Muslims behind the Ottoman sultan-as-caliph to defeat their enemies—in the Ottoman Empire and the Muslim world beyond. Reflecting on the power of Islam, Enver wrote, "There is no nationality in Islamism. Just take a look at what is going on around the Islamic world." Whatever else Enver took from his time in Libya, he came away with a firm belief in the Ottoman Empire's power to deploy Islam against its enemies at home and abroad.[21]

Between October 1911 and November 1912, the Young Turk officers and Arab tribesmen prosecuted a remarkably successful guerrilla war against the Italians. Despite superiority in numbers and modern weapons, the Italians were unable to break out of their fortified positions in the coastal plain to occupy the Libyan interior. Arab bands inflicted high casualties on the Italians, killing 3,400 and wounding over 4,000 in the course of the year. The war also took a toll on the Italian treasury, whereas the Ottomans were spending as little as 25,000 Turkish pounds (the Turkish pound was worth approximately £0.90 or $4.40) a month to support Enver in his siege of Derna. For a moment, it looked as though the Young Turks' gamble in Libya might succeed and the Italians would be driven back to the sea.[22]

Unable to win in Libya, the Italians expanded the conflict to other fronts. They knew the war would only end when the Ottoman government relinquished Libya to Italian control in a formal peace treaty. To pressure Istanbul to sue for peace, Italian naval vessels attacked Ottoman territory across the eastern Mediterranean. They bombarded the Lebanese port of Beirut in March 1912, and Italian soldiers occupied the Dodecanese (an Aegean archipelago dominated by Rhodes and today part of Greece) in May of that year. In July, the Italian navy dispatched torpedo boats into the Dardanelles. Finally, the Italians played the Balkan card. Greece, Serbia, Montenegro, and Bulgaria had entered into alliances against their former Ottoman suzerain. Each had territorial ambitions in the remaining Ottoman territory in the Balkans—in Albania, Macedonia, and Thrace. The Italian Crown was related by marriage to King Nicholas I of Montenegro, and the Italians encouraged the Montenegrins to declare war on the Ottoman Empire on 8 October 1912. It was only a matter of time before the other Balkan states followed suit.

The imminent threat of war in the Balkans provoked a crisis reaching from Istanbul to Libya. By defending remote provinces like Tripoli and Benghazi, the Ottoman government had left the empire's Balkan heartland exposed. Idealism quickly gave way to a new realism. Ten days after Montenegro declared war, the Ottoman Empire concluded a peace treaty with Italy in which it relinquished the Libyan provinces to Italian rule. The *fedaî* officers, though ashamed to abandon their Libyan comrades, left the Sanussi brotherhood to carry on the guerrilla war unassisted and made haste back to Istanbul to join in the national struggle for survival that became known as the First Balkan War.

THE BALKAN STATES HAD ALL ONCE BEEN PART OF THE OTTOMAN Empire. In the course of the nineteenth century, nationalism took hold among the diverse ethnic and religious communities of south-eastern Europe. The European powers actively encouraged these nationalist movements as they sought to secede from the Ottoman Empire, creating volatile client states. The Kingdom of Greece was the first to secure full independence in 1830 after a decade of war. Serbia gained international recognition as a principality under Ottoman suzerainty in 1829 and secured full independence in the 1878 Congress of Berlin. Also at Berlin, Montenegro gained its independence, and Bulgaria secured its autonomy under Ottoman rule, achieving full independence in September 1908. None of the independent Balkan states was satisfied with the territory under its control—each aspired to lands still under Ottoman rule in Albania, Macedonia, and Thrace. The Ottomans, for their part, had grown dismissive of their former Balkan subject peoples' claims and underestimated the danger they posed to Ottoman rule in the empire's last remaining European provinces.

Ottoman complacency was shattered as the Balkan states seized the opportunity that the Italian-Turkish War presented to satisfy their territorial ambitions. In October 1912, Montenegro, Serbia, Greece, and Bulgaria declared war on the Ottoman Empire in quick succession. From the outset the Balkan allies enjoyed numerical and strategic superiority over their former Ottoman overlords. The combined forces of the Balkan states totalled 715,000 men, compared to only 320,000 Ottoman soldiers in the field.[23]

The Greeks used their maritime supremacy over the Ottomans to advantage. Not only did they annex Crete and occupy a number of Aegean islands, but they also used their navy to prevent the Ottomans from rein-forcing their troops by sea. On 8 November, Greek forces took Salonica, the birthplace of the Young Turk Revolution. They also occupied much of southern Albania. The Serbs and Montenegrins attacked Macedonia and Albania from the north, completing the conquest of those territories. Kosovo fell to the Serbs on 23 October.

The Bulgarians faced the most heated engagements with the Turks. They managed to break through the first Ottoman line of defence in Kirklareli on 24 October and the second line in Lüleburgaz on 2 November before pressing on to Çatalca, just forty miles from Istanbul. The Ottoman de-fenders in Edirne (ancient Adrianople, a city in modern Turkey near Greece and Bulgaria) were left surrounded and under siege when the Porte sued for an armistice in early December 1912. Within two months of surrendering Libya to Italian rule, the Ottoman army had been thoroughly routed and looked certain to lose the last of its European provinces.

The Ottoman government was headed by the Liberal prime minister Kamil Pasha. The CUP and the Liberals were long-standing rivals, and Kamil Pasha had deliberately excluded the CUP from his cabinet. Facing imminent military defeat, the Liberals and Unionists took diametrically op-posed views. The Liberals advocated peace to avoid further territorial losses and to protect Istanbul from risk. The Unionists, on the other hand, called for a vigorous renewal of war to recover essential Ottoman territory—Edirne first and foremost. When the Unionists criticized the conduct of the war, Kamil Pasha ordered a clampdown on CUP branches, closed their newspa-pers, and arrested a number of leading Unionists.

Enver was caught up in these military and political tensions when he returned to Istanbul from fighting the Italians in Libya. "I find myself in a totally hostile environment," he wrote at the end of December 1912. "The whole cabinet, as well as the minister of war, are being very friendly, but I know they are having me followed by spies." He made a number of visits to the front at Çatalca and came away convinced that the Ottomans were in a better position than the Bulgarians. Not surprisingly, Enver became an out-spoken advocate of continuing the war to relieve Edirne. "If the cabinet sur-renders Edirne without any effort, I will quit the army, I will openly call for war and I do not know—or rather don't wish to say—what I might do."[24]

Convinced that Kamil Pasha was on the verge of a peace deal that would surrender Edirne to foreign rule, Enver took drastic action. On 23 January

1913, ten armed conspirators galloped through the cobbled streets of Istanbul to the offices of the Sublime Porte. As they burst into the cabinet meeting, Enver and his men exchanged gunfire with the grand vizier's guards. Four men, including the minister of war, Nazım Pasha, were killed in the shoot-out before Enver pressed his pistol to Kamil Pasha's head to demand the grand vizier's resignation. "It was all over in a quarter of an hour," Enver later confided. He then made his way to the palace to inform the sultan of his actions and to seek the nomination of a new grand vizier. Sultan Mehmed V named a veteran statesman and former general, Mahmud Şevket Pasha, to form a national unity government. Within four hours of the notorious "raid on the Sublime Porte", a new cabinet had been appointed, tasked with restoring stability to the war-shattered politics of the Ottoman Empire.[25]

Though its members had led the coup against Kamil Pasha's government, the CUP still did not exploit the opportunity to seize political power. Mahmud Şevket Pasha was sympathetic to the CUP, but he was no Unionist. The new grand vizier was encouraged to create a non-partisan coalition to provide stability and unity after the factionalism and military disasters of the recent past. Only three Unionists were appointed to his cabinet, all of them moderates. The future triumvirs of the Ottoman Empire—Talat, Enver, and Cemal—remained out of government for the moment. Cemal accepted the post of military governor of Istanbul, Talat continued as secretary general of the CUP, and Enver went to war.

When war resumed, it went badly for the Ottoman Empire. The armistice expired without agreement between the belligerents on 3 February 1913. With key cities under siege and no line of communication to resupply or relieve them, the Ottomans watched helplessly as, one by one, their last European possessions fell to the ambitious Balkan states. The Greeks took the Macedonian town of Janina (Ioannina in modern Greece) on 6 March. Montenegrin forces pinned down Ottoman defenders in Işkodra (Shkodër in modern Albania). Yet the cruellest blow came when the Bulgarians starved the defenders of Edirne into capitulation on 28 March, a moment of profound national crisis for the Ottoman Empire as a whole.

Mahmud Şevket Pasha offered an immediate truce shortly after the fall of Edirne. Negotiations resumed between the Ottomans and the Balkan states in London at the end of May, and a full peace treaty was concluded under British mediation on 30 May 1913. In the Treaty of London, the

Ottoman government signed away 60,000 square miles of territory and nearly 4 million inhabitants, surrendering all its European possessions except a small portion of Eastern Thrace, the hinterlands of Istanbul, defined by the Midye-Enez Line. As in the Italian-Turkish War, the Ottomans had suffered total defeat.

Losing Libya was nothing compared to ceding Albania, Macedonia, and Thrace. Since being conquered from the Byzantine Empire five centuries earlier, these European territories had been the economic and administrative heart of the Ottoman world. They ranked among the most prosperous and developed provinces in the empire. The loss of revenues was compounded by the high costs of the First Balkan War to the Ottoman treasury. Thousands of refugees needed resettlement, and disease swept their squalid camps. The government also faced tremendous expenses to rebuild the Ottoman army after the losses in men and materiel incurred through two failed wars.

Perhaps the greatest obstacle the Ottomans faced was one of public morale. It was bad enough to lose a war to a relatively advanced European power like Italy, but neither the Ottoman army nor the general public could accept defeat at the hands of small Balkan states that had once been part of their empire. "The Bulgar, the Serb, the Greek—our subjects of five centuries, whom we have despised, have defeated us," wrote Yusuf Akçura, a Young Turk intellectual. "This reality, which we could not conjure up even in our imaginations, will open our eyes . . . if we are not yet entirely dead." Throughout the nineteenth century, pessimistic Europeans had labelled the Ottoman Empire the "sick man of Europe". Even the most optimistic Young Turks could not rule out the sick man's demise by the end of the First Balkan War.[26]

Defeat polarized politics in Istanbul. The CUP had justified its coup d'état against Kamil Pasha's Liberal government in January 1913 as a necessary measure to prevent the loss of Edirne. Now that Edirne had fallen, the Liberals were determined to settle old scores and drive the Unionists from politics. Cemal, a leading Unionist politician and military governor of Istanbul, deployed agents to monitor everyone he suspected of plotting against the (non-partisan) government. Despite his best efforts, Cemal was unable to protect the grand vizier. On 11 June, just days after the signing of the Treaty of London ceding Edirne, gunmen shot Mahmud Şevket Pasha dead outside the Sublime Porte.

The Unionists turned the turmoil following the grand vizier's assassination to political advantage. Cemal unleashed a purge that broke the power of the Liberals once and for all. Scores were arrested, twelve leaders were given swift trials and executed on 24 June, and a number of leading opposition figures abroad were condemned to death in absentia. Dozens more were sent into exile. Once they had eliminated their Liberal opponents, the Unionists took power. Ever since the 1908 revolution, the Young Turks had chosen to stay out of government. Finally, in 1913, they were determined to rule.

The sultan invited Said Halim Pasha, a Unionist and member of the Egyptian royal family, to form the next government in June 1913. The most influential Young Turks emerged in national leadership positions for the first time in Said Halim's cabinet. Enver, Talat, and Cemal were all promoted to the rank of "pasha", the highest grade in both civil and military service. Talat Pasha entered the cabinet as minister of interior. Enver Pasha emerged as one of the most powerful generals in the army and in January 1914 was made minister of war. Cemal Pasha remained governor of Istanbul. After 1913 they would emerge as the ruling triumvirate of the Ottoman Empire, more powerful than the sultan or his grand vizier (i.e., the Ottoman prime minister).

The CUP rose to uncontested power when the Unionist-led government recovered Edirne in July 1913. This was, in fact, a gift from Bulgaria's Balkan rivals. The tenuous division of spoils between the victorious states following the First Balkan War was undone when the European powers recognized Albania's declaration of independence. Austria and Italy in particular supported the creation of Albania as a buffer to contain Serbia and prevent it from becoming a new maritime power on the Adriatic. The European powers forced Serbia and Montenegro to withdraw from the Albanian territory they had conquered in the First Balkan War. The Serbs, frustrated by the loss of Albanian lands, sought satisfaction in Macedonian territory held by Bulgaria and Greece. The Bulgarians, convinced they had done most of the fighting against the Turks, refused to cede any territory to the Serbs and rejected Russian efforts at mediation. On the night of 29–30 June 1913, the Bulgarians attacked Serb and Greek positions in Macedonia, sparking the Second Balkan War.

Bulgaria found itself taking on all its Balkan neighbours, as Romania and Montenegro allied with Greece and Serbia against Bulgaria. Overextended, the Bulgarians were forced to redeploy their troops away from the Ottoman frontier to staunch their losses against Greece and Serbia. It was precisely the opening that Enver had been hoping for—yet still he encountered resistance from Said Halim Pasha's government, ever fearful that further military adventures could provoke the demise of the empire. "If those officially charged with governing lack the courage to order the army into battle," Enver wrote, "I will make it march without orders." Enver finally received his orders and led a detachment of cavalry and infantry across the recently demarcated border towards Edirne.[27]

As the Ottoman forces approached Edirne on 8 July, they came under fire from the Bulgarian defenders. Enver held his troops back until, persuaded the Bulgarians were evacuating the city, he was able to enter Edirne the following day unopposed. He dispatched a cavalry unit to pursue the retreating Bulgarians while reinforcing Ottoman positions in the war-devastated city. The joy of liberating Edirne was tempered by the humanitarian disaster that confronted the Ottoman soldiers. Enver described the horrors of "the poor Turks squatting in their ruined houses, the elderly with atrocious scars, the orphans reliant on government charity, the thousands of atrocities which I encounter at every step".[28]

Over the month of July, Ottoman troops reoccupied most of Eastern Thrace as Bulgaria suffered defeat at the hands of its Balkan neighbours. On 10 August, Bulgaria sued for peace, leaving Edirne and Eastern Thrace securely in Ottoman hands. Enver was celebrated once again; the "Hero of Freedom" was now declared the "Liberator of Edirne". The public response across the empire was euphoric. For its role in securing victory after so many humiliating defeats, the CUP gained unprecedented support from the Ottoman public. Noting how he had gained the admiration of the entire Muslim world for this exploit, Enver gloried in his latest triumph. "I am happy as a child," he confided to his German friend Hans Humann, "for having been the only one who could leap into Edirne in just one night."[29]

BUFFETED BY WAR AND POLITICAL TURMOIL, THE YOUNG TURK REGIME failed to live up to the liberal ideals of the 1908 revolution. The Unionists responded to external threats and internal challenges by tightening their grip on those provinces that remained indisputably under Ottoman control. The government adopted a number of policies intended to combat the centripetal forces pulling the empire apart by centralizing government more efficiently. The rule of law, including such unpopular measures as taxation and conscription, would be applied with equal rigor across all provinces of the empire without exception. And all Ottomans would be pressed to use Turkish in their official interactions with the state.

These centralizing measures targeted the Arab provinces, in a bid to prevent the emergence of separatist nationalist movements that might lead the Arabs to follow the Balkans into independence. Increasingly after 1909, the Ottoman Turkish language displaced Arabic in schools, courtrooms, and government offices in the provinces of Greater Syria and Iraq. Senior government appointments went to Turkish officials, while experienced Arab civil servants were left to fill lower-level jobs. Predictably, these unpopular measures drove many loyal Arab subjects, disappointed by the authoritarian turn of the Young Turk Revolution, to form civil society organizations to oppose "Turkification". Not yet nationalist, these pre-war "Arabist" societies called for greater Arab cultural and political rights within the framework of the Ottoman Empire. In the course of the Great War, however, a growing number of these Arab activists aspired to outright independence.

Arabist societies were established in Istanbul and in the Arab provinces. Arab members of the Ottoman parliament played an active role in the meetings of the Istanbul-based Arab-Ottoman Brotherhood Association and the Literary Club, which debated cultural matters of common concern. Reform societies were created in Beirut and Basra, and the National Scientific Club opened in Baghdad. These societies met openly, with the full knowledge of the Ottoman authorities, and came under the full scrutiny of the secret police.[30]

Two of the most influential Arabist societies were established beyond the reach of Ottoman censors and police. The Young Arab Society, also known as al-Fatat (from its Arabic name, Jam'iyya al-'Arabiyya al-Fatat), was founded by a group of Syrian Muslims in Paris in 1909. Al-Fatat sought Arab equality within the framework of an Ottoman Empire reconceived as a binational Turco-Arab state, on the model of the Austro-Hungarian Habsburg Empire. As Tawfiq al-Natur, one of the founders of the party, recalled, "All that we, as Arabs, wanted was to have the same rights and obligations in the Ottoman Empire as the Turks themselves and to have the Empire composed of two great nationalities, Turk and Arab."[31]

In Cairo, a group of like-minded Syrian émigrés established the Ottoman Decentralization Party in 1912. In a direct rejection of Young Turk centralizing policies, the Cairo-based Arabists argued that the Ottoman Empire, with all its ethnic and racial diversity, could only be ruled through a federal system that conceded significant autonomy to the provinces. They took for their role model the decentralized government of Switzerland, with its autonomous cantons. Yet the Decentralization Party upheld the unity of the empire under the Ottoman sultanate and advocated the use of Turkish alongside the local language of each province.

The Unionists viewed the proliferation of Arabist societies with mounting concern. At the height of the Balkan Wars, the Young Turks were in no mood to compromise with demands for decentralization or dual-monarchies. When, in February 1913, the Beirut Reform Society published a manifesto calling for administrative decentralization, the Ottoman authorities clamped down. On 8 April 1913, police closed the offices of the Beirut Reform Society and ordered the organization to disband. The influential members of the society called for a citywide strike and organized petitions to the grand vizier protesting the closure. Several society members were arrested for agitation. Beirut entered a period of intense political crisis that lasted one week until the prisoners had been released and the strike brought to an end. But the Beirut Reform Society never reopened its doors, and its members were forced to meet in secret as Arabism went underground.

Faced with mounting Ottoman opposition, the Arabists took their cause to the international community. Members of al-Fatat in Paris decided to convene a meeting in the French capital, in order to enjoy the freedom to discuss politics without fear of Ottoman repression and to raise international support for their demands. Invitations were dispatched to Arabist societies in the Ottoman Empire, Egypt, Europe, and the Americas. Despite the best efforts of the Ottoman ambassador in France to prevent the meeting from taking place, twenty-three delegates from across the Arab provinces of the empire—eleven Muslims, eleven Christians, and one Jew—arrived in Paris to take part in the First Arab Congress, which opened before an audience of 150 observers on 18 June 1913.

Tawfiq al-Suwaydi, a native of Baghdad, was one of only two Iraqi delegates to the Arab Congress (Suwaydi's friend, the Jewish delegate Sulayman Anbar, was also from Baghdad). All of the other participants hailed from Greater Syria. Suwaydi was a recent convert to Arabist politics. "I knew I was an Arab Ottoman Muslim," he later reflected, "though I only possessed the most ill-defined sense of myself as Arab." Fluent in Turkish, Suwaydi had completed a law degree in Istanbul in 1912 before moving to Paris to continue his legal studies. While in Paris, he fell in with a group of Arabists who "profoundly influenced" his political views. Suwaydi joined al-Fatat and played a key role in organizing the Arab Congress.[32]

"The First Arab Congress," Suwaydi recalled, "turned out to be the theater for a grand quarrel among three distinct factions." The first group was the "Muslim Arab youth", who sought "to enjoy rights equal to those accorded Turkish subjects of the empire". The second faction comprised the Arab Christians, "who were full of bitter hatred for the Turks". Suwaydi dismissed the third faction as "fence sitters", men he saw as opportunists who were unable to "choose between loyalty to the Turks and loyalty to the Arabs" and would ultimately side with whatever party best advanced their material interests.

In six days of sessions, the congress agreed on ten resolutions framing the delegates' reform agenda. They demanded Arab political rights and the active participation of Arabs in the administration of the Ottoman Empire through decentralization. They demanded that Arabic be recognized as an official language of the empire and that Arab deputies be allowed to address parliament in their native tongue. They sought to restrict military service to the recruits' home provinces "except in very exceptional circumstances". The congress also passed a resolution expressing delegates' "sympathy with the demands of the Ottoman Armenians that are based on decentralization", a measure bound to raise concerns in Istanbul. The delegates resolved to share their decisions with both the Porte and governments friendly to the Ottoman Empire. The congress drew to a close on the night of 23 June.

The congress could not have chosen a more difficult moment to open negotiations with the Young Turks. The Ottomans had signed the Treaty of London (30 May) marking the end of the First Balkan War, with the loss of Albania, Macedonia, and Thrace, and Grand Vizier Mahmud Şevket Pasha had been assassinated on 11 June. The Unionists were in the midst of purging their Liberal opponents from government as the congress adjourned in Paris and were assuming power for the first time. Yet the meeting in Paris posed too great a threat to be ignored. If the Ottomans failed to respond, the Arabists would almost certainly turn to the European powers for support, and France had made no secret of its interests in Syria and Lebanon.

The Young Turks dispatched their secretary general, Midhat Şükrü, in a damage-control exercise to engage congress delegates in negotiations towards an agreed reform agenda. Tawfiq al-Suwaydi was suspicious of the Midhat

Şükrü mission, which he claimed met with the fence sitters with "the express purpose of contacting said participants and drawing them over to the side of the Ottoman government". Yet the Ottoman mediators managed to conclude a reform agreement that went some way towards addressing the resolutions of the Arab Congress. The Paris Agreement offered to expand Arab participation in all levels of Ottoman government and to extend the use of the Arabic language and confirmed that soldiers would serve "in nearby countries".[33]

The Porte invited delegates of the Arab Congress to Istanbul to celebrate the Paris Agreement. The three delegates who accepted the invitation were given a warm reception in the imperial capital, where they met with the Crown Prince, Sultan Mehmed Reşad, Grand Vizier Said Halim Pasha, and the ruling triumvirate of Enver, Talat, and Cemal. They were treated to lavish dinners and exchanged warm words of Turkish-Arab brotherhood with men at the highest level of the Ottoman government.

Formal dinners and gracious speeches could not mask the fact that the Ottoman government was doing nothing to implement the reform agenda for the Arab lands. As Tawfiq al-Suwaydi concluded, "Those familiar with the internal state of affairs in the Ottoman Empire were of the belief that these phenomena were nothing more than stalling maneuvers and, when the time was right, a means of bearing down on those who had organized the Arab Congress." The delegates returned to Beirut empty-handed in September 1913. Arabist ambitions, raised by a flurry of activity, were ultimately disappointed. And, as Suwaydi suggested with the benefit of hindsight, the organizers of the Arab Congress were marked men. Within three years of the Arab Congress, several of their number met their deaths at the gallows for their Arabist politics.[34]

IN THE COURSE OF FIVE YEARS, THE OTTOMAN EMPIRE HAD ENDURED a revolution, three major wars against foreign powers, and a number of internal disorders ranging from sectarian massacres to separatist revolts—each of which threatened further foreign intervention. It is hard to overstate the magnitude of Ottoman losses during that period. The empire had surrendered the last of its possessions in North Africa and in the Balkans, together with millions of its subjects, to European rule. The resulting state of emergency drove Ottoman reformers to abandon their liberalism in a desperate bid to preserve the empire from total collapse. The constitutional movement of 1908 that challenged the sultan's absolutism evolved through successive crises into a yet more autocratic government by the end of 1913, led by three idealistic Unionists: Enver, Talat, and Cemal.

The liberation of Edirne had given the Ottoman Empire new hope for a better future. The Ottoman army had proven its ability to regain lost land. "Now we have an army to which one can entrust the interest of the country with confidence," Enver exulted, "and which is one thousand times more capable of fulfilling its duty than at the start of this depressing war, in spite of all the losses we have suffered." Much though the territorial losses in North Africa and the Balkans were to be lamented, the Ottoman Empire had emerged as a contiguous territorial mass spanning the Turkish and Arab provinces. The coherence and logic of such an Asian Muslim empire might better withstand internal and external challenges than had the old Ottoman Empire.[35]

The Unionists had hopes for a better future but saw threats both within and outside Ottoman frontiers. They were concerned that the Arabs might succumb to their own nationalist movement and saw Armenian ambitions as an existential threat to the Ottoman Empire. The provinces in eastern Anatolia that had been the focus of Armenian reform demands, endorsed by the European powers, represented the vital heartland of the Turkish provinces. The interaction between the Armenian communities across the Russo-Turkish frontier exacerbated the danger of Armenian separatism to the Ottoman Empire.

The Young Turks saw Russia as the single greatest threat to Ottoman survival. With its territorial ambitions in eastern Anatolia, the straits, and the Ottoman capital itself, Russia openly sought the demise of the Ottoman Empire. Great Power ambitions could only be contained by the Ottomans in partnership with a friendly European power. The Ottoman Empire entered the fateful year of 1914 in search of such a defensive alliance. That search would ultimately draw the Ottomans into the Great War.

The Peace Before the Great War

SPRING BROUGHT A NEW WAVE OF OPTIMISM TO THE OTTOMAN EMPIRE in 1914. Victory in the Second Balkan War and the recovery of Edirne and Eastern Thrace had done wonders for national confidence. After years of wartime austerity, the Ottoman economy was the first beneficiary of peace. Demobilized soldiers returned to the workforce. Farmers predicted record harvests. A building boom was reported in towns across the Turkish and Arab provinces. Trade resumed with renewed vigour once the sea lanes were cleared of warships and mines. With the expansion of foreign trade came novel inventions of the modern age that, within the year, would be converted from civilian to military use.

The advent of the automobile shattered the tranquillity of Istanbul's streets. Until 1908, cars had been banned from the Ottoman Empire. When they were finally permitted after the Young Turk Revolution, the pioneers of Ottoman motoring encountered many obstacles. By and large, the streets of the empire were unpaved. Garages to service and fuel cars were few and far between. And there was no highway code, with chauffeurs disagreeing over such basic issues as the side of the road on which they should drive. Not surprisingly, very few cars had been sold in the Ottoman Empire since 1908. By the end of 1913, when there were already 1 million cars on the road in the United States, American consular officials estimated there were no more than 500 automobiles in the Ottoman Empire as a whole—with 250 of those in Istanbul. In a remote provincial town like Baghdad, you could literally count the number of cars on one hand. Yet by mid-1914, the imperial capital was beginning to experience its first traffic jams as "limousines, touring cars, motor trucks, gasoline driven delivery wagons and hospital ambulances" jostled for space.[1]

The airplane also made its first appearance in the Ottoman Empire in the Young Turk era. Aviation was still in its infancy: the Wright brothers had only made their first successful flight in a mechanized, heavier-than-air craft in December 1903. Six years later, aviation pioneer Louis Blériot came to Istanbul to demonstrate the marvels of flight. Blériot had recently achieved fame by flying a monoplane across the English Channel on 25 July 1909, and his visit to Istanbul was keenly anticipated. In the event, strong winds drove Blériot's airplane into the roof of an Istanbul house, and the pilot spent the next three weeks in a local hospital, recovering from his injuries.[2]

The first Turkish pilots were sent to Europe for training in 1911. By 1914, Turkish aviators were beginning to claim the skies above the Ottoman Empire. In February, Lieutenant Fethi Bey, accompanied by one of Enver Pasha's aides, Sadik Bey, attempted to fly from Istanbul across Anatolia and Syria to Egypt. Their plane, a Blériot design named the *Muavenet-i Milliye* (*National Assistance*) covered one twenty-five-mile leg, from Tarsus to Adana, in twenty minutes, at a speed in excess of sixty miles per hour. Crowds on the ground clapped as the plane flew overhead. They managed to reach Damascus safely, but their plane experienced engine problems on the flight to Jerusalem and crashed to the east of the Sea of Galilee, killing both pilots. Fethi Bey and Sadik Bey were laid to rest next to Saladin's tomb in the Umayyad Mosque of Damascus, Turkey's first airmen to die in military service. A second air mission ended in a similar result before two pilots, Salim Bey and Kemal Bey, finally managed to complete the journey from Istanbul to Egypt in May 1914.[3]

In June 1914, American aviator John Cooper demonstrated the Curtiss Flying Boat to an audience of thousands in Istanbul. Taking off from the Sea of Marmara, he flew fifteen miles at an average altitude of 1,000 feet before landing in the waters of the Bosporus between the European and Asian quarters of Istanbul. Members of the government, parliament, and imperial household witnessed the demonstration. Cooper then flew seven flights with key dignitaries in the passenger seat "amid the applause and wonder of the spectators, to most of whom this sort of aviation was an entire novelty", an eyewitness recounted. All the major Istanbul papers carried the story, with photographs, the following day.[4]

The spread of mechanized transport fed the sense of optimism growing in the Ottoman Empire in the spring of 1914. With the negotiation of a $100 million public loan from France in May, the Ottoman government secured the means to invest in major public works projects that would bring electricity, public lighting, urban tramways, intercity railroads, and modern port facilities to all of the provinces of the empire. The announcement of the French loan fed widespread expectations of a commercial and industrial boom.

The French loan was the culmination of peace negotiations brokered by the European powers to resolve the outstanding differences between the Ottoman Empire and its neighbours in the aftermath of the Balkan Wars. The injection of French investment capital promised real economic growth and served as a powerful incentive for the Ottomans to accept their losses in Albania, Macedonia, and Thrace. Yet even after the peace agreements had been signed and the French loan concluded, significant issues remained outstanding between Istanbul and Athens.

The terms of the 1913 Treaty of London concluding the First Balkan War left Greece in possession of three Aegean islands seized from Turkey. Chios and Mytilene, dominating the entry to Smyrna (modern Izmir), were within sight of the Turkish mainland. Lemnos, with its deep-water Moudros Harbour, was less than fifty miles from the straits of the Dardanelles. The Porte never accepted the loss of these islands and was unwilling to live with Greece dominating its coastal waters. While Ottoman diplomats sought European support for their government's claims for the restoration of the Aegean islands, Ottoman war planners worked to shift the balance of naval power in the eastern Mediterranean.

The Ottoman government commissioned two state-of-the-art dreadnoughts from the British shipbuilders Vickers and Armstrong in August 1911, scheduled for delivery in July 1914. The orders were placed as part of a British naval mission to help modernize the Ottoman fleet. The *Sultan Osman* and the *Reşadiye*, named for the eponymous founder of the Ottoman Empire and the reigning sultan Mehmed Reşad, were a tremendous drain on the Ottoman treasury. Appealing to Ottoman patriotism, the government funded the ships in large part through public subscription. Turkish schoolchildren were encouraged to contribute their pocket money, and fund-raising stands were erected in city squares where, for contributions of five piasters or more, loyal citizens were invited to hammer nails into massive wood blocks. While the ships became a focus of Ottoman pride, redressing the empire's naval forces after the defeats in Libya and the First Balkan War, Greece and Russia watched with mounting concern as the dreadnoughts neared completion in the spring of 1914. The massive battleships would give the Turkish navy an overwhelming advantage over the Russian Black Sea fleet and the Greek navy in the Aegean.

The Aegean islands dispute and the impending delivery of the dreadnoughts raised the prospect of war between Greece and Turkey in 1914. Officials in Greece called for a pre-emptive strike to defeat the Ottomans before they took possession of the new naval vessels. The Ottomans prepared once again to conscript their citizens for war, sending notices in April 1914 to village headmen across the empire to warn of a possible mobilization and appealing to their loyalty to Islam in a way that fed rumours of war with Christian Greece.[5]

The prospect of renewed war between Greece and Turkey sounded alarm bells in St Petersburg. The Russians, though no less concerned about the naval balance of power than the Greeks, were more immediately preoccupied with keeping Ottoman waters open for Russian Black Sea shipping: 50 percent of Russia's exports, including 90 percent of its grain exports, passed through the Turkish straits. Renewed war in the Aegean would result in an Ottoman closure of the straits and the bottling of Russian trade, with catastrophic consequences for the Russian economy. Russia thus exercised its diplomacy to keep Greece from going to war with Turkey, while putting pressure on Britain to delay delivery of the ships to the Ottoman navy.[6]

RUSSIAN DIPLOMACY ENTAILED ULTERIOR MOTIVES. CONVINCED THAT the demise of the Ottoman Empire was imminent, the tsar and his government wished to stake a claim to those territories of key strategic value to Russia in any future partition of Ottoman lands by the European powers. Russia's top priorities included reclaiming Constantinople for Orthodox Christianity after nearly five centuries under Turkish Muslim rule and controlling the straits linking Russia's Black Sea ports to the Mediterranean. St Petersburg was thus determined to prevent any war that might result in Ottoman territory coveted by Russia from passing into Greek or Bulgarian hands. The Russian Council of Ministers met in February 1914 to consider the occupation of Constantinople and the straits and concurred that the best opportunity would arise in the context of a general European war. Tsar Nicholas II approved his cabinet's recommendations in April 1914 and committed his government to creating the necessary forces to occupy Istanbul and the straits at the earliest possible opportunity.[7]

While planning to annex the Ottoman capital, the Russians were also looking to consolidate their position in Ottoman territory in eastern Anatolia. The eastern borderlands of the Ottoman Empire shared frontiers with Russia's volatile Caucasus provinces and gave access to north-western Iran, a zone of rivalry between Russia and Great Britain. Eastern Anatolia also corresponded to the six provinces that the European powers had identified as the territory inhabited by the Armenians: Erzurum, Van, Bitlis, Harput, Diyarbakır, and Sivas. Perhaps 1.25 million Armenians lived on the Russian side of the border, and as many as 1 million Armenians resided in the six Ottoman provinces of eastern Anatolia recognized by the international community as Turkish Armenia. The tsar's government had used the defence of indigenous Armenian rights as a pretext to intervene in Ottoman affairs since 1878. Because of Russia's ambitions in Ottoman territory, its efforts exacerbated tensions between the Ottomans and the Armenians.[8]

Real tensions had re-emerged between Armenians and Kurds in the years following the Young Turk Revolution. Some of the Armenians who fled the violence of the 1890s attempted to reclaim their homes and villages after the 1908 revolution. Some Kurdish tribesmen who had occupied properties abandoned by the Armenians refused to recognize the claims of prior owners. Already in 1909, land disputes between Armenians and Kurds had led to violence, and the Kurds enjoyed the upper hand. The nomadic Kurds were much better armed than the sedentary Armenians, and Ottoman officials seldom took the side of the Christian Armenians over the Muslim Kurds. The situation was aggravated when Ottoman troops were redeployed from eastern Anatolia to fight in the Libyan and Balkan wars and when Armenian conscripts were sent to the Balkan front in 1912. Armenian farmers were left to their own defences in an increasingly tense conflict with the Kurds.[9]

Russia stepped into the power vacuum in June 1913, with reform proposals for greater Armenian autonomy in eastern Anatolia. Drawing on Sultan Abdülhamid II's 1895 reform edict for the Armenians, the Russian plan called for the six eastern provinces of the Ottoman Empire to be consolidated into two semi-autonomous provinces administered by foreign governors-general nominated by the Great Powers. The proposal also called for provincial councils composed of an equal number of Muslim and Armenian deputies. European and Ottoman diplomats alike viewed the proposals with grave misgivings as a prelude to partition in Anatolia, with Russia staking a claim to the eastern provinces. St Petersburg reinforced its diplomacy by proposing a troop mobilization not just along the Russo-Turkish frontier but also inside Ottoman territory in the city of Erzurum itself—ostensibly to defend the Armenians. To forestall militarizing the situation, the Porte agreed to a revised reform proposal with the Russian government, which was signed on 8 February 1914.

The Armenian reform proposal only deferred conflict with Russia and exacerbated the Young Turks' problems with the Armenians. The Ottoman government viewed the reform plan as a prelude to Armenian statehood and an existential threat. The Young Turks were determined to prevent the implementation of the reform plan at all costs. Talat Pasha, the minister of interior and one of the ruling triumvirs, began to plan extraordinary measures to remove the Armenians from the six provinces and thus obviate the need for such reforms.[10]

Negotiations between the Young Turk government and the Russians revealed just how isolated the Ottoman Empire had become in the international arena. The Porte was all too aware of the danger Russia posed to the territorial integrity of the empire. While normally the Ottomans could rely on Britain or France to hold Russia's ambitions in check, those three powers were now allies in the Triple Entente. Neither Britain nor France could be counted on to side with the Ottoman Empire. In dangerous times, the Ottomans needed a strong friend. The leading candidate was Germany.

GERMAN-OTTOMAN FRIENDSHIP RAN RELATIVELY DEEP. IN 1898, Kaiser Wilhelm II made a state visit to the Ottoman Empire. Starting in Istanbul, he travelled across the Turkish and Arab provinces, visiting key cities and historic sites. In Damascus, the kaiser famously pledged Germany's perpetual friendship to the Ottomans in particular and to the Muslims of the world in general: "May the Sultan and his 300 million Muslim subjects scattered across the earth, who venerate him as their Caliph, be assured that the German Kaiser will be their friend for all time."[11]

Wilhelm's declaration of amity was not entirely disinterested. In his rivalry with the older, more established British Empire, the kaiser saw opportunities for Germany to extend its influence in partnership with the Ottoman Empire. Wilhelm believed friendship with the Ottoman sultan, who was also recognized as caliph, or successor to the Prophet Muhammad as leader of the global Muslim community, would make Muslims around the world more sympathetic to Germany than to any other European power. With over 100 million Muslims under British rule in India, the Persian Gulf, and Egypt, Germany saw the potential to deploy Islam as a weapon against the British, should the need arise.

Turkey also held a geostrategic position of importance for Germany. At the time of the kaiser's visit, Britain and Russia were locked in an intense rivalry for predominance over Central Asia that came to be known as the "Great Game". The Turkish provinces of eastern Anatolia were a gateway to both Persia and Central Asia. Germany could become a player in the Great Game and put pressure on both Britain and Russia through an alliance with the Ottomans.

The southern frontiers of the Ottoman Empire reached the Persian Gulf. Here Germany hoped to encroach on a jealously guarded British lake. In the course of the nineteenth century, the British had managed to check the Ottomans and European powers alike through a system of exclusive treaties binding the Arab rulers in the Trucial States (today, the United Arab Emirates), Oman, Qatar, Bahrain, and Kuwait to the British Crown. Following the kaiser's 1898 visit to the Ottoman Empire, Germany sought to exploit its new partnership with the Turks to challenge Britain's monopoly over the Persian Gulf by means of a railway linking Berlin to Baghdad.

Following the kaiser's visit, Germany secured a concession in December 1899 to build a railway across Turkey to Basra on the Persian Gulf via Baghdad. Construction on the line began in 1903; by 1914, it linked Istanbul to Ankara and the Mediterranean coast near Adana. The railway had run into unexpected difficulties in two mountain chains in Cilicia, however, and fallen well behind schedule. While most of the line in Anatolia was complete, great lengths of the railway remained under construction in Syria and Iraq.[12]

The first train pulled out of the station in Baghdad with little fanfare on 1 June 1914. The line ran northward for 38.5 miles to an empty spot in the desert named Sumaykha. Undeterred by the lack of public interest in the train to nowhere, the railway company printed timetables and distributed them to government offices, foreign consulates, clubs, and hotels.

Work continued apace, and in October 1914 the line reached the town of Samarra. The northbound train departed Baghdad once each week at 10 a.m. and covered the seventy-four-mile distance in four hours, at an average speed of just under twenty miles per hour. The return train departed Samarra for Baghdad each Thursday morning at 10 a.m. The dream of a direct link between Baghdad and Berlin remained remote; yet the project served to bind Germany and the Ottoman Empire closer during a turbulent time in European affairs.[13]

Deepening ties between Berlin and Istanbul provoked a crisis in European affairs with the appointment of a German military mission to the Ottoman Empire at the end of 1913. Grand Vizier Said Halim Pasha asked Kaiser Wilhelm II to nominate an experienced general to lead a team of mid-ranking German officers to assist in the reform and reorganization of the Ottoman army in the wake of the Balkan Wars. The kaiser nominated the Prussian Otto Liman von Sanders for the job. Liman was at the time commander of the 22nd Division of the German army, based in Kassel. He had served for years on the general staff and had travelled widely but had no prior experience in the Ottoman Empire. Liman accepted the commission without hesitation and set off by train for Istanbul in mid-December 1913.

Shortly after his arrival, Liman met with Sultan Mehmed Reşad, the grand vizier, and the leading triumvirate of Young Turks. The German general was impressed by Interior Minister Talat's "charm" and "attractive personality" and remarked that Cemal Pasha, commander of the First Army Corps, "combined great intelligence with a very determined attitude". However, he fell out with Enver Pasha almost immediately. No doubt Enver, celebrated months earlier as the "liberator of Edirne", resented having a German officer hold the Turkish army to account. While Liman was very critical of the deplorable state in which he found the Ottoman army, with its ragged uniforms, pestilential barracks, and underfed and unpaid soldiers, he did not see these as Enver's failings. Rather, the German general believed Enver had been promoted beyond his experience and ability. The issue came to the fore in January 1914, when the Committee of Union and Progress named Enver minister of war. The astonished Sultan Mehmed Reşad seemed to speak for Liman when he read of the appointment in the newspaper: "It is stated here that Enver has become Minister of War; that is unthinkable, he is much too young."[14]

The Russian government had opposed the appointment of the German military mission from the outset. St Petersburg's opposition developed into a crisis when Cemal Pasha handed over to Liman command of the Ottoman First Army Corps, with responsibility for the security of Istanbul and the straits. For the Russians, this was tantamount to Germany seizing control of territory in which St Petersburg had a vested interest. The tsar's government threatened to occupy the eastern Anatolian city of Erzurum to redress such a change in the balance of power.

Britain and France were determined to prevent Russian retaliatory measures that would almost certainly lead to a premature partition of the Ottoman Empire. Yet the British were in a difficult position. After all, since 1912 a British admiral, Arthur Limpus, had led a seventy-two-man naval mission to the Ottoman Empire and served as commander in chief of the Ottoman navy. Rather than seek the disbanding of the German military mission, British diplomats suggested Liman might take control of the Second Army Corps and so relinquish control of the army in Istanbul and the straits. Liman, unwilling to compromise his commission due to political pressure, rejected all efforts to transfer his command to a different army corps. In the end, the kaiser came up with a solution by promoting Liman to a rank too high for command of an army corps. Liman became a field marshal, and command of the First Army Corps passed to an Ottoman officer. Germany and the Ottoman Empire had weathered the crisis together, strengthening the bonds between the two states.[15]

BY THE SUMMER OF 1914, THE OTTOMAN EMPIRE WAS SWINGING manically between the optimism of its economic boom and the crises in its foreign relations. The contradiction was resolved, catastrophically, with the assassination of the Austrian crown prince, Archduke Franz Ferdinand, in the Bosnian city of Sarajevo on 28 June 1914. The assassination activated the web of open and secret alliances that divided Europe into two belligerent blocks. The fact that the Ottoman Empire lay outside that treacherous network of alliances was of no comfort to the Porte. The looming prospect of a European general war raised the imminent threat of a Russian annexation of Istanbul, the straits, and eastern Anatolia—and the ultimate dismemberment of the Ottoman Empire among the Entente Powers. France was known to covet Syria, Britain had interests in Mesopotamia, and Greece wished to expand its grip over the Aegean. The Ottomans alone had no chance of defending their territory against so many enemies.

Weary of war and in need of time to rebuild its military and economy, the Ottoman leadership had no wish to enter a general European conflict. Rather, it sought an ally to protect the empire's vulnerable territory from the consequences of such a war. The Ottomans' turn to Germany was not a foregone conclusion. A fascinating aspect of Ottoman diplomacy during the July Crisis was the Porte's openness to concluding a defensive alliance with virtually any European power.

The three Young Turk leaders had different views on potential allies. Enver and Talat were known to lean towards an alliance with Germany, while Cemal believed that only an Entente Power could exercise restraint over Russian ambitions in Ottoman territory. He was himself a Francophile, and there were good reasons to look to the French for a defensive alliance. France was the Ottomans' chief financial creditor since the conclusion of the $100 million public loan in May 1914. Should France demur, Cemal saw Britain as a good alternative. For most of the nineteenth century, Britain had been the staunchest proponent of preserving the territorial integrity of the Ottoman Empire. More recently, Britain had assisted with the restructuring of the Ottoman navy, through the Limpus naval mission and the construction of new ships of the line for the Ottoman fleet. Since becoming minister of marine, Cemal had worked closely with the British naval mission and respected its professionalism. It was thus natural that Cemal would look to either Britain or France to secure the assurances his government needed for the protection of the territorial integrity of the empire.

In early July 1914, shortly after the assassination in Sarajevo, Cemal visited France on the government's invitation to attend French naval manoeuvres. He took advantage of his visit to Europe to meet with the Ottoman officers liaising with the British shipbuilders, who were putting the finishing touches to the new Ottoman dreadnoughts. The officers reported to Cemal that "the English were in a very peculiar frame of mind. They seemed to be always searching for some new excuse for delaying the completion and delivery of the warships." Cemal instructed his officers to return and take delivery of the ships as soon as possible, leaving any final fittings for the Ottoman shipyards in Istanbul to complete.[16]

After attending the French fleet review in Toulon, Cemal Pasha returned to Paris to call on the French Foreign Ministry. In his discussions with the director of political affairs, Cemal came straight to the point: "You must take us into your Entente and at the same time protect us against the terrible perils threatening us from Russia." In return, Cemal promised Turkey would be a faithful ally in helping France and Britain "forge an iron ring around the Central Powers". The French diplomat responded cautiously that his government could only enter into an alliance with the Ottomans with their allies' approval, which seemed "very doubtful". Cemal recognized the response for a refusal. "I understood perfectly that France was convinced that it was quite impossible for us to escape the iron claws of Russia, and that under no circumstances would she vouchsafe us her help." On 18 July, Cemal left Paris to return to Istanbul empty-handed.

On 28 July 1914, one month after the assassination in Sarajevo, the Habsburg Empire declared war on Serbia. What began as a Balkan conflict quickly dragged Europe's greatest military powers into total war. Russia, bound by an alliance to Serbia, responded by threatening war with Austria-Hungary. Germany stood by its partner Austria, and Russia's allies Britain and France entered the fray. By 4 August, the Triple Entente was at war with Germany and Austria.[17]

The outbreak of war in Europe provoked alarm across the Ottoman Empire—from the cabinet offices of the Sublime Porte through the towns and countryside of Anatolia and the Arab lands. The need for a defensive alliance to assure the territorial integrity of the empire became critical. The Young Turks knew from Cemal's reports that there was no prospect of such an agreement with France. His trust in Britain was likewise soon to be betrayed.

On 1 August, three days before declaring war on Germany, the British government requisitioned the two dreadnoughts commissioned by the Ottomans. The news stunned Cemal Pasha, who, as minister of marine, had viewed the new ships as the cornerstone of Ottoman naval reform. He recalled his discussions with the Ottoman naval officers in Paris and realized that the repeated British delays "had been nothing but pretexts which . . . revealed the design England had long cherished of making these ships her own". Given that the ships had been paid for in full, to a great extent through public contributions, the British decision to requisition the ships was treated as a national humiliation in Turkey and ruled out the possibility of any accord between Britain and the Ottoman Empire. The very next day, 2 August 1914, the Ottomans concluded a secret treaty of alliance with Germany.[18]

The Austrians first proposed drawing the Ottoman Empire into the Triple Alliance in mid-July 1914. Vienna hoped to isolate Serbia and to neutralize Bulgaria by concluding an agreement with Istanbul. The Germans at first rejected the idea. Both the German ambassador to Istanbul, Baron Hans von Wangenheim, and General Liman von Sanders, the head of the German military mission, believed the Ottomans would prove more of a liability than an ally in both diplomatic and military terms. Turkey, Wangenheim wrote to Berlin on 18 July, "is today without any question still worthless as an ally. She would only be a burden to her associates, without being able to offer them the slightest advantage."[19]

Enver, Talat, and Grand Vizier Said Halim Pasha argued the case for a German-Ottoman alliance with Wangenheim through the latter part of July. They warned that the Ottomans would be forced to seek the support of the Entente Powers through an alliance with Greece if Germany would not come to terms with them. When Wangenheim reported back to Berlin, Kaiser Wilhelm II came down in favour of concluding an agreement with the Ottoman Empire. After two decades of cultivating German-Ottoman friendship, the kaiser was appalled at the idea of driving the Turks into the arms of the Russians and the French. On 24 July, Wilhelm instructed his ambassador in Istanbul to comply with the Ottoman request immediately. "A refusal or a snub would amount to her going over to Russo-Gallia," the kaiser exclaimed, "and our influence would be gone once and for all!"[20]

By 27 July, the Germans and Ottomans had worked out the terms of a secret defensive alliance against Russia. The eight articles of the strikingly simple document would come into effect only in the event of Russian hostilities against either side—which, with the German declaration of war on Russia on 1 August, was a near certainty at the time of signing. Crucially, Germany pledged to protect the territorial integrity of the Ottoman Empire against Russian ambitions. The treaty placed the German military mission under the authority of the Ottoman government in return for assurances that the mission would have "an effective influence over the general conduct of the army". The alliance was to last until the end of 1918, with scope for renewal by agreement of both sides. The one condition that Germany did not commit to paper was that, on entering the war, the Ottomans would open military operations immediately against either Russia or the British in Egypt in a bid to rouse Muslim subjects in their empires to rise up against the Entente Powers.[21]

On the eve of signing the pact with Germany, Enver Pasha, as minister of war, called for a general mobilization. All men between the ages of twenty and forty-five were required to register for the draft, and all reservists were told to report to their units. The mobilization hit the Ottoman public like a bombshell, though it demonstrated to their German allies that the Young Turks intended to uphold their commitments. Yet the Ottomans, who had been so impatient to conclude a defensive alliance, were in no hurry to enter a world war.

A SPECTACULAR CRASH IN AUGUST FOLLOWED THE ECONOMIC BOOM of the first half of 1914. With young men called up for military service, there would be no labourers to tend the fields or work in the factories. Trade prospects, once so promising, collapsed in the certain knowledge that all Ottoman ports would be closed to shipping by the hostilities. Army quarter-masters began to requisition food, livestock, and materiel to provide for the needs of the army under full mobilization. Turkish families began to plan for the worst. After three wars in quick succession, they knew how badly further conflict would upset their lives.

Irfan Orga, a native of Istanbul, was only six years old in 1914. The war shattered the prosperity he had known all his young life. Some of his earliest memories were of heated family discussions after the outbreak of war in Europe. He remembered sneaking out of bed one evening that summer to eavesdrop on the adults. "It was very still and I could hear every word of the conversation. My father appeared to be attempting to persuade my grandmother to sell our house!" "Nonsense!" his grandmother retorted. "Why should a war in Europe make any difference in our lives?"

Orga's father astonished his family by declaring his intention to sell not just the family home but their carpet-exporting business as well. "It is necessary to sell it, if we are to survive at all," he explained. "There are so many difficulties, labour, export, bad representation abroad; now the war in Europe writes finis to all my hopes of markets there. If Turkey comes in—and in my opinion she will—I shall have to go." His father, only twenty-six years old, knew he would face conscription in the event of war. "It is better to get rid of it now, and if one day I come back—well, with our name it is easy to build the business again." A stunned silence fell over the family.

"These conversations were the first hint of the changes that were to come," Orga reflected. In due course both the family home and business were sold to provide the food and capital Orga's father believed they would need to see them through what threatened to be a long and devastating war for Turkey. Even these precautions proved insufficient to protect the Orga family from the extreme poverty caused by the conflict.[22]

Trade to the Ottoman Empire ground to a halt on 3 August, when the government closed the straits. The harbour master informed all foreign governments that the Ottoman navy had laid mines at the entrance to both the Bosporus from the Black Sea and the Dardanelles from the Mediterranean, as well as extinguished all navigational lights and removed signal buoys. Between 4 August and 26 September, the Ottomans operated a tug service to convey vessels safely through the minefields. On 27 September, the tug service was discontinued, and the straits were definitively closed to commercial shipping. The effect on Ottoman trade was immediate and catastrophic, although the Russians felt the pain too. The severing of maritime access from the Black Sea to international markets left hundreds of their ships filled with grain and other supplies trapped in the Black Sea.[23]

The German navy was the first to seek entry into the restricted straits. Shortly after declaring war on France, the German Mediterranean squadron set off for the coast of North Africa to disrupt the transport of troops from Algeria to France. The *Goeben*, a heavy battleship, and the light cruiser *Breslau* bombarded the coastal cities of Bône (modern Annaba) and Philippeville (modern Skikda) on 4 August. The raid inflicted casualties and provoked panic along the coastline of North Africa. The British, who had declared war on Germany that same day, ordered their Mediterranean fleet to sink the German ships and were joined by the aggrieved French fleet in hot pursuit of the *Goeben* and *Breslau* as they set off towards the eastern Mediterranean.

The German admiralty had already given orders to the commander of the naval squadron, Rear Admiral Wilhelm Souchon (whose French surname revealed his Huguenot ancestry), to make for Turkish waters. In a meeting with Germany's ambassador and the head of the military mission, Liman von Sanders, in Istanbul on 1 August, Enver Pasha specifically requested the dispatch of German warships to Ottoman waters before concluding the defensive alliance with Germany. This would compensate for the loss of the dreadnoughts requisitioned by Britain earlier that day and tip the naval balance of power with Russia in the Black Sea. Ambassador Wangenheim secured Berlin's consent in the expectation that the German ships would be used to draw Turkey into the war and open a new front with Russia.

The Germans had clear interests in sending their ships into Turkish waters. They knew their vessels were outgunned by the British and the French, and the *Goeben* had boiler trouble. If left in open waters, the German ships faced certain destruction. Moreover, Chancellor Theobold von Bethman Hollweg asserted that the presence of German warships in Turkish waters would "render Ottoman neutrality untenable". The inevitable crisis would force the Porte back onto its secret alliance with Germany, which would demand immediate Ottoman action against either Russia in the east or against Britain in Egypt. Either way, the German ships would be in Ottoman waters to open new fronts against the Entente, shifting the balance of power in Germany's favour.[24]

The Ottomans turned the German naval crisis to advantage. Though Enver had requested the dispatch of the German ships in the first place, he did so without his government's authority, and the Porte initially refused the approaching warships haven. In a predawn meeting with Ambassador Wangenheim on 6 August, Prime Minister Said Halim relented, laying out his government's conditions for allowing the *Goeben* and *Breslau* to enter the straits. Said Halim insisted that the German ships could do nothing to jeopardize Ottoman neutrality in the rapidly expanding European conflict. He then went on to present six demands of Germany that represent the earliest statement of Ottoman aims for the First World War.

Said Halim first demanded that Germany assist the Ottomans in the abolition of the capitulations—a series of ancient bilateral treaties that conferred trade privileges and extraterritorial legal rights to Europeans living and working in Ottoman domains. The Ottomans had conferred the capitulations at the height of their power on the then weaker European states to facilitate trade relations. The earliest capitulations were awarded to Italian city-states in the fourteenth century, and the system was extended to Britain and France in the sixteenth century. By the twentieth century, when the Ottoman Empire was far weaker than its European neighbours, the capitulations had evolved into unequal treaties that compromised Ottoman sovereignty in important ways. The Ottomans hoped to take advantage of a major European war to be rid of them and wanted German support in a unilateral action that they knew would provoke outrage in the courts of Europe.

Two of Said Halim's conditions addressed recent Ottoman losses in the Balkan Wars. The Ottomans were determined to secure agreements with Romania and Bulgaria before entering hostilities against the Triple Entente to ensure that its Balkan neighbours would not threaten Turkish Thrace or Istanbul. The grand vizier sought German assistance both in concluding the "indispensable understandings with Romania and Bulgaria" and in negotiating "a fair agreement with Bulgaria" for an equitable division of "possible spoils of war". Second, should Greece enter the war on the side of the Entente Powers and be defeated, Germany would assure the return of the three Aegean islands of Chios, Mytilene, and Lemnos to Turkish sovereignty.

The Ottoman government also sought territorial gains at Russia's expense. In the event of a victory over the Entente, the Porte wanted Germany to "secure for Turkey a small correction of her eastern border" that would "place Turkey into direct contact with the Moslems of Russia". The Ottomans wanted back the three provinces ceded to Russia in 1878. They also wanted Germany to withhold any peace agreement with the defeated European powers until any Ottoman territory occupied in the course of the war had been evacuated by foreign troops and returned to Ottoman sovereignty—basically, a restatement of the territorial guarantees central to the German-Turkish treaty of alliance. Finally, Said Halim asked the German ambassador to ensure that Turkey would receive "an appropriate war indemnity" for its efforts.[25]

The German ambassador had little choice but to concede to the grand vizier's demands on the spot. It was the middle of the night, the German ships were fast approaching, and most of the conditions only applied in the event of Ottoman assistance to a German victory. Yet in conceding to Ottoman demands, Wangenheim set a precedent of the weaker Ottoman partner forcing important concessions from its German ally that would continue until the end of the war.

On the afternoon of 10 August, the German ships appeared off the Turkish coast. Enver Pasha sent a telegram to the commander of the Ottoman forts at the Dardanelles, ordering him to allow the *Breslau* and *Goeben* to enter the strait. The next morning, a Turkish torpedo boat was dispatched to guide the ships safely through the recently mined waters to a secure anchorage inside the Dardanelles. No sooner had the German ships entered the Dardanelles than the British and French ambassadors called on the grand vizier to protest against the decision to allow the German ships into Ottoman territorial waters as an infringement of Ottoman neutrality.

That evening, 11 August, the Young Turk triumvirate met at the grand vizier's house for dinner. Only Enver knew of the dramatic events that had just unfolded in the Dardanelles. "Unto us a son is born!" he exclaimed with a peculiar smile, to the general confusion of his colleagues. Enver, in many ways the most outspoken advocate of an alliance with Germany, greeted the arrival of the German ships with the same delight he would show the birth of a son. As he briefed his colleagues on the arrival of the *Breslau* and *Goeben*, he set out the political problems the empire now confronted. According to the laws of war, the Ottoman government had two options to preserve its neutrality: it could demand the German ships leave Ottoman waters within twenty-four hours, or it could disarm and intern the German ships in an Ottoman port.[26]

There was no question of the Ottomans expelling their German ally's ships from Turkish waters to face certain destruction by the British and French fleets waiting offshore. When the grand vizier and his ministers subsequently broached the subject of disarming the ships with the German ambassador, Wangenheim refused outright. The Ottomans then proposed as a compromise solution that the Germans transfer the ships to Turkish ownership through a fictive sale. Before the ambassador could secure Berlin's approval, Cemal Pasha issued an official communiqué to the press on 11 August, announcing the "purchase" of the *Goeben* and *Breslau* by the Ottoman government for 80 million marks—a figure Cemal seemed to have plucked from the air. The German ships would thus replace the dreadnoughts *Sultan Osman* and *Reşadiye* requisitioned by the British navy.

The announcement of the sale of the ships to the Ottoman navy was a public relations coup for both the Young Turks and the bemused German government. Turkish anger against Britain for "stealing" the warships the Ottoman government had commissioned and paid for was transformed into gratitude to Germany for providing the modern warships the Ottoman navy needed. But the Young Turks came out of the deal well too, having trumped the British and French by securing modern warships that gave the Turks mastery over Russia's Black Sea fleet. Ambassador Wangenheim was left to explain the fait accompli to his government in Berlin as the *Breslau* and *Goeben* were renamed *Yavuz Sultan Selim* and *Medilli*, Admiral Souchon was appointed commander of the Ottoman fleet, and the German sailors were integrated into the Ottoman navy. Best of all, from the Ottoman perspective, the German ships shifted the naval balance of power to the Ottomans' advantage and deepened their ties to Germany without forcing Istanbul to abandon its neutrality in the expanding global conflict.

HAVING WEATHERED THE CRISES OF AUGUST 1914, THE OTTOMANS were in an advantageous position. They had secured an alliance with a great European power to protect their territory from Russian aggression. They had mobilized their armed forces to make the European powers take note of Turkey. They had acquired the modern warships that shifted the naval balance of power in both the Aegean and the Black Sea to Turkey's advantage. Through it all, Istanbul managed to avoid getting entangled in the spreading war itself. Ideally, the Ottomans would have liked to preserve their neutrality for the duration of the European conflict. This would have left the Central Powers to wear down the Entente armies and allowed the Turks to wait until the prospect of an Austro-German victory seemed likely before entering the fray, thus to secure their war aims with least risk or expense in men and materiel.

Germany demanded a far more active involvement of its Ottoman allies. From the moment the German ships were transferred to Ottoman ownership, Berlin pressed the Turks to join the war. The only question facing German war planners was how best to use their Ottoman partner in the expanding war effort. Some argued the Turks should open a new front against the Russians to undermine the Russian war effort against the Central Powers. This would free the German army to deploy more of its forces to the western front to confront Britain and France. Those closest to the Ottomans understood Istanbul's hesitation to take on the Russians. Since 1711, the Ottoman Empire had lost each of its seven wars against Russia, and in the immediate aftermath of the Italian and Balkan wars, it had no confidence of victory against its most dangerous neighbour. Should Turkey attack Russia in 1914 and lose, it knew it faced certain dismemberment.

Others argued that Ottoman forces could be used to best effect in a swift attack on British positions in Egypt. If the Ottomans could secure the Suez Canal, they would disrupt British communications with India and cut the supply of men and materiel not just from India but also from the dominions of Australia and New Zealand. German war planners were under no illusions about the strength of British defences along the canal. However, they believed the Ottomans could deploy a secret weapon to undermine British positions.

In addition to his role as emperor of the Ottoman state, the sultan held the religious office of caliph, or leader of the global Muslim community. The Germans wanted to play on the religious enthusiasm of Egypt's 12 million Muslims, as well as the millions of Muslims in British and French colonies in Asia and Africa, to weaken the Entente Powers from within their own empires. An attack on Egypt, combined with a declaration of jihad, or Islamic holy war, could provoke an uprising among Egypt's restive population that would make Britain's position in that country untenable—or so the argument ran.

John Buchan's popular novel *Greenmantle*, first published in 1916, captured the European fascination with the latent power of Islamic fanaticism. "Islam is a fighting creed, and the mullah still stands in the pulpit with the Koran in one hand and a drawn sword in the other," Sir Walter Bullivant, the spymaster in Buchan's novel, asserted. "Supposing there is some Ark of the Covenant which will madden the remotest Moslem peasant with dreams of Paradise?" Variants of this fictive conversation, which Buchan set in the Foreign Office at the end of 1915, had been taking place for real in government offices in Berlin. They called it "Islampolitik", and many Germans believed that the Ottoman Empire's greatest contribution to the war effort would come through "Islam politics".[27]

The prophet of Germany's Islampolitik was Baron Max von Oppenheim. Born to a banking dynasty in 1860, Oppenheim had the personal resources to fund his fascination with the Orient. He made his first trip to the Middle East in 1883 and travelled widely across the region as a scholar and an adventurer. In 1892 he moved to Cairo, which served as his home base for regional travels until 1909. He was a prolific author, and his four-volume classic study of Arabian tribes, *Die Beduinen*, remains a standard reference today. T. E. Lawrence, later celebrated as "Lawrence of Arabia", was one of his readers. Though dismissed by German diplomats for having "gone native," Oppenheim gained the trust of Kaiser Wilhelm II, who gave the maverick Orientalist the official title of *Legationsrat* (chief legal counsel) in 1900. Each summer, when Oppenheim visited Germany, the kaiser met with him for a briefing on the state of the Muslim world—a part of the world in which Wilhelm took personal interest since his triumphal Ottoman tour of 1898.

Deeply hostile to the British Empire, Oppenheim was one of the first to advocate using Germany's budding friendship with the Muslim world as a weapon against it. As early as 1906, Oppenheim predicted, "In the future Islam will play a much larger role. . . . [T]he striking power and demographic strength of Islamic lands will one day have a great significance for European states." The Baron wanted to harness that strength to Germany's advantage. When war broke out in August 1914, Oppenheim established a jihad bureau in Berlin to produce pan-Islamic propaganda to instigate revolts in French North Africa, Russian Central Asia, and, the jewel in the crown, British India with its 80 million Muslims. Oppenheim assured the chancellor that even if the rebellions failed to materialize, the mere threat of a Muslim uprising in India would "force England to [agree] to peace terms favourable to us".[28]

Though frequently dismissing this tactic as "jihad made in Germany", many overtly secular Young Turks also believed that religious fanaticism could be deployed against the Entente. Enver had come to appreciate the power of Islam when he fought in Libya in 1911. Before setting out for Libya, he called for a guerrilla war against the Italians. Once on the ground, he increasingly viewed the conflict in terms of jihad. In his letters, Enver had described the Libyan volunteers as "fanatical Muslims who see death before the enemy as a gift from God" and frequently noted their devotion to him as the son-in-law of the caliph. His colleague Cemal also saw Islam as a bond between Arabs and Turks and thought a religious war would strengthen those ties. Cemal argued, "The majority of Arabs would not hesitate to make any sacrifice in this great war for the liberation of the Mussulman Khalifate." Influential members of the Unionist leadership were thus convinced that jihad, a powerful weapon in the early period of Islam, could be revived to serve as a source of strength in the impending conflict with the European Great Powers.[29]

Whatever hopes the Young Turks had invested in jihad, they remained committed to keeping the Ottoman Empire out of the war for as long as possible. Across the months of August and September 1914, Turkish officials gave their excuses to the increasingly impatient Germans. Mobilization, they argued, remained incomplete. Were the Ottomans to attack Russia before their army was at full strength, they would risk the sort of defeat that would make them more of a liability than an ally to the Central Powers. The Ottomans made clear to the Germans that they still saw Russia as posing an existential threat to their empire. The Young Turks did not disclose to their new allies, however, that in their bid to address the Russian threat, they had even proposed a secret alliance to the Russians themselves—one that would necessarily have led to a rupture with Germany.

Enver Pasha, the most outspoken advocate of Turkey's alliance with Germany, first proposed a secret treaty with Russia. On 5 August, just three days after concluding the secret agreement with the Germans, Enver stunned the Russian military attaché to Istanbul, General M. N. Leontiev, by proposing a defensive alliance with Russia. Grand Vizier Said Halim and Enver's Young Turk colleague Talat Pasha joined the negotiations and drew the Russian ambassador to the Porte, M. N. Giers, into the discussion. They sought Russian guarantees of Ottoman territorial integrity and the return of the three Aegean islands and Bulgarian-held western Thrace, lost in the Balkan Wars. In return, the Ottomans would give full military support to the Entente war effort and dismiss all German officers and technicians then at work in the Ottoman Empire. Enver, Talat, and Said Halim succeeded in convincing the Russian ambassador and military attaché of the sincerity of their offer, and the two Russian officials threw their full support behind the proposed alliance with Turkey.[30]

The Ottoman ambassador to St Petersburg, Fahreddin Bey, pursued the question of a Turko-Russian alliance with the Russian government. He explained to Foreign Minister Sergei Sazonov that the Ottomans sought territorial guarantees and a Russian pledge to withhold support for Armenian nationalist aspirations in eastern Anatolia. Sazonov, however, was unpersuaded by the Young Turks and his own ambassador in Istanbul alike. He refused to abandon the Armenian reform project and put little faith in Enver's promises to break with Germany. Sazonov would concede at most, with the support of Russia's allies Britain and France, an Entente guarantee of Ottoman territorial integrity in return for Ottoman neutrality in the war. Such a guarantee would do nothing to restore Ottoman losses in the Aegean or Thrace and would not protect the Ottomans from Russian ambitions after the war.

The fact that Sazonov upheld the Armenian reform project only reinforced Ottoman fears of future plans for the dismemberment of the empire. The German offer remained the best deal on the table, and by the end of August the Ottomans reverted to their special relationship with the Central Powers. That the Young Turks approached the Russians at all demonstrated the lengths to which they were willing to go in order to stay out of Europe's war.

GIVEN THE COURSE OF HOSTILITIES IN AUGUST AND SEPTEMBER 1914, the Ottomans had every reason to take caution before entering the conflict. The German war of movement that had led to the swift occupation of Belgium and a rapid advance on Paris ground to a halt in the decisive Battle of the Marne (5–12 September). The belligerents began to dig the trenches that would prove one of the defining features of the static warfare on the western front. The other hallmark of the Great War was already apparent by September: unprecedented casualty rates. French dead and wounded exceeded 385,000, and German casualties surpassed 260,000 on the western front alone. German forces destroyed an entire Russian army in the Battle of Tannenberg in late August, inflicting 50,000 casualties and taking 90,000 prisoners. The Russians fared much better against the Austrians, who suffered over 320,000 casualties and 100,000 captured in the Galicia campaign (Russian losses were also incredibly heavy in Galicia, with over 200,000 casualties and 40,000 POWs). Austria also launched an unsuccessful attack on Serbia in August 1914 in which Habsburg losses of 24,000 well exceeded those of Serbia, whose population was less than one-tenth the size of Austria-Hungary's. British casualties by November 1914 reached 90,000 dead and wounded, exceeding the total size of the original seven divisions of the British Expeditionary Force. In less than six weeks of fighting, the Entente and Central Powers had suffered well over 1 million casualties. It was enough to give the Young Turks pause.[31]

German patience with Ottoman procrastination snapped in September 1914. With German forces tied down on the western front and the Austrian army gravely weakened by fighting against both Russia and Serbia, the Central Powers urgently needed the Ottomans to open a new front against the Russians. The Young Turks continued to promise to enter the war while making demands for funds and war materiel. In mid-September the German minister of war, General Erich von Falkenhayn, refused to honour any further "requests for officers, artillery, and ammunition . . . until the Ottoman Empire was at war with Germany's enemies". As far as Berlin was concerned, the transfer of the *Goeben* and *Breslau* gave the Ottoman navy the perfect instruments to initiate hostilities with Russia and establish naval supremacy in the Black Sea. An attack on Russia would shatter Ottoman neutrality and draw the Turks into Europe's war. At that point, the sultan could proclaim the jihad on which German war planners placed great hopes of undermining the Entente Powers through their Muslim colonies. The challenge for Germany was to force the Ottomans to overcome their hesitation and attack the Russians.[32]

A key impediment for the Ottomans was money. They needed substantial funding to maintain their high level of mobilization and enter into military action. In mid-October, Minister of War Enver Pasha came to the negotiating table, offering an immediate naval attack on Russia in return for financial support. Enver also promised to contain the Russians in eastern Anatolia and to mount an attack on British positions in Egypt; in addition the sultan would declare a holy war against the Entente Powers. The Germans were quick to accept the Ottoman offer and dispatched 2 million Turkish pounds in gold to Istanbul, to be released on the opening of hostilities with Russia. The Germans promised a further 3 million pounds to be disbursed over the next eight months, after the Ottomans had formally entered the war. This funding gave Ottoman war planners the financial stability with which to prosecute their own ambitious war plans.

On 24 October, Minister of Marine Cemal Pasha drew up the fateful orders authorizing Admiral Souchon to conduct manoeuvres in the Black Sea. Enver Pasha gave Souchon a second set of orders, instructing the fleet to attack Russian naval forces. The admiral agreed to keep Enver's orders sealed until instructed by radio to open the envelope and carry out the instructions. Yet the initiative had now slipped from Ottoman hands as the reflagged German ships sailed into the Black Sea on 27 October.

Souchon might well have been seconded to the Ottoman navy, but he owed his full loyalty to the kaiser. When Enver failed to radio Souchon, the German admiral took the initiative and opened hostilities against the Crimean Black Sea fleet on 29 October, sinking a gunboat and a minelaying vessel. The *Goeben* also shelled the Russian city of Sevastopol. The following day, the Ottoman government issued a statement condemning a Russian attack on the Turkish fleet. Russia, then Britain and France recalled their ambassadors from Istanbul before declaring war on 2 November.

The Ottoman Empire was at war. All that remained was to raise the banner of jihad. This was not the first time the Ottomans had used religion to mobilize their subjects for war. As recently as 1877, Sultan Abdülhamid

II had raised the banner of the Prophet Muhammad to declare jihad against the Russians. Yet the circumstances in 1914 were different. This time, the sultan would be rallying the Muslims of the Ottoman Empire and the world beyond Ottoman frontiers to wage war on some non-Muslims—Russians, Britons, Frenchmen, Serbs, and Montenegrins, in the first instance—but not on others, namely, the empire's allies Germany and Austria. A group of twenty-nine Islamic legal scholars met in Istanbul to deliberate and drafted five legal opinions (fatwas, or in Turkish, *fetvas*) authorizing jihad. The five fatwas were formally sanctioned by the sultan and presented to the leading political, military, and religious authorities in a closed session on 11 November. Only then, on 14 November, was the call for holy war read out in public to a large crowd gathered outside the Mosque of Mehmed the Conqueror in the sultan's name. The crowd roared its support.[33]

The Ottoman authorities could be confident that Arabs and Turks within the empire would respond to the sultan's call. They would have to wait to see if the jihad would have wider repercussions as the whole world mobilized for war.

THREE

A Global Call to Arms

IN THE FIRST WEEK OF AUGUST 1914, NEWS OF WAR SPREAD AROUND the world at the speed of the telegraph. Drummers and buglers roused martial spirits in towns and the countryside across five continents. With their countries bound by secret treaties and mutual defence pacts, it seemed only natural that men in Europe would answer the call. Some did so with jingoistic enthusiasm, others with grave reservations about fighting enemies they had, as yet, no reason to hate.

As Britons and Frenchmen volunteered to fight the Germans, governments in London and Paris turned to their empires for assistance. Though they had even less cause for hostility towards the Central Powers, Canadians, Australians, and New Zealanders rallied to the British Crown with no less a sense of duty than any other of King George V's subjects. After all, the men of the "white dominions" were settlers who traced their origins back to the British Isles, and the British Crown was their head of state. When called on by their king, Canadians, Australians, and New Zealanders felt duty-bound to serve.

The same could not be said of the men of Asia and Africa—colonial subjects of Britain and France who, in the main, resented their foreign rulers. As Britain turned to India and France called up the Army of Africa, war planners had good reason to question the loyalty of their colonies. Germany was actively promoting colonial rebellions against the Entente Powers—particularly among Muslims. The majority of the world's 240 million Muslims in 1914 lived under colonial domination, nearly all of them subjects of an Entente Power: 100 million under British rule, 20 million in French colonies, and a further 20 million within the Russian Empire. The entry of the Ottoman Empire into the war alongside the Central Powers in November 1914 and the sultan's call for jihad against Britain, France, and Russia placed Muslim loyalties towards the Entente very much in doubt. Had the Ottomans succeeded in their appeal to global Islam, they could have tipped the balance to the Central Powers' advantage.[1]

As it was, the Ottomans faced a major challenge on their own home front, mobilizing their war-weary society to confront the gravest threat in the empire's six-century history. In the aftermath of the wars in Libya and the Balkans, men of military age had been discretely fleeing the Ottoman Empire to avoid the draft. In 1913, emigration to North and South America increased by 70 percent over previous years. American consular officials claimed that most emigrants were young men evading military service. War rumours in the first half of 1914 accelerated emigration of young Muslim, Christian, and Jewish men from across the empire until, with the order for

Recruiting for the "Holy War" near Tiberias. The Ottoman Empire mobilized for war on 1 August 1914. Village headmen were instructed to encourage martial enthusiasm by "beating drums, showing joy and gladness." This official Ottoman photograph captures recruitment teams at work with drums and banners in the Palestinian town of Tiberias.

general mobilization, the Ottoman government prohibited men of military age from leaving the country.[2]

On 1 August, the Ministry of War dispatched Enver Pasha's call to arms by telegraph across the empire. Village headmen and leaders of town quarters posted notices in public squares and on mosque doors. "Mobilization has been declared," the posters trumpeted. "All eligible men to arms!" All men, Muslims and non-Muslims alike, aged twenty-one to forty-five, were given five days to report to the nearest recruiting office. Local officials were told to encourage martial enthusiasm by "beating drums, showing joy and gladness and not despair and neglect".[3]

No amount of drum beating or official displays of joy could overcome the foreboding among Arab villagers when mobilization was first announced. A Shiite Muslim cleric in the southern Lebanese village of Nabatiyya captured the public dismay in his diary on 3 August 1914:

> The people were deeply troubled and agitated by the news [of general mobilization]. They gathered in small groups in public spaces, astonished and bewildered, as if confronting the Day of Judgement. Some wanted to flee—but where could they go? Others wanted to escape, but there was no way out. Then we heard that war had broken out between Germany and Austria on one side, and the Allies on the other side. This only increased the fear and alarm of the outbreak of a murderous war that would devour the cultivated lands and the dry earth.[4]

Similar reactions were recorded across the Ottoman Empire. Shops closed in Aleppo on 3 August in response to the mobilization orders. As one resident noted, "Great uneasiness prevails throughout this city." In the Black Sea port of Trabzon, the American consul recorded, "The decree of general mobilization came like a thunderbolt." Though anyone evading conscription faced the death penalty, many young men preferred to take their chances and go into hiding rather than face what they believed to be a more certain death fighting with the Ottoman army.[5]

In the imperial capital Istanbul, the call to arms was announced in each quarter by the town crier, popularly known as "Bekçi Baba". In daytime, Bekçi Baba delivered water to urban neighbourhoods. At night, he served as watchman over the streets of the quarter. It was Bekçi Baba who sounded the alarm when fire broke out, and it was Bekçi Baba who summoned men for war.

Irfan Orga remembered how his father was called to war by Bekçi Baba. The mobilization that had started in the summer of 1914 accelerated after the Ottoman entry into the war, with ever-older men being called up. Orga went outside into the November cold with his father to hear the crier's announcement and watched as Bekçi Baba rounded the corner and stopped beneath the street lamp "to shout his shattering news": "Men born between 1880 and 1885 must report to the recruiting centre within the next forty-eight hours. Who fails to do so will be prosecuted."

One of the men of the household shouted out, "What does it mean, Bekçi Baba?"

"War! War! Don't you know your country is at war?" he roared.[6]

The capital's recruitment centres, flooded with men of military age, were in a state of confusion. Harassed officials bellowed instructions to civilians, who were herded like cattle, hungry, hopeless, and apathetic. It could take days for conscripts to be processed for service. Once assigned to their units, men were allowed to return home to collect their possessions and say good-bye to their families. In each district of the city, a noisy band went house to house to collect the young men departing for war. A soldier would hand the Ottoman flag to the new recruit as he came out of his house, while others leaped and shouted along with the band's music to drown out the women's tears. Yet the soldiers departing for war had their own lament. "When they were leaving their homes the band played a song of unbelievable sadness," Orga recalled, and everyone started to sing,

> O warriors, yet again I must set out as a lonely stranger
> My sighs and tears are too much for even the mountains
>   and stones to bear[7]

In this way, house by house, the Ottomans expanded their standing army from 200,000 to nearly 500,000 men and officers before the outbreak of hostilities in November 1914. In the course of the war, some 2.8 million Ottoman men would serve under arms—about 12 percent of the total population of 23 million—though the Ottoman army never exceeded a maximum of 800,000 men at any one time.[8]

The figures for the other Central Powers and the Entente forces dwarfed the Ottoman numbers. Austria called up 3.5 million men in 1914—yet was chronically under-strength. In the course of the war, Germany mobilized some 13.2 million men, or 85 percent of the male population aged seventeen to fifty; Russia managed to recruit between 14 and 15.5 million men; France raised 8.4 million men, nearly 500,000 of them from the colonies; and Great Britain mobilized over 5.4 million men for the army and Royal Navy—one-third the pre-war male labour force. Little wonder that the European powers put so little store by Ottoman military might.[9]

THE RAPID EXPANSION OF ITS ARMED FORCES PLACED THE OTTOMAN government under tremendous financial strain. The economic disruptions of mobilization were devastating. Men active in agriculture, trade, and industry were forced to leave their jobs to join the army, reducing productive manpower to a drain on government resources as once tax-paying workers became soldiers on government pay, requiring room and board. The closure of the Dardanelles and the wartime threat to shipping brought the ports to a standstill. Hundreds of thousands of soldiers and the transport of supplies for the war effort clogged the roads and railways essential to domestic and international trade, producing shortages of food and consumer goods. Inflation set in at once, and the threat of hunger hung over Ottoman cities, as nervous citizens began to hoard.

These disruptions to the Ottoman economy led to a major reduction in economic productivity and thus in government revenues. By contemporary estimates, revenues fell from $63.2 million in the last six months of 1913 to $50.2 million in the last six months of 1914, a drop of 20 percent. With spending so far outstripping income, the Ottomans faced a budget deficit that consular officials predicted would exceed $100 million in 1914—basically wiping out in one stroke the benefits of the French loan of May 1914.[10]

International confidence in the Ottoman economy was already low before the country went on a war footing. No sooner had the Ottomans announced the mobilization of their troops than European banks began to recall loans made to local financial institutions. In trade cities in the Arab and Turkish provinces, Parisian bankers demanded immediate repayment in gold of outstanding loans in the first week of August 1914. The sudden drain of bullion caused panic in commercial circles across the empire. Depositors made a rush on Ottoman banks to try to recover their holdings. In Istanbul alone, banks paid out over $9 million to depositors in the month of August.

To prevent capital flight, on 3 August, the central government introduced a moratorium on banking transactions, initially for one month but extended quarterly until the end of the war. Under the moratorium, debtors had to repay only 25 percent of their obligations, and banks allowed account holders to withdraw no more than 5 percent of their deposits each month. These measures relieved pressure on borrowers but totally paralyzed the banking system and the economy as a whole. Banks would make loans only to the government. In commercial centres like Aleppo, Beirut, Harput, Izmir, and Istanbul, the moratorium led to the closure of "practically all businesses and industries", according to American consular officials in those cities.[11]

The Ottomans turned to their allies in Germany for financial assistance with their war effort. In return for the Ottoman entry into the war, Germany had pledged £2 million in gold and a further £3 million to be paid in instalments over the eight months following the Ottoman entry into the war. These grants helped restore Ottoman reserves and allowed the government to print paper money secured against gold. Germany also provided up to an estimated £29 million in military materiel and assistance, including essential arms and ammunition, during the war.[12]

The Ottoman treasury resorted to extraordinary wartime measures to raise government revenues to offset the cost of the war. On 9 September, the Ottoman Empire declared its economic independence from the European powers by unilaterally abrogating the capitulations—one of the Porte's original war aims. The measure provoked condemnation in European capitals and widespread celebration among members of the Ottoman general public, who decorated their homes and shops with flags and banners to celebrate their government's getting one over on the Western powers. The abolition of the capitulations was the first tangible benefit of the European conflict for Turkey, and 9 September was declared a national holiday. In Edirne, Istanbul, and Kütahya, crowds swelled public squares in patriotic demonstrations.

Once the capitulations had been abolished, the Ottomans passed a law with effect from 1 October 1914, to tax not just foreign residents and businesses in Turkey but thousands of Ottoman citizens who had secured tax-free status as protégés of Western powers. This measure reportedly raised "several million dollars" for the Ottoman treasury.[13]

Requisition was another form of extraordinary taxation, applicable to Ottoman subjects and foreigners alike. The law required the government to

offer fair compensation for all property claimed by the state, though in practice the government fixed prices and offered receipts rather than payment
in cash. Owners could assume that they had lost anything requisitioned.
Ottoman subjects were forced to deliver their horses, livestock, and crops as
mounts and food for the army.

Officials burst into shops to requisition on the spot those food prod-
ucts and commodities they believed useful to the war effort. Requisitioning
could be used as a form of extortion, as shopkeepers were ordered to deliver
goods they did not possess and thus had to buy from government suppliers
at set prices. Foreign businesses in the Ottoman Empire also suffered significant losses due to requisitioning. In Syria, a local governor seized Singer
sewing machines as a "contribution" to the provincial regiment's uniform
factory. In Adana and Baghdad, governors requisitioned hundreds of cases
of kerosene from the Standard Oil Company. Consular officials estimated
the Ottoman government raised over $50 million through requisitioning in
the first six months of mobilization.[14]

Ottoman citizens remained the main target of new tax levies. Christians
and Jews, subject to conscription but not fully trusted by Ottoman Muslims
as soldiers, were given the option of paying an exorbitant fee of forty-three
Turkish pounds ($189.20) to be exempted from military service. In April
1915 the government raised the exemption fee to fifty pounds ($220). This
tax netted the treasury an estimated $12 million in the nine months follow-
ing mobilization. The government also introduced new taxes on popular but
non-essential consumer goods like sugar, coffee, tea, cigarettes, and alcoholic
beverages that were raised from time to time over the course of the war. The
government increased agricultural tithes from 10 to 12.5 percent. Pre-ex-
isting taxes were increased by as much as 70 percent for war purposes, and
"voluntary contributions" were squeezed from individuals and businesses for
patriotic and military aid organizations.[15]

These extraordinary taxes raised tens of millions of dollars for the Ottoman war effort in the short term while irreparably damaging the Ottoman
economy in the longer run. In 1914, however, the Ottomans were only
concerned with the very short term. Like all of the belligerents at the outset
of the conflict, they expected a quick and decisive outcome. If victorious,
they would have the means to set the economy right; if defeated, they
faced the certainty of partition, and the occupying powers would inherit
the land's economic woes. The Ottomans could have had no illusions about

the life-and-death struggle ahead, and they threw everything they had into securing victory.[16]

As the Ottomans mobilized their troops in early August 1914, the British and French called on their empires to assist in the war effort. In response to the French call, soldiers from Senegal, Madagascar, and Indochina boarded ships for the western front, though the largest contingent of all was the Armée d'Afrique (Army of Africa). First dispatched for service on the western front, colonial soldiers from North Africa would later serve on the Ottoman front—in the trenches on both sides.

The Army of Africa comprised the colonial regiments of Algeria, Tunisia, and Morocco. Mobilization in a colonial context was particularly delicate. The French had to persuade the men of North Africa to make war on Germany, a country with which they had no grievance, in defence of an empire that had reduced them to second-class citizens in their own homelands. The task was made all the more difficult by German propaganda and the Ottoman declaration of jihad, which played on Islamic loyalties to turn the Muslims of North Africa against the French.

The first colonial regiments in North Africa were founded in Algeria in the early nineteenth century. The colourful Zouave light infantry, named for the Berber Zuwawa tribe, captured the world's imagination with their dashing uniforms of baggy red trousers, blue tunics, and red *chechias*, or fezzes. In Europe and America in the mid-nineteenth century, elite Zouave regiments of Western soldiers dressed in exotic kit were created on the Algerian model. Both the Union and Confederate armies in the American Civil War fielded such Zouave units. In the course of the nineteenth century, French recruits increasingly replaced native Algerians in the Zouaves, until they were an all-European force. By the twentieth century, there were five Zouave regiments in Algeria and one in Tunisia. Other European units in the Army of Africa included the Chasseurs d'Afrique, a cavalry corps, and the famous French Foreign Legion.

Arab and Berber soldiers excluded from the Zouaves were recruited to native army units: the Algerian and Tunisian *tirailleurs*, or riflemen, popularly known as the "Turcos", and the Spahi cavalry. While the soldiers in these units were nearly all natives, their officers were almost exclusively French. Algerians could only reach the rank of lieutenant and could account for no more than half the total lieutenants at any time (though in practice Algerians never reached parity with French lieutenants). The French enjoyed pre-eminence over Algerians of equal rank.[17]

Given the colonial context and the limits the French placed on native soldiers, it is remarkable that Arab and Berber men enlisted at all. One Algerian veteran's experiences suggest that the army was viewed as a steady job in an economy that provided very limited opportunities for working men. Mustafa Tabti, an Arab tribesman from the hinterlands of Oran with no formal education, signed up for the Algerian Rifles in 1892 when only sixteen years old, driven by curiosity and the wish "to play with gunpowder". When he concluded his first term of duty, he returned to civilian life as a small grocer. He struggled for seventeen years between shopkeeping and agricultural work before re-enlisting at the age of thirty-seven as a corporal in the 2nd Algerian Rifles. With tensions building in Europe in the early 1910s, the French began to recruit aggressively in North Africa, offering enticing bonuses and pay packages to Arabs and Berbers. In addition to food, shelter, and a regular salary, the army gave a man a certain position in society enjoyed by neither a small grocer nor a sharecropper.[18]

Until the 1910s, the Army of Africa was entirely volunteer, recruited from the European and indigenous communities of Algeria, Tunisia, and Morocco. Faced with pressure to expand its military, the French government decided in 1912 to introduce conscription to North Africa. Many in Paris and Algiers had opposed this measure, fearing it would lead native Algerians either to revolt or, worse, to demand equal citizenship rights with Frenchmen as the price for serving in a conscript army. For once, the military planners overcame the objections of the colonial lobby and put in place the mechanics for a draft. The decree of 3 February 1912 limited the number of conscripts to just 2,400 men, chosen by lottery. To ensure the support of Muslim notables, the French ensured a right of replacement, by which more affluent Algerians might pay a fee to exempt their sons from military service. The right of replacement made the draft all the more objectionable to Algerians of modest means, who rose in protest against its introduction. "We would rather die than let our children be taken away," Algerian families protested. Yet the draft lottery proceeded regularly each year after 1912, despite popular protest. On the eve of war in 1914, of 29,000 Algerian soldiers in French service, 3,900 were conscripts.[19]

When news of Germany's declaration of war on France reached Algeria on 3 August 1914, patriotic Frenchmen flooded the streets of Algiers in a mass display of patriotism. They sang "The Marseillaise" and the "Chant du Départ," another French Revolutionary–era war song with the refrain

> The Republic is calling us
> Let us vanquish or perish
> For her [the Republic], a Frenchman must live
> For her a Frenchman must die

The French in Algeria adapted the final line to implicate native Algerians in this vision of sacrifice: "For her a Frenchman must die, for her an Arab must die." Sharing in a moment of enthusiasm, Messali Hadj, a native of Tlemcen, noted how "musically speaking, all of these patriotic tunes stirred [Arab Algerians] profoundly".[20]

Germany fired its first shots against France when the battle cruisers *Breslau* and *Goeben* attacked the ports of Philippeville and Bône (Skikda and Annaba in independent Algeria). Shortly before dawn on 4 August, the *Breslau*, flying the British ensign, fired 140 rounds into the centre of Bône, hitting port facilities, the railway station, some of the main streets of the city, and a steamship in the harbour. A man named André Gaglione was killed, the first French casualty of the Great War. An hour later, the *Goeben* appeared off the coast of Philippeville under the Russian flag and fired twenty shells into the town, striking the railway station, the barracks, and a gas plant and killing a further sixteen people. Both ships then withdrew from the North African coast and made their way, pursued by the British and French fleets, into Ottoman waters, where they played a key role in Turkey's entry into the war. No reason was given for the attacks, though it was widely believed the Germans were trying to disrupt the movement of troops from North Africa to France and hoped to undermine Algerian confidence in the French.

The German attacks provoked widespread outrage and encouraged Europeans and native Algerians to volunteer for the army. The outbreak of the war coincided with the holy month of Ramadan, when Muslims fast from sunrise to sunset, so the recruitment of native Muslims began in earnest only towards the end of August, when the month of fasting had ended. Recruiting teams of French and Arab soldiers made the rounds in the towns and villages of Algeria on market days. They paraded through public places to the rhythm of drummers and the shrill piping of the *ghaita*, a double-reed horn. The rhythmic music and colourful uniforms always attracted a crowd, but the recruiting officers focused on unemployed workers and peasants. "The sergeant-major brought the music to an end once it had achieved the desired effect," Messali Hadj recalled. "An Arab sergeant would take the floor and elaborate with great eloquence all of the benefits that volunteers would enjoy. His propositions were most attractive, particularly to those with empty stomachs." Their parents, on the other hand, "lived in anguish" at the prospect of losing their sons to foreign wars.

The worst fears of many North African parents were realized within weeks. The Army of Africa suffered heavy casualties almost immediately after the start of the war. Corporal Mustafa Tabti, who had re-enlisted in 1913, was among the first sent into battle in France. He captured his experiences in verse, recorded by an Algerian army translator while Tabti was recovering from wounds in hospital. Composed shortly after the events of September 1914, Tabti's poem gained wide circulation among North African soldiers on the western front. He would have been one of the very first poets of the Great War.[21]

Tabti crossed the Mediterranean from the western Algerian port of Oran to Sète, where the Algerian Rifles disembarked and continued their journey towards the battlefield by rail. Tabti celebrated the bravura with which the Algerians viewed the prospect of battle:

> "Men," we thought to ourselves, "no fear, let's show our pluck,
>   here is our pleasure."
> "We Arabs are made of magnanimity and gunpowder!"

The North African troops were dispatched to the Belgian frontier, where they first saw battle in Charleroi on 21 August. Nothing had prepared the North African poet for the violence of the battle that followed.

> Listen to my story, friends: What an atrocious day for us at
>   Charleroi, my brothers!
> With cannon and a torrential rain of bullets they shattered us from
>   mid-afternoon prayer-time (*Asr*) to sunset prayers (*Maghrib*)

As the battle wore on over the following days, the casualties on both sides mounted. "The dead lay in countless piles," Tabti recalled. "They laid the Muslim beside the non-believer in a common grave."

> Artillery, fired from afar, set aflame earth and stone alike, my Lords!
> We perished in great numbers, by bayonets and bullets that buzzed
>   from all sides
> Leaving us no respite, they followed our tracks over six consecutive
>   days, my Lords!
> They charged us with the impetuosity of a torrent, my Lords! In
>   Belgium they give no respite.

The French and their North African forces managed to inflict losses on the Germans before retreating. "We shattered them," Tabti boasted. "Wherever you direct your step, you encounter a burial ground filled by them [i.e., the Germans]." Yet the memory of the North African dead—"from Oran, Tunis, Morocco and the Sahara"—weighed heavily on the Algerian war poet.

> The sight of so many young men mowed down has melted my
>   heart. My lords! Dead, these heroes remain in the solitude of
>   the countryside.
> They perished without anyone reciting the profession of faith for
>   them, Lords! They lay exposed to the wild beasts, eagles and
>   birds of prey.
> In their memory, I sing with sadness, Lords! Were you made of
>   stone, you would spill tears for them.

The Battle of Charleroi proved a futile butchery that decimated the ranks of North African regiments alongside those of the regular French army. Battalions of 1,200 infantrymen were cut down to less than 500 in a single day's fighting—initial casualty rates among the Turcos ran to 60 percent dead and wounded. As experienced soldiers fell, they were replaced by raw recruits with inadequate training who panicked under the blistering fire and suffered yet higher casualty rates. When the French retreated from Charleroi to regroup for the defence of Paris, the North African soldiers were redeployed to the Marne, where they played a key role in halting German advances—though again they suffered terrible casualties. In all, some 6,500

North African soldiers died between August and December 1914 alone, and thousands more were wounded.[22]

Inevitably, word of the massive losses on the western front trickled back to North Africa. Such terrible casualties fed rumours that North African soldiers were being used as cannon fodder to spare French soldiers from the worst of the fighting. Spontaneous protests against recruitment and conscription broke out across rural Algeria in September and October 1914. Families refused to deliver sons called up for conscription, and bands set on recruitment teams in the open countryside to release volunteers before they reached the barracks.

The uprisings served as a reminder to the French of the trouble that a religious uprising inspired by the Ottoman declaration of jihad might produce. Faced with nationwide resistance, the authorities had to divert 1,600 soldiers from European battlefields to Algeria to restore order. Several soldiers were captured by the insurgents and murdered before the army regained control and resumed the recruitment of fresh troops for the western front. Despite local resistance, the recruitment gangs proved effective. In the course of the war, over 300,000 North Africans—180,000 Algerians, 80,000 Tunisians, and 40,000 Moroccans—served in the French army on both the western and the Ottoman fronts.[23]

THE BRITISH ALSO CALLED ON THEIR EMPIRE TO CONTRIBUTE TROOPS to the war effort. When Britain declared war on Germany on 4 August 1914, three of its dominions—Australia, Canada, and New Zealand—followed suit that very same day. Each country began to mobilize its soldiers for war, imagining they would be defending Britain in the European theatre. The overwhelming majority of Canadians did serve on the western front (aside from a handful who served on riverboats in the Mesopotamia campaign or with medical units in Salonica). Yet most of the volunteers from Australia and New Zealand first saw service on the Ottoman front. They mobilized at the same time as Turks, Arabs, and North Africans, global soldiers who turned Europe's conflict into a world war.

On the opposite side of the globe from the theatre of conflict, Australia and New Zealand responded to the outbreak of war in Europe with no less a sense of duty to the empire than any Briton. In Australia, the leader of the opposition Labour Party, Andrew Fisher, captured the spirit of the moment when he pledged his country's support to the "last man and last shilling". Early in August 1914, the Commonwealth of Australia mobilized the Australian Imperial Force, and the Dominion of New Zealand called up the New Zealand Expeditionary Force. Their combined forces came to be known as the Australian and New Zealand Army Corps, the celebrated Anzacs.

Both Australia and New Zealand had sent contingents to support Britain in the Boer War (1899–1902). But this first experience of fighting foreign wars in no way prepared the men of the Antipodes for the violence of the Great War. Of 16,000 Australians sent to South Africa, only 251 were killed in action; more soldiers—267 men in total—died of disease. New Zealand experienced similar casualty rates: of 6,500 soldiers, 70 were killed in action, 23 died accidental deaths, and 133 perished from disease. Drawing on the recent memory of the Boer War, Kiwis and Aussies volunteered in great numbers, looking for adventure and foreign travel, imagining no doubt that nearly all would return crowned with glory.[24]

The Australian and New Zealander contingents comprised both cavalry and infantry. Most volunteers for the cavalry were from rural areas and came with their own horses—some of the more than 16 million horses to be caught up in the Great War. Cavalry volunteers had the option of enlisting with their own mounts and received £30 for the horse if it passed muster. The horse then came under army ownership and was branded with a government insignia and a number burnt into its hoof. A military horse, known to cavalrymen as a "remount", had to fit strict criteria: it must be a gelding or mare, aged four to seven, well muscled, no taller than 15.2 hands, of sound disposition, and calm under fire. The Australian "New South Waler" fit the bill perfectly, a hybrid of thoroughbred and draught horse stock.[25]

The men of the New Zealand Expeditionary Force came from all parts of the country and all kinds of backgrounds. They were farmers and mechanics, shepherds and bushmen, clerks and teachers, stockbrokers and bankers. They joined because all of their friends joined. For some, war held the prospect of a big adventure. Others volunteered out of patriotism towards Britain and the British Empire. None had the slightest idea where they would end up fighting, but after six weeks of training, they were ready to go. Trevor Holmden, a young lawyer from Auckland, remembered how he and his fellows marched from their training camp on One Tree Hill down to the transport ships in the harbour:

Auckland turned out en mass to see us go and although most people were glad to get rid of the last hooligan element we were thought to include, we all thought we were heroes and I think bore ourselves as such. Personally, I took great pleasure and pride in the march and the whole affair was certainly very dramatic and martial, when with bands playing and flags flying we . . . passed from the world we knew through the great iron gates that shut off the Queen's wharf and so on to the ships which were to carry us God knows where.[26]

Given the relatively small size of their populations, Australia and New Zealand could contribute a limited number of troops to the war. Australia had a population of 5 million and New Zealand only 1 million in 1914. Only Australian men aged eighteen to thirty-five and New Zealanders aged twenty-one to forty who stood 5 feet, 6 inches or taller and were in good health were eligible for service. By the end of August, the Australians had raised a force of 19,500 men (17,400 infantry and 2,100 cavalry) commanded by nearly nine hundred officers. In addition to a small campaign force of 1,400 men dispatched to occupy German Samoa, the main body of the New Zealand Expeditionary Force, comprising nearly 8,600 men and over 3,800 horses, was assembled in less than three weeks.[27]

The troop transport ships were delayed by reports of a German naval squadron believed to be operating in the South Pacific. Though the volunteers had completed training by late September, the ten transport ships only set off from Wellington on 16 October, escorted by a Japanese warship and two British vessels. Frank Holmden found himself on the *Waimana* along with 1,500 men and six hundred horses "packed like sardines". They sailed for Australia, where they joined forces with the Australian Imperial Force and, on 1 November, sailed from Albany in south-western Australia, their destination still unknown. Only after the Anzac convoy was under way did the Ottoman Empire enter the Great War on 2 November. Rather than sail on to Britain, the men of Australia and New Zealand would disembark in Egypt to fight on a Middle Eastern front.

As the British and French drew their empires into the European war, they were forced to examine the loyalties of the Muslim subjects under their rule. The Algerians had long-standing grievances with the status quo, which denied citizens' rights to native Arabs and Berbers. Indian Muslims were restive after decades of declining influence in the British administration and increasingly declared allegiance to the Ottoman sultan in his role as caliph of the global Muslim community. Three decades of British occupation had given rise to a nationalist movement in Egypt, whose bid for independence had been frustrated at every turn. Some feared, with good reason, that colonial policies had so alienated Muslims in India and North Africa that they might side with the enemies of Britain and France in the hope of securing independence through a German victory.[28]

As the crossroads of the British Empire, Egypt was crucial to the war effort. The Suez Canal was Britain's vital communications link to India, Australia, and New Zealand. Egypt's military bases served as both a training ground for imperial troops and a staging post for operations in the Middle East. Were Egyptian nationalists to take advantage of the war in Europe or pious Muslims to respond to the declaration of jihad and rise in rebellion, the consequences for Britain's overall war effort would be disastrous.

When war broke out in Europe in August 1914, the government of Egypt had already adjourned for the summer months. The khedive, Abbas II Hilmi, was in Istanbul on holiday, and the legislative assembly was in recess. The prime minister, Hussein Rushdi Pasha, was forced to make decisions during a rapidly evolving crisis without conferring with his head of state. On 5 August, the British pressured Rushdi Pasha into signing a document that essentially committed Egypt to a declaration of war against the king's enemies. Far from securing Egyptian loyalty for Britain's war effort, news of the decree antagonized the Egyptian people. "The deep-seated distrust, common to all classes of the population towards the Occupying Power [i.e., Britain], expanded into a sentiment of bitter, if silent, hatred," a British officer then serving in Egypt recalled. "Through an involuntary and despised association with Great Britain, Egypt had been dragged into a struggle, of which the origin was obscure to her and the objectives unknown."[29]

Between August and October, British censors shielded the Egyptian public from the worst reports from the front. The news from Istanbul was also subject to British censorship—until the Ottomans entered the war on 2 November 1914. Though under British occupation and de facto administration since 1882, Egypt was still legally part of the Ottoman Empire and had been since 1517. The khedive was an Ottoman viceroy, appointed by the Ottoman sultan, and paid an annual tribute to the Ottoman treasury. As

Germany's ally, the Ottomans were now the enemies of the British Crown. Egypt was thus caught in the contradictory position of being a loyal Ottoman vassal state and, in line with the 5 August decree, a country at war with the Ottomans at Britain's behest. Britain's position was hardly less complicated. The Ottoman entry into the war meant that Britain occupied enemy territory and that the 13 million residents of Egypt were now hostile aliens.

On the same day the Ottomans entered the war, the British declared martial law in Egypt. There was no public reaction, but the British authorities remained concerned about Egyptian loyalties. Unwilling to involve Egyptian soldiers in a fight where bonds of religion would almost certainly outweigh respect for the colonial authorities, the British decided to exempt the Egyptian people from the war entirely. On 6 November, the military commander in Egypt, General Sir John Maxwell, made the following pledge: "Recognizing the respect and veneration with which the Sultan is regarded by the Mahomedans of Egypt, [Great Britain] takes upon herself the sole burden of the present war without calling upon the Egyptian people for aid therein."[30]

Veteran Egyptian politician Ahmad Shafiq claimed that Maxwell's announcement "rocked public opinion" in Egypt, ever mistrustful of British intentions after more than three decades of occupation. While pledging to spare the Egyptian people from any involvement in the war, the British imposed strict restrictions on impeding the work of their forces in Egypt or providing succour to Ottoman efforts. Moreover, the British would soon find they could not keep their promise to take on the burden of the war without Egyptian assistance. Egyptian soldiers would serve in the defence of the Suez Canal, and Egyptian workers would in due course be recruited to labour gangs on both the western and the Middle Eastern fronts of the Great War.[31]

Although Britain had secured public order, it had yet to resolve the legal contradictions entailed by its position in Egypt. On 18 December, Britain unilaterally decreed Egypt's secession from the Ottoman Empire as a British protectorate, bringing to a close 397 years of Turkish rule. The following day, the British deposed the ruling khedive, who was deemed too sympathetic to the Ottoman cause, and installed the eldest living prince of the Egyptian ruling family, Husayn Kamil, in his place. Now that Egypt was no longer a vassal state, the British gave its ruler the title "sultan"—a titular promotion that flattered Egypt's new ruler by putting him on an equal footing with the Ottoman sultan. With a compliant new ruler who owed his position to the imperial power, the British were free to concentrate on securing Egypt, and the Suez Canal in particular, from Ottoman attack. While many of the British soldiers in Egypt had already been sent to serve on the western front, reinforcements were soon to arrive in Egypt from Australia, New Zealand, and India.

INDIA, UNDER CROWN RULE SINCE 1858, WAS THE CENTREPIECE OF the British Empire. The Raj was headed by a British viceroy who ruled over some 175 princely states that gave allegiance to the crown as their suzerain. With its own civil service and army, India was a state within the British imperial state. One-quarter of India's 255 million inhabitants were Muslims— over 65 million in all. German intelligence had identified the disgruntled Muslims of India as the Achilles' heel of the British Empire and hoped to use the Ottoman call for jihad to provoke uprisings that would destabilize the Raj and speed Britain's defeat on the western front.[32]

On the outbreak of war in 1914, Britain had two imperatives in South Asia: to recruit as many Indian soldiers to the war effort as possible and to preserve the loyalty of Indian Muslims against Ottoman and German jihad propaganda. To advance both aims, George V, the British "King-Emperor", issued a proclamation to the "Princes and people of India" on 4 August. He explained Britain's reasons for declaring war on Germany and called for India's support for the imperial war effort. Much to the British government's relief, the Indian ruling elite responded to the king's appeal with effusive declarations of loyalty. "The loyalty of the Indian Muslims to the King-Emperor," the Aga Khan asserted, "is proof against any attempt of German diplomacy in the Near East or elsewhere to create a bastard Pan-Islamic sentiment in favour of the 'mailed fist' made in Germany." Muslim princes across India repeated his views in public statements.[33]

The Ottoman entry into the war and the sultan's declaration of jihad threatened to bring disorder to the Raj. Popular loyalties were divided between the sultan-caliph and the king-emperor. To ensure the support of Indian Muslims, King George V gave assurances that Britain and its allies would protect Mecca and Medina—the holy cities of Arabia—the Red Sea port of Jeddah, and the shrine cities of Mesopotamia from attack. The king's pledge helped preserve Indian Muslim support for the British war effort. Yet, as with their promise to spare Egyptians the burden of the war, the British would find that their pledge to shield the Hijaz from the dangers of the conflict would come under pressure.

Following the king's declaration about the Muslim holy sites, Indian Muslim notables proved effusive in their support of the British war effort. The nawabs of Bhopal, Ranpur, Murshidabad, and Dhaka, along with the nizam of Hyderabad, all affirmed that the sultan had misled Muslims with his "erroneous" call to jihad and insisted that Indian Muslims had a duty to support Great Britain. The Aga Khan went so far as to withdraw his recognition of the Ottoman claim to caliphate: "Now that Turkey has so disastrously shown herself a tool in German hands she has not only ruined herself but has lost her position as Trustee of Islam and evil will overtake her."[34]

The Council of the All India Muslim League passed a resolution in November 1914 asserting "the participation of Turkey in the present war" had no impact on the "loyalty and devotion" of Indian Muslims to the British Empire. The council affirmed its confidence "that no Mussalman in India will swerve even to a hair's breadth from his paramount duty to his sovereign," the king-emperor. Similar resolutions were passed by mass meetings of Muslim notables across India in November 1914.[35]

Muslim loyalty confirmed, Britain turned next to mobilizing Indian troops for the war. India responded to George V's call with more volunteers for the war effort than all other colonies and dominions combined. Between 1914 and the end of 1919, some 950,000 Indians signed up for military service, and another 450,000 served as non-combatants, for a total of 1.4 million men sent abroad to participate in the war effort as soldiers, workers, medics, and other auxiliaries. Soldiers of the Indian army fought on every front of the war—over 130,000 on the western front alone. Yet their greatest contribution to the British war effort came in the Middle East, where nearly 80 percent of Indian soldiers served—in Gallipoli (9,400 men), in Aden and the Persian Gulf (50,000 men), in Egypt (116,000 men), and overwhelmingly in Mesopotamia (nearly 590,000 men).[36]

Following the example of British India, where Muslim rulers had spoken out so eloquently against the sultan's declaration of jihad, the French mobilized loyal Muslim notables to denounce the Ottoman entry into the war on religious grounds. Starting at the top, the French secured endorsements from the bey of Tunis and the sultan of Morocco, who exhorted their soldiers to fight valiantly for the French and called on their people to submit to and obey the colonial authorities. The muftis of the Maliki and Hanafi schools of Islamic law in Algeria made explicit reference to the position of Muslims in India, the Caucasus, and Egypt in opposing the sultan's call for jihad. Other religious leaders—heads of religious fraternities, judges, and other notables—declared their loyalty to the Allied cause, condemned the Germans and their Young Turk protégés, and dismissed the sultan's claim to caliphal authority and his right to declare jihad on behalf of the Muslim community. The colonial authorities published dozens of such declarations in Arabic, with translations judiciously edited by French scholars. The propaganda war both for and against the Ottoman jihad was being fought by European Orientalists—British, French, and German.[37]

THE GERMANS HAD SOME SUCCESS IN THEIR EFFORTS TO WIN MUSLIM enemy combatants over to jihad against Britain and France. They recruited Islamic activists like Shaykh Salih al-Sharif to the cause. Born in Tunis to Algerian exiles from French rule, Salih al-Sharif was an Islamic scholar and descendant of the Prophet Muhammad. Salih al-Sharif left his native land in 1900 in protest against French rule. The Tunisian activist came to the attention of the Young Turk leadership in 1911 during the Libyan War, in which he served under Enver. It was Salih al-Sharif who reportedly declared jihad against Italy, giving the war its overtly religious overtones. Enver, already impressed by the power of Islam to mobilize resistance to European encroachment, recruited al-Sharif to his intelligence organization, the Teşkilât-i Mahsusa.[38]

In 1914 Salih al-Sharif moved to Berlin, where he joined a new propaganda unit under the German Foreign Ministry, the Nachrichtenstelle für den Orient (Intelligence Office for the East). The Tunisian activist visited the western front to appeal directly to Muslim soldiers fighting for Britain and France across the trenches. He drafted a number of pamphlets, published in both Arabic and Berber, which were dropped over enemy lines in areas held by North African soldiers, along with news of the sultan's declaration of jihad. A number of North African soldiers deserted from French lines in response to this overtly Islamic appeal.[39]

As the Germans began to take Muslim prisoners on the western front—some eight hundred by the end of 1914—they created a special facility called Halbmondlager (Crescent Moon Camp) at Wünsdorf-Zossen, near Berlin. The camp's German commanders spoke Arabic with the prisoners. Camp

Prisoners at Zossen. The Germans established a special camp for Muslim prisoners of war at Wünsdorf-Zossen, near Berlin, where they actively recruited volunteers for the Ottoman war effort. Many later served under Ottoman colours on Middle Eastern fronts. Here a group of North African soldiers captured from French lines are reviewed by one of their own officers in the Zossen camp.

food was fully compliant with Islamic dietary requirements. The camp even had an ornate mosque, paid for by Wilhelm II himself, to provide for the spiritual needs of Muslim POWs—and to prove the kaiser's good intentions towards the Muslim world.

Ahmed bin Hussein, an elderly farmer from Marrakech, was one of eight Moroccan soldiers who surrendered to German forces in the battlefields of Belgium. From the moment the men declared themselves to be Muslims, he claimed, the German captors "showed us due respect. . . . Everybody was patting our shoulders and giving us food and beverages." He was sent to a special camp for Muslim POWs—no doubt the Halbmondlager. "They even made a favor for us, and gave us a kitchen. Pork was not to be given to us. They gave us good meat, pilaf, chickpeas etc. They gave three blankets, underwear, and a new pair of shoes to each of us. They took us to the baths once in every three days and cut our hair." The conditions in camp were a great improvement over what he had experienced in the French army and at the front.[40]

A parade of Muslim activists passed through the Zossen camp to pro-mote jihad propaganda among a (literally) captive audience. The Tunisian activist Salih al-Sharif was a frequent visitor and edited an Arabic-language newspaper for inmates called, appropriately enough, *al-Jihad*. A number of North African activists and notables visited the camp to meet the inmates and win them to the Central Powers' cause. These guest speakers lectured inmates on why fighting with the Allies was an act against religion and why joining the Ottoman jihad against the enemies of Islam (i.e., Britain and France) was a religious duty.[41]

Hundreds of POWs volunteered for the Ottoman army—among them the Moroccan farmer Ahmed bin Hussein. After he had spent six months in the special POW camp for Muslim soldiers, a German officer arrived, ac-companied by an Ottoman officer named Hikmet Efendi. "Whoever wants to go to Istanbul," they declared, "raise [your] hand." Twelve Moroccan and Algerian soldiers volunteered on the spot. "Others were afraid," Ahmed bin Hussein added. They were given civilian clothes and passports and sent on to Istanbul to join the Ottoman war effort.

It is impossible to say how many Muslim prisoners volunteered for Ot-toman service out of conviction and how many to get out of a POW camp. Whatever their motives, Indian and North African soldiers left Germany for Istanbul in a steady stream to join the sultan's war. Mobilized for a second time, as Muslim rather than colonial soldiers, they would re-enter the rap-idly expanding world war on its Middle Eastern fronts.[42]

BY THE TIME THE OTTOMANS DECLARED WAR, THE MEN WHO WOULD fight in the Middle East had been mobilized and were making their way to fronts at every point along the Ottoman Empire's exposed frontiers. North Africans had already fought and died in the thousands on the western front, and a fraction of their ranks held in German POW camps would change sides and join the Ottomans. Anzac cavalry and infantry were sailing across the Indian Ocean towards Egypt. Some soldiers from India were making their way up the Persian Gulf towards Mesopotamia, while others were sail-ing past Ottoman Yemen en route to Egypt. Ottoman soldiers were concen-trating in eastern Anatolia and Syria in advance of drives against Russian positions in the Caucasus and British lines in Egypt. Europe's war had come to the Middle East.

FOUR

Opening Salvos

Basra, Aden, Egypt, and the Eastern Mediterranean

THE OTTOMAN EMPIRE WAS BORN OF WAR, ITS FRONTIERS DRAWN through centuries of conquest and conflict. However, only in November 1914, as the Ottomans entered the first global war, did they face the threat of war on all their frontiers at once. With over 7,500 miles of borders and coastlines spanning the Black Sea, the Persian Gulf, the Red Sea, and the Mediterranean, the Ottomans presented their enemies with many points vulnerable to attack.

No sooner had the Ottomans entered the war than they came under Allied assault at disparate points in their far-flung empire. The naval vessels of the Entente Powers fired the first salvos even before war had been formally declared. British warships in the Red Sea bombarded an isolated one-hundred-man fort at the head of the Gulf of Aqaba on 1 November 1914. Two days later, British and French ships stationed off the Dardanelles subjected the outer defences of the straits to a blistering bombardment. In just twenty minutes of shelling, the Allied ships hit an ammunition storage depot, destroying the Seddülbahir Fort and dismounting its guns. The Ottomans were unable to respond to these attacks, immediately demonstrating both the vulnerability of their coastline and the Entente's naval supremacy.[1]

The Entente Powers believed Turkey was the weak link in the Central Alliance and the easiest belligerent to knock out of the war. As the conflict on the western and Russo-German fronts settled into stalemate, only the Ottoman front held the prospect of a quick Allied victory. The Entente Powers were confident the Turks would buckle rapidly under the combined onslaught of Britain, France, and Russia. In the opening days of Turkey's war, both Russia and Britain sent troops to secure a foothold inside the lightly defended peripheries of the Ottoman Empire.

RUSSIA WAS THE FIRST TO ATTACK THE OTTOMANS WITH GROUND forces. Immediately after the Goeben and Breslau bombarded their Black Sea ports and shipping on 29 October, the Russians sent a detachment across the Caucasus frontier into eastern Anatolia. Russian intelligence suggested that, with only 70,000 to 80,000 soldiers in the Erzurum region, the Ottomans did not have the forces to threaten Russian positions in the Caucasus. Consequently, the Russians limited their ambitions to securing a buffer zone along the frontier, allowing their commanders to commit more troops to the battle against Germany and Austria.

Russian General Georgy Bergmann led his soldiers into Ottoman territory at dawn on 2 November 1914. Over the next three days, the Russians advanced without encountering any significant resistance. By 5 November, the Russians had secured a salient running parallel with their own frontier some fifteen miles deep. Their mission fulfilled, Bergmann ordered his troops to fortify their positions along the heights overlooking the Pasin Valley, some fifty miles from the fortified town of Erzurum.

Perhaps the ease with which the Russians had occupied Turkish territory had gone to the Russian commander's head, for without consulting headquarters he decided to exceed his orders and continue his conquest deeper into Erzurum Province. He ordered his soldiers to move on to the strategic village of Köprüköy bridging the Aras River, halfway between the Russian frontier and Erzurum.

Bergmann did not know that the Turkish high command had been following the Russian advance with growing concern. On 4 November, Enver Pasha, the Ottoman minister of war, had sent a telegram to Hasan Izzet Pasha, the Turkish commander in Erzurum, proposing an Ottoman counter-attack against the invading Russians. Though concerned that his Third Army was under-strength, Hasan Izzet Pasha knew better than to question the judgment of his superiors and dispatched a large force to engage the

Russians. They met on the banks of the Aras River on the evening of 6 November in what would prove the first Ottoman battle of the Great War.[2]

Corporal Ali Rıza Eti was a medic with one of the units sent to fight the Russians at Köprüköy. Eti was an educated man from a village near the eastern Turkish town of Erzincan. When called up for military service, he was twenty-seven years old and married, with one son. Eti had much to live for but was willing to give his life fighting the Russians. His father, a veteran of the 1877–1878 Russo-Turkish War, had been deeply scarred by the Ottoman defeat. In 1914, Eti went to war to settle old scores.[3]

Eti's unit was sent into combat at dawn on 7 November. The soldiers made slow progress over roads turned to mud by the cold autumnal rains. As they approached the front at Köprüköy, the artillery grew more intense, and gunfire rained down on the frightened soldiers. In his diary, Eti tried to capture the sound of the bullets: *cıv, cıv, cıv.* "As it was my first day [of fighting] I was very afraid of dying. With each *cıv* I broke out in a sweat from my teeth to my toenails." As the Ottoman soldiers advanced into position, they could no longer stand in the intensive firing. The fighting went on well into the night. At 3:00 a.m., Eti and his comrades pitched their "half-patched" tent and tried to get some sleep in the terrible cold. "We shivered until morning," he wrote.

Fighting resumed early the next day. Russian artillery subjected the Turkish lines to intense shrapnel fire, the spray of sharp metal fragments cutting down men and work animals. "While writing this line a shrapnel shell '*ciiib!*' burst on the hill above me. The dead are scattered around like a weeping willow." Because the fighting was too intense for the medics to get to the wounded, Eti grabbed a Mauser rifle and went to join the fighting at the front line. "Rıza Efendi, get down flat and bring ammunition with you," his captain shouted. Armed with two boxes of cartridges and his medical supplies, Eti took aim and fired at the Russian soldiers on the hills opposite. With characteristic precision, he claimed to have fired eighty-three rounds of ammunition and killed a Russian lieutenant and three other soldiers, adding regretfully, "The other shots were wasted."

The Turkish soldiers held their positions against a Russian attempt to outflank them. Their captain, to encourage his men, went around distributing fresh ammunition. "Their bullets don't touch us," he shouted in a display of ill-timed bravura. At that moment, he was shot in the neck, fell to his knees, and died before his downcast soldiers. "Come comrades, we aren't making war for this captain's sake, but for God's sake," another officer shouted, opening fire on the Russians. Snapped out of their despondency, the Turkish soldiers fought for their lives, as their artillery took the measure of the Russian lines. A series of well-aimed artillery shells killed and wounded scores of Russian soldiers and forced the survivors into retreat. "At ten o'clock," Eti recorded, "the enemy was retreating from all fronts. Everyone is overjoyed."

As the fighting died down, Eti resumed his work as a medic, recovering the wounded from the battlefield and dispatching them to the rear. The medics recognized many of their friends among the dead and wounded and were appalled by this first experience of the casualties of war.

After they had finished their work among the Turkish lines, Eti ventured to the former Russian positions to take a closer look at the man he had killed. The Russian lieutenant lay where he had fallen. Eti expressed no sympathy for "the guy" he had shot (he consistently referred to him by the derogatory Turkish word for "man", *herif*) and took his revolver, satchel, binoculars, and sword. Inside the satchel he found a bundle of letters, a lavender-scented handkerchief, a glove, a flask, and some Russian money. "Quite a godsend," Eti mused. He gave the binoculars to his regimental commander, the sword to the doctor, and the satchel to the commander's adjutant. Reflecting on his squadron's losses on their first day of combat—one captain and five men "martyred" and thirty-six wounded—Eti concluded, "We lost the dreams of battle that we had carried inside us this morning."

Through determined resistance, the Turkish infantry succeeded in holding its lines. The Russians made a last assault on 11 November and lost 40 percent of their forces in the attempt. With their ammunition running low and facing determined Ottoman attacks on both flanks, the Russians were forced into retreat under fire. Bergmann's troops fell back to the line they had originally secured on 5 November, some fifteen miles into Ottoman territory. Both sides paid a heavy price for Bergmann's adventure. According to Turkish figures, the Ottomans suffered over 8,000 casualties in the November offensive (1,983 dead and 6,170 wounded) and lost an additional 3,070 soldiers taken prisoner and nearly 2,800 deserters. The Russians lost 1,000 dead in battle, 4,000 wounded, and another 1,000 who died of exposure. Bloodied, the two sides reinforced their positions before the first snowfalls rendered the highlands of the Caucasus all but impassable, assuming that neither side would resume the fight before the spring. Enver Pasha, encouraged by "this comparatively satisfactory beginning", would soon come to the Caucasus himself to renew the fight with Russia. For the moment, however, the Ottoman high command was preoccupied with a British invasion in Mesopotamia.[4]

THE CITY OF BASRA IS STRATEGICALLY SITUATED ON THE SHATT AL-ARAB, a river running between the confluence of the Tigris and Euphrates and the head of the Persian Gulf. It was the last port accessible to ocean-going steamers on the Shatt and served as the commercial gateway between Mesopotamia and the Persian Gulf. A few miles south of Basra, the Shatt also marked the boundary between the Persian and Ottoman empires (as it does between Iran and Iraq today), the border lying midway between the riverbanks. The Persian reaches of the Shatt were of particular interest to the British, for the Anglo-Persian Oil Company had struck oil in commercial quantities there in May 1908.

In May 1901, the Devon-born millionaire William Knox D'Arcy had secured a sixty-year concession to explore for oil in Persia. His company enjoyed the financial support of a British syndicate and the political backing of the Royal Navy, which was determined to secure a reliable source of fuel for its fleet as it shifted from coal to oil. After striking oil near the southern Persian city of Ahwaz, Anglo-Persian sought a location for a refinery with access to the sea to export its petroleum, settling on the island of Abadan in the Shatt al-Arab, 140 miles to the south of the oil field. Abadan provided an ideal site to build a refinery, with direct access to the sea lanes. And the owner of the island, Shaykh Khazaal of the nearby town of Muhammerah (now the Iranian city of Khorramshahr), was a British protégé.

With 20,000 horsemen at his command, the Arabic-speaking Khazaal was a powerful local leader. In 1902, Britain had pledged to protect Shaykh Khazaal's mini-state in return for his adherence to the British treaty system binding most of the Arab rulers in the Persian Gulf. Now that oil had been discovered, Britain placed an even higher premium on its friendship with the shaykh. The British Resident in the Gulf, Sir Percy Cox, was dispatched to Muhammerah to negotiate a lease with Khazaal for the necessary land on Abadan Island for a refinery, storage tanks, and dock. In July 1909, they concluded a ten-year agreement for £6,500 cash in hand and a loan of £10,000. The pipeline was laid, the refinery built, and oil began to flow from Abadan in 1912.[5]

Between oil, trade, and a century-old position of supremacy in the Persian Gulf, it was natural that Britain would choose Mesopotamia as its prize in any post-war partition of the Ottoman Empire. Even before opening negotiations with Russia and France, the British had already sent an expeditionary force to secure its claim to Basra.

British plans to invade Basra were made in strict secrecy by London and India in September and October 1914. Given the reverence Indian Muslims showed the Ottoman sultan as the caliph of Islam, the British feared that a premature attack on the sultan's domains might provoke religious riots. The challenge was to pre-position British troops near Basra ahead of an Ottoman declaration of war, without their deployment being seen as a hostile act against the still-neutral Ottoman Empire. This meant keeping the deployment secret even from the commander and troops who would take part in the campaign.

When Brigadier General Walter Delamain boarded ship in Bombay on 16 October to sail as part of the Indian Expeditionary Force (IEF) to the western front, he received his orders under seal with strict instructions to wait seventy-two hours before reading and acting on them. After three days at sea, Delamain opened his orders and learned that he was to command a brigade of the 6th Poona Division of the Indian army, designated IEF D, for service in the Persian Gulf. The 5,000 soldiers and their mounts (1,400 horses and pack mules) had been grouped in four shallow-draft transports that could navigate some of the shallower waters of the Gulf. Delamain was to proceed immediately to Bahrain to await further instructions.

Delamain reached Bahrain with his brigade on 23 October. He was met by Sir Percy Cox, the former Resident in the Gulf, who had been assigned as chief political officer to IEF D. Only after he reached Bahrain did Delamain learn that he was to proceed to the Shatt al-Arab to secure the Anglo-Persian oil refinery and storage tanks at Abadan and protect the pipeline from Turkish attack. Delamain was to enlist the support of Britain's Arab allies at the head of the Gulf—Shaykh Khazaal, Kuwaiti ruler Shaykh Mubarak al-Sabah, and Ibn Saud in eastern Arabia. So long as they remained neutral, Delamain's orders decreed, he was to avoid "any hostile action against the Turks without orders from the Government of India". Once the Ottomans had declared war, however, Delamain was free to "take such military and political action" as would strengthen his position "and, if possible, [to] occupy Basra". After six days at anchor, Delamain was ordered to proceed to the mouth of the Shatt on 29 October—the same day the Ottoman fleet initiated hostilities against Russia in the Black Sea. Word of the campaign's departure from Bahrain reached Basra quickly, setting off a flurry of military and political preparations.[6]

FROM THE MOMENT THE BRITISH TROOP TRANSPORTS ARRIVED IN Bahrain, rumours had begun to circulate in Basra of an imminent attack. Now that Europe's distant war was on their doorstep, the townspeople were unsure of what they wanted. The outgoing British consul, Reader Bullard, reported "strong anti-Russian and anti-British feeling" in Basra at the end of October. However, the town lived on trade, and its economy would be gravely undermined if it were isolated from the rest of the Persian Gulf by Ottoman hostilities with Britain.[7]

Loyalties towards the Ottomans were lukewarm at best. Many of the town's notables openly opposed Young Turk policies they deemed inimical to Arab interests. A group of like-minded leaders in Basra had formed the Reform Society in 1913, one of the most influential Arabist societies in Iraq. Like al-Fatat and the Decentralization Party, the Basra Reform Society advocated Arab cultural rights and greater autonomy in a decentralized Ottoman Empire. The leader of the movement was Sayyid Talib al-Naqib.

The most prominent personality in pre-war Basra, Sayyid Talib was first elected to the Ottoman parliament in 1908. After initial cooperation with the Committee of Union and Progress (CUP), he grew increasingly outspoken in favour of Arab cultural and political rights. In the course of his parliamentary career, he made dangerous enemies among the Turkish nationalists in the CUP. The Unionists, believing Sayyid Talib had separatist aspirations for Basra, openly threatened the local leader. Although Reform Society candidates swept the 1914 Ottoman parliamentary elections in the province of Basra, Sayyid Talib did not dare travel to Istanbul to take up his seat for fear the Unionists might assassinate him.[8]

Sulayman Faydi, another native of Basra elected to the Ottoman parliament in 1914 on the Reform Society list, remembered how the British tried to recruit Sayyid Talib to collaborate in their occupation of Basra. Drawing on the good offices of their ally Shaykh Khazaal, British officials invited Sayyid Talib to a secret meeting in Muhammerah in the crucial days before IEF D reached the Shatt. In return for his cooperation, they offered to name

Sayyid Talib governor general over the province of Basra under British protection, with tax-free privileges and British development assistance. Sayyid Talib declined, arguing that he was unwilling to trade one master for another, the British for the Ottomans.[9]

Rather than follow his neighbours into the British "trucial" system, Sayyid Talib decided to throw in his lot with the Ottomans instead. His decision was complicated by the fact that the Unionists had issued a warrant for his arrest on charges of treason. In a desperate bid to prove his loyalty and reverse his fortunes, Sayyid Talib sent a telegram to Enver Pasha pledging to secure the support of Saudi ruler Ibn Saud for the defence of Basra from British invasion. The Unionists had nothing to lose from this initiative and suggested that if he were successful, Sayyid Talib might be rewarded with the governorship of Basra for his efforts.

The British, already concerned about Arab loyalties, had been working to pre-empt any Ottoman initiative to recruit Gulf shaykhs to their cause or to rally Arab tribes to a global jihad against the Entente. On 31 October, the Political Resident in the Gulf, S. G. Knox, issued a proclamation to the "rulers and shaikhs in the Persian Gulf and their subjects" announcing the Ottoman entry into the war. "Your relations with Great Britain are of long standing," Knox reminded Britain's Arab allies, "and I take this opportunity of assuring you that, in this struggle, we shall do our utmost to preserve for you your liberty and religion." To reinforce this point, on 3 November the British concluded a formal agreement recognizing Kuwait's independence from the Ottoman Empire under British protection. In return, the ruler of Kuwait, Shaykh Mubarak, pledged to work with Shaykh Khazaal, Ibn Saud, "and other reliable Shaikhs" to help "liberate Basrah from Turkish possession".[10]

Sir Percy Cox, IEF D's chief political officer, was in constant contact with Britain's Arab allies, coordinating actions to ensure local support for the invasion of southern Mesopotamia. On 5 November, Cox dispatched a proclamation to the Arab rulers at the head of the Gulf to advise them of the approach of British forces, which he claimed had been sent to the Shatt "to protect [Britain's] commerce and friends and expel the hostile Turkish troops". The British had the Gulf stitched up well before Sayyid Talib al-Naqib launched his initiative to win Ibn Saud to the Ottoman cause.[11]

As he rode from Basra to Muhammerah, Kuwait, and the Najd, Sayyid Talib al-Naqib found every local leader in the Gulf opposed to his Ottoman initiative. Shaykh Khazaal tried to persuade his friend Talib to reconsider Britain's terms. The ruler of Kuwait threatened to place Sayyid Talib and his colleagues under house arrest on Britain's instructions. "If you try to prevent me from leaving Kuwait," the irate al-Naqib threatened Shaykh Mubarak, "I will fire two shots with my revolver, the first one at you and the second one at myself." Though Sayyid Talib and a small group of his friends did manage to slip out of Kuwait, it took nine days of intensive riding to reach Ibn Saud at al-Burayda in the Qasim region of north-central Arabia.[12]

The Saudi ruler received his guests with sympathy and hospitality. Ibn Saud did not hide the fact that he was in correspondence with the British, whom he claimed were urging him to preserve his neutrality (Britain would only formalize treaty relations with him in 1915). Ibn Saud was clearly torn. Given the importance of religion to his own movement, he could not be seen to support the non-Muslim British at the expense of his Arab Muslim brothers in Basra. Yet Ibn Saud was wary of antagonizing the British, given their powerful presence in the Gulf. And so he procrastinated, in the hope that the matter would resolve itself before he was forced to take sides.

Ibn Saud waited nine days before mobilizing a group of five hundred horsemen to ride towards the head of the Gulf. The Saudi leader, who could ride night and day when the cause was urgent, travelled only four hours a day with Sayyid Talib's delegation. On reaching its first post station in late November, the Saudi force learned that Basra had already fallen to the British. The news hit the men of Basra "like a bolt of lightning", Sulayman Faydi recorded. "The shock was particularly violent for Sayyid Talib, who knew the depths of English hatred for him." However, the resolution of the crisis must have been a relief to Ibn Saud. He expressed his sympathies to the men of Basra and returned to pursue his own priorities in central Arabia.[13]

The fall of Basra left Sayyid Talib an exile. He had failed the Ottomans and alienated the British. He rode back to Kuwait and surrendered to the British. He was sent to India for the duration of the war, which all sides imagined would be quite brief. Yet the British occupation of Basra initiated a far longer campaign in Mesopotamia than Sayyid Talib had ever anticipated.

ON 5 NOVEMBER, GREAT BRITAIN DECLARED WAR ON THE OTTOMAN Empire. At dawn the next day, British units of the Indian Expeditionary

Force entered Turkish territorial waters in the Shatt al-Arab. The sloop HMS *Odin*, a hybrid warship that combined steam engines with sailing masts, took up position inside the mouth of the Shatt and opened fire on the Turkish gun emplacements on the Fao Peninsula. Within an hour, the fort's commander had been killed, and the Ottoman soldiers—some four hundred men in all—abandoned the position. Delamain landed five hundred men to destroy the guns and establish a secure telegraph line from Fao to India by underwater cable. The action was not without its difficulties. Strong tidal streams disrupted the landing craft, and the muddy banks of the Shatt estuary compounded the difficulty of getting men, horses, and cannon ashore in the absence of any docks or jetties. However, the quick and decisive action, achieved without any British casualties, augured well for the British campaign.[14]

Delamain left a company of soldiers to protect the telegraph station at Fao and moved up the Shatt with the rest of his brigade to secure the oil facilities at Abadan. He landed his troops at Saniyya on the Turkish banks of the river upstream from the refinery. Without adequate lighters, it took two days to ferry men, their mounts, and materiel from the transport ships to the shore. Transport issues would plague the Mesopotamia campaign. In the absence of proper roads, everything had to be moved by river; yet the river was shallow and full of obstructions placed by the Ottomans, and its muddy banks complicated movements on and off ship. However, from their encampment at Saniyya, the soldiers of IEF D were well positioned to protect Abadan from Ottoman attack.

Delamain decided to wait until reinforcements arrived before attempting to move upriver towards Basra. The Ottomans mounted an attack on Anglo-Indian positions on 11 November, inflicting the first casualties on IEF D before retreating under fire. The Indian and British troops had to defend themselves in an alien environment that discouraged bold movements. Sudden drenching rainstorms turned the banks of the Shatt into quagmires of mud, while strong winds whipped up sandstorms that cut all visibility and signal communications. Mirages proved one of the most perplexing natural phenomena for the troops, making visual identification on the battlefield almost impossible. As Edmund Candler, a journalist embedded with IEF D as an "official eyewitness" recalled, mirages made it "difficult to tell if the enemy [were] on horse or on foot, or to make any estimate of their numbers. There is not a cavalry regiment with the Force which has not at some time or other mistaken sheep for infantry." Caution seemed to dictate waiting until the expeditionary force was strengthened before advancing up the Shatt.[15]

Reinforcements arrived on 14 November. Lieutenant General Sir Arthur Barrett reached the Shatt with the remainder of the 6th Indian Division to take command of IEF D. With enough troops both to protect Abadan and march on Basra, Barrett was confident he could resume hostilities without undue risk. He had valuable support from the Royal Navy, which had dispatched a number of shallow-draft warships to the Shatt. The naval vessels were capable of both transporting the forces and shelling Ottoman positions with their heavy guns. With the Ottomans reeling from the sudden appearance of the invasion force, Barrett wanted to strike before the defenders had the chance to regroup and confront the invaders.

The British attacked Ottoman lines the day after Barrett arrived and drove the defenders from their positions, leaving over 160 dead and wounded men on the field. Two days later, on 17 November, they engaged the Ottomans at Sahil in heavy rains followed by sandstorms. Both sides suffered losses—nearly 500 British and Indian dead and wounded, and an estimated 1,500 to 2,000 Ottoman casualties—before the Anglo-Indian army took the Ottoman lines and forced the defenders to retreat a second time. In his dispatches, Barrett claimed the operations had "proved the superiority of our troops over the Turks" and the "demoralization" of the Turks after their "severe losses".[16]

After a string of swift defeats, the Ottomans decided their position in Basra was untenable and abandoned the city on 21 November. As soon as the government authorities had left, rioters swept the city to destroy government offices and plunder businesses. John Van Ess, acting American consul in Basra, sent a letter by river courier appealing to the British commander "to send a force sufficient to guard against pillage". Basra had succumbed to total lawlessness: "All yesterday the Arabs have been robbing the places vacated by the government and there has been continual firing."[17]

The Royal Navy sloops *Espiègle* and *Odin* were dispatched immediately to Basra to secure the waterfront until the troops could arrive overland the following day. On 23 November, Barrett made a ceremonial entry into Basra, where the British flag was raised over the city centre to mark the town's passage from Ottoman to British control. Sir Percy Cox drafted a rousing proclamation that he read to the gathered townspeople in his English-accented Arabic: "The British Government has now occupied Basra, but though a state of war with the Ottoman Government still prevails, yet we have no enmity or ill-will against the populace, to whom we hope to prove good friends and protectors. No remnant of Turkish Administration now remains in this region. In place thereof the British flag has been established—under which you will enjoy the benefits of liberty and justice both in regard to your religious and your secular affairs." Cox's proclamation confused the British and the Basrans alike. The British were unsure how much liberty they wanted to concede to the people of Basra, and the people of Basra had no idea just how long the British would remain. For many, after centuries of Ottoman rule, it was hard to imagine that the Turks would not eventually return. So long as there remained any chance of an Ottoman restoration, the local townspeople would keep their distance from the British for fear of later reprisals.[18]

Once in Basra, the British had effectively achieved their objectives in Mesopotamia. They had driven the Ottomans from the head of the Persian Gulf and protected the strategic oil facilities in Abadan. Sir Percy Cox made a strong case for pursuing the retreating Ottoman forces to seize Baghdad but was overruled by military planners and the Government of India. Instead, the British authorized a limited advance to the town of Qurna, at the juncture of the Tigris and Euphrates, which would place the whole of the Shatt al-Arab under British control.

The campaign for Qurna began on 3 December. Royal Navy vessels carried the soldiers to a safe landing spot four miles south of the town. As the invaders marched up the left bank of the Shatt, they encountered growing opposition from Ottoman defenders, who managed to halt the Anglo-Indian force before withdrawing across the Tigris. Clearly the Ottomans hoped to buy time to regroup by putting the river between themselves and IEF forces. But when the invaders managed to secure a pontoon bridge across the Tigris, the Ottomans knew their position was untenable. Just before midnight on 6 December, a small river steamer carrying three Turkish commanders made its way towards the British ships with all lights blazing and sirens blaring to negotiate their surrender. The handover took place on 9 December, when the governor of the province of Basra, Subhi Bey, delivered the town of Qurna to the commander of the Indian Expeditionary Force and surrendered, along with forty-five officers and 989 soldiers, becoming a prisoner of war.[19]

British operations in the Shatt al-Arab had been deceptively easy. Quick victories were secured with remarkably light British casualties. Fewer than 100 British and Indian soldiers were killed and some 675 wounded in the fighting between Fao and Qurna. The Ottomans, on the other hand, suffered some 3,000 dead and wounded—four times the number of British casualties. Such relatively easy gains gave the British a distorted sense of their own abilities and led them to underestimate their Ottoman foe.[20]

Having secured their position in Basra, the British settled down to administer the region. As occupiers, the British were bound by the laws of war to preserve the institutions of the Ottoman state. The unwillingness of the local inhabitants to cooperate with the new authorities, however, compromised their work. The British continued to attribute this recalcitrance to local fear of a possible return by the Ottomans. Yet it might just as well have reflected a native dislike for the foreign occupiers—an antipathy reinforced by British security measures in Mesopotamia.

Private William Bird, a soldier in one of the Dorset Battalions of IEF D, described a typical village search near Basra in January 1915. Anglo-Indian soldiers would approach a village at dawn, break down all doors not answered on the first knock, "make prisoners of all the male occupants, then search everything and everywhere for arms". The British practiced rough justice among villagers suspected of resisting their occupation. "Those who attempt to run away are caught by our ring of men outside the village," Bird noted. "They are treated as combatants and meet their end on the scaffold. And of course those who shoot at us are either shot or captured and hung in the market square." Such measures were unlikely to win the affections of the native inhabitants of Basra Province.[21]

Nor did the British hold out a vision of greater political freedoms to win over the people of Basra. When the viceroy of India, Lord Hardinge, visited Basra and Qurna in February 1915, he toned down Cox's sweeping promise of "liberty and justice", offering instead "a more benign administration" and restored prosperity. Rather than greater autonomy or self-rule, the British occupation seemed to promise a British administration. Sayyid Talib al-Naqib had not been mistaken: the people of Basra had exchanged masters, British for Ottoman.[22]

AFTER SEEING OFF DELAMAIN'S BRIGADE FOR SERVICE IN THE PERSIAN Gulf, the remainder of the Indian Expeditionary Force had continued on its course to Egypt. The fleet called in to the Arabian port of Aden before entering the Red Sea. The port was the centre of a tiny colony (eighty square miles) conquered by the British and annexed to their Indian empire in 1839. The Royal Navy originally used Aden as a base for operations against piracy. With the opening of the Suez Canal in 1869, Aden proved the ideal location for a coaling station for steamships running between Britain and India. Like Hong Kong, Aden developed into one of the essential stepping stones in Britain's maritime empire and an important trade emporium in its own right.

In the second half of the nineteenth century, the British had concluded a series of treaties with the tribes in the territories surrounding Aden, creating a special zone of influence known as the Aden Protectorate. The protectorate comprised nine distinct mini-states with their own autonomous rulers, British protégés whose combined territory added up to 9,000 square miles of coastal territory on the southernmost tip of Arabia. The Aden Protectorate abutted the Ottoman province of Yemen. Between 1902 and 1905, an Anglo-Turkish Boundary Commission demarcated the frontier between the two territories. With the Ottoman entry into the war in 1914, this was suddenly transformed into a hostile border and the second point of engagement between Britain and the Ottoman Empire.

The border between Ottoman Yemen and the Aden Protectorate met at the Bab al-Mandab straits, the gateway to the Red Sea. The southernmost point of Ottoman territory was Shaykh Said, where the Turks maintained a series of hilltop forts with guns dominating the sea lanes. The British held Perim Island, a five-square-mile rock facing Shaykh Said in the Bab al-Mandab straits, some one hundred miles west of Aden.

In early November, British intelligence reported the Turks were massing troops in Shaykh Said. Analysts speculated the Ottoman forces intended to open hostilities against British positions in the Aden Protectorate or even to occupy Perim Island. Given the strategic importance of the Red Sea waterways to the British Empire at war—all troop ships from New Zealand, Australia, and India had to pass through the Bab al-Mandab to reach the Suez Canal—British war planners in India decided to disperse Ottoman troops and disable their guns at Shaykh Said. Fresh troops were dispatched from India to Aden on 2 November to secure Britain's island in the straits.

On the morning of 10 November, British ships off Perim opened fire on Ottoman positions on the hilltops of Shaykh Said. Lieutenant H. V. Gell, a signaller in the 69th Punjabis, was impatient for the bombardment to end so that he and the rest of the landing party could go ashore for their "first action". The men boarded landing ships and were towed to shore by a slow-moving tugboat, while Turkish gunners fired with increasing precision from the heights overlooking the beach. As they rowed the final stretch to shore, a shell struck within yards of Gell's boat, killing a young Indian reservist. The other men made it to land safely, where they regrouped and waited for orders to begin their attack on Ottoman positions. Taking shelter from intensive fire, the Anglo-Indian landing party waited over four hours before beginning their ascent towards Turkish positions. "There was very little firing then," Gell recalled, "only a few stray bullets now and then."[23]

By the time the Anglo-Indian forces reached the first ridge, they found the Ottomans had abandoned their positions. No doubt the bombardment from British ships, combined with the advance of landing parties, had convinced the defenders that their position was untenable. Given the quantities of clothes, arms, and ammunition left behind, the Ottomans clearly retreated in panic. "The only pity was they got away," Gell noted in his diary. "Their numbers were estimated at about 500." While Gell had no knowledge of Ottoman casualties (he did not see any Turkish dead), he reported five Indian and British soldiers killed and eleven wounded in the operation. The Anglo-Indian force spent the night at Shaykh Said and destroyed all surviving Ottoman gun emplacements before withdrawing to their ships and resuming their journey westward to Egypt on 11 November.

While the operation at Shaykh Said was a military success, it raised political difficulties that would bedevil the British in Aden for the remainder of the war. Military officials in India had drawn up the plans without consulting the authorities in Aden, who had been engaged in delicate negotiations to isolate the Ottomans in Yemen. Much of the diplomacy had targeted Imam Yahya, leader of the Shiite Zaydi community in the northern highlands around Sanaa (the capital of Yemen today). The imam had struck a truce with the Ottomans in 1911 and agreed to rule the province of Yemen in alliance with Istanbul in 1913. Though Imam Yahya was in no position to break with the Ottomans, he was keen to establish cordial relations with the British.[24]

The bombardment of Shaykh Said changed everything. "The Imam [Yahya] was incensed, and the [Ottoman] Governor-General of Sana broadcasted a manifesto depicting the ulterior motives of Great Britain, who was bent on annexation," Harold Jacob, a British official in Aden, wrote. "Our action had aided the Turkish propagandists." The imam, for his part, claimed "the affair of Sheikh Said [had] aroused Arab suspicion everywhere." Rather than securing Britain's position in South Yemen, the attack on Shaykh Said had actually left Aden more vulnerable. It was easy enough to drive five hundred soldiers from an isolated coastal fortification. It would prove much harder to defend the 9,000 square miles of the Aden Protectorate from the 14,000 Ottoman soldiers stationed in Yemen, reinforced by Imam Yahya's retainers.[25]

The Ottoman guns at Shaykh Said did not in fact threaten British shipping. The Bab al-Mandab is twenty miles wide at its narrowest, so British ships never needed to pass within range of Turkish guns. Turkish mines and German submarines posed a far greater danger to shipping, and to combat those threats took sea power, not land forces. The Royal Navy dispatched warships to impose a blockade on Turkish ports along the length of the Red Sea coast and to keep the sea lanes open to friendly shipping. Their success could be measured in the scores of cargo ships and troop transports conveying goods and soldiers from the empire through the Red Sea to the Suez Canal and the war zones beyond.

STARTING IN SEPTEMBER 1914, EGYPT WAS FLOODED WITH THOUSANDS of soldiers from Britain and the dominions. The East Lancashire Territorial Division, sent to relieve the professional army in Egypt for service on the western front, was the first to arrive in late September. The Indian Expeditionary Force from Bombay reached Egypt towards the end of October, its soldiers posted to cities in the Suez Canal Zone. The first wave of 30,000 Anzacs completed their journey from New Zealand and Australia to Alexandria in early December. Thousands of reinforcements followed in the ensuing weeks and months. The railway lines between Alexandria and Cairo were clogged with troop trains moving armies of men and horses to camps around Cairo. The Australian Infantry settled to the west of Cairo in Mena, near the Pyramids, the Australian Light Horse in the leafy southern suburb of Maadi, and the New Zealanders in Zeitoun Camp, to the north of Cairo, near Heliopolis.

The influx of imperial troops helped to stabilize a tense situation in Egypt. Since the outbreak of the war, Egypt had been shaken to its political foundations by a series of momentous events: the Ottoman declaration of war and the caliph's call for jihad, the severance of Egypt's centuries-old ties to the Ottoman Empire, the deposal of Khedive Abbas II, and the accession of Sultan Husayn Kamil under British protection. The people of Egypt had grown weary of the British occupation after nearly thirty-two years and looked on Germany as a possible deliverer. German victories over British forces on the western front, such as the Battle of Mons in Belgium (23–24 August 1914), only encouraged such hopes. The British authorities feared subversion by German and Turkish spies, rebellion by Egyptian nationalists, and religious rioting by the "excitable" masses.[26]

The sudden arrival of thousands of foreign soldiers convinced the local population that the British position in Egypt was too strong to challenge. The Anzac training camps surrounded the city of Cairo with tens of thousands of cavalry and infantrymen stirring the desert dust with training and manoeuvres. To impress the townspeople of Cairo, who might not have seen the soldiers at drill in their suburban camps, the British authorities ordered the newly arrived troops to parade through the heart of the city. "We had a great march through the winding streets of Cairo some days ago," Gordon Harper, a cavalryman from Canterbury, New Zealand, wrote in a letter home. "We penetrated all the old Cairo native quarters through miles of alleys and slums and variegated stinks." Harper grasped the political significance of the parade: "The idea was to impress the natives who simply swarm here, with our strength, as they still have a traditional and spiritual connection with the Turks. . . . The effect was very interesting. The route was packed with fezzed men and veiled women who watched us closely without the semblance of a smile or a cheer, but every indication is that they are petrified with British rule."[27]

British and imperial soldiers became tourists when on leave from their camps. Soldiers posed for photographs on horse and camel before the Sphinx, pestered by hucksters with artful forgeries of pharaonic antiques. They were lured into shops in the bazaars with signs that played on Anzac humour: "Don't go elsewhere to be cheated, Australians. Come here!" and "English and French spoken; Australian understood". The Egyptian tourist trade, ever quick to adapt to a changing clientele, renamed hotels and restaurants after every township in Australia and New Zealand. Among the new venues were the Balclutha Bar and the Waipukurau Reading Rooms.[28]

The European quarters surrounding the Ezbekiya Gardens catered to the leisure activities of the foreign soldiers in Cairo. Officers gathered in the restaurants and terraces of the grand hotels surrounding the park, like the famous Shepheards, the New Hotel, and the Bristol. The common soldiers frequented the cafés and bars in the narrow side streets to the north of the park, known as the "Red Blind Quarter" or the "Wozzer" (from the Arabic street name Wasaa), Cairo's red-light district.

The packed bars and brothels of the Red Blind Quarter, filled with soldiers seeking relief from the tedium of camp life and desert drill, proved a volatile environment. Tired of waiting to be sent to war, sick of the "vile doctored liquor" sold to them in cheap bars, and bearing grudges against the prostitutes that had given many soldiers venereal diseases (for which there was no real cure at the time), the imperial forces became a threat to law and order the longer they stayed in Cairo.[29]

Anzac troops rioted in central Cairo on at least two occasions in 1915. On the eve of their departure for Gallipoli in April and again in July of that year, drunken soldiers attacked the brothels of the Red Blind Quarter. Different reasons were given for the outbreaks of violence: soldiers accusing whores of robbery, or seeking revenge for having contracted venereal diseases, or even claiming a racist attack on a Maori soldier. On each occasion, soldiers destroyed the personal effects of prostitutes, throwing linens and furniture from the windows into the streets below. Wardrobes and chests too big to fit through the windows were carried to the tops of the five-story buildings and thrown from the roofs. The crowds that gathered to watch the spectacle piled the furniture and set it alight. Fire quickly spread to the buildings overlooking the narrow alleyway.[30]

In April 1915, when the British authorities dispatched mounted military police to restore order, they confronted a drunk and angry mob of soldiers who refused to obey orders. "All sorts of things were being thrown at the police," one eyewitness reported, "kettles, bits of furniture." The police fired warning shots over the rioters' heads before shooting into the crowd. "Four or five dropped, but the others simply went on facing the police (who were about 5 yards away) as if nothing had happened." Fire trucks were dispatched to bring the flames under control. When they turned their jets of water on the rebellious soldiers, the rioters attacked the fire hoses, disabling the truck. At this point, British soldiers were called to the scene and took up firing positions, "back row standing, second row kneeling, front row lying down. The officer in command warned the crowd in the street that he must fire if it didn't disperse and it dispersed at once," an eyewitness recounted. "Three rows of men like that are not the sort of thing you care to face when you are unarmed." The riot broke up around 8 p.m., with five Anzac soldiers wounded and fifty under arrest. British reports gave no figures for Egyptian casualties in the April troubles, though several houses were burned to the ground. Yet more houses were burned down in the July 1915 riots.[31]

For the residents of Cairo, these dangerous disorders contributed to growing hostility towards the dominion troops—and the British occupation that had brought them to Egypt. In his account of the riots in the Red Blind Quarter, veteran Egyptian politician Ahmad Shafiq expressed dismay that soldiers would stand by and watch their comrades set fire to brothels without intervening and that the Anzac soldiers showed so little concern for the lives of the women inside. "Had these events happened in any other circumstances than the war, they would have ignited a major revolt," Shafiq concluded. "Those soldiers, particularly from the dominions, treated the Egyptians with crudeness and contempt."[32]

The influx of imperial troops, rather than stabilizing things, was making a tense situation in Egypt worse. Yet the people of Egypt would continue to play host to British and imperial forces for years to come. Their country was an important staging post, training ground, and medical base for soldiers who would fight in Egypt, Gallipoli, and Palestine in campaigns that would last to the very end of the war. Egypt's northern ports, Alexandria and Port Said, also served as important maritime bases for British and French shipping as they asserted their mastery over the eastern Mediterranean.

AFTER THE OTTOMANS ENTERED THE WAR IN NOVEMBER 1914, BRITAIN and France imposed a blockade on the Aegean coastline from the Thracian port of Dedeağaç (the modern town of Alexandroupoli in north-eastern Greece) to the island of Samos, south of the Turkish port of Smyrna (modern Izmir). The combined Allied fleet, known as the Eastern Mediterranean Squadron, reached a full strength of eighteen battleships, forty destroyers, fifteen torpedo boats, twelve submarines, and twenty monitors (shallow-draft warships with heavy cannons that were notoriously unseaworthy). The squadron was based in Moudros Harbour on the disputed island of Lemnos, just fifty miles from the Dardanelles.[33]

At the start of the European conflict, Ottoman sea defences along the straits were outdated and inadequate. Shortly after the Germans and Young Turks concluded their secret alliance on 2 August, German ships began to ferry men and materiel to the Dardanelles to reinforce the straits. The Allied bombardment of the Dardanelles on 3 November 1914, which destroyed much of the Seddülbahir Fort at the entrance to the straits, set back their work. The Ottomans and Germans redoubled their efforts. Hundreds of German soldiers and military engineers designed and built new batteries along the European and Asian shores, installing powerful guns to deter ships from entering the strategic waterway. The aged warship *Messoudieh*, built in 1876 but armed with heavy cannons, was anchored inside the Dardanelles with its guns pointing out to sea. Turkish ships laid hundreds of mines in neat rows running southward from the Narrows at Çanakkale and around the Black Sea entrance to the Bosporus. Powerful searchlights were placed on the headlands to expose shipping at night, and a Marconi radiotelegraph system was installed to provide modern communications between military posts.

The Ottomans concentrated their Mediterranean fleet in the Dardanelles to protect their capital city, Istanbul, from Allied attack. The two German warships transferred to the Ottoman fleet in August 1914, the *Breslau* and *Goeben*, were deployed to the Bosporus to protect Istanbul from the north and to attack Russian ports and shipping in the Black Sea. By the time Turkey entered the war in November, the Bosporus and Dardanelles were much better defended from naval attack. However, the Germans and Ottomans recognized that the straits were not impregnable. The German admiral overseeing the works reported in December 1914 that he believed a strong Allied fleet could still break through the Dardanelles' defences with the loss of four or five ships.[34]

The Ottomans' infantry served as their ultimate deterrent against an Allied attack on Istanbul. Both the Germans and the Ottomans believed the Allies needed to land troops in order to occupy Istanbul—they could not do so by naval power alone. In order to secure the capital and its hinterlands, the Ottomans concentrated the largest part of their army in the straits and in Thrace. Between the Ottoman First Army (160,000 men), which counted some of the most experienced Turkish troops among its ranks, and the Second Army (80,000 men), the Turks could boast a force of nearly 250,000 soldiers—half of the armed forces mobilized by November 1914—to defend the capital from an Entente landing.[35]

With the Turkish navy confined to the straits, Ottoman coastal towns on the Aegean and the Black Sea were highly vulnerable to Allied attack. In both the seas, Entente warships disrupted economic activity and lines of communications. Russian warships bombarded the Black Sea port of Trabzon on 17 November 1914, spreading panic and inflicting "a great deal of loss in life and property", according to the American consul who witnessed the attack. Between November 1914 and March 1915, the Russians attacked Trabzon six times, sinking ships, damaging the city, and driving the townspeople to seek refuge in the surrounding countryside. The Russians also shelled the Turkish coal mines in Zonguldak to disrupt a vital energy source for Turkish and German ships. In the Aegean, the British and French opened fire on the port of Izmir, where a number of merchant vessels had been trapped by the blockade. In retaliation, the Ottomans seized three British ships as prizes of war and sank them at the mouth of the harbour to obstruct entry by Allied war vessels. This left six other steamships from the United States, Greece, Bulgaria, the Netherlands, and Germany bottled up for the duration of the war.[36]

In the coastal region of Cilicia, where Turkish Anatolia borders the Syrian lands, the Ottomans feared for the security of their railway lines. With the closure of all maritime lines of communications, the railways played a particularly important role in the transport of troops, materiel, and supplies from the provinces to the front—in the Caucasus, Mesopotamia, and Syria. The port of Mersin, linked to the Baghdad Railway through neighbouring Adana, had no sea defences at the start of the war. Some 16,000 troops, as well as large shipments of ammunition, were reported to have passed through the Mersin-Adana railway line at the end of November 1914. Unable to mount any deterrence to Allied vessels, the Ottomans were forced to submit to the humiliation of French warships entering Mersin with impunity, impounding and destroying ships at will.[37]

The Gulf of Alexandretta, due east of Mersin, was another crossroads of rail and maritime communications. The Baghdad Railway reached the Mediterranean coast at this point, though in 1914 the line remained isolated from Adana by unfinished tunnels in the Taurus Mountains and from Aleppo by on-going works in the Amanus Mountains. This meant that passengers and cargo had to disembark the trains and be transported around the mountain obstructions to resume their rail journey from the other side of the unfinished tunnels. These inconveniences notwithstanding, Alexandretta served as a transit point for tens of thousands of Turkish troops running between Syria, Mesopotamia, and Anatolia.

In December 1914, the British light cruiser HMS *Doris* entered the Gulf of Alexandretta to bombard the railway line from the sea. On Sunday morning, 20 December, the warship opened fire near the village of Dörtyol. "Shot after shot was fired at the railroad line," H. E. Bishop, the American consular agent in Alexandretta, reported, "the ship slowly proceeding along the coast towards Alexandretta." Shortly after midday, the ship entered Alexandretta Harbour under a white flag and sent a tender ashore to deliver an ultimatum to the town's officials. Explaining that the railway lines served to transport Ottoman troops to fronts where they threatened British forces (particularly in Mesopotamia), the British commander demanded that the Ottoman authorities surrender all rail stock and war materiel for a British landing party to destroy on shore. Should the authorities fail to comply, the *Doris* would bombard all administrative, rail, and port facilities with her heavy guns. Any civilian casualties would be the responsibility of the Ottoman authorities, the British having discharged their obligations under the Hague Convention of 1907 by giving fair warning before firing on the unfortified port.[38]

Cemal Pasha, one of the ruling CUP triumvirs, had just assumed his new wartime commission as commander in chief in Syria. When he received word of the British ultimatum from the district governor of Alexandretta, he responded impulsively with a counterthreat. He refused out of hand to surrender rolling stock or war materiel to the captain of the *Doris*. As a nation at war, he agreed the British were within their rights to fire on government buildings. However, for each Ottoman government building damaged by the British navy, he threatened to retaliate by ordering the immediate destruction of a like number of English properties and institutions in Syria. Yet more inflammatorily, Cemal informed the British commander that he had interned scores of British subjects in Syria since the outbreak of the war. He now threatened to shoot an English subject for every Ottoman citizen killed in any hostile action taken by the *Doris* against the city of Alexandretta.

Cemal's provocative response escalated the Alexandretta Incident into a full-scale crisis that was defused by American diplomacy. The United States was still a neutral power in the Great War (it would remain so until April 1917) and enjoyed cordial relations with the Ottoman Empire. The Americans also agreed to represent the interests of the Entente Powers within Ottoman domains. Both the British and the Ottomans seemed open to American mediation to get them out of the deadlock of ultimatum and threats of retaliation.

Working with the Turkish and German officials in Alexandretta, US Consular Agent Bishop secured a twenty-four-hour grace period to negotiate a resolution. Since Cemal Pasha was unwilling to evacuate the civilians of Alexandretta, the local governor hoped to avoid bombardment at all costs. The British commander, for his part, was very concerned about avoiding the retaliatory killing of British subjects. Bishop reported to the captain of the *Doris* that "there were no troops in Alexandretta and that according to . . . local officials all munitions of war had been already removed to the interior" (in a confidential aside, Bishop noted that he later discovered "there *were* other munitions of war here at the time"). Bishop suggested that the Ottomans could be brought to accept the destruction of two locomotives, ostensibly "the only materiel of war at Alexandretta", which would fulfil the *Doris*'s mission of disrupting military communications.

"After consultation held between an officer from the ship, the Governor of the city, and the writer," Bishop later reported, "it was decided that the engines would be run into an open space and would be blown up in the presence of a representative of the ship and myself." The *Doris* provided the high explosives for the job, and a party of four officials—an Ottoman captain, the harbour master, a warrant officer from the *Doris*, and the American consul—set off at 9:30 p.m. to witness the destruction of the two forlorn locomotives. Charges were detonated, "luckily without injury to anyone", and on inspection the two locomotives were declared "sufficiently damaged to prohibit their further operation". Consul Bishop concluded his report with some irony: "At 10:45 we again arrived at the railroad pier whereupon the Commander of the British landing party informed the writer that the Captain of the ship had signaled his thanks for having witnessed fairplay, the British stepped into the steamboat, shoved off and the incident was closed."

The British made a more lethal demonstration of their mastery of the seas when they dispatched a submarine to sink the *Messoudieh* at its anchorage in the Dardanelles. On an exceptionally clear and calm Sunday morning in December, a British submarine negotiated four miles of minefields undetected to fire a torpedo into the bow of the aged Ottoman cruiser. At 11:55 a.m., a terrible explosion rocked the *Messoudieh*, shrouding the vessel in smoke. As the haze cleared, the *Messoudieh* fired two salvos from its heavy cannons in a blind effort to retaliate against its hidden attacker, until it began to list too heavily to continue. With a sudden jerk, the Ottoman warship capsized. According to one eyewitness, the cruiser sank in no more than seven minutes. Anchored in shallow waters close to shore, the *Messoudieh* settled on the seabed with much of her hull exposed. As dozens of sailors clung to her gun ports and hull fittings, boats put out from shore to rescue survivors. The operations went on late into the night while engineers drilled escape hatches through her hull. Between fifty and one hundred men were reported to have died in the attack.[39]

The enemy submarine's successful evasion of an extensive minefield and the sudden loss of a major warship came as a terrible shock to the Ottoman authorities. Vice Admiral Johannes Merten, the German officer in command at the Dardanelles, grudgingly acknowledged, "It was a mighty clever piece of work." Yet most of all, the attack on the *Messoudieh*, combined with previous shelling of Turkish positions in the Dardanelles, served as a warning to the Ottomans that the Allies were preparing for a larger campaign against the straits.[40]

TWO MONTHS INTO THE WAR, THE VULNERABILITY OF THE OTTOMAN Empire was clear to both the Entente and the Central Powers. The Turks had proven incapable of defending all of their frontiers from attack, and given the territorial spread of the Ottoman Empire, it was not realistic to expect that they could. They had been forced into retreat at every point of the compass: in the Caucasus, in Basra, in Yemen, and in the Aegean and Cilicia. The Russians had seized territory in Anatolia, while the British had stripped the Ottomans of their autonomous province of Egypt, excluded the Ottomans from the Persian Gulf, and secured total naval supremacy in the Red Sea and (in partnership with the French) in the Mediterranean. With tens of thousands of imperial soldiers arriving in Egypt each month from Australia, New Zealand, and India and a growing naval presence in the Aegean, the Entente Powers were building an unassailable position against the Ottomans.

Under growing German pressure, the Ottomans decided to go on the offensive. They needed victories to rally the morale of their soldiers and citizens alike. And they had yet to put the sultan's call to jihad to the test.

FIVE

Launching Jihad

Ottoman Campaigns in the Caucasus and the Sinai

IN THE OPENING WEEKS OF THE WAR, THE OTTOMANS HAD SUFFERED a string of minor defeats around the fringes of their vast empire. Yet their army remained fully intact, and the Turks had yet to play the wild card of jihad against the Allies. In fact, many in the German high command believed that the Ottomans' greatest contribution to their war effort would come less from the Turkish army than from the internal uprisings Ottoman military action might provoke among Muslims under French colonial rule in North Africa, under the British in Egypt and India, and under the Russians in the Caucasus and Central Asia. At the very least, the threat of such internal rebellions might force the Entente Powers to deploy troops in Asia and Africa to preserve the peace in their Muslim territories, relieving the pressure on the Germans on the western front and the Germans and Austrians on the eastern front.

Since mid-September 1914, this pressure had grown severe. The concerted French and British counteroffensive on the Marne (5–12 September) had brought the German war of movement to a halt and resulted in trench warfare. Stalemate in western Europe left Germany fighting a two-front war, when German war plans had called for a quick victory in France to free the German army to relieve Austria and throw its full weight against Russia. The Austrians needed all the assistance they could get on the eastern front. In August and September 1914, Austria-Hungary suffered critical defeats to the

Serbs in the Balkans and to the Russians in the eastern Austro-Hungarian territory of Galicia. Austrian losses in Galicia alone reached 350,000 men. As Austria faltered, German war planners began to pressure their Ottoman ally to initiate hostilities against Britain and Russia.[1]

The Germans pressed their Ottoman allies to engage the Russians and British in places that would most assist the German and Austrian war effort. General Liman von Sanders, commander of the German military mission to Turkey, suggested sending five Ottoman army corps (approximately 150,000 men) across the Black Sea to Odessa to relieve Austrian positions in Galicia and press Russian forces between the Austrians and the Turks. Berlin favoured an expedition against British positions along the Suez Canal, both to cut imperial maritime communications and to exploit Egyptian hostility to the British occupation. The kaiser and his military chiefs hoped that by striking such bold blows against the Entente, the Ottomans might inspire Muslims across Asia and Africa to take up the sultan-caliph's call for jihad.[2]

The Young Turks had their own agenda and hoped to use the war to recover lost territory in both Egypt and eastern Anatolia. British-held Egypt and the "three provinces" (*Elviye-i Selâse*) taken by the Russians in 1878 were Ottoman Muslim lands. The Young Turks were confident their soldiers would fight to recover Ottoman territory and hoped their successes would encourage local Muslims to rise up against the Russians and British.[3]

In mid-November 1914, Enver Pasha, Ottoman minister of war, invited his colleague Cemal, the minister of marine, home for a private meeting. "I want to start an offensive against the Suez Canal to keep the English tied up in Egypt," Enver explained, "and thus not only compel them to leave there a large number of Indian divisions which they are now sending to the Western Front, but prevent them from concentrating a force to land at the Dardanelles." Towards this end, the minister of war offered Cemal the commission to raise an army in Syria to lead the attack on British positions in the Sinai. Cemal accepted the commission with alacrity and promised to set off within the week.[4]

On 21 November, Cemal boarded a train at Istanbul's Haidar Pasha Railway Station to begin his journey to Syria. The station was crowded with members of the cabinet, leading Ottoman statesmen, and the diplomatic corps, in the caustic words of US Ambassador Henry Morgenthau, "to give this departing satrap an enthusiastic farewell". Carried away by their war enthusiasm, the patriotic crowd hailed Cemal prematurely as the "saviour of Egypt". Just before the train pulled away, Cemal pledged to his supporters that he would not return "until I have conquered Egypt". Morgenthau, no fan of the Young Turks, found "the whole performance . . . somewhat bombastic".[5]

Enver Pasha took it on himself to lead the attack on Russia. He had no interest in German plans for an operation on the north shore of the Black Sea, far removed from Ottoman frontiers. He focused instead on the lost "three provinces" of eastern Anatolia. Enver believed that a sizeable Muslim population in the Caucasus would respond enthusiastically to an Ottoman offensive. Moreover, Enver believed Turkish forces had taken the measure of the Russian Caucasus Army. The Russians had already initiated hostilities against the Turks on the Caucasus frontier. The Ottomans' recent success in turning back the Russian advance at Köprüköy had stirred Enver's ambitions. On 6 December, Enver called on Liman von Sanders to announce he was sailing that night for the Black Sea port of Trabzon to lead an attack on the Caucasus frontier. As Liman later recalled, "Map in hand Enver sketched to me the outline of the intended operations by the Third Army. With one army corps, the Eleventh, he meant to hold the Russians in front on the main road, while two corps, the Ninth and Tenth, marching by their left were to cross the mountains by several marches and then fall on the Russian flank and rear in the vicinity of Sarikamisch. Later the Third Army was to take Kars." The plan Enver outlined was fraught with risks. The mountainous terrain and inadequate roads compromised troop movements, supply lines, and lines of communication. When Liman raised his concerns, Enver insisted that these issues "had already been considered and that all roads had been reconnoitered".[6]

Bringing his meeting with Liman to a close, Enver played to Berlin's deepest hopes for the Ottoman jihad. As the German general recorded, Enver "gave utterance to phantastic, yet noteworthy ideas. He told me that he contemplated marching through Afghanistan to India. Then he went away." Liman did not rate Enver's chances of success very highly, but he wasn't going to get in his way.

Two of the ruling Young Turk triumvirs set off to lead the first Ottoman ground campaigns against the Entente Powers. Perhaps, had they focused their efforts on a single campaign, they might have stood a chance of success. The rush to take on two Great Powers with inadequate preparation condemned both campaigns to catastrophic failure.

ENVER PASHA SAILED THE BLACK SEA FROM ISTANBUL TO TRABZON, where he disembarked on 8 December. Accompanied by two of his closest German advisers, Colonel Paul Bronsart von Schellendorf and Major Otto von Feldmann, he made his way overland to the headquarters of the Ottoman Third Army in the garrison town of Erzurum. Many in the Ottoman high command complained that the Germans had too much influence over their minister of war. Indeed, the broad outlines of Enver's bold plan to defeat the Russian Caucasus Army can be traced back to his German advisers.

In late August 1914, German forces performed a perfect flanking operation against the Russians in Tannenberg, East Prussia. While the Germans engaged Russian troops along the front line, they dispatched infantry and artillery by road and rail around the Russians' left flank, cutting their supply and communications lines and encircling the tsar's troops. By the time the Russians realized the danger they were in, it was already too late. The Germans destroyed the Russian Second Army, inflicting 30,000 casualties and taking 92,000 men prisoner in what would prove the most complete German victory of the First World War. Enver hoped to adapt German tactics to lead the Ottoman army to a similar triumph against Russian forces in the Caucasus.[7]

Enver, an impetuous man, had made his career through bold, high-risk initiatives. A historic leader of the 1908 revolution, an architect of the 1911 Ottoman-led jihad in Libya, leader of the 1913 raid on the Sublime Porte who forced the prime minister to resign at gunpoint, and "liberator of Edirne" in the Second Balkan War, Enver believed in taking action and had little doubt in his own judgment and abilities. He clearly believed he could lead an army to victory against Russia and that such a victory would be of the greatest benefit to the Ottoman war effort. The Turks would not only regain territory lost to Russia in 1878 but could discourage further Russian ambitions in Ottoman territory—particularly in the straits and Istanbul. And, as Enver suggested to Liman von Sanders, a glorious battlefield victory might just trigger Islamic enthusiasms in Central Asia that would open the road to Afghanistan and India.

Ottoman commanders in the field had their doubts that the battle plan developed in Tannenberg at the height of summer could be applied to the very different setting of the Caucasus Mountains in winter. The Germans, operating very close to well-stocked bases, had relied on roads and railways to move large numbers of troops into position to complete the encirclement of Russian forces at Tannenberg. The unpaved roads and footpaths in the mountainous highlands of eastern Anatolia were practically impassable to wheeled traffic in winter. With mountain peaks in excess of 3,000 metres, winter snows 1.5 metres in depth, and temperatures plunging to –20°C, only soldiers with special training and equipment could survive, let alone prosecute a successful war, in such hostile conditions. Yet even the most sceptical Ottoman officers believed Enver was lucky and just might be able to secure a victory against all the odds.[8]

In the course of the summer of 1914, Enver had consolidated Ottoman forces in the Caucasus region of eastern Anatolia into the Third Army, headquartered in Erzurum. In September, the XI Corps was redeployed from its base in Van to join the IX Corps in Erzurum, and in October the X Corps was transferred secretly from Erzincan to bring the Third Army to fighting trim. By the time Enver reached Erzurum in December 1914, the total strength of the Third Army was around 150,000 men (including Kurdish irregular cavalry and other auxiliaries). That gave the Turks a campaign force of some 100,000 to use against the Russians, while holding the remainder in reserve to secure Erzurum and the Caucasus frontier from Lake Van to the Black Sea—nearly three hundred miles in all.[9]

The commander of the Ottoman Third Army, Hasan Izzet Pasha, had reviewed Enver's battle plan and given his qualified support for the attack on Russian positions. He argued that his men needed proper provisions for a winter campaign, including cold-weather clothing, sufficient food, and stores of ammunition. To Enver, such sound logistical considerations were but delaying tactics on the part of an overly cautious commander. He placed his trust instead in an ambitions officer named Hafız Hakki Bey, who wrote Enver in secret to claim he had reconnoitred the roads and passes and was convinced they could be used in winter by infantry with mountain guns (light artillery that could be transported by mules). "The commanders here do not support the idea [of a winter campaign] because they lack persistence and courage," he wrote to Enver. "Yet I would undertake this task if my rank were adjusted accordingly."[10]

When Enver arrived to launch the campaign, Hasan Izzet Pasha tendered his resignation as commander of the Third Army. He simply did not believe the campaign could succeed without adequate provisions for the soldiers. Given his knowledge of the surrounding area, Hasan Izzet Pasha was a loss to the Ottoman war effort in the Caucasus. Yet Enver had lost confidence in the general and, in accepting his resignation, took personal command of the Third Army on 19 December. He also promoted the ambitious Hafız Hakkı Bey and put him at the head of the X Corps. Commanding officers with little or no experience of formal military campaigns and very limited knowledge of the dangerous terrain were now in charge, as Enver issued orders for the fateful attack on the Russian railhead at Sarıkamış, to begin on 22 December.

As Enver's campaign came to eastern Anatolia, the Armenians found themselves on the front line, their loyalties divided between the Russian and Ottoman empires. In 1878, a sizable Armenian population in the three provinces of Kars, Ardahan, and Batum had passed from Ottoman to Russian rule. While the tsarist government had proven no more accommodating of Armenian separatist aspirations than the Turks, St Petersburg played on a common Christian identity (notwithstanding the deep doctrinal divides between Russian and Armenian Orthodoxy) in a bid to turn the Armenians against the Muslim Turks.

Russian and Turkish religious politics in the Caucasus had a certain symmetry, with the tsarist government hoping to foment a Christian uprising against the Turks, just as the Ottomans sought to exploit Muslim solidarity to provoke jihad among Caucasian Muslims against Russia. In the Russian Caucasus, the Armenian National Council had worked closely with the tsarist government even before the outbreak of war to recruit four volunteer regiments to assist a Russian invasion of Turkish territory. Russian consular officials and military intelligence concurred that such Armenian volunteer units would encourage Ottoman Christians to assist a Russian invasion, and in September 1914 Russia's foreign minister, Sergei Sazonov, signed orders to smuggle Russian arms to Ottoman Armenians ahead of Turkey's anticipated entry into the war. A number of prominent Ottoman Armenians crossed the frontier to join the Russian war effort, though most held back, fearing their involvement in such regiments would jeopardize the safety of Armenian civilians under Ottoman rule.[11]

In the summer months of 1914, Ottoman officials kept a watchful eye on the Armenians of eastern Anatolia. In July and August, while Ottoman war mobilization was at its height, the Armenian men of Van, Trabzon, and Erzurum reported for duty while the civilian population remained, by all accounts, loyal. Yet the Russians reported over 50,000 deserters from the Ottoman army, most of them Armenians, crossing over to Russian lines between August and October 1914.[12]

Amid mounting concern over Armenian loyalties, the Young Turks convened a meeting in Erzurum in October, at which they proposed an alliance with the Armenian nationalist parties, the Dashnaks and Hunchaks. The Ottomans pledged to establish an autonomous Armenian administration comprising several provinces in eastern Anatolia and any territory conquered from Russian Armenia in return for assistance against the Russians from Armenian communities in both Russia and Turkey. The Armenian nationalists declined, arguing that Armenians should remain loyal to the governments under which they lived on both sides of the Russian-Ottoman border. This reasonable response only fed Ottoman doubts about Armenian loyalties.[13]

Relations between Armenians and Turks deteriorated rapidly after the outbreak of the war. Corporal Ali Rıza Eti, who had served in a medical unit during the Battle of Köprüköy, grew increasingly hostile to the Armenians he encountered at the front. Towards the end of November, the Russians deployed their Armenian volunteer units in eastern Anatolia. They engaged Ottoman forces from Van, a major centre of the Ottoman Armenian community, along the Aras River—no doubt with the deliberate intention of encouraging Armenians to defect from Ottoman ranks. Many did: Corporal Eti claimed that Armenians in groups of forty or fifty deserted to join with Russian forces. "Obviously they will inform the enemy of our positions," Eti reflected.[14]

In November, Eti's unit marched through a number of deserted villages whose Armenian residents had gone over to the Russians and whose Muslim inhabitants had fled or been killed by the invaders. "When the Armenians of this area sided with the Russian Army," he wrote in his diary on 15 November, "they showed great cruelty to those poor villagers." He described desecrated mosques littered with animal carcasses and the pages of broken

Qurans carried by the wind down empty streets. The anger in his writing is palpable.[15]

As word of Armenian defections gained circulation, Turkish soldiers grew increasingly violent towards the Armenians in their midst. Eti mentioned casually how a Turkish soldier's weapon "discharged" and struck down an Armenian comrade. From Eti's account, it hardly sounded like an accident. "We buried the guy," he wrote dispassionately. There was no suggestion of disciplinary action for the killing of a fellow Ottoman soldier. Increasingly, Armenians were no longer seen as fellow Ottomans.[16]

IN THE DAYS LEADING UP TO THE TURKISH OFFENSIVE, ENVER PASHA made the rounds to review his troops. The Third Army commander's message to Ottoman soldiers was sobering. "Soldiers, I have visited you all," he declared. "I saw that you have neither shoes on your feet nor coats on your backs. Yet the enemy before you is afraid of you. Soon we will attack and enter the Caucasus. There you will find everything in abundance. The whole of the Muslim world is watching you."[17]

Enver's optimism for his army's chances of success stemmed from a series of favourable developments on the Caucasus front. With winter fast approaching, the Russians did not believe the Ottomans would attempt hostilities before spring. They took the opportunity to redeploy surplus troops from the Caucasus to more pressing fronts, reducing the size of the army in eastern Anatolia. The Turks, on the other hand, had managed to transfer the X Corps without the Russians' knowledge. These troop movements gave the Ottomans a numerical advantage over the Russians, with some 100,000 Turkish troops facing fewer than 80,000 Russians.[18]

With the Russians bedding down for the winter, Enver hoped a surprise attack would catch the enemy with his guard down. To preserve the element of surprise, Ottoman forces needed to move quickly into Russian territory. Enver ordered his men to leave their heavy packs behind and to carry only their weapons and ammunition with a minimum of provisions. While lightening his soldiers' load, Enver's order also meant his troops carried no fuel, tents, or bedding and only half rations. Enver hoped to billet and feed his men off the Russian villages they would conquer on their way to Sarıkamış. "Our supply base is in front of us," was Enver's mantra.[19]

Most Russian forces were dispersed inside Ottoman territory, along the salient they had seized in the fighting in November. Their supply centre at Sarıkamış was practically undefended, with only a handful of frontier guards, militiamen, and railway workers to protect their sole line of supply and communications, as well as their only line of retreat through the mountain valleys back to Kars.

This was Enver's dream: to send a large force around the Russian right flank both to cut off the railway line and to seize the town of Sarıkamış, surrounding the Russian Caucasus Army, which, severed from its only line of retreat, would have no choice but to surrender to the Turks. Once Sarıkamış was secured and the Russian Caucasus Army destroyed, the Ottomans could retake Kars, Ardahan, and Batum—the three provinces lost in 1878—unopposed. Such brilliant Ottoman victories would stir the Muslim populations of Central Asia, Afghanistan, and India beyond. The conquest of one strategic railhead opened such remarkable possibilities for both the Ottoman Empire and the ambitious Young Turk generalissimo.

In his battle plan, issued on 19 December, Enver assigned distinct objectives to each of the three corps (each comprising 30,000 to 35,000 soldiers) of the Third Army. The XI Corps was ordered to engage Russian forces along the length of its southern front as a diversion to provide cover for the IX and X corps while they manoeuvred around to the west and north towards Sarıkamış. The IX Corps was to follow an inner loop and descend on Sarıkamış from the west, while the X Corps took the outer loop, sending one division (roughly 10,000 men) north towards Ardahan and two divisions to cut the railway line and descend on Sarıkamış from the north. Operations were scheduled to begin on 22 December.[20]

After a period of unseasonably fair weather, the winter snows began to fall on the night of 19–20 December. A major snowstorm struck on the morning of 22 December, as the Ottoman Third Army went into action. Carrying only flat bread for rations, dressed in light uniforms without proper coats to protect them against the cold, and shod with inadequate footwear for the harsh terrain, the Ottoman soldiers set off under the most adverse conditions to fulfil the superhuman tasks Enver had set them.

Ottoman forces of the XI Corps opened hostilities along the south bank of the Aras River to divert Russian forces from the west of Sarıkamış, where the Ottoman IX and X corps planned to outflank Russian positions.

Corporal Ali Rıza Eti watched from the medics' tents as the Russians returned fire, inflicting heavy casualties and driving the Turks into retreat. As the Ottomans fell back, Eti grew concerned that the advancing Russians would capture his medical unit.

Eti heard many stories of near escapes from the Russians told by incoming wounded. When one Turkish-held village fell to the Russians, a group of sixty Ottoman soldiers took refuge in a hayloft. They were discovered by three Russian Muslim soldiers of a Kazak regiment who, after making the Turks prove they were Muslim by showing their circumcised penises, left them in hiding. "Brothers, be quiet and wait here," the Kazaks explained, "we are leaving now." Such fraternization between Muslim soldiers across battle lines met with Eti's full approval.[21]

Christian fellow feeling between Armenians and Russians, however, continued to infuriate Medical Corporal Eti. On the first day of battle, he saw two Ottoman Armenian soldiers cross over to Russian lines and a third shot and killed in the attempt. Turkish soldiers blamed the Armenians not just for defecting but for providing the Russians with intelligence on Ottoman positions and numbers. "Isn't it natural that the Russians would gain information from the Armenians who flee from the army every day?" he reflected bitterly. "I wonder if anything will be done to the Armenians after the war?"[22]

Armenian soldiers in Ottoman ranks faced an intolerable situation. They were actively recruited by Armenians in Russian ranks and knew their lives were in danger the longer they stayed among Ottoman soldiers whose mistrust was growing murderous. Eti reported that in every battalion between three and five Armenians were shot daily "by accident" and mused, "If it goes on like that, there won't be any Armenians left in the battalions in a week."[23]

The XI Corps faced heavy resistance from Russian troops. The front line was too long for the Turks to mount more than a modest assault at any given point, and in the first days of the attack, they not only failed in their efforts to force the Russians north of the Aras River but were driven back towards their own headquarters in Köprüköy. Though their casualties mounted, the XI Corps succeeded in drawing the fire of Russian troops, providing the necessary diversion for the IX and X corps to execute their flanking operation. In the opening days of the campaign, these two Ottoman army corps achieved remarkable successes.

The Ottoman X Corps, commanded by Hafız Hakki Bey, raced northward to capture territory from the Russian right flank. They cut through the Russian salient and proceeded northward across the frontier to lay siege to the lightly defended garrison town of Oltu. The Ottomans surprised a Russian colonel along the way, who surrendered with the 750 soldiers under his command. Yet the Ottomans faced some nasty surprises of their own. Caught in heavy fog outside Oltu, one Turkish regiment mistook another for Russian defenders and battled for four hours against its own troops, incurring over 1,000 Ottoman casualties through friendly fire. However, by the end of the day, the Ottomans had succeeded in driving the Russian defenders out of Oltu. Here at least, the Ottoman soldiers found food and shelter as promised, and they set about looting the conquered town.[24]

True to form, the headstrong Hafız Hakki followed his victory in Oltu by pursuing the retreating Russians with all of his forces rather than making his way eastward to join up with Enver Pasha and the IX Corps in their attack on Sarıkamış. Given the difficulties of communications in the mountainous terrain, this spontaneous change of plan placed the whole campaign in jeopardy.

Enver Pasha accompanied the IX Corps on its treacherous course towards Sarıkamış. The determined Ottoman soldiers made their way through narrow mountain paths obstructed by snowdrifts, covering forty-six miles in just three days. The cold took its toll, as the men were forced to sleep in the open, without tents and only the scrub they could scavenge for firewood in subfreezing temperatures. In the morning light, groups of men could be found lying in circles around the remains of fires that proved no match for the cold, their corpses blackened by the ice. Over one-third of the men of IX Corps never reached the Sarıkamış region.

Yet Enver drove his men onward to the outskirts of Sarıkamış, where they paused on 24 December to consolidate before the final attack on the garrison town. The Turks, interrogating their Russian prisoners, learned there were no troops to defend Sarıkamış at all except for a few rear units without artillery. Realization of how weakly the strategic town was fortified reaffirmed Enver's conviction that his frozen and exhausted troops were within striking distance of total victory.[25]

The Russians only learned the full extent of the Turkish assault on 26 December, when they captured an Ottoman officer and secured copies of Enver's war plans. They now knew that the X Corps had been redeployed to the Third Army and that the Ottomans enjoyed a sizable numerical advantage. They had learned of the fall of Oltu and that Ottoman troops were not only advancing on Ardahan but due to arrive shortly in Sarıkamış. The Muslim population between the Black Sea port of Batum and Ardahan had risen in revolt against the Russians—precisely the religious enthusiasm the Ottomans hoped to provoke and the Russians most feared. The Russian generals were, according to historians of the campaign, "almost in a state of panic . . . convinced that Sarıkamış would be lost and that the bulk of the Caucasian army would be cut off from their line of retreat to Kars". The Russian commanders ordered a general retreat in a desperate bid to save their army, or at least some part of it, from total defeat.[26]

Fortune favoured the Russians, as the Turkish battle plan began to unravel. After a remarkable start, the weather and human error began to take their toll on the Ottoman expedition. Blizzards swept the high peaks of the Caucasus, making the mountain paths all but impassable to those on the march. In zero visibility, with windswept snow hiding the mountain tracks, many men got separated from their units, thinning the ranks. The lack of proper roads, the extreme weather, and the high mountains played havoc with Ottoman communications. Worse yet, one of Enver's generals, Hafız Hakki Bey, had disregarded his orders and was pursuing a small Russian force that led him miles away from Sarıkamış.

Enver dispatched urgent orders to Hafız Hakki Bey to break off his pursuit of Russian forces and fall back into line with the original battle plan. The commander of X Corps entrusted the assault on Ardahan to one of his regiments (as set out in the original battle plan) and personally led the two other regiments of X Corps to join in Enver's assault on Sarıkamış. Hafız Hakki set off on 25 December and promised to meet Enver the following morning. He was at that point thirty miles away from the Sarıkamış front and had to cross the high massif of the Allahüekber Mountains, rising 3,000 metres above sea level, in the full fury of winter. The next nineteen hours were nothing short of a death march. One of its survivors described the hardships the soldiers suffered: "We climbed with great difficulty, yet were orderly and disciplined. We were very tired and exhausted. When we reached the plateau, we were hit by a strong blizzard. We lost all visibility. It was impossible to help let alone talk to each other. The troops lost all order. Soldiers ran anywhere to seek shelter, attacking any house with smoke coming from its chimney. The officers worked very hard, but they could not force the soldiers to obey." The cold was beyond human endurance, driving some of the soldiers mad: "I still remember very clearly seeing a soldier sitting in the snow by the side of the road. He was embracing the snow, grabbing handfuls and stuffing it into his mouth as he trembled and screamed. I wanted to help him and lead him back to the road, but he kept shouting and piling up the snow as if he did not see me. The poor man had gone insane. In this way we left 10,000 men behind under the snow in just one day."[27]

On 25 December, Enver Pasha convened a meeting of his Turkish officers and German advisors to take stock of the situation. The Russians had begun to retreat from their front line along the Aras River to fall back on Sarıkamış. Reinforcements were being sent down the railway line to offer assistance to the retreating Russians, who still believed their cause was lost. While their commanders were still in disarray, this meant that large numbers of Russian soldiers were descending on Sarıkamış from the north and the south. If the Ottomans did not act soon, they might lose the chance to take the town while it was still relatively undefended.

In the meeting, IX Corps commander Ihsan Pasha and Şerif Ilden, the chief of staff, were given a grilling by Enver and his German advisors. When, they wanted to know, would the Ottoman expedition be in a position to take Sarıkamış? Ihsan Pasha presented his commanders with the hard truths of the Third Army's position. They had lost all contact with Hafız Hakki and the X Corps, who were at that point marching over the Allahüekber Mountains, and could not say with any confidence when they would be in position to join an attack on Sarıkamış. Only one IX Corps division was currently available within striking distance of the town. "I don't know what the requirements of the campaign are," Ihsan Pasha concluded. "If your orders could be carried out with one division, then the 29th Division is ready for your orders."[28]

After hearing from his Turkish officers, Enver asked his German advisers for their opinions. They shared full responsibility with Enver in drafting the original battle plan and had fed his ambition to replicate the German victory in Tannenberg on the Caucasus front. They advised Enver to wait until Hafız Hakki arrived with his troops before attacking. Yet Enver was not for waiting. He knew that the longer he delayed, the more Russian troops his own soldiers would face. Moreover, once his soldiers had taken Sarıkamış, they would have roofs over their heads and food to eat. Each night his army spent in the open left hundreds more soldiers dead from exposure. His officers believed Enver was driven to action by an unspoken rivalry with Hafız Hakki, fearing that the X Corps commander might reach and occupy Sarıkamış before him. Enver, always at the front, cherished that particular trophy for his own glory.

In the end, Enver Pasha overrode all his advisers and ordered his troops to begin their attack the next morning, 26 December. This fateful decision proved the turning point in the Ottoman campaign. From that moment forward, every Ottoman attack lacked the manpower to prevail or to retain any ground won against Russian counter-attacks.

It is to the credit of the tenacity of the Ottoman soldiers that each of the objectives of Enver's unrealistic plan was achieved—however briefly. Hafız Hakki's men, after crossing the forbidding Allahüekber Mountains, reached the railway between Kars and Sarıkamış and cut that vital line of communication—though with insufficient men to hold it against Russian reinforcements from Kars. Ottoman troops captured the town of Ardahan but, with insufficient forces to hold the city, lost it within a week. The once victorious Turkish soldiers of the X Corps found themselves surrounded, and the 1,200 survivors of the original force of 5,000 were forced to surrender to the Russians. Ottoman troops even managed to penetrate into Sarıkamış itself, though the price they paid in lives lost overshadowed that short-lived accomplishment.

The IX Corps's first attacks on Russian positions in Sarıkamış were repelled with heavy losses by the town's defenders on 26 December. That night, Hafız Hakki Pasha and the exhausted survivors of the march over the Allahüekber Mountains finally reached their positions near Sarıkamış. Given the losses the IX Corps had suffered and the deplorable state of the X Corps after its forced march, Enver decided to suspend operations for thirty-six hours to consolidate his forces.[29]

The decisive battle for Sarıkamış was fought on 29 December. By that time, the cold had decimated Ottoman numbers. From an original strength of more than 50,000 men, the Ottoman IX and X corps together numbered no more than 18,000, and those survivors were in no condition to fight. Russian numbers in Sarıkamış had risen to over 13,000 defenders in the town, with more artillery and machine guns than the Turks had, in well-defended positions. With these heavy weapons, the Russians succeeded in repelling determined Turkish attacks throughout the day.

Enver made one last attempt to take Sarıkamış with a night attack on 29 December. This time, his forces swept into the garrison town, engaging

Ottoman prisoners in Ardahan. One detachment of the Ottoman Caucasus Army succeeded in capturing the town of Ardahan from Russian forces during the Sarıkamış campaign but, with insufficient forces to hold the city, was forced to surrender in early January 1915 in what was touted as the first Russian victory on the Caucasus front.

the Russian defenders in hand-to-hand combat with bayonets in the dark. Most of the Turkish soldiers were killed or taken prisoner, though a determined squad of several hundred men succeeded in occupying the Russian barracks in the centre of the town. For one night, a small part of Enver's army could claim to have occupied a small part of Sarıkamış. By morning, Russian forces surrounded the barracks and forced the Turkish soldiers to surrender. An entire Ottoman division was lost in the offensive.

The Russians soon realized how weak the Ottoman attackers were and, recovering from their initial loss of composure, went on the offensive. Now the Ottoman Third Army, rather than the Russian Caucasus Army, was in imminent danger of encirclement and destruction.

In the first two weeks of January 1915, Russian forces drove the Ottomans back, recovering all of the territory they had surrendered in the opening days of the campaign. In the process, they destroyed the Third Army, corps by corps. The IX Corps was surrounded by the Russians and forced to surrender on 4 January. The chief of staff, Şerif Ilden, recorded that there were only 106 officers and eighty soldiers with him at the IX Corps' head-quarters when he surrendered to the Russians. Hafız Hakki led the X Corps into a retreat under fire but managed to avoid total destruction, and after sixteen days, some 3,000 survivors reached the security of Turkish lines.[30]

As the IX and X corps collapsed, the XI Corps took the brunt of the Russian counter-attack. At one point during their retreat from Russian territory, Turkish troops were surprised when an alien cavalry force charged the Russian left flank and scattered the enemy. They were a group of Circassian villagers who, learning of the sultan's declaration of jihad, immediately rode out to support the Ottoman troops. It was, for Medical Corporal Ali Rıza Eti, who witnessed the Circassian attack, further proof of Muslim solidarity in the Great War. The XI Corps completed its retreat to Turkish lines by mid-January, with 15,000 of the original complement of 35,000 soldiers. But the Ottoman Third Army had been destroyed. Of the nearly 100,000 soldiers sent to battle, only 18,000 broken men returned.[31]

Enver Pasha narrowly managed to escape capture and returned to Istanbul in disgrace, though neither Enver nor Hafız Hakki faced any disciplinary hearing for what some of their officers condemned as criminal neglect. In fact, before leaving Erzurum for the imperial capital, Enver promoted the rash Hafız Hakki from colonel to major general, with the title of pasha, and placed him in command of what remained of the Third Army (he died two months later of typhus). The defeat was too terrible for the Young Turks to acknowledge, and according to Liman von Sanders, the destruction of the Third Army was kept secret in both Germany and the Ottoman Empire. "It was forbidden to speak of it," he later wrote. "Violations of the order were followed by arrest and punishment."[32]

The repercussions of Sarıkamış would be felt for the remainder of the war. Without an effective army in eastern Anatolia, the Ottomans were unable to defend their territory from Russian attack. Ottoman vulnerability heightened tensions between Turks, Kurds, and Armenians in the frontier zone with Russia. And whatever enthusiasm for jihad Muslims in the Russian Empire might have shown in the early stages of the Sarıkamış campaign, the totality of Ottoman defeat ruled out the prospect of an Islamic uprising on the Russian front.

The magnitude of the Ottoman defeat served to encourage Russia's Entente allies in their plans for an attack on the Dardanelles to seize Istanbul and take the Turks out of the war once and for all.[33]

ONE MONTH AFTER THE OTTOMAN DEFEAT AT SARIKAMIŞ, CEMAL PASHA led an attack on the British in the Suez Canal. The contrast between the deserts of Egypt and the blizzards of the Caucasus could not have been more extreme, though the arid wastelands of Sinai were no more hospitable to a campaign force than the high mountains around Sarıkamış.

After his very public proclamations in Istanbul's central train station on 21 November 1914, no one could accuse Cemal of hiding his intention to lead an expedition against Egypt. Given the obstacles any such expedition would encounter, the British dismissed Cemal's pledge to "conquer" Egypt as empty rhetoric. They did not think Cemal could raise an army in Syria large enough to threaten British forces in Egypt. Even if he did succeed in putting together a large campaign force, no proper roads crossed the Sinai, which had few sources of water and almost no vegetation. The logistics of providing food, water, and ammunition for a large campaign force crossing such inhospitable terrain were forbidding. And even if they were to overcome all of those obstacles and reach the canal, Ottoman forces would still face a body of water hundreds of metres wide and twelve metres deep protected by warships, armoured trains, and 50,000 troops. The British position looked unassailable.

British calculations were not wrong. Cemal faced serious constraints in mobilizing a campaign force in Syria. In December 1914, the Ottomans needed all their soldiers in Anatolia to reinforce the ill-fated Caucasus frontier and to protect Istanbul and the straits. Cemal would be reliant on the regular soldiers of the Arab provinces, reinforced by irregular volunteers from local Bedouin, Druze, Circassian and other immigrant communities. Of the 50,000 combatants at his disposal, Cemal would be able to deploy no more than 30,000 for the Suez campaign, as the rest would be needed to man garrisons across the Arab provinces. Moreover, the Ottoman commander would have to retain 5,000 to 10,000 soldiers in reserve, to protect or reinforce the initial campaign force. This meant Cemal would have only 20,000 to 25,000 Ottoman soldiers with which to take on a dug-in British force at least twice that size—a suicidal proposition.[34]

To succeed, Cemal counted on a sequence of improbable events. "I had staked everything upon surprising the English," Cemal later recorded. If caught by surprise, he hoped the English might surrender a stretch of the Canal Zone that the Ottomans could reinforce with "twelve thousand rifles securely dug in on the far bank". From such a bridgehead, Cemal planned to occupy the key town of Ismailia, raising Ottoman numbers on the west bank of the canal to 20,000. And the Ottoman occupation of Ismailia, he believed, would inspire a popular uprising in Egypt against British rule—the jihad that the sultan had called for. In this way, Cemal argued, "Egypt would be freed in an unexpectedly short time by the employment of quite a small force and insignificant technical resources."[35]

Cemal's rash plan had the full support of the Germans, who still harboured high hopes for the Ottoman-led jihad. Moreover, Germany placed a high priority on cutting the Suez Canal. Between 1 August and 31 December 1914, no fewer than 376 transport ships transited the canal, carrying 163,700 troops for the Allied war effort. While the British were not totally reliant on the canal for troop transport—the rail system linking Suez to Cairo and the Mediterranean ports could have served this purpose—it was a vital artery for war and merchant ships traveling from the Indian Ocean to the Mediterranean. So long as the canal was operating, Britain could derive full benefit from its empire for the war effort. Any Ottoman attack on Suez that slowed this imperial traffic or forced Britain to concentrate troops for the defence of Egypt that might otherwise be deployed to the western front was of direct benefit to the German war effort.[36]

From the moment Cemal reached Damascus on 6 December, he set to work mobilizing the men and resources to undertake the perilous crossing of the Sinai. His regular forces numbered some 35,000 soldiers, primarily young men from the Arab provinces of Aleppo, Beirut, and Damascus and the autonomous districts of Mount Lebanon and Jerusalem. To bolster his numbers, Cemal appealed to the patriotism of tribal leaders across the Arab lands to join the attack on the British and liberate Egypt from foreign rule.

Druze prince Amir Shakib Arslan was a serving member of the Ottoman parliament in 1914. When he learned of Cemal's plans, Arslan applied to Istanbul for release from his parliamentary duties to lead a detachment of Druze volunteers for the Sinai campaign. He met with Cemal and promised to raise five hundred men for the war effort, though the Young Turk leader asked for no more than one hundred. Arslan came away from his interview convinced Cemal "thought that disorganized volunteers would not be of great value to the war". Yet Arslan claimed his Druze volunteers exceeded all expectations, outperforming regular soldiers in riflery and horsemanship in the Damascus military depot. Instead of the month's training initially

Ottoman soldiers in Palestine before the first attack on the Suez Canal. Cemal Pasha assembled the main body of his expeditionary force for the assault on the Suez Canal in Syria and Palestine in January 1915. Large bodies of troops combining Ottoman regulars and tribal volunteers mustered in shows of patriotism intended to raise public support for the war effort in the Arab provinces.

envisaged, the Druze volunteers were dispatched without delay by train to join the campaign.[37]

In December 1914 and January 1915, a heterogeneous army was assembling in the fortified desert frontier town of Maan (today in southern Jordan), some 290 miles south of Damascus. Maan, on the pilgrimage route from Damascus to Mecca, was also a major depot on the Hijaz Railway. Here Arslan found a "unit of volunteers from the people of Medina, and another unit of mixed Turks from Romania, and Syrian Bedouin and Albanians and others", including Kurdish cavalry from the Salahiyya district of Damascus.

Wahib Pasha, the governor and military commander of the Red Sea province of the Hijaz (which included Mecca and Medina, the birthplace of Islam), headed the largest force in Maan. Arslan claimed that Wahib Pasha brought 9,000 soldiers from the Ottoman garrison in Mecca, though there was a notable absence among his levies. Cemal Pasha had written Sharif Husayn ibn Ali, the chief Ottoman religious authority in Mecca, Islam's holiest city, asking him to contribute a detachment of forces under the command of one of his sons. Cemal hoped that the sharif would lend his religious authority to the Suez expedition and prove his loyalty to the state. Sharif Husayn replied courteously to Cemal's request and sent his son Ali with Wahib Pasha when the governor set out from Mecca. However, Ali went no further than Medina, promising to catch up with Wahib Pasha as soon as he had mobilized his full volunteer force. Cemal noted with concern that Sharif Husayn's son never left Medina.[38]

The main body of the Ottoman Expeditionary Force assembled in January 1915 in Beersheba (today in southern Israel), near the Ottoman-Egyptian frontier. Here Ottoman and German planners worked to prepare the logistics of the expedition. The chief of staff of the Ottoman VIII Corps, Colonel Friedrich Freiherr Kress von Kressenstein, positioned supply depots every fifteen or so miles between Beersheba and Ismailia, where the headquarters of the Suez Canal were based. In each depot, engineers dug wells and built dykes to trap the winter rains to provide adequate water facilities for the army. Medical facilities and food stores were pre-positioned in each depot. Over 10,000 camels were requisitioned from Syria and Arabia to provide transport between depots, and provisional telegraph lines were laid to provide instant communications.

The greatest challenge facing the Ottoman expedition was the transport of twenty-five pontoons designed for crossing the Suez Canal. The pontoons, made of galvanized iron, ranged from 5.5 to 7 metres in length and 1.5 metres in width. Ottoman soldiers, aided by camels and mules, pulled these flat-bottomed boats on specially devised trailers, laying boards over the soft sand to keep the trailer wheels from getting stuck. Ottoman soldiers practiced pulling the unwieldy craft overland and making bridges with the boats.

The British seem to have had little appreciation of the campaign force taking shape in Syria. A French priest, whom the Ottomans had expelled from Jerusalem, was the first to give detailed intelligence on Cemal's preparations. The British interviewed the priest in the Canal Zone on 30 December. The priest knew the Syrian Desert intimately from his many years of archaeological work and spoke fluent Arabic. He claimed to have seen as many as 25,000 men assembling in Damascus and Jerusalem with extensive materiel, including boats, wire, and telegraph equipment, all making their way towards Beersheba. Provision was being made for water, and biscuit cooked in Damascus was being stored in depots in Sinai. At first the British dismissed his comments as ridiculous, but the more detail he gave, the more seriously they took his report.[39]

The British and French began to deploy airplanes for the first time in the war in the Middle East in an attempt to secure aerial confirmation of the French priest's report. It was the Ottomans' good fortune that the central regions of Sinai, where the ground was firmest and best suited for marching an army, was also the furthest from reach of aerial surveillance, affording the Suez campaign a surprising degree of secrecy on the eve of its departure. British planes based in Ismailia were too short-range to penetrate into central Sinai, while French seaplanes operating from Port Said and the Gulf of Aqaba could only view the northern and southern extremities of the Sinai Peninsula, where the smaller Turkish contingents were concentrated. The Ottomans and Germans had yet to deploy aircraft to support their own troops, leaving the Allies in control of the skies.

When the first echelon of Ottoman forces set out from Beersheba towards the canal on 14 January 1915, the British had little idea of either where they were or where they were headed. The main body of Ottoman forces marched through the centre of the Sinai, while two smaller detachments diverged, one heading along the Mediterranean coast from El Arish and the other passing through the desert fort of Qalaat al-Nakhl. Each man carried light rations of dates, biscuit, and olives not to exceed one kilo in weight, and water was carefully rationed. The troops found the winter nights too cold to sleep, so they marched through the night and rested during the day. It took twelve days to cross the desert, with the loss of neither a man nor a beast along the way—a tribute to the detailed planning behind the Suez campaign.

In the last ten days of January, French seaplanes began to report alarming concentrations of Turkish troops within those areas their planes had the range to reach. The low-flying aircraft returned to base with wings shredded by the ground troops' gunfire. Reports of enemy forces concentrated at several points around the Sinai Peninsula drove the British to reassess their defences along the canal.[40]

The Suez Canal runs one hundred miles from Port Said on the Mediterranean to Suez on the Red Sea. The canal joins two large saltwater lakes whose twenty-nine miles of marshy shores were ill-suited to military movements, and British engineers flooded ten miles of low-lying shores on the east bank of the canal, thus reducing the total distance to defend to seventy-one miles. The British decided to take advantage of the depressions on the north-eastern banks of the canal to flood a twenty-mile stretch, further reducing the area to be defended to just fifty-one miles of the canal. British and French warships deployed to key points along the canal, between Qantara and Ismailia, to the north of Lake Timsah, and between Tussum and Serapeum, to the north of the Great Bitter Lake, where the British believed an attack would be most likely. Indian troops were reinforced by Australians and New Zealanders, as well as a battery of Egyptian artillery.[41]

With some incredulity, British forces waited to see what the Ottomans would try to do next. H. V. Gell, the young signals officer who had taken part in the action off Aden, was posted to the northern Suez Canal near Qantara. Though eager enough to "see some action", Gell makes clear in his diary that neither he nor his commanders had any idea what the Ottomans were up to. He recorded a series of minor skirmishes and false alarms in the last days of January 1915. While patrolling the West Bank of the canal in an armoured train on 25 January, he received an urgent message from brigade headquarters: "Return camp immediately. Kantara being threatened in earnest by real enemy." False alarm. On 26 January, while British positions came under artillery fire from Turkish guns, Gell was dispatched to a post several miles south of Qantara. "Hear 3000 enemy are reported near Ballah," he noted. Increasingly concerned by reports of enemy soldiers in the Sinai, the British did not know where the Ottomans were, what their numbers were, or where they planned to attack. To that extent at least, Cemal Pasha had achieved a degree of surprise.[42]

As a precaution, the British withdrew all their troops to the western shores of the Suez Canal. They left dogs chained at regular intervals on the east bank of the canal to bark at any approaching men. In the event of a night attack, airplanes would be of no use in spotting troop movements, and old-fashioned guard dogs would have to do.[43]

On 1 February, Ottoman commanders issued the orders for the attack. To maintain the element of surprise, "absolute silence must be preserved by both Officers and men. There must be no coughing, and orders are not to be given in a loud voice." Soldiers were to wait until they had crossed from the east to the west bank of the canal to load their weapons, presumably to avoid accidental gunshots that would alert the British defenders. Cigarette smoking was also forbidden—a hardship for the nerve-bitten soldiers. All

Ottoman troops were to wear a white band on their upper arms as a distinguishing mark to avoid friendly fire. As a play on the symbolism of jihad, the password for the attack was "The Sacred Standard".

"By the Grace of Allah we shall attack the enemy on the night of the 2nd–3rd February, and seize the Canal," the orders explained. While the main body was to attempt a crossing near Ismailia, diversionary attacks were to be made in the north near Qantara and to the south near Suez. Further, a battery of howitzers was to take up position near Lake Timsah to fire on enemy warships. "If it gets the opportunity, [the heavy artillery battery] is to sink a ship at the entrance of the Canal." Seizure of the canal was but one part of the operation. Sinking ships to obstruct the canal was a far more realistic objective than the capture of well-entrenched British positions on the canal.[44]

The day before the attack, a sudden wind blew up, causing a heavy sandstorm that obstructed all vision. A French officer later claimed, "It was a terrible ordeal just to keep one's eyes open." The Ottoman and German commanders took advantage of the cover provided by the sandstorm to move their troops forward towards the canal at a point just south of Ismailia, before the wind died down for a clear night. The conditions were perfect for the attack.[45]

"We arrived at the canal late at night," Fahmi al-Tarjaman, a Damascene veteran of the Balkan Wars, recalled, "moving quietly with no smoking or talking allowed."

> No one was to make a single sound walking across the sand. A German came along. We were to lower two of the metal boats in the water. The German took one to the other bank and returned after about an hour. He picked up the second one filled with soldiers and also took it across to the other side. As each boat was filled he would drop the soldiers on the other side of the canal. In this way, by taking the full boats over and returning empty he took two hundred and fifty of the soldiers to stand guard around the work site to prevent anyone from interfering.[46]

The crossing took more time than the Ottoman commanders had expected, and by daybreak they were still assembling the pontoon bridge across the canal. Silence on the west bank of the canal confirmed the Turkish attackers' belief that they had crossed an undefended stretch of the canal. A group of jihad volunteers from Tripoli in Libya, who called themselves the Champions of Islam, broke the silence, shouting slogans to encourage each other. In the distance, dogs started barking. And suddenly, as the sixth boat joined the pontoon bridge, the western bank of the canal erupted in machine-gun fire.[47]

"The bullets were all over, hitting and exploding in the water and making the water of the canal churn like a kettle of boiling water," Fahmi al-Tarjaman recounted. "The boats were hit and started sinking and most of our men could not shoot back although those who could did. Those who could swim saved themselves but those who could not drowned and went down with the boats." Tarjaman and a group of soldiers ran from the exposed coastline "faster than we had ever run before". He saw a group of armoured ships coming up the canal with their guns pointing towards Ottoman positions. "Above us planes began bombarding us, along with the ships from the water." A telegraph operator, Tarjaman set up his equipment from the relative shelter of the dunes behind the canal and "made contact with the troops behind us to apprise them of the situation while the guns at the canal continued all the while dropping shells on us".[48]

Some of the heaviest firing against Ottoman positions came from an Egyptian artillery battery that had dug into a position high on the west bank of the canal with a commanding view over the Ottoman pontoon bridge. Ahmad Shafiq, the veteran Egyptian statesman, recounted how First Lieutenant Ahmad Efendi Hilmi ordered his battery to wait until the Turks had crossed the canal before opening fire but lost his life in the crossfire. Hilmi was one of three Egyptians killed and two wounded in the defence of the canal. The members of the 5th Artillery Battery were later decorated by Egyptian Sultan Fuad for their heroism. But Shafiq was quick to remind his readers, "The participation of the Egyptian Army in the defense of Egypt contravened the English pledge [of 6 November 1914] to bear the responsibility of the war themselves, without any assistance from the Egyptian people." However much the Egyptians celebrated the valour of their soldiers, they resented the British dragging them into a war in which Egypt had no cause to fight.[49]

In the course of the battle on 3 February, British gunships destroyed all of the Ottoman pontoons. Those Turkish soldiers who had succeeded in crossing the canal were either captured or killed. Unable to fulfil the primary objective of securing a bridgehead over the canal, the Ottomans now focused their efforts on trying to sink Allied shipping to obstruct the waterway. The heavy howitzer battery got the measure of the British ship HMS *Hardinge* and scored direct hits on both funnels, damaging her steering and forward guns and knocking out her wireless communications. In imminent risk of sinking, *Hardinge* raised anchor to retreat to the safety of Lake Timsah, beyond the reach of Ottoman artillery.

The Ottoman battery turned next to the French cruiser *Requin* and pounded the ship with dangerous accuracy. Only when the French spotted a puff of smoke marking the location of the Ottoman guns were they able to return fire and silence the howitzers. Meanwhile, lighter artillery levelled accurate fire on the British ship *Clio*, which took several direct hits before it too managed to locate the Ottoman guns and destroy them.[50]

By early afternoon, all Ottoman ground attacks had been repulsed by the British, and most of the Turkish artillery batteries had been destroyed. In his headquarters, Cemal Pasha convened a meeting of Turkish and German officers. The Turkish commander of the VIII Corps, Mersinli Cemal Bey, argued that the army was no longer in any position to continue fighting. Cemal's German chief of staff agreed and proposed an immediate end to the fighting. Only Mersinli Cemal Bey's German chief of staff, Colonel von Kressenstein, insisted on pursuing the offensive to the last man. He was quickly overruled by Cemal Pasha, who argued that it was more sensible to preserve the Fourth Army for the defence of Syria and called for a retreat to begin as soon as darkness fell.[51]

The British, expecting the attack to be renewed on 4 February, were surprised to see that the bulk of the Turkish force had disappeared overnight. As British forces patrolled the east bank of the canal, they surprised isolated detachments of Turkish soldiers who had not been informed of the retreat. However, the British decided not to chase the retreating Ottomans, still not knowing how many men were in the campaign army and fearing that the whole expedition might prove a sort of trap to draw British forces into an ambush in the depths of the Sinai. The Ottomans, for their part, relieved to see that the British forces were not in pursuit, slowly made their way back to Beersheba.

Casualties for both sides were relatively low. The British lost 162 dead and 130 wounded in the fighting on the canal. Ottoman casualty figures were higher. The British claimed to have buried 238 Ottoman dead and taken 716 prisoner, though many others were believed to have died in the canal itself. Cemal gave Ottoman losses as 192 dead, 381 wounded, and 727 missing.[52]

IN THE AFTERMATH OF DEFEAT IN THE CAUCASUS AND ON THE SUEZ Canal, Ottoman commanders in the ministry of war were determined to recover Basra from the British. The speed of the Anglo-Indian army's conquest of southern Iraq had caught the Young Turks by surprise and revealed their vulnerability in the Persian Gulf region. The challenge was to retake Basra and repel the British from Mesopotamia with the fewest regular Ottoman troops possible. Enver Pasha, the minister of war, entrusted the mission to one of the leading officers in his secret intelligence service, the Teşkilât-i Mahsusa (Special Organization). His name was Suleyman Askeri.

Born in the town of Prizren (in modern Kosovo) in 1884, Suleyman Askeri, son of an Ottoman general and graduate of the elite Turkish military academy, was the consummate military man. Even his surname, Askeri, meant "military" in Turkish and Arabic. His revolutionary credentials were impeccable. As a young officer, Askeri served in Monastir (today the town of Bitola in modern Macedonia) and took part in the Young Turk Revolution in 1908. He subsequently volunteered as an officer in the guerrilla war against the Italians in Libya in 1911. In Libya, he served as liaison between Enver's forces in Derna and the Turkish chief of staff in Benghazi. He joined the Teşkilât-i Mahsusa during the Balkan Wars and rose through its secretive ranks to reach second in command under Enver in 1914. By some accounts rash and impetuous, Askeri was a commander in Enver's mould. He devised complex war plans and dreamed of glorious victories over the empire's enemies.[53]

Between 1909 and 1911, Askeri commanded the Ottoman gendarmerie in Baghdad. This experience made him the Young Turks' resident expert on Mesopotamia when the Ottomans entered the war. After the Anglo-Indian conquest of Basra and Qurna, Askeri pressed for a counter-attack to drive the invaders back to the Gulf. He fully expected that a successful campaign in Basra would encourage the zeal of Muslims from the Arab world to Central Asia, blow life into the Ottoman jihad plans, and put pressure on British India and the Russian Caucasus. Convinced he was the man for the job, Enver and his colleague Talat Pasha, the minister of interior, appointed Askeri governor and military commander of the province of Basra on 3 January 1915. The ambitious officer set off for his post immediately.

Askeri recognized his challenge was to raise a force to expel the British, drawing on a minimal number of regular Ottoman soldiers. His solution was to recruit a substantial force of tribal levies from Basra and its surrounding regions. No doubt Askeri hoped to re-create the dynamic he had witnessed in Benghazi during the Libyan War, of tribal levies rallying to the sultan's banner to fight European imperial forces. He reinforced the religious appeal of jihad against the empire's enemies with payments to tribal leaders. With little or no time to train his new recruits, Askeri led his mixed force to engage the British.

Within days of his arrival in Mesopotamia, on 20 January 1915, Askeri was seriously wounded in a skirmish with British troops on the Tigris ten miles north of Qurna. He was evacuated to Baghdad for medical treatment. Yet the zealous Turkish commander refused to let his injuries deter his efforts. His officers continued to recruit tribesmen to serve with the Ottoman army. Askeri met regularly with his commanders to plan the liberation of Basra. Knowing the British had the majority of their forces in Qurna—the strategic junction of the Tigris, Euphrates, and Shatt al-Arab waterways—and that the region around Qurna was still flooded and practically impassable to infantry, Askeri and his officers planned to bypass Qurna to attack the smaller British garrison at its headquarters in Basra instead.

Still recovering from his wounds, Askeri returned to the front in April 1915 to command the assault on Basra. He led a mixed force of 4,000 Turkish regulars and perhaps 15,000 Arab tribal irregulars. As it passed to the west of British positions in Qurna, the Ottoman campaign force was spotted by scouts, who alerted British headquarters in Basra on 11 April. A combined Anglo-Indian force of 4,600 infantry and 750 cavalry took up well-entrenched positions to the west of Basra in Shaiba (in Arabic, Shuayba) to repel Suleyman Askeri's forces.

The Ottomans established their base in woodlands south-west of Shaiba. At dawn on 12 April, they launched their attack, with the convalescent Askeri watching the battle from his headquarters in the woods. Mobile artillery fired on British positions and machine-gunners raked the trenches as wave after wave of Turkish infantry tried to break through British lines. As the sun rose in the sky, both armies found themselves firing on mirages, their vision confused by the moisture and bright sunlight. The well-trained Ottoman soldiers fought with great discipline, but as the day wore on the tribal irregulars increasingly abandoned the field.[54]

Suleyman Askeri's faith in Bedouin "holy warriors" was to be disappointed. The tribes of Iraq felt little loyalty towards the sultan or reverence for him as caliph. Nor did they see the British as a particular threat. Many of the Arab rulers at the head of the Persian Gulf—like the shaykhs of Kuwait, Qatar, and Bahrain—had actively sought British protection against Ottoman rule. Thus, while the Bedouin went to war with Suleyman Askeri's forces, they did so opportunistically, retaining the right to change sides if fortune favoured the British. The longer the battle continued without a breakthrough, the less the tribesmen were persuaded of the merits of the Ottoman cause.

The British went on the offensive the next day. Without airplanes at their disposal, they had no sense of the battlefield (the Battle of Shaiba was one of the last a British army would enter into without prior aerial reconnaissance). The dust, heat, and mirages left British commanders in a state of confusion. They could not see the retreat of the Arab irregulars, and the Turks who remained behind fought with fierce determination. Major General Sir Charles John Mellis, the British commander, was on the verge of retreating when he received news that his troops had managed to break through the Turkish lines. "I never want to go through the anxiety of some of that time," he later wrote his wife. "Reports came in to me of heavy losses on all sides and doubt if further advance was possible. I had thrown my last man into the fight—still it hung very doubtful."[55]

After seventy-two hours of battle, the exhausted Anglo-Indian forces did not pursue the retreating Ottoman army. Both sides had suffered heavy casualties in the three days of fighting, the Ottomans reporting 1,000 dead and wounded while the British suffered 1,200 casualties at Shaiba. The British medics were left to face the human cost of war when the battle ended. One medical officer recalled how "cartloads of dead and wounded Turks were brought in all mixed up. It was horrible beyond description."[56]

Though the British left them to withdraw in peace, the battle-weary Turks did not enjoy a respite in their retreat. All along the ninety-mile road upriver towards their garrison at Khamisiya, Bedouin tribesmen harried the defeated Ottoman infantry. The Turkish officers were convinced that many of the tribesmen now attacking them were the same "volunteers" who had deserted them in the heat of battle at Shaiba. For Askeri, the perfidy of the Arab tribes compounded the humiliation of defeat. He gathered his Turkish officers at Khamisiya to vent his rage over the Bedouin and their role in the Ottoman defeat. There was to be no repetition of the Libyan War, of Young Turks fighting side by side with Arab tribesmen against a foreign enemy. There was to be no greater Islamic uprising spreading from liberated Basra down the Persian Gulf to enflame India. His dreams of glory shattered, Suleyman Askeri took his pistol and ended his own life in Khamisiya.

Shaiba was a very significant encounter. The Ottomans would never make another attempt to recover Basra, and British oil interests on the Persian side of the Shatt al-Arab were secured for the remainder of the war. The threat of an uprising by the Arab tribes and towns against the Anglo-Indian occupation in Basra Province was, for the moment, neutralized. German and Turkish hopes that a decisive Ottoman victory would promote a broader jihad against the Entente Powers were also dashed, and British fears on that score were put to rest. On reflection, British commanders declared Shaiba "one of the decisive battles of the War."[57]

The combination of heavy casualties and the suicide of their commander gravely undermined morale among the ranks in the Ottoman army in Mesopotamia. Rather than expel the British from Basra, Suleyman Askeri's failed attack had left Mesopotamia more vulnerable to further invasion. The Indian Expeditionary Force, still at full strength and encouraged by its victories, took advantage of Turkish disarray to extend its conquests deeper into Iraq. In May, the Anglo-Indian force advanced towards Amara on the Tigris and Nasiriyya on the Euphrates. The Ottomans had to respond in haste to protect Baghdad from invasion—a task made all the more difficult by the defeat at Shaiba and the continued shortage of manpower as they tried desperately to rebuild their shattered Third Army in the Caucasus.

BETWEEN DECEMBER 1914 AND APRIL 1915, THE OTTOMANS TOOK the initiative on three fronts without success. In the Battle of Sarıkamış, the Ottoman Third Army was nearly destroyed, while Cemal Pasha managed to retreat from the first assault on the Suez Canal with nearly all of his Fourth Army intact. Suleyman Askeri's attempt to regain Basra also ended in failure. These campaigns revealed Ottoman commanders to be unrealistic in their expectations and the average Ottoman soldier to be incredibly tenacious and disciplined under even the most extreme conditions. These battles also revealed the limits of the sultan's call for jihad. Where Ottoman troops suffered defeats, local Muslims were discouraged from rising against the Entente Powers. By dealing the Ottomans a decisive defeat, the Allies believed they could lay to rest the threat of jihad once and for all.

Drawn into a false complacency about the limits of Ottoman military effectiveness, the Allies considered a major campaign to knock the Turks out of the war. They turned their focus on the Ottoman capital, Istanbul, and the straits that guarded the sea lanes to that ancient city—the Dardanelles. In fact, it was the Ottoman offensive in Sarıkamış that first led British war planners to consider an invasion of the straits.

SIX

The Assault on the Dardanelles

THE BRITISH WAR COUNCIL MET IN LONDON ON 2 JANUARY 1915 TO consider an urgent request for assistance from the commander in chief of the Russian army. Convened by the prime minister, Herbert Henry Asquith, the council assembled key cabinet ministers to guide the progress of the British war effort. Though technically only a committee of the British cabinet, the War Council had developed into a decision-making body in its own right, reporting policy decisions to the cabinet as faits accompli. The civilians in the council were forceful personalities: Winston Churchill, the first lord of the Admiralty, David Lloyd George, the chancellor of the Exchequer, Sir Edward Grey, the foreign secretary, among others. Yet the dominant voice in council deliberations belonged to a military man: Field Marshall Horatio Herbert Kitchener, the secretary of state for war.

Lord Kitchener, whose prominent moustache and pointing finger became iconic on 1914 British army recruitment posters, was the empire's most famous soldier. He had led the British to victory in the Battle of Omdurman, reconquering the Sudan in 1898. He had commanded British forces in the Second Boer War (1899–1902) and served as commander in chief of the army in India until 1909. He was very much a warrior among civilians in the War Council.

In their meeting of 2 January, the council focused on the volatile situation in the Russian Caucasus. Grand Duke Nicholas, the supreme commander of Russian forces, had met with the British military attaché in St Petersburg to apprise him of Russia's precarious position. The news from

Sarıkamış was just filtering in, and reports from as recently as 27 December suggested the Turks were on the verge of encircling the Russian army in the Caucasus. Nicholas sought Kitchener's commitment to launch an offensive against the Ottomans to relieve the pressure.

The politicians in Whitehall could not know that, even as they discussed the Turkish threat in the Caucasus, the Russian army was on the verge of total victory over Enver's forces. The War Council did not want to refuse the request of an allied power and agreed to commit British forces to an offensive against the Ottomans. As soon as the meeting was over, Kitchener sent a telegram to St Petersburg to assure the grand duke that British forces would "make a demonstration against the Turks". With this fateful decision, Britain initiated planning for the Dardanelles campaign.[1]

FROM THE OUTSET, KITCHENER ADVOCATED A NAVAL OPERATION against the Turks. He did not believe Britain could spare any soldiers from the Western front; however, a number of British and French warships in the eastern Mediterranean could be called into service against the Ottomans. The challenge was to find a coastal target that posed enough of a threat to Ottoman interests that Istanbul would redeploy troops away from the Caucasus in response to an attack. The Royal Navy had already bombarded Turkish positions in Mesopotamia, Aden, the Gulf of Aqaba, the Gulf of Alexandretta in the north-east corner of the Mediterranean, and the outer forts of the Dardanelles with no noticeable impact on Ottoman troop movements. Kitchener believed a new attack on the Dardanelles might serve the purpose if it seemed to threaten the Ottoman capital itself. "The only place that a demonstration might have some effect in stopping reinforcements going east," Kitchener wrote Churchill, "would be the Dardanelles"—the gateway to Istanbul.[2]

Kitchener instructed Churchill, as first lord of the Admiralty, to consult with his admirals on the feasibility of such a naval "demonstration" against the Dardanelles. In his communications with the naval commanders in the eastern Mediterranean, Churchill raised the stakes, seeking their views not just on a naval bombardment but also on the feasibility of threatening Istanbul itself by "forcing of the Straits by ships alone"—in other words, an operation to run warships through the heavily armed and mined Dardanelles into the Sea of Marmara to threaten Istanbul.

The Dardanelles run forty-one miles from the Mediterranean to the Sea of Marmara. In their efforts to protect Istanbul from invasion by sea, the Ottomans and Germans concentrated their efforts on the fourteen-mile stretch from the Mediterranean to the Narrows, where the European shores are only 1,600 yards from the Asian coast. Gun batteries along this strategic leg of the straits were modernized and reinforced. The Ottomans and their German allies placed searchlights to hinder night-time operations. They stretched underwater nets to obstruct the movement of enemy submarines. And they laid hundreds of mines in a bid to make the straits impassable.

Admiral Sackville Carden, British naval commander in the eastern Mediterranean, replied to Churchill on 5 January, arguing that while it would not be easy to overcome Ottoman defences, the straits could be forced by "extended operations with a large number of ships". Admiral Carden went on to draft a four-stage plan to force the straits, calling first for the "reduction of the forts at the entrance". This would allow British and French ships to broach the mouth of the straits and provide cover for minesweepers as they cleared a safe path. The second stage of operations called for "the destruction of the inside defenses as far as Kephez", a point four miles inside the straits. After the British had secured control of the broadest part of the straits, they would proceed next towards the Narrows, where the mine fields were concentrated and the shore batteries were closest to the shipping lanes. In the fourth and final stage of the operation, the fleet would clear remaining minefields, destroy defences beyond the Narrows, and proceed down the remaining twenty-seven miles of the Dardanelles to enter the Sea of Marmara. Carden proposed to achieve these ambitious goals in a matter of weeks with naval force alone. Churchill submitted Admiral Carden's sketchy plan to the War Council for approval on 13 January.[3]

By the time the War Council met to consider Carden's plan, the Russians had already defeated Enver's army on the Caucasus front and no longer needed British help. Yet the prospect of a major naval victory in the Dardanelles and the occupation of the Ottoman capital had captured Kitchener's imagination. With the western front in total deadlock, there was a greater prospect for a breakthrough in the east. The string of Ottoman defeats between November 1914 and January 1915—in Mesopotamia, Aden, the Gulf of Alexandretta, and Sarıkamış—convinced many in Whitehall that the Ottomans were on the brink of collapse. Were the

Allies to force the straits and take Istanbul, they could knock Turkey out of the war once and for all.

Istanbul was a prize, but the straits linking the Mediterranean to the Black Sea would be a great strategic asset for the war effort. With the straits under Allied control, Britain and France could deploy soldiers and materiel through the Black Sea to coordinate attacks with their Russian allies against Germany and Austria from the east. Russian grain, freed from the closure of the straits, could feed British and French troops on the western front. Recognizing the risks involved, Kitchener reassured more sceptical colleagues in the War Council that, in case of failure, the ships could simply be withdrawn. Such was the attraction of a campaign that required no ground forces.

Hoping for a breakthrough that might hasten the end of the war, the War Council approved Admiral Carden's plan on 13 January. The Royal Navy was ordered "to prepare for a naval expedition in February, to bombard and take the Gallipoli peninsula, with Constantinople as its objective."[4]

Immediately after deciding to open a new front in the Middle East, the British briefed their Entente allies. Churchill contacted his French counterpart to apprise him of British plans in the Dardanelles. The French government gave its full support and pledged a naval squadron, under British command, to assist in the campaign. And on 19 January, Churchill advised Grand Duke Nicholas that rather than undertaking a minor "demonstration", Britain would seek to force the Dardanelles and take Istanbul. Churchill asked the Russians to reinforce the Anglo-French campaign with a simultaneous attack from the Black Sea against the northern straits of the Bosporus. The Russians pledged to send their naval forces into the Bosporus as soon as the British fleet reached the Sea of Marmara.

THE RUSSIANS HAD EVERY INTEREST IN ASSISTING THE ALLIED CAMPAIGN in the straits. They had waited for a general European conflict to provide the opportunity to seize Istanbul and the straits. Now that the opportunity was at hand, they were concerned lest another power—particularly Greece—should send troops into Istanbul before they had secured their claim. While the Russians had pledged their support for a joint attack on the straits, they invested far more energy in trying to secure their claim to Constantinople by diplomacy than by military means.[5]

The planning of the Dardanelles campaign thus had the unintended consequence of initiating wartime negotiations between the Allies for the partition of the Ottoman Empire. Against the background of the An-glo-French naval attack on the Dardanelles, the tsar's government would formally seek its allies' recognition of Russian claims to Turkish territory. On 4 March 1915, Russian foreign minister Sergei Sazonov wrote to the am-bassadors of Britain and France seeking Allied agreement on "the question of Constantinople and of the Straits" in line with "the time-honored aspira-tions of Russia". Sazonov spelled out the boundaries of the territory Russia sought: the city of Istanbul; the European shores of the Bosporus, the Sea of Marmara, and the Dardanelles; and Ottoman Thrace up to the Enez-Midye Line (the boundary imposed on the defeated Ottomans at the end of the First Balkan War in 1912). This would have left the Asian side of the straits, the Asian half of Istanbul, and the Asian coasts of Marmara under Ottoman rule but ensured Russian domination over the vital waterways linking the Black Sea and the Mediterranean.

As no British or French interests were particularly compromised by Rus-sia's bold demands, London and Paris proved forthcoming. On 12 March, Britain conceded what it termed "the richest prize of the entire war" to Rus-sia, while reserving the right to stake its own claims to Ottoman territory in due course. France already knew what it wanted from Ottoman domains: it demanded Syria (including Palestine), the Gulf of Alexandretta, and Cilicia (the coastal region around the south-eastern Turkish city of Adana) in re-turn for recognizing Russian claims to Constantinople and the straits. These claims and Britain's deferral were formalized in a series of documents ex-changed between 4 March and 10 April 1915 that came to be known as the Constantinople Agreement—the first of several wartime partition plans for an Ottoman Empire that proved far more resistant to defeat than its enemies ever anticipated.[6]

IN LATE JANUARY AND EARLY FEBRUARY, THE ALLIES MASSED THEIR fleets outside the straits. By agreement with the Greek government, the Brit-ish and French secured the "loan" of Moudros Harbour on the disputed is-land of Lemnos, some fifty miles from the Dardanelles, to serve as their base of operations. The British also occupied the smaller islands of Imbros and Tenedos (known today by their Turkish names, Gökçeada and Bozcaada), both within sight of the Turkish coastline on either side of the mouth of the Dardanelles. Given that Turkey had never recognized Greek claims to these islands, seized in the First Balkan War, the Allied presence at the mouth of the Dardanelles did not compromise Greek neutrality (Greece only entered the war on the side of the Entente Powers in June 1917).

Allied war planners soon recognized they would need to deploy some ground forces as part of any naval manoeuvre in the Dardanelles. British intelligence reports claimed there were 40,000 Turkish troops on the Gallipoli Peninsula. Even if these Ottoman soldiers retreated in the face of a major naval attack, the British and French would need to secure the abandoned fortifications along the Dardanelles if the straits were to remain safe for Allied shipping. They would also need an occupation army to hold Istanbul once it fell. The difficulty was in persuading Lord Kitchener to divert infantry from the western front for an eastern campaign.

As Kitchener warmed to the potential benefits of the Dardanelles campaign for the overall war effort, he came round to the need to involve the army. However, he still urged Churchill to rely first and foremost on naval power to force the straits. The war lord viewed the infantry units as provisionally on loan for a short campaign in Turkey before returning to the western front, where Kitchener believed they were most needed. The ground forces were thus to be held in reserve until the navy had forced the straits. On this basis, in late February Kitchener ordered the British commander in Egypt to dispatch 36,000 Anzac troops to join 10,000 men of the Royal Naval Division at Moudros. The French too began to assemble ground forces for the Dardanelles campaign. The Eastern Expeditionary Corps (Corps Expéditionnaire d'Orient), combining European units, colonial soldiers, and Foreign Legionnaires—18,000 men in all—was mobilized and dispatched to the straits in the first week of March.

As tens of thousands of Allied soldiers and sailors converged on the Dardanelles, the "demonstration" was increasingly turning into a campaign—one that the Entente Powers could ill afford to lose. Kitchener's argument that the British could break off an unsuccessful attack with no loss of prestige no longer seemed to hold water. With the opening salvo against the outer forts of the Dardanelles in February 1915, the British made such a big show that there would be no turning back without a serious loss of face.

In the deep harbour of Moudros, an impressive armada had assembled that brought industrial-age war craft to the Middle Eastern front. The British dispatched their very first aircraft carrier to the Dardanelles. The Ark Royal was a converted merchant ship fitted with two cranes to deploy seaplanes from a workshop in its hull to the water's surface for take-off and to retrieve them after landing. The Ark Royal's six seaplanes would provide aerial reconnaissance for operations in the Dardanelles until landing strips could be built on Lemnos and Tenedos for heavier aircraft with greater range. Among the fourteen British and four French battleships, the massive *Queen Elizabeth* stood out as the largest and most modern ship of the line, a "super-dreadnought" brought into service that same year. Its eight 15-inch guns were the most powerful cannons in the eastern Mediterranean, capable of firing a one-ton shell over a distance of eighteen miles. The lesser dreadnoughts and older fighting ships boasted 12-inch guns—shorter in range but still powerful. Another seventy ships crowded the harbour, including cruisers, destroyers, submarines, minesweepers, and torpedo boats. The combined firepower of the Anglo-French fleet totalled 274 medium and heavy cannons.

Naval operations opened on 19 February 1915. The Allied fleet's first object was to destroy the outer forts of the Dardanelles—around Seddül-bahir on the European side and Kum Kale on the Asian coast—and their nineteen outdated guns. The modern British dreadnoughts had far greater range than the Turkish guns. They opened fire on the forts from five to eight miles offshore with total impunity. After scoring what appeared to be a number of direct hits on Ottoman positions, the British ships approached closer to shore to examine the damage. Only then did the Turkish gunners return fire, forcing the British ships to retreat to a safe distance to reconsider their tactics.

News of the allied bombardment of the straits, however unsuccessful, provoked panic in Istanbul. The Ottoman government and the palace prepared to abandon the capital city and relocate to the Anatolian town of Eskişehir, halfway between Istanbul and Ankara. The treasury had already begun moving its gold reserves to Anatolia for safekeeping. The Turks' reaction encouraged the hope in London that a successful forcing of the straits might provoke a political crisis in Istanbul that would topple the Young Turk government and lead to a quick Ottoman capitulation. Kitchener, for one, had always counted on a successful assault on Istanbul sparking such a revolution.[7]

High seas and bad weather delayed the resumption of hostilities for five days. On 25 February, Admiral Carden renewed the bombardment of Turkish positions from closer in. In so doing, he exposed his ships to enemy fire. The dreadnought *Agamemnon* was severely damaged by Turkish shelling. However, in the course of the day's bombardment, the other ships managed to silence the Turkish guns in the outer forts on the Asian and European sides of the Dardanelles. The Turkish defenders abandoned their positions under the blistering Allied gunfire. When parties of Royal Marines landed on the southern tip of the Gallipoli Peninsula to destroy any remaining guns, they made their way to the forts unopposed and reboarded their ships after demolishing gun emplacements in total safety.[8]

Allied ships could now enter the mouth of the Dardanelles without fear of shelling from the guns of the outer fortresses. This left Admiral Carden free to proceed to the second stage of the campaign: minesweeping operations and the destruction of the inner defences from the mouth of the straits to Kepez Point. Had the British moved quickly, they would have found the Dardanelles defended by relatively few Turkish ground forces. However, faulty intelligence and bad weather slowed the British campaign and gave the Turks precious time to reinforce their position.

Strong winds and rough seas prevented British and French ships from engaging in the delicate work of mine sweeping for days on end between late February and mid-March. When the weather permitted the minesweepers to work, the British and French battleships entered the straits to protect the trawlers from artillery on shore. The Allies were frustrated in their efforts to destroy the fixed shore batteries lining the inner coasts of the Dardanelles. The guns had been well placed and were practically invisible—and unreachable—from sea level. The heavy shells of the Allied battleships ploughed into the earth around the emplacements, burying the guns without damaging them. Once the ships withdrew, the Ottomans and Germans dug out the emplacements and restored the shore batteries to working order.[9]

However frustrating the British and French found their duels with the shore batteries, the new mobile artillery the Germans had introduced in the Dardanelles proved the greatest hazard to Allied shipping. "Those nasty cannons make no smoke, are very small, highly mobile, and I have no advice to offer in locating them," a French naval officer complained. The mobile howitzers fired from behind the hillsides flanking the straits and dropped shrapnel onto the unprotected decks of Allied ships, inflicting

Turk battery, Gallipoli. Turkish gunners deployed mobile artillery from behind the hills overlooking the straits of the Dardanelles to devastating effect on Allied shipping. As one French naval officer noted, these "nasty cannons make no smoke, are very small, highly mobile, and I have no advice to offer in locating them."

heavy casualties. One direct hit during minesweeping operations claimed twenty French sailors' lives on the cruiser *Améthyst*. Only reconnaissance aircraft could locate the mobile canons. However, before the British pilots could report the howitzers' positions to the ships below, the gun crews would have already moved their pieces to new locations to renew their lethal fire on the invading ships in total safety.[10]

The minesweepers were no more successful in locating mines than the battleships were in finding mobile batteries. British intelligence reported the Turks had laid mines from the mouth of the Dardanelles to the Narrows. Actually, the Ottomans sensibly chose to concentrate their limited resources further north in the narrowest reaches of the Dardanelles, making the waters between Kepez Point and the Narrows impassable to hostile traffic. This meant the allies wasted weeks trawling the broadest part of the Dardanelles, where there were no mines. One French naval officer suspected the Germans of having deliberately misled the Allies: "In spite of our very precise information (probably of Boche provenance) on the position, number and density of the lines of mines, *we have yet to find a single one*," he fumed in his diary. "So what the devil have we been doing here since February 25?"[11]

In a month of operations, the Allied fleet had made little headway against Ottoman batteries, and its minesweepers had come back empty-handed. In London, Winston Churchill was growing impatient. "If success cannot be obtained without loss of ships and men, results to be gained are important enough to justify such a loss," he telegraphed Admiral Carden on 11 March. "Every well-conceived action for forcing a decision, even should regrettable losses be entailed, will receive our support." Admiral Carden responded to Churchill's pressures by issuing orders on 15 March to attack the inner forts and force the Narrows. Yet the pressure took its toll on Carden, who collapsed on 16 March and had to be shipped out to Malta for medical treatment. He was succeeded by his second in command, Vice Admiral J. M. de Robeck, who gave orders to commence operations on the morning of 18 March.[12]

ON THE CLEAR, CALM MORNING OF 18 MARCH, THE ANGLO-FRENCH fleet entered the straits to launch what one German officer described as "the greatest battle which had ever taken place between floating ironclads and land batteries". At 11:00 a.m., the super-dreadnought *Queen Elizabeth* led a squadron of the six largest British ships inside the mouth of the straits, opening fire on the Ottoman forts, in the words of one eyewitness, "at a truly terrifying rate". The British ships maintained an intense level of fire against Turkish positions. "The forts were replying in fine style, despite the fact that . . . it seemed impossible that men could live under conditions as existing in and about the forts." The deserted wooden houses in the towns of Çanakkale and Kilitbahr caught fire and burned throughout the day. For ninety minutes the two sides exchanged blows without either achieving a decisive advantage.[13]

At 12:30, four French warships eagerly joined the battle and took the lead towards Kepez Point. As they moved up the straits, the French ships came under intense crossfire from the fortresses at the Narrows, the shore batteries, and the mobile howitzers. Over the next hour, the *Suffren* and *Bouvet* took several direct hits but continued to fire tenaciously. As Turkish fire began to slow after one hour of fierce cannonades, the French squadron was ordered to withdraw to be replaced by fresh British ships.

That was when things started to go badly wrong for the Allies. As the *Bouvet* turned to make its way out of the straits, it was carried downstream by the strong current and struck a mine in Erenköy Bay, off the Asian shores of the Dardanelles. The explosion blew a massive hole in the hull of the warship, which instantly listed to starboard. Its masts horizontal, seawater boiling as it filled the ship's smokestacks, the *Bouvet* capsized within two minutes, its three propellers still turning in the air. Nearly all of the ship's crew of 724 men were trapped in the overturned hull when it suddenly plunged to the ocean floor. "It seemed as though no one, not even God, could stop the ship's fatal movement," one French officer recorded in his diary. "If I live one hundred years I will never forget the horror of watching the *Bouvet* sink." It was all over in a matter of minutes. Only sixty-two men survived.[14]

The mines in Erenköy Bay had caught the Allies completely by surprise. The Ottomans, having observed British and French ships manoeuvring in Erenköy Bay during their weeks of sweeping operations, had laid a new row of twenty mines across the mouth of the bay on the night of 7–8 March. These had totally escaped the notice of Allied mine sweepers and

Sinking of *Irresistible*. One string of twenty Ottoman mines laid across Erenköy Bay claimed four Allied ships of the line—among them HMS *Irresistible*—in the catastrophic naval engagement of 18 March 1915. The Royal Navy succeeded in rescuing most of *Irresistible*'s crew before Turkish gunners finally sank the foundering ship.

aerial reconnaissance alike. As it was unclear what had sunk the *Bouvet*—artillery, a drifting mine, or a torpedo sent from shore—several British warships also came to grief in Erenköy Bay. Around 4:00 p.m., the British battleship *Inflexible* struck a mine, and almost immediately afterwards the *Irresistible* hit another, which destroyed her rudder and left her drifting out of control. *Ocean*, sent to *Irresistible*'s assistance, detonated yet another mine. One row of twenty mines had claimed four ships of the line.

Turkish gunners, seeing one ship sink and three others in distress, smelled victory and redoubled their efforts, firing on the stranded vessels. A well-aimed shell struck the magazine of the French ship *Suffren* and set off a huge explosion that killed twelve sailors and nearly sank her before the magazine could be flooded to prevent further explosions. The *Gaulois* was also badly damaged by artillery fire and started taking on water. The *Queen Elizabeth* suffered five direct hits. As soon as the stricken *Inflexible* had retired from the straits and the surviving crewmembers of *Ocean* and *Irresistible* had been rescued from their disabled vessels, Admiral de Robeck raised the flag for a general recall of all ships.

One battery took particular satisfaction at the Anglo-French fleet's distress. The guns of the ill-fated *Messoudieh*, torpedoed by a British submarine in December 1914, had been salvaged from the seabed and mounted in an improvised fortification named after the sunken ship. Survivors of the ship's gun crews, reunited in the Messoudieh Battery, fired until their ammunition stores were nearly emptied. Şefik Kaptan, the *Messoudieh*'s gunnery officer, recalled his intense joy as he watched the defeated Allied fleet disengage. "The battle was won," he exulted. "We had helped avenge the loss of our ship." Turkish gunners continued to fire on the drifting *Ocean* and *Irresistible* until both ships joined the *Bouvet* (and the *Messoudieh*) on the ocean floor.[15]

When the last Allied ship limped out of the Dardanelles, the Turks could hardly grasp the scale and significance of their accomplishment. It was, in fact, the first Ottoman victory of the Great War. Jubilant gun crews in the straits leapt to the parapets of their batteries, shouting the traditional Ottoman cheer: "Padişahım Çok Yaşa!" "Long live my Sultan!" But the reaction in Istanbul and the other cities of the Ottoman Empire was muted. The American ambassador in Istanbul noted how police had to go from door to door to encourage the townspeople to display flags to celebrate the victory. There were no spontaneous demonstrations or victory parades.

Hakki Sunata, a young lieutenant in the Ottoman army, learned of the naval victory while sitting in a coffeehouse writing letters to his friends. He later remarked how, on the day, "we knew very little about the battle" and "could not comprehend the extent of the enemy's losses. I suppose, at the beginning, even the government could not grasp the significance and so refrained from presenting it as a big victory." The General Headquarters did issue a series of reports to the Istanbul press on the day's fighting, noting the ferocity of the Allied attack and the heroism of the Turkish forces in defending the motherland against the world's greatest navy. Yet the Ottomans did not quite believe the battle had ended and fully expected the Allied ships to return the following day to resume their campaign.[16]

The British and French, for their part, were stunned by the magnitude of their defeat. Three battleships had been sunk, and three others were so badly damaged that they were effectively out of service; over 1,000 lives had been lost, and hundreds of men had been wounded. The total strength of the Allied battle fleet was reduced by one-third in a single day's action with no significant damage inflicted on Ottoman positions. Though the British and French were not to know it, the Ottomans came out of the battle practically unscathed. Their inner gun batteries were largely intact, the minefields between Kepez Point and the Narrows remained undisturbed, and they had suffered fewer than 150 casualties. The defeat of 18 March spelled the end of the naval campaign in the Dardanelles and set in motion plans for the ground campaign.[17]

BACK IN LONDON, THE WAR COUNCIL MET ON 19 MARCH TO TAKE stock of a very unfavourable situation. Following the debacle in the Dardanelles, Sir Ian Hamilton, commander in chief of the infantry units comprising the Mediterranean Expeditionary Force, convinced Lord Kitchener that the straits could not be forced by the navy alone. A large ground force needed to take the Gallipoli Peninsula and silence the guns to permit ships to enter the straits and advance on Istanbul. It was out of the question that the British might break off hostilities at the straits in the aftermath of such a terrible defeat. Nor could the Royal Navy afford to suffer another such setback. Though long opposed to committing the army to a major campaign beyond the western front, Kitchener saw no alternative. "You know my views," Kitchener replied to Hamilton, "that the passage of the

Dardanelles must be forced, and that if large military operations on the Gallipoli peninsula are necessary to clear the way, they must be undertaken, and must be carried through." Kitchener committed 75,000 infantry to the campaign.[18]

At this point, Russia dropped out of the Allied assault on the Ottoman capital. As the British and French ships had failed to reach the Sea of Marmara, the tsar's forces felt no obligation to attack the northern straits of the Bosporus. Aside from minor demonstrations on the Black Sea coast, the Russians did little to relieve the Allies in the Dardanelles. The British official history of the Gallipoli campaign generously noted that "the fear of a Russian landing detained three Turkish divisions in the Bosporus till almost the end of June", troops that otherwise could have been dispatched to defend the Dardanelles.[19]

The Allies gave themselves one month to prepare for the invasion of the Gallipoli Peninsula. It was not nearly enough time to plan and coordinate what would prove the greatest seaborne landing yet attempted. However, the Allied war planners knew that the longer they took, the better prepared the Ottomans and their German allies would be to repel such an invasion. Thanks to the delays in naval operations, the Turks had already enjoyed a month's head start to reinforce their position on the peninsula. The challenge facing British war planners was to devise an offensive over the next four weeks that would overwhelm the best-laid defences the Ottomans and Germans could assemble within the same time frame.

The invaders faced the greater challenge. The logistics and planning involved in a combined naval and ground operation are infinitely complex. Transport ships had to be assembled to convey troops, mobile artillery, ammunition, work animals, food, water, and supplies to the battlefront. A beach landing calls for large numbers of landing craft and lighters. British officers scoured Mediterranean ports to buy every small craft available, paid for in cash. (The requisition officers' efforts to buy boats of course alerted Turkish and German intelligence to an imminent landing operation.) Piers and pontoons had to be constructed and transported to the landing beaches, and military engineers had to practice assembling these dock facilities under adverse conditions. Medical personnel and facilities needed to be prepared to receive the wounded, and hospital ships had to be positioned to transport serious cases to medical centres in Malta and Alexandria. The list of details, each essential in its own right, seemed unending.

The diversity of the invasion force further complicated planning. No battlefield in the Great War would prove more global than Gallipoli. The Mediterranean Expeditionary Force numbered some 75,000 men from around the world. In addition to British troops—Welsh, Irish, Scottish, and English—there were volunteers from the Dominion of Newfoundland, Australians and New Zealanders (with both Pakeha and Maori units), Gurkhas and Sikhs, Frenchmen, Foreign Legionnaires hailing from around the world, and colonial troops from across Africa—Senegal, Guinea, Sudan, and the Maghrib. Soldiers were mutually reliant on men with whom they could barely communicate. Without a clear battle plan to guide the movements of each and every unit, the expeditionary force risked dissolving into a veritable Tower of Babel.[20]

Although their task was simpler than that of the invaders, the stakes could not have been higher for the Ottoman defenders. They rightly saw Gallipoli as a struggle for the survival of their empire. Enver Pasha, back in Istanbul after leading the Third Army to total defeat in the Caucasus, knew he could not afford to lose again. Victory would require total organization and clear lines of communication between units spread over a wide area of the Asian and European shores of the straits. In the last week of March 1915, Enver decided to reorganize the different divisions in the Dardanelles into a unified force—the Fifth Army. Overlooking his past differences with the head of the German military mission to Turkey, Enver swallowed his pride and appointed Otto Liman von Sanders commander in chief of the new Fifth Army, tasked with the defence of the Dardanelles. Liman set off immediately for the town of Gallipoli to set up his headquarters. "The British gave me four full weeks before their great landing," Liman later recorded in his memoirs. "The time was just sufficient to complete the most indispensable arrangements."[21]

The Ottoman Fifth Army numbered some 50,000 men, only two-thirds the size of the invading force. Yet it takes fewer men to defend a beachhead than to invade it—if they are stationed in the right places. Liman's challenge was to second-guess British plans in order to concentrate Ottoman forces where the invaders were most likely to land. He deployed two divisions (roughly 10,000 men each) on the Asian side of the Dardanelles and concentrated three divisions on the Gallipoli Peninsula. Yet the peninsula is sixty miles long and presented Ottoman war planners with many vulnerable points to defend.

After careful consideration, Liman and his Turkish commanders identified three areas on the Gallipoli Peninsula most vulnerable to Allied attack:

Cape Helles, Arıburnu, and Bulair. The southernmost tip of the peninsula around Cape Helles favoured a seaborne landing because Allied warships could fire on the coast from three sides at once. The beaches to the north at Arıburnu (which would soon come to be known as Anzac Cove) provided an easy landing spot at a point only five miles distant from the Dardanelles. Were the Allies to secure the line from Arıburnu to the town of Maidos (the modern town of Eceabat) on the straits, they could effectively cut off the southern reaches of the peninsula, trapping the Ottoman defenders. Yet Liman was convinced that Bulair, far to the north where the peninsula narrows to just two miles' width, was the place of greatest vulnerability. A successful landing at Bulair would sever the entire peninsula and give the Allies a position to dominate the Sea of Marmara and thus cut vital shipping lines of supply and communications with the Ottoman Fifth Army in the straits. Following his analysis of the threat, Liman decided to post one division in each of these vulnerable points—Cape Helles, Arıburnu, and Bulair.

Ottoman officers set their men to work digging defensive trenches and laying wire along key beaches to obstruct landings. British aircraft regularly flew over Gallipoli and directed naval bombardment towards any worksites or Turkish troop concentrations, forcing the Ottomans to do most of their defensive work at night. By mid-April, the defenders had installed miles of trenches with hidden machine-gun emplacements and artillery batteries to repel any landing by sea. The work continued right up to the eve of an invasion that, judging by the massing of ships and soldiers in Moudros Harbour, the Ottomans knew to be imminent.

AFTER THE TEDIUM OF CAMP LIFE IN EGYPT, MOST ANZAC SOLDIERS were glad to board ship for Gallipoli. The only soldiers with a regret were the cavalry, who were forced to leave their horses behind. Given the hilly topography of Gallipoli, there was no prospect of a cavalry charge, and their mounts remained in Egypt.

The men penned letters home full of anticipation of battlefield glory. Corporal Mostyn Pryce Jones of the New Zealand Canterbury Battalion wrote to his mother, marvelling at the view as his vessel entered Moudros on 16 April—the scores of transport ships carrying "British, French, Australians and N.Z. troops all eager for the fray" and the "hundreds of cruisers, dread-noughts, super dread-noughts, submarines, torpedo destroyers and torpedo boats, all making a wonderful picture". He took pride and comfort in this visible display of power. "It makes you realize the great might and strength of <u>OUR</u> Empire and you can even feel a thrill of pride run through you as you realize that you yourself are a part (if a very insignificant one) of this vast and magnificent brotherhood of people." Jones and his comrades believed they were embarked on the adventure of a lifetime.[22]

The commanders of the Mediterranean Expeditionary Force actively promoted the idea of the approaching battle as an adventure. The night before the landing the commander in chief, Sir Ian Hamilton, addressed a proclamation to the "soldiers of France and the King" in which he described the battle ahead as "an adventure unprecedented in Modern war". To some extent, this show of bravura was meant to raise the men's courage. Yet it also reflected the illusions of military commanders who in many cases were as inexperienced with "modern war" as the men they led.

For the Turks, Gallipoli was no adventure. It was a matter of life or death. Colonel Mustafa Kemal, commander of Ottoman troops at Arıburnu, famously strengthened his officers' resolve in his pre-battle address: "I don't order you to attack, I order you to die. In the time which passes until we die other troops and commanders can take our places." For tens of thousands of Turkish soldiers, the future Atatürk's words were tragically prophetic.[23]

BY THE TIME THE MOON HAD SET IN THE EARLY MORNING HOURS OF Sunday, 25 April, the Allied warships were nearing their positions to launch the troop landings. The ships observed total silence under blackout conditions to avoid alerting the Turks of their approach. The actual landing sites remained a tightly guarded secret among the Allied commanders. They hoped by ruse and surprise to overwhelm the defenders and secure a beachhead to land the rest of the invasion force in relative safety.

To trick the Ottomans, the British and French prepared feints at the northern and southern extremities of the battle zone. The French sent a number of ships to Besika Bay on the Asian coastline south of the Dardanelles, where they were to feign a major landing in a bid to detain Ottoman troops far from the actual landing beaches. The British unwittingly played to Liman von Sanders's fears by organizing a feint at the northern extremity of the Gallipoli Peninsula off Bulair. Liman had positioned a division to protect the Bulair lines and went in person to observe British manoeuvres.

These feints tied up two Ottoman divisions that might otherwise have been dispatched to the actual landing zones.

For the landings, the Mediterranean Expeditionary Force was divided into three groups. The British were assigned the principal landing site around Cape Helles on the southern tip of the Gallipoli Peninsula. British troops were to coordinate landings at five different beaches around Helles. The French were to secure the Asian shores of the Dardanelles around Kum Kale to prevent the Ottomans from firing on British troops landing across the straits. Once the British had secured their beaches, the French were to re-embark from Kum Kale to reinforce the British in Cape Helles. The Australians and New Zealanders were dispatched to the area around Arıburnu to check any Turkish reinforcements and threaten the Ottoman rear in the Helles area. By attacking in so many positions at once, the Allies hoped to confuse the Turks, who would not know where to concentrate their forces to repel the invaders, and to get as many men ashore in as short a time as possible to overwhelm Ottoman defences.

In the predawn hours, the first wave of invaders descended on rope ladders from the high decks of the warships to the rowboats waiting below to take them ashore. Small steamboats towed strings of four rowboats from ship to shore, leaving sailors to row the final hundred yards or so to the beach. The soldiers, packed tightly into their designated landing craft, were totally exposed to gunfire and shrapnel. To protect the troops from shore fire, the British and French warships unleashed "a mass of fire and smoke" on the beaches at 4:30 a.m. "The noise was awful and the air full of powder," a British naval officer later wrote. The warships kept up the shelling until the landing craft were within half a mile of the shore.[24]

For the Ottoman defenders, who had long anticipated an invasion, the ships' cannonade was a call to arms. Turkish officers blew their whistles and ordered their men to take up defensive positions. The ships' fire was concentrated on a handful of small beaches, from two or three directions at once, inflicting terrible damage on Turkish positions. "The shoreline was covered with heavy black smoke, tinged with blue and green," Major Mahmud Sabri recalled. "Visibility was zero." Major Sabri described how naval cannon fire destroyed gun positions, levelled communication trenches, and turned "foxholes, meant to protect lives," into "tombs". Shrapnel "as big as eggs" inflicted heavy casualties among the Turkish soldiers waiting in their trenches. Yet far from provoking panic among the Turkish defenders, the heavy gunfire seemed only to steel their determination to repel the invaders. "With dead and dismembered comrades at their side, without worrying about being outnumbered or the nature of the enemy's fire, our men waited for the moment they could use their weapons." As the warships ceased fire to allow the landing craft to approach the beaches, surviving Ottoman soldiers waited patiently and took aim.[25]

The main British landing point was at V Beach, between the old fortress of Seddülbahir and the ruined lighthouse at Cape Helles. Royal Marines had landed there with impunity on 25 February to destroy surviving cannons after the naval bombardment of the outer forts. Since February, the Ottomans had made every effort to reinforce the position, which was shaped like a natural amphitheatre overlooking the bay. The challenge for the British war planners was to land enough troops to overcome the stiff opposition they expected to encounter. Tows of four rowboats could only deliver 120 to 130 men at a time, and the British could only manage six tows for V Beach—a maximum of 800 men. The invaders needed to find a way to land many more men on V Beach.

The classically trained British officers found their solution in Homer. Legend and archaeology placed the site of the Trojan War near the Asian shores of the Dardanelles. Captain Edward Unwin of the Royal Navy suggested that "after the manner of the wooden horse of Troy, a harmless-looking collier, filled with all the troops she could carry" could be run ashore. Not only would the sight of a steamship running towards the beach at full speed distract the defenders, but a refitted collier, or coal ship, could hold at least 2,100 men. Once grounded, the ship would provide a sheltered landing platform for soldiers and serve as a jetty for future operations. The suggestion was approved immediately, and the collier *River Clyde* was refitted to serve the purpose. Its hull was reinforced, heavy guns were mounted on its bows to provide cover fire to protect landing troops, and sally ports were cut into the sides of her hull to facilitate the rapid debarkation of the soldiers she carried.[26]

On the morning of 25 April, the *River Clyde* made her way towards V Beach with Captain Unwin at the helm. He watched as the light steam launches before him struggled against the strong current of the straits to deliver their tows to the landing site. The beach was still shrouded in smoke from the naval bombardment and totally quiet. Standing next to him on the bridge was Lieutenant Colonel Williams of the General Staff, keeping a minute-by-minute log. At 6:22 a.m., the *River Clyde* ran aground in the exact position charted for the landing. "No opposition," Colonel Williams recorded optimistically. "We shall land unopposed." He spoke too soon. Three minutes later, as the tows reached the shore, the disciplined Turkish defenders opened fire. "Hell burst loose on them," Williams recorded at 6:25. He watched, appalled, as one of the landing craft drifted past the *River Clyde* with every soldier and sailor on board dead. Only a handful of the first eight hundred men made it ashore unscathed to take shelter behind the first row of dunes.[27]

Major Mahmud Sabri described the scene from the perspective of the Turkish trenches:

> The enemy approached shore in life-boats. When they came into range, our men opened fire. Here, for years, the colour of the sea had always been the same, but now it turned red with the blood of our enemies. Whenever the flash of (our) rifles was spotted, the enemy plastered the area with artillery and machine-gun fire. This failed to reduce the intensity of our fire.
>
> In the hope of saving their lives, some of the enemy jumped from life-boats into the sea. From shipboard, their commanders used flags to order life-boats to take shelter behind promontories, but there was no escape. In spite of enemy shelling and machine-gun fire, our men continued to hit their targets, and the dead rolled into the sea. The shoreline of [V Beach] filled with enemy corpses, lined up like rows of broad-beans.[28]

The *River Clyde*, conceived of as a Trojan horse, was now reduced to a sitting duck. The ship had grounded in waters too deep to land the 2,100 men waiting anxiously inside its hull. The crew had towed a number of lighters and a small steamboat to rig a pontoon bridge on which the landing troops might run from ship to shore. The crew had a terrible time manoeuvring the boats into place in the strong current off the Dardanelles. G. L. Drewry, a midshipman on the *River Clyde*, braved the gunfire and leapt into the water to rig a workable pontoon bridge. The shooting from shore was so intense that when he tried to lift a wounded soldier from the water, the stricken man was shot to pieces in Drewry's arms. Incredibly, Drewry managed to work on the pontoon bridge without getting shot. All the while, the Turkish defenders trained their guns on the grounded collier. Two shells ripped into

No. 4 hold, killing several men. Turkish marksmen fired at the ship's port-holes, killing those straining for a look at the battle scene.

Whatever the carnage aboard the *River Clyde*, the death toll reached a peak on the pontoon bridge. The Turks trained their guns on the narrow causeway and mowed down the Munster and Dublin Fusiliers before they even managed to reach the shore. "I stayed on the lighters and tried to keep the men going ashore but it was murder and soon the first lighter was covered with dead and wounded," Drewry recounted. Echoing Mahmud Sabri's comments, Drewry was appalled to see the sea stained red with soldiers' blood. "When they got ashore they were little better off for they were picked off many of them before they could dig themselves in."

One thousand men attempted the pontoon bridge before their commanders brought the suicidal landing to a halt. The handful that made it to shore alive took shelter behind sand dunes, where they waited for nightfall. The current later dislodged the precarious pontoons, breaking the bridge to land. The remaining soldiers, sheltering in the reinforced hull of the collier, waited until evening for the firing to die down before repairing the bridge and resuming their operations. They only risked the gunfire outside to ferry the wounded from the tenders back onto the ship.[29]

British forces suffered heavy losses in the W Beach landing as well. Nearly 1,000 British soldiers sat anxiously on the benches of their landing craft as they approached the beach below the ruined Helles lighthouse, still smouldering from the after-effects of the intensive naval bombardment. They faced a company of well-entrenched Turkish defenders—perhaps 150 men in all. When the landing craft were just fifty yards from shore, Major Haworth of the Lancashire Fusiliers recalled, "an awful rifle and maxim gun fire broke out from the cliffs" overlooking the bay. He noted how the "courageous sailors" continued to row the landing craft into shore "while they and our men were being hit". As the boats neared the beach, Major Haworth ordered his troops to disembark in order to escape the gunfire. They found themselves chest deep in water. Many of those subsequently wounded by Turkish fire sank under the weight of their heavy packs (each man carried two hundred rounds of ammunition and three days' provisions) and drowned.[30]

Once ashore on W Beach (later renamed Lancashire Landing), Haworth's company was pinned down by lethal crossfire. One of the captains accompanying him was mortally wounded. Tracing the gunfire to a trench at the crest of a hill, Haworth ordered his company to storm the position. As they made their way up the steep slope, the British officer watched men on either side of him fall dead and wounded. Haworth was nearly killed when a Turkish defender fired at close range and took the top off his right ear. The British officer shot the man dead with his revolver as he continued towards the hilltop position. "Just as I reached the trench there was a terrific explosion—the trench was mined and I and those near me were sent hustling down to the bottom of the cliff again." Dazed, Haworth collected the forty survivors of his company to take shelter at the foot of the hills, where, for the rest of the day, they were picked off by sniper fire. Six of his men were killed or wounded before Haworth himself was shot in the back. Paralyzed by his wound, Haworth was left in the horrific company of the dead and wounded until nightfall, when medics could reach the beach.[31]

The British had relatively easy landings on other Helles beaches. On Morto Bay, the landing party encountered only a handful of Turkish defenders and easily established their position. The Turks had not anticipated a landing at X Beach either and had left only one platoon to guard the spot. The invaders secured the beach with relatively light losses.

The landing parties at Y Beach found their position entirely undefended. Within fifteen minutes, 2,000 men had cleared the beach and scaled the steep heights onto the plateau. However, as they prepared to move southward to reinforce British positions around Helles, they discovered the steep banks of Zığındere, or Gully Ravine. The inaccurate maps used by British war planners made no mention of this impassable obstruction. Not only was the landing party prevented from relieving beleaguered British forces further south, but the troops found themselves with the ravine at their backs when Ottoman units mounted a stiff counter-attack later that afternoon. Caught on the plateau with nowhere to retreat to and faced with determined Turkish assaults through the night, the British suffered over seven hundred casualties before they were able to evacuate Y Beach the following morning.

As the day wore on, waves of British reinforcements landed. The invaders began to drive the Ottoman defenders back from the Helles coastline, relieving the pressure on V and W Beaches, where the British had suffered such high casualties. As night fell, fresh British troops began to disembark on those deadly beaches as well. The crew of the *River Clyde* reassembled the jetty, and between 8 p.m. and 11:30 p.m. the remaining troops disembarked past the wounded and the dead. The defenders continued to fire onto the landing beach "with shell, shrapnel and every other nasty thing", but the fire was much less intense and "little harm was done", according to Midshipman Drewry, observing from the *River Clyde*.

After a terrible day of fighting, the Turkish defenders watched waves of fresh British soldiers landing with mounting concern. One of the defenders at V Beach wrote his superior officer with growing urgency to request reinforcements or permission to withdraw. "Send the doctors to carry off my wounded. Alas! Alas, my captain, for God's sake send me reinforcements because hundreds of soldiers are landing." On W Beach, Turkish forces charged British positions with bayonets twice that night before falling back to their rear lines.[32]

By dawn on Monday, 26 April, the British held four of their five landing sites; they evacuated Y Beach later that morning to redeploy its surviving troops to other positions. At the end of their first day in Gallipoli, the British had managed to secure a beachhead, but at a terrible price. The intensity of Ottoman resistance had caught them by surprise and denied the British their ambition of reaching the high ground of Achi Baba (Elçı Tepe), five miles inland. And despite the men and materiel deployed in Gallipoli over the rest of 1915, the British never would reach Achi Baba.

FRENCH FORCES INITIALLY MET LITTLE RESISTANCE WHEN THEY LANDED on the beaches of Kum Kale. At 5:15 a.m., the French fleet opened fire on Ottoman positions along the coast. Their cannonade was longer than intended, as the landing parties were delayed by currents far stronger than anticipated (as the British had encountered at Helles). The French turned the two-hour delay to advantage, reducing Kum Kale to rubble and driving the defenders back to the east bank of the Menderes River. By the time the Senegalese troops stormed the beaches at 10:00 a.m., only one machine gun remained to harry the troops, and it was soon silenced by naval gunfire. French forces occupied the town of Kum Kale by 11:15, ensuring that the British landing at Helles would not be attacked from that position.[33]

The landings at Kum Kale continued throughout the day. By 5:30 p.m., all men and artillery were ashore. French forces consolidated their position in Kum Kale to face Turkish troops massing in the neighbouring town of Yeni Şehir. As night fell, the Turks mounted the first of four attacks on French positions. Bayonet charges gave way to intense and confused hand-to-hand fighting. Casualties on both sides mounted. While the French were able to retain their hold on Kum Kale, they began to question the wisdom of attempting to take Yeni Şehir. Their occupation of the Asian coast was meant to be temporary, and every casualty in Kum Kale meant one less fighter to reinforce the British on the Gallipoli Peninsula, where they would be most needed.

On the morning of 26 April, a party of eighty unarmed Ottoman soldiers—Greeks and Armenians—advanced towards French lines under the white flag of surrender. They were taken as prisoners of war. Shortly afterwards, hundreds of Turkish soldiers walked openly towards French lines, though these men were armed, with bayonets fixed. The French, believing the soldiers intended to surrender, allowed the men to approach to persuade them to lay down their arms. A French officer named Captain Rockel went forward to negotiate and disappeared into the crowd, never to be seen again. Turkish soldiers took advantage of the confusion to penetrate French lines and take up positions inside the occupied village of Kum Kale. Others jostled with French soldiers and managed to seize two machine guns. When word of the situation reached the French commander, General Albert d'Amade, he ordered his troops to open fire. The French found themselves under fire from houses behind their own lines and shooting into groups of mixed French and Turkish soldiers—it was total chaos. The French fought into the early afternoon to recover Kum Kale, bombarding the houses held by Turkish troops. The French summarily executed a Turkish officer and eight soldiers in retaliation for the (presumed) killing of Captain Rockel under the white flag of a parley. By sowing confusion, the Turks had confined the French to Kum Kale and inflicted heavy casualties on the invaders.[34]

As French losses mounted and the British need for reinforcements in Helles grew more acute, the Allied commanders decided to withdraw from Kum Kale on 26 April. Under the cover of darkness, all French troops and materiel were re-embarked, along with 450 Turkish prisoners of war. On the morning of 27 April, they crossed the straits to land at V Beach via the now secure landing jetty attached to the *River Clyde*. French forces in Gallipoli were stationed on the right, or eastern, side of Allied lines, overlooking the straits of the Dardanelles, and the British were concentrated on the western part of the line, overlooking the Aegean. Together they consolidated a front line to challenge strong Ottoman defensive positions that lay between the invaders and the strategic high ground of Achi Baba, which dominated the southern reaches of the Gallipoli Peninsula.[35]

THE FIRST WAVE OF AUSTRALIAN TROOPS SET OFF FOR THE ARIBURNU coast at dawn on 25 April. Their intended landing site was a stretch of beach to the north of a rocky promontory known as Gaba Tepe (Kabatepe). However, the planners had once again miscalculated the strength of the currents off the Gallipoli coastline, and the steam launches with their tows of four landing craft drifted well off course, landing a mile or more north of the landing site in a small bay to which the invaders gave their name—Anzac Cove. The sailors guiding the tows had difficulty working out their positions in the early morning light against an unfamiliar coast. This meant that the troops, when they landed, faced a totally different landscape than planned and an extra ridge to scale to reach the high plateau. The confusion resulting from this mistake would plague the Anzac landing for the rest of the day.

Ottoman sentries spotted the lighters as they approached the shore. Journalist C. E. W. Bean, who accompanied the Australian force as official historian, noted in his diary the time, 4:38 a.m., when he first heard the sound of rifle fire from the shore—"first a few shots, then heavy and continuous". The

Australian troops landing at Anzac Beach on the morning of 25 April 1915. The troopers, "jammed together like sardines in the boats", were vulnerable to gun and artillery fire from Ottoman defenders. The photographer, Lance Corporal A. R. H. Joyner, survived Gallipoli only to die on the western front in December 1916.

landing parties felt exposed as they neared the shore, "jammed together like sardines in the boats, while the Turks blazed away merrily at us from the top of a big hill just skirting the shore", one Australian soldier in the first wave recalled. The soldiers were in a hurry to get out of the landing craft as they watched their comrades killed and wounded at random around them.[36]

Once the men were ashore, the carefully scripted battle plan began to unravel. The landing craft, carried off course by the current, had not only landed in the wrong place but in the wrong order. Soldiers were separated from their commanding officers, and units got intermixed. Under fire and fired up, the Australian soldiers fell in with the nearest officer, fixed bayonets, and began to charge up the first ridge of hills to drive back the Ottoman defenders. As one Australian infantryman wrote home, "The lads cheered every inch of the way, which I really believe helped to dishearten the Turks, for when we got near the top, they jumped out of their trenches and ran like old Harry to their second line of trenches, a distance of half a mile or more." The quick and successful bayonet charge gave the Australian troops a false sense of confidence, for the Ottomans were already beginning to prepare to repel the invaders.[37]

Mustafa Kemal Bey had his headquarters within a few miles of Anzac Cove. When he first heard about the landing, the Ottoman commander dispatched a cavalry squadron to observe and report back. At 6:30 a.m. his commanding officers issued orders for Mustafa Kemal to dispatch a battalion (roughly 1,000 men) against the invaders. Drawing on his own intelligence reports, Mustafa Kemal knew he needed to deploy an entire division (about 10,000 men) to repel an invasion of such magnitude. He gave orders for the Ottoman First Infantry Regiment and a mounted battery to prepare for battle before heading off in person to assess the situation at the front.[38]

Eight thousand Australian soldiers had landed at Anzac Cove by 8 a.m. At 10:45, the first New Zealand troops reached the shore. The invaders had faced heavy opposition in the northern and southern extremities of the landing sites, where well-entrenched Ottoman gunners deployed shrapnel and machine guns to lethal effect. One tow landing to the north was devastated by machine-gun fire, and only 18 of 140 men reached the shore uninjured. Those landing closest to Gaba Tepe faced intense shrapnel from Ottoman batteries in the heights. Yet by mid-morning the main body of Anzac forces had secured the central stretch of beaches and driven the Ottoman defenders from the first and second ridges overlooking Anzac Cove. While making

Mustafa Kemal in Gallipoli. The future Ataturk emerged
as one of the greatest Ottoman commanders of the First
World War, serving in Gallipoli, Edirne, the Caucasus,
Palestine, and Syria. He would later become the founding president of the Turkish Republic.

his way to the front, Mustafa Kemal encountered a group of retreating Ottoman soldiers who had run out of ammunition. He ordered them to fix
bayonets to their bulletless rifles and hold their position.

The Ottoman commander correctly assessed the vulnerability of the Anzac position. Though they had managed to land a large number of soldiers,
the Australians and New Zealanders held "an unfavourable and very wide
front . . . cut up by a number of valleys which were obstacles. For this reason
the enemy was weak on nearly every part of his front." Moreover, Mustafa
Kemal had great confidence in the fighting power of his soldiers. As he
organized his troops to counter-attack, he reflected, "This was no ordinary
attack. Everybody in this attack was eager to succeed or go forward with the
determination to die."

The strength of the Turkish riposte caught the Anzacs by surprise. Just
before noon, "strongly reinforced, [the Ottomans] commenced a desperate
counter-attack, supported by artillery, and machine guns, and having our

range to a nicety, they gave us the hottest time of our lives", an Australian soldier later wrote. As fresh New Zealand soldiers reinforced Anzac positions, the invaders entrenched and "settled down" for a firefight that "raged incessantly the whole night through". Ottoman forces had the benefit of mobile artillery and rained shrapnel and machine-gun fire on the invaders, who began to suffer very high casualties.[39]

New Zealand corporal Mostyn Pryce Jones shed all of his illusions about the adventure of war in his first day of combat. Landing at mid-morning, his unit advanced up a steep valley under a hail of shrapnel. "Our men were dropping one after another but then gamely stuck to it, finally gaining the firing line." Jones was demoralized by the growing number of casualties. "You cannot possibly imagine how horrible it is to see your chums and comrades, just before laughing and joking, dropping round you with all kinds of horrible wounds." By the end of the day, only 86 of 256 men in Jones's company made roll call—the rest were dead, wounded, missing, or simply divided from the rest of their unit by the chaos of Anzac Beach.[40]

As the day wore on, a growing number of isolated soldiers abandoned the firing line to return to the coast. Having left their heavy packs on the beach in order to scale the steep slopes overlooking the landing site, the soldiers, hungry and thirsty after an intense day of fighting, were also running low on ammunition. These tired and demoralized men made their way down the main valleys to the beach below, soldiers reduced to stragglers.

The Turkish defenders took every advantage of the confusion and disarray among the Anzac troops. In perhaps the boldest initiative of the day, a group of Ottoman soldiers penetrated Australian lines, pretending to be Indian troops serving in one of the British imperial units. As the Australians were expecting a detachment of Indian reinforcements, the Turks' ruse worked better than they could have dared hope. Word came down the line that a party of Indians had arrived and requested a meeting with one of the Australian officers. A lieutenant named Elston, accompanied by an interpreter, went along to meet the "Indians". They asked for a more senior officer "to discuss matters", and an adjutant named Captain McDonald was sent to join them. "Presently a message came that they wanted to see the Colonel." When the commanding officer, Colonel Pope, arrived, he found Elston and McDonald "in parley with 6 soldiers who had rifles and bayonets fitted" and began to suspect a trap. As the colonel approached the group, the Turkish soldiers closed round the Australians. Pope managed to escape under fire, but Elston, McDonald, and the corporal were all taken prisoner, a coup reported in the Istanbul papers the following day. The Australian journalist, C. E. W. Bean, fascinated by this story, noted, "How easy it would be for any Oriental to dress up as an Indian and come along the beach—not one of our men would have distinguished him."[41]

By the end of the first day, some 15,000 Anzac troops had landed around Arıburnu. They had suffered a casualty rate of 20 percent, with 500 dead and 2,500 wounded. They had sent every available man into battle and had no fresh soldiers in reserve. In the course of an intense day's fighting, the Anzacs had secured a beachhead but had not managed to achieve half of their objectives in the face of determined Ottoman defence. As the valleys and beaches filled with stragglers, the Anzac commanders believed their position was growing untenable, with insufficient soldiers left to hold their front line. Were the Ottomans to mount a major counter-attack the next day, the Anzac commanders feared, the chances of preventing a disaster were remote. Weighing their options, the commanders decided to request boats to evacuate all soldiers from Arıburnu.[42]

Sir Ian Hamilton, commander in chief of the Expeditionary Force, met with his commanding officers through the night of 25–26 April to consider their options. The Allies had suffered very heavy casualties, though they had managed to complete the landings. Although none of the landing parties had achieved the high ambitions set for the first day, Hamilton believed the worst was behind them now that all of the Allied soldiers were ashore. By all reports, the Ottomans too had suffered heavy losses and were being made to divide their forces to fight the Allies at several points simultaneously. By securing their positions, the Allies hoped to wear down the resistance and morale of the Ottoman defenders. Any attempt to re-embark Anzac forces—a two-day operation—would have the opposite effect, encouraging the Turks and leaving the retreating soldiers vulnerable to Ottoman attack.

Hamilton decided to decline the Anzac commanders' request to evacuate their troops. "There is nothing for it but to dig yourselves right in and stick it out," Hamilton explained. "Make a personal appeal to your men . . . to make a supreme effort to hold their ground." To reinforce the point, Hamilton added in a postscript, "You have got through the difficult business. Now you have only to dig, dig, dig, until you are safe." To compensate for the lack of field artillery, Hamilton ordered the fleet to open fire on Turkish positions beyond Anzac trenches to give the Australians and

New Zealanders time to consolidate their positions. As the sun rose on 26 April, the dreaded Turkish counter-attack did not materialize. Both sides, it seemed, needed time to reorganize before returning to battle.[43]

FROM THE FIRST DAY OF THE GROUND WAR IN GALLIPOLI, THE Ottomans and invaders proved remarkably well matched. Both sides showed tenacity and courage in what was a first experience of battle for nearly all participants. Yet the events set in motion on 25 April would demand far more tenacity and courage in the months of terrible violence yet to come. And the commanders on both sides would face difficult decisions, balancing the deployment of troops in the straits against other pressing demands for forces on other fronts. For the Allies, the western front was always the higher priority. For the Ottomans, the Dardanelles would take top priority as key to the empire's struggle for survival.

Yet the Ottoman war planners did not enjoy the luxury of concentrating single-mindedly on the defence of the straits. The Young Turks faced urgent demands for military resources on several fronts at once—especially in the Caucasus, where Russo-Armenian cooperation threatened the Ottomans in a region of particular vulnerability. In addressing that threat, the Young Turks would resort to means for which they have been accused of crimes against humanity down to the present day.

SEVEN

The Annihilation of the Armenians

By the spring of 1915, the Ottomans faced invasion on three fronts. Since their conquest of the Basra region of southern Iraq in the final months of 1914, Anglo-Indian troops had posed a grave threat at the southern gates of the Ottoman Empire. In the east, the Ottoman Third Army was in total disarray in the aftermath of Enver Pasha's ill-conceived Sarıkamış campaign against the Russians in December 1914 and January 1915. To the west, British and French fleets had mounted sustained attacks against the Dardanelles, and Allied infantry had managed to secure several beachheads on both sides of the straits. There were good grounds for the panic that swept the imperial capital in March 1915. The empire's collapse appeared imminent.

With the onset of spring, the respite provided by winter's natural defences was coming to an end. The deep snows of the Caucasus had started to melt. The winter gales in the Aegean had given way to calm and stable conditions in Gallipoli. The Ottomans' enemies were once again on the move, and by April 1915 the empire confronted the gravest combination of challenges in its history.

The Young Turks had very limited means to confront these concerted threats. They struggled to rebuild the Third Army to defend the Caucasus against Russian attack while concentrating every available unit for the defence of the Dardanelles, leaving almost no regular forces to repel the British from Mesopotamia. The Ottomans mobilized their population for total war, stepping up conscription and deploying police and gendarme units to reinforce regular infantry (the gendarmes were a mounted rural police force).

Enver's secret security force, the Teşkilât-i Mahsusa, mobilized Kurds, Bedouin tribesmen, and released prisoners to serve as irregulars. And when, in the spring of 1915, the Young Turks declared the entire Ottoman Armenian population a dangerous fifth column, the Unionists even mobilized average citizens to assist in their annihilation.

In the aftermath of defeat by the Russian army at Sarikamiş, the survivors of the Ottoman Third Army were devastated by an invisible enemy—disease. Between October 1914 and May 1915, as many as 150,000 soldiers and civilians in north-eastern Turkey succumbed to contagions, far exceeding the 60,000 Turkish soldiers who died in the Battle of Sarıkamış.[1]

Soldiers carried a host of infectious illnesses. After weeks of exposure to the elements, their immune systems gravely weakened, they contracted typhoid and dysentery from the contaminated food and water they scavenged. The unwashed soldiers were infested with lice and fleas that carried typhus. While billeted in towns and villages in eastern Anatolia, Ottoman soldiers infected the civilian populations. Passing from soldiers to civilians and back again, these lethal diseases spread, reaching epidemic proportions in the opening months of 1915.

The Ottoman medical authorities in Erzurum, already struggling to treat the wounded, were totally overwhelmed by the sick. As the military hospital provided only nine hundred beds, the authorities were forced to commandeer every school, mosque, and government building in Erzurum to accommodate the sick and wounded. Up to 1,000 new patients were admitted daily, with the total number of sick patients in Erzurum reaching a maximum of 15,000 at the height of the crisis. Food and medical supplies were rapidly depleted, compounding the miseries of the sick and wounded. Patients sometimes went two or three days without food. In Erzurum, soldiers actually died of starvation in hospital. Nor did the authorities have sufficient firewood to heat these improvised medical facilities in the dead of winter. These conditions contributed to the plight of the sick and wounded—and to a shockingly high mortality rate.[2]

The American missionary school in Erzurum was converted into a four-hundred-bed facility that the medical missionary Dr Edward Case found more conducive to the spread than the treatment of disease. The patients were densely packed into rooms with straw mattresses on the floor, making it impossible to isolate or quarantine those who were contagious. Without disinfectant or other sanitary measures to combat disease, the hospitals themselves rapidly became the centres of transmission. Between December 1914 and January 1915, Dr Case reported as many as 60,000 deaths (civilians and soldiers combined) in Erzurum—this in a town whose pre-war population numbered only 60,000. Nor was Erzurum unique. The American consul in Trabzon estimated that over the winter of 1914 and 1915, between 5,000 and 6,000 soldiers and civilians had died of typhus in the Black Sea port town, where local doctors claimed the mortality rate from the disease reached 80 percent at the height of the epidemic.[3]

These conditions put medical workers in as much danger as their patients. At one point between thirty and forty doctors were confined to the "contagious hospital" in Erzurum, according to Dr Case, "all sick with the typhus, nearly half of whom, or more, died from the disease". After two months in these insalubrious wards, Case himself contracted typhus, though he did recover. Case was more fortunate than many: the US consul in Trabzon claimed that over three hundred doctors and medical personnel died in north-eastern Turkey between October 1914 and May 1915. As more medical personal took ill and perished, there were fewer available to treat the sick and wounded, whose suffering and mortality increased accordingly.

The dead weighed heavily on the living during the winter of 1915. Dr Case described the horror he witnessed in Erzurum: "The dead were so numerous they forbade their burial by day, and at night they were carried naked by the wagon-load to the trenches, their clothing having been taken from their backs. I saw a trench or rather a large hole half-filled with dead bodies in every position, just as they had been thrown in like rubbish, and half-uncovered, their heads, arms, legs and even parts of their bodies showing. Others were later thrown in on top of them, and all covered up. It was a terrible sight to see." Case even saw dying men being laid in mass graves, to expire where they would be buried. Faced with the sheer magnitude of the dead and dying, the living were losing their sense of compassion.[4]

Medical Corporal Ali Rıza Eti, who had served at Sarıkamış, was posted to the Erzurum military hospital at the height of the epidemic. He was made chief orderly of the quarantine section when the previous incumbent contracted typhus. Eti found the work exhausting and, given his exposure to hundreds of men with contagious diseases, dangerous. He applied repeatedly to be transferred to a different job, without success, as more sick and wounded crowded the hospital, filling beds vacated by those who had recently died. After his time at the front, Eti knew and sympathized with these men. He grew increasingly angry at the suffering of the common soldier. And he came to focus his anger on the Armenians as scapegoats for Turkish wartime suffering.

Already in his time on the Sarıkamış front, Eti had developed a deep hostility towards the Armenians. He regularly accused them of disloyalty to the Ottomans, of crossing lines to join with the Russians, and of providing the enemy with information on Ottoman positions. He had reported the "accidental" deaths of Armenian soldiers by their fellow Ottoman soldiers with seeming satisfaction. But only while serving in the hospital did Eti have the opportunity to act on his deepening hatred.

The death of a soldier from Eti's hometown proved the catalyst for his rage against Armenians. The wounded man told Eti that he had been evacuated from the front only to be abandoned in an isolated ditch by an Armenian orderly in the transport corps. After two days in the extreme cold, the Turk suffered frostbite to both hands and feet. The medics in Erzurum tried to save the man's life and amputated his limbs, but he died the next day. "Imagine how contemptible the Armenian soldier was" who had abandoned the wounded Turk in a ditch, Eti raged. "Could we be brothers and fellow citizens after this war? For my part, no! It is easy for me to take my revenge. I will just make three or four of the Armenians in the hospital drink poison."[5]

Corporal Eti resorted to cruelty rather than murder in his personal campaign against the Armenians. In January 1915, he abused his position in the medical service to dismiss and banish Armenian workers. "I dispatched three Armenians, one from Van and one from Diyarbakır, to be stripped and robbed [i.e., by rural marauders, who usually killed their victims]. This is what you call Turkish revenge," he gloated. He fired four Armenian women and replaced them with Turkish women. "And I assign the most dangerous tasks to Armenian orderlies," he noted with grim satisfaction.[6]

Though he never claimed to have actually killed an Armenian himself, Ali Rıza Eti clearly wished the Armenians dead. Nor was he alone. Defeat at Sarıkamış and the devastating impact of contagious disease had left the Ottomans more vulnerable on their eastern front than ever. The divided loyalties of some Armenians had tarred all Armenians in the eyes of many

Turks. The Young Turk leadership began to contemplate permanent solutions to the "Armenian problem".

IN THEIR SHORT TIME IN POWER, THE YOUNG TURKS HAD OVERSEEN massive population transfers. Territorial losses in the Balkan Wars had driven waves of destitute Muslim refugees to seek shelter in Ottoman domains. Without the resources to address this humanitarian crisis, the Turkish leadership created space for the Balkan refugees by deporting thousands of Ottoman Christians to Greece. A government committee then oversaw the reallocation of the houses, fields, and workshops of deported Ottoman Christians to resettled Balkan Muslim refugees. These "population exchanges" were regulated by formal agreements concluded between the Porte and the Balkan states—ethnic cleansing with an international seal of approval.[7]

The deportation of ethnic Greeks from the Ottoman Empire served several purposes. Deportation not only freed up homes and workplaces for the resettlement of Balkan Muslim refugees but also allowed the Ottomans to expel thousands of citizens of questionable loyalty. Tensions over the Aegean islands that threatened renewed war between Greece and the Ottoman Empire in the first six months of 1914 had left Ottoman Greeks vulnerable and exposed. The population exchanges initiated after the Balkan Wars had provided an internationally sanctioned solution to the empire's "Greek problem".

What started as a controlled exchange of border populations between belligerents evolved into a systematic expulsion of ethnic Greeks from Ottoman lands generally. Though there are no precise figures for the deportations, several hundred thousand Greek Orthodox Christians were forcibly relocated before and during the First World War. The deeper into Ottoman domains the deportations were conducted, the more the government had to rely on violence and intimidation to achieve its aims. Greek Orthodox Christian villagers in western Anatolia, far from the troubled Balkans, resisted the state's efforts to uproot them. Gendarmes rounded up villagers, beat the men, threatened to kidnap women, and even killed Ottoman Greeks who resisted deportation. Foreign consuls, appalled by the violence against Christian civilians, reported dozens killed in some villages. Yet the expulsion of Ottoman Greeks could be carried out with relatively low levels of killing because there was a Greek state to which they could be deported.

The same could not be said of Ottoman Armenians. A minority in every province of the Ottoman Empire, the Armenians were concentrated in three areas of particular sensitivity during the First World War. Istanbul, threatened with imminent Allied invasion, was home to the largest concentration. In Cilicia, overlooking the Gulf of Alexandretta, the Ottomans suspected the Armenian community of making common cause with the Allied fleet. In the Caucasus, a minority of Armenian activists compromised the standing of the community as a whole when they allied themselves with Russia against the Ottoman Empire. The Young Turks believed the Armenians posed a far greater threat to the Ottoman Empire than the Greeks because some Armenians hoped to create an independent homeland in Ottoman territory with Allied support.

One of the Ottoman government's first acts after entering the First World War was to abrogate the February 1914 Armenian Reform Agreement with Russia. The agreement called for a reorganization of the six easternmost Ottoman provinces bordering Russia into two administrative units under foreign governors to provide an autonomous homeland for the Armenians. The Ottomans had opposed this reform agenda, which they viewed as a prelude to the partition of the Turkish heartland of Anatolia—a plan to create an Armenian state in lands with a sizable Muslim majority under Russian patronage. What they had signed under duress in February 1914, the Ottomans were relieved to annul on 16 December of the same year.[8]

In the aftermath of defeat at Sarıkamış, the Young Turks began to consider extreme means of addressing the threat they believed Armenian national aspirations posed to their territory. In February 1915, Dr Bahaeddin Şakir, operational chief of the Teşkilât-i Mahsusa and a member of the Committee of Union and Progress (CUP) Central Committee, returned to Istanbul from the Caucasus front. Armed with reports and documentation gathered in the field, Şakir met with the powerful interior minister, Talat Pasha, and another Central Committee member, Dr Mehmed Nazım. Şakir spoke of the necessity to address "the enemy within" because of "the oppositional stance that the Armenians had taken toward Turkey and the assistance that they were affording to the Russian army". Though there is no transcript of their meetings—those contemplating atrocity seldom leave a written record—Ottoman documents and contemporary memoirs suggest these three

Young Turk officials made key decisions initiating the annihilation of the Armenian community of Turkey between February and March 1915.[9]

THE HAPLESS ARMENIAN COMMUNITY OF ISTANBUL PLAYED INTO THEIR enemies' hands by the open show of support they gave to the Allied campaign against the Ottomans and Germans.

Grigoris Balakian was an Armenian priest studying theology in Berlin in 1914. When war broke out in Europe, Balakian wanted to return immediately to Istanbul. The Armenians in Berlin tried to dissuade Balakian. "Many advised me to go to the Caucasus and join the Armenian volunteer groups, and then cross over into Turkish Armenia" with an invading Russian army, he recalled. Balakian wanted nothing to do with the Armenian brigades in Russia, which he saw as a threat rather than a support to Armenian communities in the east, but his friends in Berlin dismissed Balakian's concerns. "Caught up in their nationalist sentiment, they were loath to miss this unique opportunity to redress the wrongs committed by the Turks against the Armenian people," Balakian recalled.[10]

On his arrival in Istanbul, Balakian made a point of telling the Ottoman immigration officials that he was returning from Berlin and expressed his support for the German war effort and Turco-German relations. One customs official, who warmed to Balakian's expression of loyalty, counselled the Armenian priest: *"Effendi*, give your compatriots in Constantinople, whose views are completely opposite yours, a little advice so that they will renounce their love for Russia. They have gone to such extremes in their affinity and love for the Russians, French, and

Grigoris Balakian, 1913. An Armenian priest, Balakian was one of 240 Armenian communal leaders arrested in Istanbul on the night of 24 April 1915. He survived the death marches to bear witness to a genocide he termed the "Armenian Golgotha".

English that on the day that the Russians win, the Armenians smile . . . but when the Russians have been defeated, they are sad. This much sincerity will cause them much trouble later on." Within days of his arrival, Balakian was concerned to see the custom official's observation vindicated by the Istanbul Armenians' open display of support for Allied wartime successes.

With the onset of the Allied attack on the Dardanelles, the Armenians made no effort to hide their celebration of imminent delivery from Turkish rule. "After all, weren't the mighty English and French fleets already in the Dardanelles," Balakian asked rhetorically. "And after all, wasn't Constantinople on the verge of falling in a couple of days?" He watched in dismay as Armenians gathered each day in anticipation of witnessing "the majestic British fleet pass toward the Bosporus, its mission to save the Armenians, of course". Balakian claimed his compatriots "believed that the historic hour had come for the realization of their age-old national dreams and hopes", leaving Ottoman Armenians "in a state of unprecedented euphoria" at a moment when Ottoman Turks faced an existential threat. It was a formula for violence.[11]

Already in Cilicia Talat Pasha and his colleagues were initiating the first measures against the Armenian community. The area around Alexandretta was particularly vulnerable to naval attack, as the HMS *Doris* had demonstrated by shelling railway lines and rolling stock in Dörtyol and Alexandretta in December 1914. Allied warships continued to blockade and bombard the Cilician coastline and had deployed spies ashore. Armenian activists were suspected of assisting these foreign agents and providing information on depleted Ottoman troop numbers across the region. Minister of War Enver Pasha followed these developments with mounting concern. "My only hope is that the enemy has not discovered our weakness" in Cilicia, Enver confided to German field marshal Paul von Hindenburg. Unable to raise the number of Ottoman troops in the region, Enver and Talat opted to forcibly relocate the suspect Armenian communities instead.[12]

In February 1915, the Ottomans began to deport Armenians from Dörtyol and Alexandretta (in Turkish, Iskenderun) to the Adana region. On the model of the Greek population exchanges, Muslim refugees were then resettled in the forcibly vacated Armenian properties. The deportations relieved Turkey's security concerns in the Gulf of Alexandretta. However, no provision was made for the welfare of the dispossessed Armenians, who were forced to rely on their coreligionists in Adana to survive. The state's indifference revived memories of past massacres, and fear swept the Armenian communities of eastern Anatolia.[13]

Activists in the village of Zeytun, some sixty-five miles north-east of Dörtyol, responded to these first deportations by plotting an uprising against the Ottomans. In mid-February, a group of Armenian rebels travelled from Zeytun to Tiflis (Tbilisi in modern Georgia) to seek Russian arms and support. They claimed to have as many as 15,000 men ready to rise up against the Ottomans. Many still lived in the flawed belief that a full-fledged rebellion might prompt an Allied intervention on the Armenians' behalf. However, the Russians were in no position to deliver arms, let alone send troops, to assist the Armenians in Cilicia, so far from their own frontiers.[14]

At the end of February, an anxious group of Armenian notables from Zeytun alerted the Ottoman authorities that activists were plotting a revolt. The Christian leaders hoped by this show of loyalty to protect their community from attack, but their revelations only served to unleash the very reprisals the Armenians most feared. Ottoman soldiers were dispatched to Zeytun to conduct mass arrests. Many young men fled their homes for the countryside, where they joined growing bands of Armenian rebels and army deserters preparing for a confrontation with their government.

An armed Armenian band ambushed Ottoman gendarmes near Zeytun on 9 March, killing a number of soldiers (reports vary between six and fifteen killed) and taking their weapons and money. The attack served as a pretext for the total deportation of Zeytun's Armenian community. Soldiers sealed off the town and placed its Armenian notables under arrest. Between April and July, every one of Zeytun's Armenians was deported to the central Anatolian town of Konya, and Muslim immigrants were resettled in their place. Stripped of their possessions and given little or no food or protection along the way, over 7,000 Armenians were left homeless in Konya. Some 1,500 of the Zeytun Armenians died from starvation and disease that summer before suffering a second deportation to Syria.[15]

ON THE EVE OF THE ALLIED LANDINGS IN THE DARDANELLES IN APRIL 1915, Talat Pasha and his colleagues shifted their focus from Cilicia to Istanbul. They aimed to decapitate the political and cultural leadership of the Armenian community in advance of a possible invasion of the capital to prevent the Armenians from making common cause with the invaders.

Turkish police arrested 240 notables—politicians, journalists, members of Armenian nationalist parties, professionals, and religious authorities—in a night-time sweep on 24 April. They worked from a blacklist compiled with the assistance of Armenian collaborators. The knock at the door came late at night. Many of those arrested were still in their nightclothes when they reached prison.

The Armenian priest Grigoris Balakian was one of those arrested on the night of 24 April. He, like all the others, was caught by complete surprise. Policemen escorted him to a "blood-red bus" waiting in the street below. The captive priest was taken with eight of his friends by ferry from the Asian to the European districts of Istanbul. "The night smelled of death; the sea was rough, and our hearts were full of terror," he recalled. Balakian and his fellows were deposited at the central prison, where they met up with other Armenian detainees. "They were all familiar faces—revolutionary and political leaders, public figures, and nonpartisan and even antipartisan intellectuals." Busloads of new arrivals joined the group through the night "in a state of spiritual anguish, terrified of the unknown and longing for comfort". The next day, the Armenian detainees could hear the distant reports of Allied cannons supporting the Gallipoli landings and wondered if the ominous thunder would spell their doom or their delivery.[16]

For Armenians, the arrest of the political and intellectual leadership in Istanbul on 24 April initiated the systematic destruction of the Armenian communities of Anatolia. The date has since gained international recognition as the Armenian Genocide Memorial Day. For the Ottomans, however, the war against the Armenians had begun four days earlier with the Armenian uprising in the eastern Anatolian town of Van.[17]

VAN WAS A MAJOR MARKET TOWN DIVIDED INTO ARMENIAN AND Muslim quarters. Lying near the shores of Lake Van, the old town was a walled city with four gates, built against a massive outcrop of rock rising two hundred metres above the plain. A citadel built by Suleyman the Magnificent crowned the promontory and dominated the town. The narrow winding streets were lined with two-story houses that gave onto markets, mosques, and churches. There were a number of government buildings in the south-eastern part of the town, along with a police station and gendarmerie.

In the course of the nineteenth century, Van spread beyond the walls of the old city to the fertile lands to the east. Orchards and high mud-brick walls surrounded the houses in the Garden District. A number of foreign consulates—British, French, Iranian, Italian, and Russian—as well as the Catholic and Protestant missions, had taken premises in the Garden District. It was a remarkably cosmopolitan mix for a provincial town whose population a French demographer estimated to number only 30,000 souls in the 1890s: 16,000 Muslims, 13,500 Armenians, and 500 Jews. The townspeople shared a strong sense of civic pride. Gurgen Mahari, a native son, described Van as "a miraculous green-haired enchantress from a fairy tale" in his classic novel *Burning Orchards*.[18]

The Armenian community in Van and the surrounding villages was large and politically active. Given its strategic location near both the Persian and Russian frontiers, it was inevitable that Van would prove a flashpoint between the Ottoman state and its Armenian citizens.

The governor of Van was Cevdet Pasha, a committed Unionist and Enver's brother-in-law. In March 1915, Cevdet ordered gendarmes to search Armenian villages for hidden weapons and to arrest anyone suspected of bearing arms against the empire. These searches led to violent pogroms against Armenians in the villages surrounding Van. In a bid to decapitate the leadership of the Armenian community, Cevdet allegedly ordered the deaths of three leaders of the Armenian nationalist Dashnak Party in Van. Two of the Armenian leaders—Nikoghayos Mikaelian, better known as Ishkhan (the Armenian word for "prince"), and Arshak Vramian, a member of the Ottoman parliament—were murdered. The third leader, Aram Manukian, mistrusted Cevdet and chose not to respond to an invitation from the governor to call on him in his offices. When he learned of the disappearance and presumed murder of his two comrades, Aram went underground to prepare the Armenians of Van to resist imminent massacre.[19]

Rafael de Nogales was a Venezuelan soldier of fortune who volunteered for the Ottoman army more out of a sense of adventure than from conviction. Enver Pasha met de Nogales in Istanbul and offered him a commission in the depleted Third Army shortly after the defeat at Sarıkamış. In March, the Venezuelan reached the Third Army headquarters in Erzurum, where officers were more concerned with fighting typhus than the Russians. Eager to see action, de Nogales volunteered for the Van gendarmerie, the only unit then engaged in active combat on the Russian front. His journey from

Erzurum to Van took de Nogales through the tense conflict zone between Ottomans and Armenians. He arrived on the day the Armenians of Van rose in revolt against Ottoman rule.

On 20 April, de Nogales and his escort came to a stretch of road on the north-western corner of Lake Van strewn with "mutilated Armenian corpses". They could see columns of smoke rising from the villages on the south shores of the lake. "Then I understood," he later wrote, as if the event had long been expected. "The die was cast. The Armenian 'revolution' had begun."[20]

The following morning, de Nogales witnessed a brutal massacre in the Armenian quarter of the village of Adilcevaz, on the north shore of Lake Van. Ottoman officials, assisted by Kurds and "the rabble of the vicinity", broke into Armenian homes and shops, systematically robbing and killing all the men. When de Nogales, wearing the uniform of an Ottoman officer, approached an official and demanded that he put a stop the killing, he was astounded when the man replied "that he was doing nothing more than carry out an unequivocal order emanating from the Governor General of the province [i.e., Cevdet Pasha] . . . *to exterminate all Armenian males of twelve years of age and over*". As de Nogales had no authority to override the orders of a civil official, he withdrew from the massacre, which went on for another ninety minutes.[21]

From Adilcevaz, de Nogales crossed Lake Van in a motor boat, reaching the village of Edremit on the outskirts of Van after nightfall. "Burning villages that bathed the sky in scarlet" lit the shoreline. Edremit was a war zone, its houses and churches in flames, the smell of burning flesh in the air and the rattle of gunfire punctuating the roar of destruction. He spent the night in Edremit and witnessed running gun battles between Kurdish and Turkish irregulars and the sorely outnumbered Armenians.

At noon, de Nogales set out from Edremit for Van under escort. "To right and left of the road circled screaming flocks of black vultures, disputing with the dogs the putrefied Armenian corpses thrown about on every side," he recalled. By the time he entered Van, the uprising was already two days old, and the old town was in the hands of the Armenian insurgents. The castle overlooking the old town remained in Ottoman hands, and from those heights Turkish forces were able to subject Armenian positions to artillery fire day and night. As an artillery officer, this duty now fell to de Nogales. He set up his headquarters in the castle's mosque and mounted its tall minaret to observe the accuracy of fire.

For twenty-one days, de Nogales took part in the Ottoman campaign against the Armenians of Van. "I have rarely seen such furious fighting as took place during the siege of Van," he reflected. "Nobody gave quarter nor asked it." As the battle wore on, he witnessed atrocities committed by Armenians and Ottomans alike. His memoirs of the siege of Van swing between sympathy and revulsion for both sides.

Russian forces slowly made their way from the Persian frontier, driving back the Ottomans in their effort to relieve the Armenian defenders in Van. For the Russians, the uprising facilitated their occupation of strategic Ottoman territory. The approach of Russian troops forced Cevdet Pasha to order the Muslims of Van to evacuate the city on 12 May. The last Ottoman soldiers withdrew from the citadel on 17 May. Armenians from the Garden District were finally able to link up with their compatriots in the old city. Together, they set fire to the Muslim neighbourhoods and all government buildings in advance of the arrival of the first Russian soldiers on 19 May.[22]

The Russians appointed the Dashnak leader Aram Manukian as governor of Van. Manukian established an Armenian administration in the town, complete with a militia and police force—measures that, in the words of an Armenian historian, "stimulated the Armenian political consciousness and reinforced the convictions of those who foresaw a liberated and autonomous Armenia under Russian protection"—everything the Ottomans most feared.[23]

The Turks, for their part, were not reconciled to the loss of Van and attacked Russian and Armenian positions relentlessly. The Russians, overextended, were driven into retreat. On 31 July, the Armenians were advised to prepare their belongings and abandon their homes. An estimated 100,000 Armenians withdrew with the Russians in what came to be known as the Great Retreat. Still the Russians and Ottomans fought over Van, the town exchanging hands three times over the summer of 1915 before Russian forces captured and ultimately retained the town in the autumn of 1915—by which time very little of Van was left standing and very few Armenians in eastern Anatolia were left alive.

By facilitating the Russian occupation of Van in return for the right to govern the Van region, the Armenians had confirmed the Young Turks' suspicion that they constituted a fifth column and posed a threat to the territorial integrity of the Ottoman Empire. Moreover, the timing of the uprising, so close to the Allied landings at Gallipoli, convinced the Young Turks that the Armenians and the Entente Powers had coordinated the attacks. As Cemal Pasha wrote in his memoirs, "A fact, in my opinion absolutely irrefutable, is that at the moment when the Dardanelles campaign was at its crisis, the Armenians were ordered by the French and English Commanders-in-Chief of the Forces in the Eastern Mediterranean to rise." Though there is no evidence to support Cemal's allegations, the Unionists were convinced that the Armenians were in league with the Allies. With the fall of Van, the Ottomans began to implement a series of measures to eradicate the Armenian presence not just from the six provinces of eastern Anatolia but from Asiatic Turkey as a whole.[24]

THE DEPORTATION OF ARMENIANS WAS CONDUCTED OPENLY BY government orders. The Young Turk leadership had secured an early recess of the Ottoman parliament on 1 March 1915, which left Interior Minister Talat Pasha and his colleagues a free hand to enact law without parliamentary debate. On 26 May 1915, within a week of the Russian entry into Van, Talat submitted a bill to the Ottoman Council of Ministers. The government swiftly approved Talat's "Deportation Law", which allowed for the wholesale relocation of the Armenian population of the six provinces of eastern Anatolia to undisclosed locations away from the Russian front.

At the end of May, the Interior Ministry issued orders to provincial and district governors bearing Talat's signature, calling for the immediate deportation of all Armenians. Announcements were posted in the main streets of towns and villages across eastern Anatolia, giving the local Armenian community between three and five days' notice of what was presented as a temporary relocation for the duration of the war. Armenians were encouraged to deposit any possessions they could not carry with the government for safekeeping.[25]

Alongside these publicly declared measures of forced displacement, the Young Turks issued secret orders for the mass murder of Armenian deportees. The extermination orders were not written down but were communicated orally to provincial governors either by their author, CUP Central Committee member Dr Bahaeddin Şakir, or by other CUP officials. Any provincial governor who asked for written confirmation of the orders or otherwise opposed the mass murder of unarmed civilians faced dismissal and even assassination. When one district governor in Diyarbakır Province demanded written notice before carrying out the massacre of

Mehmed Talat Pasha in 1915. One of the triumvirate of Young Turks who came to dominate the Ottoman government after 1913, first as minister of interior and later as grand vizier, Talat authorized the measures leading to the Armenian genocide.

Armenians from his district, he was removed from office, summoned to Diyarbakır, and murdered en route.[26]

More compliant governors faced the task of recruiting armed gangs to kill the deportees. They were assisted by Enver's secret intelligence service, the Teşkilât-i Mahsusa, which mobilized violent criminals released from prison, Kurdish bands with a long history of antagonism towards the Armenians, and recent Muslim immigrants from the Balkans and Russian Caucasus to assist in the slaughter. Even average Turkish villagers were reported to have contributed to the killing of Armenian deportees, some to rob them of the clothing, money, and jewellery they had brought for their sustenance in exile, others because government officials had convinced them that the killing of Armenians contributed to the Ottoman jihad against the Entente Powers. The Armenian priest Grigoris Balakian recounted a conversation with a Turkish captain who claimed "government officials" had sent gendarmes "to all the surrounding Turkish villages and in the name of holy jihad invited the Muslim population to participate in this sacred religious obligation" of massacring Armenians.[27]

Evidence of this "two-track approach" of an open deportation decree and secret annihilation orders came to light in the post-war testimony of government officials. A member of the Ottoman Council of Ministers testified in 1918, "I've learned of a few secrets and have come across something interesting. The deportation order was issued through official channels by the minister of the interior [i.e., Talat] and sent to the provinces. Following this order the [CUP] Central Committee circulated its own ominous order to all parties to allow the gangs to carry out their wretched task. Thus the gangs were in the field, ready for their atrocious slaughter. "28

The massacres followed a standard pattern across Anatolia. A set number of days after deportation notices were posted, Armenians were driven from their homes by gendarmes with fixed bayonets. Males aged twelve and older were separated from their female relations and killed. In smaller villages, the men were often killed within sight or hearing of their horrified womenfolk, but in larger towns they were marched away to where their murder would not be witnessed, particularly by foreigners. After the Armenian men had been separated from them, the women and children were escorted out of town under armed guard. According to survivors' accounts, some of these caravans faced robbery and wholesale massacre; others were marched from town to town, with the sick, infirm, and elderly killed as they fell behind. The ultimate destination for survivors were desert settlements in Syria and Iraq: Dayr al-Zur (Der Zor in Turkish) and Mosul, towns reached by perilous treks across open desert.

The architects of the genocide—Talat and his advisers Dr Mehmed Nazım and Dr Bahaeddin Şakir—aimed to ensure that Armenians were driven entirely from the six eastern provinces and totalled no more than 10 percent of the population in any part of the empire. In this way, the Armenians would never attain the critical mass needed to secure independent statehood within Ottoman domains. Yet reaching this reduced demographic profile would require the annihilation of the vast majority of Ottoman Armenians. This was achieved through the combination of bloody massacres conducted by armed gangs and the high attrition rate through death marches across the desert.29

The Armenians of Erzurum and Erzincan were among the first to be deported in May 1915. After two months of marching, the survivors reached the town of Harput, some 125 miles away. The American consul there met with the deportees in the encampment the government provided for their short stay. "There are very few men among them as most of them have been killed on the road," Consul Leslie Davis noted. "The system that is being followed seems to be to have bands of Kurds awaiting them on the road to kill the men especially." The women were "almost without exception ragged, filthy, hungry and sick. That is not surprising in view of the fact that they have been on the road for nearly two months with no change of clothing, no chance to wash, no shelter and little to eat." The starved women mobbed the guards who brought them food, only to be beaten back with clubs "hard enough to kill them". Desperate mothers offered their children to the American consul in the hope that he might spare them from further horrors. "By continuing to drive these people on in this way it will be possible to dispose of all of them in a comparatively short time," Davis reflected. "The entire movement seems to be the most thoroughly organized and effective massacre this country has ever seen."[30]

In June, Talat extended the deportation policy to "all Armenians without exception" in all eastern provinces of Anatolia. Towns like Erzincan, Sivas, Kayseri, Adana, Diyarbakır, and Aleppo became reception centres for waves of Armenian deportees destined for Dayr al-Zur, Mosul, and Urfa. Each leg of the march was marked by unspeakable atrocities for the Armenian deportees. "We were living through days of such unheard-of horror, it was impossible for the mind to fully comprehend," Father Grigoris Balakian recalled. "Those of us still alive envied those who had already paid their inevitable dues of bloody torture and death. And so we survivors became living martyrs, every day dying a few deaths and returning to life again."[31]

GRIGORIS BALAKIAN HAD MADE THE FIRM DECISION TO SURVIVE THE annihilation of the Armenians in order to bear witness to the suffering of his people for future generations. Taken from the comfort of his home in Istanbul on the eve of the Gallipoli landings, Balakian was dispatched with 150 other notables to the central Anatolian town of Çankiri, north-east of Ankara. When Talat issued his orders for the general deportation of Armenians on 21 June, Balakian negotiated a massive bribe of 1,500 gold pieces with the local officials to spare the small group of Armenians in Çankiri from deportation. The payment bought the Armenian priest and his companions a seven-month reprieve that spared them from the worst months of the massacres. Yet when finally deported to Dayr al-Zur in February 1916, Balakian and his comrades confronted gangs and villagers who had come to view the murder of Armenians with equanimity.

Marching along the roads on which thousands of Armenians had already met their deaths, Balakian engaged the officers accompanying his caravan in conversation. The Ottoman gendarmes were willing to answer any questions, as they did not believe the Armenians they were "guarding" had long to live. One of the most forthcoming was Captain Shukri, who by his own admission had overseen the killing of 42,000 Armenians.

"Bey, where have all these human bones along this road come from?" Balakian asked the captain disingenuously.

"These are the bones of Armenians who were killed in August and September. The order had come from Constantinople. Even though the minister of the interior [i.e., Talat] had huge ditches dug for the corpses, the winter floods washed the dirt away, and now the bones are everywhere, as you see," Captain Shukri replied.

"Upon whose orders were the massacres of Armenians committed?" Balakian probed.

"The orders came from the Ittihad [i.e., Unionist] Central Committee and the Interior Ministry in Constantinople," Captain Shukri explained. "This order was carried out most severely by Kemal . . . vice-governor of Yozgat. When Kemal, a native of Van, heard that the Armenians had massacred all his family members at the time of the Van revolt, he sought revenge and massacred the women and children, together with the men."[32]

Balakian's questions did not upset the captain. He seemed to enjoy filling the long hours on the road in conversation with the Armenian priest, inured to the evil he recounted: of the thousands of men hacked to death, of 6,400 Armenian women systematically robbed of their possessions and murdered along with their children, actions he consistently referred to as "cleansing" (*paklamak* in Turkish). The mass-murdering Ottoman officer even seemed to develop an affection for the Armenian priest, offering to protect him from all harm if only he would convert to Islam.

Through conversations with Turkish officers, Balakian learned every aspect of the Armenian tragedy from the government's perspective. In his exchanges with survivors encountered along the way, the priest also deepened his knowledge of the Armenian experience of the genocide. He wove both perspectives together in his remarkable memoirs, first published in Armenian in 1922, thereby discharging his duty as a witness to what Balakian dubbed the "Armenian Golgotha".

Surviving the genocide was easier said than done. By preserving cordial relations with his captors and, in his own words, putting his trust in God, Balakian lived one day at a time, always at risk of sudden death. During the length of their forced march, the priest and his fellows confronted the magnitude of the horror that had befallen the Ottoman Armenian community:

the bodies of the dead, the pleas of starving survivors, the shame of those who had converted to Islam to save their lives. He recorded the details in his diary as the caravan made its way across Anatolia to Cilicia towards the Syrian Desert. The accounts of other survivors of the Armenian genocide confirmed much of what he wrote.

Fear of violent death that might come at any moment without warning compounded the daily experience of brutality, exhaustion, and deprivation. Many Armenians chose to take their own lives rather than face the cruelty of strangers. Even Grigoris Balakian, who had vowed to survive, was driven to contemplate suicide. When accosted by an armed gang near the Halys River, Balakian and his comrades agreed to dive into the torrential waters in the event of "inescapable disaster", as many had done before them. "Surely this deep grave of tens of thousands of Armenians would not refuse to take us too into its flowing turbid currents . . . and save us from harrowing and cruel deaths, at the hands of these Turkish criminals," he recalled. Only Balakian's presence of mind in negotiating the caravan's way past the gang spared them all on that occasion.[33]

Manuel Kerkyasharian, who called himself M. K., was only a nine-year-old boy when he watched his mother dive from a bridge into the turbulent waters of the Euphrates. Natives of Adana, M. K.'s family had been deported to the Mesopotamian settlement of Ras al-Ayn (in modern Syria). An only child, M. K. saw his family robbed by armed gangs and beaten by the gendarmes sent to escort them. His mother's feet swelled painfully from the extensive marching, but she struggled to keep up with the caravan, knowing the fate of those who fell behind.[34]

One night, when she knew she could walk no further, M. K.'s mother made a terrible request of her husband: "Lead me to the river's edge. I am going to throw myself into the water. If I stay, the Arabs will kill me with torture." Her husband refused, but a neighbour understood her fears and carried M. K.'s mother on his back to the banks of the swollen Euphrates. Her young son and a priest followed them to the river, but M. K. averted his eyes when she threw herself into the torrent. When he turned back, he saw his mother briefly before the current carried her away.

Within two days of his mother's death, M. K.'s father died in his sleep. The young boy was now an orphan with no one to care for him. The barefoot boy's feet swelled until he was unable to walk. He watched as soldiers killed a number of women and children who, like him, had been left behind by the caravan. He was robbed of his remaining clothes down to his under-pants and abandoned by the roadside alone—hungry, thirsty, and terrified.

The Armenian priest Grigoris Balakian encountered many such orphans along the way. At Islahiye, near where M. K. was orphaned, he encountered an eight-year-old boy begging with his eleven-year-old sister, both nearly naked and dying from hunger. The elder sister explained "in a schoolgirl's proper Armenian" how all the other members of their family of fourteen had died, leaving the two children to fend for themselves. "How I wish we hadn't survived," she sobbed.[35]

Buffeted by forces beyond his control, young Manuel Kerkyasharian did survive. He found himself among Arabs and Kurds, people whose lan-guages he did not speak and whose actions he did not understand. Some gave him food and clothing; others stoned and robbed him. He witnessed acts of terrible brutality and crossed plains covered with Armenian corpses. He was rescued by four Kurdish women who found him wandering on the open road and took him back to their village as a domestic servant. He spent the remainder of the war years moving among the Kurdish villages on the Turkish-Syrian frontier, living off the kindness—and fleeing the cruelty—of strangers.

One evening, M. K. saw a distant hilltop village in flames. The Kurd then sheltering him explained it was the Assyrian village of Azak, one of several Christian villages being sacked. "Hey, child of disbelievers. Did you see?" the Kurd gloated. "All of the Armenians of Turkey and all of the dis-believers of Turkey have been liquidated. The burning village is an infidel (*gavur*) village and they are all being burned alive." The Kurd added that there were no Christians left in Turkey, just to scare M. K. "And me," M. K. recalled, "I believed it."[36]

Like the Armenians, the Assyrian Christians of the Ottoman Empire were accused of making common cause with Russia at the outset of the Great War. The Assyrians are a Christian ethnic group who speak dialects derived from ancient Aramaic. For centuries they lived among the Kurdish communities in the border regions of the modern states of Turkey, Syria, Iran, and Iraq. The Nestorians, Chaldeans, and Syrian Orthodox Christians are the main Assyrian denominations.

The Assyrian communities of the Ottoman Empire suffered from the same periodic massacres as the Armenians, including the events of 1895 and 1896 and the 1909 Adana killings. In search of Great Power protection, the Assyrians also put their trust in Russia. After the Ottoman entry into the Great War, the Assyrians were accused of collaboration with the Entente Powers and targeted by the Young Turk regime for annihilation. An estimated 250,000 Assyrian Christians, out of a pre-war population of 620,000, were killed in the course of the First World War. For the child M. K., it seemed credible that the Assyrians and Armenians might be eliminated entirely from Ottoman domains as part of one big plan.[37]

As he moved between the villages of south-eastern Anatolia, M. K. encountered a number of Armenian children and young women who, like him, had taken refuge among the Kurds. Many had been collected from the death marches and taken to work in the homes and farms of the Kurdish villagers. M. K. met several young Armenian women who had married into the families of their Kurdish protectors. That was how Heranuş Gadarian survived the genocide.

Heranuş was born into a respected family in the eastern Anatolian village of Habab, a large Armenian community of over two hundred households, with two churches and a monastery. Her father and two uncles emigrated to the United States in 1913, the year Heranuş started school. As soon as she learned to write, she composed a letter to her father that he carried in his wallet until the day he died. "We all keep hoping and praying that you are well," she wrote on behalf of all her siblings. "And we are going to school every day, and we are trying very hard to be well-behaved children," all written in what Father Balakian would have called a schoolgirl's proper Armenian.[38]

In her third year of school, the gendarmes raided Heranuş's village. They killed the Armenian headman in front of the terrified villagers before rounding up all the other men. Her grandfather and three uncles were taken away and never heard from again. The gendarmes then led the women of the village to the nearby market town of Palu, where they were shut into a church. The women heard terrible screams from outside the church walls. One girl climbed a high window to observe. Heranuş never forgot the horror the girl described: "They're cutting the men's throats, and throwing them into the river."

From Palu, the women and children of Habab joined the throngs of Armenians on the death marches across Anatolia towards the Syrian Desert. "During the march," Heranuş later recalled, "my mother was so anxious to avoid the back of the line that she walked very fast, and because we couldn't

Armenian widows, Turkey, September 1915. News of systematic massacres against Armenians filtered out of Turkey and had already been taken up by European and American newspapers by the autumn of 1915.

keep up with her, she pulled us with her hands. At the back of the line we could hear people crying, screaming, pleading." At the end of the first day's march, Heranuş's pregnant aunt became ill and fell to the back of the line. The gendarmes killed her on the spot with their bayonets and left her by the roadside. "The elderly, the infirm, the ones who couldn't walk—throughout the march they'd kill them with their bayonets and leave them lying there, just where they fell."

As they made their way towards Diyarbakır, the caravan crossed a river in the town of Maden. Heranuş saw her paternal grandmother throw two of her orphaned grandchildren who could no longer walk into the water, pushing their heads under the surface before throwing herself into the madly rushing water, "this deep grave of tens of thousands of Armenians", as Grigoris Balakian had observed.

When they reached the town of Çermik Hamambaşı, the local inhabitants surrounded the miserable survivors, looking for healthy children to work in their homes. A gendarme on horseback asked for Heranuş, while a man from a neighbouring village asked for her brother Horen, but their mother refused outright. "No one can take them from me. I'll never give them up," Heranuş's mother screamed.

Heranuş's maternal grandmother tried to persuade her to surrender the children for their own safety. "My girl," she pleaded with Heranuş's mother, "the children are dying one by one. No one's going to come out of this march alive. If you give these men your children, you'll save their lives." While the women of her family pursued this terrible debate, the men simply seized the children—the gendarme on horseback taking Heranuş, the other man seizing Horen. Her mother held on for as long as she could against the man on horseback, but once she relinquished her grip, she lost her daughter forever.

The gendarme took Heranuş to a farm outside Çermik, where she found eight Armenian girls from her home village of Habab, each snatched from the death march. The girls were left in a fruit orchard where they were fed and well treated. At the end of the day, the mounted policeman returned to collect Heranuş and took her to his home near Çermik. He and his wife were childless, and the gendarme treated her like a daughter. His wife, however, was jealous of the affection her husband showed the young Armenian girl and constantly humiliated Heranuş by reminding her she was only a servant girl. They gave Heranuş a Turkish name, Seher, and taught her Turkish.

Though she had lost her freedom and identity, Heranuş survived under her new Turkish name. And while many of her family members died under deportation, a surprising number survived. Her brother Horen, taken the same day as Heranuş, worked in a neighbouring village where he was known as Ahmet the Shepherd. One of her aunts, her mother's prettiest sister, who had been abducted and married by a Kurdish horseman, not only survived but managed to track down Heranuş in her new home. Most astonishingly, her mother survived the march to Aleppo, where she remained for the rest of the war and was reunited with her husband, who travelled from the United States in search of his devastated family. However, the Gadarians never saw their daughter Heranuş again.[39]

Heranuş completed the process of her Turkification when, aged sixteen, she married one of the gendarme's nephews. Her marriage certificate listed her as Seher, daughter of the gendarme Hüseyin and his wife Esma. Seher spent the rest of her life as a Turkish housewife and raised her children as good Muslims.

Grigoris Balakian encountered several Armenians who had converted to Islam to avoid massacre. The change was hardest for adults to accept, but children were more adaptable. Hundreds, probably thousands, of young Armenians integrated into Turkish society, where their origins were almost forgotten—but not quite. Years after the war, ethnic Turks still referred to these converts as "the leftovers of the sword".[40]

GRIGORIS BALAKIAN DECIDED TO ABANDON THE DEATH MARCH BEFORE commencing the fatal desert crossing to Dayr al-Zur. He met two Armenian coachmen serving in the Ottoman transport corps who had just come from Dayr al-Zur and, astonished to encounter a living Armenian priest, did everything in their power to dissuade Balakian from attempting the march. "How can I tell you so you will understand?" they asked in desperation. "It is impossible for human language to describe what those who went to Der Zor experienced." Yet the Armenian coachmen attempted to capture the horror in words:

> Thousands of families put on the road from Aleppo, to be sent to Der Zor; of these, not even five percent reached Der Zor alive. Because bandits in the desert . . . in groups on horseback and armed with spears, attacked these defenseless people; they killed, they abducted, they raped, they plundered, they selected those appealing to them and carried them off, subjecting those who resisted to horrific tortures, before picking up and leaving. Because it was forbidden and impossible to turn back, those who survived had no choice but to go forward and were subjected to new attacks and plundering. Not even five percent reached Der Zor.[41]

As the coachmen detailed the horrors, they finally succeeded in convincing the Armenian priest that his only chance of survival lay in a carefully planned escape from his Ottoman captors. After divulging his plans to his closest companions, Father Balakian fled the caravan in early April 1916 in the company of an Armenian tobacco smuggler to seek shelter in the Amanus Mountains.

The German railway company was still hard at work to complete the tunnels through the Amanus Mountains. The Taurus and Amanus mountain chains had proved the final obstacle to the completion of the Berlin-to-Baghdad railway. The line was critical to the Ottoman war effort in Mesopotamia and Palestine, and Enver, as minister of war, had given the

German railway company a free hand to recruit whatever labour it needed to complete the long tunnels through the dense mountains. Thousands of Armenians who had fled the death marches found refuge in the tunnel works of the Amanus. Balakian claimed that as many as 11,500 were working on the line in early 1916. They performed heavy labour for subsistence wages, but work on the railway was preferable to the death marches. Here, Grigoris Balakian, who had cast off his priest's robes and shaved his patriarchal beard, began his flight from the genocide.

With his fluent German, Balakian soon gained the protection of the Austrian and German engineers working on the line and secured a job as a surveyor. Yet there was no security on the railway line. In June 1916, Turkish officials rounded up nearly all of the Armenian workers for immediate deportation against the protests of the German railway engineers, who argued that the Armenian workers were essential to complete the railway. Balakian was one of 135 "specialists" spared this latest death march. The few Armenians spared deportation came under increasing pressure to convert to Islam. For Balakian, conversion was not an option. With the assistance of his German colleagues, the Armenian priest fled to another workstation on the railway line under an assumed German identity (Balakian wrote warmly of the humanitarian efforts of German and Austrian civilians but found the German military men no less hostile to Armenians than the Young Turks). For the remainder of the war, Balakian moved clandestinely or under assumed identities to elude deportation. In this way, the exiled priest survived measures that, by his own estimate, had led to the extinction of three-quarters of Ottoman Armenians by the end of 1915.

THERE IS NO AGREED FIGURE FOR THE NUMBER OF OTTOMAN CHRISTIANS massacred in the course of the Great War. Whereas the population exchanges with Greece were achieved with relatively little killing, hundreds of thousands of Armenians and Assyrians died in the deportations that began in 1915. The debate persists into the twenty-first century as to whether the mass murder of Armenians between 1915 and 1918 was an unintentional consequence of war or a deliberate policy of extermination. But even those who deny the Armenian genocide acknowledge that between 600,000 and 850,000 Armenian civilians perished as a result of wartime measures. Armenian historians argue instead that deliberate state policy resulted in the deaths of between 1 million and 1.5 million Armenians—making this the first modern genocide.[42]

There is no doubt that members of both the Armenian and the Assyrian communities had made common cause with the Ottomans' wartime enemies. In the spring of 1915, the empire faced invasion on three fronts simultaneously: in the Dardanelles, on the Caucasus frontier, and in Mesopotamia. While helping to explain why the Young Turks unleashed such unprecedented violence against their Christian subjects, this in no way justifies the crimes against humanity that ensued.

The bitter irony is that the annihilation of the Armenians and other Christian communities in no way improved the security of the Ottoman Empire. The Allies never mounted an attack on the Cilician coast to justify the deportation of Armenians there. The deportations actually undermined the Ottoman war effort in Mesopotamia when Armenians working on the Berlin-to-Baghdad railway were condemned to a death march. The extermination of Armenian communities in eastern Anatolia did nothing to protect the Caucasus from Russian invasion. Tsarist forces met little resistance in conquering the fortress town of Erzurum in February 1916. The Russian army swept through the Black Sea port of Trabzon and the market town of Erzincan later that year—defeats that could not be blamed on Armenian collaborators after the deportations.

It was in the Dardanelles that, against the odds, the Ottomans succeeded in defending their territory against the combined armies of France, Britain, and the dominions through the courage and determination of their soldiers—not through the annihilation of minority communities.

EIGHT

The Ottoman Triumph at Gallipoli

THE CAMPAIGN IN GALLIPOLI EVOLVED QUICKLY FROM A WAR OF motion to the static warfare of trenches. The Allies had succeeded in landing some 50,000 able-bodied men, after the dead and wounded were accounted for. Yet they had failed to achieve the ambitious tasks the war planners had set for them. The British were supposed to roll the Ottoman defenders back and secure the high ground of Achi Baba some five miles inland, from which point they would dominate Turkish positions on the Dardanelles. The Anzac troops were not only to seize the ridges overlooking the beaches around Arıburnu but also to secure the high plateau across the peninsula to Maidos on the Dardanelles, cutting all Ottoman lines of communication and resupply. Had they managed to achieve these tasks, the Allies would have been in a position to silence the shore batteries in the Dardanelles and open the path to the British and French warships to force the straits and seize Istanbul. Instead, they encountered stiff resistance from the Turkish defenders, who drew lines around Anzac Cove and Cape Helles and doggedly refused to let the invaders pass.

Three times the British and French tried to break through Turkish lines on the tip of the Gallipoli Peninsula to seize the strategic village of Krithia and the Achi Baba heights. And three times they failed. In the First Battle of Krithia, on 28 April, the British and French suffered 3,000 dead and wounded (a 20 percent casualty rate) for little or no territorial gain. The Allies launched their second attempt just nine days later (6 May), and after three days of battle had lost 6,500 men (nearly 30 percent of forces engaged) for 600 yards of territory. The third and final Battle of Krithia

(4 June) resulted in 4,500 British and 2,000 French casualties for gains of 250 to 500 yards along a one-mile front. The road to Krithia cost the Allies 20,000 casualties per mile. They simply could not sustain the effort.[1]

The defence of Gallipoli had exacted a terrible toll on Turkish forces as well. The Ottomans suffered losses on a par with Allied casualties in the three battles for Krithia and fared yet worse in their own attacks on the British and French lines. Under orders from Enver Pasha to drive the invaders back into the sea, the Ottomans mounted determined attacks on Allied lines. The first assault on British positions in Helles on the night of 1–2 May resulted in 6,000 Ottoman casualties, and in a second night attack in the same area on 3–4 May, the Turks lost another 4,000 soldiers—losses of 40 percent in just ten hours.

The Ottomans made one further massive assault on the night of 18 May, mobilizing 50,000 infantrymen in a bid to drive the Australians and New Zealanders from their Arıburnu beachhead. British reconnaissance aircraft had reported the troop concentrations, and the Anzac soldiers were ready and waiting. In seven hours of combat, the Ottoman initiative failed completely, leaving over 10,000 dead and wounded strewn across the landscape between enemy lines. The soldiers at Gallipoli were learning what their comrades on the western front already knew from bitter experience: attackers stood no chance against well-entrenched defenders with machine guns.[2]

After a month of horrific violence on the Gallipoli Peninsula, stalemate ensued. Both sides dug in to hold the lines for which tens of thousands had fought, suffered terrible wounds, and died. The Australians and New Zealanders held their tiny beachhead at Anzac Cove, while the British and French established a line across the toe of the Peninsula no more than three miles from Cape Helles. While the Turks had failed to drive the invaders into the sea, they had succeeded in preventing the Allies from reaching the high ground. Contained within their narrow enclaves, the Entente armies were subjected to regular artillery, shrapnel, and gunfire from well-hidden snipers, while British and French ships bombarded Turkish positions with their heavy guns. It was trench warfare with all of the attendant horrors known to the soldiers on the western front.

THE BRITISH GOVERNMENT REVIEWED THE SITUATION IN GALLIPOLI with mounting concern. The campaign was not going as planned. The naval venture that Winston Churchill advocated had been abandoned after the disastrous attempt to force the straits on 18 March, and the limited ground campaign Lord Kitchener approved had foundered in the face of determined Ottoman defence. Casualties had been high, the number of able-bodied soldiers on the ground was insufficient to achieve victory, and the sea lanes between Alexandria and Lemnos (the island that served as Allied headquarters for the Dardanelles campaign) were no longer secure.

The Ottomans first exposed the vulnerability of British warships on 13 May in a surprise attack on the *Goliath*. The aged British battleship was at anchor in Morto Bay (inside the Dardanelles near the southern tip of the Gallipoli Peninsula), providing cover for French forces, when the Turkish torpedo boat *Muavenet-i Milliye* reversed down the Dardanelles towards the Allied anchorage. As it was moving slowly, stern first, the officers on watch mistook the Ottoman boat for a British vessel, an illusion shattered when the Turkish vessel fired three torpedoes into *Goliath*'s hull. The British battleship sank in two minutes, taking 570 of its crew of 700 men down with her, while the Turkish torpedo boat slipped away with impunity.

Landing an artillery piece at Gallipoli. The logistical challenges of the Gallipoli campaign were unprecedented, with men and materiel being delivered by sea under relentless fire from Ottoman defenders.

The arrival of German U-boats later in the month of May transformed the balance of naval power in the Dardanelles. The Allies could hardly complain. British, French, and even Australian submarines had been deployed in the Dardanelles since the British sank the Ottoman battleship *Messoudieh* in December 1914. An Australian sub, the *AE2*, managed to clear the underwater barriers to reach the Sea of Marmara on 25 April 1915. Two British submarines, the *E11* and *E14*, also navigated the treacherous straits and spent weeks cruising the Sea of Marmara, sinking transport and supply ships carrying reinforcements and provisions to Ottoman forces in Gallipoli. Yet the Allies suffered high losses to their submarine fleets because of underwater hazards in the straits and the confines of the Sea of Marmara. A Turkish torpedo boat sank the Australian *AE2* within days of her arrival in Marmara, and by May the French had lost two submarines—the *Saphir* and the *Joule*—to submarine nets and mines.[3]

German U-boats had a much easier time picking off British ships in the open waters of the Aegean. On 25 May, the German submarine *U-21* torpedoed and sank the British battleship *Triumph* while she was firing on Ottoman positions near Anzac Cove. The ship was struck shortly after midday, within full sight of both armies—a triumph for the Turks and a terrible blow to morale for the Australians and New Zealanders ashore. In the twenty minutes that *Triumph* took to sink, most of her crew was rescued, though seventy-five sailors and three officers died in the wreck. Two days later, the same German submarine sank HMS *Majestic* off Cape Helles, with the loss of forty-nine men. The capsized hull of the battleship, propped up by her masts on the coastal shelf, served as a reminder of the failure of the Allied navies in the Dardanelles campaign. For with the sinking of three ships of the line in quick succession, the Royal Navy was forced to withdraw all heavy battleships from the Dardanelles. Henceforth, naval support for ground operations would be provided by monitors (shallow draft vessels built for shore bombardment) and smaller ships less susceptible to submarine attack. Yet the submarine hazard remained to plague French and British troop carriers and supply ships running between Alexandria and Moudros Harbour, further complicating the campaign.[4]

SUCCESSIVE FAILURES IN GALLIPOLI PROVOKED A POLITICAL CRISIS IN Britain. In May 1915, Liberal prime minister H. H. Asquith was forced into a wartime coalition with the Conservative Party. The new cabinet reflected changes in political fortunes. Arthur James Balfour, a member of the Conservative Party, took Winston Churchill's place as first lord of the Admiralty. Churchill, condemned for his role in the unsuccessful naval campaign in the Dardanelles, was demoted to chancellor of the Duchy of Lancaster, becoming essentially a minister without portfolio. A new body, the Dardanelles Committee, was created to oversee the Gallipoli campaign, taking the place of the old War Council. The Dardanelles Committee held its first meeting on 7 June 1915 to decide the future of the campaign.

Lord Kitchener was still secretary of state for war and still the most influential voice in the meeting. (It is ironic that, to this day, Churchill takes the blame for Gallipoli when Kitchener was so clearly the campaign's most influential decision maker.) He presented the Dardanelles Committee with three options. Britain and its allies could abandon the Gallipoli campaign altogether. They could dispatch a major army to conquer the peninsula. Or they could continue to reinforce the small expeditionary force under Sir Ian Hamilton in the hope of making slow but steady progress towards the eventual conquest of Gallipoli.

The members of the committee ruled out retreat from Gallipoli. They feared the admission of defeat would turn the undecided Balkan states against the Entente Powers and, in the words of the British official historian of the campaign, "almost certainly lead to risings all over the Moslem world", a reflection of how much the Ottoman call for jihad continued to preoccupy Entente war planners. Yet the members of the committee had difficulty in deciding between a major campaign force and the status quo, largely because they did not know how large a force might be needed to overwhelm the Turks in Gallipoli or how long it would take to dispatch such a force. Every delay gave the Ottomans and their German allies precious time to build up their defences further and to make Gallipoli impregnable.[5]

In the end, Kitchener came down on the side of dispatching a large body of reinforcements to prosecute a vigorous campaign in the Dardanelles. The commander in chief of the Mediterranean Expeditionary Force, Sir Ian Hamilton, had requested three fresh divisions (a British division in World War I numbered between 10,000 to 15,000 men) to enable Allied forces to break out of the confines of Anzac Cove and complete the conquest of the Gallipoli Peninsula. The Dardanelles Committee agreed to the dispatch of these three divisions in the meeting of 7 June, and at the end of June Kitchener decided to send two further divisions—five divisions in all—to give Hamilton the surge he needed for victory in Gallipoli. The first units would reach the front by the beginning of August.

OVER THE SUMMER OF 1915, BRITISH AND FRENCH SOLDIERS trans-formed the rural landscape of Gallipoli into a complex grid of trenches. In the French sector, soldiers marched towards the front down a broad communications trench optimistically dubbed the "Avenue de Constan-tinople", while those returning from the firing line came down a parallel trench known as the "Avenue de Paris". The English too gave whimsical names to their trenches. "Regent Street" ran south from the front line past "Piccadilly Circus" into "Oxford Street," and a particularly complex intersection of trenches was christened "Clapham Junction" after London's largest rail crossroad. Dozens of smaller trenches were named for the regi-ments whose men had fought and died there: "Lancashire Street," "Mun-ster Terrace", "Essex Knoll", "Worcester Flat". The most ironic names were reserved for the front line itself: "Hyde Park Corner", "Main Street", and, bleakest of all, "Hope Street".[6]

The ironic names did little to mask the violence of the trenches. Those who served both on the western front and at Gallipoli found the Turkish front by far the more relentless of the two. "It is much worse here than in France, in the view of all those who have seen the two fronts," French cor-poral Jean Leymonnerie wrote home in June 1915. Britons were of the same view. "In France, apart from full-dress attacks, an infantryman may live for many months without once firing his rifle, or running the remotest risk of death by a rifle bullet," A. P. Herbert claimed. "But in those hill-trenches of Gallipoli the Turk and the Gentile fought with each other all day with rifle and bomb, and in the evening crept out and stabbed each other in the dark. There was no release from the strain of watching and listening and taking thought."[7]

Life in the trenches assaulted every one of a soldier's senses—sight, sound, taste, smell, and touch. Trench warfare undermined the physical and mental health of those not killed or wounded. Herbert's description of the British experience in the trenches of Gallipoli held equally true for the Turks. Invaders and defenders shared the squalor and horrors of trench warfare equally.

From the moment a soldier arrived in Gallipoli, he lived with the sound of artillery. The Allies, however, were most exposed. Ever since the German submarines had driven the British battleships away from the mouth of the Dardanelles, Ottoman gunners on the Asian shores of the straits had fired with impunity, hitting French lines with particular severity. On the Gallipoli Peninsula, the Turks held the high ground overlooking both Helles and Anzac Cove and kept up a steady stream of shrapnel and artillery fire. "Since we were positioned on the top of Alcitepe (Achi Baba), we were able to fire artillery wherever we wanted," an Ottoman artillery officer claimed. "We were able to make war in a way that suited us." The British and French were frustrated in their efforts to locate Ottoman gun emplacements. The Turks used camouflage, decoy cannons firing smoke charges to attract Allied fire, and their mobile howitzers to defy Allied efforts to silence their guns. The Ottomans and their German allies fired at will among the densely packed invaders in Helles and Anzac. Sometimes heavy, sometimes light, sometimes near, sometimes far, artillery harried the soldiers day and night, an unpredictable threat that claimed a steady stream of casualties on both sides of the conflict.[8]

Turkish soldiers, Gallipoli. Combatants on both sides of the trenches lived in similarly exposed conditions and were just as likely to be struck down by illness as by shrapnel and bullets.

In the course of the Gallipoli campaign, the Turks taught the invaders the art of sniping. At first the Allied troops were terrified by these invisible killers. Ottoman marksmen, camouflaged with green face paint and hidden in terrain they knew far better than the invaders, infiltrated behind enemy lines in both Helles and Anzac Cove after the landings, "content to lie there and pick off the infidels till they too died", A. P. Herbert wrote. "They were very brave men." Snipers had a terrible impact on the invaders' morale. "Nothing in their training had prepared them for it," Herbert continued. "They hated the 'blinded' feeling it produced; it was demoralizing always to be wondering if one's head was low enough, always to walk with a stoop; it was tiring to be always taking care; and it was very dangerous to relax that care for a moment." As one soldier reflected in verse,

> All day long the snipers sniped,
> All day long the bullets piped,
> And men dropped one by one.[9]

In time, the invaders recovered from their initial shock and developed into proficient snipers in their own right. Sergeant G. T. Clunie of the Wellington Mounted Rifles found himself exchanging fire with a Turkish sniper within days of arriving in Gallipoli in mid-May 1915. "I had a very interesting duel this morning," he noted in his diary on 16 May. "I put my head up and very nearly had it shot off, so I got to another position and watched and presently I saw him in a bush just behind the Turk trench at 200 yards. So I got to it and so did he. We must have fired about ten shots each and at last I hit him and he died there but by Jove he gave me a narrow go for it." Clunie made no attempt to hide his glee at killing an enemy sniper. Over time, the Turks came to respect the abilities of Allied marksmen. "We were shocked by the fact that the enemy was such a good shooter," Ibrahim Arikan reflected in his diary. "Although we went hunting the enemy, they were hunting us." Yet the invaders continued to live in fear of the invisible killer who might strike at any moment.[10]

One of the most surprising claims made by British and Anzac troops was that women were active in the battlefield as snipers. There is no record of women serving with the Ottoman army in the First World War, and in view of the segregation of the sexes in Ottoman society, it seems incongruous to say the least. Yet given the number of British and Anzac claims of women snipers killed, wounded, or arrested, it is hard to dismiss the phenomenon merely as a soldier's myth. A British medic noted in his diary that a wounded Turkish female sniper had been admitted to the hospital in Cape Helles, "she having been shot in the arm"—though he did not claim to have seen the woman himself. One private from New Zealand gave an eyewitness account: "We got a female sniper, but she was shot before we knew she was a woman. There have been a lot of women snipers about. They are good shots." Private John Frank Gray of the Wiltshire Regiment, who was engaged in operations against snipers around Chocolate Hill, near Anzac Cove, claimed the discovery of women snipers was his unit's "queerest find of all". He wrote that the women were armed and hiding in trees, alongside male colleagues. "Some of the women wore trousers, like the men, and some wore full, grey-coloured skirts. They were as thin as could be, and looked as if they had had nothing to eat for months." There is no telling, on the basis of these accounts, if women actually were involved in the fighting or Allied soldiers were justifying violence against Turkish women by alleging they were combatants.[11]

In addition to the relentless dangers of artillery and snipers, the Allies and the Turks regularly dug mines under each other's trenches to kill from below. Corporal Leymonnerie was awakened around midnight, his ear to hard ground in his dugout, by the distinct sound of digging in the ground beneath him. As he listened, he heard the regular blows of a pick. "It had to be the Turks," he concluded, "digging a sap to blow up our fort." He quickly found a safer spot to sleep. "The one thing I fear is to end my days blown sky high over the trenches." He never rested easy in that section of the trenches, fearing the Turks might detonate a charge beneath him at any moment.[12]

Lieutenant Mehmed Fasih was more afraid of being buried alive by an underground explosion than of being blown sky high. The punctilious young officer noted in his daily log that the enemy had detonated a mine so powerful that he had felt the ground heave under his feet. "It occurred where I had heard sounds [of digging] a few days back," he recorded. "7 men are missing." Later that afternoon, one of the missing men managed to extricate himself from the debris, much to the Ottoman lieutenant's relief. "There is no worse death than that," Mehmed Fasih reflected. "To face slow death while fully conscious! . . . My God, spare everyone from such a fate."[13]

The weeks spent in the trenches were periods of waiting, punctuated by major attacks. The Ottomans and the Allies alternated in taking the initiative, leaving soldiers on both sides of the trenches in a state of perpetual tension. "We were afraid of being attacked," Jean Leymonnerie wrote after a period of duty in the French front line, "but I admit we were much more afraid of having to make an attack ourselves." The greatest risks in trench warfare came with the desperate run across no-man's-land, though it was nonetheless terrifying to hear the enemy swarming your lines.[14]

Sergeant Moriarty of the Royal Munster Fusiliers survived the Turkish night attack on 1 May. "They crept right up to our trenches (they were in thousands) and they made the night hideous with yells and shouting Allah, Allah." The Munsters fought for their lives as waves of Ottoman soldiers charged their position. "When the Turks got to close quarters the devils used hand grenades and you could only recognize our dead by their Identity Discs," the round dog tags that British soldiers wore around their necks. Moriarty fought through the night to behold at dawn the horrible sight of hundreds of Turkish dead covering the ground before the British trenches. "I am sure I will never forget that night as long as I live," he reflected.[15]

The Australian war poet Harley Matthews was haunted by the Ottoman war cry "Allah", an alien sound that pricked the nerves of all Allied soldiers:

> We heard them gathering on the hills again
> They called and whistled, bugles blew.
> "Allah!" they cried. Then feet came thudding on.
> "Allah!" Up on the left the firing grew,
> In one gust it came down to us. "Stand to!
> Here they come. Fire!" Once more
> We fire at shouts and shadows—and then . . . gone
> They are gone now, all melted as before.[16]

For all soldiers, the experience of "going over the top" proved the ultimate baptism of fire—and a trauma that survivors would never forget. "Life in the trenches would be very agreeable," French corporal Leymonnerie reflected ironically, "were it not for the bayonet charges, which are terrible. The men are mowed down by the many machine guns and the excellent Turkish marksmen before they even hoist themselves over the parapet."[17]

Robert Eardley was a Territorial soldier from Manchester who reached Gallipoli in June. His first attack on Turkish lines came on 12 July, and he remembered each passing second before the fatal order with precision:

Anzac soldiers in a bayonet charge at Gallipoli. In trench warfare, the attacking army always suffered the highest casualties.

"The moments appeared like hours—the suspense—then the officer, his eyes glued on his watch following that finger (of death) slowly, so slowly, but surely moving to destruction—maybe a second left to live—for this is sacrifice—this is the moment when all hearts are sad and heavy—when you will hear some muttering a prayer—at your side you will notice some poor fellow dreading the approaching time knowing that 'death' creeps slowly but surely from 'over there'." The anxious soldiers tried to raise one another's spirits with empty words totally out of measure with the gravity of the moment.

"Cheer up chum!"

"Shake, old mate, good luck, hope for the best," and with a final shake of the entire frame of body, the order is given.

"Over lads and the best of luck."

Eardley climbed out of the relative safety of the trenches into the line of fire. He ran across no-man's-land, bayonet fixed, and marvelled at his own survival (he suffered only a flesh wound to the leg and grazed his nose on a broken bayonet), while his comrades fell dead and wounded around him. To hear the wounded call out for help, to give "a last handshake to a dying chum, as long as I live I shall never forget my first experience—those few moments of hell".[18]

Each attack littered the battlefield with hundreds and thousands of fallen soldiers. Unburied between enemy lines, in the intense heat of summer, the decomposing bodies infused the Gallipoli Peninsula with an intense stench of death. In the early weeks of the conflict, the Ottomans and the Allies agreed to local ceasefires lasting three or four hours to recover and bury the corpses. On 24 May, the British and Ottomans observed a nine-hour armistice along the Anzac front following a massive Turkish attack that left thousands of dead. Each side agreed the ceasefire was necessary but suspected the other of using the hiatus to advantage, to survey the other's trenches and move men and materiel into a favourable position before the resumption of hostilities. After the ceasefire of 24 May, no further break in fighting was agreed to, and the dead began to pose a growing threat to the morale—and the health—of the living.

"The trenches are filthy and at parts of the parapet men are buried with their feet projecting over the parapet, dead for days, and on either side the dead lie unburied in the sweltering heat," wrote Bartle Bradshaw, a young officer with the Border Regiment, in a letter home. "We do our best to cover them with lime, the stench is awful and when you realize that what sleep you get is in half yards between the dead and that you eat what meals you get in the same space, and that if you stop waving a piece of food about for a moment . . . " Bradshaw left his sentence incomplete because he did not want to write that if a soldier stopped waving his food around, it was soon swarmed by flies—the same flies that covered the dead.[19]

A. P. Herbert captured this particular horror of the trenches in his poem "Flies", written in Gallipoli in 1915:

> The flies! Oh, God, the flies
> That soiled the sacred dead.
> To see them swarm from dead men's eyes
> And share the soldiers' bread.
> Nor think I now forget
> The filth and stench of war,
> The corpses on the parapet
> The maggots on the floor.[20]

Clouds of flies carried sickness to the living from the dead. Soldiers on both sides of the lines suffered from the whole range of air- and waterborne diseases. The absence of proper latrines left soldiers who feared to expose themselves to sniper fire to relieve themselves in the same trenches where they fought, ate, and slept. Dysentery reached epidemic proportions. Raymond Weil, a French artillery officer, noted with growing concern the spread of disease among his troops. The inoculations given French soldiers against cholera and typhoid gave no protection against fevers and gastric disorders. "In recent days, there has been so much illness that even the officers' ranks have been reduced to nothing," Weil noted in his diary. Despite severe restrictions on sick leave, thousands of soldiers had to be evacuated from the front, dehydrated and too weak to walk, let alone to fight. At the height of summer, hundreds of sick men were evacuated from Gallipoli each day. They were sent to hospital facilities at Moudros until they were well enough to return to battle.[21]

Living and fighting in the confines of the trenches strained the mental health of the soldiers. Unlike at the western front, which provided opportunities for soldiers to take leave in towns and villages removed from the fighting, there was no relief from the violence at Gallipoli. Even when swimming in the sea, the invaders were exposed to random shelling that maimed and killed men desperate for a break from the fighting. Nor could they take refuge in sleep. The continual shriek of artillery, the percussion of impact, and the relentless demands of the front left the men no peace to slumber. Soldiers' journals frequently note how little they slept. "My men are tired," Jean Leymonnerie wrote, "and I am too, though I am holding up." He managed only two hours of sleep that night, between 2:30 and 4:30 a.m. It was the same on the Ottoman side. "Only manage 2 to 3 hours of sleep throughout the night and have awful nightmares," Mehmed Fasih noted.[22]

As the weeks wore on, the daily anxiety and sleeplessness took their toll, as a growing number of men succumbed to nervous breakdowns or shell shock. A sergeant with the British field ambulance corps first witnessed a case of "nerves" on 14 June, just seven weeks into the campaign. Henry Corbridge was horrified by the "mental cases, pathetic sights they are, with vacant stare and glassy look, and partial paralysis, some are raving". One case, a giant of a man "who had lost his reason, not a scratch on him", needed eight men to restrain him during evacuation to a hospital ship. Over the course of the summer, Corbridge noted ever more cases of shell shock. By mid-August he was recording five times more mental cases than wounded.[23]

Ottoman soldiers too suffered from shell shock. Ibrahim Arıkan, a volunteer from the Ottoman gendarmerie, was astonished to find his bat-tle-hardened commander sitting in a foxhole with the shakes. "Ibrahim, my son, where are you going?" the captain asked him. Arıkan knew something was wrong when the captain, who normally swore at his soldiers, addressed him as "my son". The captain was disoriented and asked Arıkan to accom-pany him. "He had lost his reason and willpower," Arıkan recalled. "His hand was shaking so violently that he was unable to hold his rifle." Even the hardest men cracked under the relentless bombardment at Gallipoli.[24]

Months of combat came to shape how the invaders and defenders saw each other. Whereas the popular press and propaganda had stirred deep hatred for the Germans in the early months of the war, the British, French, and Anzac soldiers had no prior antagonism towards the Ot-tomans. Allied soldiers gave nicknames to the Turks. The British referred to the Ottomans as "Abdul" or "Johnny Turk"; the French spoke of "Monsieur Turc". Even the Ottomans had a nickname for their own soldiers—Meh-medçik, or "Little Mehmed"—though they showed no such tenderness to the invaders, whom they branded "the English" or "the French" or simply *duşman*, "the enemy".

The trenches were at some points so close that the two sides could hear each other speak. Living at such close quarters had a humanizing effect on the men, and in periods of calm they would throw treats across to the enemy trenches. A Turkish soldier remembered throwing cigarettes, raisins, hazel-nuts, and almonds into the Anzac lines. The invaders reciprocated with cans of fruit and jam by way of thanks. Emin Çöl found it remarkable that no one ever mixed dirt with the gifts or followed a treat with a hand grenade. The exchanges were made with genuine goodwill.[25]

This is not to suggest the Allies and Ottomans were engaged in anything short of total warfare. Both sides committed atrocities, but there were also acts of compassion across enemy lines. Sergeant Henry Corbridge of the medical corps recalled treating an Ottoman prisoner who had saved a British soldier's life. The Briton, a sergeant with the Essex Regiment, accompanied the wounded Turk to the dressing station to ensure his protector was well

A Royal Irish Fusilier teasing Turkish snipers in Gallipoli by holding his helmet above the trench on his rifle.

treated. The Turkish soldier had been shot in the arm and leg while helping the British sergeant, who had been pinned down by crossfire between the lines. Corbridge and his orderlies "saw that the Turk didn't go short of any comforts which we could give him" while in hospital.[26]

Private Robert Eardley of the Lancashire Fusiliers had the extraordinary experience of rescuing, and being rescued by, the same Ottoman soldier in the course of battle. In early August, the Lancashires attacked Turkish lines astride the Krithia road in the southern tip of Gallipoli. Private Eardley took part in a bayonet charge that overran the Ottoman front line. Once again he was amazed at his own survival, as he saw comrades fall dead and wounded on either side as they dashed across no-man's-land. When he reached the Ottoman trench, Eardley came between a British soldier and a wounded Turk who lay defenceless on the ground.

"Here you get out of my way—he has killed my mate and I am going to stick him," the Briton growled.

Eardley reasoned with his comrade, arguing that it was a cowardly act to kill a defenceless man.

"Put yourself in his place chum—one never knows—cheer up old pa—don't do it, that's a good fellow," he cajoled.

Eardley managed to prevent the angry Lancashireman from killing the Turkish soldier. He found himself alone in the trench with the wounded Ottoman. The two men could not communicate in words, but the Turk made clear to Eardley that he was in terrible pain. "Poor fellow," Eardley muttered to himself, as he bandaged the man's gaping head wound. He settled the injured soldier in a safe spot away from the line of fire, put a coat under his head as a pillow, and sat with him for a spell, "exchanging signs and glances". When Eardley was called to take up sentry duty he gave the wounded man a drink of water and a cigarette. "I could see by his eyes that he appreciated the kindness and as the old saying goes 'one good turn deserves another'."

The Lancashire Fusiliers did not hold the Turkish trenches for long. A massive Ottoman counter-attack drove the British troops back to their original lines. Eardley was left in one of the occupied Turkish trenches to cover the retreat of his comrades. He watched as his area was overrun by hundreds of Ottoman soldiers charging with bayonets fixed. "The excitement was intense—beads of perspiration on my forehead—our foe galloping on in one great effort to sweep us off the face of the earth." He was surprised by a Turkish soldier who hurdled the parapet, bayonet first. "I felt a sharp piercing sensation—a burning feeling at the back of my left shoulder. I knew I had got the bayonet. . . . I distinctly felt the thrust and drawing out." Eardley fell face forward to the bottom of the trench among the dead and wounded, where, suffering from shock and loss of blood, he lost consciousness.

Eardley was awakened hours later by the sensation of dirt being shovelled onto his back. As he struggled to stand up, dizzy and disoriented, Eardley found himself surrounded by hostile bayonets pointed towards his chest. He had no doubt they intended to kill him. But before his captors had the chance to strike, a wounded Turkish soldier with a bandage around his head leapt into the trench and protected Eardley with his own body. The Briton immediately recognized his deliverer. The injured Turk was himself quite weak—he had presumably just been rescued by his comrades in their recent counter-attack—but he clung to Eardley for all he was worth and shouted for a sergeant.

When the Ottoman sergeant finally arrived, the wounded Turk told his story. "Away they jabber," Eardley recalled, unable to understand a word of what his protector was saying but recognizing from the expression on the sergeant's face that his chances of survival were rapidly improving. Finally, the sergeant turned and spoke to him in broken English: "'English get up, no one will harm you—you would have died only for this soldier—you gave him water, you gave him smoke and you stop bleed (wound from bleeding)—you very good Englishman,' and patted my back all over." Before being led away, Eardley took leave of his Turkish friend. "I shook hands with this Turk (and would give all I possessed to see this man again). As our hands clasped I could see he understood for he lifted his eyes and called 'Allah' and then kissed me (I can feel this kiss even now on my cheek as if it was branded there or was part of my blood)." They never saw each other again. Jostled through a hostile crowd of Ottoman soldiers, Eardley was taken up to a communications trench for interrogation. Further on, a hostile soldier dealt Eardley a blow to the chin that knocked him out. He later came to among a handful of other wounded British prisoners. It was a rude reminder that for most Turkish soldiers, Eardley's English uniform marked him as the invading enemy, the *düşman*. But Eardley's days in combat were over. He would spend the next three years alternating between confinement and heavy labour as an Ottoman prisoner of war.[27]

THE TRENCHES WERE TAKING THEIR TOLL ON THE INVADERS. BRITISH and French soldiers were killed by enemy fire or taken prisoner by the Ottomans in steady stream, with a far greater number evacuated from Gallipoli to be treated for wounds, disease, or shell shock. Hospital facilities in Moudros, Malta, and Alexandria were filled, and a growing number of passenger ships were recommissioned as floating hospitals to cope with the sick and wounded. Many of those who remained in the trenches were too sick with dysentery to fight but could not be spared from the already thinned Allied lines. Meanwhile, Enver Pasha continued to deploy fresh Ottoman troops from Anatolia and the Arab provinces to reinforce Ottoman lines on the Gallipoli Peninsula. Were it not for the five new divisions that Kitchener had dispatched to Gallipoli, the invaders would have been in an untenable position. On 3 August, the first units of Kitchener's New Army began to arrive at Anzac Cove to help launch the new offensive to secure the Gallipoli Peninsula once and for all.

The commander in chief of the Mediterranean Expeditionary Force, Sir Ian Hamilton, had spent weeks refining plans for the August offensive. He recognized that the Allies were in a disadvantageous situation in both Helles and Anzac Cove. The Turks held the high ground overlooking both Allied positions, and the invaders could not break through the Ottoman trenches to reach the high ground beyond. The British needed to break out of the confines of the positions occupied since the 25 April landings, and Hamilton chose to concentrate his forces to the north of the Gallipoli Peninsula, at Anzac Cove and Suvla Bay.

The plans for the August offensive were complex. The campaign would begin with diversionary attacks to distract Ottoman forces far from the main battlefield. Allied troops in Helles were to attack Ottoman positions south of Krithia in a feint to prevent Otto Liman von Sanders, the German general commanding Ottoman forces in the Dardanelles, from redeploying soldiers from the toe of the peninsula to Anzac. The attacks in Helles were to be made without any reinforcements, drawing on the war-weary troops who were already in position. Hamilton concentrated three of the new divisions that Kitchener provided to the northern front in Gallipoli. He directed two divisions to the weakly defended beaches of Suvla Bay to the north of Anzac Cove. He hoped to get as many new troops as possible safely ashore by deploying them where they were least expected. In this way, he hoped to restore movement to the Gallipoli campaign, quickly marching fresh and healthy soldiers unconfined by trenches across open terrain to outflank Ottoman positions in the high ground over Anzac Cove, in the area the Turks referred to as Anafarta.

One fresh division was dispatched to the Anzac front to take part in a multi-front attack on the Sari Bair Ridge. This ridge, punctuated by three distinct peaks—Battleship Hill (Düz Tepe in Turkish), Chunuk Bair (Conkbayırı) and Hill 971 (or Kocaçimen Tepe)—dominated the surrounding landscape and was viewed by the Allied commanders as the gateway to the Dardanelles. New Zealand major Fred Waite summarized the war planners' thinking: "Win the Ridge and we should win the Narrows," the heavily fortified section of the Dardanelles. "Open the Narrows to the Navy, and Constantinople was ours!" Were the Ottomans to be driven from these hilltops, their position would be untenable, and once the Suvla and Anzac divisions joined forces, the entire Ottoman Fifth Army would be cut off and forced to surrender. "The whole plan has been admirably conceived by Sir Ian Hamilton," Australian lieutenant Oliver Hogue wrote in a letter to his wife, Jean, "and the Staff work has been excellent down to the minutest detail. It now only remains to be seen if our tactics are equal to our strategy."[28]

The British mounted the first diversionary attack in Helles on 6 August. This was the battle in which Robert Eardley was taken prisoner. The carnage he witnessed in the Lancashires' charge was replicated across the front, as Ottoman gunners decimated the ranks of British attackers. On the first day of operations, the British suffered 2,000 casualties among the 3,000 men involved, then on 7 August sustained a further 1,500 casualties, for virtually no territorial gains. The Ottomans suffered even higher casualties, with 7,500 dead, wounded, or missing in the fighting at Helles between 6 and 13 August. However, the diversion failed to achieve the Allies' aim of pinning down Ottoman forces away from the main front. Liman von Sanders correctly interpreted the Helles attack as a feint and deployed reinforcements from the southern front to face the attack further north.[29]

A second diversion planned for Lone Pine, to the south-east of Anzac Cove, was no less costly to both sides. The Australians mounted a successful bayonet charge that dislodged the Ottomans from their front-line trenches in a position the Turks referred to as Kanlısırt (Bloody Ridge). Between 6 and 10 August, Turkish and Australian soldiers engaged in hand-to-hand combat in what the Ottomans remembered as one of the most fiercely contested battles of the Gallipoli campaign. Lone Pine stands out in Australian memory as well. "Of all those battles fought by our troops at Anzac, none was more fierce, and few were more bloody, than that waged at Lone Pine," wrote trooper William Baylebridge. Turkish records show nearly 7,500 dead, wounded, or missing. The Australians reported 1,700 casualties. The territory gained by the attack hardly justified the losses, though here at least the Australians managed to pin down a sizable Ottoman force to facilitate the main offensives further north against the Sari Bair Ridge and Suvla Bay.[30]

Australian casualties in three other feints were far worse where inadequate artillery fire had failed to dislodge Ottoman machine guns. Two lines of attackers were mowed down almost to a man in the midnight assault on the Ottoman position known as German Officers' Trench. The dismounted Australian Light Horse managed to seize three Turkish trenches in Dead Man's Ridge before they were expelled with heavy losses by an Ottoman counter-attack. But it was the Australian attack on the Nek that came to emblematize the callous waste of life at Gallipoli. After watching the first wave of 150 men mowed down by Turkish gunfire within yards of their trenches, Australian officers blindly followed orders and sent two further waves over the top to near certain death. At least 435 of the 450 men who attempted to storm the Nek fell dead or wounded, without inflicting a single Turkish casualty. It was a high price to pay to distract the Ottomans from the main area of attack at Sari Bair.[31]

The main Anzac force launched its attack on the three peaks of the Sari Bair Ridge under the cover of night on 6 August. Four columns made their way up the steep valleys surrounding Hill 971 and Chunuk Bair in the course of the night. After two days of intensive fighting, a combined force of New Zealanders, Australians, Gurkhas, and Britons failed to dislodge the Turks from Hill 971 but managed to seize the central peak of the ridge, Chunuk Bair. It was the greatest achievement of the offensive but proved more than the Allies could hold. From the top of Hill 971, which dominated Chunuk Bair, the Ottomans subjected the invaders to heavy artillery fire until they managed to retake the peak in a determined counter-attack on the morning of 10 August. After four days of fighting, the Anzac troops looked in vain for relief from the two divisions that had landed at Suvla and been expected to join forces with them.

By all accounts, the Suvla Bay landing was a squandered opportunity. The British managed to land two divisions—over 20,000 men—with relatively few casualties on a beach defended by no more than 1,500 Ottoman soldiers. Disorganization and delay combined to turn a successful landing into a failed offensive.

On the night of 6 August, British warships transported two divisions of Kitchener's New Army recruits into position around Suvla Bay, some five miles north of Anzac Cove. Those battalions that landed on the southern horn of the bay had a smooth ride, touching down in modern landing craft whose ramps afforded the troops dry feet as they hit the beach. However, those troops assigned to the central coastline inside Suvla Bay faced uncharted hazards in the pitch black of the moonless night. In the darkness, many of the landing craft lost their bearings and motored southward from the designated landing site into treacherous reefs. As the landing craft grounded on shoals and reefs, some of the troops found themselves debarking in neck-deep water; others were delayed for hours while their boats were refloated. And all were in the wrong location. To compound the difficulties, the defenders set off flares that exposed three British destroyers at anchor, discharging thousands of soldiers. Ottoman headquarters were alerted, and the element of surprise was lost before the landing had even begun.

As the sun rose, the invaders spent the first precious hours trying to regroup rather than pressing on to the lightly defended high ground overlooking the Suvla Plain. Several battalions had seen action overnight and suffered casualties, though most of the units were at full strength. However, the delays in getting soldiers ashore meant that the navy was late in landing artillery and provisions. With little water and no cannons to support them, the British officers decided to limit their aims to securing those hills nearest the landing site—disregarding the objectives set out in Hamilton's carefully crafted plans. Worse yet, with their unauthorized delays, the British officers gave their Turkish counterparts time to dispatch reinforcements. Liman von Sanders redeployed units from Helles and Bulair to counter the Suvla threat. And he appointed the energetic Colonel Mustafa Kemal as commander of the Anafarta front, which dominated both Suvla and Anzac.

After twenty-four hours ashore, the British commanders decided to give their men a day's rest. The inexperienced New Army recruits were exhausted after a sleepless night's landing and a full day of fighting. They had lost one hundred officers and 1,600 men, dead and wounded. They had gone short of food and water in the summer heat. And their artillery had still not been fully unloaded. After so many soldiers had died in precipitous attacks without sufficient artillery cover, the British officers refused to move from their secured beach positions until their men had recovered and had the means to deal with what they erroneously believed to be strongly held Turkish positions. And so the British did not fight on 8 August. Instead, they spent the day swimming and resting. Ironically, had the British commanders attacked immediately, their admittedly tired troops would have faced no significant opposition. As Liman noted in his memoirs, the delay gave him the time he needed to redeploy troops to contain this latest invasion. The British would pay dearly for their day's rest.[32]

When battle resumed on 9 August, Turkish numbers had reached near parity with the invaders'. The Ottomans had been left in possession of the high ground, giving them a tactical advantage over the invaders. And the Ottoman troops were seasoned veterans fighting on their own terrain, facing inexperienced recruits armed with unreliable maps. "The Suvla scheme, as planned by the Commander-in-Chief [Sir Ian Hamilton] was already doomed to failure," the British official history of the campaign concluded.[33]

The British and Ottomans fought pitched battles all day on 9 and 10 August, each side suffering heavy casualties. At one point on 9 August, the artillery was so intense that the brush caught fire and, whipped to high temperatures by the winds, burned British and Turkish wounded alive while their comrades were unable to reach them. Though the British suffered fewer casualties on 10 August, they made no progress in gaining ground from the Turks. Nor were they any closer to providing relief to the beleaguered Anzac troops fighting for the Sari Bair Ridge. After four days of fighting around the peak of Chunuk Bair, the British withdrew to their original lines in Anzac Cove. They had lost 12,000 men and had no further reserves to keep up the fight. Taking the three fronts involved in Hamilton's "break-out" offensive—Helles, Anzac, and Suvla—the Allies had suffered a total of 25,000 casualties in just four days. The Ottomans were also stretched to the breaking point but had managed to hold their positions despite losses on a par with those suffered by the Allies.

Though the joint Suvla-Anzac attack had already failed by 10 August, the Allies continued to pursue the offensive. On 12 August, a party of fifteen officers and 250 men from the Norfolk Regiment, all drawn from the royal estate in Sandringham, disappeared without a trace; they are believed to have fallen behind enemy lines and been cut down to the last man. Finally, by 15 August the offensive had ground to a halt, leaving the Ottomans in firm possession of the high ground over each of the three Gallipoli fronts and the Allies with a longer front line to defend and no place to break through the determined Ottoman defences.[34]

The Suvla and Anzac offensives had ended in total failure, and the Allied position in Gallipoli was weaker than before. Hamilton claimed to have lost 40,000 men—sick, wounded, and dead—since 6 August, leaving him with a total fighting force of only 68,000 men to defend a much longer front line. With the addition of Suvla Bay, the Allied front now stretched 23,000 yards. On 17 August, Hamilton requested 45,000 reinforcements to bring his depleted units back up to full strength, plus an additional 50,000 fresh troops. Kitchener, who believed that the five divisions he had just sent to Gallipoli should have been more than enough to secure victory, was unwilling to entertain this new request. He wrote back to Hamilton on 20 August to explain that a "big push" was planned on the western front and warned, "No reinforcements of importance can be directed from the main theatre of operations in France." Without reinforcements, Hamilton replied, he would have to relinquish either Anzac or Suvla.[35]

ALLIED LOSSES AT GALLIPOLI AND THE FAILURE TO FORCE THE Dardanelles began to influence the volatile politics of the Balkans—to the Central Powers' advantage. After a year of indecision, Bulgaria broke its neutrality to conclude a war pact with Germany and Austria in September 1915. German advances against Russia and Turco-German successes in the defence of the straits convinced Bulgaria's government that the Central Powers would prevail in the Great War. Bulgaria entered the conflict on 15 October when it joined the Austro-German campaign against Serbia.

Bulgaria's entry into the war proved nothing short of catastrophic for Allied efforts in the Dardanelles. Serbia and Greece requested 150,000 soldiers to protect them from the Central Powers. A Franco-British campaign force had to be mobilized at short notice to send to Salonica in north-eastern Greece, with many of its units to be drawn from Gallipoli. Rather than receiving the major reinforcements he required to hold his position, Hamilton had to accept a depletion of his garrison as whole divisions were siphoned off for service in the Balkans.

The Central Powers' overwhelming advances in Serbia transformed the Turkish position in Gallipoli. With the conquest of the Serbian city of Nis on 5 November, Germany and Austria were able to establish a direct rail link from Belgrade to Istanbul (though damage to the rails delayed regular service until January 1916). The Ottoman Empire's European allies were at last free to dispatch cannons and ammunition directly to Turkey, providing a dramatic change in the balance of power in Gallipoli. The British and French viewed the new developments with growing apprehension. Their war-weary and depleted units would now be coming under more regular and more powerful shelling.

By October 1915, then, the British government was facing a moment of decision in the Dardanelles. The failure of the August offensive had gravely compromised the Allies' position in Gallipoli. Between losses on the western front and the dispatch of another campaign force to Salonica, there were no soldiers to spare for the Gallipoli campaign. Shelling and sniping continued to claim Allied casualties regularly, and the spread of disease weakened those left holding the trenches. The Turks, meanwhile, were only strengthening their positions with powerful new artillery and fresh troops from Anatolia. After months of terrible losses, the British and French faced the very real prospect of total defeat. Better to cut their losses through a successful evacuation than lose everything by trying to hold an indefensible position.

Lord Kitchener first put the idea of evacuation to Sir Ian Hamilton in a telegram on 11 October. "What is your estimate of the probable losses which would be entailed to your force if the evacuation of the Gallipoli Peninsula was decided on and carried out in the most careful manner?" Hamilton was appalled. "If they do this they make the Dardanelles into the bloodiest tragedy of the world," he confided to his officers. Hamilton feared that, while the first contingent of troops might get away unnoticed, it would prove impossible to hide a total evacuation from Turkish observers, and the depleted ranks ashore would be overwhelmed and cut down by the Ottomans. In his reply to Kitchener, Hamilton gave his personal estimate that the Allies would suffer losses of between 35 and 45 percent, adding that his General Staff estimated 50 percent losses.[36]

Hamilton's pessimistic assessment notwithstanding, the Dardanelles Committee (the British cabinet subcommittee overseeing the conduct of the Gallipoli campaign) increasingly viewed evacuation as inevitable. Yet after the repeated failures of the Gallipoli campaign, they were not confident in Sir Ian Hamilton to oversee the evacuation. The commander in chief of the Mediterranean Expeditionary Force was relieved of his command on 16 October, and General Sir Charles Munro was appointed to take his place. Some still advocated pursuing the campaign in Gallipoli—Kitchener in particular—arguing that, given the hardening of lines on the western front, Gallipoli still offered the best opportunity for victory over the Central Powers and that failure to secure the straits risked leaving Russia isolated and facing certain defeat. However, even the advocates of the Gallipoli strategy recognized that a new offensive would have to wait until the winter storms had passed. And it was not clear that the Allies could hold their positions against determined Ottoman attacks through the winter. It would take a major investment of men and materiel to hold these positions—resources that were desperately needed on other fronts. The commanders needed to make a decision, and soon.

When Sir Charles Munro reached Gallipoli at the end of October, he was shocked by what he saw in the three Allied enclaves. "It's just like Alice in Wonderland," he commented to a staff officer, "curiouser and curiouser." In

Helles, Anzac, and Suvla, he asked the local commanders if they believed their men could hold their positions against Turkish reinforcements with German heavy guns. The most his divisional commanders could promise was that the men would do their best. It was enough to convince Munro that evacuation was the only solution, but he needed to persuade Kitchener. When Munro reported his findings back to Whitehall, the Dardanelles Committee decided to dispatch Kitchener to assess the situation for himself.[37]

Kitchener sailed from France to Gallipoli determined to avoid withdrawal at all costs. He regretted not having sent more troops earlier in the campaign and remained convinced that a breakthrough was more likely in the east than on the western front. Yet when he arrived at the headquarters of the Mediterranean Expeditionary Force in Moudros, Kitchener found himself surrounded by advocates of evacuation. It only took a visit to the front-line positions on the Gallipoli Peninsula to win the minister of war over to the inevitability of evacuation.

On 13 November, the prime mover of the Dardanelles campaign finally visited the front to which he had sent so many British, French, and colonial troops. If they bore him any ill will, the troops did not show it, receiving Kitchener with rousing cheers at every stop he made. He paid a quick visit to headquarters at Helles and mixed with French troops at Seddülbahir. He stretched his legs at Anzac, climbing the steep slopes up to Russell's Top and visiting the front-line trenches at the Nek, where so many men of the Australian Light Horse had been sent to futile deaths. From a hilltop at Suvla Bay, Kitchener looked across the Salt Lake towards the Sari Bair Ridge—the elusive Kocaçimen Tepe and Chunuk Bair, where the New Zealanders had achieved what many would claim was the greatest, if short-lived, victory of the entire Gallipoli campaign. He saw Gallipoli, and he understood: "The country is much more difficult than I imagined," Kitchener was later to write to the Dardanelles Committee, "and the Turkish positions . . . are natural fortresses which, if not taken by surprise at first, could be held against very serious attack by larger forces than have been engaged." It would take more men than the British could afford to overwhelm the Ottomans in Gallipoli, and so they would have to go.[38]

EVACUATING WAS EASIER SAID THAN DONE. THE LATE AUTUMN WINDS had already wreaked havoc with Allied positions. Gales had swept away many of the precarious landing piers set up in Helles, Anzac, and Suvla, and a British destroyer, the HMS Louis, had been blown ashore and wrecked in Suvla Bay. November rains later flooded the trenches, creating misery for soldiers on both sides of the battlefield. Unless there was a break in the weather, it would be impossible to load men, animals, and guns onto boats.

The Allied commanders were particularly anxious to preserve secrecy about their plans for an imminent evacuation. Were the Ottomans or their German allies to learn of the withdrawal, it was feared they would unleash a devastating attack on the retreating forces. Their task was compromised by the bitter debate raging in the British parliament in London, in which members demanded a clear statement from the government: Would they evacuate Gallipoli or not? Those debates, covered in the British press, made it into Ottoman newspapers as well. "The enemy is in flight!" a young lieutenant exclaimed to Mehmed Fasih on 19 November. "They are giving up their Gallipoli Campaign." Fasih was sceptical at first but gradually came to believe the Ottoman newspaper reports that the debates in the British parliament presaged the "eventual withdrawal of English from Çanakkale". However, his Ottoman and German superiors discounted the British reports as a deliberate disinformation campaign to obscure a new assault on the Dardanelles. Still, the open discussion of top-secret military manoeuvres only made the British commanders more fraught over the dangers of evacuation.[39]

Though the end of the campaign was in sight, the two armies continued to bombard each other's trenches, inflicting a steady stream of casualties. The conditions were miserable, and morale was flagging on both sides. The low point was reached at the end of November, when a three-day gale flooded trenches before turning into a blizzard and deep frost that left those soldiers most exposed to the elements suffering from frostbite. Turks and Britons actually drowned in flash floods that swept the trenches at Suvla. Yet the Turks took comfort in the steady stream of heavy weaponry and artillery shells from Austria and Germany. On 9 November, Lieutenant Mehmed Fasih noted in his diary the "sweet news" that "three hundred railway wagons" with howitzers and ammunition from Germany had reached Ottoman territory. "Instead of 22 hours, we shall be able to bombard [the] enemy for 70 hours," he wrote. The growing disparity in firepower gave the Allies every incentive to accelerate their withdrawal from a losing battlefield.[40]

Evacuation of guns and personnel from Suvla, December 1915. British troops were no less vulnerable when withdrawing from Gallipoli than they had been in the original landings.

After the violent storms of late November, Gallipoli witnessed three weeks of perfect calm. On 7 December, the British cabinet made the final decision to evacuate the Suvla and Anzac beachheads as soon as possible but to retain the Allied position at Helles for the moment. The embarkations began almost immediately. There were 77,000 British and imperial soldiers at Suvla and Anzac on 9 December. Within eleven days, all British forces on the two northern beachheads would be gone.

Allied commanders took a number of measures to hide the evacuation from the Turks. All soldiers and artillery were embarked from the beaches after dark. The long December nights provided nearly twelve hours of cover. In daylight, the Royal Naval Air Service maintained a continuous aerial patrol over Anzac and Suvla to keep enemy aircraft at a distance. Mehmed Fasih watched as four Allied aircraft intercepted a single German plane to prevent it from flying over Anzac Cove in mid-December. In this way, the Allies managed to clear tons of precious war materiel from the beaches of Gallipoli in advance of evacuating troops.[41]

The British did everything to preserve the look of normalcy, keeping a standard level of activity on the beaches and controlling the number of vessels coming and going from the shore. They varied the level of firing from the trenches, following intense bombardment with prolonged periods of almost complete silence, to keep the Ottomans guessing. The strategy worked. "Front lines completely silent," Fasih noted in his diary at dawn on 24 November. By nightfall, he was genuinely puzzled. "Front is quiet. Very occasionally, shots fired by infantry. Almost no grenades." By the next day, officers and men, confused by the continued Allied restraint, were nervous. "Our men, especially the old soldiers, are worried," Fasih recorded on 25 November. "They have tried to provoke the enemy by deliberately taking risks when firing at his positions. There has been no response." The anxious Ottomans dispatched patrols to spy on the British and continued to fire on enemy trenches in a bid to stir a reaction. Suddenly, on 28 November, after four days of quiet, the British opened up with an intense barrage on Ottoman positions. "This sudden activity has a bad effect on me," Fasih recorded. "Presence of what we had thought gone is not something to look forward to!" Judging by Fasih's meticulous diary, the Turks, puzzled by the Allies' unpredictable behaviour, did not suspect an evacuation was underway. If anything, the Ottomans came to believe the British were about to launch a fresh attack.[42]

The final evacuation from Anzac and Suvla took place over two nights and was completed in the early hours of 20 December. Though they had anticipated as many as 25,000 casualties, every last soldier was evacuated without a single fatality. The withdrawal was carefully choreographed, with volunteers manning the front trenches, firing occasional shots towards Ottoman lines to maintain the semblance of normalcy. Escape routes were marked in flour on the dark soil of Gallipoli to ensure the last men could find their way to the beaches in the dark. When the last man was safely embarked, Allied ships opened fire on those guns and ammunition that had to be left behind, setting off a massive explosion. The Turks responded by opening fire on the empty trenches and beaches, much to the wry satisfaction of the retreating invaders.

The final decision to abandon Helles followed shortly after the successful evacuation of Anzac and Suvla. On 24 December, orders were given to withdraw from the toe of the Gallipoli Peninsula. The task had been made harder by the success of the prior evacuation. The Ottomans were on the alert for any sign of a retreat, and Liman von Sanders gave orders to launch a full assault in the event of an evacuation from Helles. However, the British and French managed to coordinate a complete withdrawal of their troops over a two-night period and succeeded in getting the last man off Helles Point by 3:45 a.m. on 9 January 1916.

As dawn broke after both withdrawals, Turkish patrols were amazed to find that the enemy had fully evacuated its positions. The departing Anzacs had left some nasty surprises behind. "Devices, some worked by candles, some by tins of water rigged up to fire old and broken rifles hours after the last man had left the trenches," a machine-gunner from New Zealand wrote home. "Bombs which exploded on a spring being released are in all sorts of odd places. Altogether the first party of Turks that came over were due to have a few casualties." They did. Ibrahim Arikan's men set off a number of hidden bombs as they reclaimed the vacated beaches. "We suffered many losses," he lamented.[43]

The departing invaders left behind enormous quantities of supplies that provided much welcome booty to the cold and hungry Ottoman soldiers. Men who had stripped the dead for warm clothes were amazed to find thousands of tunics, trousers, and coats left in piles on the beaches. Ibrahim Arikan walked through the abandoned British tents marvelling at the supplies the invaders had left behind. One tent "was like a market place, full of tiles, zinc, plates, bicycles, motorcycles, forks, spoons and so on". On shore he "saw food and clothing supplies piled as high as apartment buildings. There was enough supply to meet the needs of an army corps for an entire year." Hakki Sunata and his men took over one of the abandoned tents and feasted on British marmalade, cheese, oil, and milk.[44]

The men in Emin Çöl's unit were in high spirits the morning after the British had left. One of the men, a born comic, slapped a British hat on a comrade and pretended to interrogate him.

"Jonnie, why did you stay behind?"

The "Briton", getting into character, asked a comrade to be his "translator".

"I fell asleep," he said, to general hilarity.

"What did you do when we began to fire on you with our new heavy artillery," the "Turk" asked. The "Briton" silently buried his face between his knees in response. Then he raised his head and replied cryptically, "Had those guns gone on for another day or two, it wouldn't have been us who escaped from here."

"Who would it have been, then?" pressed his Turkish interrogator.

"It would have been our souls." And all of the soldiers around collapsed into the hysterical laughter of men who couldn't believe they had survived the carnage of war and won.[45]

At 8:45 a.m. on 9 January, Liman von Sanders wrote jubilantly to the Ottoman minister of war, Enver Pasha, to inform him, "God be thanked, the entire Gallipoli Peninsula has been cleansed of the enemy." The Gallipoli campaign was finally at an end.

THE GROUND CAMPAIGN IN GALLIPOLI LASTED 259 DAYS, BETWEEN the landings on 25 April 1915 and the final evacuation from Helles on 9 January 1916. The invasion force that Lord Kitchener had hoped to keep to 75,000 men had swelled to nearly half a million by the end of the campaign—410,000 Britons and 79,000 French. The Turkish army peaked at 310,000 men in Gallipoli (many of them wounded once or more and returning to service).

Of the roughly 800,000 men who fought in Gallipoli, over 500,000 were wounded, taken prisoner, or killed in the conflict. The casualty figures were neatly divided between defenders and invaders in the eight-and-a-half-month struggle for mastery of the Dardanelles: 205,000 British and dominion casualties, 47,000 French and imperial soldiers, and between 250,000 and 290,000 Ottomans. As many as 140,000 men died in Gallipoli: 86,500 Turks, 42,000 British and dominion troops, and 14,000 French and imperial soldiers.[46]

These losses weighed heavily on the British, for whom Gallipoli proved a total defeat. The campaign was a drain on men and materiel while total warfare was being waged on the primary front in France. There was to be no conquest of Istanbul, no collapse of Germany's Ottoman ally, and no Black Sea route linking Russia to her Entente allies. Rather than hastening the end of the Great War, Gallipoli actually lengthened it considerably. The Turco-German alliance was stronger than ever. Direct rail communications facilitated the flow of men, money, and weapons between them. And Allied war planners' fear of jihad among colonial Muslims was more acute in the aftermath of a brilliant Ottoman victory. The Ottomans were a foe the British would have to mobilize more armies to defeat—most immediately in Mesopotamia.

For the Turks, a historic victory compensated for the losses at Gallipoli. In defending the straits against the Allies, the Ottoman army emerged from the shadow cast by the Balkan Wars of 1912 and 1913 and the string of defeats that marked the start of the Great War in Basra, Sarıkamış, and the Suez Canal. Victory at Gallipoli proved the Turks capable of fighting and winning in modern warfare against the greatest powers of the day. Moreover, a new generation of fighting commanders emerged from Gallipoli who would go on to lead the Ottomans to new victories against the British.

As they withdrew from their trenches, the Tommies and Anzacs left notes for the Ottomans, promising to meet again. An Australian war poet captured his countrymen's grudging respect for the Turks who had beat them back:

> I reckon the Turk respects us, as we respect the Turk;
> Abdul's a good, clean fighter, we fought him, and we know.
> And we've left him a letter behind us to tell him we found him so.
> Not to say, precisely, "Goodbye" but "Au revoir"!
> Somewhere or other we'll meet again, before the end of the war!
> But I hope it'll be a wider place, with a lot more room on the map,
> And the airmen over the fight that day'll see a bit of a scrap![47]

They were as good as their words. Many of the same soldiers on both the British and Ottoman sides who fought in Gallipoli would face each other again in Palestine before the war was over.

NINE

The Invasion of Mesopotamia

Victory at Gallipoli freed thousands of Ottoman soldiers for service on other crucial fronts. With the imperial capital secured, Enver Pasha could finally satisfy his field officers' urgent demands for reinforcements. The ravaged Ottoman army in the Caucasus received seven infantry divisions to ward off the Russian threat. Cemal Pasha's forces in Syria and Palestine had been depleted for service in the Dardanelles; four divisions were dispatched to the Levant to restore the Fourth Army to full strength. In Mesopotamia, the Ottomans had fielded ill-trained and poorly supplied troops to face the Anglo-Indian juggernaut. The deployment of two experienced and disciplined divisions from Gallipoli to Baghdad, it was hoped, would shift the balance of power in Mesopotamia in the Ottomans' favour.[1]

The Ottoman position in Mesopotamia had deteriorated alarmingly in the aftermath of Suleyman Askeri's defeat at Shaiba in April 1915. High rates of desertion among Iraqi recruits exacerbated losses through heavy battlefield casualties, leaving Ottoman forces severely under-strength. Ottoman commanders in Mesopotamia had no choice but to go from town to town rounding up deserters under the threat of exemplary punishment. Turkish officers, who regarded Arab recruits as unreliable in the best of circumstances, had few illusions about the military value of deserters reconscripted by force. They would be surprised, however, by the ferocity of Iraqi deserters' resistance to the recruiting parties sent to reclaim them for the Ottoman war effort.[2]

Starting in May 1915, the towns and villages of the Middle Euphrates rose in rebellions that ran on for the final two years of Ottoman rule over southern Iraq. The first rebellion broke out in the city of Najaf, a pilgrimage site for Shiite Muslims and a refuge for hundreds of Iraqi deserters who sought asylum within the walls of the shrine city. Iraq's Shiite communities had grown increasingly disaffected with their Sunni Ottoman rulers, resentful of being drawn into a global war that increasingly disrupted their lives. The clampdown on deserters brought matters to a head, and when the Ottoman governor in Baghdad dispatched a large force to Najaf under an Iraqi officer named Izzet Bey to round up malingerers hiding in the ancient city's quarters, resentment boiled over into rebellion.

The Ottoman commander announced a three-day amnesty for all deserters who handed themselves in. Given that desertion was punishable by death, Izzet Bey had reason to hope the Iraqis would take advantage of the reprieve and return to military service voluntarily. Yet most of the deserters had fled from Najaf before Izzet Bey's arrival, and few if any remained in the town to surrender.

After three days, the Ottoman commander decided to send his troops to conduct house-by-house searches. The Ottoman soldiers outraged the conservative women of Najaf by checking under their veils to ensure they were not men hiding in women's clothes. The townspeople protested this assault against the honour of their women and waited for the right moment to exact their revenge.[3]

On the night of 22 May 1915, a band of deserters descended on Najaf with their guns blazing and laid siege to the government buildings and army barracks. The townspeople made common cause with the rebels, as deserters from the surrounding countryside converged on Najaf to make a stand against the Ottomans and the global war they had imposed on the unwilling people of Iraq. The battle raged for three days, while the rebels systematically destroyed government offices and records. All communication between Najaf and other administrative centres was severed, as tribesmen in the surrounding countryside cut lines and uprooted telegraph poles. With the surviving Ottoman soldiers and officials besieged in a handful of government buildings, the heads of the town quarters sent criers through the streets of Najaf calling on merchants to open their stores and resume business as usual.

Alarmed, the governor in Baghdad sent a delegation to confer with the townspeople. In a meeting with the town's leaders, the Ottoman delegates reminded the Najafis that the Ottoman Empire faced a "life or death war" against infidel invaders and that it was every Muslim's religious duty to assist in this struggle. For their part, the Najafis placed full responsibility for the situation on the Ottomans themselves and stubbornly refused all of the delegation's requests. In the end, the Ottomans were left to negotiate the safe withdrawal of their besieged soldiers and officials from Najaf and appointed a skeleton administration to keep the semblance of Ottoman rule over the shrine city. However, the people of Najaf took over effective government, with the town gaining a high degree of independence from Ottoman rule.

Encouraged by Najaf's example, several other key towns in the Middle Euphrates region rose in rebellion against the Ottomans in the summer of 1915. For the people of Karbala', another Shiite shrine city, rebellion became a matter of civic pride. "Are the people of Najaf better than us, or braver, or more manly?" they asked rhetorically. Once again a group of deserters launched a rebellion on 27 June, burning down municipal buildings, schools, and even a new hospital in Karbala'. Two hundred houses in one of the new quarters of the town were put to the torch, driving the mostly Persian inhabitants to take refuge in the older quarters. Rebels and Bedouin from nearby tribes began to fight amongst themselves over the distribution of plunder as chaos descended on Karbala'. Once again, the Ottomans were forced to negotiate a controlled handover to local rule.[4]

The Ottomans put up a desperate fight in the town of al-Hilla but found themselves outnumbered by waves of Bedouin and deserters. In al-Samawa, the town's notables broke their pledge of loyalty, sworn on the Quran to the district governor, when they learned of the approach of British forces in August 1915. A detachment of ninety local soldiers deserted en masse, while the townspeople and Bedouin turned on the Turkish soldiers in their midst. An entire cavalry detachment of 180 men was stripped of their weapons, horses, and clothes and driven from town stark naked. Similar events took place in al-Kufa, al-Shamiyya, and Tuwayrij. In the end, their futile efforts to force deserters to return to active service cost the Ottomans the Euphrates basin.

WHILE THE OTTOMANS FACED INTERNAL REBELLION, THE BRITISH continued their relentless advance in Mesopotamia. Following its victory at Shaiba in April 1915, the Indian Expeditionary Force had received fresh troops and a new commander, General Sir John Nixon. Under orders to secure the whole of the Ottoman province of Basra, Nixon prepared to advance up the Tigris to the strategic river port of Amara.[5]

With a population of some 10,000, Amara lay nearly ninety miles north of Basra. After several weeks of preparation and planning, Nixon ordered the 6th Division into action under the command of Major General Charles Townshend. To break through Turkish lines north of Qurna, Townshend deployed hundreds of small native river craft as improvised troop transports supported by British steamboats armed with cannons and machine guns. This unlikely armada, dubbed "Townshend's Regatta", set off for Amara at dawn on 31 May. Between the artillery bombardment provided by the heavier ships and the massed charges from men in native boats, the British managed to break through Ottoman positions north of Qurna and proceed upriver unopposed by the retreating Ottoman defenders. The advancing British army found itself fighting on friendly territory. Arab villages along the Tigris flew white flags to demonstrate their good intentions towards the new conquerors as the Ottoman retreat degenerated into a demoralized rout.

On 3 June, the advance guard of Townshend's Regatta reached the outskirts of Amara, where they found an estimated 3,000 Turkish troops attempting to withdraw in advance of the Anglo-Indian army. A British river steamer with a crew of only eight sailors and armed with a 12-pound gun cruised up to Amara unchallenged by the Turkish defenders. The sudden appearance of a boat under the British ensign so demoralized the Turks that eleven officers and 250 men surrendered on the spot, while more than 2,000 Ottoman troops retreated upriver. General Townshend arrived by steamer later that afternoon and raised the Union Jack over the customs house, claiming victory in Amara before the main body of 15,000 troops had even reached the town. The surrender of hundreds of Turkish and Arab soldiers to an advance party they could have overcome easily reflected the collapse of Ottoman morale.[6]

Following the capture of Amara, Nixon planned to advance up the Euphrates to occupy Nasiriyya and thereby complete the British conquest of the province of Basra. Nasiriyya was a new town established in the 1870s to serve as the market centre of the powerful Muntafik tribal confederation; like Amara, it had a population of some 10,000. Nixon hoped to win over the powerful Euphrates Bedouin tribes by dealing the Turks a defeat and believed that the Ottomans posed a clear and present danger to British troops in Qurna and Basra so long as they held a garrison at Nasiriyya.

Nixon's forces, under General George Gorringe, began their advance on Nasiriyya on 27 June.

The lower Euphrates was far more treacherous to navigate than the Tigris. In the course of the summer, the river typically dropped in depth from five feet in June to three feet by mid-July and became impassable by August. To secure ships of sufficiently shallow draft, the British were forced to recommission several obsolete paddle steamers to carry their troops upriver towards Nasiriyya. One of the British ships, the *Shushan*, was first commissioned for the relief of General Gordon at Khartoum in 1885. These ancient British steamboats struggled to cross a series of marshlands through ill-marked channels that grew alarmingly shallower week by week.

Despite the outbreak of rebellions in Najaf and Karbala', the Ottomans mounted a spirited defence against the British on the lower Euphrates. With some 4,200 Turkish troops assisted by Bedouin tribesmen in well-defended positions outside Nasiriyya, they initially outnumbered the invaders. Unwilling to proceed against superior numbers, Gorringe called for reinforcements and held his position until the third week of July, when his force reached full strength with 4,600 infantrymen. The diminishing river, parts of which were closed to navigation by late July, had delayed the dispatch of extra troops. With no prospect of further reinforcements by river, Gorringe had to make do with the forces at hand.

The British had mounted preliminary attacks on Ottoman positions outside Nasiriyya in early July. Ali Jawdat, a native of the northern Iraqi city of Mosul, was one of the Ottoman troops resisting the British advance. Jawdat was a professional soldier who had graduated from both the Baghdad military high school and the elite Harbiye military academy in Istanbul before taking his commission in the Ottoman army. Despite his military training, however, Jawdat had mixed loyalties. He had grown disenchanted with the Young Turk government and, like many educated elites in the Arab provinces, aspired to greater Arab autonomy within the Ottoman Empire. He was a founding member of al-Ahd (the Covenant), a secret society established after the 1913 Arab Congress in Paris. The military equivalent of al-Fatat, the Young Arab Society, al-Ahd was particularly strong in Iraq, where it attracted many of the brightest young Arab officers. Like al-Fatat and the De-centralization Party, al-Ahd called for Arab autonomy within a reformed Ottoman state rather than outright independence for fear of European colonial domination. With the outbreak of the Great War, Jawdat threw himself into the defence of the Ottoman Empire against the Entente Powers with all of the loyalty and determination of his Turkish compatriots.

In 1915, Ali Jawdat had served with Suleyman Askeri in the Battle of Shaiba. He retreated with Askeri to Nasiriyya and, after his commander's suicide, was put in charge of an Ottoman detachment near that town. The Ottomans were assisted by the powerful Bedouin leader Ajaymi al-Sadun, whose tribesmen filled the thin Ottoman ranks confronting the British invaders. The tribesmen asked the Ottomans to provide them with ammunition, and Jawdat was tasked with giving the Bedouin what they needed for the defence of Nasiriyya.

When Gorringe's forces attacked Turkish lines on the Euphrates, Jawdat watched as the Bedouin irregulars took the measure of the situation and turned against the Ottomans. He saw tribesmen assault Ottoman soldiers to steal their rifles and ammunition. He saw his soldiers fall dead and wounded under intense British gunfire. "The Ottoman soldiers were caught between two fires," Jawdat later wrote, "from the Bedouin and the British." Isolated from the main Ottoman lines, Jawdat was himself ambushed by Bedouin

British boat bridge across the Euphrates at Nasiriyya, guarded by Indian soldiers. The Ottomans abandoned Nasiriyya to the British after a day's intense fighting on 24 July 1915, redeploying their troops to the Tigris for the defence of Baghdad.

tribesmen, who disarmed and robbed him before he was captured by the British in the village of Suq al-Shuyukh, near Nasiriyya.[7]

Judging by Ali Jawdat's experiences, the Ottomans were in no position to retain the lower Euphrates against a sustained attack. There simply were not enough regular Ottoman soldiers to withstand the British, and the Bedouin would side with whomever they believed was stronger. While it was common for Turkish officers to criticize their Arab and Bedouin soldiers as unreliable, Jawdat's experiences are all the more telling, coming from a native of Iraq with strong Arabist leanings. Jawdat was dispatched to Basra, where he was held as a prisoner until later in the war, when the British had more use for Arab activists.

The British attack on Nasiriyya itself opened on 24 July with salvos of artillery fired from steamships. British and Indian troops then stormed the defenders' trenches in waves of bayonet charges. The Ottomans held their ground, forcing the invaders to fight for every yard gained. The fighting raged until nightfall. The Turkish defenders, having suffered 2,000 casualties and 950 soldiers taken prisoner, withdrew under cover of darkness. At dawn the next morning, a delegation of townspeople rowed out to the British boats to offer Nasiriyya's surrender. After suffering heavy casualties of their own, the British were relieved not to have to fight another day.[8]

With the occupation of Nasiriyya, the British had secured the entire Ottoman province of Basra. Yet General Nixon wanted to press on to take the strategic town of Kut al-Amara. Situated in a bend in the Tigris, Kut was the terminus of the Shatt al-Hayy channel that linked the Tigris to the Euphrates just south of Nasiriyya. British intelligence reported that the 2,000 Ottoman troops who had retreated from Nasiriyya had fallen back on Kut, where they joined forces with a garrison of 5,000 men with the potential to threaten British positions in both Amara and Nasiriyya. Nixon argued that Britain's control over the province of Basra would not be secure so long as the Ottomans retained Kut.

A growing division was emerging between British officials in London and India on war policy in the Middle East. Although an integral part of the British Empire, India had its own government, headed by the viceroy, Lord Hardinge, and its own army. That army served the empire loyally, dispatching troops to the western front and Gallipoli as well as leading the campaign in Mesopotamia. However, the Government of India needed to preserve a garrison to ensure its own domestic security. With German agents working in Persia and Afghanistan and threatening jihad in the Muslim north-western provinces of India, the viceroy was concerned about preserving a credible deterrent at home. Given India's importance to the empire, London fully shared the viceroy's concerns.

The Government of India differed with the British government in London, however, on the deployment of troops. For London, the top priority remained the western front, with Gallipoli a secondary concern and Iraq practically an afterthought. Mesopotamia was far more important to the Government of India than it was to London. Territory gained in Iraq extended the Raj's own sphere of influence in the Persian Gulf, and many of the political officials attached to the Indian army in Mesopotamia envisaged Iraq one day coming under the Government of India's control. Thus, the viceroy, unwilling to dispatch significant new forces for fear of compromising the security of India, wanted the return of Indian regiments from the western front to reinforce and extend the Raj's gains in Mesopotamia. Officials in London, satisfied with the status quo in Iraq, argued instead for a "safe game in Mesopotamia", in the words of the secretary of state for India, Lord Crewe.[9]

Following the occupation of Nasiriyya, the Government of India urged London to authorize the occupation of Kut as "a strategic necessity". The viceroy went on to request the deployment of an Indian army unit, the 28th Brigade then serving in Aden, to reinforce Nixon's numbers in advance of an assault on Kut. It was a reasonable request, though, given Britain's tenuous position in South Yemen, not one London was in a position to concede at that moment.[10]

THE TRUTH OF THE MATTER WAS THAT THE 28TH BRIGADE WAS desperately needed in Yemen to prevent the strategic port of Aden from falling to the Turks. The British assault on Shaykh Said in November 1914 had only served to weaken Britain's position in Yemen. Officials in India and London had made the decision to destroy the Turkish guns overlooking the entry to the Red Sea without consulting the British Resident in Aden. Colonial officials in Yemen thought the attack ill-advised as it alienated Imam Yahya, the Yemeni ruler in Sanaa, who saw it as an assault on his territory. Although Imam Yahya was nominally an ally of the Ottoman Empire, the British had hoped to preserve cordial relations with him. Those hopes were dashed in February 1915, when the imam wrote to Colonel Harold Jacob, the First Assistant Resident in Aden, to reaffirm his loyalty to the Ottoman Empire and, by implication, his hostility to Britain.[11]

Turkish forces crossed into the territory of the Aden Protectorate, supported by Imam Yahya, in February 1915. At first, British officials dismissed the Turkish troop movements as posing little or no threat to their position in Aden. Yet, as Ottoman forces in Yemen grew and Turkish agents recruited a growing number of tribal leaders to their cause, the British became increasingly concerned. By June, British intelligence reported Ottoman strength at six battalions (an Ottoman battalion numbered between 350 and 500 men)—Turkish forces outnumbered the British. On 1 July, the Ottomans attacked one of Britain's key allies in the town of Lahij, less than thirty miles from Aden.[12]

The sultan of Lahij, Sir Ali al-Abdali, was a semi-independent ruler of one of the mini-states within the British Protectorate of Aden. Though he had been on the throne for less than a year, the British saw him as one of their leading allies in southern Yemen. When Lahij came under threat of Ottoman invasion, the British Resident in Aden mobilized his small and inexperienced garrison to repel the Turkish forces. An advanced unit of 250 Indian troops with machine guns and 10-pound artillery set off for Lahij overnight on 3 July, reaching the town early the following morning. The main body of Welsh and Indian troops followed a few hours later and found themselves marching in the extreme heat of the Yemeni summer. Two of the Welsh soldiers died of "heat apoplexy" on the march, and even the Indian soldiers began to collapse from exposure. The exhausted troops staggered into Lahij before sunset on 4 July to find the town in a state of sheer chaos.

Night fell on Lahij as Arab tribesmen loyal to the sultan fired their weapons into the air. At that moment, a Turkish column entered the central town square, totally unaware of the British presence in their midst. The British captured the Ottoman commander, Major Rauf Bey, and seized a number of Turkish machine guns before the Ottomans had time to react. Once the Turks got the measure of the situation, they went on the offensive, mobilizing a bayonet attack on the British troops. In the chaos, an Indian soldier mistook the sultan of Lahij for a Turk and killed the very ally the British had intended to protect.

The four hundred British troops in Lahij, heavily outnumbered by the Ottomans and their tribal supporters, beat a hasty retreat. Exhausted by their forced march to Lahij and the pitched battle they had fought through the night, the British soldiers only just managed to reach Aden with their forty Turkish prisoners after losing fifty men in combat and another thirty to heat-stroke. In addition, the British left behind all of their machine guns, two of their mobile artillery pieces, three-quarters of their ammunition, and all their equipment. And the Turks were left in full possession of Lahij, within striking distance of Aden.

The road to Aden lay open to the Ottoman army. Turkish troops advanced from Lahij to the township of Shaykh Uthman, just across the harbour from Aden. As Major General Sir George Younghusband, commander of the 28th Brigade, noted, from Shaykh Uthman the Ottomans were "within easy artillery range of the port buildings, ships, residential quarters, Club, Government House, and ships in harbour". Worse yet, the wells and treatment plant that provided Aden with all of its drinking water were in Shaykh Uthman. Unless the British could drive the Ottomans out of the neighbouring township, their position in Aden was untenable. And the loss of Aden, both for the security of British shipping and for British standing in the Arab world, was inconceivable.[13]

The Government of India made an urgent request for relief forces from Egypt to reinforce the British position in Aden. The British government swiftly complied, and on 13 July 1915 General Younghusband received his orders to proceed directly to relieve Aden at the head of the 28th Brigade. The troops reached Aden five days later and disembarked at night to hide their arrival from the Turks. On 21 July, British forces crossed the causeway between Aden and Shaykh Uthman and drove the Ottoman troops back to Lahij in a surprise attack. While British casualties were light, the Ottomans lost some fifty men killed and several hundred taken prisoner.

Younghusband fortified the British position in Shaykh Uthman and decided to hold his ground. Having regained control over Aden's water supply, he refused to extend his lines or put his men in jeopardy by going on the offensive. "It is too hot for one thing and for another it does not seem wise at this juncture to leave a strong fortress to go forth on precarious adventures in the desert," he wrote to the British commander in chief in Egypt. This was the situation at the end of July when Lord Hardinge requested that the 28th Brigade be dispatched to the Mesopotamian front to assist in the conquest of Kut al-Amara. Needless to say, the War Cabinet in London denied the viceroy's request. With an estimated 4,000 Ottoman troops in Lahij, the

Aden garrison of 1,400 men was even then insufficient to hold the strategic port without reinforcements—an uncomfortable situation that would endure until the end of the war.[14]

To make matters in Yemen worse, as in Gallipoli the Turks had asserted control over the front. The British had proved too weak to protect the rulers and territory of their Aden Protectorate. Even more than the loss of territory, the loss of face in the Arab and Muslim world concerned officials in London, Cairo, and Simla. As Acting British Resident in Aden Harold Jacob concluded, Britain's "failure to defeat the Turks before Aden was the supreme cause of our loss of prestige in the country". Ever conscious of German and Ottoman jihad propaganda, the British felt their failings in Aden were another gain for their enemies and undermined the Entente Powers' position in the Muslim world more generally.[15]

EVEN WITHOUT THE BENEFIT OF REINFORCEMENTS IN MESOPOTAMIA, General Nixon had persuaded the viceroy that the Indian army could take Kut al-Amara with the forces already at its disposal. The Turkish army in Iraq, Nixon argued, was in disarray after a string of battlefield defeats. The Anglo-Indian troops had gained in experience and won the self-confidence that came with repeated victories. Given time to recover from their fevers (even General Townshend succumbed to illness after the conquest of Amara and had to return to India to convalesce), Nixon was confident that his soldiers could resume their seemingly unstoppable advance up the Tigris. He proposed waiting until September 1915 to launch the assault on Kut, and Lord Hardinge gave his approval for the next stage of the Mesopotamia campaign.

The conquest of Kut was to be led by General Townshend, whose "regatta" had so effortlessly taken Amara. Yet Townshend had grave reservations about extending British lines. "Where are we going to stop in Mesopotamia?" he fretted. His concerns were well founded. After nearly a year in Mesopotamia, the Indian army needed reinforcements, and Townshend worried about his supply lines as British forces advanced deeper into the region. Each conquest extended lines of communication that were entirely dependent on river transport. Yet the riverboats available to the Indian army were not fit for purpose. Doubling the length of the supply line from Basra without adequate transport would place the entire expeditionary force at risk. While convalescing in India, Townshend met Sir Beauchamp Duff, the commander in chief of the Indian army, who pledged "not one inch shall you go beyond Kut unless I make you up to adequate strength". On this understanding, Townshend accepted his orders from Nixon to lead the advance on Kut and began his march upriver on 1 September.[16]

Townshend had more grounds for concern than he realized at the time. The Ottomans had appointed an energetic new commander to head their forces in Mesopotamia. Nurettin Bey was a fighting general who had served in the Ottoman-Greek War of 1897 and suppressed insurgencies in Macedonia and Yemen before the outbreak of the Great War. As one military historian concluded, the multilingual Nurettin (who spoke Arabic, French, German, and Russian) was "exceptionally talented". Tasked with protecting Baghdad from the Indian army, Nurettin worked tirelessly to rebuild his depleted divisions and managed to draw new units to Mesopotamia. A dangerous new dynamic was transforming the Mesopotamian front to Britain's disadvantage: Ottoman numbers were expanding while British forces were being progressively depleted.[17]

BRITISH AND AUSTRALIAN AIRMEN TOOK TO THE SKIES OVER THE TIGRIS to assess Turkish positions around Kut al-Amara. The aerial reconnaissance was of immense value to Townshend and his officers in planning their offensive. They saw where Turkish forces were entrenched and could plot the locations of artillery batteries with a higher degree of precision than for any previous attack in Mesopotamia. Yet it was dangerous business. The aircraft were prone to breaking down in the heat and dust of summer, while Turkish sharpshooters inflicted serious damage on planes intent on getting a closer look at their positions. On 16 September, a British plane was forced to land behind Ottoman lines, where the Australian pilot and his English observer were taken prisoner.[18]

Aerial reconnaissance showed that the Turks had established strong positions seven miles downstream from Kut at a position known as al-Sinn. Their trenches ran for miles on both sides of the Tigris between impassable marshlands, forcing the British attackers either to risk a frontal assault across open terrain or to march for miles around marshlands to outflank Ottoman lines. An obstruction laid across the river prevented British ships with artillery mounted on their decks from getting through. Nurettin had assured his troops that their positions were impregnable and that the British would not pass.

The British estimated total Ottoman strength in al-Sinn at 6,000 infantry, of which only one-quarter were Turks and three-quarters were Arabs. Townshend was confident that his force of 11,000 men, reinforced with artillery and machine guns, was more than sufficient to overcome Ottoman defences. Some of his junior officers were less sanguine. "Having seen enemy's position," Captain Reynolds Lecky wrote in his diary, "very big, strongly entrenched and well wired in, more dirty work for some of us."[19]

British troops moved into position overnight to launch a multi-front attack on Ottoman lines in the early morning hours of 28 September. The plan called for precision manoeuvres, with some units drawing fire from the Ottoman front while others circled around to outflank Ottoman positions. However, in the predawn dark, several of the British columns got lost and delayed among the marshes. Forced to attack in broad daylight, the British not only lost the crucial element of surprise but also found themselves exposed to heavy artillery and machine-gun fire. "Had a beastly day," Captain Lecky recorded in his diary, "lost a lot of men. The Turks fairly caught us in one place with their shrapnel. They had evidently ranged it to the foot and kept putting them right on top of us. . . . One of our machine-guns about five yards from me got a direct hit which smashed the mounting to pieces. Spent all night digging in and by daybreak we were dead tired." As Lecky's account confirms, Ottoman forces put up a determined defence of their lines and inflicted heavy casualties on the exposed British attackers. The two armies battered each other from dawn to sundown. While the exhausted British forces settled in to hold their gains overnight, the Ottomans silently withdrew to the town of Kut. Captain Lecky noted with respect, "The Turks cleared in the night, a very masterly retreat, not a thing left."

The British took several days to advance from the abandoned Ottoman lines at al-Sinn to the town of Kut. The barrier the Ottomans had erected across the river obstructed shipping long after it had been breached, and the low water level in the river further hindered navigation. There were also far more wounded than British planners had allowed for, and they needed to be transported downstream to medical facilities in Amara and Basra before the British renewed hostilities with the Turks for control of Kut.[20]

In the end, the Turks did not force the British to fight further for Kut. British aerial reconnaissance reported on 29 September that the Ottomans had abandoned the town and completed an orderly retreat upriver towards Baghdad. On the one hand, this was good news, as the British could occupy Kut al-Amara unopposed. Yet in victory Townshend had failed: the Ottomans had slipped through his net and retreated with their artillery and most of their forces intact. Each British failure to surround and destroy the Ottoman army in Mesopotamia gave the Turks the opportunity to regroup, drawing the Indian army ever deeper into Iraq and further extending its lines of supply and communications. The Indian Expeditionary Force grew more vulnerable with every battle it won in Iraq.

THE BRITISH VICTORY AT KUT IN OCTOBER 1915 COINCIDED WITH the growing recognition in London that the Dardanelles campaign had failed. Many politicians feared the adverse consequences of a British defeat in Gallipoli for their standing in the Muslim world. The British cabinet believed that failure in the Dardanelles would deal their enemies a propaganda victory for their jihadist politics. Inevitably, some politicians came to see the occupation of Baghdad as a remedy for the reputational risks of evacuation from Gallipoli.

The commanders in the field were of two minds. General Nixon believed not only that his forces could take Baghdad but that their position in Mesopotamia would not be secure until they did. General Townshend, who had led the 6th Poona Division to victory in Amara and Kut, argued that the British should consolidate their hold over the extensive territory they had already conquered. While his soldiers could quite possibly take Baghdad from the Turks, they would need significant reinforcements to hold the city and to assure lines of communication stretching hundreds of miles along the fickle Tigris from Baghdad to Basra. The operation required no less than two full divisions of fresh troops, Townshend maintained.

On 21 October, the Dardanelles Committee, the British government's war committee for operations in the Middle East, debated options in Mesopotamia. Lord Curzon took Townshend's line that Britain would do best to consolidate its gains from Basra to Kut. An influential troika of ministers, including Foreign Secretary Lord Grey, First Lord of the Admiralty Arthur Balfour, and Winston Churchill (demoted after Gallipoli to the minor cabinet post of chancellor of the Duchy of Lancaster but still a powerful voice in government), agreed with Nixon and called for a full occupation of Baghdad. Lord Kitchener, the military man, advocated a middle line between these two positions, calling for a raid to destroy Ottoman forces in Baghdad followed by a strategic retreat to more defensible British positions. "If Baghdad is occupied and Gallipoli evacuated," Kitchener argued, "a force of 60–70,000 Turks might be sent" to retake Baghdad, and Townshend would need several divisions to retain the city against such an army. Perhaps Kitchener's influence over the cabinet was waning after repeated failures in the Dardanelles, for he gathered little support for his position. As the official historian of the campaign concluded, the politicians saw in Baghdad an opportunity "for a great success such as we had not yet achieved in any quarter and the political (and even military) advantages which would follow from it throughout the East could not easily be overrated".[21]

In the end, the Dardanelles Committee was unable to come to a decision. In not explicitly forbidding an advance on Baghdad, however, it tacitly approved whatever action the most determined might pursue. And the most determined—General Nixon, Viceroy Lord Hardinge, and their supporters in the cabinet, Grey, Balfour, and Churchill—were for taking Baghdad. The secretary of state for India, Austen Chamberlain, conceded and, with the cabinet's blessing, sent a telegram to Lord Hardinge on 23 October giving General Nixon authorization to occupy Baghdad and promising to dispatch two Indian divisions from France to Mesopotamia as soon as possible.[22]

For the first time since the outbreak of the war, the Ottoman army in Mesopotamia had the commanders and troops with which to confront the Anglo-Indian invaders. Ottoman forces in Mesopotamia and Persia were reorganized into the Sixth Army in September 1915, and the venerable Prussian field marshal Colmar Freiherr von der Goltz was appointed commander in chief. Aged seventy-two when he took up his appointment, Goltz Pasha and his German staff officers received a hero's welcome on arrival in Baghdad in December 1915.

The Prussian commander enjoyed important advantages over his predecessors in Iraq. The Turkish generals under his command had gained valuable experience in fighting against the British, and with the arrival of two new divisions in Mesopotamia, the Sixth Army was reaching parity with British forces in Mesopotamia. The battle-hardened Ottoman 51st Division, composed entirely of Anatolian Turks, was a more disciplined force than the Indian army had yet encountered in Iraq.

The arrival of these new forces in the autumn of 1915 made quite an impression on the people of Baghdad, as one resident recalled: "The town crier went through the markets of al-Kazimiyya [a district of Baghdad] calling on the people to gather on the riverbank to welcome the Turkish forces that were arriving. When the people went out they found the river covered in an amazing number of rafts, each filled with soldiers. The troops disembarked from their rafts and set off marching in ranks to music. The people raised their voices in cheers and the women ululated to greet the soldiers." The balance of power was shifting in Mesopotamia, as the Ottomans came to enjoy both a numerical and a qualitative advantage over the battle-weary ranks of the Indian army.[23]

Townshend's task was to take Baghdad with the forces under his command—in all, some 14,000 men. A further 7,500 British troops were distributed among garrisons stretched from Basra to Kut al-Amara on the Tigris and to Nasiriyya on the Euphrates. The promised Indian divisions were not expected to reach Basra before January 1916. While the string of victories had certainly given the Anglo-Indian troops confidence, the months of marching and fighting, compounded by the hardships of the Iraqi summer and the prevalence of disease, had taken their toll. Many of the British units under Townshend's command were well under-strength, and he was beginning to have concerns about the loyalties of his Indian Muslim soldiers.

Ottoman propagandists actively played on Islamic loyalties to try to split British ranks. The government press in Baghdad printed leaflets in Hindi and Urdu calling on Indian Muslims to abandon the "army of disbelievers" and join their brothers in faith in the Ottoman army. They reminded Muslim soldiers that Salman Pak, where the Turks had entrenched for the defence of Baghdad, was revered as the burial place of one of the Prophet Muhammad's most faithful companions, Salman (*pak* means "pure" in Persian and Turkish—thus, "Salman the Pure").[24]

These leaflets had some effect as the British generals detected a growing reticence among the Muslim sepoys to advance against the "holy place" of Salman Pak. Isolated cases of mutiny had already been reported. In October 1915, Captain Lecky recorded that four Muslim soldiers on picket watch close to Turkish lines had cut the throat of their commander and fired on British positions before crossing over to Ottoman lines. After that incident, the 20th Punjabis were dispatched for service in Aden "owing to desertions". The British feared further mutinies in response to Ottoman propaganda focusing on the shrine of the Prophet's companion. In order to diminish the religious significance of the place, the British systematically referred to Salman Pak by its classical Sassanid name, Ctesiphon.[25]

At the very heart of the Ottoman defences lay the Arch of Ctesiphon, a colossal monument dating from the sixth century that even today remains the largest brick vault ever constructed. For months, the Turks had been preparing their positions around the great arch. Their front line stretched over six miles, broken up by fifteen earthwork fortresses, or redoubts, armed with cannons and machine guns. A complex network of communication trenches enabled the movement of men and supplies to and from the front, and enormous water jugs installed at regular intervals ensured defenders would not go thirsty. About two miles behind the front line, another well-constructed set of trenches defined the Turkish second line. The crack 51st Division was held in reserve in this second line of trenches. These defences were as close to impregnable as the Ottoman commander Nurettin and his officers could manage in the time between their retreat from Kut in October 1915 and the British advance the following month.

British commanders had no reliable information on Ottoman forces defending Baghdad. Estimates of Turkish numbers ranged from 11,000 to 13,000 in the lead-up to the assault on Salman Pak. In early November, Nixon and Townshend began to receive contradictory reports about Ottoman reinforcements sent from Syria or the Caucasus to Baghdad but discounted them as unreliable. To compound their uncertainty, Nixon had ordered a halt to reconnaissance flights over enemy lines on 13 November after losing another of his precious airplanes to enemy fire. Nixon and Townshend assumed that either their numbers were at parity with Ottoman forces or the Ottomans slightly outnumbered them. However, their experience of Turkish defenders collapsing under pressure gave British commanders confidence that they could prevail even against slightly superior numbers.[26]

On the eve of battle in November 1915, Townshend ordered two aircraft aloft for a last, long-range overview of the enemy's positions. The first pilot returned safely, reporting no changes in Ottoman lines. The second pilot, flying to the east of Ctesiphon, was troubled by significant changes on the ground and evidence of considerable reinforcements. As he circled back for a closer look, Ottoman troops shot holes in his engine, forcing him to land behind enemy lines, where he was taken prisoner. Though the pilot refused to answer his captors' questions, they took the map on which he had marked the position of the 51st Division—the first reliable intelligence on Ottoman reinforcements. As a Turkish officer recorded, "The map containing this priceless information fell, not into the hands of the enemy commander . . . but into those of the Turkish commander."[27]

The downing of the British plane not only prevented Townshend from learning that his troops were dangerously outnumbered by an Ottoman force of more than 20,000 men but also did a great deal to raise morale among the Turkish troops. "This little event was taken for a happy omen that the luck of the enemy was about to change," the Turkish officer noted. And so it was.

IN THE EARLY MORNING HOURS OF 22 NOVEMBER, THE BRITISH MOVED against the Ottoman front line. Four columns of troops advanced under the mistaken belief that they still enjoyed the element of surprise. The illusion was quickly shattered as the defenders opened fire with machine guns and artillery as the British came into range. "Almost directly under fire from guns," Captain Lecky recorded in his diary, along with the names of his comrades killed in the first onslaught. "Rifle fire incessant until about 4 p.m. Fighting very severe."

The British and Ottomans engaged in bayonet charges and hand-to-hand combat for hours before the British finally took the Ottoman front-line trenches. Yet no sooner had the British secured the front than the Ottomans mounted a fierce counter-attack with some of their most experienced troops from the 51st Division. The fighting raged well into the night as the casualties mounted on both sides. "A dreadful day," Lecky concluded, "dead and wounded everywhere and no means of getting them in." By the end of the first day of fighting, British losses reached 40 percent of their forces, and the Ottomans lost nearly 50 percent of theirs, leaving commanders on both sides profoundly depressed.[28]

The fighting continued for a second day on 23 November, with both armies facing a growing crisis with their wounded troops. "All day getting in wounded," Captain Lecky recorded, "hundreds still un-treated, no stretchers, no morphia, no opium, nothing for them." Still the two sides battled at close quarters deep into the night. "About 10 p.m.," Lecky recorded, "while

Turkish infantry in Mesopotamia launching a counter-attack. The Ottomans deployed experienced front-line troops for the defence of Baghdad who surprised the British invaders with the intensity of their counter-attacks. Both sides suffered casualties of between 40 and 50 percent in the decisive battle of Salman Pak in November 1915.

creeping along the Dorsets' trench we were heavily attacked. Wounded had an awful bad time, they were still lying out in open behind trenches. Our guns were close up, firing point-blank, and one could hear the [Turkish] officers urging the enemy on, a devil of a night."

For three days, the Ottomans held the Anglo-Indian army at bay. The British managed to retain the Ottoman front line but lacked the troops to overwhelm the defenders in the second line of trenches. The number of untreated wounded posed a growing problem for the British in particular (the Ottomans were able to evacuate their wounded to nearby Baghdad). The British had not anticipated such heavy casualties and were woefully unprepared to treat the thousands of grievously injured soldiers. Captain Lecky described "men with shattered legs and no legs at all being brought in on great coats. Their sufferings were beyond description." The relentless fighting, the piteous groans of the wounded, and the rumours of Turkish reinforcements combined to sap the morale of Townshend's army.

By 25 November, Townshend and his commanders recognized their position was untenable. The Indian army was outnumbered and overextended.

They had gone to battle with a fixed number of troops and no reserves to back them up. The earliest reinforcements would not reach Mesopotamia before January. They had to preserve as many able-bodied soldiers as possible to defend British positions between Basra and Kut al-Amara and urgently needed to evacuate the wounded. Townshend required every riverboat at his disposal to carry the thousands of wounded downstream, leaving the able-bodied, exhausted after three days of intense fighting, to undertake every soldier's nightmare: a retreat under enemy fire.

THE BRITISH RETREAT FROM SALMAN PAK MARKED A DECISIVE TURNING point in the Mesopotamia campaign. The Ottomans were quick to take the offensive—both on the battlefield and in the propaganda war.

Relations between the Ottomans and their Iraqi citizens had reached a low point with the British advance up the Tigris in September and October 1915. The residents of Baghdad had openly begun to mock the caliph, Sultan Mehmed Reşad, and his armed forces, chanting,

> Reşad, you son of an owl [a bird of misfortune], your armies
> are defeated
> Reşad, you ne'er-do-well, your armies are on the run.[29]

With the towns of the Middle Euphrates growing bolder in their revolt against the Ottomans and the natives of Baghdad increasingly defiant, the Ottomans decided to relaunch their jihad efforts, this time targeting the disaffected Shiite population of Iraq. The Ottoman government played on popular religious enthusiasm by unfurling "the Noble Banner of Ali" to win the support of the Shiites of Iraq for the unpopular war effort.[30]

Ali ibn Abi Talib was the cousin and son-in-law of the Prophet Muhammad and the fourth caliph of Islam. Since the first century of Islam, Shiite Muslims have revered the Caliph Ali and his descendants as the only legitimate leaders of the Muslim community (indeed the word "Shiite" derives from the Arabic name for Ali's supporters, *Shiat Ali*, or the "Party of Ali"). This made Shiites unresponsive to the Sunni Ottoman sultan's decrees as caliph, or spiritual leader of the global Muslim community.

The Ottomans hoped to mobilize the Iraqi Shiite community through its reverence for the Caliph Ali to join the fight against the British invaders.

Towards this end, they engaged in the outright chicanery of parading an impressive flag as a relic endowed with special powers associated with the Caliph (or in Shiite nomenclature, Imam) Ali. Government agents circulated among the shrine cities of Shiite Iraq, describing the banner as a sort of secret weapon that had brought faithful Muslim generals victory over infidels in every battle fought under Imam Ali's standard.

The Noble Banner of Ali was entrusted to a high-ranking Ottoman official who, accompanied by a detachment of cavalry, carried it from Istanbul to Iraq in the autumn of 1915. It was rumoured that the delegation distributed gold to secure the support of the more materialist Bedouin tribal leaders along the way. The delegation went first to the city of Najaf, burial place of Imam Ali and the political centre of Shiite Iraq. Revolt had first broken out there against the government in May 1915. The Ottomans planned to unfurl the banner over the mosque in which Imam Ali is buried, in Muharram, the holiest month of the Islamic calendar to Shiites.

The banner was revealed to enthusiastic crowds in Najaf on the eleventh day of Muharram, which corresponded with 19 November on the Western calendar. Shiite notables waxed eloquent on the renewed call for jihad against the British infidels, or "worshippers of the cross"—a reference not just to the British soldiers' Christian faith but to the medieval wars of the Crusades that had pitted Christians against Muslims in the eastern Mediterranean.

The fortunes of war favoured the myth of the banner. In the ten days it took for the flag to travel from Najaf to Baghdad, the Ottoman army achieved its first victory against the British. The deputy governor in Baghdad was quick to draw the connection in his speech to the townspeople who turned out to welcome the mystical flag. "No sooner had this Noble Banner left Najaf than the enemy was brought to a halt and failed in his grand attack on Salman Pak," Shafiq Bey intoned, and the crowd roared its approval. The anxious citizens of Baghdad took comfort in the Ottoman army driving the British away from their city and dared to hope for victory—even if it took divine intervention.

WHILE THE AUTHORITIES RAISED THE NOBLE BANNER OF ALI IN IRAQ, a group of Ottoman officers had resumed their jihad in the Libyan Desert. In May 1915, Italy had entered the Great War in alliance with the Entente

Powers. The Young Turks seized the opportunity to subvert Italy's precarious position in Libya, which the Ottomans had been forced to cede in 1912. By promoting religious extremism in the frontier zone between Libya and Egypt, the Ottomans and their German allies hoped to undermine both Britain and Italy through their North African colonies. Their partner in jihad was the head of the Sanussi religious fraternity, Sayyid Ahmad al-Sharif al-Sanussi.[31]

Sayyid Ahmad had led Sanussi forces in the Italian-Turkish War of 1911. The Sanussi order was a powerful Sufi (or mystical Islamic) brotherhood based in Libya, with a network of lodges across North Africa and a membership spanning the Arab world. Leader of the Sanussi brotherhood since 1902, Sayyid Ahmad had continued the fight against the Italians even after the Ottomans ceded Libya to Rome's rule in 1912. His standing as head of a transnational Muslim mystical order and his reputation for fighting foreign invaders made Sayyid Ahmad a powerful partner for the Ottoman jihad effort.

In January 1915, two influential Ottoman officers set out on the perilous journey from Istanbul to Libya. The head of mission was Nuri Bey, brother of the minister of war, Enver Pasha. He was accompanied by Jafar al-Askari, a native of the northern Iraqi city of Mosul. A graduate of the Ottoman military academy who completed his training in Berlin, Askari was also a founding member of the Mosul branch of the secret Arabist society al-Ahd. Like many of his Arabist fellow officers, he was a staunch opponent of the British and French in their quest to conquer and carve up the Ottoman and Arab lands. He would defend Ottoman territory against European encroachment, but he would also defend Arab rights against Turkish domination. Jafar al-Askari was comfortable with his mission to assist the Sanussi.

Nuri and Jafar went first to Athens, where they purchased a small steamship and a quantity of arms to take with them to Libya. To elude enemy warships in the eastern Mediterranean, they made their way to Crete to await favourable conditions for a dash to the Libyan coast. They instructed their skipper to convey them to an isolated stretch of beach between the Libyan town of Tobruk and the Egyptian border town of Sallum. They landed in February 1915 at a point on the Libyan coast some twenty miles from the Egyptian frontier and immediately made contact with Sayyid Ahmad.[32]

The Ottoman officers found the Sanussi leader preoccupied with a difficult balancing act. On the one hand, he needed to preserve good relations with the British in Egypt to keep open the only supply route for his movement, which was hemmed in by Italian enemies to the west and the French in Chad to the south. The British openly courted Sayyid Ahmad to keep the peace on Egypt's western frontier. Yet the Ottomans were there to remind him of his duty, as an influential Muslim leader, to promote jihad against foreign invaders. "There is no doubt that in his heart he favored the Ottomans," Jafar al-Askari claimed, "but it always proved impossible to dispel that Arab leader's general mood of gloom, suspicion and apprehension."

The Sanussi tribesmen made for a highly irregular army. Some were organized along tribal lines. Others were drawn from theology schools, including the four-hundred-man elite Muhafiziyya corps of religious scholars who served as Sayyid Ahmad's bodyguard. "Their constant recital of the Qur'an in a loud, low throaty drone through their period of guard duty presented an awesome spectacle of piety which deeply struck everyone who witnessed it," Jafar al-Askari recalled. It was up to him, along with some twenty Arab and Turkish officers, to organize these irregulars into a standard military force before unleashing them against the British in western Egypt. In light of their battlefield performance, even the British would later acknowledge that Askari "was an excellent trainer of men".[33]

After months in eastern Libya, the Ottoman commanders were impatient for the Sanussi to launch an attack. Frustrated by Sayyid Ahmad's indecisiveness, Nuri Bey prompted some of the Sanussi leader's subalterns to lead a raid on British positions in late November 1915. Sayyid Ahmad was furious that his officers had acted without his authority, but the Ottomans were delighted when, on 22 November, the Sanussi attacks drove the British into retreat. The British abandoned their frontier posts at Sallum to fall back to Marsa Matruh, 120 miles to the east.

The Sanussi movement gained momentum as Bedouin of the Awlad Ali tribe joined in the attack on British positions. A detachment of the Egyptian Camel Corps crossed lines to join the growing Arab movement against the British. Fourteen native officers of the Egyptian coastguard and 120 men deserted to the Sanussi cause with their arms, equipment, and transport camels. Following these defections, the British withdrew Egyptian artillery units of "doubtful" loyalty from Marsa Matruh as a precaution. These developments encouraged Ottoman aspirations to provoke a broader Egyptian uprising against the British and raised morale among the Sanussi fighters.

The British moved quickly to contain the threat posed by the Sanussi jihad. Some 1,400 British, Australian, New Zealand, and Indian troops were dispatched to Marsa Matruh to serve in the newly formed Western Frontier Force, reinforced by artillery, armoured cars, and aircraft. Their mission was to re-establish British control over the Libyan frontier and to prevent Sayyid Ahmad from inciting a broader revolt in Egypt and the Arab world in the dangerous month of December 1915, when the British were feeling particularly vulnerable in both Gallipoli and Mesopotamia.

On 11 December, units of the Western Frontier Force set out from Marsa Matruh to attack Arab forces encamped sixteen miles to the west. As the British infantry drew within range of their guns, the Sanussi opened fired, pinning the foot soldiers down until their artillery and cavalry could relieve them. The fighting went on for two days, the Arabs attacking with great discipline. Scattered by accurate cannon fire, the tribesmen were finally driven back by the Australian Light Horse on 13 December. Both sides suffered relatively light losses in their first skirmish, though the head of British intelligence for the Western Frontier Force was killed.[34]

The British launched a second surprise attack on Sanussi positions at dawn on Christmas Day 1915. The sudden appearance of enemy forces provoked panic among the Arab tribesmen. By the time Jafar al-Askari reached the front, he found his soldiers, in his words, "retreating in a manner suggesting more a rout than an orderly withdrawal". Working to re-establish discipline in his lines, Askari made a grim assessment of the situation at sunrise: "I could see that our position was surrounded by the enemy on all sides." He could make out two infantry battalions approaching from the west, a large cavalry force on his right flank, and a large column marching down the road from Marsa Matruh in his general direction, while a British warship moored in the bay fired with increasing accuracy on Arab positions. "It was a thoroughly terrifying sight," Askari confessed, "and I had the greatest difficulty in keeping the men in their positions."

In a day of intense fighting, the British drove Arab forces into retreat from their hilltop positions. Jafar al-Askari narrowly escaped capture, though the New Zealanders seized his tent and all of his papers. "At sunset we beat a retreat," Askari recorded, "abandoning our dead and wounded to the mercy of the enemy, having exhausted or lost all our food and ammunition." The defeat took its toll on the Arab fighters' morale, and the Ottoman officers recorded a "steady trickle of desertions".

The British had secured victory, but they had yet to destroy the Sanussi army, which had grown to some 5,000 men. With his Arab tribesmen in possession of the coastline from Sallum to the British garrison town of Marsa Matruh, Sayyid Ahmad enjoyed some significant advantages. German submarines plied the Libyan and Egyptian coastlines, providing guns, ammunition, and cash to the Ottoman officers advising the Libyan campaign. Moreover, news of the British evacuation from Gallipoli and reversals in Mesopotamia had many in Egypt looking to the Sanussi uprising with hope for deliverance from a hated British colonial order.

BRITISH WAR PLANNERS WERE FAR MORE CONCERNED ABOUT THE reversals they had suffered in Mesopotamia than the challenges posed by a handful of Sanussi zealots in Egypt's Western Desert. The unbeaten 6th Poona Division had been turned back at Salman Pak and driven into a retreat under fire. And the British commanders in Mesopotamia lacked the forces to protect Townshend's defeated army. Until the promised reinforcements reached Basra, the British barely had enough troops to hold the towns they had occupied in the first year of campaigning.

After a relentless week of marching under fire, the weary Indian and British soldiers filed into the familiar streets of Kut al-Amara on 2 December. Situated in a horseshoe bend of the Tigris, Kut was a prosperous town, the centre of the local grain trade with an international commerce in liquorice root. Its mud-brick courtyard houses stood several stories tall, with intricate carved wooden decorations. Among its larger public buildings were government offices, two mosques, one with a fine minaret, and a large covered market that the British requisitioned to serve as a military hospital. A mud-brick fortress dominating the river to the north-east of the town became the cornerstone of the British line of defence stretching across the neck of the peninsula on the left bank of the Tigris.

Some of Townshend's officers questioned the wisdom of retiring to Kut. Given its location, the town was certain to be surrounded and besieged by the Ottomans. This placed not just the Indian army but the civilian population of Kut in mortal danger. While the townspeople had surrendered to the British without a fight, their cooperation could not be relied on in a prolonged siege. Weighing the alternatives of expelling the civilians, with the ensuing humanitarian crisis of making 7,000 townspeople homeless, and forcing the residents to share the hardships of a siege, Townshend and his commanders decided that leaving the residents of Kut in their homes would be the lesser of two evils. Events were to prove them wrong.

Townshend accepted the inevitability of a siege, believing it would be of short duration. The survivors of Salman Pak, combined with the garrison at Kut, gave Townshend a force of 11,600 combatants and 3,350 non-combatants, with sixty days' rations. He was confident that his troops could withstand a few weeks of siege until the promised reinforcements reached Mesopotamia in January to relieve his position and resume the conquest of Iraq.

The Turkish advance guard reached Kut on 5 December. Nurettin Pasha's forces began to take up positions around the town. By 8 December, Kut was encircled. The Ottomans, after a year of losing ground to the Anglo-Indian army in Mesopotamia, had turned the tide of battle. With the Noble Banner of Ali flying over the Tigris, the Ottoman army sensed victory was within reach.

TEN

The Siege of Kut

FROM THE MOMENT THE YOUNG TURKS ENTERED THE GREAT WAR, THE British had viewed the Ottomans as the weakest link in the Central Powers' chain of command. War planners in Whitehall had counted on a quick defeat of the Ottoman Empire for the breakthrough that had eluded Entente forces on the western front. Little in the Ottoman army's performance in the first six months of the war challenged these views. Allied shipping attacked Ottoman coastlines with impunity, the British secured control over Basra Province with relative ease, and the campaigns the Ottomans chose to launch, in the Caucasus and Sinai, had ended in abject failure.

The Dardanelles campaign proved a major turning point. The Turks held their ground under relentless Allied pressure and forced the invaders into a humiliating evacuation. Suddenly, the British were on the defensive and forced to cede territory to Ottoman initiatives. Turkish forces had invaded the British protectorate in South Yemen and posed a threat to the vital port of Aden. Libyan tribesmen, commanded by Ottoman officers, had overrun Egypt's western frontier, forcing the British to cede over 120 miles of coastline. And in Mesopotamia, Nurettin Bey had cornered an entire British division in Kut al-Amara.

None of these Ottoman attacks posed a significant threat to Allied war efforts in their own right. The British were confident they would ultimately prevail over Arab tribesmen in Yemen and Egypt's Western Desert. They viewed the siege of Kut as an unfortunate delay in the inevitable conquest of Baghdad. Of far greater concern to the British was how defeat in Gallipoli and setbacks in Yemen, Libya, and Mesopotamia played on public opinion across the Muslim world. They believed that German propagandists work-ing across the Middle East and South Asia exploited each Ottoman victory. They feared confronting religious fanaticism at the front and Muslim upris-ings in the colonies. In this sense, the British and Germans had themselves proven more responsive to the caliph's call to jihad than had his Ottoman subjects or Muslims across the Middle East, North Africa, and South Asia.[1]

To put the risk of jihad to rest, the British believed they needed to reas-sert their dominance over the Ottomans—by regaining lost territory, reliev-ing the troops in Kut, and resuming their conquests in Ottoman lands. The Turks had to be denied any further victories at all costs.

And yet there were real limits to what the British, faced with the relent-less attrition on the western front, could commit to the Ottoman front. In February 1916, Germany unleashed a major new offensive against French positions at Verdun. The German chief of general staff, General Erich von Falkenhayn, embarked on what he termed a "war of attrition," not so much to take Verdun as to bleed the French army to death in defence of the posi-tion. Enduring heavy artillery bombardment that reached up to forty shells per minute in some sectors, the French withstood the German offensive for ten months. By the time the Germans abandoned their assault in Decem-ber 1916, they had suffered nearly as many casualties (337,000 dead and wounded) as the French (377,000 dead and wounded). The British needed to preserve numbers on the western front to reinforce their French allies and deny the Germans the critical breakthrough that would win them the war.

The dilemma confronting war planners in Paris and London was how to balance the deployment of forces to deny the Ottomans a major victory that might blow life into the jihad effort without drawing troops from the life-and-death struggle on the western front. In the relief of Kut, they simply got the balance wrong.

The dangers of life under siege were immediately apparent to the defenders in Kut al-Amara, who must have felt like the proverbial fish in a barrel. "The Turks set about drenching the place with shells," G. L. Heawood, a junior officer attached to the Oxfordshire and Buckingham-shire Light Infantry recalled, "and when they got closer they swept all the flat ground with machine gun fire; from this day the river bank sniping also got serious." As the British struggled to deepen their trenches against the relentless fire, the Ottomans drove their saps ever closer to the British lines. "During these early weeks the Turks made no actual assault, but they got up very close, and we had some rather anxious nights," Heawood confessed, as Turkish lines reached to within one hundred yards of British positions.[2]

Field Marshal Colmar Freiherr von der Goltz, the German commander of the Ottoman Sixth Army, visited the front at Kut and met with Nurettin Bey to discuss strategy. The two commanders disagreed fundamentally. Nurettin, ever the fighting general, wanted to storm Kut and defeat the British outright. Goltz, determined to preserve his forces from needless losses, argued for a tightening of the siege to starve the British into surrender. As the two were unable to resolve their differences, Nurettin waited until Goltz left to inspect the Persian front before sending his troops into battle.[3]

The Ottoman commander launched his attack on Kut on Christmas Eve. Artillery blew great holes in the mud-brick walls of the fortress as British and Indian troops struggled to repel waves of determined Turkish infantry charging their trenches. Heawood's unit faced the brunt of the Turkish offensive: "After dusk they kept assaulting and bombing all through the night. . . . They had obtained a footing in one bastion of the Fort, and a temporary barricade had been built up out of hay bales, store tins, flour bags, and everything that could be got handily. The enemy were on one side and our people on the other and bombing at this barricade went on most of the night and all the heavier casualties of Christmas were here." The casualties were heavy on both sides, but as was so often the case in the Great War, the attackers suffered the most. As dawn broke over Kut on Christmas morning, the Turkish dead and wounded lay in piles stretching from the British trenches back to the Ottoman lines. Many of the British survivors wrote of their attempts to assist the Turkish wounded pinned down by the gunfire between enemy lines. In the end, they threw bread and water bottles to those soldiers within range and suffered the groans of the injured until, with time, death brought silence to the terrible battlefield. Weeks later, many of the Ottoman dead still lay where they had fallen on Christmas Eve.

After the battle of 24 December, Nurettin Bey made no further efforts to storm British positions. Falling in line with Goltz's strategy, he ordered a tightening of the siege instead, cutting Kut off from all supply lines and subjecting the fortified areas to sustained artillery, machine-gun, and sniper fire. Yet when Goltz returned from the Persian front, he was appalled at the losses the Ottomans had sustained in the Christmas Eve assault and set in motion Nurettin's reassignment to the Caucasus front. He was replaced in early January by the well-connected Halil Bey, a cousin of Enver Pasha, the minister of war.

The British too had suffered casualties in the Christmas Eve attack, and the commander in Kut, General Charles Townshend, questioned how long he could withstand such a siege. On the experience of his first weeks in Kut, the British commander calculated that daily losses in excess of seventy-five dead, wounded, or sick would reduce his army from its current strength of 7,800 to 6,600 effectives by 1 January and to only 5,400 by 15 January. Still in contact with headquarters by wireless telegraph, Townshend convinced his superiors of the need for swift action to relieve his army while it was still strong enough to contribute to its deliverance.[4]

British reinforcements were already gathering in Mesopotamia. The first to arrive was General George Younghusband's 28th Brigade. Leaving Aden secure from further Ottoman attacks, Younghusband's brigade was more urgently needed to address the crisis in Mesopotamia. They disembarked in Basra on 2 December. The new commander of the relief force, Lieutenant General Sir Fenton Aylmer, arrived that same week. General John Nixon, commander of the Mesopotamian Expeditionary Force (MEF), gave Aylmer his orders on 8 December: to defeat the Ottomans on the Tigris and relieve Townshend at Kut. There was no longer any consideration of conquering Baghdad.

With two divisions of the Indian army en route from France to Mesopotamia, Aylmer was confident that by February 1916 he would have the manpower to achieve his objectives. Yet the besieged Townshend did not believe he could wait until February for relief. With each passing week, he saw his strength reduced while the Ottoman army enjoyed steady reinforcement. Time was of the essence; it was imperative to strike before the Indian army in Kut was overwhelmed by superior Ottoman forces.

Mindful of the political consequences of a defeat in Mesopotamia so soon after the failure in Gallipoli, the British high command came to share Townshend's fears. With only three brigades at his disposal—some 12,000 men in all—Aylmer ordered General Younghusband to advance against Ottoman positions on the Tigris on 3 January 1916. Younghusband, dismayed at having to engage the Ottomans before the relief force was at full strength, later declared in his memoirs that his orders had been "a very grave mistake.

This premature advance was responsible for all the tragedies which followed each other during the next four months."[5]

THE OTTOMAN ARMY HAD ESTABLISHED SEVERAL LINES OF DEFENCE between Aylmer's relief column and Townshend's forces in Kut. Two Ottoman divisions had been sent to reinforce the garrison in Baghdad. By January 1916, the Sixth Army enjoyed numerical superiority over British forces on the Tigris—by British estimates, the Turks had around 27,000 soldiers in the field, whereas the combined forces of Aylmer's relief column and Townshend's besieged units did not exceed 23,000 men. If the British were confident of victory, it was only because they continued to underestimate their enemy.

Aylmer's relief force first engaged the Ottomans on 7 January near the village of Shaykh Saad, some twenty-five miles downstream from Kut. The Turkish trenches extended for miles on either side of the river, forcing the British to make frontal attacks over flat ground under heavy and accurate rifle, machine-gun, and artillery fire. The British suffered over 4,000 casualties before taking the Turkish trenches in four days of intense fighting. Despite their losses, the British claimed victory and set up their base camp in Shaykh Saad. Aylmer telegraphed General Townshend in Kut, who retained telegraphic communications with the outside world throughout the siege, to announce that the relief column was advancing on both sides of the Tigris. After thirty-five days under siege, this news caused "great rejoicings" among the soldiers trapped at Kut, noted army chaplain Reverend Harold Spooner in his diary.[6]

Four days later, Aylmer's forces engaged the Ottomans at a tributary of the Tigris known as al-Wadi. Fighting in heavy rain and strong winds, the British forces succeeded in driving the Ottomans back a second time. The British lost over 1,600 men, dead and wounded, reducing Aylmer's column to just 9,000 men. Still they pressed on to face the most formidable Ottoman positions yet at Hanna, a narrow stretch of land between impassable swamps and the Tigris.

On 21 January, Aylmer ordered his troops into a frontal assault across open ground on well-entrenched Ottoman positions. The attackers slipped and stumbled in the slick of mud left by days of heavy rain, facing intense Turkish gunfire without so much as a shrub for cover. For the first time in the Mesopotamia campaign, the British suffered higher casualties than they were able to inflict. After two days of battle, they had no choice but to give up and retreat from "the Hannah position of hideous memory", in General Younghusband's words. Having failed in his first bid to relieve Kut, General Aylmer was forced to wait for further reinforcements to rebuild his depleted ranks before making a second attempt.[7]

"I fear it looks as though our relieving force are not strong enough to push through and are digging themselves in . . . and awaiting reinforcements," Reverend Spooner noted in his diary in Kut on 23 January. After hopes of imminent relief, the troops had to come to terms with several more weeks of withstanding the siege. "Bad look out as no doubt the Turks will be heavily reinforced by then," Spooner predicted, "but are we downhearted? No-o-o-o," he concluded in best British tradition.

The rainclouds that had so hindered Aylmer's relief operations had a silver lining. The downpour had swelled the Tigris, flooding both the Turkish and British front-line trenches at Kut and forcing both sides to withdraw to positions separated by as much as 2,000 yards of water. The damp conditions caused misery all around but ruled out any Turkish assaults or surprise attacks until the water level had fallen again. Townshend's challenge was to preserve his force in fighting trim until the river had receded and the relief column arrived.

Townshend's first priority was to reduce his forces' consumption. On 22 January, he ordered all rations cut by half. These restrictions applied to the 6,000 townspeople of Kut as well as to his forces, for all mouths had to be fed from the same limited supplies. He then ordered British troops to conduct a house-by-house search to requisition food stores. The soldiers uncovered nine hundred tons of barley, one hundred tons of wheat, and nineteen tons of cooking butter, or ghee. Though the searches outraged the civilians of Kut, the requisitioned supplies, when combined with British stores and served in half rations to soldiers and townspeople alike, extended the food supply from twenty-two to eighty-four days.[8]

The cut in their food rations was but the latest hardship inflicted on the residents of Kut. Their shops in the covered market had been commandeered to provide a hospital for sick and wounded soldiers. Their homes were constantly violated, as British soldiers knocked holes through their walls to provide safe passages protected from gunfire and stripped the woodwork from their houses for firewood. Civilians were exposed to the same lethal gunfire as the soldiers, rendering daily chores life-threatening. Reverend Spooner witnessed the desperate grief of the townspeople mourning a woman shot dead while fetching water from the river. The poor woman was but one of nearly nine hundred civilian casualties of the siege.

The natives of Kut were trapped between the British, who suspected them of passing intelligence to the Ottomans, and the Turks, who considered them collaborators for harbouring the British in their town. The besieging Turks fired on any civilians who tried to flee Kut. The Ottomans had only one use for the townspeople: as mouths hastening the depletion of the British army's finite provisions.

Rationing imposed differential hardships on the British and Indian soldiers in Kut. The Hindu soldiers were vegetarians who, for reasons of both religion and taste, refused the meat ration that supplemented the increasingly reduced bread and vegetable supplies. The Muslim soldiers also refused meat as the British exhausted the supply of beef and lamb and began to slaughter their work horses and mules to feed the troops. Townshend initially preserved a higher flour and vegetable ration for his Indian troops, while soliciting dispensation from both Hindu and Muslim religious authorities in India to permit his soldiers to eat the meat ration. Yet the reduced rations took their toll. With fewer calories in their daily diet, Indian soldiers suffered the effects of exposure to the cold and damp, took ill, and died in greater numbers than the carnivorous British soldiers.

The Ottomans continued to play on the racial divisions in Townshend's army. British soldiers found thousands of the propaganda leaflets turned out by the government press in Baghdad, printed in Hindi and Urdu, when exploring the front-line Turkish trenches abandoned by flooding. According to Reverend Spooner, these leaflets were tied to stones to be thrown into the British lines to exhort "native troops to kill their officers (English), mutiny and come over to the Turks and be under the protection of Allah, telling them they would be far better treated and have more pay".

A small minority of Indian soldiers accepted the Turkish invitation. Already at the end of December, General Townshend was reporting "certain unsatisfactory incidents" among his Indian troops. Other soldiers were more explicit. "Several times during the siege I heard of Indians (Mohammedans) who had left our trenches and deserted to the Turks," British artilleryman W. D. "Gunner" Lee recounted, "but some who were caught in attempting to escape from our lines were shot before their regiments." The evidence suggests that only a small fraction of Indian troops actually crossed over to Ottoman lines—no more than the seventy-two men listed as "missing" by the end of the siege. Yet clearly not all Indians were willing to die for the British Empire.[9]

WHILE BRITISH FORCES STRUGGLED TO RELIEVE THE BESIEGED TROOPS in Kut, the authorities in Egypt still faced a crisis on their western frontier with Libya. In January 1916, Sir John Maxwell, British commander in Egypt, urged the War Office in London to authorize a campaign to regain territory lost to Sanussi forces two months earlier. Reasserting British control over the Western Desert, while not yet a military necessity, he argued, was advisable on political grounds. The evacuation of imperial troops from Gallipoli, combined with Sanussi gains in the Western Desert, had encouraged Egyptian activists to question British strength and resolve.

With London's approval, Maxwell formed the Western Frontier Force to re-establish British control over Egypt's territory up to the Libyan border. Taking advantage of the growing number of imperial troops at his disposal since the evacuation of Gallipoli, Maxwell assembled a large and diverse force of British, Indian, Anzac, and even South African infantry. Combining such modern technology as aerial reconnaissance and armoured cars with horse and camel cavalry better suited for desert sands, the Western Frontier Force employed both traditional and modern war craft.

The Arab tribesmen fighting with Sayyid Ahmad al-Sanussi were trained and led by Ottoman officers under the command of the Minister of War Enver Pasha's brother, Nuri Bey, and the Iraqi Jafar al-Askari. The Ottoman high command had dispatched Nuri and Jafar with clear orders "to penetrate Egyptian territory and sow alarm and confusion there, tying down as many British soldiers as possible in the process". The Ottomans and their German allies saw the religious authority of Sayyid Ahmad, as leader of the Sanussi mystical order, as a distinct asset in the jihad effort. Their successes at the end of 1915 had alarmed the British and enflamed Egyptian nationalists.[10]

In January 1916, Sanussi forces were encamped at Bir Tunis, some twenty miles south-west of the British garrison in Marsa Matruh. Jafar al-Askari knew an attack was imminent when he saw a British airplane fly over his positions. He posted sentries around the Sanussi encampment and instructed them to be vigilant. After torrential rainfall on the night of 22 January, one of Askari's Turkish officers woke him at dawn to warn that "a long enemy column composed of infantry, cavalry, artillery and armoured cars" was advancing towards Sanussi positions. The rains the Turks had cursed overnight proved a blessing: the armoured cars got bogged down in mud and bought the Arab tribesmen a bit of time to prepare.

Fighting raged at Bir Tunis all day on 23 January. The Ottoman-led irregulars surprised the British with their discipline under fire. Nuri led a team of camel-mounted machine-gunners to attack the British right flank, while Jafar al-Askari led an attack on the British cavalry. Sayyid Ahmad, the Sanussi leader, withdrew with most of his guard to a safe position twenty miles further south. The Sanussi front line grew thinner as it extended to over five miles in the course of the day, allowing British forces to break through the Arab army's centre and capture its abandoned encampment. The tents, with all their contents, were put to the torch, but Sayyid Ahmad's army had once again escaped with most of its forces intact.[11]

General Maxwell had ample forces at his disposal to address the Sanussi threat. The Turco-Arab army, on the other hand, was losing numbers the longer the campaign continued. "Our manpower had been much diminished by the rigours we had endured," Jafar al-Askari recalled. "Fighting men would join up or disappear in proportion to the quantity of food and ammunition available. There was no permanent core and nothing to detain these holy warriors if they wanted to leave." As ever, Arab tribesmen made fickle soldiers.

After their retreat from Bir Tunis, Sayyid Ahmad and his Sanussi followers parted company with Nuri and Jafar. The Sanussi fighters went south to occupy the oasis towns of the Western Desert, stretching from Siwa near the Libyan frontier to Farafra and Bahariya, where they were within striking distance of the Nile valley but beyond the reach of British forces. Jafar and Nuri continued their efforts to harry the British along the Mediterranean coastal plain. However, with fewer than 1,200 men and only one quick-firing cannon and three machine guns left at their disposal, the Ottoman-led force posed an ever smaller threat to the growing British army.

The British pursued the retreating Arab army to Aqaqir, fifteen miles south-east of the coastal village of Sidi Barrani. Here, on 26 February, Jafar al-Askari unwittingly made his last stand against the British. As enemy forces surrounded their positions, Nuri withdrew his regular army battalion to avoid capture—he did not consult with Jafar before abandoning him to face the British alone with his small detachment. A courier managed to deliver a message informing the incredulous Jafar of Nuri's withdrawal shortly before he found himself surrounded by British forces.

The ensuing melee was like a scene from the Crimean War: officers charging on horseback, sabres drawn. His right arm disabled by a deep saber wound, Jafar found himself fighting on foot after having his beloved mare shot from beneath him. The British commander, Colonel Hugh Souter, was in turn flung at Jafar's feet when his mount was shot and killed. "Before I was able to make another move," Jafar wrote, "the enemy horsemen were all around me and I had collapsed from heavy loss of blood." Jafar al-Askari was taken prisoner and shown all of the honours due a high-ranking officer.

The Battle of Aqaqir marked the end of the Turco-Sanussi threat to British rule in the Western Desert. The Western Frontier Force advanced unopposed to reclaim the port of Sallum to re-establish the frontier with Libya. "The effect in Egypt was excellent," the authors of the British official history noted, "and the unrest in the Alexandria district [where pro-Sanussi demonstrations had broken out] was greatly diminished." With their prestige restored in the northern coastal region, the British were able to concentrate on securing the western oases. Between March 1916 and February 1917, the British succeeded in driving Sayyid Ahmad and his forces out of the oases one by one.[12]

In Cairo, Jafar al-Askari recovered from his wounds in a military facility attached to the POW camp in Maadi. He was received by the sultan of Egypt, Husayn Kamil, and by the British commander, Sir John Maxwell. He was most surprised to meet many friends and comrades, Arab officers of the Ottoman army taken prisoner in the Mesopotamian and Sinai campaigns. Many of those he met shared his Arabist political leanings, like his old friend and colleague Nuri al-Said, whom the British had captured in Basra. British intelligence placed great stock in exploiting their nationalist aspirations to advance their own war aims.

With the threat of a Sanussi-led jihad in Egypt contained, British war planners were once again free to concentrate on the relief of General Townshend's forces in Kut al-Amara.

AS THE SIEGE WORE ON, THE BELLIGERENTS OCCASIONALLY RELENTED in their hostility. After a particularly hard rainfall, frozen Tommies came out of their flooded trenches to warm up over a game of football, oblivious of the omnipresent threat of Turkish gunfire. Reverend Spooner claimed, "The Turkish snipers became so interested in the game that they stopped sniping and watched" until the Britons finished playing. Another of Spooner's anecdotes captured a rare exchange of trench humour. A Turkish soldier, hard at work on the trenches, occasionally waved his shovel towards British lines, as if to say, "Cheeroh ye British." After watching the Turk make several waves, a British soldier took up his rifle and put a bullet through the taunting spade. "There was no work for some time," Spooner recounted, "when slowly and in a very tired way up came the spade again with a bandage on its head!"[13]

Such lapses in hostilities were an exception to the Ottomans' relentless efforts to tighten the siege of Kut. One morning in mid-February 1916, a low-flying Fokker monoplane circling over the skyline captivated the bored soldiers and townspeople of Kut. "Everybody was interested as it was obviously a very fast machine," Major Alex Anderson recalled. "It circled round the south of the town and then when it had turned north-west again, it was seen to drop something that shone in the sun for a moment—in fact four such things were seen to drop and interest increased." Until this point, aircraft had only been used for aerial surveillance. This was the first time the people in Kut had witnessed an aerial bombardment.

When the high explosive bombs hit the ground, the soldiers were too stunned to react. In the first raid an artillery piece was shattered, and sentries were buried in their trenches. A residence in the village took a direct hit, though astonishingly no one inside was killed. From that day forward, monoplanes (dubbed "Fritz" by the British, who assumed the pilots to be German) made regular air raids on Kut, dropping high-explosive bombs of up to one hundred pounds in weight. One of Fritz's bombs struck the British hospital in the covered bazaar, killing eighteen and wounding thirty. Aerial bombardment added significantly to the tightening of the siege of Kut.[14]

After weeks of relentless gunfire, an unnatural silence fell over Kut on 18 February. The British, confused at first, feared the ceasefire presaged a fresh assault. Only on the following day did they realize that the halt in hostilities reflected the Ottomans' shock on learning of the fall of Erzurum.

THE RUSSIAN CHIEF-OF-STAFF IN THE CAUCASUS, GENERAL NIKOLAI Yudenich, had anticipated the inevitable troop redeployments that would follow the Allied withdrawal from Gallipoli. He predicted Enver would take the opportunity to rebuild the Ottoman Third Army. Each of the eleven divisions guarding the Ottoman Caucasus frontier was under-strength, left to guard hundreds of miles of mountainous terrain. Yudenich decided to strike while the Ottomans were still weak and destroy the Third Army before Enver had the chance to reinforce it.

General Yudenich began planning his campaign in strict secrecy. He shared limited details with his officers on a need-to-know basis and kept his soldiers in total darkness. To divert the attention of both his own soldiers and the Ottomans, he promised lavish celebrations of the Russian Christmas and New Year holidays that, set by the Eastern Orthodox calendar, fell on 7 to 14 January 1916. He also spread rumours of Russian plans to invade Persia to further confuse Ottoman intelligence. This disinformation campaign did the trick, and the Ottomans settled down for the winter, confident that the Russians would not attempt to attack before the spring, by which time they expected to be reinforced to full strength. Turkish commanders no doubt believed the Russians shared their aversion to fighting in the dead of the Caucasus winter after the experience of Sarıkamış in December 1914.[15]

The Russians certainly had learned lessons from Enver's ill-planned Sarıkamış campaign. As part of his war preparation, Yudenich ordered winter uniforms for his infantry. All soldiers were issued fur coats, lined trousers, felt boots, thick shirts, warm gloves, and caps. He even ordered firewood so that each soldier could be issued two short logs as protection from the cold that had killed so many Ottoman soldiers in the barren Caucasian mountains. Crucially, Yudenich had observed how easy it was to surprise an unsuspecting enemy in the dead of winter. Enver had caught the Russians unprepared at Sarıkamış and in the ensuing panic had nearly forced a Russian surrender. Yudenich hoped, through careful preparation and total secrecy, to succeed where the Ottomans had failed.

War came to Köprüköy for the third time as the Russians launched their invasion on 10 January 1916. The Ottomans had driven back tsarist forces here in the opening days of the war in November 1914, and the defeated Third Army had assembled here as it fell back from the failed bid on Sarıkamış in January 1915. The strategic town on the Aras River guarded the eastern entry to Erzurum. Given the concentration of Ottoman troops around Köprüköy, Yudenich opened his campaign with a diversion to the north of the town on 10 January, followed by a second diversionary attack along the Aras on 12 January. The Ottomans fought back with determination, committing five of the nine divisions around Köprüköy to repelling the Russians. This reduced their strength in Köprüköy itself to just four divisions when the Russian general unleashed his main attack on the town on 14 January. The Turks put up a determined defence, but when they faced encirclement, the Ottoman garrison withdrew from Köprüköy on the night of 16 January. Russian troops occupied the town the following day.

The defeat at Köprüköy took a heavy toll on the Ottoman Third Army. Out of an original force of 65,000 on the Caucasus frontier, only 40,000 men completed the retreat to Erzurum. Still, they fell back on positions the Ottomans believed impregnable. Two rings of fortifications—some fifteen modern forts and batteries in all—surrounded the town of Erzurum, protecting it from the east. Moreover, by mid-January Enver had dispatched seven divisions from the Dardanelles to reinforce the Third Army. The first units were expected in Erzurum in early March. The Ottomans were confident of repelling the Russian Caucasus Army in the spring. The Russians were determined to seize Erzurum before the Third Army could be reinforced.[16]

Rather than rush headlong against strong Ottoman positions, Yudenich prepared carefully for the assault on Erzurum. He ordered the road from Köprüköy widened to enable motor vehicles to transport artillery to the front. The Russian railway was extended from Sarıkamış to the pre-war Turkish border at Karaurgan. The Siberian Air Squadron was dispatched to provide aerial reconnaissance for the first time on the Caucasus front. While these preparations were underway, Yudenich and his officers finalized their plans for attack.

Ottoman defences had been built to protect Erzurum from attack from the direction of Köprüköy. Rather than suffer heavy losses trying to force a frontal assault, Yudenich and his officers decided to concentrate on the mountainous terrain to the north of Erzurum, where the Ottomans, relying on the difficult topography, had fewer fortifications. Seizure of four north-eastern fortifications would open the road to Erzurum from the north.

The Russians opened their attack on 11 February with an artillery barrage, followed by night assaults on two of the northernmost fortresses guarding the area around Erzurum. An Armenian officer, Colonel Pirumyan, commanded the attack on the fortress of Dalangöz and took it after hours of violent hand-to-hand battles. The Russians continued their assault the following day, picking off the Ottoman perimeter forts one by one. The defenders began to abandon their positions to fall back onto the town. By 15 February, Russian aerial reconnaissance reported intense movement within Erzurum and the departure of baggage trains heading west. It was clear that, after the shock of the Russian assault, the defences around Erzurum had collapsed, and the Ottomans were in full retreat.

On the morning of 16 February, a Cossack cavalry regiment galloped into Erzurum. The moment captured the imagination of the Russians and their allies after eighteen months of static trench warfare and catastrophic losses on both the western and eastern fronts. Here at last was a moment of glory, of men on horseback driving the enemy into headlong retreat. As Russian forces flooded into the once proud fortress town, they took 5,000 Ottoman soldiers prisoner. Over the next two days, the Russians pursued the retreating Ottomans, taking another 5,000 prisoners. Combined with 10,000 Ottoman casualties and perhaps 10,000 deserters, the Third Army had been reduced to just 25,000 effectives. Yudenich had achieved total success. He had destroyed the Third Army and extended Russian conquest deep into Turkish territory long before Ottoman reinforcements had the time to reach the Caucasus front.

The Russian Caucasus Army took advantage of Ottoman disarray to extend its conquests, taking Muş and Bitlis, near Lake Van, between 16 February and 3 March. The Black Sea port of Rize was captured on 8 March, and Trabzon fell on 18 April. When Turkish reinforcements finally reached eastern Anatolia, they found the Ottoman position in total disarray.

It was little wonder that the Ottoman soldiers in Mesopotamia were shocked into a day of silence when news reached them of the fall of Erzurum. Sobered by the greatest territorial loss the Ottomans had yet suffered in the war, they redoubled their efforts to achieve victory in Kut. Whenever the Turks dealt the British relief force a setback, they posted billboards with large inscriptions in French reading, "Kut is vanquished. Time to go home." The British, not to be outdone, responded with signs of their own: "What price Erzurum? Watch your back."[17]

OVER THE MONTH OF FEBRUARY, WAVES OF REINFORCEMENTS WERE shipped from France to Basra to join the MEF. They arrived piecemeal, often separated from their artillery or horses in the haste of their transport. The chaos of the docks turned Basra into a bottleneck, where units were held up for weeks while sorting their guns and horses before setting off for the front. Inadequate river transport meant that most troops had to march the two hundred miles from Basra to the front line near Kut. In this way, General Aylmer, commander of the British relief force in Mesopotamia, received the two divisions he had been promised to reinforce his depleted ranks—but far too slowly and unevenly to achieve numerical superiority over Turkish forces.

Aylmer faced a difficult decision. Ideally, he would wait until all of his reinforcements had arrived before engaging the Ottomans. However, with each passing week, fresh Ottoman troops were also reinforcing the Sixth Army, while Townshend and his men in Kut grew weaker and sicker due to shortages of food and medicine. Aylmer's dilemma was to pick the optimal moment to strike on the basis of incomplete information about the relative balance of powers. He chose to resume the offensive in early March 1916, as the siege entered its third month. Rather than pick up where he left off on the Tigris, Aylmer proposed a bold surprise attack overland towards the Shatt al-Hai channel to the south of Kut. His target was the high ground of the Dujaila redoubt, the Ottomans' last major defensive point before Kut.

To preserve the crucial element of surprise, Aylmer proposed to march his troops overnight to strike Dujaila at dawn. With the vantage point secured, he hoped to open a safe passage for Townshend's forces from the southern reaches of Kut, across the Tigris, to link up with the relief column. Had Aylmer's troops followed the plan, they might well have succeeded, for the Turkish lines at Dujaila were all but abandoned on the night of 7 March, when the Tigris Corps set off for battle.

But the disoriented British columns, crossing uneven and unfamiliar terrain in the dark, were delayed in their night march. At sunrise on 8 March, the attackers were still 4,000 yards from the Dujaila redoubt. The British commanders assumed the Ottomans would have seen their columns arriving across the flat ground in the early dawn light. Believing his forces had lost the element of surprise, Aylmer feared his men would be exposed to heavy gunfire from the Ottoman lines. The British commander didn't realize that the Turkish trenches in Dujaila were empty, and the Ottomans were totally unprepared to repel an attack.

Aylmer knew from bitter experience how many casualties he risked in storming well-entrenched Ottoman lines over flat ground. He ordered his officers to hold their troops back and subject the Ottoman positions to an intense artillery bombardment to silence Turkish guns before ordering their men to attack. British gunners opened fire at 7:00 a.m. and kept up their bombardment for three hours. Instead of protecting his soldiers from enemy fire, the barrage alerted Ottoman commanders of an imminent attack, and they flooded Dujaila with troops. By the time the British were ordered into battle, the empty trenches at Dujaila had been filled.

Ali Ihsan Bey was the commander of Ottoman forces to the south of Kut. He had arrived from the Caucasus in February 1915 and spent his first month in Mesopotamia drilling his soldiers to fight in this alien new environment. He had gone to bed on 7 March with no reports of unusual enemy activity. He was first advised of the British offensive early the next morning, when one of his battalion commanders informed him of the artillery barrage.

As soon as he realized the gravity of the situation, Ali Ihsan conferred with the commanders of his mountain artillery and machine-gun companies. He showed them the location of British forces on a map. "I told them to answer the enemy artillery and to fire on any enemy troops as they marched" towards Turkish lines. He then gave orders to the commander of the Ottoman 35th Division, a unit made up of conscripts from Iraq whose "discipline, order and training" he doubted. They were instructed to fight to the last man in defence of the hills to the north of Dujaila. "I told them that I would execute anyone who attempted to run away, and knowing of my reputation from the Caucasus front, everyone believed me." He placed his trusted Anatolian soldiers at the very centre of the redoubt, confident that they would hold the line.[18]

Ali Ihsan Bey threw every unit under his command into Dujaila while the British artillery kept up the barrage. "The enemy did not send their infantry forward while their artillery was firing on us," the Ottoman commander noted. "We benefited from this mistake and all of our troops managed to arrive" at the redoubt before the British launched their infantry assault. He expressed his full gratitude to the British generals for giving him three hours to get his men into position.

Abidin Ege, a Gallipoli veteran whose unit had been deployed to Mesopotamia, was in the Ottoman front line when the British infantry began to charge. He watched as thousands of English and Indian soldiers crossed the plain, wondering how he could stop so many attackers with only one battalion. "The distance between us and the enemy was only 800 meters. Both sides started firing and the battle began. The enemy made every effort to reach us, but their forces were melting under the heat of our fire." Turkish casualties were mounting as well—Ege reported "martyrs" falling all around him. Yet they succeeded in holding their lines until reinforcements arrived in the afternoon. By evening, the British could no longer sustain the attack and withdrew. "We had an absolute victory against the enemy," Ege boasted, "yet we lost half of our battalion."[19]

The assault on Dujaila, known to the Turks as the Battle of Sabis Hill, was a crucial victory for the Ottomans. British casualties were nearly three times higher than Ottoman losses. The magnitude of the Ottoman victory proved a great boost to Turkish morale and left the British despairing of ever relieving Townshend and his increasingly weakened army in Kut. Nowhere was this despair felt more acutely than inside Kut itself. "After hearing our heavy guns firing almost unceasingly for 3 days and 3 nights and to hear them getting closer and closer—the forces here all ready to sally forth—the bridge ready for the Sortie etc.," Reverend Spooner confided to his diary, "it was cruel to know our Relieving Force had failed again."[20]

The Ottoman commander, Halil Bey, tried to capitalize on the collapse of the defenders' morale. On 10 March, Halil sent a messenger to General Townshend inviting him to surrender. "You have heroically fulfilled your military duty," Halil wrote in French. "From henceforth, there is no likelihood that you will be relieved. According to your deserters, I believe that you are without food and that diseases are prevalent among your troops. You are free to continue your resistance at Kut, or to surrender to my forces, which are growing larger and larger." Townshend declined Halil's offer, but it made him think. In his report to London, the British commander in Kut asked permission to enter negotiations with the Turks if there was any doubt of his position being relieved by 17 April, when his food supplies would be nearly exhausted.[21]

THE GLOOM SPREAD FROM MESOPOTAMIA TO WHITEHALL. JUST THREE months after the humiliating retreat from Gallipoli, the British faced catastrophic defeat in Iraq. The War Committee's concerns reached far beyond the welfare of Townshend and his soldiers to Britain's position in the Muslim world more generally. The British government feared that Ottoman victories risked provoking pan-Islamic revolts in India and the Arab world. In their bid to forestall disaster, the British cabinet was willing to consider even the most unrealistic of schemes.

Lord Kitchener proposed two measures to secure the release of Townshend and his troops, each more unlikely than the other. Perhaps inspired by the wave of popular rebellions against Ottoman rule in the Middle Euphrates—in the Shiite shrine cities of Najaf, Karbala', and their environs—Kitchener suggested the dispatch of agents provocateurs to stir mass uprisings against the Ottomans to create trouble behind Turkish lines. If the movement grew big enough, Halil Bey might be forced to deploy troops away from Kut to suppress an internal revolt, weakening his lines enough to allow the relief force to break through.

Kitchener's second plan was yet cruder. Convinced of the inherent corruption of Turkish officialdom, he proposed offering a massive bribe to a senior Ottoman commander to turn a blind eye to Townshend's withdrawal from Kut with all of his forces. Kitchener asked British officials in the Cairo Military Intelligence Office to give him their best man for the mission—both to raise a popular rebellion and to bribe an Ottoman commander. With none of the higher officers willing to risk their reputations on such an ill-conceived assignment, the commission fell to a low-ranking intelligence officer, Captain T. E. Lawrence. Lawrence spoke Arabic, had extensive contact with Arab officers of the Ottoman army held in British POW camps in Egypt—including Jafar al-Askari and Nuri al-Said—and had the self-confidence to believe he could succeed in such an improbable mission.[22]

Lawrence sailed from Egypt on 22 March and reached Basra on 5 April. The relief column, under a new commander, General Sir G. F. Gorringe, was about to launch another effort to break through Ottoman lines that would meet with no more success than the previous attempts. Lawrence knew he had little time to launch an Arab revolt if it was to have any influence on the relief of Kut. After briefings with the British intelligence officers in Iraq, including Sir Percy Cox and Gertrude Bell, Lawrence arranged meetings with influential Arabists in Basra. His first appointment was with Sulayman Faydi.

Sulayman Faydi, a noted Arabist and former member of the Ottoman parliament from Basra, had worked closely with Basra's leading political notable, al-Sayyid Talib al-Naqib, and had accompanied Sayyid Talib on his ill-fated mission to secure Ibn Saud's support for the Ottoman war effort in October and November 1914. After accompanying Sayyid Talib to Kuwait, where he surrendered to the British and was exiled to India, Faydi returned to Basra to live under British occupation. Cut off from the Ottoman world and his former Arabist friends and colleagues, Faydi opened a small business and turned his back on politics.[23]

Before heading to Iraq, Lawrence had met with Nuri al-Said and other Ottoman prisoners in Cairo known to have Arabist political leanings. When Lawrence asked members of the secret Arabist society al-Ahd to suggest people he should consult in Iraq, all spoke highly of Faydi. Lawrence took notes. When the two men met, Lawrence was well briefed.

Lawrence arranged to meet with Faydi in the offices of British military intelligence in Basra. The Iraqi was struck by the Briton's good looks and fluent Arabic, spoken with a heavy Cairene accent. Yet everything Lawrence said made Faydi uncomfortable. The English officer knew too much about the Iraqi Arabist for Faydi's peace of mind.[24]

"Forgive me for asking," Faydi ventured, "but have we met before? If so, I cannot recall the occasion."

"No, we have never met before, but I know everything about you and your activities," Lawrence replied.

"How do you know me, and to what activities do you refer?" Faydi parried, nonplussed. Only when Lawrence mentioned his Arabist contacts among Ottoman POWs in Cairo did Faydi understand how the Englishman knew so much about his past.

Lawrence finally came to the point. The Arabs, he argued, wanted their independence from Turkish rule. The British, at war with the Ottoman Empire, wanted to help the Arabs achieve their independence to advance their own war aims against the Ottomans. The British government was willing to provide the guns and the gold to facilitate a popular uprising against the Ottomans in Iraq. "And, given my trust in your abilities," Lawrence concluded, "I want you to organize this revolt."

Faydi was aghast. "You are gravely mistaken, sir, in asking me to undertake this mighty task. I have no influence in Basra, and no tribal backing. No one would follow such an individual." Faydi suggested the exiled Sayyid Talib would be much better for the job. But Lawrence, knowing the British government would never consent to releasing Talib, whom they viewed as a dangerous nationalist, ruled out the suggestion. Moreover, Lawrence had a very short list of potential leaders for an Arab revolt in Iraq. He was determined to win Faydi over to his cause.

After a long and frank exchange, Faydi remained unconvinced by Lawrence's proposal. The only concession that Lawrence could secure was Faydi's agreement to meet with three of his Arabist contacts, former Ottoman officers held prisoner by the British in Basra, to sound out their views before giving his final decision on the Briton's offer. One of the officers was Ali Jawdat, who had been captured by the British on the Euphrates in July 1915.

The Iraqi Arabists spent four hours together, deliberating Lawrence's extraordinary proposition—to mount a tribal revolt against Ottoman rule with British support. They had no reason to trust the British, whose imperial presence in Egypt and India gave little grounds for confidence in Lawrence's claims of a disinterested British policy in Iraq. They had even less reason to trust their fellow Arabs—particularly the Bedouin tribesmen. Jawdat's own experiences of Bedouin treachery in the Euphrates campaign would have made him a most unwilling partner in any project involving Arab tribesmen. By the end of their meeting, the three officers urged Faydi to reject Lawrence's offer in no uncertain terms.

Faydi returned to the British intelligence office to give Lawrence his final refusal. The two parted on amicable terms. In a subsequent report, Lawrence described "Suleiman Feizi" as "too nervous to give any prospect" of leading the proposed revolt. Though Lawrence did not say so in writing, Faydi's refusal put paid to the first of Kitchener's improbable missions—to raise an Arab revolt behind Ottoman lines to draw pressure away from the siege of Kut. Lawrence set off for the front by steamboat the next day, meditating on how best to bribe an Ottoman commander.[25]

THE BRITISH RELIEF FORCE, UNDER THE COMMAND OF GENERAL George Gorringe since Aylmer's failure at Dujaila, resumed the attack on Ottoman positions on 5 April 1916. It drove the Turks back from the narrow defile at Hanna, where Aylmer's troops had been checked in January, only to be stopped by the Ottomans eight miles upstream at Sannaiyat, with heavy losses. The British had to wait another eight days before resuming hostilities, with diminishing confidence of success.

The situation in Kut was growing desperate. The besieged soldiers were beginning to show advanced signs of malnutrition. Their daily bread

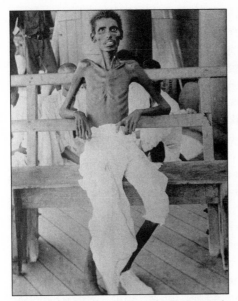

A weakened survivor of the siege of Kut. Hindu and Muslim Indian soldiers who refused horsemeat on religious grounds until the final weeks of the siege nearly starved to death. This emaciated sepoy was photographed after he had been liberated during an exchange of British and Ottoman prisoners.

rations had been cut over the weeks to six ounces, supplemented by one pound of horsemeat per day, which only the British troops accepted. "Poorly and emaciated as the British soldiers are looking," Reverend Spooner noted on 9 April, "the Indian troops are looking far worse." Following the setback to the relief force at Sannaiyat, Townshend cut his rations again to five ounces of bread and meat. By 12 April, the starved Indian soldiers, given formal dispensation by both Hindu and Muslim religious authorities, began to eat horsemeat. General Townshend advised the commanders of the relief force that his food stores would be depleted by 23 April but that he would have enough horses to provide meat until 29 April. After that date, there would be no more food at all.

To buy time for further military operations, the British found innovative ways to deliver food to Kut. Having witnessed the advent of aerial bombardment, the defenders in Kut became the first to receive food aid by airdrop. The effort was condemned to failure by the inclement weather, the weight limits that early aircraft could manage, and the poor aim of the pilots. "Aeroplanes arriving all day dropping supplies," Spooner noted on 16 April. "Seaplanes too but these latter are bad 'droppers' and as often as not their parcels go into the Tigris or into the Turkish trenches!" Abidin Ege, watching from Turkish lines, noted that each airplane carried three sacks of provisions and that aircraft had made drops from morning to evening on 16 April. "Two sacks of flour were dropped into our trenches," he remarked, confirming Spooner's observation about "bad droppers". The planes managed 14 drops that day, but the total of 2,500 pounds of food provided less than five ounces per head for 13,000 soldiers and 6,000 civilians. Airdrops alone would not suffice to save the besieged in Kut.[26]

The relief force mobilized for one last drive on Kut. On 17 April, the British attack on Ottoman positions in Bait Isa was driven back by an overpowering Ottoman counter-attack. Abidin Ege described how the British forces "collapsed" before the Turkish onslaught. "The enemy withdraws and we pursue them. We advanced until we reached the enemy's main trenches." Checked at Bait Isa, the relief force made its final assault on 22 April, with a bloody attack on Ottoman lines at Sannaiyat, some fifteen miles from Kut, that was decisively repelled. By late afternoon, both sides had called a truce to recover their wounded. The recovery operations went on until sundown, as the Turkish and British stretcher-bearers ferried their comrades back to their own lines. It was as though both sides recognized that the time for hostilities had now ended.

In four months of fighting to free the 13,000 troops in Kut, the relief force had suffered over 23,000 casualties. On 22 April, General Gorringe and his officers called a halt to operations. Their exhausted and demoralized troops could do no more.

In a desperate last bid to buy time, the British reinforced a steamship with steel plates to try to run food and medicine through the Ottoman blockade to Kut. Weighed down by her armour and 240 tons of supplies—enough to feed the garrison at Kut for three weeks—the *Julnar* could only manage five knots against the current. Crewed by volunteers, the relief vessel set off at night on 24 April. The defenders in Kut were advised of the vessel's mission and assigned to provide artillery cover against Turkish trenches along the riverbanks where the *Julnar* hoped to pass. The ship never got within reach of Kut's guns. The Ottomans had stretched a cable across the Tigris and the slow-moving *Julnar* was caught like a fish in a net five miles short of her destination.

Major G. L. Heawood was with the artillerymen in Kut waiting for the steamship to arrive. "We heard the running escort of rifle and artillery fire and could eye-follow it up, when it abruptly stopped about four miles to the East, and we soon could guess the worst." The Ottomans took possession of the ship and all its precious stores. The captain was executed, his crew taken prisoner, and Kut's fate sealed.

On 26 April, General Townshend was authorized to enter into negotiation with Halil Bey to agree on the terms of surrender.

THE MONTHS OF WITHSTANDING THE SIEGE HAD TAKEN THEIR TOLL on General Townshend, who was in no state to negotiate surrender with the Turks. "I am ill in body and in mind," he wrote to his commander, General Percy Lake. "I have had my share of responsibility and I consider that you should conduct these negotiations." In fact, none of the British top brass wanted to involve themselves in discussions that were certain to end in an unprecedented humiliation for the British army. Rather than dirty his own hands with the surrender, Lake instructed Townshend to initiate talks with Halil and offered the services of Captain Lawrence from the Cairo Military Intelligence Office and Captain Aubrey Herbert, a brilliant linguist and intelligence officer celebrated for his derring-do.[27]

In his first meeting with Halil on 27 April, Townshend tried to buy his troops' freedom with cash and trophies. If Halil would allow the Anglo-Indian soldiers to withdraw on parole (i.e., pledge not to take up arms against the Ottomans), he would surrender his forty cannons and pay 1 million pounds. The Ottoman commander said he would need to refer the financial offer to Enver, though he made clear his own preference for an unconditional surrender. Townshend returned to Kut discouraged, knowing that Enver and his German advisers craved the total victory more than the cash. "This comes of negotiating with starvation at the gate," he wrote to Lake, trying to convince his superior to take over the discussions. Yet the commander in chief of the MEF refused to get personally involved, offering once again the services of Captains Herbert and Lawrence.

The young intelligence officers set off to meet Halil Bey at dawn on 29 April. Under a white flag, they approached the Turkish trenches, where they waited for hours, chatting amicably with the enemy soldiers. "The Turks showed us their medals, and we were rather chagrined at not being able to match them," Herbert grumbled. Eventually, Lawrence, Herbert, and their superior, Colonel Edward Beach, were blindfolded and taken across Turkish lines to Halil's headquarters. Beach and Herbert were taken on horseback, but Lawrence, who had injured his knee, could not ride and was separated from the others. He arrived after Herbert had already started discussions with the Ottoman commander.[28]

Fluent in French, Herbert spoke for the British delegation. He and Halil had already met at a dance at the British embassy in Istanbul before the war. "He was quite a young man for his position, I suppose about thirty-five, and a fine man to look at—lion-taming eyes, a square chin and a mouth like a trap," Herbert noted. The British began discussions with a plea for clemency for the Arab population of Kut. "I said that the Arabs with Townshend had done what weak people always do: . . . because they feared him, they had given him their service." Halil made clear that the native inhabitants of Kut, as Ottoman subjects, were not a matter of British concern. Ominously, Halil refused to give any assurance that there "would be no hanging or persecution".

Herbert waited until Lawrence arrived to bring the discussion to the terms of Townshend's surrender. The Ottoman commander dashed any hopes the Britons might have held of buying Townshend's way out of Kut. To broach the delicate subject of the bribe, Beach instructed Herbert "to say that we would willingly pay for the maintenance of the civilians and the Arabs of Kut". Given Halil's evident disregard for Kut's townspeople, whom he saw as outright collaborators with the British army, Halil "brushed this [non-starter] aside".

Halil made one request of the British. He asked them to provide ships to transport Townshend and his men to Baghdad. "Otherwise they would have to march," Halil reasoned, "which would be hard on them." Halil promised to return the riverboats to the British as soon as the prisoners had been transferred to Baghdad. Conversing with Herbert and Lawrence in English, Colonel Beach explained that the British did not have enough shipping for their own men and could not possibly agree and that Herbert should simply say that he would refer the matter to General Lake. No doubt Halil or one of the men in his retinue understood sufficient English to grasp Beach's point. If the British demonstrated so little concern for the safe transport of their sick and ailing soldiers, the Ottomans could hardly be expected to evince more.

The Ottoman commander showed temper only once in the course of their negotiations. He had received word that Townshend had ordered all of his artillery destroyed earlier in the day. "Khalil was angry and showed it," Herbert recorded. "He said he had a great admiration for Townshend, but he was obviously disappointed at not getting the guns." It was to be expected that Townshend would prevent his guns from falling into enemy hands to be used against British forces. However, in destroying his cannons, Townshend had denied Halil a trophy, which hardened the Ottoman commander's position.

The junior British officers were in no position to bargain with the victorious Ottoman commander. Once Kitchener's financial inducement had been rejected, Herbert and Lawrence had nothing more to offer. They did not realize that Townshend, having failed in his own attempt to bribe Halil two days earlier, had conceded an unconditional surrender that very morning. Kut was in Ottoman hands; Townshend and his men were already prisoners of war. Halil revealed nothing of these momentous events to his British guests. Recognizing that Captains Lawrence and Herbert had no particular authority and nothing new to put on the table, Halil brought the interview to a close with a yawn. "He apologized and said he had had a lot of work to do," Herbert recorded in his diary. It had been an eventful day for Halil.

THE STARVED AND EMACIATED SOLDIERS IN KUT ASSEMBLED AT MIDDAY on 29 April to face their captors. "So ended the long period of fighting, waiting and hoping, suspense and anxiety, and starving," Major Alex Anderson wrote. "The impossible and unthinkable had happened and one felt stunned." Yet there was some sense of relief mixed with the shock. After 145 days under siege, relentless gunfire, and progressive starvation, the British and Indian soldiers were glad to be at the end of their ordeal. They imagined conditions as prisoners of war could be no worse than what they had already endured.

The depression on the British side was matched by elation in the Turkish lines. "Everyone is smiling with joy and happiness," Abidin Ege, the Gallipoli veteran, recorded in his diary on 29 April. "Today was declared the 'Kut Bayram' [lit., 'Kut Holiday'] and will henceforth be a national holiday." He marvelled at the scale of the Ottoman victory: five generals, four hundred officers, and nearly 13,000 men were taken prisoner. "The English have never faced such a defeat anywhere." Ege's claims were quite accurate. With a loss of 13,309 men in total, Kut was the British army's worst surrender ever: 277 British officers, 204 Indian officers, 2,592 British soldiers, 6,988 Indian soldiers, and 3,248 Indian support staff.[29]

By midday on 29 April, the British and Indian soldiers were impatient for the arrival of the Ottoman troops. At around 1:00 p.m., a great cry went up—"Here they come!"—and everyone scrambled for a view. Gunner Lee, watching from a gun emplacement, saw "columns of them" approach via the ravaged fortress of Kut, "dark masses of troops that appeared to be running. They were some distance from us yet. . . . I was amazed at their eagerness to get to us," Lee wrote. "It was only the sharp commands of their officers that prevented them from running into Kut in disorder."

The Turkish soldiers were quick to fraternize with the men they had fought for so long. They handed out cigarettes to Tommies too weak to smoke them. Gunner Lee used every scrap of language at his disposal—"French, Turkish, Arabic with a little of the 'Cockney' language thrown in"—to try to communicate with his captors. He found that many of the Ottomans he met were veterans of Gallipoli in search of Australians. Perhaps in response to the letters the Anzacs had left in their trenches before evacuating, the Turkish soldiers "seemed anxious to renew their acquaintance with our Colonials with the idea of starting another 'little war'". The officers too got into long conversations with their Turkish counterparts. T. R. Wells, an officer in the Royal Flying Corps, engaged two Turkish officers in conversation from 7:30 p.m. until midnight, "telling many interesting details of recent events".[30]

The end of the siege brought only horror to the townspeople of Kut. Much as Captain Herbert had feared, the Ottomans treated them to summary justice. Reverend Spooner reported that many of those suspected of working with the British were hanged on tripod gallows and "left to be slowly strangled to death. These people were various Jews or Arabs who had interpreted for us, or who the Turks imagined had given us assistance in various ways. Among them were the Sheik of Kut-el-Amara and his sons." Gunner Lee was appalled by "the crying and awful wailing of the Arab women and children" in the days after the Ottoman entry into Kut. By the time the British troops were marched out of the town four days later, one officer claimed, half the town's inhabitants had been shot or hanged, and "the trees were dangling with corpses".[31]

The British and Ottoman commanders agreed to exchange their invalid prisoners. Some 1,100 British sick and wounded were traded for a similar number of Turks. The rest of the POWs were told to gather their belongings and prepare to depart for Baghdad. Common soldiers were allowed two blankets and a change of kit, while officers were allowed as much as two hundred pounds of kit and tents. The officers and remaining invalids not exchanged were placed on steamships for the trip—many on the ill-fated *Julnar*. Due to lack of vessels—and the British unwillingness to provide transport—most common soldiers were forced to march the one hundred miles from Kut to captivity in Baghdad.

The Turkish commandant drew up orders for British officers to read to their men. They were to prepare for a march of several hundred miles through desert country and to carry as little kit as possible. There would be no transport and no protection for stragglers. Those who fell behind would face a terrible death at the hands of the Bedouin Arabs. As Gunner Lee recalled, "Every man there listening realized that he was going to be up against it on this long trek." The officers were then separated from their men. It was a terrible moment for the common soldiers. "Some of the older men were weeping as they marched past us," Colonel L. S. Bell Syer recorded in his diary, "particularly those of the Rajputana, who said that in being taken from the British Officers they were leaving all possible hope of protection."[32]

As the first British prisoners reached Baghdad, they found the city in a festive mood. Talib Mushtaq was a high school student at the time. A native Arab of Iraq, he was an ardent Ottoman patriot who longed to enlist in the army to defend his homeland against invasion. He joined the crowds to watch the British prisoners arrive. "All of Iraq celebrated," he remembered, "and Baghdad was festooned with flags and lanterns and palm leaves." He watched as steamboats carrying prisoners tied up along the riverbank. "I easily scaled one of these ships and saw for myself those unfortunate prisoners who had fought against people for whom they had no enmity." He went up to an English sergeant he found on deck, "gaunt and exhausted, his body emaciated by the effects of hunger after months under siege in the town of Kut". Though Mushtaq spoke no English, he found the sergeant spoke a few words of Arabic.

"How are you?" Mushtaq asked.

"Fine, fine," the Englishman replied in Arabic.

"How did you find the Turkish army?" Mushtaq continued.

"The English bang . . . bang stronger, but no bread," the man replied in broken Arabic.

"I understood what he was trying to say," Mushtaq added, "that the English had stronger weapons and artillery, but that they were forced to surrender because they had run out of food."[33]

In Baghdad, the prisoners were sorted by rank and ethnicity. Enver Pasha came to review them and gave them a promise that would soon become notorious. "Your troubles are over now, my dears," he reassured the weak and hungry prisoners. "You will be treated as the honoured guests of the Sultan." It soon became apparent that the sultan drew clear distinctions among his guests.[34]

Indian Muslim officers received the best treatment. They were separated from their British and Hindu colleagues, housed in the most comfortable accommodation, given fine food and cigarettes, and taken to the city's mosques for prayer. "The Turks seem to be getting at them," Colonel Bell Syer noted with justified suspicion. Every British Indian officer recruited to serve in the Ottoman army was a propaganda victory for the sultan's jihad.[35]

A related jihad initiative was the battalion of Algerian recruits posted to Baghdad to reinforce the sultan's appeal to colonial Muslims. These North African soldiers had been recruited to serve with the French army on the western front. Taken prisoner by the Germans in Belgium and France, the Algerians had enjoyed special privileges in the Muslim-only POW camp in Zossen-Wünsdorf, near Berlin, known as the Halbmondlager (Crescent Moon Camp). Recruited in Berlin by Turkish officers, some 3,000 North Africans found themselves in Baghdad, encamped near the British POWs. Few soldiers of the Great War could match the experience of these North Africans, who had served with both the Entente and the Central Powers in Africa, Europe, and Asia.[36]

No sooner were they in Baghdad, however, than many of the North African soldiers questioned their decision to change colours. A number of Algerians called on the American consul in Baghdad to seek his help. "Some say they came on the promise of the Sultan that they would be treated splendidly and that they would fight against 'unbelievers'," Consul Charles Brissel reported, "while others say they were sent here by the Germans. However, they all unite in saying that they were deceived." The American consul could do little for volunteers in Turkish uniform aside from giving them small sums of money. Many were subsequently dispatched to fight against the Russians on the Persian frontier.[37]

Indian Muslim officers received much better treatment than the common North African infantryman—and the consideration paid dividends to the Ottoman jihad effort. In August 1916, the local press in Iraq noted that the sultan had received a group of seventy Indian Muslim officers taken prisoner at Kut. Claiming that the officers were unwilling warriors in "the campaign against the Empire of the Caliph", the sultan returned their swords as a mark of his personal respect. "This imperial favor so affected them," the newspaper reported, "that they all expressed their wish to serve the Empire."

If this story was true, it meant that the Ottomans had succeeded in recruiting nearly all Indian Muslim officers taken prisoner in Kut (only 204 Indian officers, Hindu and Muslim combined, had been captured there).[38]

The 277 British officers were well treated, with privileges in accordance with their rank. Each officer was given a living wage by the Ottoman authorities and allowed a servant to do his shopping and cooking. Accommodation was always basic, but officers had a roof over their heads and a modicum of comforts. When transported from Baghdad to their ultimate place of internment in Anatolia, the officers travelled by rail, steamship, and horseback. In exchange for their word of honour not to attempt to escape (parole, in military parlance), officers enjoyed extensive freedom to move about the towns of their detention. They were even allowed to receive mail and care packages from home.[39]

E. H. Jones, a young lieutenant imprisoned in the central Anatolian town of Yozgat, detailed how British officers filled their days in captivity. "Our chief problem was how to pass the time," he wrote. "We had four-a-side hockey tournaments and (when the Turks allowed) walks, picnics, tobogganing, and ski-ing. For indoor amusement we wrote dramas, gay and serious, melodramas, farces and pantomimes. We had an orchestra of prison-made instruments, a prison-trained male-voice choir and musicians to write the music for them."[40]

The treatment of British officers stands in stark contrast to the brutality meted out to the common soldiers. Their story is less well documented because so few of the "other ranks" survived the death marches to tell their story. Those who lived were reticent about describing the horror they had witnessed. "Of the sufferings and the terrible brutalities endured by the troops on this march or of the awful scenes that we witnessed when marching through the stricken Armenian areas, I will not deal with here," Gunner Lee wrote in the conclusion to his memoir of the siege. Flight Sergeant J. McK. Sloss of the Australian Flying Corps was more forthcoming. "It was a horrible sight to see our boys driven along by rifle-butt and whip. Some of them were beaten until they dropped. One naval brigade man never rose again. If you said anything you were whipped yourself." While marching "the road of death", Sergeant Jerry Long confronted a sympathetic Ottoman officer with his fears: "I told him that our party numbered less than half of the original . . . and we were beginning to think that the policy of the Turkish Government was to have us marched around until we were all dead."[41]

The treatment of the Kut POWs has often been compared to the Armenian death marches—not least by the survivors themselves. They crossed the same forbidding terrain, under Ottoman guards indifferent to their welfare, without any of the primary necessities to survive: water, food, clothing to protect them from the sun, or footwear for walking across such harsh terrain. They were subject to attack by villagers and tribesmen, who fell on stragglers left behind to die on the open road.

Yet the Kut and Armenian death marches were different. The Ottomans drove Armenians across the Syrian Desert in a coordinated policy of extermination. The prisoners of Kut were not slated for killing, but no effort was made to preserve their lives. For the most part, the Ottoman guards seemed to care little if their POWs survived or perished. This indifference is easy to explain. The thousands of sick and starving Britons and Indians who emerged from the siege of Kut were a drain on resources. The Ottomans lacked the means to provide for such a large number of needy prisoners. They were short of medicine and food for their own soldiers and felt no responsibility for the welfare of enemy combatants who, until recently, had been invading their country. Those whose weakened condition left them unfit for service the Ottomans drove to their deaths—and they were in the majority. Of the 2,592 British rank and file led into captivity from Kut, more than 1,700 died in captivity or on the death marches—nearly 70 percent. The figures for Indian "other ranks" are less precise, but no fewer than 2,500 of the 9,300 Indian soldiers and support staff perished in Ottoman captivity.[42]

The survivors from Kut were put to work on the railway line between Anatolia and Baghdad. Indian soldiers were concentrated at the railhead at Ras al-Ayn, while British troopers were sent to work in the tunnels in the Taurus and Amanus Mountains. Work on the railway tunnels had nearly ground to a halt since the Armenians had been rounded up and deported to the killing fields of the Syrian Desert. The Armenian priest Grigoris Balakian encountered a column of British and Indian prisoners from Kut at the Bahçe railway station in the Amanus Mountains in mid-summer 1916.

The first group of two hundred British and Indian soldiers reached Bahçe after nightfall, moving through the darkness like "living ghosts . . . humpbacked, in tatters, covered in dust and reduced to skeletons", recalled Balakian. They called out to Balakian and the other men who met them as they arrived at the worksite. "Are there any Armenians among you?" they asked. "Give us a piece of bread. We haven't had anything to eat for days." The incongruity of the situation was not lost on Balakian and his comrades. "We were dumbfounded that they spoke English . . . that they were British . . . distant friends sharing our fate, asking us for bread. . . . What an irony indeed!"[43]

The men, in no condition when they arrived to undertake hard labour in the tunnels, were given a week's rest to rebuild their strength. During that time, Balakian and his small group of Armenian survivors met and conversed with the British prisoners—fellow travellers in every sense of the word. "When the British officers finished their heartrending stories of desert suffering, they told us, with great compassion, of the frightful scenes [of massacred Armenians] they had witnessed in Der Zor." Balakian concluded that the Ottomans "had treated the British prisoners just as they had treated the many thousands of Armenian deportees—without fear of any subsequent accountability".

THE BURDEN OF ACCOUNTABILITY FELL ON THE BRITISH CABINET AS soon as news of the surrender of Kut reached the British press. Coming so soon after the failure in Gallipoli, the fall of Kut redoubled pressure on the government of Liberal prime minister H. H. Asquith to convene not one but two commissions of enquiry—one on the Dardanelles and the other on Mesopotamia. The Mesopotamia Commission opened proceedings on 21 August 1916. Over the next ten months, it held sixty meetings before producing its report. The resulting document was so damning of both the cabinet and the Government of India that the politicians delayed publication for two months. "I regret to have to say," concluded Lord Curzon, the influential former viceroy of India and member of the War Cabinet, "that a more shocking exposure of official blundering and incompetence has not in my opinion been made, at any rate since the Crimean war."[44]

The report of the Mesopotamia Commission was published on 27 June 1917 and heatedly debated in parliament the following week. The secretary of state for India, Austen Chamberlain, tendered his resignation as a result. Ironically, by the summer of 1917, Baghdad was already in British hands. Yet that delayed victory would not bring back the 40,000 men lost in the mismanaged Mesopotamia campaign up to the fall of Kut. Their sacrifice, like that of the dead and wounded of Gallipoli, had served to lengthen rather than shorten the Great War.

Whatever the consequences in Westminster, the war planners feared the reverberations across the Muslim world of two such great Ottoman victories over the British. In Cairo, the Arab Office was furiously engaged in countering the religious authority of the Ottoman sultan and caliph by promoting a strategic alliance with the next highest religious authority in Ottoman domains and in the Islamic world as a whole: the sharif of Mecca, Husayn ibn Ali of the Hashemite descendants of the Prophet Muhammad.

ELEVEN

The Arab Revolt

THE BRITISH WARTIME ALLIANCE WITH THE SHARIF OF MECCA WOULD be concluded after months of increasingly anxious negotiations, with both sides driven by wartime fears. Sharif Husayn had reason to believe the Young Turks sought his overthrow and possibly his murder. Moreover, to realize his ambitious goal of carving an independent Arab kingdom from Ottoman domains, he needed Great Power support. The British feared their recent string of defeats to the Ottomans would encourage colonial Muslims to rebel against the Entente Powers. War planners in Cairo and Whitehall hoped that an alliance with the custodian of Islam's holiest shrines would neutralize the appeal of the Ottoman sultan-caliph's jihad at a moment when Britain's military credibility was at its lowest point since the start of the war.

AS A CENTURIES-OLD POLITICAL OFFICE, HELD EXCLUSIVELY BY ARAB descendants of the Prophet Muhammad (who were distinguished by the title "sharif"), with authority over Islam's holiest city and the annual Muslim pilgrimage, the amirate of Mecca was a unique institution in the Arab and Islamic worlds. The amirs of Mecca, appointed by the Ottoman ruler, were second in religious authority only to the sultan in his role as caliph. Despite the overtly religious nature of the office, the amirs of Mecca were intensely political men. The Ottomans played on the ambitions of rival branches of the reigning Hashemite dynasty to prevent the incumbent from ever gaining too much independence from Istanbul. A charismatic Arab ruler with religious legitimacy could pose a grave threat to Ottoman rule in Arab lands.[1]

Sharif Husayn was no stranger to Ottoman intrigue. He was born in Istanbul in 1853, where his father was detained at the sultan's pleasure. He moved to the Arabian province of the Hijaz, home to Islam's holiest cites, Mecca and Medina, after his father's death in 1861 to grow up among the Bedouin, as was customary among the sharifs of Mecca. Exiled to Istanbul in his own right in 1893, Sharif Husayn raised his four sons—Ali, Abdullah, Faysal, and Zayd—in the imperial capital in a home overlooking the Bosporus. In the aftermath of the Young Turk Revolution in 1908, Sultan Abdülhamid II named Sharif Husayn to the amirate in order to deny the revolutionary Committee of Union and Progress its first choice for the post. Although he was the compromise candidate, Sharif Husayn managed to survive Abdülhamid II's overthrow in 1909 to entrench his position in Mecca.

With the rise of the triumvirate of Ismail Enver, Ahmed Cemal, and Mehmed Talat in 1913, relations between Sharif Husayn and the Unionists began to deteriorate. From his office in Mecca, the sharif actively resisted Young Turk measures to centralize Ottoman rule in the Hijaz. He obstructed all efforts to apply a new administrative reform law to the province and fought plans to extend the Hijaz Railway from Medina to the seat of the amirate in Mecca. Such measures would undermine the autonomy of the amir of Mecca and, in the case of the railway, hurt the local economy by depriving camel drovers of their fees for transporting Muslim pilgrims between Medina and Mecca. In opposing these Young Turk initiatives, Sharif Husayn knew he was courting dismissal. Yet rather than bow to Istanbul's pressures, the sharif began to consider rebellion. Knowing that Great Britain had given its support to the ruler of Kuwait in 1899 when he sought his independence from the Ottomans, Sharif Husayn dispatched his son Abdullah to Cairo to open discrete negotiations with British officials there.

In February and April 1914, Sharif Abdullah met with Lord Kitchener, then consul general in Egypt, and his Oriental secretary, Ronald Storrs. Abdullah took the opportunity to probe the British position on the deepening tensions between Istanbul and Mecca. "When I asked him to tell me whether, in the event of a rupture, the Sherif could count upon any support from Great Britain," Abdullah recalled, "Kitchener replied negatively, on the plea that British relations with Turkey were friendly and that, in any case, the dispute was an internal matter in which it would not be proper for a foreign Power to intervene." Abdullah was quick to remind Kitchener how friendly relations had not prevented the British from intervening in an internal matter between Kuwait and the Sublime Porte in 1899. The display of wit drew a laugh from Kitchener but not a change of policy, and the consul general rose to take his leave. Yet both Kitchener and Storrs were impressed by Abdullah and would remember his visit months later when, following the outbreak of the Great War, relations with Turkey were no longer so friendly.[2]

In September 1914, the British expected the Ottomans to enter the war on Germany's side at any moment. A venerated Muslim ally would be a great asset in a war against the Ottomans. Storrs suggested to his superiors "that by timely consultation with Mecca we might secure not only the neutrality but the alliance of Arabia in the event of Ottoman aggression". He wrote to Kitchener, who had been recalled to London and appointed minister of war, to suggest renewing contacts with the sharifs of Mecca. Kitchener responded with alacrity, instructing Storrs to send a reliable messenger to Abdullah to ascertain, in the event of an Ottoman declaration of war, if "he and his father and Arabs of the Hejaz would be with us or against us".[3]

Following the Ottoman entry into the war, both the Turks and the British actively courted the loyalty of the amir of Mecca. As he was the highest-ranking Muslim official in the Arab world, the Ottomans sought Sharif Husayn's endorsement of the sultan's jihad. He temporized, pledging his personal support but refusing a public declaration for fear of provoking enemy reprisals. A blockade of Red Sea ports by the Royal Navy, he argued, would cut the vital supply of food to the Hijaz and lead to famine and tribal rebellion. However clever his excuse, Sharif Husayn's refusal created a crisis for the Young Turks. They planted groundless stories in the Ottoman press asserting that Sharif Husayn had "proclaimed the call to Holy War throughout the Hejaz" and that "the tribes are everywhere answering the call". In private, they plotted Sharif Husayn's overthrow.[4]

While the Young Turks pressed Sharif Husayn to support the Ottoman jihad, the British were, in the words of an early Arab nationalist, determined to "rob the call to Holy War of its principal thunderbolt" by striking an agreement with Sharif Husayn themselves. In November 1914, Storrs wrote to Sharif Husayn's son Abdullah in Kitchener's name to secure a tacit alliance: if the sharif and the Arab peoples would give their support to the British war effort, Kitchener pledged Britain's guarantee of Arab independence and protection from external aggression. Sharif Husayn instructed his son to respond that the Hashemites would adopt no policies hostile to Great Britain but that his position not to break with the Ottomans constrained him for the moment.[5]

The Hashemites were as noncommittal with the British as they had been with the Ottomans. Were he to rebel against the Ottomans and fail, Sharif Husayn faced certain death. He needed to assemble sufficient forces to ensure the success of his rebellion. The amir also had to define the ambitions of his movement. Did he wish to secure the autonomy of the Hijaz alone, or did he aspire to lead a greater part of the Arab world? He had to answer these questions before entering into detailed negotiations with the British.

THE BAKRI FAMILY WERE RESPECTED MEMBERS OF THE DAMASCENE notability and old friends of the Hashemite sharifs. When their son Fawzi was drafted into Ottoman service, they used their influence to secure his assignment to the bodyguard of the amir of Mecca. Though he would be far from home, he would be even further from the fatal fronts to which Arab conscripts increasingly were deployed—in the Caucasus, Mesopotamia, and the Dardanelles.

In January 1915, on the eve of Fawzi's departure for the Hijaz, his younger brother Nasib inducted him into the secret Arabist society al-Fatat. Founded in Paris in 1909, al-Fatat had played a key role in organizing the First Arab Congress in 1913. Since then, al-Fatat had returned to Syria, though it was driven underground by Ottoman repression. So secret was the society that the elder brother had been totally unaware of his younger brother's political activities. The young Syrian nationalists entrusted Fawzi with a verbal message for Sharif Husayn that was too dangerous to commit to paper.[6]

Fawzi al-Bakri reached Mecca in the last week of January. He waited until he found himself alone in Sharif Husayn's company to whisper his message into the amir's ear: Nationalist leaders in Syria and Iraq planned to launch a revolt against the Ottomans to attain Arab independence. Many were senior officers in the Ottoman army. Would Sharif Husayn agree to lead their movement, and if so, would he receive a delegation in Mecca to coordinate their efforts? The amir stared out a window and made no response, as though he had not heard the question. The subtle messenger withdrew to allow the elder statesman to ponder the matter in private.

Sharif Husayn of Mecca (ca. 1854–1931). Following an extensive correspondence with British officials in Egypt, Sharif Husayn declared the Arab Revolt on 5 June 1916.

Shortly after Fawzi al-Bakri delivered his message, Sharif Husayn was confronted with incontrovertible evidence of the Young Turks' plots against him. The sharif's retainers had searched a trunk carrying the correspondence of the Ottoman governor of the Hijaz, Vehip Pasha, and discovered government documents outlining plans for Sharif Husayn's overthrow and murder. The revelations forced the sixty-one-year-old ruler of Mecca to reconsider his wartime neutrality. He had to choose between total loyalty to the Ottomans and revolt in alliance with Great Britain. Yet he wanted more information before deciding.

Sharif Husayn dispatched his son Faysal on an information-gathering mission to Damascus and Istanbul. The diplomatic Faysal was the ideal candidate for the commission. A loyal but critical Ottomanist who had served in parliament as a member from the Hijaz, Faysal was known to be a supporter of the empire. Ostensibly, Faysal was to meet with the sultan and the grand vizier to present his father's complaints against Vehip Pasha and the Young Turks' plans for Sharif Husayn's overthrow. The astute Faysal would know by their reaction if his father had a future in the Ottoman system. Yet Faysal's visits to Damascus, on his way to and from the imperial capital, were of equal importance to the amir. He was to make contact with members of the secret Arabist societies to confirm Fawzi al-Bakri's message and assess their preparedness for a revolt.[7]

Faysal reached Damascus in late March 1915 en route to Istanbul. Cemal Pasha, governor general of Syria and commander of the Fourth Army, invited the amir's son to stay in his mansion. Faysal gave his apologies, having already accepted the hospitality of the Bakri family. He spent his days with Ottoman officials, discussing the course of the war. Cemal had recently returned from his failed first bid on the Suez Canal and sought to secure the

Hashemites' support for a second attack. At night, Faysal met with leading members of the Arabist societies in the relative security of the Bakri home.

Convinced he was sympathetic to their cause, the Arabists shared their aspirations with the Meccan prince. They wanted to break with the Ottoman Empire but feared European designs on their territories. France in particular had made no secret of its ambitions in Syria. They wanted assurances of Arab independence before rebelling against the Ottomans. Faysal reciprocated the Arabists' trust by divulging the main lines of the Hashemites' secret negotiations with the British and Kitchener's offer—of British guarantees of Arab independence in return for an alliance against the Ottomans. By the time he resumed his journey to Istanbul, Faysal had been inducted into both the secret military society al-Ahd and the civilian al-Fatat movement. He left the Arab activists to ponder the implications of British support for an Arab revolt against the Ottoman Empire.

In Istanbul, Faysal met with the sultan and his grand vizier, as well as the Young Turk leadership. The mood in the imperial capital was tense in early May 1915. The Allies had secured beachheads in Cape Helles and Anzac Cove, and the state had initiated its first actions against Ottoman Armenians. The Young Turks had only marginally more confidence in Arab loyalties than in the Armenians. Against this background, Faysal presented his father's complaints against the Ottoman governor of the Hijaz.

The Ottoman leaders expressed their regrets for the "misunderstandings" surrounding Vehip Pasha's letters without entirely dismissing the threat to Sharif Husayn's rule. Talat and Enver urged the Hashemites to throw their full support behind the Ottoman war effort. Were the amir of Mecca to endorse the sultan's call for jihad and dispatch his tribal supporters to assist in a new Sinai campaign, his security of life and tenure in Mecca would be ensured. Enver and Talat drafted letters reinforcing these points for Faysal to take back to his father. The young prince left Istanbul in mid-May 1915, with a clear understanding of the Ottoman government's position: Sharif Husayn needed to give his total loyalty or face elimination.

On his return to Damascus, Faysal found the Arabists had been active in his absence. The members of the secret societies believed Lord Kitchener's pledge might provide the necessary assurances of Arab independence to justify a revolt against the Ottomans, but they wanted an unequivocal commitment to specific territory within clearly defined boundaries. They set out their conditions in a document that came to be known as the Damascus Protocol.

The Damascus Protocol set the boundaries of the Arab world within natural frontiers. The northern frontier ran from Mersin on the Cilician coast along the plains at the foot of the Anatolian plateau (defined by towns in southern Turkey today—Adana, Birecik, Urfa, and Mardin) all the way to the Persian border. The eastern boundary followed the Persian-Ottoman frontier down to the waters of the Persian Gulf. The Arabian Sea and Indian Ocean defined the southern boundaries, as the Red Sea and Mediterranean defined the western boundaries. Claiming all of Greater Syria, Mesopotamia, and Arabia, the Arabists were willing to concede the port of Aden to continue under British colonial rule. The Damascus Protocol also called for a special relationship with Britain, defined by a defensive treaty of alliance and "economic preference".[8]

The Arabist leadership authorized Sharif Husayn to negotiate Arab independence with Great Britain along the lines set out in the protocol. If he gained British acceptance of their territorial demands, the Arabists pledged to respond to Sharif Husayn's call for a revolt and to recognize the amir of Mecca as "king of the Arabs" if their revolt were successful. Faysal added the Damascus Protocol to the correspondence he carried from Enver and Talat in Istanbul to take back to his father in Mecca. His mission complete, Faysal returned with all of the information his father needed to decide which cause to back: the Ottoman war effort or the Arab bid for independence.

On Faysal's return to Mecca on 20 June 1915, Sharif Husayn convened his sons in a war council. For a week they weighed the risks of taking sides in the Great War. They decided to put the terms of the protocol to the British authorities in Cairo before making the fateful decision between Ottoman jihad and Arab revolt.

Sharif Husayn's son Abdullah drafted a letter to his contact in Cairo, Oriental Secretary Ronald Storrs. He now claimed to speak on behalf of "the whole of the Arab nation" in seeking British support for Arab independence from Ottoman rule. Yet Abdullah sought reassurances that Britain would accept certain "fundamental propositions" as the basis for negotiating a wartime alliance. In his letter of 14 July 1915, Abdullah reproduced the terms of the Damascus Protocol verbatim and asked "the Government of Great Britain to answer them positively or negatively in a period of thirty days". So began the exchange of proposals collectively known as the Husayn-McMahon Correspondence, which would prove the most sweeping—and controversial—of Britain's wartime agreements for the post-Ottoman Middle East.[9]

WARTIME EXIGENCIES SHAPED THE TERMS AND TIMING OF THE Husayn-McMahon Correspondence. When Abdullah's letter reached Ronald Storrs in July 1915, the British were still confident of defeating the Ottomans in Gallipoli and taking the imperial capital. And the British found the sharif's territorial claims excessive. "His pretensions are in every way exaggerated," Sir Henry McMahon, the British high commissioner in Egypt, wrote to London. Yet the failure of the August offensive in Gallipoli, when the Ottomans withstood the Allied landings in Suvla Bay, forced the British to reconsider their eastern war strategies. The British were keen to keep the door open to Sharif Husayn and his sons and to the tantalizing prospect of a major internal rebellion.[10]

McMahon addressed his response to Abdullah's letter to the amir of Mecca directly. "We have the honour to thank you for your frank expressions of the sincerity of your feeling towards England," he began his letter of 30 August. He reconfirmed Kitchener's earlier pledge of support "for the independence of Arabia and its inhabitants, together with our approval of the Arab Khalifate when it should be proclaimed". He refused, however, to get drawn into discussions of boundaries, arguing that it was "premature to consume our time in discussing such details in the heat of war".

The tone of Sharif Husayn's response to McMahon, dashed off by return post on 9 September, left little doubt of the amir's position. He protested the "ambiguity" and "tone of coldness and hesitation" with which the high commissioner refused to commit on Arab boundaries. He disavowed personal ambition and claimed to speak on behalf of the Arab people as a whole. "I am confident that your Excellency will not doubt that it is not I personally who am demanding of these limits, which include only our race [i.e., the Arabs], but that they are all proposals of the people," Sharif Husayn insisted in his convoluted prose.

Confirmation of the sharif's claims of speaking on behalf of Arab aspirations more widely came from an unlikely source. An Arab lieutenant in the Ottoman army deserted to British lines in Gallipoli in August 1915. A native of the northern Iraqi town of Mosul and a member of al-Ahd, Muhammad Sharif al-Faruqi knew the details of the Damascus Protocol and that the amir of Mecca was in discussion with the high commissioner in Cairo. He confirmed that the Arab officers who were members of secret societies had renounced their loyalty to the Ottoman sultan and sworn allegiance to Sharif Husayn, who would lead them in a revolt to achieve Arab independence. By October, Faruqi had been transferred from a prison camp in the Dardanelles to Cairo for questioning by British intelligence officers. Everything he said convinced the British that Sharif Husayn was in fact the leader of a broad-based Arab movement ready to rise in revolt against the Ottoman Empire.[11]

As the Allies' position in the Dardanelles grew increasingly untenable, British officials in Cairo resumed negotiations with the Hashemites with a new sense of urgency. Evacuation of Gallipoli would deal the Turks a major victory and free whole Ottoman divisions for redeployment to other fronts. Under these circumstances, an agreement with the Hashemites took on added importance. Sir Henry McMahon recognized he would have to respond to the sharif's territorial claims in order to strike a deal. In his letter of 24 October 1915, the high commissioner sought to square British and French interests in the Middle East with the territorial ambitions of the protocol.

The British government's first concern was to preserve its special relations with the Arab shaykhdoms of the Persian Gulf. The rulers of Oman, the Trucial States, Qatar, Bahrain, and Kuwait, as well as Ibn Saud in central and eastern Arabia, were British protégés bound by treaties dating back to the early nineteenth century. Sir Henry McMahon thus pledged his government's support of the sharif's boundaries "without prejudice to our existing treaties with Arab chiefs".

With the Mesopotamia campaign, the British had drawn the Ottoman provinces of Basra and Baghdad into their Persian Gulf sphere of interest. Without staking an explicitly colonial claim to Iraq, Sir Henry asserted that "the established position and interests of Great Britain" necessitated "special administrative arrangements" to secure the provinces of Baghdad and Basra "from foreign aggression, to promote the welfare of the local populations and to safeguard our mutual economic interests"—in essence, the integration of Mesopotamia into Britain's trucial system in the Persian Gulf.

Finally, Sir Henry had to ensure he made no commitments to the Arabs that would contravene prior Anglo-French agreements. In March 1915, the French government had asserted its claim to annex Syria together with the region of the Gulf of Alexandretta and Cilicia up to the Taurus mountain range as part of a post-war settlement, which its British and Russian allies formally recognized. He knew that the full French demands would scuttle any agreement with Sharif Husayn and that any paring down of French claims would provoke the fury of Paris.[12]

Where clarity would prove counterproductive, Sir Henry McMahon opted for obscurity. The high commissioner withheld British recognition of "the two districts of Mersina and Alexandretta and portions of Syria lying to the west of the districts of Damascus, Homs, Hama and Aleppo" from the territory claimed by the Arabs on the spurious grounds that those territories were not "purely Arab". It was a transparent bid to detach Arab territory from British pledges to the sharif that would bedevil future relations between Britain, France, and the Arab world—not least over whether this formula included Palestine among the lands slated for independent Arab rule. Yet such was the commitment the British high commissioner made to Sharif Husayn. "Subject to the above modifications," Sir Henry asserted, "Great Britain is prepared to recognize and support the independence of the Arabs in all the regions within the limits demanded by the Sharif of Mecca."

In subsequent correspondence exchanged between 5 November 1915 and 10 March 1916, Sir Henry McMahon concluded a wartime alliance with Sharif Husayn of Mecca. The weeks that passed between their letters were punctuated by British defeats in both the Dardanelles and Mesopotamia. McMahon's letter of 14 December followed both the British cabinet's decision to evacuate the Suvla and Anzac positions in Gallipoli (7 December) and the beginning of the siege of Kut al-Amara (8 December). The high commissioner's letter of 25 January 1916 followed the final evacuation of Gallipoli (9 January). Unsurprisingly, McMahon's last letter, dated 10 March, noted British victories over the Sanussi tribesmen in Egypt and Russian victories in Erzurum without mentioning the impending surrender at Kut. He must have felt his hand weakened by this string of British defeats.

Knowing that he was negotiating with a beleaguered Britain, Sharif Husayn drove a hard bargain. Instead of seeking recognition of Arab independence, the amir increasingly wrote of an "Arab kingdom" and of himself as its chosen leader. Yet the amir of Mecca consented to significant territorial compromises. He claimed "the Iraqi *vilayets*" as integral parts of the future Arab kingdom but consented to leave "those districts now occupied by the British troops" under British administration for "a short time" in return for "a suitable sum paid as compensation to the Arab Kingdom for the period of occupation".

French claims to Syria were harder for the amir to accept. The Syrian provinces, he insisted, were "purely Arab" and could not be excluded from the Arab kingdom. Yet in the course of their exchange, Sharif Husayn conceded he wished "to avoid what may possibly injure the alliance of Great Britain and France and the agreement made between them during the present wars and calamities". However, he warned McMahon, "at the first opportunity after this war is finished . . . we shall ask you for what we now leave to France in Beirut and its coasts". The remainder of the correspondence focused on the material needs for a revolt: the gold, grain, and guns to sustain the future Arab war effort against the Turks.

Sir Henry McMahon could not have done better. He succeeded in concluding an agreement with the sharif of Mecca excluding Syrian territory claimed by the French and the Iraqi provinces the British wished to retain. The fact that the boundaries of the territories conceded in the Husayn-McMahon Correspondence were vague was an advantage in wartime Anglo-Arab relations. In the interest of Anglo-French relations, though, a more precise agreement on the post-war partition of Arab lands was needed.

THE BRITISH GOVERNMENT WAS BOUND TO SEEK FRENCH AGREEMENT on promises made to Sharif Husayn. The foreign secretary, Sir Edward Grey, had previously recognized France's special interest in Syria. In October 1915, after authorizing McMahon's territorial concessions to Sharif Husayn, the Foreign Office requested that the French government send negotiators to London to put some clearly defined boundaries to French claims in Syria. The French foreign minister designated the former consul general in Beirut, Charles François Georges-Picot, to negotiate with Sir Mark Sykes, Lord Kitchener's Middle East adviser, in drafting a mutually acceptable post-war partition of Arab lands.[13]

The fact that the British and French were dividing amongst themselves lands that Sharif Husayn was claiming for the future Arab kingdom has led many historians to denounce the Sykes-Picot Agreement as an outrageous example of imperial perfidy—none more eloquently than Palestinian historian George Antonius: "The Sykes-Picot Agreement is a shocking document. It is not only the product of greed at its worst, that is to say, of greed allied to suspicion and so leading to stupidity: it also stands out as a startling piece of double-dealing." Yet for Britain and France, whose past imperial rivalries had nearly led them to war, the Sykes-Picot Agreement was an essential exercise for France to define precisely the territories it claimed in Cilicia and Syria and for Britain to stake its claim in Mesopotamia—the lands Sir Henry McMahon tried to exclude from his pledge to Sharif Husayn.[14]

There are many misconceptions about the Sykes-Picot Agreement. A century later, many still believe the agreement set the borders of the modern Middle East. In fact, the map as drawn by Sykes and Picot bears no resemblance to the Middle East today. Instead, it defined areas of colonial domination in Syria and Mesopotamia in which France and Britain were free "to establish such direct or indirect administration or control as they desire[d]".[15]

In the "blue area", France laid claim to the eastern Mediterranean coastline stretching from Mersin and Adana, around the Gulf of Alexandretta and southward through the shores of modern Syria and Lebanon to the ancient port town of Tyre. The French also claimed an extensive part of eastern Anatolia to a point north of Sivas and to the east of Diyarbakır and Mardin—all towns comfortably inside the modern Turkish Republic. In the "red areas", the British secured recognition of their claim to the Iraqi provinces of Basra and Baghdad.

The vast lands between the blue and red areas were divided into separate zones in which Britain and France would exercise informal influence. Zone A placed the major inland cities of Syria—Aleppo, Homs, Hama, and Damascus, as well as the northern Iraqi city of Mosul—under indirect French control. The British claimed informal empire over Zone B, which spanned the deserts of northern Arabia from Iraq to the Sinai frontiers of Egypt. These two zones were to be part of "an independent Arab State or a Confederation of Arab States . . . under the suzerainty of an Arab chief"—a formula that fell well short of Sir Henry McMahon's pledges to Sharif Husayn.

The one area on which the British and French could not agree was Palestine. They could not resolve their conflicting claims and anticipated that Russian ambitions would further complicate negotiations. Sykes and Picot decided to paint the map of Palestine brown, to distinguish it from the red and blue areas, and proposed an "international administration" whose ultimate shape would only be decided in negotiations with Russia, the "other Allies, and the representatives of the Shereef of Mecca"—the only explicit mention of Sharif Husayn in the Sykes-Picot Agreement.

In March 1916, Sykes and Picot travelled to Russia to secure their Entente ally's agreement to their partition plan. In addition to their earlier claims to the straits and Constantinople, confirmed in the 1915 Constantinople Agreement, the tsar's ministers sought British and French recognition of the annexation of the Turkish territories that the Russian army had recently overrun—Erzurum, the Black Sea port of Trabzon, the shattered city of Van, and Bitlis—as the price for their acquiescence to the terms of Sykes-Picot. With Russia's support secured by May 1916, the Allies had achieved a comprehensive agreement on the post-war partition of the Ottoman Empire. And for the moment, they managed to keep the whole matter secret from their Arab allies, Sharif Husayn and his sons.

In the early months of 1916, while the Entente Powers concluded their secret post-war plans for the Middle East, pressure was building on Sharif Husayn and his sons. Cemal Pasha, the commander of Ottoman forces in Syria, planned a new attack on British positions in Egypt and demanded that the Hashemites supply tribal levies to demonstrate their loyalty to the Turkish war effort. The commander of the Ottoman Fourth Army had begun to doubt Hashemite intentions and the loyalties of the Arabs generally. Under the pressure of total war, Cemal's authoritarianism in the Syrian lands hardened into a reign of terror that would further undermine Ottoman rule in the Arab provinces.

Early in his tenure as wartime governor general of the Syrian provinces, Cemal Pasha was confronted with irrefutable evidence of Arab disloyalty to the Ottoman Empire. After entering the war, the Ottoman authorities ordered the seizure of the archives of the British and French consulates for the intelligence they might contain. In Beirut and Damascus, Ottoman officials reaped a rich harvest. The French consular papers contained voluminous correspondence from members of secret societies—including many who had taken part in the First Arab Congress in Paris in 1913—seeking French support for Arab aspirations ranging from greater autonomy to outright independence under French protection. Muslim and Christian notables were implicated in the documents. The list read like a who's who of Syria's educated elites, including parliamentarians, journalists, religious figures, and army officers.

Initially, Cemal Pasha decided to take no action on the incriminating documents. He had come to Syria with the ambition of leading an Ottoman army in an inspiring attack on the Suez Canal that would provoke an

Egyptian uprising against British rule. He believed the Arabists were a marginal political movement that would be neutralized by Ottoman successes on the battlefield. Political trials would only undermine public morale, at a time when Cemal hoped to promote unity of purpose in taking the fight to British-occupied Egypt.[16]

The failure of the Ottoman attack on the Suez Canal in February 1915 led to a hardening of Cemal's attitude towards the Arabists. Many of the Arab irregulars who had promised to join the war effort had remained on the sidelines to witness Cemal's humiliating retreat from the Sinai. The Hashemites were notably absent in the campaign, having failed to rally the tribes of the Hijaz to the sultan's banner.

Moreover, Ottoman failure had fed public doubts about the empire's future. Ihsan Turjman, an Arab soldier from a middle-class family in Jerusalem, recorded in his diary a conversation with three friends, two of whom were commissioned officers in the Ottoman army. In late March 1915, following the failed attack on the Suez Canal, the four men discussed the course of "this miserable war" and "the fate of this [Ottoman] state. We more or less agreed that the days of the state are numbered and that its dismemberment is imminent." As Arab citizens began to anticipate the demise of the Ottoman Empire, the threat posed by secret nationalist societies grew in significance. Cemal Pasha decided to eliminate the Arabist threat.[17]

Falih Rıfkı, a brilliant young journalist from Istanbul, witnessed Cemal Pasha's repression at first hand. Rıfkı had risen through the ranks of the grand vizier's offices and come to the attention of the Young Turk leadership through his weekly columns in the leading Istanbul daily newspaper *Tanin*. He covered the Balkan Wars, where he met Enver. As minister of interior, Talat Pasha appointed Rıfkı as his personal secretary. When Cemal left Istanbul to become governor general of Syria and commander of the Fourth Army, he specifically requested that Rıfkı be seconded to his general staff as head of intelligence. He reached Jerusalem some time in 1915.

Cemal's headquarters in 1915 were in a German guesthouse on the Mount of Olives, overlooking the walled city of Jerusalem. The commander had his back to Rıfkı, who joined a nervous crowd assembled outside Cemal Pasha's door. He was in a fierce mood, reading correspondence, signing paperwork, and barking orders to his staff. "Tell my aide-de-camp to call in the notables from Nablus," Cemal ordered.

The terrified group of twenty men hesitated at the threshold of Cemal's office to say a quick prayer before entering. They took up position before the large window overlooking Jerusalem and its surrounding countryside. Cemal made no effort to acknowledge their presence as he continued working at his desk. Rıfkı had no idea what the men were accused of, but he knew from their anxious expressions that they feared for their lives. After keeping the notables waiting for what must have seemed to them an eternity, the commander in chief slammed his papers on his desk and turned to face them.

"Are you aware of the gravity of the crimes you have committed against your sovereign state?" he asked in am imperious voice.

"In God's name, forgive us," the men murmured in despair. Cemal cut them short with a look.

"Do you know the punishment for such crimes?" Cemal continued. "You deserve to be hanged." Rıfkı saw the blood drain from the anxious men's faces. "Yes, hanged—but give thanks to the merciful generosity of the Sublime Porte. I will be satisfied, for the moment, to exile you and your families to Anatolia."

Relieved to have been spared the gallows, the notables prostrated themselves in prayers of thanks for their deliverance. "You may retire," Cemal Pasha said, bringing the meeting to a close. The notables fled the room in disorder.

As his office cleared, Cemal turned to welcome Rıfkı to his new post with a broad smile. He must have discerned the journalist's discomfort after witnessing the meeting with the notables of Nablus and the arbitrary justice meted out for their unnamed crimes. "What do you expect!" Cemal Pasha shrugged. "Here, one has to behave this way!"[18]

Starting in 1915, the Ottoman authorities began to exile large numbers of Arab citizens of questionable loyalty. Cemal Pasha took much of the credit for this policy. "There are people I have personally exiled everywhere," he once boasted with a smile to Falih Rıfkı. The primary targets were men suspected of Arabist leanings and Arab Christians whose churches had enjoyed the Great Power protection of Russia or France.

Unlike the Armenian deportations, exile in the Arab provinces was not a prelude to massacre or a death march. Rather, it was a way of neutralizing the threat an individual posed to the state by disconnecting him from "dangerous" friends and associates. Men in exile were forced to live off their personal resources and, when these were depleted, became totally reliant on the Ottoman government. Their friends and families went to great lengths to demonstrate loyalty to the government to help secure the return of their exiled loved ones. The Ottoman authorities had exiled an estimated 50,000 people by the end of the war.[19]

Villages already depopulated by conscription were increasingly diminished by the new policy of exile. The impact on trade and agriculture was devastating, as shops closed and fields lay idle in farms worked by exhausted women, children, and the elderly. Nature compounded the catastrophe of war when clouds of locusts descended on Greater Syria. "Locusts are attacking all over the country," Ihsan Turjman noted in his diary in March 1915. "The locust invasion started seven days ago and covered the sky. Today it took the locust clouds two hours to pass over the city" of Jerusalem. "God protect us from the three plagues: war, locusts and disease, for they are spreading through the country," he prayed.

The Syrian lands had suffered from locust plagues in the past, but the invasion of 1915 was unprecedented in both its intensity and geographic extent. In a desperate bid to halt the infestation, the Ottoman authorities ordered all citizens aged fifteen to sixty to collect twenty kilograms (forty pounds) of locust eggs each week to be delivered to government depots for destruction—or face a stiff fine. The people of Jerusalem took the levy seriously. Six weeks after the locusts first appeared, Turjman noticed the shops in Jerusalem were closed "since most people were out collecting locusts' eggs".

Government measures were totally inadequate to contain the locust threat. Clouds of the insects continued to ravage farms and orchards through the summer months and deep into autumn. Harvests were ravaged, with regions of Syria reporting losses of 75 to 90 percent of crops. What survived the locusts went to feed the army—or was hoarded by the fortunate few. The inevitable result was a critical food shortage. Hunger began to spread across the towns and villages of Palestine, Syria, and Lebanon.

By December 1915, there was no flour in the markets of Jerusalem. "I haven't seen darker days in my life," Ihsan Turjman recorded in his diary. "Flour and bread have basically disappeared since last Saturday. Many people have not eaten bread for days now." He witnessed crowds of men, women, and children jostling for flour near the Damascus Gate. As their numbers swelled, fighting erupted. "We have so far tolerated living without rice, sugar, and kerosene. But how can we live without bread?"

In 1916, hunger turned to starvation. Locusts, war requisitioning, and hoarding, compounded by failures in the transport and distribution of food, combined to create a famine that claimed between 300,000 and 500,000 civilian lives in Syria and Lebanon between 1916 and the end of the war. In the Syrian lands, the famine and other wartime hardships came to be synonymous with the war; the population called them *Seferberlik*, the Turkish word for "general mobilization". The Great War was *Seferberlik*, that series of misfortunes that began with general mobilization and led inexorably to crop failure, inflation, disease, famine, and death among non-combatants on an unprecedented level.[20]

A Syrian émigré on a clandestine mission for the French travelled through Syria and Lebanon in April 1916, where he witnessed the suffering at first hand. He met survivors who had fled dying villages in search of food. He found countless skeletons of victims of the famine, left unburied where they had fallen by the roadside. In conversation with a disillusioned Arab officer in Damascus, he accused the Ottomans of deliberately provoking starvation as a way to purge the state of its "disloyal" Christians. "They put the sword to the neck of the Armenians, as they intend to annihilate the [Christian] Lebanese by starvation, so that they never trouble their Turkish masters again."[21]

Enver Pasha insisted that "the Allied naval blockade," imposed in the opening months of the war, was "responsible for this famine." British and French vessels refused to permit any ships to enter Syrian ports—even those carrying humanitarian relief. Enver reportedly approached the Vatican in 1916 with a proposal to distribute food aid in Syria and Lebanon. Speaking to the papal envoy to Istanbul, Enver acknowledged that the Ottomans did not have enough supplies to feed both the army and the civilians in Syria. He urged the Vatican to persuade the British and French to allow at least one ship to deliver food each month, to be distributed by any agency the pope might appoint for the task to reassure the Allies the food would not go to Turkish soldiers. Yet nothing came of Enver's papal initiative. Like many Ottomans, Enver believed the Allies were deliberately starving the Syrians to weaken resistance to invasion or to encourage rebellion against the empire.[22]

Enver had good grounds to fear rebellion in the Syrian provinces. Ottoman losses combined with wartime hardship turned many Arab citizens against the sultan's government. It fell to Cemal Pasha, as governor of Syria, to suppress the Arab threat. He hoped by show of exemplary justice to decapitate any Arab movement that might make common cause with the empire's enemies. He also wanted to intimidate Syrian elites from engaging in separatist politics. For, as Turkish journalist Falih Rıfkı surmised, "the [Committee of] Union and Progress was the mortal enemy of all nationalists and independence movements among all of the minority communities, be they Albanian, Armenian, Greek or Arab".[23]

IN JUNE 1915, CEMAL PASHA ORDERED THE FIRST WAVE OF ARRESTS OF Arab political activists. He established a military court and put the activists on trial. By August 1915, the court had completed its investigations. Cemal Pasha instructed the judges to impose the death penalty on any suspect found guilty of membership in a secret Arabist society or of conspiring with the French against the Ottoman Empire. Thirteen men were convicted and sentenced to death (though two of the sentences were later commuted to life imprisonment).

The first hangings took place in Beirut on 21 August 1915. Ottoman soldiers sealed the central Burj Square to civilian traffic. Soldiers and policemen filled the square as the condemned men were led in the dark of night to the gallows. News of the hangings spread quickly through the Arab provinces. Word reached Jerusalem by the end of the month. "I do not know any of these patriots," Ihsan Turjman wrote in his diary on 1 September, "but I was deeply shaken by this news." Turjman felt a national bond to the Arabs executed by the Turks. "Farewell to you, brave compatriots," he saluted. "May our souls meet when your noble objectives are realized."[24]

These first hangings proved but the beginning of a reign of terror. In September 1915, Cemal Pasha ordered the arrest of dozens more men implicated in the documents seized from the French consulate. They were taken to the Lebanese mountain village of Aley, on the Beirut-Damascus highway. Between their sessions before the military tribunal, the suspects were tortured to reveal the names of other members and the aims of their societies. Those who had not yet been arrested went underground or tried to flee. Repression worked. In a matter of weeks, the Arabist movement that had confidently set the boundaries of Arab independence in the 1915 Damascus Protocol (that served as the basis of Sharif Husayn's territorial claims in the Husayn-McMahon Correspondence) was broken and on the run.

D AMASCUS WAS A DANGEROUS CITY WHEN S HARIF H USAYN'S SON F AYSAL returned in January 1916, hoping to coordinate an uprising with the authors of the protocol. Faysal had taken precautions. He travelled with a band of fifty armed retainers that he now presented to the suspicious Ottoman authorities as the vanguard of the Hijaz volunteers his father, Sharif Husayn, had pledged for the next Ottoman attack on the Suez Canal. Cemal Pasha welcomed Faysal and his retainers, extending to his Hashemite guests the hospitality of the governor's headquarters.

On his visits to the household of the Bakris, whose son Nasib had eluded Cemal's dragnet, Faysal learned of the fate of the Arabist movement in

Enver Pasha (centre) and Cemal Pasha (to Enver's left) in Jerusalem, February 1916. The two Young Turk leaders travelled across Syria, Palestine, and the Hijaz in early 1916 to assess war preparedness in the Arab provinces.

Damascus—of the redeployment of Arab regiments away from their home provinces to the intense fighting in Gallipoli and Mesopotamia, of the civilians exiled to Anatolia with their families, and of the dozens of prominent citizens on trial before the military tribunal in Aley charged with treason. Faced with a transformed political situation, Faysal put aside all plans for revolt. He worked instead to build Cemal Pasha's trust and secure the release of the imprisoned Arabists. His father's deepening antagonism towards the Young Turk leadership, however, undermined Faysal's efforts.

The Young Turk leaders pressed Sharif Husayn to contribute tribal volunteers for their next attack on the Suez Canal. Enver and Cemal took the train to Medina in February 1916 to review Hashemite forces and urge the dispatch of *Mujahidin* (soldiers of jihad) from Islam's holy lands. In response, the amir wrote to Enver Pasha the following month to give his preconditions for endorsing the sultan's jihad. Sharif Husayn's letter sounded more like the work of an Arab nationalist than a servant of the sultan. He demanded an amnesty for all Arab political prisoners currently on trial. He called for a decentralized administration for Greater Syria, with administrative autonomy from Istanbul. And he sought hereditary rights for his family to the amirate of Mecca, with all the traditional privileges of that office restored.

Enver was brutally direct in his response. "Such matters are outside your concerns, and it will gain you nothing to persist in requesting them," he warned. He reminded the amir of his duty to the state to provide soldiers for the war effort to be commanded by his son Faysal, "who will remain the guest of the Fourth Army until the end of the war". The sharif, unbowed by Enver's threat to hold Faysal hostage, entrusted his son to the Young Turk's safekeeping, his conditions unchanged. He had, as yet, no idea how brutal the Young Turks would prove against those they suspected of Arab separatist aspirations.[25]

In April 1916, the Ottoman military tribunal in Aley concluded its deliberations. Dozens of the defendants were convicted of "treasonable participation in activities of which the aims were to separate Syria, Palestine and Iraq from the Ottoman Sultanate and to constitute them into an independent State". While everyone knew that treason carried the death penalty, many of those convicted came from prominent families and had held high office, as members of parliament or in the Ottoman senate. It seemed unthinkable that the government would hang such prominent citizens like common criminals.[26]

The Hashemites were outspoken on behalf of the Aley convicts. Sharif Husayn addressed telegrams to the sultan, to Cemal Pasha, and to Talat Pasha, pleading for clemency and warning against the death penalty on the grounds that "blood will cry for blood". Faysal, back in Damascus, urged mercy for the Aley convicts in his regular meetings with Cemal. Yet the Young Turk leader was deaf to their arguments, determined to set an example that would deter Arab separatism once and for all.

Without warning, twenty-one men were hanged in the predawn hours of 6 May 1916 in the central squares of Beirut and Damascus. Even the Turkish journalist Falih Rıfkı, who witnessed the hangings in Beirut, had sympathy and admiration for the condemned. "Most of those hanged in Beirut were young nationalists," he recalled. "They went from their cells to the noose with their heads held high, singing the Arab hymn." Later that day, Rıfkı travelled to Damascus, where seven men had been hanged before sunrise. He was astonished to see the notables of Damascus proceed with a banquet in Cemal Pasha's honour fifteen hours after the Arabists had faced the gallows. "No mourning in Damascus," Rıfkı reflected. "Poets, professional flatterers, orators—everyone expressed the country's gratitude to the great man who saved Arabia from its wayward children."[27]

To Arab nationalists, Cemal Pasha was no hero. In the aftermath of the hangings, they branded him Cemal Pasha al-Saffah, the "blood shedder". To the Hashemites, Cemal was nothing short of a murderer. Faysal was with the Bakri family when a breathless runner brought them news of the hangings. The government had printed a special issue of the official newspaper, listing the name of each of the condemned and the crimes for which he was executed. Faysal broke the shocked silence when he flung his headdress to the ground and tramped it underfoot, shouting an oath of revenge: "Death has become sweet, O Arabs!"[28]

THERE WAS NO LONGER ANY REASON FOR FAYSAL TO REMAIN IN DAMASCUS. Cemal's repression ruled out any political action in the Syrian provinces. Revolt was conceivable only in the Hijaz, where tribesmen outnumbered the isolated Ottoman troops. Yet before he could return to the Hijaz, Faysal needed to secure Cemal Pasha's permission to leave Damascus. On the least suspicion of disloyalty, Faysal feared he and his men could find themselves joining their martyred friends on the gallows.[29]

Faysal used a ruse to secure Cemal Pasha's permission to return to the Hijaz. The Hashemite prince claimed to have received a message from his father confirming that the Hijaz volunteer unit was at full strength and ready to join up with Cemal's forces in Syria. The Young Turks no doubt believed Sharif Husayn had been intimidated into compliance by the public hangings in Beirut and Damascus. Faysal was authorized to return to Medina to lead the Hijazi *Mujahidin* into Damascus in person.

Cemal Pasha had not been entirely taken in by Faysal's story. Faysal had pleaded for the condemned Arabists too energetically. The commander of the Ottoman garrison in Medina had accused Sharif Ali and the Hijazi detachment of interfering in military matters. Sharif Husayn's correspondence with Enver and Cemal bordered on the treasonous. Yet the benefits of the sharif of Mecca's endorsement for the Ottoman jihad outweighed the risks of permitting the hostage sharif to return to the Hijaz.

Sharif Faysal left Damascus on 16 May. Before he departed, Cemal Pasha presented him with a gift. Victorious Ottoman soldiers had captured the British Lee Enfield rifle, originally issued to a soldier of the 1st Essex Regiment, at Gallipoli. "Booty of the Dardanelles Campaign" was inscribed on the barrel in gold letters in Ottoman Turkish. The war trophy was no doubt intended to reinforce the Hashemite's belief that the Ottomans would win the war. Yet Faysal was quick to turn the weapon against the Ottoman Empire.[30]

As a precaution against Hashemite double-dealing, Cemal decided to dispatch one of his most trusted generals, Fahri Pasha, to take command of the garrison in Medina. Fahri was "well known for his reliability and patriotism," Cemal claimed. Others accused him of atrocities against Armenians. At the first sign of trouble, Fahri was to seize the sharif and his sons and put the civil affairs of Mecca under the authority of the Ottoman governor of Medina.[31]

ON THE EVE OF THE ARAB REVOLT, THE ANGLO-HASHEMITE ALLIANCE offered far less than both sides originally believed they were securing on first entering into negotiations. The British were not the invincible power they had appeared to be in early 1915, when first setting off to conquer Constantinople. The Germans had inflicted terrible casualties on the British on the western front, and even the Ottomans had dealt them humiliating defeats. Sharif Husayn and his sons had every reason to questions their choice of ally.

Yet the Hashemites were in no position to bargain. All through their correspondence with the high commissioner in Egypt, Sharif Husayn and his sons had presented themselves as leaders of a pan-Arab movement. By May 1916 it was apparent that there would be no broader revolt in Syria and Iraq. The most the sharifs could do was challenge Ottoman rule in the Hijaz. Success depended on their ability to mobilize the notoriously undisciplined Bedouin to their cause.

Arguably, the alliance survived because the Hashemites and the British needed each other more in the summer of 1916 than ever. Sharif Husayn had strained relations with the Young Turks to the breaking point; he knew they would seize the first opportunity to dismiss—even murder—him and his sons. The British needed the sharif's religious authority to undermine the Ottoman jihad, which officials in Cairo and Whitehall feared recent Turkish victories had strengthened. Whatever the results of a Hashemite-led revolt, the movement would at least weaken the Ottoman war effort and force the Turks to divert troops and resources to restore order in the Hijaz and possibly in other Arab provinces. For their own reasons, both the British and the Hashemites were in a hurry to launch the revolt. Once Faysal had returned to the Hijaz, they did not have long to wait.

On 5 June, Faysal joined his brother Ali outside Medina to begin operations against the largest Ottoman garrison in the Hijaz. Fahri Pasha had already arrived to take command of Ottoman forces numbering over 11,000 men. With only the 1,500 tribal volunteers Ali had mobilized for the Sinai campaign at their disposal, the Hashemites were in no position to take the railhead. Instead, they held Fahri Pasha's forces to Medina, leaving their father and brothers to operate with relative impunity in Mecca, some 210 miles to the south.

After four days of skirmishes around Medina, the Hashemites made their intentions clear. Sharif Husayn's eldest son, Ali, sent an ultimatum to Cemal Pasha on 9 June setting out a series of demands for his family's continued loyalty, the sincerity of which was undermined by the tight deadline he offered the Young Turks. "Twenty-four hours after receipt of this letter a state of war will exist between the two nations," Turkey and the Arabs, he warned.[32]

It fell to Sharif Husayn to fire the opening shot of the Arab Revolt from his palace in the holy city of Mecca. On 10 June 1916, the amir of Mecca took up a rifle—quite possibly the same trophy from Gallipoli that Cemal had given Faysal—and fired once at the Ottoman barracks to initiate the uprising. The Hashemites were at war with the Turks in the name of the Arab peoples. It remained to be seen how the Arab world would respond.[33]

HASHEMITE FORCES SECURED MOST OF MECCA WITHIN THREE DAYS. The governor, Ghalib Pasha, had withdrawn to his summer residence in the highlands of Taif sixty miles east and taken most of the Mecca garrison with him, leaving only 1,400 soldiers to guard the holy city. One hilltop fortress held out against the amir's forces for four weeks, firing shells into Mecca to disperse the Arabs. A number of shells hit the Great Mosque, setting fire to the canopy over the Kaaba, Islam's holiest shrine. Fragments from another shell struck the name of the third caliph, Uthman ibn Affan, from the facade of the building. As the eponymous founder of the Ottoman dynasty was also named Uthman (Osman in Turkish), Sharif Husayn's son Abdullah claimed that the people of Mecca took this as "an omen of the imminent fall of the Osmanli [i.e., Ottoman] power". Eventually, the besieged gunners in the hilltop fort ran out of food and ammunition and were forced to surrender on 9 July, leaving Mecca in Hashemite hands.[34]

Shortly after Sharif Husayn fired his opening shot on 10 June, 4,000 Bedouin horsemen of the Harb tribe descended on the Red Sea port city of Jeddah under the command of their leader, Sharif Muhsin. The 1,500 Ottoman soldiers initially repelled the attackers with machine guns and cannon fire, dealing a heavy blow to Bedouin morale. Two Royal Navy warships assisted the Arab attack, subjecting Ottoman positions in Jeddah to sustained cannonades. British airplanes bombed and strafed Turkish troop positions. Attacked from land, sea, and sky, the defenders surrendered on 16 June.

Sharif Husayn's second son, Abdullah, had moved with a small band of seventy camel-mounted retainers to the outskirts of Taif shortly before the outbreak of the revolt. The governor, Ghalib Pasha, invited Abdullah to his palace to discuss rumours of an imminent uprising. "You see how the people of Taif are leaving their homes with their children and as many of their goods as they can carry," the governor remarked. Taking a Quran from the shelf, he urged Abdullah to tell him "the truth about these rumours of the revolt". Abdullah bluffed his way out of a difficult position. "Either they are not true, or it is a revolt against both you and the Sherif, or against you by the Sherif and the people. If the latter explanation were true, should I have come to you now, and put myself into your hands?"[35]

When Abdullah left the governor's residence, he gave orders to his men to sever the telegraph lines and prevent any couriers from leaving Taif by road. At midnight on 10 June, he ordered his troops, reinforced by tribesmen from the surrounding countryside, to attack the Ottoman positions. "Our attack was made with great violence," he recalled. The Bedouin were quick to break through the Turkish front lines, returning "with some prisoners and some loot". However, their discipline broke at sunrise when the Turkish artillery began to fire on Arab positions. Many of the tribesmen "deserted to their homes in disorder". Fearful that his forces would collapse were he to attempt further assaults, Abdullah reorganized his troops to place Taif under siege.

Bedouin irregulars armed with rifles were no match for Ottoman regulars with field artillery and machine guns. After five weeks of stalemate, the British shipped Egyptian artillery batteries to Taif to reinforce Abdullah's position (in yet further violation of General Sir John Maxwell's 1914 promise not to involve the Egyptians in the British war effort). In mid-July, the Egyptian gunners began a sustained artillery attack that overwhelmed the Ottoman defenders. The Turks held out until 21 September, when Ghalib Pasha was forced into an unconditional surrender. "The following day, the Ottoman flag was officially hauled down from the fortress and the Arab flag hoisted," Abdullah recorded. "It was a very impressive sight." The Ottoman governor, shattered by the experience of siege and defeat, did not share the Hashemite's sense of history. "This is a great catastrophe," Ghalib Pasha lamented. "We were brothers, and now we are enemies."[36]

By the end of September, Sharif Husayn and his sons had captured Mecca and Taif, as well as the Red Sea ports of Jeddah, Rabigh, and Yanbu. They had taken more than 6,000 Ottoman soldiers prisoner with relatively few casualties on either side. The following month, Sharif Husayn unilaterally declared himself "king of the Arab lands," and his sons assumed the princely title "amir". (The British, discomfited by the announcement, were only willing to recognize Husayn as king of the Hijaz.)

News of the revolt spread across the Arab world and generated growing excitement among those disillusioned by the Ottoman conduct of the war. In Jerusalem, where the Ottoman authorities suppressed news of the revolt for weeks, Ihsan Turjman noted the auspicious event in his diary on 10 July.

"Sherif Hussein Pasha declared rebellion against the state," he wrote incredulously. "Could this be the beginning?" Turjman could not hide his enthusiasm. "Every Arab should be pleased about this news. How can we support this state after it killed our best youth? They were hanged in public squares like common criminals and gangsters. May God bless the sherif of Hijaz and strengthen his arm. And may your campaign spread to every corner of the Arab lands, until we get rid of this cursed state."[37]

Muhammad Ali al-Ajluni was a young officer in a Syrian regiment billeted in Anatolia. In Ajluni's experience, the war had turned Ottomans against one another. Turkish soldiers refused to mix with Arab comrades in both the mosque and the officers' mess and made racist remarks about their skin colour, deriding Arabs as "blacks". The suffering the government inflicted on innocent civilians appalled him. From his post in Tarsus on the Cilician coast, he saw trainloads of Syrians sent into exile by Cemal Pasha's administration. "We saw the pain and sorrow etched in the expression of each and every one of them," he remembered. Worse yet were the lines of Armenian deportees heading in the opposite direction towards the Syrian Desert—women, children, and the elderly driven by guards "into whose hearts mercy never found its way". Given his wartime disillusionment with the Ottoman Empire, Ajluni was elated by news of Sharif Husayn's revolt. "It restored our shaken confidence and drew broad new lines of hope and strength. It was a new dawn for the Arabs." He vowed on the spot to make his way to the Hijaz to join the revolt, whatever difficulties he might encounter.[38]

News of the Hashemite revolt ignited heated debates among Arab officers in the Ottoman army. One of Ajluni's closest friends tried to dissuade him from deserting. By allying with the imperial British and calling for total independence from the Ottoman Empire, he argued, the sharif's movement exposed the Arab world to European domination. Many Arabist officers preferred to remain within a reformed Ottoman Empire that gave greater autonomy to the Arab provinces; they spoke of a Turco-Arab dual-monarchy on the model of the Austro-Hungarian Empire. While Ajluni considered his friend's arguments carefully, he remained committed to the sharifian cause. Yet, as their debate demonstrated, the appeal of the Arab Revolt was not universal among Arab Ottomans.

The Hashemite revolt split public opinion across the broader Muslim world. The Indian Muslim press denounced the sharif for leading the Arabs in rebellion against their caliph. Mosques in the volatile North-West Frontier Province of India echoed with imams' curses against Sharif Husayn and his sons. On 27 June, the All-India Muslim League passed a resolution condemning the Hashemite revolt in the strongest terms, suggesting Sharif Husayn's actions had given real cause for jihad. British officials in India, who had consistently opposed the British high commissioner in Egypt, Sir Henry McMahon, in his negotiations with Sharif Husayn, now argued the revolt had backfired and that Indian Muslims appeared more inclined to support the Ottomans as a result.[39]

The Hashemites faced bigger problems closer to home. Initial successes left King Husayn and his sons holding towns and cities around Mecca and on the Red Sea coastline without the forces to retain them. The initial enthusiasm of their Bedouin volunteers evaporated quickly. Drawn to the revolt by the authority of the sharif of Mecca and the opportunity to raid Ottoman government property, they had no ideological commitment to the movement for Arab independence. Once the first battles had been won and the towns taken, the tribesmen took their booty and went home. This forced King Husayn's sons to draw on every friend and favour to recruit fresh tribal soldiers with the promise of guns and regular pay that only the British could provide.

In Medina, Fahri Pasha was poised to launch a counter-attack. His army was at full strength, and communications with Damascus were running smoothly. Without dynamite, the rebels had no means to cut the Hijaz Railway, which continued to provision Fahri's garrison. On 1 August, a new amir of Mecca descended from the train to full state honours. The Young Turks had named Sharif Ali Haydar, head of a rival branch of the Hashemite dynasty, to replace the renegade Husayn on 2 July. Fahri Pasha aimed to install him in Mecca in time for the Hajj pilgrimage season in early October.

There were two routes from Medina to Mecca. The inland route was more direct but led through waterless and difficult terrain effectively impassable to armies. The coastal route via the Red Sea ports of Yanbu and Rabigh, though much longer, was punctuated by watering holes that could sustain men on the march. To protect Mecca, the Hashemites had to control Yanbu and Rabigh. As the Ottomans set forth from Medina in early August, Faysal took up positions blocking the road to Yanbu, and his brother Ali occupied

Rabigh. They were in the right locations but needed regular soldiers, in addition to the tribal volunteers, to withstand the Ottomans. Unless they were reinforced quickly, the Hashemites faced imminent defeat—with catastrophic consequences for Arab and British interests alike.

British war planners in London, Cairo, and Simla (the summer capital of British India) weighed the risks of sending British troops to reinforce the Hashemites. The Government of India argued that the introduction of British troops into the Hijaz would provoke a violent reaction from Indian Muslims, who would see them as "infidel" soldiers "desecrating" the sacred soil of the Hijaz to fight the faithful legions of the caliph. The Arab Bureau in Cairo believed the sharif's forces were on the verge of collapse and that an Ottoman triumph in Mecca would critically discredit the British in their Muslim colonial territories. Either way, Britain's exposure in the Hijaz risked provoking jihad. The compromise position was to reinforce the sharif's army with Muslim volunteers.

The natural recruiting grounds for Muslim soldiers were the British POW camps in India and Egypt. In the course of interrogating Arab Ottoman prisoners, the British encountered many committed to the Arabist cause. Muhammad Sharif al-Faruqi, whose testimony was influential in confirming Sharif Husayn's claims to speak on behalf of a broader Arab movement, has already been mentioned. Others included the Iraqi officers Nuri al-Said and Ali Jawdat, captured in the Mesopotamia campaign, and Jafar al-Askari, taken prisoner near the Libyan frontier in the Sanussi campaign. The sharif's declaration of Arab independence was enough to convince many of these officers to disavow their loyalty to the sultan and join the Hashemite revolt. Nuri al-Said led the first detachment from Egypt to the Hijaz on 1 August 1916. Ali Jawdat, released on parole in the city of Basra, was recruited by British officers and sent to India to persuade other POWs from the Mesopotamia campaign to sign onto the sharif's army. Jawdat succeeded in persuading thirty-five officers and 350 soldiers to volunteer for the Arab Revolt. They left Bombay in early September and were greeted by Nuri al-Said on arrival in Rabigh.[40]

However, not every Arab POW was committed to the Arabist cause. After these first detachments of ideologues set off, the British emptied their POW camps in Egypt and India to ship potential Arab recruits to the Hijaz campaign—with very mixed results. Two ships set off from Bombay at the end of November carrying ninety officers and 2,100 men. When the ships arrived off Rabigh, sharifian recruiters were dismayed to find that only six officers and twenty-seven enlisted men agreed to join the Arab army. The rest either had no wish to make war on fellow Muslims or feared Turkish retribution for their treason if they were captured. After ten days of persistent effort by Arab volunteers already in sharifian service, the transport ships continued up the Red Sea to deposit their unwilling recruits in POW camps in Egypt.

Arab officers and soldiers who abandoned Ottoman service in favour of the sharif's cause made a contribution to the revolt that exceeded their limited numbers. Their military training and their fluency in Arabic recommended them for both training and commanding Bedouin recruits. Yet their limited numbers meant they were insufficient to hold in check the threat posed by Fahri Pasha, whose army continued to advance towards Yanbu and Rabigh. As the Muslim pilgrimage season approached, Whitehall began to reconsider dispatching British troops to reinforce Hashemite positions. The British were galvanized into action when France offered to send Muslim troops to assist the campaign in the Hijaz.

The French seized on the pilgrimage season to appoint an armed escort for North African pilgrims to Mecca. The escort evolved into a full-fledged military mission to the Hijaz and a French offer of assistance to the sharif's forces. The French military mission set off alarm bells among British colonial officers. The British high commissioner in Cairo, Sir Henry McMahon, telegraphed London to "greatly deprecate" the French offer of troops "as it will rob us of very great political advantages which Sharif's success will hereafter give us". In fact, the French were less interested in securing advantages in Arabia than in ensuring that the sharifian cause did not endanger French interests in Syria. They sent officers to Arabia to keep an eye on the British and protect everything France was promised in the Sykes-Picot Agreement.[41]

Command of the French military mission fell to Colonel Edouard Brémond, who had served with distinction in Morocco and was fluent in Arabic. He arrived in Jeddah on 21 September at the head of a mixed military and civilian delegation and two hundred North African pilgrims. Not to be outdone, the high commissioner in Cairo dispatched Ronald Storrs to escort the Egyptian ceremonial delegation for the pilgrimage. It gave Storrs the opportunity to discuss military strategy both with Colonel Brémond and with Hashemite commanders in the field. All were convinced that sharifian forces remained too weak to hold off Fahri Pasha and his Ottoman regulars.

If Arab soldiers could not be recruited in sufficient numbers from British POW camps, the next best option was to deploy Muslim colonial soldiers to the Arab Revolt. The British drafted Egyptian artillerymen into the Hijaz campaign—their pledge to the Egyptian people effectively abandoned under the constraints of total war. A first detachment of 250 men was sent via the Sudan. The total Egyptian contingent would reach over 960 men by December.[42]

The French military mission never exceeded British numbers, despite the large number of North African (Muslim) soldiers serving in the French army. When asked by Britain's War Office to contribute a Muslim artillery battery and the greatest possible number of military specialists—machine-gunners, sappers, signallers (particularly those fluent in Arabic), and doctors—the French were embarrassed to admit they lacked such expertise among their Muslim soldiers. By the end of 1916, the French mission in Arabia numbered no more than twelve officers (almost entirely French) and under one hundred infantrymen (almost entirely Muslim). At its height, the French force reached a total of forty-two officers and 983 men, many of whom remained in Port Said without ever setting foot in Arabia.[43]

Though these colonial soldiers made an important contribution to the Arab cause, neutralizing the Ottoman advantage in artillery and machine guns, their numbers were too limited to address the looming threat of Ottoman forces from Medina, who continued their relentless advance towards the Hashemites' coastal positions across the autumn months of 1916.

The Ottoman threat grew critical in early November when the Turkish column drove Faysal and his troops from their camp in Hamra, in the hill country behind the Red Sea port of Rabigh. Without sufficient Muslim soldiers at hand, officials in Cairo and London reconsidered the pros and cons of dispatching British regulars to reinforce the sharifian cause. The British military opposed the idea, claiming it would take more troops than they could spare to hold the Red Sea coast against Fahri Pasha's army. In London, Sir William Robertson, chief of the Imperial General Staff, suggested that 15,000 British soldiers would be required just to hold the Red Sea village of Rabigh. The military commander in Egypt, Lieutenant General Sir Archibald Murray, did not believe he could spare such numbers without putting the defence of the Suez Canal at risk. He decided to seek the advice of the one British junior officer who had met with Faysal and knew at first hand the situation at Rabigh and Yanbu.

Back in Cairo after his ill-fated attempt to assist in the relief of Major General Charles Townshend's forces in Kut, Captain T. E. Lawrence made his first visit to the Hijaz in October 1916. An intelligence officer in the Arab Bureau, he had invited himself on one of Oriental Secretary Ronald Storrs's missions to Jeddah and taken the opportunity to travel inland from Rabigh to meet with Sharif Husayn's sons and inspect their positions. The British commanders did not rate Lawrence's knowledge of military strategy, but they valued his local knowledge and, after his travels from Rabigh to Faysal's camp in Hamra, believed he could provide crucial intelligence to help make the difficult decision about whether to send British troops to the Hijaz.

In his classic history of the Arab Revolt, Lawrence provides a unique eyewitness account of Hashemite positions in the desperate autumn months of 1916. In Rabigh, he met with Ali and several Arab officers formerly in Ottoman service—Nuri al-Said of Iraq, Aziz Ali al-Misri of Egypt, and Faiz al-Ghusayn of Syria—who were training the sharif's regular army units. After several days' ride on camelback, Lawrence reached Faysal's camp at Hamra. He found Faysal discouraged and his troops demoralized. They had been starved of arms, ammunition, and cash. To date, the only assistance Faysal's force had received was the battery of Egyptian artillery whose crews expressed their "resentment at having been sent so far away into the desert to serve in an unnecessary and toilsome war". He concluded that foreign soldiers, Muslim and European alike, were ill-suited for the Hijaz campaign.[44]

When asked his opinion by officials in Cairo, Lawrence warned against dispatching British troops to the Hijaz. Any expeditionary force would only rouse suspicions that the British had imperial ambitions in Arabia. "If the British, with or without the approval of the Sharif, disembarked an armed force at Rabigh powerful enough to take possession of the groves and organize a position there," the Arabs, he concluded, "would, I am convinced, say 'We are betrayed' and scatter to their tents." Instead, Lawrence recommended providing Ali and Faysal with the necessary gold to retain their Bedouin soldiers' services ("Nothing else would have performed the miracle of keeping a tribal army in the field for five months on end," Lawrence claimed) and to limit British involvement to air support and technical advisers. The British commanders found Lawrence's view—that the Arabs should be left to fight the Arab Revolt—extremely convenient and agreed to limit Britain's involvement accordingly.[45]

When Lawrence returned to Arabia at the start of December, the situation had deteriorated to such an extent that he must have questioned the soundness of his own advice. A Turkish surprise attack caught the Arab army unawares, and the Bedouin fighters, in Lawrence's words, "melted into a loose mob of fugitives riding wildly through the night towards Yenbo". With the road to Yanbu now open before the Turkish column, Faysal had ridden in with 5,000 troops to fill the gap. He had delayed the Turkish advance, but his position was untenable. The Turks had managed to isolate Faysal's forces from his brother Ali's troops in Rabigh to the south. Thus separated, neither Arab unit could withstand the Ottoman army. Once the Turks had recovered the Red Sea coast, they would face no obstacle in retaking Mecca from Sharif Husayn's forces.[46]

Lawrence rode with Faysal as he ordered his forces to retreat to the date groves of Nakhl Mubarak, just six hours by camel ride from Yanbu. During these manoeuvres the Hashemite prince first suggested to Lawrence that he dress in Arab clothes so that the Arab fighters would treat him as though he were "really one of the leaders" and so that he could move around the camp without his dishevelled British officer's uniform "making a sensation" among

Sharif Faysal's camp at dawn, Nakhl Mubarak, near Yanbu. T. E. Lawrence photographed the encampment shortly before Faysal's retreat to Yanbu, when the Arab Revolt faltered in December 1916.

the tribesmen. Faysal dressed Lawrence in wedding finery given to him by an aunt—a mark of favour, no doubt, but unlikely to make the Englishman less of a sensation as he moved among the Bedouin. Faysal also gave Lawrence a rifle—the Gallipoli trophy Cemal had presented to him months earlier in Damascus. Lawrence immediately burned his initials and the date into the stock of the Lee Enfield: "T.E.L., 4-12-16." He then left Faysal and rode back to Yanbu to sound the alarm.

Back in port, Lawrence telegraphed the Royal Navy commanders in the Red Sea to warn that Yanbu was "gravely threatened". Captain William Boyle promised to mobilize British ships off the port within twenty-four hours. Good to his word, Boyle assembled an impressive fleet of five warships to defend Yanbu. They were hardly ships of the line—Boyle described his own vessel, the *Fox*, as "almost the slowest and oldest ship commanded by a Captain in the Navy"—but their guns were more powerful than any of the field artillery the Turks had at their disposal.

As the British naval vessels assembled off Yanbu, the Turks mounted another successful attack against Faysal's forces. Three battalions of Ottoman infantry descended on Nakhl Mubarak, supported by field artillery, and the Bedouin army collapsed into a disorderly rabble. Egyptian gunners kept up a spirited cannonade with the defective artillery the British had contributed to the Hashemite cause—"old rubbish thought servicable for the wild Arabs", in Lawrence's estimation. Without sights, range finders, or high explosives, the Arab artillery's chief deterrent was the noise the cannons made. It gave the Ottomans pause and the retreating Arabs courage, allowing Faysal to withdraw his forces from Nakhl Mubarak without significant casualties. They fell back onto Yanbu, completing the Arab surrender of the highlands to Ottoman forces. "Our war seemed entering its last act," Lawrence recalled.

The streets of Yanbu were crowded with thousands of Arab fighters digging in for a last stand. The defenders raised earthwork walls to slow the Ottoman advance that few could have hoped would hold against a determined assault. The Royal Navy provided the only real deterrent to the Ottoman occupation of Yanbu. The vessels' imposing bulk, every gun pointing ashore, and the eerie beams of searchlights criss-crossing the plains in the dark served as a warning against attack by day or night.

By the time they reached the outskirts of Yanbu on 11 December, the Ottomans were a spent force. Though they had enjoyed a string of victories against Faysal's army, weeks of campaigning in the inhospitable Arabian highlands had taken their toll. The army's ranks had been depleted through illness, and its transport animals had been weakened by overwork and underfeeding. The soldiers fought on hostile terrain, with Bedouin tribesmen attacking the Ottomans' rear and cutting their supply lines. They could have continued chasing the Arabs but could not afford to take on the Royal Navy. Hundreds of miles from their base in Medina, the isolated Ottoman battalions would receive no relief if they suffered serious casualties in Yanbu; they would be forced to surrender. "So they turned back," Lawrence recorded. "And that night, I believe, the Turks lost their war."[47]

THE OTTOMAN ARMY WAS SOON DRIVEN BACK FROM YANBU. BRITISH aircraft subjected the Turks' camp in Nakhl Mubarak to sustained aerial bombardment. Rather than suffer further attrition, they began to withdraw their forces to positions surrounding Medina. Sharif Husayn's son Abdullah pinned the Ottomans down with a force too small to lay siege to Medina but big enough to prevent deployment beyond the limits of the town. Here Fahri Pasha would remain for the duration of the war.

Rather than risk their forces in direct assault on Ottoman defences in Medina, the Hashemites opted for a war of movement. In coordination with their British and French advisors, the sharifian commanders planned to move north up the Red Sea coast to take the port of Wajh. With the Royal Navy on hand to supply Arab forces from the Red Sea, the move would also facilitate attacks on the Hijaz Railway to sever Medina's fragile supply line. What could not be taken by conventional means might best be conquered by guerrilla methods.

British war planners were relieved to see the Ottomans withdraw and leave the Hashemites in possession of their gains in the Hijaz. The Turks had been denied an important victory that would have reinforced their call for jihad by restoring Ottoman control over Mecca and the key cities of the Hijaz. The fact that the Hijaz had been stabilized without the deployment of British troops was an added bonus. Not only were Indian Muslim concerns assuaged, but the British simply had no spare forces by the end of 1916. The British had launched a major campaign against German positions on the Somme on 1 July and suffered their highest casualties in a single day—58,000 dead and wounded. As in Verdun, the Battle of the Somme was one of attrition that dragged on for months without a decisive result. By its end in mid-November 1916, the British had suffered 420,000 casualties and the French a further 194,000 dead and wounded. Estimates of German casualties at the Somme range from 465,000 to 650,000. Faced with such losses on the western front, the British were ever unwilling to draw down their forces in Europe for Middle Eastern battlefields.

The British, spared from deploying soldiers to support Sharif Husayn in the Hijaz, were pleased to give material assistance to their Arab allies. By the end of 1916, the British government had provided nearly 1 million pounds in gold to the sharifian cause. They provided a flight of aircraft under British pilots, both for surveillance and to keep German-supplied Ottoman planes away from the Bedouin, who harboured an entirely healthy dread of aerial attack. Along with the French they provided as many Muslim regular forces as they could muster and a handful of European officers as technical advisers in such arts as railway demolition.

Once the spectre of Hashemite defeat had lifted, British and French war planners came to view the Arab Revolt as a distinct asset in the Great War. As early as July 1916, the War Committee had based new strategic objectives for its forces in Egypt on the strength of early Hashemite gains in Hijaz. The committee instructed the commander in chief in Egypt, General Murray, to establish British control along a line extending across northern Sinai from El Arish on the Mediterranean to the tiny port of Aqaba on the eastern head of the Red Sea. British war planners maintained that these measures would "threaten communications between Syria and the Hejaz, and encourage Syrian Arabs" in support of the Arab Revolt. So began the fateful link between the Hashemite revolt in Arabia and the British campaign in Palestine that, between them, would ultimately spell the downfall of the Ottoman Empire.[48]

TWELVE

Losing Ground

The Fall of Baghdad, the Sinai, and Jerusalem

WITH THE OUTBREAK OF THE ARAB REVOLT IN THE HIJAZ, WAR planners on both sides of the conflict focused their attention on the Syrian lands. The Allies were intent on drawing Syria (which at that time referred to the territory of the modern states of Syria, Lebanon, Israel, Palestine, and Jordan) into a broader Arab revolt to give momentum to the Hashemite movement and to force the Ottomans to fight on hostile terrain. The Central Powers, on the other hand, were confident of their position in Syria. Aside from the first attack on the Suez Canal in February 1915, the Fourth Army had yet to see action and was at full strength. The Ottomans believed their forces in Syria were sufficient to contain the Hashemite revolt in the Hijaz and threaten British communications along the Suez Canal, which remained vulnerable to Turkish attack through the Sinai Peninsula.

Although Cemal Pasha's first attack on the Suez Canal ultimately ended in failure, the Ottoman army retained control of virtually all of the Sinai Peninsula. Though the Sinai was an integral part of British-occupied Egypt, the War Cabinet was unwilling to divert the necessary troops to recover and protect the largely uninhabited Sinai Desert from future Turkish attacks. The top British priorities were to preserve stability in the Nile valley and to maintain the flow of men and materiel through the Suez Canal. The west bank of the canal became the front line of British defence in Egypt, and the Ottomans were left undisturbed in the rest of the Sinai.

By early 1916, the Ottomans had transformed the Sinai into a launching pad for sustained hostilities against British forces along the Suez Canal. Cemal Pasha, commander of the Fourth Army, had worked closely with his German advisors to reinforce Ottoman positions. He extended the railway southward from Beersheba, the small inland market town to the south-east of Gaza, to the Egyptian frontier at al-Auja and beyond into the Sinai. The railway permitted the rapid transport of men and materiel into the heart of the Sinai. Here Cemal established a network of bases with wells to provide water for men and animals. Roads linked the Ottoman bases, and a crack desert force patrolled the Sinai under a German commander.

Cemal no longer dreamed of driving the British from Egypt as a whole. Instead, he planned to advance until his artillery was within range to strike the Suez Canal. The Ottomans could attack shipping and close the vital waterway from positions five miles from its banks, disrupting imperial communications without exposing their soldiers to well-entrenched British defences. When Enver Pasha inspected the Palestine frontier in February 1916, he approved Cemal's strategy and promised reinforcements.

The minister of war was true to his word. On his return to the Ottoman capital, Enver dispatched the battle-hardened Third Infantry Division from Gallipoli to Palestine. He also secured material support from the Central Powers. In April 1916, the Germans assigned a flight of aircraft to Ottoman headquarters in Beersheba. The state-of-the-art planes—powerful Rumplers and Fokker monoplanes that had proved the scourge of the western front—gave the Turks air superiority over the Sinai. Later that same month, the Austrians dispatched two batteries of field artillery to the Sinai front. The 15-cm howitzers gave Ottoman forces the firepower to challenge the British in the field. Reinforced with the latest military technology, Cemal began to plan a second attack on the Suez Canal Zone in earnest.[1]

Meanwhile the British had grown increasingly concerned by the Turkish menace to the Canal Zone. In February 1916, the commander of the Egyptian Expeditionary Force (EEF), Lieutenant General Sir Archibald Murray, proposed an "active defence" based on the fortification of strategic oases and crossroads in northern Sinai. Murray's plan called for the occupation of the Qatiya oasis, some thirty miles to the east of the canal. Part of a network of brackish watering holes, Qatiya was of critical strategic importance in the largely waterless Sinai wastes. Once Qatiya was secured,

Murray proposed to advance along the Mediterranean coast to the port of El Arish and to occupy a line running inland from El Arish to al-Kussaima, south of Beersheba. Murray argued persuasively that it would take far fewer men and resources to contain the Turks within the forty-five-mile stretch between al-Arish and al-Kussaima than along the full ninety-mile stretch of the canal itself.[2]

The chief of the Imperial General Staff, General Sir William Robertson, saw the wisdom in denying the Sinai oases to the Turks. However, with the British facing major setbacks on the western front and struggling to relieve the ill-fated garrison at Kut, he was unwilling to commit to a broader campaign in Sinai or Palestine than the troops already in Egypt might safely prosecute. On 27 February 1916, Robertson authorized the occupation of Qatiya and the surrounding oases and deferred the decision on advancing towards El Arish to a later date.

In March 1916, the British began to extend a standard-gauge railway line eastward from the canal town of Qantara towards Qatiya. Alongside the railway, the British also laid a pipeline to provide a reliable supply of fresh water. The 13,000 men of the Egyptian Labour Corps, working on short-term contracts, undertook the back-breaking work of building the railway and pipeline in the relentless desert heat. Following in the tracks of a caravan route, the line extended at the rate of four miles per week and reached the perimeter of the Qatiya oasis by late April.

The Ottomans moved swiftly to disrupt British progress. The German commander of the Turkish Desert Force, Colonel Friedrich Freiherr Kress von Kressenstein, led 3,500 soldiers in a bold raid on British forces protecting the railhead. At dawn on 23 April, the Ottomans swept through British positions in the oases surrounding Qatiya. Attacking in the early-morning fog, the Ottomans enjoyed total surprise and, after several hours of intense fighting, secured the surrender of nearly an entire British cavalry regiment. According to the official British account, only one officer and eighty soldiers managed to escape capture (a cavalry regiment typically numbered some twenty-five officers and 525 men). Von Kressenstein's force withdrew from Qatiya with impunity. The attack did not long disrupt progress on the railroad, but the Turks had succeeded in rattling the British, and as Cemal Pasha recorded, it "raised the confidence of our troops to a remarkable degree".[3]

Ottoman cavalry charge. Turkish mounted forces played a key role in the Sinai battles, including the Ottoman victory over British forces at Qatiya in April 1916.

Following the Ottoman attack on Qatiya, the British advance across northern Sinai was led by the Anzac Mounted Division. Composed of the New Zealand Mounted Brigade and units of the Australian Light Horse, the mounted division combined battle-seasoned Gallipoli veterans and fresh recruits. Mounted troops were essential in desert terrain inaccessible to motor vehicles. In fact, the British were forced to diversify their cavalry with camel units to give chase to Ottoman forces operating in the region's vast sand traps. The Sinai campaign thus presented a unique contrast between twentieth-century air power, nineteenth-century cavalry tactics, and Bedouin-style camel warfare.[4]

British progress on the railway and pipeline proceeded through the intense summer heat of 1916. Workers, troops, and horses all suffered from temperatures that often exceeded 50°C, from shortages of potable water, and from swarms of flies that plagued man and beast alike. They took comfort in the belief that the Ottomans were unlikely to risk another attack in the mid-summer heat. Yet the cavalry forces remained on high alert, patrolling deep in the desert to ensure there would be no repeat of the humiliation at Qatiya.

After repeated delays in the long-anticipated second attack on the Suez Canal, the Ottomans and their German allies were impatient to proceed. Cemal had deferred the second Sinai campaign in the hope that Sharif Husayn would contribute a detachment of volunteers from the Hijaz. The outbreak of the Arab Revolt in June 1916 dashed those hopes and created a new hostile front in the Arab provinces. Cemal believed success against the British in Sinai would undermine the appeal of the Hashemite uprising in the Arab provinces, and he gave Colonel von Kressenstein the green light to launch the long-delayed second attack on the Canal Zone in the dead of summer, when the British least expected it.

The Turks attacked British positions at Romani, near Qatiya, in the early morning hours of 3 August. With only 16,000 men, Colonel von Kressenstein headed a much smaller force than the British had anticipated. In a feat of remarkable endurance, the soldiers had managed to transport artillery across the desert sands to compensate for their small numbers with heavy firepower. To catch British forces by surprise, von Kressenstein timed his advance to coincide with the return of one of the light horse patrols to base, literally tailing the Anzac cavalry home. Although they did not catch the Australians totally unawares, Ottoman forces overpowered the Anzac post and forced them into retreat, capturing strategic high ground before sunrise.

Once alerted, the British flooded Romani with reinforcements to repulse the Turks. As the day wore on and the Turkish soldiers ran short of water and ammunition, hundreds were forced to surrender. Remarkably, von Kressenstein succeeded in extricating most of his forces and his heavy guns from a losing battle, driving his exhausted soldiers into a rapid retreat with Anzac cavalry in hot pursuit. The British commanders, determined to capture and destroy von Kressenstein's expeditionary corps, sent their aircraft aloft to guide the pursuers. However, the Ottomans drove back a final attack at the Bir al-Abd wells before completing their withdrawal to the safety of al-Arish, still securely in Turkish hands.

The Ottomans were soundly defeated in the Battle of Romani. They had lost an estimated 1,500 soldiers dead and wounded and another 4,000 taken prisoner, while British losses were just over 200 killed and 900 wounded. Yet the British viewed Romani as an incomplete victory. British commanders deemed it a critical failure that von Kressenstein had been allowed to withdraw with the majority of his forces and artillery intact after suffering the type of defeat that gave ample opportunity for the destruction of his force. While Romani represented the final Ottoman attack on British positions in Egypt, the Turks still retained the forces and artillery to defend their Palestine frontier.[5]

THE BRITISH ADVANCE IN THE SINAI IN THE SUMMER OF 1916 coincided with the launch of the Arab Revolt in the Hijaz. It is worth recalling that the first two months of the Arab Revolt were remarkably successful, with Hashemite forces defeating the Ottomans in Mecca, Taif, Jeddah, Rabigh, and Yanbu. The War Committee in London began to see the potential to coordinate the Arab Revolt and the Sinai campaign to make the Ottoman position in southern Syria and Palestine untenable. Whereas in February 1916 the chief of the Imperial General Staff had authorized only limited operations to Qatiya to defend the Suez Canal, in July 1916 the War Committee ordered Murray's forces to occupy the Sinai from al-Arish to the Red Sea port of Aqaba "since a force established at these places would directly threaten the Turkish communications between Syria and the Hejaz, and encourage Syrian Arabs" to revolt against the Ottomans.[6]

The methodical General Murray advanced in line with the construction of the Sinai railway and pipeline. By December 1916, the railhead had reached the wells of Mazar, within forty miles of al-Arish. With all of the necessary supplies stockpiled at the railhead and sufficient camels mobilized to deliver food, water, and ammunition to an army fighting in the barren desert, the British prepared to attack the Ottoman garrison.

Ottoman commanders assessed the situation in al-Arish with mounting concern. Their aerial reconnaissance had followed the British railway's progress and the concentration of troops and supplies. Moreover, they knew their garrison to be within easy range of British warships cruising off the Sinai coast. The 1,600 Ottoman defenders could not hope to hold their position against naval firepower and over four divisions of British infantry. On the eve of the British attack, the Ottomans fell back from al-Arish to better-defended positions along the Palestine frontier. The Royal Flying Corps reported Turkish lines abandoned, and on 21 December the first British troops occupied the strategic town unopposed.

The British position was far from secure. Aerial reconnaissance revealed heavily fortified Ottoman positions down the al-Arish valley in the village of Magdhaba. So long as the Turks remained in Magdhaba, they would pose a threat to the British rear. The Anzac cavalry and Imperial Camel Brigade were dispatched to drive the Turks from Magdhaba on 23 December. It was a race against time. With no water between al-Arish and Magdhaba, the mounted soldiers had to take the village before sundown; otherwise, the parched soldiers and their mounts would be forced to withdraw to El Arish for water. By early afternoon, when their anxious commander, the Australian general Sir Harry Chauvel, was on the verge of calling off the attack, a combined cavalry and camel assault broke through Ottoman lines.[7]

"To our surprise," a camelier (a soldier of the Camel Corps) recalled, "several of the Turks jumped from their trenches to shake hands with us." It was a strange moment of fraternizing between men who had last met in the Dardanelles. "Put it there, old chap," an Australian private said to a Turkish prisoner wearing a Gallipoli campaign medal. "I was there myself, and it was such a hell of a place that you have my sympathy." The Australian then pinned the Turkish medal on his own chest and helped himself to the prisoner's tobacco before advancing on another Ottoman position. Nearly 1,300 Ottoman soldiers surrendered as the British completed their occupation of the al-Arish valley.[8]

The British completed the reconquest of the Sinai on 9 January 1917, with the capture of the town of Rafah on the Ottoman-Egyptian frontier. In a day of intense fighting, forces of the Anzac Mounted Division succeeded in encircling the Ottoman trenches and forcing their surrender. Following their retreat from Rafah, the Ottomans abandoned their ambitions in Egypt to protect their position in Palestine.[9]

A question mark hung over the ultimate objective of the EEF. A new British prime minister, David Lloyd George, came to office in December 1916 following a cabinet crisis over the conduct of the war. A Liberal like his predecessor, H. H. Asquith, heading a coalition government with the Conservatives, Lloyd George sought a quick and decisive victory that would rally the government and the public behind his leadership. He argued for a vigorous campaign against the Ottomans in Palestine, convinced the conquest of Jerusalem would give British public opinion a much-needed boost after the ghastly losses at Verdun and the Somme. Lloyd George's generals, on the other hand, were loath to deploy more troops outside the western front, where they knew the war would be won or lost. The primary mission of the

EEF, the generals argued, was the defence of Egypt. The military men won the argument, and two days after the EEF's victory in Rafah, the War Cabinet ordered General Murray to defer large-scale operations in Palestine until the autumn of 1917 and to dispatch one division of his forces to France.

Expelled from Sinai, the Ottomans established a defensive line running inland from Gaza on the coast to the oasis town of Beersheba. Between January and March 1917, Ottoman reinforcements were deployed to the twenty-mile front protecting southern Palestine. A cavalry unit from the Caucasus and an infantry division from Thrace joined Cemal's forces in a determined bid to preserve Palestine from a future British attack.[10]

AT THE START OF 1917, AS THE EEF GROUND TO A HALT ON THE Palestine frontier, the Mesopotamian Expeditionary Force (MEF) resumed its offensive on the Tigris. What began as a cautious advance designed to wear down the Ottoman Sixth Army ended in the first major British victory in the Middle East—the conquest of Baghdad.

Repeated assaults to relieve Kut had left both British and Ottoman forces depleted and exhausted by the time Major General Charles Townshend surrendered in April 1916. Having failed in their objective, the British had neither the forces nor the incentive to resume their attack on Ottoman lines on the Tigris, and the Turks themselves were too worn down to take the offensive against the weakened British forces. Both sides reinforced their positions, tended to their sick and wounded, and lapsed into relative inactivity while their respective higher commands were preoccupied with more critical threats on other fronts.

Almost immediately after their victory in Kut, the Ottomans faced the menace of a Russian attack on Baghdad. In early May 1916, General Nikolai Baratoff, commander in chief of the Russian armies in Persia, occupied the border town of Qasr-i Shirin and threatened Turkish positions across the frontier in Khaniqin—just one hundred miles from Baghdad. Halil Pasha, who had been rewarded for his victory in Kut with command over the Ottoman Sixth Army, redeployed his forces from the Tigris front for the defence of Khaniqin, reducing his numbers around Kut to 12,000 men.

The British made Halil's task easier. Sir William Robertson, the chief of the Imperial General Staff, confirmed British aims in Mesopotamia after the fall of Kut as "defensive", and he informed the MEF commander, "We do not attach any importance to the possession of Kut or to the occupation of Baghdad." He recommended the British maintain "as forward a position as can be made secure tactically" to minimize the effect of the fall of Kut on Britain's reputation and to force the Ottomans to retain troops on the Tigris that might otherwise be redeployed to confront the Russian column threatening Baghdad. But Robertson had no intention of authorizing hostilities against Ottoman positions on the Tigris.[11]

With the British taking a passive line, Halil threw everything he had at the Russians and stopped Baratoff at Khaniqin on 1 June 1916, driving Russian forces back in a bid to occupy the Persian towns of Kermanshah (1 July) and Hamdan (10 August). The Ottoman surge into Persia worried both the Russians and the British but left Halil Pasha's defences in Baghdad dangerously under-strength. They never recovered and would leave Halil struggling to contain the British threat as reinforcements began to arrive in Mesopotamia from India and Egypt.

In August, the British appointed a new commander to the MEF. Major General Sir Stanley Maude had been wounded in France and was the last man off the beach in the Suvla Bay evacuation at the end of the Gallipoli campaign. An aggressive commander, Maude was determined to take the offensive on the Tigris front. Across the summer and autumn of 1916, he managed to build up a formidable force in Mesopotamia. He secured two fresh infantry divisions, raising the MEF to a fighting strength of more than 160,000 men, of which over 50,000 were deployed to the Tigris front (with the remainder distributed between British positions in Basra and on the Euphrates). As Maude's army expanded, Halil's contracted. Worn down by illness, desertion, and casualties incurred in the regular exchanges of fire between Turkish and British lines, the Sixth Army suffered above all from a lack of reinforcements. Maude's intelligence reported no more than 20,000 Ottomans deployed around Kut, though in fact their numbers were far fewer—perhaps only 10,500.[12]

The British advance base on the Tigris at Shaykh Saad was a hive of activity in the autumn of 1916. New riverboats expanded freight capacity to over seven hundred tons per day to the Tigris riverhead. To speed supplies to the front near Kut, the British constructed a light railway line from Shaykh Saad to the Shatt al-Hayy (the channel connecting the Tigris at Kut to the Euphrates at Nasiriyya). Running beyond the reach of Ottoman artillery, the railway was operational in September 1916 and had reached the banks of the Shatt al-Hayy by early 1917. To improve the transport of supplies and ammunition from railhead to front, Maude ordered hundreds of Ford vans that proved surprisingly effective even after the rains had reduced the terrain to mud.

Despite these advantages, the War Committee in London remained cautious. The chief of the Imperial General Staff, General Robertson, believed Baghdad would be very difficult to take and even harder to hold, given the length of the lines of supply and communication to the Persian Gulf. Moreover, he dismissed the capture of Baghdad as of "no appreciable effect on the war". As late as September 1916, Robertson's orders to Maude ruled out an advance. Yet the MEF commander kept his war plans to himself. In November, he secured permission for offensive operations against Ottoman positions on the Shatt al-Hayy. He refused to commit to a date for the start of operations and even kept his plans from his own staff and commanders. As it turned out, they did not have long to wait.

On 10 December, General Maude wired his superiors in India and London that his preparations were complete and the start of operations against the Shatt al-Hayy was imminent. If surprised by the short notice, the War Committee would have been astonished by the reason for Maude's haste. The MEF commander was superstitious. Maude believed 13 was his lucky number and had decided to launch his offensive on 13 December with the 13th Division in the vanguard.[13]

The third and final battle for the devastated town of Kut opened with British artillery on 13 December. The campaign dragged on for over two months along a twenty-mile front. Maude's men suffered heavy casualties in frontal assaults on well-entrenched Turkish positions, while superior British artillery cut down the Ottoman ranks. Yet the Turks continued to hold their lines and counter-attack with remarkable tenacity. In mid-February 1917, they repulsed a full frontal assault on the Sannaiyat trenches, forcing the British back with terrible losses.

The battle for Kut reached its climax on 23 February, when the British managed to secure a bridgehead across the Tigris. To distract the defenders, Maude ordered assaults on the Sannaiyat trenches and near Kut itself. With Ottoman troops massed to repel the British at these two points, Maude managed to catch the Turks by surprise five miles upriver from Kut with an advance guard securing a bridgehead at the Shumran Bend. The handful of Turkish defenders there put up a determined fight but were soon overcome by British artillery fired from very short range. By the time the Ottoman commanders realized the danger, they were unable to send enough men to stem the flood of hostile troops crossing the pontoon bridge.

As British cavalry, infantry, and artillery raced across the river, Ottoman commanders recognized their situation was untenable. At risk of encirclement and capture, Halil Pasha ordered an immediate retreat—from all twenty miles of positions his forces held on the left bank of the Tigris. The success of the Ottoman retreat stemmed largely from the order with which it was carried out. The main body of Ottoman troops withdrew with their guns and as many of their supplies as they could carry. A rear guard held the route until the main body had passed, then followed behind to protect the retreating force from enemy assault. Arnold Wilson, a political officer from British India, estimated the retreating Ottoman column at no more than 6,200 men, pursued by a British force in excess of 46,000 infantry and cavalry.[14]

As the Anglo-Indian army occupied the left bank of the Tigris, Captain W. Nunn of the Royal Navy led his gunships up to Kut al-Amara, where he anchored on the night of 24 February. The following morning he sent a party ashore. They found the place deserted and ran up the Union Jack. Though the ruined town held no more strategic value for the Mesopotamia campaign than any other bend in the river, it held great symbolic value for Maude and his men. Restoring the British flag went some way towards redeeming the failures that had led to Townshend's surrender ten months earlier. Yet for the residents of Kut, who had endured siege and the severity of Ottoman reprisals after Townshend's surrender, every change of flag had spelled devastation. They could not have viewed the return of the British with much confidence in their future.

After successfully eluding the British infantry and cavalry, the retreating Ottoman army came under attack from the Royal Navy. Hundreds of miles from the sea, Captain Nunn's squadron of five gunboats sped upriver to overtake Halil's XIII Corps. They met the Ottoman rear guard entrenched at a hairpin bend in the Tigris. For several miles, the British gunboats faced intense artillery and machine-gun fire at near point-blank range. All five ships suffered direct hits and heavy casualties but still managed to get past the rear guard in pursuit of the retreating Ottoman army.

Nunn's squadron caught up with the main body of Halil's forces on a stretch of river running parallel to the line of retreat. Firing with all their guns, the ships wreaked havoc among the exhausted and demoralized Turkish soldiers. An Allied pilot who flew over the area described the scene as "a spectacle amazing and horrible. Dead bodies and mules, abandoned guns, wagons and stores littered the road, many of the wagons had hoisted the white flag, men and animals, exhausted and starving, lay prone on the ground. Few of these, if any, survived the attentions of the Arab tribesmen, hanging round like wolves on their trail.I turned home sickened."[15]

By sunset, the British naval squadron overtook retreating Turkish river vessels and managed to capture or destroy them all, including several steamships the British had surrendered to the Ottomans earlier in the campaign. The Turkish hospital ship *Basra* ran up the white flag and transferred hundreds of seriously wounded Turkish prisoners, along with several Britons, to British care. At the end of the day, Nunn anchored to allow his men to tend to their own dead and wounded and patch their battered ships, miles ahead of the nearest British soldiers.[16]

In two and a half months of fighting, General Maude had shattered Halil's defences. He had broken through hitherto impregnable Turkish lines, taken some 7,500 prisoners, and reduced the four Ottoman divisions on the Tigris front to under 5,000 men while preserving his own forces at near full strength. His ships controlled the river, and his aircraft dominated the skies. Maude knew the Ottomans had insufficient forces to defend Baghdad against British occupation. However, he was still operating under orders from London that barred an advance on that city. The MEF commander could only report to London and request new orders.

THE COMMANDERS IN LONDON WELCOMED THE GOOD NEWS FROM Iraq but were divided over how best to take advantage of Maude's successes. The surrender at Kut still cast a long shadow over British aspirations in Mesopotamia, and the chief of the Imperial General Staff was risk-averse. He accepted that Maude's army could occupy Baghdad but questioned its ability to keep the city, fearing the Ottomans would return with strong reinforcements and threaten an isolated British army with yet another siege. With no troops to spare from any front and fearing the effects on Muslim public opinion were the British to suffer another humiliation at the hands of the sultan-caliph's "holy warriors", General Robertson was unwilling to authorize Maude to do more than "establish British influence in the Baghdad *vilayet* [province]". While he instructed Maude to "press enemy in direction of Baghdad" and even to "raid" the city with his cavalry if doing so proved opportune, Robertson's orders of 28 February warned against "being compelled later to fall back for any reason" because of the "objectionable political effect" that any such retirement might produce.[17]

In the ensuing exchange of telegrams, the commander in chief in India, General Charles Monro, argued enthusiastically for a rapid occupation of Baghdad while the Turks were in disorder. It would deny the Turks a strategic concentration point to menace British interests in Basra and Persia and would greatly increase British prestige in the Islamic East. Maude also reasoned with Robertson, outlining the advantages for the British military position in Iraq to be gained from the occupation of Baghdad. One other concern weighed on the War Committee's minds. The Russians were proposing a spring offensive in Mesopotamia, with operations against Mosul, Samarra, and Baghdad. Were the Russians to get to Baghdad first, one British official reasoned, "it would nullify the Sykes-Picot agreement".[18]

The weight of these arguments drove General Robertson to revise his orders to Maude. In a telegram addressed to the MEF commander on 3 March, he conceded that "the feasibility of occupying Baghdad forthwith" was "probably greater" than he had first believed. Without actually ordering Maude into Baghdad, he agreed to leave the final decision to Maude's own judgment but reiterated all of his old fears: "In brief, our object should be to attain greatest possible result from your recent victory and at the same time to avoid overdoing things to such an extent as to incur repetition of the old communication trouble, or, after a definite occupation of Baghdad, to be compelled to withdraw."

After this pause to sort his marching orders, Maude led his army upriver towards Baghdad. On 6 March they reached Salman Pak, where Townshend had been driven into retreat at the end of 1915, unopposed. They marvelled at the ancient arch of Ctesiphon, the most visible landmark for miles around, and examined the elaborate Ottoman trench network prepared for the defence of Baghdad and subsequently abandoned. Turkish commanders had decided to concentrate their defences on the Diyala River, one of the tributaries of the Tigris downstream from Baghdad. The British were surprised by the intensity of Turkish resistance on the Diyala, which held Maude's column in check for three days during which both sides suffered heavy casualties. But the Diyala position was no more than a holding operation. Halil recognized that Baghdad could not be defended against Maude's superior numbers and firepower.

Inside Baghdad, Ottoman civil and military officials did their best to preserve order while preparing to evacuate the city. For Talib Mushtaq, the Baghdad schoolboy who had chatted with British POWs from Kut, it was inconceivable that the Turks would abandon Baghdad to foreign occupation. On the eve of the evacuation, Mushtaq and his brother were called to the office of the deputy governor, an old family friend, who, "with emotion and pain etched on his face", sent the two boys under police protection to rejoin their family in the nearby town of Baquba, where their father served in the civil administration. "We are now evacuating Baghdad," the deputy governor explained, "and the Turkish army is retreating on all fronts. The English Army is likely to enter Baghdad tomorrow or the day after." Mushtaq was incredulous. "How could we evacuate Baghdad?" the patriotic teenager asked. "How could we allow the hooves of English horses to defile the soil of this sacred homeland?" But the deputy governor was adamant, and the two boys were taken from school and dispatched under escort to their frantic parents in Baquba.[19]

The illusion of normalcy was shattered shortly after midnight on 11 March, when the Ottomans and their German allies began to destroy military installations in Baghdad. German engineers severed the steel cables securing the wireless masts, which came crashing to the ground. Heavy explosions rocked the city as the derricks, cranes, and water tanks of the Baghdad Railway Company were dynamited. One by one, the main government offices were blown up, and the pontoon bridge across the Tigris was torched. Oscar Heizer, the American consul in Baghdad, watched the systematic destruction of Ottoman Baghdad from his rooftop. As the Ottoman state withdrew, disorder took its place. "Looting of the market and bazaars by the Kurds and Arabs of the lower class began immediately," he noted in his consular log.[20]

By morning, the looting had reached such proportions that Consul Heizer, accompanied by an armed retainer, set off on horseback in search of the British advance guard. By 9:30, he encountered a detachment of Indian lancers led by a British major and accompanied them into the centre of the city. The streets were crowded with people, Heizer noted, "many of

The fall of Baghdad. An Indian army transport section moves along New Street during the entry of British forces into Baghdad on 11 March 1917.

whom had just before been looting, but were now looking virtuous and cheering the troops". The lancers proceeded to the main bazaars, where they found men, women, and children stripping the last of the goods from shop shelves. The looters also stripped the windows, doors, and woodwork of many houses. The major drew his revolver and fired several shots in the air, scattering the looters, who were beaten by the lancers as they fled past Baghdad's new masters.

General Maude waited until the town had been secured before making a low-key entry later that afternoon. The Union Jack that enthusiastic soldiers had raised over the citadel earlier in the day was lowered, to be hoisted anew over the clock tower of the Turkish barracks following Maude's entry. However, the conqueror of Baghdad was barred from making any official statement without government approval. Back in London, the British cabinet tasked Sir Mark Sykes, Lord Kitchener's Middle East advisor and coauthor of the Sykes-Picot Agreement, with drafting a formal proclamation in Maude's name. As Arnold Wilson tartly remarked, the document "bears in every line the mark of [Sykes's] ebullient orientalism".[21]

The proclamation opened in high rhetorical style, reassuring the people of Baghdad, "Our armies do not come into your cities and lands as conquerors or enemies, but as liberators."

> Since the days of [the 13th-century Mongol conqueror] Hulagu your city and your lands have been subject to the tyranny of strangers, your palaces have fallen into ruins, your gardens have sunk in desolation, and your forefathers and yourselves have groaned in bondage. Your sons have been carried off to wars not of your seeking, your wealth has been stripped from you by unjust men and squandered in distant places.[22]

Printed in both English and Arabic and distributed freely in Baghdad, Maude's proclamation failed to persuade Iraqis that the British were anything other than the latest in a long line of strangers to subject their country to despotism. As Talib Mushtaq recalled, "After his entry into Baghdad, General Maude announced that he had not come as a conqueror but as a savior and a liberator. What shameful lies and deceit, for the people of Baghdad and of Iraq as a whole saw with their own eyes how the English treated the Iraqis as slaves or as captives. So where was the freedom? Where was the salvation?"[23]

These were small considerations to the British War Committee. After a string of catastrophic failures on the Ottoman front, the British had finally scored a major victory. Baghdad might have been of little or no strategic value to the overall war effort, but any victory was welcome, and Baghdad, city of *The Arabian Nights*, was an exotic prize. For the Ottomans, the fall of Baghdad was a grave reversal. The ancient capital of the Abbasid caliphate (750–1258 CE) was also the intended terminus of the Berlin-to-Baghdad railway and the launching pad for Ottoman post-war ambitions in the Persian Gulf. With the loss of Baghdad, coupled with their losses to the Russians in eastern Anatolia, including the garrison town of Erzurum and the Black Sea port of Trabzon, the fall of Mecca and Jeddah to the Hashemites in the Hijaz, and their recent setbacks in the Sinai, the Ottomans once again were being pressed back on all their frontiers.

THE BRITISH VICTORY IN BAGHDAD ENCOURAGED THE WAR CABINET to reassess its strategy in Egypt. Since taking the Sinai border town of Rafah in January 1917, the Egyptian Expeditionary Force had been under orders to defer further operations until the autumn. Yet Allied war planners were reconsidering their approach to the war as a whole. On 26 February 1917, British and French generals had met in the English Channel port of Calais to review the global strategy for the war. In a bid to regain the initiative, the Allies decided to take action against the Central Powers on several fronts simultaneously—on the western front, in Macedonia, and in Mesopotamia—in a coordinated spring offensive. With Maude's occupation of Baghdad on 11 March, the timing was opportune for the EEF to play its part.

The Allies were further encouraged when the United States joined their ranks by declaring war on Germany on 2 April 1917. It took a great deal to overturn American isolationism. After all, Woodrow Wilson successfully ran for re-election in 1916 on the slogan "He kept us out of the war." However, a combination of unrestricted German U-boat attacks on Atlantic shipping (the sinking of the passenger ship SS *Lusitania* off the coast of Ireland on 7 May 1915 claimed 128 Americans among the 1,201 lives lost) and revelations of German overtures to conclude an alliance with Mexico in the event of American entry into the war sufficed to secure America's adhesion to the Allied cause. Though far from a military power in 1917—America's peacetime army numbered under 100,000 men—the country's mighty industrial base and large population promised to revive the Entente's fortunes on the western front, encouraging British war planners to fresh action in the Middle East.[24]

The EEF was ready for action. Railway construction had continued apace in the opening months of 1917, reaching Khan Yunis, fifteen miles south of Gaza, by the third week of March. The water pipeline was not far behind. A large stockpile of ammunition and supplies had been assembled near the front, allowing British officers to prepare for an offensive before the end of March. The British enjoyed numerical superiority over the defenders, with 11,000 cavalry and 12,000 infantry and an entire division of 8,000 held in reserve. The Ottoman garrison in Gaza numbered only 4,000 men, though another 15,000 Turkish front-line troops were stationed a few miles to the rear.

General Murray and his officers drew up a battle plan modelled on his previous engagements in the Sinai. The Anzac Mounted Division was ordered to encircle Gaza from the north, east, and south-east, both to cut the Turkish line of retreat and to block reinforcements. The infantry took up positions for a direct assault from the south. Like the Sinai battles, the attack on Gaza would be a race against time. Unless they could take the town before sunset, the parched British forces would have to retreat miles to the railhead to replenish their water supplies.

In the early morning hours of 26 March, the cavalry set out to encircle Gaza. By 10:30, the town had been surrounded by enemy troops. The infantry, however, was delayed by heavy fog, and the order to attack wasn't given until noon. British artillery opened fire, laying waste to the coastal city of 40,000. The infantry was held back by relentless sniper and machine-gun fire from Turkish lines and the difficult terrain broken up with dense hedges of cactus. Yet, while the Ottomans concentrated on the infantry assault from the south, Anzac cavalry units closed in on Gaza from the north and east. By 6:30 p.m., their defences collapsing, Ottoman forces were on the verge of surrender. To the Turks' great good fortune, a breakdown in communications meant the British commanders had no idea how close to victory their own forces were.

By late afternoon, after taking heavy casualties in a number of pitched battles around Gaza, the British ordered a general retreat. They calculated that, after the unforeseen delay in the start of battle, their men would not have enough time to secure all of their objectives before nightfall and feared their forces would be pinned down by Ottoman reinforcements advancing on Gaza. Without access to fresh water and ammunition, neither the soldiers nor their mounts would be in any condition to continue fighting a second day. Rather than risk defeat, British generals preferred to sacrifice the day's hard-earned gains to preserve their ranks.

Soldiers on both sides of the battle were equally astonished when British forces suddenly abandoned their assault on Gaza and withdrew. The retreat left the British exposed to Ottoman counter-attack, and the heavy casualties suffered while withdrawing compounded the soldiers' fury at having to abandon ground won after intense fighting. For the Ottomans, the British retreat was nothing short of a miracle, and their commanders were quick to take advantage of the opportunity to recover strategic high ground. By the end of battle on 27 March, British losses exceeded Ottoman dead and wounded.[25]

The shadow of Gallipoli hung over Gaza. "So what do you say?" a Turkish journalist asked a wounded soldier after the battle. "Do you think they'll come back?" "They can't come back, *effendi*," the Turkish soldier replied gravely. "They saw what regiment we were." The soldier meant that the British

Regimental standard presented to victorious Ottoman forces after the First Battle of Gaza, March 1917.

knew his regiment had defeated them at Gallipoli, and they would not be back for more.[26]

In his reports back to London, General Murray economized on the bad news and exaggerated his gains in this first attempt on Gaza. Claiming to have advanced fifteen miles, Murray reported that his forces had "inflicted very heavy losses" of "between 6,000 and 7,000 men" when Turkish casualties were actually under 2,500. The London newspapers, hungry for good news, published Murray's figures without question. But the soldiers in the field knew better. Briscoe Moore, a lieutenant in the Auckland Mounted Rifles, picked up a message dropped by an enemy plane shortly after the battle, which set the record straight: "You beat us at communiqués, but we beat you at Gaza."[27]

The British War Cabinet ultimately called Murray's bluff. General Robertson, chief of the Imperial General Staff, informed Murray that in light of Maude's recent occupation of Baghdad and Murray's own "success" at Gaza, he was revising his instructions for the Egyptian Expeditionary Force. Murray's immediate objective was to defeat Turkish forces south of Jerusalem, leading to the occupation of the holy city. In his telegram to Murray dated 2 April 1917, Robertson stressed the symbolic importance of the conquest of Jerusalem for the war-weary British public. "War Cabinet are anxious therefore that your operations should be pushed with all energy." In return, Robertson promised to supply all of the war materiel Murray needed to succeed.

Judging from the cautious tone and many reservations raised in his correspondence with London, General Murray had little confidence in his ability to defeat the Ottomans in Palestine and take Jerusalem. His whole strategy in the arid landscape of southern Palestine had been based on a gradual advance in line with the railway and pipeline. Even if he got past Gaza—a task that had grown more difficult with Ottoman reinforcements following the First Battle of Gaza—he had grave concerns about the rapid extension of his supply lines and access to water for tens of thousands of men and animals. Yet his orders could not be clearer, and Murray began to prepare for a second attempt on Ottoman lines at Gaza.

The Ottomans now knew where the British were concentrated to attack and made every effort to bar their route from Gaza to Beersheba. As Cemal Pasha recalled, "I decided to hold that front and prevent the English from breaking through at any cost by concentrating all the Turkish forces there." In the three weeks following the first attempt on Gaza, Cemal distributed his reinforcements along the Gaza-Beersheba line, where they built up a series of earthwork defences and trenches that subjected all approaches to Gaza to machine-gun and artillery fire.[28]

Experience had taught the British commanders that fortune favoured the defender in trench warfare. To improve his troops' chances of breaking through Turkish lines, General Murray deployed some of the most terrible weapons in the British arsenal. He stockpiled 4,000 rounds of gas-tipped artillery for the initial bombardment of Ottoman positions. Although both sides had used poison gas extensively on the western front since the Second Battle of Ypres in April 1915, it had never been used against the Ottomans. British soldiers were issued with gas masks in advance of the attack; Ottoman soldiers, of course, had none. Eight tanks were delivered in secret to the Sinai front to assist the infantry in their advances on well-entrenched Turkish lines. "We had heard much about these monstrous engines of war," an Australian in the Camel Corps recorded, "and were overjoyed at their arrival, believing that as soon as they went into action they would strike terror in the ranks of the enemy."[29]

The Second Battle of Gaza opened with a heavy bombardment on 17 April 1917. The gas shells fired were concentrated on one section of trenches but proved ineffectual. Offshore, battleships subjected Gaza to a rain of steel and fire without dislodging the defenders. When finally the British soldiers advanced on Turkish lines, they faced relentless machine-gun and artillery fire.

Frank Reid, an Australian soldier in the Imperial Camel Corps, dismounted to go into battle "under very heavy rifle and machine-gun fire". Reid watched his comrades fall around him as artillery shells burst overhead.

The Imperial Camel Corps in Sinai. Camel-mounted soldiers from (left to right) Australia, England, New Zealand, and India posed for this image, capturing the "imperial" nature of the Camel Corps.

Suddenly he heard men to his left cheering and saw one of the eight British tanks making for the Turkish trenches. He fully expected "that once the tank reached the trenches in front the Turks would surrender". Instead, the Ottoman soldiers took aim and fired on the tank with everything they had. "Huge slugs clanged against the iron plates of the tank and ricocheted in every direction. But the tank still went on."

Following in the tank's wake, the cameliers reached the first line of Turkish trenches, where they confronted a handful of Ottoman soldiers too wounded to retreat. Reid remembered the face-to-face encounters between Australians and Turks as a moment of conflict between contradictory instincts. Two cameliers came on a wounded Turkish soldier, his arms crossed over his chest.

"Bayonet the cow," yelled the first camelier.

"No, give the poor devil a chance," cried the second.

Reid watched another camelier snatch the rifle from a wounded Turk and pause. Rather than kill the bleeding man, the Australian bent down and gave him a drink of water. "Poor wretch! Wants to live like the rest of us."

British tanks destroyed in the Second Battle of Gaza. The British only deployed tanks once in the Middle Eastern campaigns, where they proved of limited value in the disastrous Second Battle of Gaza. Ottoman gunners destroyed no fewer than three of the eight tanks deployed.

He then took out his own first aid kit to dress the Turk's head wound. The compassion of the gesture was somewhat diminished when a wounded Turkish officer hobbled over to thank the Australian.

"Good," said the Turkish officer in broken English, patting the Australian on the shoulder.

"Good be damned," cried the camelier. "Go and bury yourself. I'm busy."

Reid continued to follow the tank's progress. Its crew seemed disoriented and began to drive erratically. Hit by several enemy shells, the tank suddenly exploded in flames. The Australian cameliers and English infantry-men following the tank found themselves exposed to intense fire from the Turkish trenches, the dead and wounded falling on all sides. They managed to rush the Ottoman redoubt but were soon pinned down by a Turkish counter-attack. The cameliers, along with the English infantry and the Australian Light Horse, were all driven back.[30]

Over three days of battle, the Ottomans held their lines and drove the British into retreat with heavy losses. None of the British "secret weapons" had daunted the Turks, who had not noticed the gas and managed to destroy three of the eight British tanks. The Turkish journalist Falih Rıfkı wrote lyrically about the carcasses of the "dead combat tanks" that littered the Gaza battlefield with their "enormous mass twisted and empty". When the British generals took stock of their casualties, they were forced to break off the engagement and accept a second defeat yet more terrible than the first. By nightfall on 19 April, the British had lost 6,444 casualties—three times Ottoman losses of 2,013 dead, wounded, and missing.[31]

The Palestine campaign had, for the moment, stalled. Murray's failures at Gaza cost him his job. He was replaced in July 1917 by General Sir Edmund Allenby, dispatched by Prime Minister David Lloyd George with the seemingly impossible assignment of conquering Jerusalem by Christmas. Cemal Pasha was in a far stronger position. His forces held the well-watered lands of Palestine and had confined the British to the Sinai Desert. Moreover, the Ottomans had prevented the British from making contact with the forces of the Arab Revolt. So long as the EEF and the Arab army were kept apart, the Ottomans stood every chance of preserving their position in Syria and Palestine.

As the Ottomans held the Egyptian Expeditionary Force in check, they faced renewed threats from the Arab army in the Hijaz. With Ottoman forces confined to Medina, the Hashemites were free to extend their control over the rest of the Hijaz and advance northward towards Syria. As commander of the Arab army, Sharif Husayn's son Faysal's sights were set on the Red Sea port of Wajh. His British advisers were in full agreement. The supply line from Suez to Wajh was two hundred miles shorter than that to Yanbu, and from Wajh the Arab army would be in position to attack a 250-mile stretch of the Hijaz Railway. Cutting the railway line would sever the supply line and communications to Ottoman forces besieged in Medina, hastening their surrender.

For Faysal, the march on Wajh was a recruitment opportunity. He needed to broaden tribal participation in the revolt to prevent it from collapsing. By riding northward at the head of an 11,000-strong army, Faysal knew he would make a great impression on local Bedouin and attract the allegiance of fresh tribes. He also hoped to overwhelm the eight hundred Turkish defenders at Wajh with the sheer mass of his army and secure their surrender without a fight.

The Royal Navy coordinated closely with the Arab army. To ensure the Bedouin force had sufficient water supplies, the HMS *Hardinge* deposited twenty tons of water in tanks at an agreed-on location just south of Wajh. The ship also carried an advance troop of four hundred tribesmen to land due north of Wajh. With Faysal's forces arriving from the south, this advance troop could prevent any Ottoman effort to reinforce or retreat from Wajh. Faysal and the British agreed to meet at Wajh at dawn on 23 January 1917.

The small Bedouin force disembarked to the north of Wajh with a landing party of two hundred British marines and sailors from the *Hardinge* right on schedule. They found no sign of Faysal or his army. Undeterred, some one hundred tribesmen approached the town to engage the Turkish defenders. As most of the garrison had already withdrawn to an old fort some six miles inland, the attackers quickly broke through the Turkish lines to plunder the town before the rest of the Arab army arrived. The last of the defenders took refuge in Wajh's mosque, where they held out until the building was struck by naval gunfire. The British ships then trained their guns on the old fort, driving the Ottoman soldiers into headlong retreat. By the time Faysal arrived on 25 January, two days after the scheduled start of hostilities, Wajh was securely in Arab hands. The show of strength had paid off, as tribal leaders from all around northern Hijaz now called on Faysal to offer their allegiance to the Hashemite cause.[32]

Once established in Wajh, Faysal and his British advisors went to work on disrupting the Hijaz Railway. On 20 February, the first raiding party succeeded in detonating a charge under an Ottoman train, destroying the locomotive. The attack had an immediate impact on morale in both Damascus and Medina. Cemal Pasha sent orders to the Ottoman commander in Medina, Fahri Pasha, to evacuate the city. The British, who intercepted Cemal's orders, instructed their officers in the Hijaz to redouble their attacks on the railway line to prevent an Ottoman withdrawal. So long as it was confined to Medina, Fahri's 11,000-man garrison posed no threat to Arab or British forces elsewhere. Given that Murray's Egyptian Expeditionary Force was preparing to make its first attack on Gaza, the British sought at all costs to prevent Cemal from using the Medina garrison to reinforce his positions in Palestine.

Throughout the month of March, British sappers and their Arab guides placed mines at strategic points along the Hijaz Railway. At the end of March, even T. E. Lawrence, who served as liaison between British commanders in Cairo and Faysal, tried his hand at blowing up an isolated station. Armed with a mountain gun, machine guns, and explosives, Lawrence and his team managed to disrupt traffic on the railway line for three days with the mayhem they unleashed. The attacks on the railway, combined with Fahri Pasha's determination to defend the holy city, prevented the evacuation of Medina. Yet they failed to obstruct communications and supply along the Damascus-to-Medina railway. The Ottomans proved remarkably resourceful, discovering mines before they detonated and repairing the damage of successful charges with great efficiency. It was clear that the war in the Hijaz would not be won on the railway alone.[33]

While British officers perfected their rail-blasting techniques, Faysal set about organizing a regular army to bring discipline to the Arab forces. He recruited Jafar al-Askari, an Ottoman officer captured by the British in the Sanussi campaign in Egypt, in Faysal's words, "to create a regular army capable of carrying out its military duties in an appropriate fashion". Askari was reunited with a number of fellow Iraqis, many of them members of al-Ahd, the secret Arabist society favoured by military men. They became some of Faysal's most devoted followers, ideologically committed to the cause of Arab independence.[34]

British arms and supplies began to flood the growing sharifian headquarters at Wajh. A shipment of 30,000 rifles and 15 million rounds of ammunition reached the Red Sea port. Armoured cars manufactured by Rolls Royce were unloaded and began to patrol the desert flats, providing mobile firepower. The Royal Flying Corps created a series of landing strips to permit its planes to bomb the Hijaz Railway. Gold and grain were unloaded in great quantities to pay and feed the growing numbers in the Arab army. With such reinforcements, Faysal began to consider extending his lines beyond the Hijaz into the southern reaches of Syria.

To prepare the ground for a bold move further north, Faysal dispatched three of his most trusted lieutenants on a reconnaissance journey: Sharif Nasir ibn Ali, a notable of Medina and close confidant of Faysal's; Auda Abu Tayi, leader of the powerful Huwaytat tribe; and Nasib al-Bakri, whose family introduced Faysal to the Arabist movement in Damascus. The three departed on 19 May for the Wadi Sirhan, the valley that for centuries had served as the main caravan route between central Arabia and the Syrian Desert. Each had a distinct mission. Sharif Nasir was sent as Faysal's personal representative to gain the loyalty of the Syrian tribes. Auda was to make contact with fellow tribesmen of the Huwaytat to secure camels and sheep to transport and feed the Arab army in its forthcoming operations in southern Syria. And Bakri was to make contact with Arabists in and around Damascus to gain their support for a general uprising.[35]

T. E. Lawrence asked to accompany the small expedition. Three days before they set off, Lawrence had met with Sir Mark Sykes, who had travelled to the Hijaz to brief the Hashemites on the terms of the Sykes-Picot Agreement. If, as seems likely, Sykes took the opportunity to brief Lawrence as well, the idealistic young English officer would have been appalled by the British government's double dealing. Lawrence's actions and writings make clear that he was determined to assist the Arabs in securing Syria before the French could. Sharif Nasir's expedition gave him the opportunity to act on his convictions.[36]

After a taxing journey across the desert, Sharif Nasir's expedition reached the Wadi Sirhan. After three days with the Huwaytat, the members of the group set off on their different tasks. Nasib al-Bakri went to Damascus to work with Arabists there. Lawrence reconnoitred the terrain surrounding Damascus to drum up support for the revolt, managing to blow up a railway bridge between Beirut and Damascus for good measure. Sharif Nasir and Auda Abu Tayi actively recruited tribesmen to join their movement. On 18 June, Nasir, Auda, and Lawrence reassembled at the mouth of the Wadi Sirhan (Bakri had chosen to remain in Damascus). Through the combined efforts of Auda and Nasir, some 560 Huwaytat tribesmen had joined their force. Their numbers were not sufficient to attack a major Ottoman garrison, such as the railway depot at Maan (in modern Jordan). Instead, at the end of June, the small column advanced towards the Red Sea port of Aqaba.

The port of Aqaba sits at the head of the Gulf of Aqaba, the eastern fork of the Red Sea that divides Sinai from the Hijaz. This backwater had immense strategic value. Its capture would give British forces in Egypt and the Sinai direct lines of communication with the Arab army. The conquest of Aqaba would place all of the Hijaz, except Medina, under Hashemite control. And the sharif's army would control the southern entrance to the Syrian lands. Since the opening days of the war, when the British bombarded Aqaba with impunity, the Ottomans had built strong sea defences to protect the little port. However, they had never anticipated an attack from the landward side. The mounted column led by Sharif Nasir sought to exploit this weakness.

Bypassing the garrison at Maan, the six hundred Bedouin fighters crossed the Hijaz Railway further south at the Ghadir al-Hajj station, which they sacked. Lawrence did as much damage to the railway line as possible to slow the movement of Ottoman reinforcements from Maan. He claimed to have "ruined ten bridges and many rails" before running out of explosives.[37]

On 2 July, Sharif Nasir's column surrounded a Turkish battalion sent to guard the approaches to Aqaba at a spot called Abu al-Lisan. After subjecting the Ottoman soldiers to hours of sniping, Auda led his tribesmen in a headlong rush. The Ottoman soldiers froze in horror at the sight of the galloping horsemen and took flight. By Lawrence's account, 300 Turkish soldiers were left dead or dying, with only 160 survivors taken prisoner. Only two tribesmen were killed. The success of Arab arms against the Ottomans encouraged more tribesmen to join the Hashemite movement, and the small column grew larger.

The Arab army enlisted a Turkish prisoner to draft letters to the commanders of the three isolated army outposts between Abu al-Lisan and Aqaba. The letters promised good treatment to those who surrendered and no mercy for those who resisted. The first outpost surrendered without a fight. The second outpost resisted and was taken without the Arabs suffering a single casualty. The third Turkish unit negotiated, then resisted, before finally capitulating when it found itself surrounded and fired on from all sides. The last barrier broken, Sharif Nasir's small army "raced through a driving sand-storm down to Akaba, four miles further, and splashed into the sea on July the sixth", Lawrence exulted, "just two months after our setting out from Wejh."[38]

The entry of Arab forces into Aqaba, 6 July 1917. T. E. Lawrence captured this iconic image on the day sharifian forces took Aqaba, transforming the Hashemite uprising in the Hijaz into an Arab revolt.

Victory at Aqaba was the Arab Revolt's greatest achievement to date. Sharif Nasir wrote a report to Faysal that same day, crediting the tribesmen for their courageous action. Lawrence, recognizing the significance for British war planners, set off across the Sinai for Cairo, accompanied by eight volunteers. Still dressed in Bedouin robes and headdress, Lawrence seemed to revel in the shock he caused at British headquarters in Cairo on 10 July when, mistaken for a ragged Arab, he spoke with a perfect Oxford accent. At that moment Captain Lawrence was transformed into the celebrated Lawrence of Arabia. However much the top brass frowned at his appearance, his news of an Arab victory in Aqaba made him an overnight hero. Sir Reginald Wingate, the high commissioner in Cairo, dashed a telegraph off to the chief of the Imperial General Staff, Sir William Robertson, that same night. His claims suggest that either Lawrence or Wingate himself had inflated Arab gains: "Captain Lawrence arrived Cairo today by land from Aqaba. Turkish posts between Tafilah, Maan and Aqaba in Arab hands."[39]

For the new commander of the Egyptian Expeditionary Force, General Sir Edmund Allenby, the Arab victory at Aqaba had the potential to transform the British position in Sinai. He invited Lawrence to brief him on 12 July. After relating the events of the occupation of Aqaba, Lawrence, still dressed in Bedouin robes, expounded on his ideas for a general Arab uprising against Ottoman forces from Maan in the south as far as Hama (in modern Syria) to the north, severing Turkish rail communications with Medina, Damascus, and Palestine. To support the Arab effort, Lawrence asked Allenby to invade Palestine and pin down Cemal Pasha's forces. Allenby was noncommittal. "Well," he said to close the interview, "I will do for you what I can."[40]

In fact, Allenby was captivated by what Lawrence and the Arab Revolt might do for the EEF. He wrote to the War Committee the following week to endorse Lawrence's call for cooperation between the Arab army and the Palestine campaign. Such a two-front assault, he argued, could "cause a collapse of the Turkish campaign in the Hijaz and in Syria and produce far-reaching results, both political as well as military". Of course, in order for Allenby to fulfil his part of the plan, he would need reinforcements. He asked for—and received—two fresh divisions for the EEF. Finally, to ensure seamless communications between the two forces, Allenby proposed bringing Faysal and his army under his own command. Lawrence was dispatched to Wajh and Jeddah to secure the acquiescence of Faysal and Sharif Husayn to placing the Arab Revolt under British command.[41]

As of August 1917, General Allenby was securely in command of a two-front campaign to defeat the Ottomans in Syria and Palestine. He turned his attention towards the Palestine front and prepared his army for a third attempt on Gaza.

FOLLOWING THE SURRENDER OF AQABA, THE OTTOMANS TRIED TO beat the Arab army at their own game. They actively courted the loyalty of the leading tribes of Transjordan (as the British termed the southern extremities of Ottoman Syria to the east of the Jordan River) and recruited armed militias from the local population to reinforce their overextended regular army units. By rallying the Arabs of Transjordan against Faysal's army, the Ottomans hoped to force the Hashemites to fight on hostile territory.[42]

Ottoman efforts to recruit local militias met with mixed results. In the northern districts of Transjordan, where all young men had already been conscripted into the Ottoman army, only the elderly were left to serve in the volunteer force. The Ottoman officer dispatched to Irbid to inspect the

Mujahidin (jihad-fighters) was appalled to find a corps of elderly gentlemen, "most of whom were infirm by age and degree". The military authorities ordered the Irbid volunteer force disbanded and for its members to pay a military-exemption tax instead.[43]

In the town of Amman (capital of the modern Kingdom of Jordan), the Circassian community responded enthusiastically to the Ottoman call to arms. The Circassians came to Transjordan in the late nineteenth century as refugees fleeing Russian conquests in the Caucasus. As a refugee settler community, they were actually exempted from military service. However, the Circassians were the ultimate Ottoman loyalists, and in November 1916 the head of their community, Mirza Wasfi, petitioned Istanbul for permission to form a volunteer cavalry unit "to offer their lives in sacrifice to the homeland". The Circassian Volunteer Cavalry numbered over 150 mounted fighters and played an active role in defending the Hijaz Railway and combating the forces of the Arab Revolt.[44]

A third volunteer force was formed in the southern town of Karak, seat of an Ottoman deputy governor. The hilltop town, built into a crusader-era citadel overlooking the Dead Sea, had been the centre of a major tribal revolt in 1910 that the Ottomans had put down with great violence. The townspeople of Karak did not love the Ottomans, but they certainly feared them and displayed unqualified loyalty throughout the First World War. After the outbreak of the Arab Revolt, Cemal Pasha went to Karak in person to remind the townspeople of "each Ottoman subject's duty to protect the state" and asked them to form a militia for the defence of their territory. The different tribes and clans, Muslims and Christians alike, volunteered for the militia under the command of an Ottoman colonel.[45]

The Ottomans also cultivated the loyalty of Bedouin tribes along the Transjordan frontier. Cemal Pasha invited leading tribal shaykhs to visit Damascus by train at government expense, where they were housed in hotels and treated to lavish hospitality. Commending them for their "display of friendship and service to the government", Cemal showered the tribesmen with medals and honours. In this way, members of the Ruwalla, Billi, Bani Atiyya, and Huwaytat tribes were all courted, with some success. While key tribal leaders like Auda Abu Tayi (awarded an Osmani medal, fourth class) threw in their lot with the Hashemites, others remained loyal to the Ottoman cause. Indeed, even Auda wavered in his loyalty. T. E. Lawrence confronted the Huwaytat warrior with evidence of his correspondence with

Cemal Pasha offering to swap sides. In the competition for Bedouin loyalties, the Ottomans were not to be underestimated.[46]

The Ottomans put Arab loyalties to the test immediately after the fall of Aqaba in July 1917. Fearful lest the Hashemites' shock victory turn the Arabs of Transjordan against the Ottoman state, Cemal Pasha ordered the tribal militias to mount an attack on Faysal's army in Aqaba. He promised the Bedouin volunteers all the support the Ottoman army could muster— regular infantry and cavalry, artillery and aircraft. The Ottomans gave each commander five days' food for their men and fodder for their horses. Each horseman was paid three Turkish pounds in gold, and their commanders received five gold pounds. The tribesmen responded enthusiastically and set off from Karak to assemble in the garrison town of Maan in mid-July.

Odeh al-Goussous was a notable from Karak with a distinguished record in the Ottoman civil service. Fluent in Turkish, he often served as a translator between government officials and local townsmen. The sharif of Mecca held no particular appeal to Goussous, a Christian, and he noted Sharif Husayn's overtures to the people of Transjordan with detachment. He played a leading role organizing the Karak militia. Along with more than four hundred Muslim volunteers, Goussous mobilized eighty Christians to serve in the Karaki battalion and served as their commander as they set off for battle on 17 July 1917.

Goussous watched as the tribesmen in the campaign faltered in their enthusiasm. He knew the men of the Huwaytat and Bani Sakhr tribes and understood their hesitation to fight. Rival branches of both tribes, including Auda Abu Tayi of the Huwaytat, had sided with Faysal. Were they to kill members of their own tribes in battle, the blood feuds could last for generations. Goussous also noted that the tribal militias were heading into battle with none of the support Cemal Pasha had promised them: there were no regular forces or artillery, let alone aircraft, to back them up. Cemal was trying to provoke enmity between the tribes of Transjordan and the tribes supporting the Hashemite revolt without risking any of his limited troops and resources in Maan.

The Karak militia attacked a detachment of the Arab army at al-Quwayra, a small telegraph station twenty-five miles north-east of Aqaba. The Huwaytat and Bani Sakhr Bedouin watched the engagement from the surrounding hilltops without engaging in the battle themselves. The action lasted three hours, and the Karakis claimed victory after killing nine of the

Arabs and driving the rest into retreat. The Karakis seized over 1,000 head of sheep and thirty donkeys, a few camels, and ten tents and returned to Maan triumphant. In keeping with tribal raiding practice, they treated the captured livestock as booty. They left five hundred sheep as a gift to the Ottoman army and drove the rest of the herd home to Karak as their own reward for the successful raid. The attack was trivial (Faysal's forces reoccupied al-Quwayra shortly after), but the Ottomans had succeeded in driving a wedge between the local population and the Hashemite army that would persist to the end of the war.[47]

THE OTTOMAN MINISTER OF WAR, ENVER PASHA, CONVENED HIS ARMY commanders in the northern Syrian city of Aleppo on 24 June 1917. Halil Pasha, commander of the Sixth Army in Mesopotamia, Mustafa Kemal Pasha, the hero of Gallipoli, Izzet Pasha, commander of the Caucasus Army, and Cemal Pasha, governor of Syria and commander of the Fourth Army, were all in attendance for this extraordinary meeting. As Cemal noted in his memoirs, "The meeting of four army commanders with the Chief of the General Staff to preside was not an everyday affair."[48]

Enver proposed a bold new initiative to the Turkish top brass. "I am contemplating an offensive with a view to the recovery of Bagdad," Enver explained. Towards this end, he proposed the creation of a new Ottoman formation under German command, to be called the "Yıldırım Group". Yıldırım—the word means "lightning" or "blitz" in Turkish—was to be organized along the lines of a German army group. It would combine Halil Pasha's Sixth Army and a new Seventh Army under Mustafa Kemal's command with a full German infantry division. The commander in chief would be General Erich von Falkenhayn, whose recent successes in Romania had gone some way to redeeming his reputation after his failure to break through French lines at Verdun in 1916. The German government committed £5 million in gold—extremely scarce resources in mid-1917— to ensure Yıldırım had the resources to succeed.

The Ottoman army commanders were stunned by Enver's plan. Offensive operations to recover Baghdad seemed foolhardy when the empire was threatened by attack on so many other crucial fronts. And they were appalled by the prospect of coming under German command. The Yıldırım staff was overwhelmingly German, comprising sixty-five foreign officers and only nine Turks. Relations between Germans and Turks had grown strained in the course of the war. Soldiers' diaries capture the resentment among officers and the ranks alike at what they saw as German arrogance. Mustafa Kemal warned Enver that Turkey was becoming a "German colony". Even Otto Liman von Sanders, head of the German military mission to the Ottoman Empire, thought it a mistake to dispatch officers from Germany who had no knowledge of the Ottoman Empire or Turkish culture. Reliance on interpreters to make their commands understood caused much good-will between Germans and Turks to be lost in translation.

Despite the opposition of all of his army commanders, Enver was not to be deterred. Over the summer months of 1917, the Yıldırım Group began to assemble in Aleppo for eventual deployment in Mesopotamia. Cemal continued to submit intelligence reports tracking the growing British force along the Gaza-Beersheba front and to lobby for a change in policy. For his pains, Cemal was relieved of his command over the Palestine front, which passed to von Falkenhayn. The German general, however, was not deaf to Cemal's concerns. By the end of September, von Falkenhayn was convinced of the British threat to Palestine and persuaded Enver to divert the Yıldırım Group to address the danger. On 30 September, the Yıldırım group began to move south to the Palestine front.

As the German and Turkish divisions of Yıldırım converged on Aleppo, the first of Allenby's own reinforcements began to arrive in Egypt. The politicians wanted Allenby to deliver Jerusalem as a Christmas present to the war-weary British public. The generals wanted him to achieve as much as he could with the forces at his disposal, making it very clear that he was unlikely to secure any more support. His orders were similar to those given General Maude before his advance on Baghdad: to break through Turkish lines and pursue the Turks as far as his resources permitted but to avoid getting overextended at all costs. There was to be no defeat, retreat, or Kut-style surrender.

The Egyptian Expeditionary Force now enjoyed a comfortable margin of superiority over Ottoman defenders around Gaza. The British had mobilized twice the estimated 40,000 Ottoman infantry and eight times the 1,500 mounted troops and had a three-to-two preponderance in artillery over the Turks. Yet it was not enough to simply outnumber the defenders.

The British had lost the first two battles for Gaza in frontal assaults on tenaciously defended trenches. Over the intervening months, the Turks had worked tirelessly to improve their defences. To overcome well-entrenched defensive lines, Allenby had to rely on deception.

The Third Battle of Gaza was a complex plan involving feints and ruses. British intelligence had confirmed that Ottoman defences were strongest around Gaza and weakest at Beersheba, where the defenders counted on the inhospitable terrain to deter an offensive. Allenby decided to strike there, for if he could take Beersheba, he could assure his troops of a reliable water supply and outflank Ottoman positions surrounding Gaza. Allenby's plans called for preliminary attacks to concentrate Ottoman forces in Gaza and leave Beersheba vulnerable to a surprise attack.

The British went to great lengths to mislead Ottoman commanders. The head of military intelligence, Colonel Richard Meinertzhagen, rode towards Turkish lines until Ottoman cavalry intercepted him. He provoked the enemy horsemen into a gunfight and chase in which he dropped a blood-smeared satchel with fake documents setting out British plans for an attack on Gaza. British intelligence also spread false rumours of a naval landing to the north of Gaza. The presence of British warships off the coast only lent credence to these rumours.[49]

Allenby issued his orders on 22 October, ten days before the start of operations. His plans called for moving infantry and cavalry units gradually into positions opposite Beersheba to avoid alerting the defenders to a troop build-up that could only mean a major assault. By 30 October, the attackers were in place. They struck at dawn the following morning, announcing their attack with a heavy artillery bombardment on Ottoman lines in Beersheba.

Emin Çöl, a veteran of the Gallipoli campaign, was one of the soldiers in the Turkish trenches at Beersheba. "We woke to the sound of artillery," he recalled. "We had not slept anyway." Turkish lines in Beersheba were in a deplorable state. Their narrow trenches were too shallow to provide much protection. Each fifty-metre line lay totally isolated from other Ottoman positions. There were no communication trenches to permit the safe transit of men and materiel to and from the front. Without adequate shelter from enemy artillery, Ottoman casualties instantly mounted, the dead and wounded clogging the trenches without the living having any safe means to move them. Little wonder that Çöl had no stomach for the impending battle. "What kind of war are we fighting?" he mused. "The [Ottoman] army has no working artillery, no functioning machineguns, no aircraft, no commanding officers, no defensive lines, no reserves, no telephone. The troops are fighting in total isolation of each other, and their morale has collapsed. Indeed, this army has none of the things it would need [to win]."[50]

However demoralized they might have been, the Ottoman soldiers put up a stiff defence. Marching into heavy Turkish gunfire, the British infantry managed to reach their designated positions by early afternoon but, facing sustained resistance, went no further. The British infantry dug in to positions in the hills overlooking Beersheba from the south to await further orders.

The success of the attack hinged on the cavalry. Riding twenty-five miles overnight, the Desert Mounted Corps was tasked with circling around Beersheba to enter the town from the north-east. Once again the horsemen faced a water constraint—unless they took Beersheba and its wells by sunset, men and horses would not have enough water to fight a second day. In the course of the morning, Anzac cavalry units came under heavy machine-gun fire from Ottoman defenders that slowed their progress and put the whole operation at risk. By mid-afternoon, the horsemen's chances of securing the town by sunset looked slim. General Sir Harry Chauvel, commander of the Desert Mounted Corps, decided to break with the agreed-on plan and risk a direct cavalry assault on the Turkish trenches guarding the entry to the town.

With only half an hour before the autumn sun set, the 4th Australian Light Horse Brigade got into position. Some eight hundred horsemen in two broad columns spread four hundred yards apart set off towards Turkish lines at a trot. It was the largest cavalry charge of the Great War—probably the greatest such attack in a century (the celebrated 1854 Charge of the Light Brigade in the Crimean War, by comparison, numbered under seven hundred troopers). As they came within range of Turkish guns, the cavalry accelerated to a canter and then a full gallop.

The defenders had great difficulty in taking aim against such fast-moving targets. Emin Çöl watched as the thundering cavalry approached his lines. The hundreds of horsemen swept over the first line of trenches, forcing Çöl and his comrades to take cover to avoid being crushed under the horses' hooves. Groups of cavalrymen dismounted to engage the defenders in hand-to-hand fighting. Çöl continued to fire on the British for as long as he could see them. Suddenly, though still conscious, Çöl lost his vision. He had been wounded and could feel blood flowing down his face. In the heat of battle, his friends bandaged his wounds and took him to a sheltered spot before surrendering. "They told me that two British soldiers were approaching us. They took my hand and made me come out of the trench." Now prisoner, Çöl would regain his liberty in a year, but he never regained his sight.[51]

The cavalry continued their race into Beersheba, fearful that the now retreating Ottomans would destroy the wells as they withdrew. The town was rocked by a series of heavy explosions as an ammunition dump was destroyed and rolling stock in the railway station dynamited to prevent them from falling into English hands. The horsemen saw two wells blown before they could intervene to protect the rest. With darkness falling, British forces descended on Beersheba from all sides as the Ottomans attempted to withdraw. By midnight, the town was securely in British hands as surviving Ottoman forces completed their withdrawal under cover of night.

The commanders of the Yıldırım Group were stunned by the sudden loss of Beersheba in a single day's fighting. Those soldiers who managed to elude capture fell back on Gaza, whose defences had twice withstood invasion. Yet Gaza was no safe haven. The British subjected the town to

The ruins of the main mosque in Gaza, 1917. The Ottomans had forcibly evacuated all civilians before the three British attacks on Gaza, when the town was subjected to the heaviest bombardment witnessed anywhere outside the European theatres of war.

the heaviest bombardment witnessed anywhere outside the European theatres of war. Between 27 and 31 October, ground-based artillery and naval gunfire combined to deliver over 15,000 rounds into Ottoman positions in and around Gaza. The reinforcements who took up positions in Gaza entered a living hell.[52]

British infantry attacked Ottoman positions facing Gaza on 1 and 2 November. These were feints designed to convince the defenders that the British intended a direct assault. To further confuse the situation, British cavalry held manoeuvres between Beersheba and the hill town of Hebron further north, raising Ottoman fears of a direct attack on Jerusalem. The Yıldırım commanders responded by dispatching troops to defend Gaza and Hebron, leaving central positions in their twenty-mile front between Gaza and Beersheba thinly defended. This had been Allenby's ultimate object—to force the Turks to deplete their central positions and to drive the main body of his force through the gap.

The Third Battle of Gaza entered its final act on 6 November, when Allenby unleashed the main body of his force on Turkish positions halfway between Gaza and Beersheba. In a day of intense fighting, British forces succeeded in breaching Turkish lines at several key points along a seven-mile front and penetrated nine miles inside Ottoman territory. Yet the British were amazed by the tenacity of the Turkish defence.

Australian soldiers of the Imperial Camel Corps were pinned down for two days by Ottoman forces at Tal al-Khuwaylfa, due north of Beersheba. Fighting alongside the Welsh infantry, the cameliers suffered their worst losses of the Palestine campaign. Frank Reid listed the names of his comrades cut down beside him during the days of bloody fighting: Sergeant Dan Pollard, shot through the head; Sergeant Arthur Oxford, shot in the nose; Frank Matzonas, who had only just emigrated from Riga to Australia in 1914, shot in the brain; Reg Reid, who got lost and was bayoneted in a Turkish trench—the list went on and on. "Another Camelier named Neilsen lay wounded in the open for several hours, close to the Turkish trenches. Each time he called out the Turks put a bullet into him until he was riddled with them. Murderous beggars were those Turks who lined the heights of Tel el Khuweilfe." Of course, had the memoirs of any of the Ottoman defenders at Tal al-Khuwaylfa survived, they would have said the same of the British attackers.[53]

By 7 November, the Ottomans were in full retreat. Allenby's complex plan had achieved total success. His troops entered Gaza unopposed. Indeed, there was no one left in Gaza, where Ottoman soldiers had forcibly evicted the civilian population before the start of hostilities. British soldiers walked down narrow streets without a single house left standing, Gaza having been reduced to a ghost of a city.

After losing their positions in Gaza, the Ottomans struggled to re-form into a defensive line to stop the EEF before it reached Jerusalem. But the Yıldırım Group was still in the process of formation, and Allenby's army, at near full force, had built unstoppable momentum. The Anzac Mounted Division pursued the Ottomans up the Mediterranean coastline, while British forces succeeded in capturing a vital railway junction to the south of Jerusalem on 14 November. The following day, the Anzac Mounted Division occupied Ramla and Lidda and the Australian Mounted Division took Latrun; on 16 November the New Zealand Brigade occupied the port of Jaffa. Isolated from the south and west, Jerusalem could not be defended.

ON 9 NOVEMBER, TWO DAYS AFTER ALLENBY'S FORCES ENTERED GAZA, the *Jewish Chronicle* published a new British policy on Palestine. In a brief letter to Walter Rothschild dated 2 February, Foreign Secretary Arthur Balfour issued the declaration that would come to bear his name:

> His Majesty's Government view with favor the establishment in Palestine of a national home for the Jewish people, and will use their best endeavors to facilitate the achievement of this object, it being clearly understood that nothing shall be done which may prejudice the civil and religious rights of existing non-Jewish communities in Palestine, or the rights and political status enjoyed by Jews in any other country.

The Balfour Declaration was an extraordinary commitment on the part of the British government. Its army had only just entered Palestine and was far from Jerusalem, and yet it felt sufficiently confident of success to make promises about what was still sovereign Ottoman territory.

Of course, the British had been negotiating over Ottoman territory since the very start of the war. In that sense, the Balfour Declaration was but the latest in a string of wartime partition plans, beginning with the Constantinople Agreement of March 1915, the Husayn-McMahon Correspondence of 1915 and 1916, and the 1916 Sykes-Picot Agreement. However, each of these previous partition plans had been kept secret. The Balfour Declaration was openly published in the London press. Moreover, in promising Britain's "best endeavors" to achieve the establishment for a national home for the Jews, Balfour seemed to be violating the terms of previous agreements with Sharif Husayn and the French government. To further complicate things, Sir Mark Sykes, architect of the Sykes-Picot Agreement, had lobbied the British government to lend its support to the Jewish national movement. It was Sykes who left the meeting of the British War Cabinet on 31 October 1917 to tell the Zionist leader Chaim Weizmann that the declaration had been approved. "Dr . Weizmann, it's a boy!" Sykes famously announced to the anxious Weizmann waiting outside the War Cabinet's meeting room.[54]

Like the other partition plans for the Ottoman Empire, the Balfour Declaration was a product of wartime considerations. Note that it was the War Cabinet that approved the declaration, and it did so less to support Zionism than to harness Jewish influence to the British war effort. Weizmann and his supporters had succeeded in persuading influential members of the British cabinet that the Zionist movement spoke on behalf of not just a nationalist fringe among European Jews but the political and economic might of the Jewish diaspora as a whole—the flip side of the old anti-Semitic myth of a clandestine Jewish international organization secretly controlling global finance.

In supporting Zionism, members of the British government believed they would gain the support of influential Jews in the United States and Russia. America was a late entry into the war, its traditional isolationism making it a reluctant ally, and Russia's commitment to the war had been in doubt since the February Revolution and the tsar's abdication in March 1917. Jews were believed to exercise significant influence over US President Woodrow Wilson and over Prime Minister Alexander Kerensky's provisional government in Russia. If Jewish influence could keep these two powers actively engaged in the war, then it was in Britain's interest to court Jewish favour by supporting Zionism.

Finally, many in the War Cabinet wanted to revise the terms of earlier wartime agreements, particularly the Sykes-Picot Agreement. A growing number of influential voices believed Sykes had simply given too much to the French. The British had fought too hard for Palestine to hand the territory over to an ill-defined international administration at war's end. Furthermore, the British had learned from wartime experience how a hostile power in Palestine could threaten the security of the Suez Canal. At war's end, the British wanted to ensure that Palestine came under British administration. The Zionists were natural allies in that project, their political ambitions inconceivable without a Great Power's support.

On the face of it, Lord Balfour was offering Palestine to the Zionist movement. In fact, Lloyd George's government was using the Zionist movement to secure Palestine for British rule.

JERUSALEM SURRENDERED TO THE BRITISH ON 9 DECEMBER 1917. THE Ottomans had made every effort to defend the city. Yet Allenby's advance was relentless. Though his forces had been depleted by weeks of intense fighting and his able-bodied men had been given only one day's leave (on 17 November), he never left the Ottomans time to prepare their defences. He rightly reasoned his chances of success were higher and the risk of casualties lower if he pressed the Ottomans while they were on the run and demoralized by defeat.[55]

Both sides were averse to fighting in Jerusalem. Neither the British nor the Ottomans and Germans wanted to incur the international condemnation that would inevitably result from fighting in the holy city or damaging shrines sacred to Judaism, Islam, and Christianity. As British forces progressively secured the southern, western, and northern approaches to the city, the Ottomans and their German allies decided to withdraw to the east with the remainder of the Seventh Army intact. The retreat from Jerusalem began after sundown on 8 December and was completed overnight. By sunrise on 9 December, 401 years of Ottoman rule in Jerusalem had come to an end.

The last act of the departing governor of Jerusalem was to draft a letter of surrender entrusting the holy city to the government of Great Britain. The governor left the letter with the mayor of Jerusalem, Husayn Salim al-Husayni, scion of one of the city's most respected families. The mayor, who spoke English, met with a number of British soldiers and officers too junior in rank to accept the city's surrender. Not until later in the afternoon was Major General Shea authorized by Allenby, still at his headquarters in Jaffa, to accept the surrender of the city on his behalf.[56]

Allenby made his formal entry into Jerusalem on 11 December 1917. The War Office Cinematograph Committee filmed the carefully staged

The mayor of Jerusalem encounters his first British soldiers,
9 December 1917. The mayor, Husayn Salim al-Husayni
(centre, with cane and cigarette), set out from Jerusalem under a white flag to ensure the peaceful surrender of the city
to the approaching British forces. The first soldiers he met,
Sergeants Sedgewick and Hurcomb, pictured here, were too
junior to accept the city's surrender.

event to ensure the widest possible audience for the greatest victory of the
war to date. This was, after all, Lloyd George's "Christmas present for the
British nation". Like Maude's declaration in Baghdad, Allenby's lines had
been drafted for him in London and telegraphed to Palestine. The commander in chief of the Egyptian Expeditionary Force was even ordered to
dismount before making his entry into the holy city, a gesture of humility
that would appeal to Christians in particular. The event was scripted not
just for the benefit of onlookers in Jerusalem but for the prime minister's
announcement in the House of Commons. Lloyd George did not wish to
squander the public relations coup and insisted on getting every detail of the
historic moment right.

As he entered Jerusalem, Allenby passed through an honour guard representing each of the nations whose soldiers had fought in Palestine: England, Wales, Scotland, India, Australia, and New Zealand. Twenty French and twenty Italian soldiers represented Britain's Entente allies. Among the dignitaries in Allenby's entourage were T. E. Lawrence, who had come to discuss joint strategy between the Arab Revolt and the EEF, and Charles François Georges-Picot, joint author of the Sykes-Picot Agreement.

Allenby read the proclamation in English and looked on as it was read out in Arabic, Hebrew, French, Italian, Greek, and Russian from the foot of David's Tower. The speech was brief: Jerusalem was now under martial law, though its residents would be left to pursue their "lawful business without fear of interruption", and the holy places of "the three religions" would "be maintained and protected according to the existing customs and beliefs of those to whose faith they are sacred". To reinforce this point, Allenby then received the civil and religious dignitaries of the city—a parade of patri-

General Allenby's proclamation read in British-occupied Jerusalem. The carefully scripted British entry to Jerusalem was filmed to raise morale in war-weary Britain; note the cinematographer on the rooftop in the upper right corner of the picture.

archs, rabbis, muftis, and metropolitans in exotic robes and long beards. The film reel closes with shots of Jerusalem crowds jostling with the lines of soldiers, mule-drawn wagons, motorcycles, and motor cars of the army of occupation.[57]

THE FALL OF JERUSALEM MARKED A MAJOR TURNING POINT IN THE Great War in the Middle East. By the end of 1917, the Ottomans had surrendered three cities of great symbolic value: Mecca, Baghdad, and Jerusalem. These losses—particularly the holy cities of Mecca and Jerusalem—had dealt the Ottoman jihad a severe blow. British officials in Egypt and India no longer feared reversals on the battlefield provoking religious fanaticism. More significantly, after victories over the British in Kut and Gaza, the Ottomans' lines in Mesopotamia and Palestine had been breached and their armies driven into retreat by larger, better-provisioned British campaign forces. And the British in Palestine were now in touch with the Hashemite Arab army, which, following the occupation of Aqaba, was threatening Ottoman positions in the Syrian interior.

By the end of 1917, the Ottomans had not been defeated, but their Great War ambitions had been narrowed from victory to survival.

THIRTEEN

From Armistice to Armistice

IN NOVEMBER 1917, THE BOLSHEVIKS SEIZED POWER IN RUSSIA AND sued for an immediate ceasefire with the Central Powers—an unimaginable reversal of fortunes that held the prospect of rescuing the Ottomans when their war effort, following the loss of Jerusalem, was at its nadir.

The hardships of war had brought down the Russian monarchy in the February Revolution (a name based on the old Russian calendar; the events of the "February Revolution" actually took place in March 1917). Tsar Nicholas II abdicated on 15 March, and a provisional government headed by Alexander Kerensky assumed power. The Allies at first thought the revolution might revive the Russian war effort, though political upheaval undermined military discipline from the start.

The first measure taken by the new government (Order No. 1 of 14 March 1917) was to strip Russian officers of their authority over the troops, who would be commanded thenceforth by elected "soldier soviets". Russian forces in occupied Ottoman territory were quick to comply—and chaos ensued. "Long and repeated meetings of the [Russian] soldiers took place to-day as a result of the revolution in Petrograd," the American consul in the Black Sea port of Trabzon recorded in his political log on 23 March 1917. "Excesses were feared as a result of the manifestations. Most of the shops were closed. After the election of an executive committee composed mostly of soldiers, things became much quieter."[1]

Over the spring and summer months of 1917, an uneasy calm settled over the eastern Turkish lands occupied by the Russians. The shattered Ottoman Caucasus Army, grateful for the respite, held its positions without firing a shot in anger for the rest of the year. Russian soldiers engaged in fierce political debates amongst themselves, their focus entirely on the homeland. Many questioned what they were doing on Ottoman territory at all.

The Bolshevik Party resolved the soldiers' lingering doubts when it seized power on 7 November 1917 (the "October Revolution" by the old Russian calendar). Denouncing the war as an imperialist project, the Bolsheviks sued for a negotiated peace "without annexations and indemnities". The Young Turks could hardly believe their luck. Fear of Russian territorial ambitions in the straits and Istanbul had driven the Ottoman Empire into its wartime alliance with Germany. In the course of the war, the Russian army had destroyed Ottoman defences in the Caucasus and occupied extensive territory in eastern Anatolia. Yet here was the new government of Russia pledging to withdraw from the war as soon as possible and to abandon all territory gained in its course.

The Young Turks met with representatives of the Russian Caucasus Army in the occupied city of Erzincan and concluded a formal armistice on 18 December. From the Black Sea to Lake Van, Russian and Ottoman soldiers laid down their arms while their political leaders entered into negotiations for a peace treaty. In the Russian-occupied territories of eastern Anatolia, the armistice left a power vacuum. The Russian soldiers in Trabzon acted independently of their government in Petrograd. A democratically elected "Council of Soldiers, Workers and Peasants" claimed full power and authority but had no means to exercise either. The longer soldiers went without discipline and hierarchy, the more lawless and unruly they became.

At the end of December 1917, Russian soldiers in Trabzon began to commandeer vessels to return home across the Black Sea. Many of the outgoing soldiers, who had gone months without pay, looted the town's shops to provide for their ride home. Martial law was declared on 31 December without restoring security to the port. Disorder in the city was magnified in the surrounding countryside, where armed Turkish gangs drew ever closer as the Russians withdrew. "Firing, pillaging, and panic are in the order of the day," the American consul reported at the end of January 1918. "The Turkish bands are getting more audacious, and the Russian soldiers obnoxious." Whatever relief the armistice had brought to the Ottoman army, the towns under Russian occupation longed for the return of regular government that would only come with a peace treaty.

The Central Powers met with representatives of the Bolshevik government in the German army headquarters at Brest-Litovsk. While the Russians
hoped to recover territory lost to Germany and Austria, only the Ottomans
stood to gain from the Bolshevik's pledge of a peace without annexations.
The Young Turks went to the peace table to seek not just the restoration
of the 1914 borders but to recover the *Elviye-i Selâse*, the "three provinces"
annexed by Russia in 1878: Kars, Ardahan, and Batum.

After two rounds of inconclusive negotiations, the German army resumed hostilities against Russia and marched towards Petrograd on 18 February 1918. Defenceless before the German army, Vladimir Lenin instructed
the Russian negotiators to conclude a peace deal with the Central Powers on
whatever terms they could. The Russian hand thus weakened, the Ottomans
secured the restoration of their 1914 borders and a full Russian evacuation
from the three provinces, whose ultimate disposition would be determined by
a public referendum, to be organized by the Ottomans. The Young Turks were
thus prime beneficiaries of the Treaty of Brest-Litovsk, signed on 3 March.

The Ottoman government broke the news of the treaty to the Chamber
of Deputies the day after it was signed. The politicians celebrated peace with
Russia as a prelude to a general peace and the end of the war. The favourable
terms of the treaty, restoring long-lost territories, compensated the Turkish
nation for its horrendous wartime sacrifices. It also put to rest Russia's "historic" claims to Constantinople and the straits. These gains combined to
encourage hopes that the Ottomans might yet emerge from the Great War
victorious.

THE BOLSHEVIKS WENT TO EXTRAORDINARY LENGTHS TO DISCREDIT
the policies of the deposed tsar's government. Leon Trotsky, then people's
commissar of foreign affairs, published some of the ancien régime's dirtiest
linen in the Soviet daily newspaper *Isvestia* in late November 1917. The
most sensational item was the Sykes-Picot Agreement, the secret tripartite
accord for the partition of the Ottoman Empire. Foreign correspondents in
Moscow picked up the revelations and relayed them back to their eager editors at home. The *Manchester Guardian* first broke the news of the Sykes-Picot Agreement to the English-speaking world on 26 and 28 November.

The Ottoman government seized on the revelations to denigrate the
rebel amir of Mecca, Sharif Husayn, and his son Faysal, commander of the

Arab army. In a speech delivered in Beirut on 4 December 1917, just days before the fall of Jerusalem, Cemal Pasha divulged the terms of the Sykes-Picot Agreement to a stunned audience. Casting Sharif Husayn and his sons as the dupes of the British, he laid full responsibility "for the enemy's arrival at the ramparts of Jerusalem" on the leaders of the Arab Revolt. "Had there been some prospect, however remote, of his dreams of independence being realized, I might have conceded some speck of reason to the revolt in the Hijaz. But, the real intentions of the British are now known: it has not taken them so very long to come to light. And thus will the Sharif Husain be made to suffer the humiliationof having bartered the dignity conferred upon him by the Caliph of Islam for a state of enslavement to the British." The Ottoman government distributed copies of the speech in Arabic translation to the Syrian press, and the sensational news received wide coverage. Copies of the Beirut and Damascus newspapers were sent by rail to Medina and smuggled into Mecca to complete the Hashemites' humiliation.[2]

Sharif Husayn and his son Faysal were not totally unfamiliar with the Anglo-French partition plan. After all, Sir Mark Sykes and Picot had travelled to Jeddah earlier in the year to brief the sharif and his son on the terms of their agreement. However, the British and French diplomats had been deliberately vague, knowing that full disclosure of their plans would put the Anglo-Arab alliance at risk. Sykes had led Sharif Husayn to believe that the British planned a short occupation of Iraq and would pay him rent for the time they remained there. He encouraged the sharif to see France's presence in Syria as another such short-term lease in a small patch of the Syrian coastal region. The sharif learned a great deal more about Anglo-French territorial ambitions from Cemal Pasha's speech than he had from his French and British allies.[3]

Cemal Pasha hoped to use the Sykes-Picot Agreement to persuade the Hashemites to abandon their revolt and return to the Ottoman fold with all forgiven. Such a reconciliation would have a dramatic impact on the Ottoman position in Syria and Iraq. The now well-armed Arab forces the sharif had recruited to fight the Ottomans could be turned against the British instead. Fahri Pasha's forces could be redeployed from Medina and, combined with the Caucasus Army now liberated from the Russian front by the armistice, used to recover Baghdad and Jerusalem from the British. By regaining Arab loyalties, the Young Turks believed the Ottoman Empire stood a fighting chance of surviving the war.

In December 1917, Cemal Pasha dispatched a letter to Faysal in Aqaba by secret courier. The Young Turk leader offered full Arab autonomy within the Ottoman Empire—real autonomy instead of the foreign domination outlined by the Sykes-Picot Agreement—in return for Hashemite loyalty. Faysal forwarded Cemal's letter to his father unanswered. The sharif in turn sent the letter on to Sir Reginald Wingate, British high commissioner in Egypt. Between the Balfour Declaration and the Sykes-Picot Agreement, both published in November 1917, Sharif Husayn believed his British allies owed him an explanation.

British officials in Egypt found themselves in an awkward position. They had played no part in the secret partition plans they now had to answer for on behalf of His Majesty's Government. The stakes were high, as these awkward disclosures endangered British campaigns in Mesopotamia and Palestine and threatened to destroy the Anglo-Hashemite alliance and the Arab Revolt just as it was gaining momentum.

The head of the Arab Bureau in Cairo, Commander D. G. Hogarth, addressed the sharif's concerns about the Balfour Declaration in a message dated January 1918. He reaffirmed the Allies' determination "that the Arab race shall be given full opportunity of once again forming a nation in the world" and that "no people shall be subject to another" in Palestine. However, "world Jewish opinion" favoured "a return of Jews to Palestine", and the British government supported that aspiration. "World Jewry", Hogarth assured his Arab ally, had "a political influence" in many states, and the friendship Jews tendered the Arabs was "not one to be lightly thrown aside".[4]

Wingate sought the Foreign Office's advice before responding to the sharif's questions about the Sykes-Picot Agreement. London replied on 8 February 1918 with classic diplomatic double-talk. The British government thanked the sharif for sending Cemal's letter, dismissed it as a transparent bid "to sow doubt and suspicion" between the Hashemites and the Allied Powers, and reaffirmed His Majesty's Government's "pledge in regard to the liberation of the Arab peoples".[5]

The sharif might have been concerned that the British neither confirmed nor denied the contents of the partition plans, but he and his sons had gone too far in their revolt against the Ottomans to turn back now. Cemal's letter to Sharif Husayn went unanswered. Clinging to every British statement reconfirming their support for Arab independence, Sharif Husayn and his sons persisted in their struggle against the Ottoman Empire, hoping to secure by military success what the British and French seemed intent on denying them through their secret diplomacy.

SINCE THE OTTOMAN SURRENDER IN AQABA IN JULY 1917, THE MAIN theatre of the Arab Revolt had shifted from the Hijaz to the southern frontiers of Syria. Here Faysal continued to build up his regular army under the command of Jafar al-Askari and to recruit fresh tribal irregulars. The British and French, assisted by colonial forces from Egypt and Algeria, provided technical expertise and modern firepower. A squad of armoured cars, a flight of airplanes, and a battery of 10-pound guns gave the Arab army the latest military technology to bombard Turkish lines.

From Aqaba, Faysal's army confronted the strong Ottoman garrison at Maan. One of the pilgrimage stations between Damascus and Mecca, Maan traditionally marked the boundary between Syria and the Hijaz. It was one of the larger stations on the Hijaz Railway and housed a major garrison. In August 1917, T. E. Lawrence had estimated the Ottomans "had six thousand infantry, a regiment of cavalry and mounted infantry, and had entrenched Maan till it was impregnable according to the standard of manoeuvre war". It was not the sort of position that Faysal's guerrilla army stood a chance of taking.[6]

Faced with the pressure to advance northward as General Sir Edmund Allenby's "right flank", the Arab army initially bypassed Maan to seize the highlands dominating the Jordan Valley. Led by Faysal's youngest brother, Zayd, the sharifian detachment captured the castle town of Shawbak and occupied the Ottoman administrative centre Tafila unopposed on 15 January 1918. The commander of the local garrison, Zaki al-Halabi, deserted from Ottoman service along with his 240 soldiers to join forces with the Arab army. The Turkish army, unreconciled to the loss of Tafila, made a determined bid to recover the hilltop town on 26 January but was repulsed, with heavy losses, by the sharifian detachment and its new allies. Tafila was to change hands twice in the next six weeks, with the Ottomans recovering the town on 6 March before surrendering it to the Arabs again on 18 March.[7]

In Palestine, the Egyptian Expeditionary Force (EEF) resumed its offensive. Britain's prime minister, David Lloyd George, had instructed Allenby to renew hostilities in Palestine in February 1918 and to deal the Ottoman Empire a decisive blow to force it out of the war. Rather than advance deeper into Palestine, Allenby decided to make his attack in the east. His objective was Amman, across the River Jordan, where he hoped to join forces with the Arab army and sever the Ottomans' vital rail link to both Maan and Medina. With an estimated 20,000 Turkish troops to the south of Amman, Allenby wanted to neutralize the threat on his right flank before making his final push on to Damascus.

As a first step, Allenby chose to occupy the town of Jericho in the Jordan Valley to serve as an advance base for operations in Transjordan. On 19 February, Allenby's forces began a slow and deliberate march down the steep slopes of the Jordan Valley towards Jericho. The narrow tracks were impassable to wheeled traffic, and the line of infantry and cavalry extended over five miles. Turkish gunners slowed but did not stop the British advance, and Allenby's forces entered Jericho on the morning of 21 February. Their imaginations fired by biblical accounts of Joshua and the walls of Jericho, the Anzac cavalrymen were quickly brought back to earth: "Of all the cities of the east that our men had passed through," one New Zealand cavalry officer recalled, "Jericho easily led the way as the filthiest and most evil-smelling of them all."[8]

Before crossing the Jordan, Allenby secured a safety cordon along his northern Palestine front. The EEF advanced seven miles northward to take control of the high ground around the Wadi Auja, one of the water courses to the Jordan River. In so doing, the British put their operations in Jericho beyond the reach of Ottoman artillery and forced the Turks into a long detour should they seek to reinforce their positions in Transjordan with troops from Palestine. Beginning 8 March, the operation took four days; the Ottomans grudgingly withdrew to avoid a major engagement. With British forces holding a secure line from the Mediterranean to the Jordan River, Allenby prepared to invade Transjordan.

The British commanders coordinated their invasion plans with their Arab allies. With Lieutenant Colonel Alan Dawnay, head of the newly created Hijaz Operations Staff, serving as the liaison to sharifian forces, Allenby's plan called for the Arab army to attack Maan to pin down the garrison there while the EEF seized Amman. Faysal met with his officers to agree on their plan of action. One force would attack the Hijaz Railway south of Maan and destroy the rails. A second force would do the same to the railway north of Maan. Jafar al-Askari would lead the main body of the Arab army in a direct assault on Ottoman positions in Maan, which would be cut off from the twice-severed railway line and impossible to reinforce. In this way, the garrison in Maan would pose no threat to British operations further north in Amman. T. E. Lawrence was to make contact with Allenby's forces in Transjordan and bring the powerful Bani Sakhr tribe to reinforce British positions against the Turks.

These ambitious plans relied on each party fulfilling its role on a timely basis, for there were no communications between the different forces. The British had introduced carrier pigeons into the theatre, but there was no way of coordinating actions between the different units of the Arab army operating over a fifty-mile stretch of the Hijaz Railway, let alone between the Arabs and the British, separated by hundreds of miles of open land. When things went wrong, the allies only learned of each other's setbacks at the speed of a horseman. Rumour and disinformation added to the fog of war.[9]

The Arab assault on Maan was a washout. Unseasonably cold rains drenched southern Transjordan in March 1918. Jafar al-Askari, who accompanied the raiding party tasked with destroying the railway south of Maan, recalled how "a torrential downpour soaked us to the skin and further progress became impossible. Camels and pack animals were floundering in mud, and our men were so beset that during the night some of them died of exposure to the bitter cold and rain." In the end, the attack on Maan was postponed pending more favourable conditions.[10]

Unaware of the Arab army's problems around Maan, British troops crossed the Jordan on 21 March. They advanced up the steep tracks from the Jordan Valley towards the Transjordanian highlands and the town of Salt. Seat of an Ottoman district governor, Salt was the largest town to the east of the Jordan, with a population of some 15,000 Muslims and Christians. As they approached the town on 25 March, the British paused at the sound of relentless gunfire. Rather than the battle they had imagined, the advance guard found the townsmen firing in the air, celebrating the Ottoman withdrawal as they looted the Ottoman municipality. "They had stripped the building bare," one astonished soldier recorded in his diary, "even the roof and all woodwork, leaving only the walls standing." The natives of Salt believed the British occupation spelled the end of their war and revelled in what would prove short-lived freedoms.[11]

The Ottomans had withdrawn from Salt without a fight to regroup for the defence of Amman. The new commander of the Yıldırım Group in Palestine and Transjordan was none other than Otto Liman von Sanders, who since 1913 had headed the German military mission to the Ottoman Empire. His experience proved a great asset, and the respect he showed his Ottoman officers and soldiers was reciprocated with a high degree of trust. Liman needed the full cooperation of his Ottoman troops. Were the British to seize Amman, with its strategic rail facilities, Ottoman positions further south on the Hijaz Railway would be untenable, leaving 20,000 troops in Medina and Maan in total isolation. Amman was a fight to the death for Turkish forces in both the Hijaz and Transjordan.

Liman responded to news of the British occupation of Salt by calling up all available troops to Amman. Disruptions on the railway line slowed their movement, but hundreds of reinforcements from Damascus began to flood into Amman. Some nine hundred men entrained from Maan, their movement unhindered by any Arab operations. Turkish cavalry in Palestine forded the Jordan River upstream from British positions to threaten their line of communications.

The British planned to secure their position in Salt with infantry and to attack Amman with cavalry. Their objectives were a viaduct and tunnel near Amman that, once destroyed, would disrupt rail travel for months. A strong infantry detachment based in Salt would then prevent Ottoman repair teams from making good the damage and would threaten communications between Damascus and the garrisons south of Amman. If the British were successful, the Ottomans would be forced to retreat north of Amman, effectively abandoning Medina and the southern half of Transjordan to the Hashemites.

As they advanced from Salt towards Amman on 27 March, the British encountered the same bad weather that had hindered Arab operations further south. The movement of animals and men was slowed over ground reduced to mud slicks impassable to wheeled traffic. Guns and ammunition were transferred from wagons to camels to be transported to the front. "Even camels could barely get over this ground on which they were constantly slipping," Liman recorded. "We intercepted a British wireless message complaining of this condition." By monitoring British radio communications, the Germans had a good sense of British plans and organized their defences accordingly.[12]

The 2,000 Ottoman defenders took up positions dominating every point of entry into Amman. Armed with seventy machine guns and ten artillery pieces in well-sheltered positions, they enjoyed the defender's advantage in trench warfare. The 3,000 British troops approached Amman wet and tired after a march in which several Britons died of exposure. The rains had prevented British artillery from reaching the front, and their supplies of machine guns and ammunition had been reduced to what could be transported by camel—many of which perished on the steep valley tracks made treacherous by the rains.[13]

For three days, the Turks held off determined assaults by EEF cavalry and infantry. Fighting in the same adverse weather as the British attackers, the Turks also suffered heavy casualties and began to flag. To counter any defeatism among his front-line troops, Liman von Sanders gave orders "for resistance to the last, regardless". He reminded his officers that fresh reinforcements were arriving daily from Damascus and Maan to help them weather the storm.[14]

Though the Turks believed their situation was critical, the invaders were in a far worse position. The Anzac cavalrymen, drenched from the relentless rains and sleeping in the open air, suffered from the intense cold. The rain-slicked paths were nearly impassable to horses and camels, making it ever harder for the British to supply advance troops with ammunition and rations. It also proved increasingly difficult to evacuate the growing number of wounded. After days of intense combat, the Turks showed no sign of giving up. Moreover, the British line of retreat was threatened by Turkish cavalrymen who harried their positions on the Jordan River and in Salt. By mid-afternoon on 30 March, the British commanders acknowledged they were unable to take Amman and ordered a full retreat.

The Ottomans pursued the retreating British forces from Amman back to Salt. As the British began to evacuate their wounded and pack their stores, panic swept Salt's townspeople. The plundered shell of the government building stood as a monument to their disloyalty to the Ottoman Empire, and they knew they faced certain retribution when the Turks returned. Some 5,500 Christians and 300 Muslims abandoned their homes to retreat with the British to Jerusalem. A British soldier captured in his diary their misery amidst the chaos of the British retreat: "One young man is carrying his grandfather on his back. He carries him 13 miles!!! Women and men and children are bent nearly double under the tremendous bundles and they cap the lot with a saucepan or washing bowl on their heads. Bullocks get in the way of armoured cars, camels stumble over over-loaded donkeys."[15]

The British press declared the Amman "raid" a success. The soldiers who fought in the engagement, having lost 200 dead and 1,000 wounded, knew better. As one New Zealand cavalryman summed it up, "The damage done to the enemy hardly justified the heavy British casualties suffered." Headlines trumpeting success "made the press reports, in the light of knowledge of the truth, seem more or less facetious".[16]

As British forces withdrew from Transjordan, Faysal's army resumed operations against Maan. The Ottomans' recent redeployment of troops for the defence of Amman had reduced the strength of the garrison in Maan, improving the Arab army's chances of a breakthrough against the nearly impregnable town.

The plan once again was to sever Maan from the north and south before mounting a direct assault on the town centre. Jafar al-Askari, chief of staff of the Arab army, led the assault on the northern railway station of Jarduna on 12 April. He had under his command an infantry battalion, one artillery piece, and four hundred Bedouin cavalry. They approached the station at dawn and opened fire with their 18-pound field gun. The advancing infantry came under intense gunfire from the defenders. Askari kept waiting for his Bedouin cavalry to attack and relieve the infantry. He found them "milling about aimlessly in dead ground" and stirred them to action with "an impassioned harangue pointing out that their comrades would be slain unless they came to their rescue with a diversionary assault". The tribesmen then stormed the station and forced the two hundred defenders to surrender. They looted the station, seizing weapons, ammunition, and military supplies. T. E. Lawrence and Hubert Young appeared later in the evening to blow the railway bridge to the south of Jarduna, cutting Maan off from the north.[17]

That same night, Nuri al-Said led an attack on the Ghadir al-Hajj railway station to the south of Maan. Muhammad Ali al-Ajluni commanded one of the infantry companies in the attack on the station. Their force was divided by personal grievances between two of the officers, and Ajluni, like Askari, was forced to deliver an "impassioned harangue" to restore order to the raiding party. A French artillery battery and a machine-gun team provided support, along with several hundred Bedouin horsemen commanded by the famous Auda Abu Tayi of the Huwaytat. As in Jarduna, the raiders struck at dawn, with their artillery bombarding the station for two hours. Most of the defenders surrendered early in the day, but one trench of Ottoman soldiers held out for hours before finally surrendering.

The deep hatreds provoked by the Arab Revolt surfaced at Ghadir al-Hajj. One of the Arab commanders confronted the three hundred Ottoman prisoners with an atrocity committed against a captain in his unit who had allegedly been tortured and burned alive by his Turkish captors. The commander ordered the Ottoman prisoners to select four of their own ranks to be executed to avenge the terrible death of his captain. Before he could proceed, the other Arab officers intervened to ensure the POWs received humane treatment. The raiding party then resumed its work, destroying five bridges and some nine hundred yards of track, cutting Maan from the south.[18]

With Maan's links to the outside world severed, the Arab army began an assault on the garrison town itself. On 13 April, they occupied the high ground to the west of Maan at Simna. Two days later they stormed the railway station in what proved the bloodiest encounter of the Arab Revolt. The battle for control of the station dragged on for four days, with heavy casualties on both sides. Jafar al-Askari bitterly condemned the French artillery battery, commanded by Captain Rosario Pisani of the French Mission to the Hijaz, which ran out of ammunition on the first day of fighting (actually, after the first hour of fighting, by Askari's account).

The Arab commander had little faith in his French allies, whom he accused of supporting France's share of the Sykes-Picot Agreement more energetically than the Arab war effort. "Captain Pisani used to remind us incessantly that he would be able to accompany us no farther than the Syrian frontier and that the French would not assist the Arabs beyond that point," Askari remembered. "Pisani's declarations were doubtless a reflection of France's bad intentions." T. E. Lawrence, an eyewitness to the battle for Maan, gave Pisani the benefit of the doubt. "We found Pisani wringing his hands in despair, every round expended," Lawrence wrote. "He said he had implored Nuri not to attack at this moment of his penury." Amir Faysal later telegraphed his thanks to the French Ministry of War for the "good work" of French troops in Maan, expressing his hopes that "all artillerymen will receive their reward". The leader of the Arab Revolt was more diplomatic than his Arab officers.[19]

After three days of heavy fighting, Arab forces had managed to capture three lines of Turkish trenches around Maan. The Ottoman commanders knew that with the railway line cut, they would receive no reinforcements or fresh ammunition. Some of the officers called for a fight to the last man; others wanted to open negotiations with the Arab army to discuss terms of surrender. The townspeople of Maan, knowing the Bedouin fighting with Faysal would pillage their homes and shops, stiffened the Ottoman resolve to fight. Five hundred townsmen joined forces with the Ottomans on the fourth day and renewed the battle with determination against the exhausted Arab army.

By the fourth day of battle, the Arab army was shattered. Its soldiers had gone without artillery cover for days while being strafed and bombarded by Ottoman machine guns and artillery. Their Bedouin cavalry had withdrawn two days earlier in what the regular infantry saw as a vote of no confidence. With over half their officers dead or wounded, discipline among the regular soldiers was breaking down. Reluctantly, Askari called for a retreat. Their losses at Maan—over ninety Arab dead and two hundred wounded—though paltry by the standards of the western front, were the worst the Arabs had yet suffered in the revolt.

Faced with a defeat of unprecedented magnitude, Amir Faysal and his chief of staff struggled to rebuild morale in their broken army. Faysal gave the army a rousing speech, and Jafar al-Askari reminded his men that a retreat was not a defeat and that once they had sufficient artillery, they would resume their victorious course and take Maan. These speeches helped to restore morale among the Syrians and Iraqis in the regular army, according to one of the officers present. But the damage to Hashemite prestige in Transjordan would not be restored for some time.[20]

ON 21 MARCH 1918, GERMANY HAD ACHIEVED A MAJOR BREAKTHROUGH on the western front. Peace with Russia had enabled the Central Powers to redeploy forces from the eastern front to the West, giving them a decisive local numerical advantage over the Entente Powers. German commanders decided to act before the United States, which had entered the war the previous year, had sent sufficient forces to redress the balance of power. Operation Michael targeted a relatively weak point in the British line at Saint-Quentin. After an overpowering artillery barrage, German forces attacked, sweeping the British before them. By the end of the first day of fighting, the Germans had advanced eight miles and occupied nearly one hundred square miles of French territory. These gains came at a price, and the Germans suffered heavy casualties. However, British losses were alarming—over 38,000 by the end of the day, including 21,000 taken prisoner.[21]

The EEF felt the consequences of Germany's spring offensive almost immediately. On 27 March, the British War Cabinet ordered Allenby to adopt an "active defence" in Palestine and to prepare his infantry divisions for immediate dispatch to France. By mid-1918, some 60,000 experienced infantrymen had been sent from Egypt and Palestine to France. They were replaced by fresh recruits from India—inexperienced soldiers who needed extensive training before they would be ready for battle.[22]

Before going on "active defence" and shipping his best troops to France, Allenby made one last bid on Transjordan. Given the tight constraints, the campaign was ill-timed and misconceived. To all appearances, Allenby sent his men into a trap.

Allenby's plan called for his cavalry to secure the key fords across the Jordan River and to protect three of the main tracks leading from the Jordan Valley to the Amman Plateau. Mounted troops were then to scale the valleys to reoccupy Salt. After securing their positions in Salt from counter-attack, the Anzac cavalry were to gallop back down the Jordan Valley to attack the Turkish garrison at Shunat Nimrin from the rear, forcing its surrender. Allenby's men had negotiated with the powerful Bani Sakhr tribes to block the crucial fourth track between the Jordan Valley and the Amman Plateau to complete the encirclement of Ottoman forces between Salt and the Jordan Valley. From this strong position, British forces would be well placed to occupy Amman and the high plateau.[23]

Allenby's officers thought his plans impracticable. General Sir Harry Chauvel, commander of the Desert Mounted Corps, believed the Ottomans anticipated the attack. Given frequent German intercepts of British wireless communications, this was probably true. The Bedouin might also have revealed British plans to the Ottomans. Chauvel was very uncomfortable with the prominent role Allenby's plan assigned to the Bedouin. The Australian general did not believe the tribesmen were sufficiently reliable to count on in the heat of battle. In fact, the Bani Sakhr were among the tribes of Transjordan whose loyalties were divided between the Hashemites and the Ottomans. If Allenby's men had negotiated with a branch of the Bani Sakhr that leaned to the Ottomans, their plans would have been leaked directly to Liman von Sanders.

Two things make treachery by the Bani Sakhr seem likely. First, the tribesmen played a key role in setting the date for Allenby's attack, arguing that they would only be available to cut the route to Shunat Nimrin until 4 May. Their reasons for this seemingly arbitrary date ring hollow: they claimed they would need to change encampments to resupply after that date. In forcing Allenby to launch his attack by a specific date and earlier than he had planned, the Bani Sakhr seemed to be working to the Ottomans' advantage. More damning still, the Bani Sakhr failed to materialize on the agreed date to block the strategic track to Shunat Nimrin, condemning the British plan to failure before it had even begun.[24]

THE FIRST AUSTRALIAN CAVALRY UNITS CROSSED THE JORDAN BEFORE sunrise on 30 April and took up the positions assigned to them in the battle plan. By 8:30 word of the attack reached Liman von Sanders, who unleashed a counter-attack that caught the invaders completely by surprise. Liman had managed to deploy significant new reinforcements in Palestine, including a cavalry brigade from the Caucasus and several German infantry units, in total secrecy. The Germans and Ottomans had also assembled and hidden a pontoon bridge for the rapid deployment of these troops between the west and east banks of the Jordan. On Liman's command, these forces began to cross the Jordan River to challenge the invaders.

Suddenly outnumbered, Allenby's mounted forces surrendered two of the four tracks leading from the Jordan Valley to Salt. The Shunat Nimrin track remained open to Turkish traffic with no sign of the Bani Sakhr. That left only one track in British hands for their forces to reach—or retreat from—Salt. And that route was in imminent risk of being cut off by Ottoman and German forces far stronger than Allenby had anticipated.

Fresh troops were sent across the Jordan to help secure the EEF's beleaguered positions. They engaged in heavy fighting with Ottoman forces who threatened to cut off and defeat the British force. After four days, with ammunition and rations running low, Chauvel requested Allenby's permission to retreat. Salt was abandoned for the second time, and by midnight on 4 May, all surviving forces had crossed safely back into Palestine. But the EEF had lost 214 men killed and nearly 1,300 wounded. As one British soldier concluded, "The second Es-Salt stunt was a complete muck-up."[25]

IN THE FIVE MONTHS AFTER THE FALL OF JERUSALEM, THE OTTOMANS had enjoyed an astonishing recovery. Peace with Russia had restored lost territory in eastern Anatolia and eliminated military threats in both the Caucasus and Mesopotamia. The revelation of secret wartime partition agreements had discredited the British, French, and Hashemites. The Yıldırım Group had effectively contained attacks by the Arab army in Maan and two attempts by Allenby's army on Amman. And with the German spring offensive breaking through British and French lines on the western front, the Ottomans seemed to be on the winning side of the Great War.

The impact on public opinion in Transjordan was dramatic. In Salt, townspeople volunteered to join the Ottoman army. As a French intelligence agent reported, "The headmen in the villages are registering numerous volunteers who present themselves for military service. The inhabitants say: if the English had to withdraw from Salt, when faced with such insignificant Turkish forces, they will not be able to make any further advances since the Ottoman forces are growing. This is why we must preserve good relations with the Turks and win their sympathy." Trust in Faysal's army had also been shaken. His appeals to the tribes of central Transjordan went unanswered. As a native agent for the French intelligence service explained, "The Arabs would have responded to Faysal in the following terms: You took Tafileh and you withdrew; the English took Salt twice and withdrew. If we declare war on the Turks we worry that, after massacring the troops now among us, you will abandon us."[26]

As Allenby saw off his experienced soldiers and received his new drafts, he was forced to defer further action in Palestine until the autumn at the very earliest. The only positive result for the EEF after a spring of disastrous campaigns was that the two attempts on Amman had encouraged the Ottomans to draw down their forces in Palestine to reinforce their positions in Transjordan. This was to Allenby's advantage, as the EEF's final push would be in Palestine, not Transjordan.

AS THE OTTOMANS CONTAINED ALLENBY'S FORCES IN PALESTINE, Enver Pasha launched a desperate bid to reinforce the empire's position in the Caucasus. Following the peace treaty with Russia signed at Brest-Litovsk in March 1918, Enver and his colleagues saw a window of opportunity to regain lost territory while Russia was weak with revolution and civil war. Although no longer at war with Russia, Enver never had more need for his soldiers on the eastern front.

Already in February 1918, the Ottoman army had moved to reclaim territory occupied by the Russians in the course of the war. The power vacuum in Trabzon was finally resolved on 24 February, when Ottoman troops entered the city without a fight. Quite the contrary—a Russian brass band was on hand to welcome their arrival. The energetic Turkish forces swept on towards Erzurum, which they stormed on 11 March. The short-rationed Turkish soldiers marvelled at the supplies the Russians had left behind— more than enough to feed the army as it pressed on towards the Ottomans' 1914 frontiers, which they reached on 24 March.[27]

As the Turks moved beyond the 1914 frontiers to stake their claim to the three provinces ceded to Russia in 1878 but recovered at Brest-Litovsk, they faced a dilemma. On the one hand, they sought the restoration of Ottoman territory as a matter of national priority. Yet encouraging the creation of buffer states between their empire and Russia was in the Ottomans' interest. Georgia, Armenia, and Azerbaijan, three relatively weak new states to emerge following the collapse of the Russian Empire, would be safer neighbours than the Russian giant. The challenge was to recover former Ottoman territories—Batum in Georgia, Kars and Ardahan in Armenia— without destabilizing their new neighbours on the Caucasus frontier.

Turkish troops entered Batum on 19 April and occupied Kars on 25 April. They went to work preparing the plebiscite that, in accordance with the Treaty of Brest-Litovsk, would legitimate their annexation to the Ottoman Empire. The Ottoman army organized the vote, overseen by a committee of Turkish civil servants, and achieved predictable results from the all-male electorate: a 97.5 percent vote in favour of the incorporation of the provinces into the Ottoman Empire. The process was formalized by imperial decree on 11 August 1918, in which Sultan Mehmed VI Vahieddin acceded to the wishes of the region's people to return to the "divinely protected lands" of the Ottoman Empire.

When the Ottomans went beyond the three provinces to make a bid for the Azeri capital of Baku, they faced hostility from their German allies, the Bolsheviks, and the British alike. Oil-rich Baku was the greatest prize of the Caucasus. The Germans had set their sites on the Caspian city since the start of the war and in the summer of 1918 needed its oil resources more than ever. The British, advancing through Persia, were determined to deny Baku to both the Germans and their Ottoman allies.

The Bolsheviks held tenuous control over Baku through a violent revolutionary regime shared with the Armenian nationalist Dashnak Party known as the "Baku Commune". In March 1918, the commune's forces had unleashed a pogrom against the Azeri Muslim majority, killing up to 12,000 Muslims. Half the surviving Muslim population fled the city for the relative safety of the countryside. When the Azeri Muslims appealed for help, Enver Pasha was quick to take up their cause—and to extend Ottoman influence over Caspian oil.

The Ottomans and Azeris concluded a treaty of friendship and alliance on 4 June 1918. The Azeris sought Ottoman assistance to liberate their territories from the Bolsheviks' control and requested Turkish military assistance. The Germans bristled at their Turkish allies' advance towards Baku. Following events from Berlin, Germany's military rulers, Erich Ludendorff and Paul von Hindenburg, advised Enver to withdraw his forces back to the frontiers recognized at Brest-Litovsk and to redeploy the Caucasus divisions to the Arab fronts, where they were more urgently needed. Enver blithely disregarded their "advice" and pressed on. While all was calm in Palestine, Enver seized the opportunity to secure Ottoman interests in a rapidly changing geopolitical game. From Baku, Enver reasoned, he would deploy his forces southward towards Mesopotamia and retake Baghdad.

To spearhead the "liberation" of Baku, Enver created a corps of Caucasian volunteers called the Caucasus Army of Islam. He appointed his half-brother Nuri Pasha, who had served with Jafar al-Askari in the 1915–1916 Sanussi campaign in the Western Desert, to lead this volunteer force. Given the tepid response to Nuri Pasha's efforts at recruitment, Enver was forced to transfer an Ottoman infantry division to reinforce the Caucasus Army of Islam. A first attempt to occupy Baku on 5 August was driven back by Bolshevik artillery and the sudden appearance of a British detachment. Nuri urgently requested reinforcements, and Enver dispatched two more Ottoman regiments to assist in the conquest of Baku. They finally took the city on 15 September—not to add Baku to the Ottoman Empire but to ensure that the new state of Azerbaijan would become a loyal client in the post-tsarist Caucasus.

Enver succeeded in recovering Ottoman territory in the Caucasus and in shaping the new states bordering eastern Anatolia to Ottoman advantage.

Had the Ottomans won the Great War, he might have been celebrated as a visionary statesman for securing his country's eastern frontiers. However, within days of the Ottoman entry into Baku, Allenby's forces broke through Ottoman lines in Palestine. For having diverted Turkish troops away from more critical fronts in Mesopotamia and Palestine, Enver's Caucasus campaign is remembered instead as a rash initiative that contributed to the fall, rather than the preservation, of the Ottoman Empire.[28]

BY THE SUMMER OF 1918, ALLIED FORCES ON THE WESTERN FRONT had ground the German breakthrough down to a halt. Whitehall once again encouraged Allenby to renew his offensive on the Ottoman front—so long as he could manage with his existing resources. By mid-July, Allenby informed the War Office that he planned to resume operations in the autumn. The commander of the EEF then began to plan in earnest.

Allenby was a master of deception. In the Battle of Beersheba (31 October 1917), he had made every effort to convince the Ottomans he planned a third attempt on Gaza and in so doing encouraged his enemy to weaken his defences just where Allenby planned to attack. Now, to cover his plans for a major assault on Ottoman positions on the Mediterranean coast of Palestine, Allenby made a great show of planning a third attack on Amman.

While his troops were not engaged in basic training to prepare them for the approaching campaign, Allenby had them building life-size models of horses in wood and canvas—15,000 in all. Little by little, under cover of darkness, he began to transfer cavalry and infantry units from the Jordan Valley and the Judean Hills to the coast, where they were billeted in camouflaged tents to prevent German aircraft from observing them. The wood and canvas remounts were left to take the place of the real horses while soldiers drove mule-drawn sleighs across the dry ground of the Jordan Valley to simulate the dust of cavalry manoeuvres. Engineers threw new bridges across the Jordan, and radio signals were broadcast from deserted headquarters.

The Arab army played a key role in focusing Ottoman attention on Transjordan. Jafar al-Askari's regular army had reached a strength of over 8,000 men, reinforced by British armoured cars, French artillery, Egyptian Camel Corps, and Australian and British airplanes. Sharif Nasir had rallied thousands of Bedouin irregulars sworn to support the Arab Revolt. In early September, while Askari and the bulk of his army remained in position surrounding Maan, a 1,000-man detachment of the Arab army was posted in al-Azrak, an oasis fifty miles east of Amman. Their sudden appearance helped feed rumours of an impending Arab attack on Amman, when in fact Faysal's forces had been assigned the task of cutting the railway lines at the key junction of Daraa, where the Hijaz Railway joined the Haifa spur.

The Royal Air Force launched aerial attacks on Daraa on 16 September in a bid to disrupt Ottoman communications and to encourage Liman von Sanders to focus on the defence of the Hijaz Railway. T. E. Lawrence led Arab forces in an attack with armoured cars on the railway south of Daraa, where they succeeded in destroying a bridge. The following day, the main Arab force attacked the railway to the north of Daraa with relative impunity. The Ottomans rushed to repair the line, and Liman called up reserves from the coastal port of Haifa to reinforce Daraa—playing perfectly into Allenby's deception.

In his determination to keep the details of the attack secret, Allenby waited until just three days before zero hour to brief his brigade and regimental commanders on the actual objectives of the offensive. By that time, he had managed to concentrate some 35,000 infantry and 9,000 cavalry, supported by nearly four hundred heavy artillery, on a fifteen-mile front on the Mediterranean just north of Jaffa. The Turks had no more than 10,000 men and 130 guns defending the coastline, while their positions in Transjordan were heavily reinforced in anticipation of an imminent attack.[29]

Two days before the attack was launched, an Indian soldier deserted British lines for the Ottoman trenches. Under questioning by Ottoman and German officers, he revealed everything he knew about the impending campaign—that the British intended to breach Ottoman lines on the Mediterranean in an attack beginning 19 September, which, Liman recorded, the deserter "wanted to escape". But Allenby's deception was so thorough that Liman and his officers dismissed the deserter's account as deliberate disinformation. The massing of Arab troops in al-Azrak and the attacks on Daraa convinced Liman the Allies were determined to sever his main line of communications, the Hijaz Railway, and he further reinforced his positions in Transjordan.[30]

Shortly before dawn on 19 September, the British revealed their true intentions with an intense artillery bombardment of Ottoman trenches north of Jaffa. For many of the new Indian soldiers, their first experience of battle was overwhelming, with the massed cannons firing at the rate of 1,000 shells per minute. "The fire of the artillery and the machine guns was very heavy," a Sikh soldier wrote to his father. "Our ears could hear nothing and in that place brother could not recognize brother. The very earth was forced to quake."[31]

As soon as the artillery barrage ended, British and Indian infantry stormed the devastated Ottoman trenches. After some hand-to-hand fighting in the third and fourth lines of defence, those Turks who could retreat did, and the rest surrendered. In the first two and a half hours of operations, the infantry had broken through Turkish lines and advanced 7,000 yards, clearing the way for the cavalry to invade northern Palestine.

Anzac and Indian cavalry units flooded through the breach made by the infantry and began a series of manoeuvres designed to encircle the Ottoman Seventh and Eighth armies and seize key towns. One of their first targets was the crossroads of Tulkarm. Tawfiq al-Suwaydi, who as a student in Paris before the war had helped to organize the 1913 Arab Congress, was serving as an officer with a desk job in Tulkarm when the battle erupted. He and his comrades woke "in a panic" to the sounds of the artillery bombardment. He climbed to the rooftop and could see the exchange of artillery about ten miles away, "a dreadful band of fire all the way down the front as each side bombarded the other with unrelenting ferocity". Shortly after sunrise, retreating Ottoman soldiers flooded Tulkarm, and "British forces appeared from everywhere, taking the remnants of the Turkish army captive".[32]

As British aircraft bombed Tulkarm, the civilians fled the town in terror. Suwaydi retreated with them to a neighbouring village, where he took off his officer's uniform and dressed in the clothes of a Palestinian peasant. With this simple gesture, Suwaydi joined the swelling ranks of deserters from the Ottoman army. Remaining in British occupied territory while Turkish forces retired in disorder, Suwaydi abandoned the Ottoman Great War and dreamed of returning home to Baghdad.

The British cavalry raced across northern Palestine, securing key towns and crossroads to complete the encirclement of the Ottoman Seventh and Eighth armies—the backbone of the once formidable Yıldırım Group. At dawn on 20 September, Baisan and Afula were in British hands. Bombing raids by the Royal Air Force and the Australian Flying Corps had destroyed Ottoman telephone lines. With their communications down, Turkish and German officers had no warning of British advances or of Ottoman losses.

Twenty-four hours after the start of operations, Liman was surprised in his Nazareth headquarters by the sudden appearance of British forces on

Ottoman prisoners near Tulkarm, Palestine, 22 September 1918. The surprise attack on Ottoman positions in northern Palestine on 19 September led to the collapse of the Ottoman Seventh and Eighth armies, leading tens of thousands of Turkish soldiers to surrender. Here British cavalry escort a column of 1,200 Ottoman prisoners.

the outskirts of town. The German commander only just eluded capture as the British were slowed by street-to-street fighting. "The strangest thing of all," an Indian soldier wrote home, "was that some of the enemy's aeroplanes were captured here [i.e., in Nazareth], with their airmen, that is to say the cavalry proved themselves skillful enough to catch birds with their hands." After meeting determined resistance, the British secured Nazareth on 21 September.[33]

By the third day of operations, British forces had captured the key towns in the Palestinian hill country and taken control of the main railway bridge over the Jordan River at Jisr al-Majami. Having cut every escape route from the West Bank to Transjordan, the British began to accept the surrender of tens of thousands of Turkish soldiers from the Seventh and Eighth armies, both of which were defunct by 21 September. All that remained to complete the conquest of Palestine was to secure the northern ports of Acre and Haifa, which fell to British and Indian cavalry on 23 September.

With Palestine securely in British hands, Allenby now turned to Transjordan. The New Zealand Mounted Brigade rapidly secured Salt (23 September) and Amman (25 September). The 4,000-man garrison in Maan, ordered to withdraw to Amman as part of a last-ditch attempt to rally the Fourth Army for the defence of Damascus, was intercepted by the 2nd Australian Light Horse Brigade. The Turkish soldiers agreed to surrender but, surrounded by hostile Arab tribesmen, refused to lay down their arms. Prisoners and their captors proceeded together under arms to Amman before the Turks felt secure enough from Bedouin attack to surrender their weapons.

As the Ottoman army fell back on Damascus, the Arab army and Allenby's EEF combined forces in a drive to take the Syrian capital. The Arab army stormed Daraa on the night of 26–27 September and was joined there by British forces the following day. They advanced immediately on Damascus, with Anzac and Indian cavalry circling around from northern Palestine to cut the Ottoman line of retreat towards Beirut in the west and Homs in the north. British and Arab forces advanced due north from Daraa, marching the seventy miles to Damascus in relentless pursuit of the remainder of the Ottoman Fourth Army. On 30 September, the Allies were on the outskirts of Damascus.

The politics of the Palestine campaign came to a head with the entry to Damascus. Given the many partition plans negotiated in the course of the war, political considerations had never been far from Allenby's campaign. In June, he received two Jewish battalions of Royal Fusiliers, formed with the express intention of advancing the Zionist claim to Palestine by valour and sacrifice on the battlefield. The French contributed the Détachement Français de Palestine et de Syrie to ensure that France protected its long-standing claims to Syria. One regiment of the French detachment was made up entirely of Armenian refugees rescued by the French from the famous siege of Musa Dagh. Amir Faysal was at the front of the line, with T. E. Lawrence as his advocate, to uphold Hashemite claims to rule Syria as part of a greater Arab kingdom. Stakeholders of the Husayn-McMahon Correspondence, the Sykes-Picot Agreement, and the Balfour Declaration jostled for pre-eminence as the campaign reached its climax at the gates of Damascus.[34]

To reward their Hashemite allies, the British conceded the honour of accepting the city's surrender to Amir Faysal's Arab army. However, the 3rd Australian Light Horse Brigade gained the distinction of being the first to

The 2nd Australian Light Horse Regiment enters Damascus. The Australians were the first to reach Damascus on 1 October, but for political reasons Amir Faysal's Arab army was allowed to accept the city's surrender.

enter Damascus. The cavalry unit was granted permission to traverse Damascus at dawn on 1 October to cut the Ottoman line of retreat down the main road north to Homs. It needn't have bothered. The last Ottoman troops had already boarded train for Rayak the night before and left the city in the hands of a committee of urban notables. Turkish flags had been replaced with sharifian colours in anticipation of Faysal's entry. The Australians quickly departed Damascus to take up their assigned positions and to leave the city for the sharifian army to occupy formally.

Sharif Nasir, who had served the Hashemite cause from the start of the revolt, entered Damascus on behalf of Sharif Husayn of Mecca, the self-proclaimed king of the Arabs. He was accompanied by Auda Abu Tayi and Nuri Shaalan, the two most powerful Bedouin shaykhs to support Faysal's campaign, at the head of some 1,500 Bedouin soldiers. The townspeople lined the streets to welcome the Hashemite forces as liberators, though the merchants were nervous. As they feared, the Bedouin began to raid and plunder the city shortly after entering. British and Allied forces began to make their way into the liberated city, overwhelmed by the crowds and the sense of elation among a people who rightly saw the retreat of the Ottomans as the final act in a long and terrible war.[35]

The pageantry continued over the next two days, as first General Allenby made his entry into Damascus and finally, on 3 October 1918, Amir Faysal himself arrived. Hubert Young, a British officer seconded to the Arab Revolt as a sort of understudy for T. E. Lawrence, drove out to meet Faysal in the large red Mercedes that Liman von Sanders had abandoned in Damascus. He found the Arab prince "at the head of a large band of horsemen" riding "through narrow streets thronged with exultant Damascenes" and offered to drive him back to the city's centre. Faysal declined the lift, preferring to enter Damascus on an Arab charger rather than in a German limousine.

Faysal rode straight to the aptly named Victoria Hotel for a historic first meeting with General Allenby. What should have been a moment of celebration was overshadowed by the politics of partition, as Allenby, with Lawrence as his interpreter, took the opportunity to spell out the new administrative arrangements for Amir Faysal. In line with the Balfour Declara-

Horsemen of the Arab army enter Damascus, 1 October 1918. The symbolism of this image is quite striking, as British officers in a modern motor car drive against the current of the Arab horsemen. Anglo-Arab politics were equally at cross purposes following the fall of Damascus.

tion, the Arab administration would have no status in Palestine. In deference to French interests established through the Sykes-Picot Agreement, the Arab government would have no role in Lebanon, which France would administer. In deference to French wishes, Faysal would ensure that the sharifian flag was removed from public buildings in Beirut. Finally, so long as war conditions prevailed, Allenby would exercise supreme command over all Entente-occupied Arab territory.[36]

From his meeting with Allenby at the Victoria Hotel, Faysal made his way to the town hall to receive the acclaim of the Damascene public. Yet after his meeting with Allenby, one wonders how he felt to be celebrated as the liberator of Damascus.

The British pursued the Ottomans for the rest of the month, taking all of the main cities of Syria and Lebanon. The Ottomans never managed to establish a defensive line to put a halt to the British war of movement that began on 19 September. The fall of Aleppo on 26 October marked the end of a campaign that had fulfilled all of its objectives. The destruction of the Ottoman army in Syria would force the Ottomans out of the war. This goal had been reached with remarkably few Allied casualties—5,666 killed, wounded or missing. There is no official figure for Turkish casualties in the campaign, though the British claim to have taken 75,000 prisoners.[37]

THE CENTRAL POWERS WERE IN TERMINAL DECLINE BY THE TIME OF the Ottoman defeat in Syria. More and more countries around the world were joining the Entente Powers. In July 1917, Greece declared war on the Central Powers, followed by China in August. Several South American countries either declared war on Germany or severed ties with the German state. Yet the American Expeditionary Force decisively shifted the balance of power in the Entente's favour. In the eighteen months after declaring war on Germany, the American army grew from 100,000 to 4 million men and managed to deploy 2 million soldiers overseas. Exhausted after four years of relentless slaughter, Germany and her allies could not find the men and materiel to meet the American threat.

Bulgaria was the first to fall, concluding an armistice with the French commander in Salonica on 30 September 1918. Bulgaria's capitulation severed communications between Turkey and Germany, cutting the flow of arms and supplies that had sustained the Ottoman war effort for so long. The end was in sight for the Germans as well. A string of Allied victories on the western front had German forces on the retreat. When the Young Turks learned that their German ally had approached US President Woodrow Wilson to mediate a ceasefire with Britain and France, the Ottomans knew they had no choice but to sue for peace as well.

In Istanbul, the Ottoman government was in turmoil. The Unionist cabinet headed by Talat Pasha resigned on 8 October. The ruling triumvirate—Grand Vizier Talat, Minister of War Enver, and former supreme commander in Syria Minister of Marine Cemal—who bore collective responsibility for Ottoman wartime decision-making, could only have complicated efforts to negotiate an armistice with the victorious Allies. For one week, the empire went without a government as no credible statesman could be found to lead the Ottomans into surrender. Eventually, Ahmet Izzet Pasha, who had commanded the Ottoman Army in the Caucasus, agreed to form a new government to conclude a peace agreement.

The new government dispatched its highest-ranking prisoner of war to initiate discussions with the British for an armistice. General Charles Townshend, former commander of the besieged garrison at Kut al-Amara, had spent the remainder of the war in the comfort of a villa on the Princes Islands in the Sea of Marmara. Townshend had been discredited for accepting enemy hospitality, not least when the other survivors of Kut had suffered such terrible fates. Townshend was dispatched to the island of Lesbos, where he conveyed Ottoman intentions to withdraw from the war.[38]

The commander of the British Mediterranean squadron, Admiral Sir Somerset A. Gough-Calthorpe, invited an Ottoman delegation to the island of Lemnos to receive armistice terms. The choice of venue could only have reinforced Ottoman bitterness: the island had been seized by Greece in the First Balkan War, and its port of Moudros had served as Britain's base of operations during the Gallipoli campaign. Terms were concluded in four days of negotiations, and British and Ottoman delegates signed the armistice agreement aboard the battle-scarred HMS *Agamemnon*, a veteran of the Gallipoli campaign, on 30 October.

The terms of the armistice in themselves were none too harsh. Admiral Calthorpe secured the Ottoman Empire's total surrender but left it to the politicians to impose more draconian terms through the peace treaty. The

Ottomans were to open the straits to the Allied fleet, clearing a safe passage through the minefields and placing the Dardanelles forts under Allied control. All Ottoman soldiers were to be demobilized with immediate effect and all naval vessels surrendered to the British and French. The communication network—rail, telegraph, and wireless facilities—was to come under Allied supervision. German and Austrian forces were given one month to evacuate Ottoman territory. Allied POWs and any Armenian internees were to be transported to Istanbul and "handed over unconditionally" to the Allies, but Ottoman POWs were to remain in Allied hands.[39]

Elements of the Moudros armistice would have raised Ottoman concerns for the future. The Armenians were mentioned twice, a reminder to the Ottoman authorities that they would be held accountable for wartime crimes against humanity. And there were intimations of partitions to come—in demands for the withdrawal of Ottoman troops from Cilicia, where France had staked a claim; in acknowledgment of the Allies' right to occupy "any strategic points" for their own security; and in assertions of their right to occupy any part of the six "Armenian *vilayets*" in case of

Proclaiming the armistice in central Baghdad, 31 October 1918. By the time the war ended, the British had occupied Baghdad for nearly twenty months. Already a distinct imperial separation is apparent in the stands that divided Western onlookers in suits and hats from the native crowd. Note the numerous British flags draped from building tops surrounding the square.

"disorder". By signing the document, the Turkish delegates were effectively forced to concede the Armenians had a stronger claim to the six provinces of eastern Anatolia than the Ottomans themselves.

In accordance with the terms of the armistice, hostilities ended at noon on 31 October 1918. The Ottoman war ended nearly one year after Russia's and just eleven days shy of the German surrender on 11 November. The Ottomans had surprised everyone by surviving to the final days of the war—but they had gained nothing from their tenacity. The length of the war had only imposed greater hardship and brought greater despair to the experience of defeat.

With the end of hostilities, soldiers celebrated their survival and dreamed of going home. "Now the water that had to run and the wind that had to blow, they are gone," an Indian trooper wrote his brother in Urdu. "Now we may hope for perfect calm and [that] we shall return to India in peace." He spoke for the hopes of soldiers from all corners of the earth who had struggled and survived the Great War on the Ottoman front.[40]

Conclusion

The Fall of the Ottomans

THE OTTOMANS HAD LOST THE GREAT WAR. IT WAS A NATIONAL catastrophe but not unprecedented. Since 1699, the Ottomans had lost most of the wars they had fought, and still the empire had survived. Yet never had the Ottomans faced such a constellation of interests as they did in negotiating the peace after the Great War. Caught between the conflicting demands of the victorious powers and Turkish nationalists, the Ottomans ultimately fell more as a result of the terms of the peace than of the magnitude of their defeat.

ON 13 NOVEMBER 1918, AN ALLIED FLEET NEGOTIATED THE RECENTLY cleared minefields of the Dardanelles to steam into Istanbul. The Ottoman capital, having eluded capture since the start of the war, lay defenceless before the victorious powers. Forty-two vessels, led by the dreadnought HMS *Agamemnon*, descended on the Dolmabahçe Palace, dominating the Bosporus waterfront. A squadron of biplanes passed over the British, French, Italian, and Greek warships, completing the spectacle. Admiral Somerset Gough-Calthorpe and the other officers disembarked to take possession of the city. Entente soldiers marched through the streets to the strains of military bands. Istanbul's Christian inhabitants welcomed them as heroes.

Grigoris Balakian was among the crowds watching the fleet's arrival from the Istanbul hilltops. Against all the odds, the Armenian priest had survived the genocide to make his way back to his native city in September 1918. Ever fearful of rearrest, Balakian had remained in hiding for the next two months, moving between the homes of his mother and sister, who had long since given him up for dead. He spent the days writing his account of the "Armenian Golgotha", capturing all the suffering he had witnessed at first hand and heard from others while the painful memories were still fresh. Yet he wanted to see for himself the arrival of the Allied fleet, marking the moment that Armenian wartime suffering would finally come to an end.

Making his way from the Asian to the European quarters of Istanbul, Balakian donned a redingote and top hat as a precaution to hide his identity. The Turkish boatman who rowed him across the Bosporus did not suspect he was carrying an Armenian priest. "Effendi," he lamented, "What bad times we're living in! What black days we have fallen upon! Talaat and Enver have destroyed the fatherland, picked up and fled, and left us to our fate. Who would have believed that a foreign fleet would enter Constantinople so illustriously and that we Muslims would be simple spectators"? Balakian surprised himself when he turned to comfort the man, assuring him, "These black days will pass too."[1]

Also among the crowds that day was German general Otto Liman von Sanders. He had served the Ottoman Empire for five years as head of the German mission and ultimately as commander of the Yıldırım Group in Palestine. He had narrowly escaped capture in Nazareth in September and retreated through Syria with the British in hot pursuit. In Adana, he turned over command of the remaining Ottoman forces to Turkish general Mustafa Kemal Pasha, the hero of Gallipoli. Liman then returned to Istanbul to oversee the repatriation of German forces from the Ottoman Empire in line with the terms of the armistice.

Though they viewed the day's events from very different perspectives, Liman and Balakian gave strikingly similar descriptions of Istanbul as the Allied fleet occupied the city. Greek, French, British, and Italian flags festooned the houses. Christian girls threw flowers at the victorious soldiers as they passed through the streets, while men tossed their hats in the air and embraced each other in celebration. As the day wore on, wine flowed as townspeople and occupiers fraternized. Both Liman and Balakian found the drunken revels distasteful. "None would have credited these demonstrations with any dignity," Liman sniffed, while Balakian regretted how "the Turkish capital had become a Babylon".[2]

While Istanbul's Christians celebrated, the Muslim majority watched the Allied soldiers take possession of their city in silence from behind their shuttered windows, overwhelmed by humiliation and despair. Their anger, like that of the boatman who had ferried Balakian across the Bosporus, focused on the leaders of the Committee of Union and Progress (CUP), who, having brought the whole misery of war on an unwilling populace, had fled immediately after the armistice went into effect.

In the middle of the night on 1 November, the Young Turk leadership boarded a German naval vessel in total secrecy to flee Ottoman domains. Mehmed Talat, Ismail Enver, and Ahmet Cemal, accompanied by four of their closest advisors, sailed to Odessa and made their way overland from the Black Sea coast to Berlin. Their German allies, knowing the Unionists would face victors' justice, assisted in their escape and granted the fugitives asylum. The Ottoman newspapers, on the other hand, expressed public outrage over the CUP triumvirs' flight, leaving the Turkish nation to face the consequences of Unionist policies and wartime atrocities—particularly the Armenian massacres.[3]

In the chamber of the Ottoman parliament and in the Turkish press, an open debate raged about the Armenian massacres in November 1918. Then as now, there was no agreed-on figure for the number of Armenians killed by government wartime measures. In their deliberations, members of the Ottoman parliament cited figures ranging from 800,000 to 1.5 million Armenian civilians massacred. Regardless of whether one subscribed to the high or low estimate or to some figure in between, it was clear that the genocide would cast a long shadow over peace negotiations with the victorious Entente Powers.

The Entente Powers openly condemned the Ottoman government for the Armenian massacres. America and Britain were particularly outspoken in calling for retributive justice for the Turks' wartime crimes against humanity. In order to avoid a draconian peace settlement, the new Ottoman government decided to establish military tribunals to try those accused of responsibility for the annihilation of the Armenian community. They hoped to focus international condemnation on the Young Turk leadership as the architects of the genocide rather than punishing the Turkish people as a whole.

Between January and March 1919, the Ottoman authorities ordered the arrest of three hundred Turkish officials. Among those detained were provincial governors and Unionist members of parliament as well as lower-ranking local officials. Though the police struck without warning, making their arrests in the middle of the night, many—like the triumvirate and their advisers, who were already in exile—were tried in absentia. The main military tribunal was convened in Istanbul. The trials were open to the public, with the state's evidence and court decisions published in the official gazette, the *Takvîm-i Vekâyi*.

The published indictments lay full responsibility for the mass murder of Armenian civilians on the Young Turk leadership. The prosecutors asserted, "These massacres were carried out under the orders and with the knowledge of Talat, Enver and Cemal." They quoted an official in Aleppo who claimed to have "received the order for annihilation" from "Talaat himself" and was convinced that "the well-being of the country" depended on the extermination of the Armenian population. In one telegram presented as evidence before the court, Dr Bahaeddin Şakir, the alleged architect of the genocide, demanded of the governor of Mamuretülaziz an "honest report" on the "liquidation" of Armenians from his province: "Are the troublemakers, whom you reported as being driven forth and banished, being destroyed or are they merely being driven out and sent away?"[4]

Witness testimony revealed how the mass murder was organized: the official printed orders calling for deportation were followed by oral instructions to massacre deportees. Evidence was presented of convicted murderers released from prison and mobilized in gangs to serve as "butchers of men". The prosecutors assembled compelling documentation linking Enver's secret intelligence service, the Teşkilât-i Mahsusa, to the formation of the murder gangs. And they assembled extensive evidence of mass killings, individuals claiming responsibility for the death of thousands, and provinces reporting deportations numbering in the hundreds of thousands.[5]

After months of deliberations, the courts passed death sentences on eighteen defendants for their roles in the Armenian massacres. Talat, Enver, and Cemal faced capital punishment, along with key CUP leaders such as Dr Bahaeddin Şakir and Dr Mehmed Nazım, who had followed them into exile. With fifteen of the condemned tried in absentia, only three lower-ranking officials were ultimately sent to the gallows. Mehmed Kemal, lieutenant governor of Yozgat, whom Grigoris Balakian claimed was responsible for the massacre of 42,000 Armenians, was hanged on 10 April 1919. The commander of the Erzincan gendarmerie, Hafız Abdullah Avni, was executed on 22 July 1920. The third and final execution was held on 5 August 1920, with the hanging of the district head of Bayburt, Behramzade Nusret.[6]

By August 1920, it was clear that the military tribunal was not going to bring the main perpetrators of the Armenian massacres to justice. It was equally clear that the trials would not spare the Ottoman Empire from a draconian peace settlement. Once they had outlived their usefulness, the military tribunals lapsed into inactivity. But the record of these trials provides the most extensive evidence ever compiled by the Turkish authorities on the organization and the conduct of the Armenian massacres. These records, published in Ottoman Turkish, have been in the public domain since 1919 and make a mockery of any attempt to deny the Young Turk government's role in ordering and organizing the annihilation of the Ottoman Armenian community.

UNWILLING TO WATCH THE YOUNG TURK LEADERS IN EXILE ESCAPE justice, a group of Armenian militants from the Dashnak organization took the law into their own hands. Between March 1921 and July 1922, the Dashnaks ordered a series of assassinations of key Young Turk leaders in a program known as "Operation Nemesis".[7]

The assassins struck first in Berlin, where many of the leading Young Turks had taken refuge. On 15 March 1921, a twenty-five-year-old genocide survivor from Erzincan named Soghomon Tehlirian gunned down Talat Pasha. The young assassin was arrested, tried, and acquitted by a German court on the grounds of diminished responsibility due to the mental trauma and personal losses he had suffered in the Armenian massacres. Arshavir Shiragian, a twenty-one-year-old native of Istanbul, who had already assassinated former grand vizier Said Halim Pasha in Rome on 5 December 1921, took part in a second attack in which both Dr Bahaeddin Şakir and Cemal Azmi, the murderous governor of Trabzon Province, were shot dead in Berlin on 17 April 1922.

The two surviving triumvirs, Cemal and Enver, met their deaths in the Caucasus and Central Asia. Armenian assassins tracked Cemal Pasha, wartime governor general of Syria, to the Georgian city of Tbilisi, where he was killed on 25 July 1922. He would have been surprised to learn that his killers were Armenian rather than Arab. While widely despised in Syria for his execution of Arab nationalists, Cemal is credited with having settled Armenian deportees—some 60,000 by January 1916 alone—across the Syrian provinces. Yet measures to convert Armenian survivors of the death marches to Islam, which amounted to the annihilation of the Armenians by other means, undermined his humanitarian efforts. Among the former ruling triumvirate, only Enver eluded assassination. The Young Turk leader made his last stand near Dushanbe, in the Tajik-Uzbek border regions, and was killed leading a Muslim militia in battle against the Bolsheviks in August 1922.[8]

By 1926, ten of the eighteen men sentenced to death by the Istanbul military courts for their role in the Armenian genocide were dead. The other eight, mass murderers lower down the chain of command, escaped execution, but their convictions left them feeling like marked men for the rest of their days.

THERE WAS NOTHING THE OTTOMANS COULD DO TO SOFTEN THE TERMS the Allies would impose at the Paris Peace Conference. From the very outset of the war, Britain, France, and Russia had negotiated the future partition of Ottoman domains. Though Russia had retracted its claims after the Bolshevik Revolution, new allies had taken its place. Italy and Greece, both relative latecomers to the Ottoman front (Italy declared war on Turkey in August 1915 and Greece only in June 1917), proved no less avid to acquire Ottoman territory than the tsar's government had been. In April 1919, the Italians landed troops in the Mediterranean port of Antalya, and on 15 May Greek forces occupied the port of Izmir.

When the Ottoman delegates appeared before the Supreme Council of the Paris Peace Conference in June 1919, they could have had little confidence of a sympathetic hearing. Appealing to "President Wilson's principles"—the twelfth of Woodrow Wilson's famous Fourteen Points called for "a secure sovereignty" for the "Turkish portion of the present Ottoman Empire"—they set out their vision for the post-war Ottoman Empire. In essence, they sought to retain all territory within their October 1914 frontiers, divided between areas of direct Turkish rule (in Anatolia and Thrace) and autonomous zones with a high degree of local rule under the Ottoman flag (in the Arab provinces and the disputed Aegean islands). "Nobody in

Turkey is unaware of the gravity of the moment," the Ottoman delegation's memorandum concluded. "The ideas of the Ottoman people are however well defined: It will not accept the dismemberment of the Empire or its division under different mandates."[9]

Five days after the Ottoman delegation submitted its memorandum, the Allies and Germany signed the Treaty of Versailles, on 28 June 1919. The treaty set a high benchmark for the harsh terms the victorious powers would impose on the defeated Central Powers. Germany was forced to accept responsibility for the loss and damage caused by the war. Its military was to undergo disarmament. It faced substantial territorial losses in excess of 25,000 square miles. And Germany was ordered to pay unprecedented reparations of $31.4 billion (£6.6 billion).[10]

The terms dealt the other defeated powers were hardly less draconian. The peace with Austria, signed at Saint-Germain-en-Laye on 10 September 1919, imposed the dissolution of the Austro-Hungarian Empire, forced Austria to accept responsibility for causing the war, imposed heavy war reparations, and distributed Austrian territory to a number of successor states, including Hungary, Czechoslovakia, Poland, and the Kingdom of the Serbs, Croats, and Slovenes (subsequently renamed Yugoslavia).

In November 1919, the Allies signed the Treaty of Neuilly-sur-Seine with Bulgaria, remembered in national histories as the "Second National Catastrophe" (the first had been Bulgaria's defeat in the Second Balkan War of 1913). The treaty forced Bulgaria to cede territory in western Thrace (ultimately awarded to Greece) and on its western frontiers and left the country saddled with £100 million in reparations.

The peace treaty with Hungary, signed at the Trianon on 4 June 1920, reduced the Hungarian lands of the former Austro-Hungarian Empire to 28 percent of its pre-war territory and left the landlocked state saddled with a major reparations bill.

There was little reason to expect the Ottoman Empire would face more generous terms than its wartime allies. In fact, the Treaty of Versailles signed with Germany incorporated the Covenant of the League of Nations, giving the sanction of international law to a mandate system designed expressly to allow for the partition of the Ottoman Empire. Article 22 of the covenant read, "Certain communities formerly belonging to the Turkish Empire have reached a stage of development where their existence as independent nations can be provisionally recognized subject to the rendering of administrative advice and assistance by a Mandatory until such time as they are able to stand alone."[11]

After the Turkish delegation returned to Istanbul, the victorious powers engaged in a final round of negotiations to agree on the ultimate distribution of Ottoman territory. The prime ministers of Great Britain, France, and Italy met in the Italian resort of San Remo in April 1920 to resolve the contradictions between the Husayn-McMahon Correspondence, the Sykes-Picot Agreement, and the Balfour Declaration. After six days of discussion, the three powers, with Japan as a disinterested observer, agreed that Britain would be awarded mandates over Palestine (including Transjordan) and Mesopotamia, and France would secure the mandate over Syria (including Lebanon). The Italian government withheld its formal approval of the agreement until its declared interests in Anatolia had been satisfied.

Once the Allies had agreed on the partition of the Arab lands, they turned to finalize the peace treaty with the Ottoman Empire. The terms, first shared with the Porte in May 1920, could not have been worse for the Turks. In addition to transferring all of the Arab provinces to European mandatory control, the draft peace agreement called for the partition of Anatolia and the distribution of territories with Turkish-majority populations among former subject peoples and hostile neighbours.

Eastern Anatolia was to be divided between the Armenians and the Kurds. The north-eastern provinces of Trabzon, Erzurum, Bitlis, and Van were designated an Armenian sphere of influence. These four provinces enjoyed the full freedom, under American arbitration, to secede from the Ottoman Empire and join the new Armenian Republic in the Caucasus, with its capital in Yerevan. The Kurds were offered a smaller territory on the southern frontiers of the Armenian zone, based around the town of Diyarbakır. Under the terms of the treaty, the Kurds too were given full freedom to secede from the Ottoman Empire and to establish an independent state.

In western Anatolia, the port city of Smyrna (modern Izmir) and its hinterlands were placed under Greek administration. The government of Greece was instructed to assist the local Greek community in electing a parliament that would enjoy the authority to legislate Smyrna's future union with the Kingdom of Greece. Most of Turkish Thrace, including the city of Edirne (which the Ottomans had lost in the First Balkan War and recovered in the Second), was also ceded to the Greeks. The Ottomans even lost control over the strategic waterways linking the Black Sea and the Mediterranean. The

Bosporus, the Dardanelles, and the Sea of Marmara were to be placed under an international commission that Turkey would only be allowed to join if and when it was admitted to the League of Nations.[12]

The partition of Anatolia did not end there. By separate agreement concluded between Britain, France, and Italy, the Mediterranean regions of Anatolia were to be divided between the French and Italians. The Cilician coast, reaching deep inland to Sivas, was designated a French sphere of influence. Italian claims to South-West Anatolia, including the port of Antalya and the inland city of Konya, were also recognized. Though nominally still part of the Ottoman Empire, Turkey's Mediterranean coast would effectively fall under informal French or Italian colonial rule.[13]

The draft peace treaty left very little territory to the Turks. The Ottoman Empire was effectively reduced to those parts of central Anatolia that no one else wanted: Bursa, Ankara, and Samsun on the Black Sea coast, with Istanbul as its capital. And even Istanbul was awarded to the Turks on sufferance. If the Ottomans failed to uphold their treaty commitments, the Allies threatened to retract the award of Constantinople to the post-war Turkish state.

The terms of the settlement provoked widespread opposition across the Ottoman Empire. The presence of foreign armies on Turkish soil already had engendered profound resentment. In May 1919, Mustafa Kemal Pasha, hero of Gallipoli and the nation's most respected military leader, had been sent to Samsun to oversee the demobilization of Ottoman troops in line with the terms of the armistice. Following the Italian and Greek occupations of Cilicia and Izmir in April and May 1919, Mustafa Kemal decided to disobey his orders to demobilize the army and mounted a resistance movement against the invasion of Anatolia instead. He established his base in the central Anatolian town of Ankara, where the Turkish National Movement he launched increasingly rivalled the Ottoman government in Istanbul in representing the political aspirations of the Turkish people.

Between July and September 1919, the Turkish National Movement convened two congresses, in Erzurum and Sivas, that set out its principles in a document known as the National Pact. The National Pact sought to reconcile a "just and lasting peace" with "a stable Ottoman sultanate" through a clear statement of principles. The framers of the National Pact accepted the loss of the Arab provinces and were open to arrangements to ensure free navigation of the straits. But they ruled out any partition of those territories "which are inhabited by an Ottoman [read Turkish] Moslem majority, united in religion, in race and in aim", claiming those territories "form a whole which does not admit of division for any reason". In one of its final sessions, the Ottoman parliament in Istanbul threw in its lot with the Turkish National Movement in Ankara and adopted the National Pact by overwhelming majority in January 1920.[14]

However popular the nationalists' policies were with parliamentarians, the Porte viewed the Turkish National Movement in central Anatolia as a dangerous threat to its authority. In the national crisis that followed the release of the Allied peace terms in May 1920, the Ottoman government believed it had no choice but to cooperate with the victorious powers. By accepting the victorious powers' harsh terms in the short run, the Porte hoped to secure better terms in the long run. The Turkish National Movement, on the other hand, believed the Ottomans would never recover the territory or sovereignty surrendered in the peace treaty. Mustafa Kemal and his partisans called for the rejection of the draconian terms and resistance to any partition of Anatolia.

The Porte believed the course of confrontation advocated by Mustafa Kemal and the Turkish National Movement, given the shattered state of the Ottoman military and economy, would lead to catastrophe. Resistance might even cost the Ottomans their capital city, Istanbul, given the conditions of the peace treaty. The Ottoman government charged Mustafa Kemal and several other nationalist leaders with high treason, and in May 1920 the same military court that had conducted the Armenian trials sentenced the "hero of Gallipoli" to death in absentia.

History was to prove the grand vizier and his cabinet wrong: only resistance to the peace treaty would preserve Turkish sovereignty, and Mustafa Kemal was no traitor. A committed Ottomanist, Mustafa Kemal had framed his every act in terms of preserving the sultan's state. The National Pact even used the word "Ottoman" rather than "Turk" to describe the nation. The breaking point for the Kemalists came when the Ottoman government committed the Turkish nation to the draconian peace and the partition of Anatolia under foreign occupation. In signing the Treaty of Sèvres on 10 August 1920, the Porte provoked an irreconcilable split with the Turkish National Movement. From that date forward, the Kemalists worked to bring down both the treaty and the Ottoman government that signed it.

By 1922, after an intense war on three fronts—against the Armenians in the Caucasus, the French in Cilicia, and the Greeks in western Anatolia—the Kemalists achieved total victory over all foreign armies in Turkey. After concluding an armistice with Greece on 11 October 1922, the Turkish Grand National Assembly voted to abolish the Ottoman sultanate on 1 November. After only four years on the throne, Mehmed VI (who succeeded his half-brother Mehmed V in July 1918, four months before the end of the war), the last Ottoman sultan, was sent into exile aboard a British warship bound for Malta on 17 November.

In July 1923, the nationalist government in Turkey signed a new treaty with the victorious powers in Lausanne, Switzerland, that recognized Turkey's independence more or less within its present boundaries. On the strength of that international recognition, the Turkish Republic was proclaimed on 29 October 1923, with Mustafa Kemal as the new country's first president. The Turkish parliament later awarded Mustafa Kemal the surname Atatürk (literally, "father of the Turks") in recognition of his leadership in the creation of modern Turkey.

Had the sultan's government harnessed Atatürk's movement and resisted the terms imposed by the victorious powers at Sèvres, the Ottoman Empire might well have survived within the boundaries of the modern Turkish Republic. However catastrophic their defeat in the Great War, acceptance of the draconian peace led to the fall of the Ottomans.

WITH THE END OF HOSTILITIES IN OCTOBER 1918, SOLDIERS FROM both sides of the trenches were eager to return home. The first to depart from the Middle East were the soldiers of the defeated Central Powers. In line with the terms of the armistice, Liman von Sanders oversaw the repatriation of German soldiers from Ottoman domains. Initially, German and Austrian troops already in Istanbul were shipped to Odessa to make their way home overland through Ukraine. However, the 1,200 German and Austrian soldiers with the Sixth Army in Mesopotamia took weeks to reach Istanbul, as did those serving in Syria and Palestine. Liman estimated there were 10,000 men to be shipped by late December 1918. He secured five steamships to transport them directly from Istanbul to Germany, and at the end of January 1919, Liman boarded ship with 120 officers and 1,800 men for the long journey back to their war-shattered homes. So ended the German-Ottoman alliance.[15]

There remained a large number of Ottoman troops in Allied-occupied territory. Fahri Pasha, commander of the Ottoman garrison at Medina, enjoyed the distinction of being the last Turkish general to surrender. Though under total siege since the closing months of the war, the Ottoman garrison in Medina had rationed its provisions and refused every overture to capitulate. After the armistice, the British high commissioner in Egypt, Sir Reginald Wingate, wrote to Fahri to persuade him to surrender. The stubborn Turkish general refused outright, responding, "I am an Osmanli [Ottoman]. I am a Muhammadan. I am the son of Bali Bey, and I am a soldier." Between his devotion to the sultan and his veneration for the Prophet's Mosque in Medina, Fahri had no intention of yielding his sword to an Englishman.[16]

For ten weeks after the armistice, the Ottoman garrison held out. As Arab forces threatened to storm the city, Fahri Pasha locked himself into the Prophet's Mosque with crates of ammunition and threatened to blow up the sacred shrine rather than surrender. His men, however, demoralized by weeks of privation made worse by knowledge of the war's end, began to desert their commander to surrender to the Arab army. Finally, on 10 January 1919, the zealous general was persuaded to deliver the holy city to Hashemite forces. He emerged from Medina "depressed and angry", Amir Abdullah recalled, "looking round like a caged lion, and finding no escape". He was seen off with full honours from the port of Yanbu, boarded a British destroyer, and set sail for captivity in Egypt. The evacuation of Ottoman troops took place over the following weeks under Amir Abdullah's supervision, with Arab soldiers from the Ottoman garrison pressed into the Hashemite army and Turkish soldiers sent on to Egypt, where they were detained in POW camps until they could be repatriated to Turkey.

French colonial authorities made North African soldiers recruited to Ottoman service from German POW camps pay for their wartime disloyalty. Already since Major General Stanley Maude's occupation of Baghdad in 1917, thousands of North African soldiers had passed from Ottoman service into British prison camps. They were dispatched in due course to France for repatriation. A number of camps were opened in southern France to receive "native troops" from Tunisia, Algeria, and Morocco. Those deemed of dubious loyalty were barred from returning to North Africa or fraternizing with Muslims in France. Of all Great War veterans, few fought on so many fronts, with so little incentive, as the North African POWs.[17]

Allied forces remained in service long after the armistice as an army of occupation. The Arab provinces of the Ottoman Empire were brought under an Allied Occupied Enemy Territory Administration. Inevitably, tensions emerged between local communities resentful of foreign occupiers and British and dominion forces hardened by the war and impatient to return home.

In Palestine, the killing of a New Zealand sergeant by a local villager set off a retaliatory massacre in mid-December 1918. Accounts vary, but between sixty and two hundred New Zealanders surrounded the village of Sarafand, where the sergeant's killer was believed to have taken refuge. They drove out the women, children, and elderly before attacking the men of the village. According to New Zealand sources, the vengeful soldiers killed or wounded over thirty men before setting fire to the village and a nearby encampment.[18]

General Edmund Allenby convened a formal inquiry into the massacre. In a determined conspiracy of silence, none of the soldiers in the Anzac units billeted around Sarafand would give evidence. By all accounts, Allenby was livid at the insubordination of his troops. Yet rather than impose collective punishments that might provoke further rebellion, the British general decided to order the Anzac troops back to the Egyptian border at Rafah. It was the first stage in their planned demobilization and return to New Zealand and Australia.

At Rafah the army began to kill the Anzac cavalrymen's horses. To be precise, most were killed, some were saved for the army of occupation, and a limited number in good health were set aside for sale. The troopers were given many explanations—that not enough ships were available to transport both the men and their mounts, that the horses were in no state for the long journey home, and that the animals risked carrying infectious diseases that would spread to the national herd in Australia and New Zealand. But the cavalrymen took this unexpected news badly. "The parting of the men from their horses was pathetic," Sergeant C. G. Nicol of the Auckland Mounted Rifles recalled. After years of campaigning, the bond between the troopers and their horses was stronger than many felt for their fellow man.[19]

Though strictly forbidden, many troopers preferred to kill their own horses rather than leave them for the livestock market or the butcher. The Australian soldier-journalist Oliver Hogue, a veteran of both the Gallipoli and

Palestine campaigns who wrote under the pseudonym Trooper Bluegum, captured the typical cavalryman's sentiments towards his "waler" (short for the most common breed of Australian warhorse, the New South Wales) in a poem titled "The Horses Stay Behind":

> I don't think I could stand the thought of my old fancy hack
> Just crawling round old Cairo with a 'Gyppo on his back.
> Perhaps some English tourist out in Palestine may find
> My broken-hearted waler with a wooden plough behind.
>
> No; I think I'd better shoot him and tell a little lie:
> "He floundered in a wombat hole and then lay down to die."
> Maybe I'll get court-martialled; but I'm damned if I'm inclined
> To go back to Australia and leave my horse behind.[20]

The Anzac troops were scheduled to leave Egypt for home in mid-March 1919. Before they could board ship, Egypt exploded in a nationwide uprising that detained the Australians and New Zealanders a bit longer.[21]

Egypt and the Arab lands emerged from the Great War with heightened expectations of a new era of independence. The twelfth of Woodrow Wilson's Fourteen Points assured the Arabs, along with the other subject peoples of the Ottoman Empire, "an undoubted security of life and an absolutely unmolested opportunity of autonomous development". Political activists were at work in Syria and Mesopotamia debating different political visions, freed from the constraints imposed by decades of Ottoman political repression. In Egypt, political elites knew precisely what they wanted. After thirty-six years of British occupation, they wanted Egypt's total independence.[22]

A group of prominent Egyptian politicians approached the British authorities in Cairo to request permission to present their case for independence at the Paris Peace Conference. Sir Reginald Wingate, British high commissioner, received the delegation led by veteran politician Saad Zaghlul two days after the armistice with Germany, on 13 November 1918. He heard the delegates out and promptly declined their request to attend the peace conference in no uncertain terms. The Paris Peace Conference was to decide the fate of the defeated powers and in no way concerned Egypt. When Zaghlul and his colleagues persisted in their efforts, they were arrested on 8 March 1919 and deported to Malta. The following day, Egypt exploded in demonstrations that rapidly spread nationwide and across the different social classes in a common demand for independence.

Egyptians in town and countryside attacked every visible manifestation of British imperial power. The railways and telegraph lines were sabotaged, government offices burned, and government centres confronted with huge crowds of protesters. The British dispatched soldiers to restore order, but soldiers are blunt tools for crowd control, and casualties began to mount. The Egyptians accused British soldiers of atrocities—of using live fire against demonstrators, burning villages, and even committing rape. By the end of March, 800 Egyptian civilians had been killed and a further 1,600 injured in the violence.[23]

To restore the calm, the British allowed Zaghlul to return to Egypt and lead a delegation to Paris in April 1919. Before the Egyptian delegation reached Paris, British prime minister David Lloyd George had persuaded his French and American allies that Egypt was an "imperial and not an international question". The day the Egyptian delegation reached Paris, President Wilson recognized Britain's protectorate over Egypt. The delegation was never granted a formal hearing by the peace conference. The war might have ended, but British rule in Egypt had not.

Amir Faysal's Arab administration in Damascus also faced a sceptical hearing in Paris. While the Hashemite prince believed himself entitled to Entente support after serving the Allied cause by leading the Arab Revolt against the Ottoman Empire, his claims collided with French ambitions in Syria.

Faysal presented his case for Arab independence to the Supreme Council of the Paris Peace Conference in January 1919. In light of the extensive territory Sir Henry McMahon had promised Sharif Husayn in their famous correspondence, Faysal's position was very moderate. He sought immediate and full independence for Arab kingdoms in Greater Syria (corresponding to the territory of the modern states of Syria, Lebanon, Jordan, Israel, and the Palestinian Authority) and the Hijaz, then ruled by his father King Husayn. He accepted foreign mediation in Palestine to resolve conflicting Arab and Zionist aspirations. And he acknowledged British claims to Mesopotamia, while expressing his belief that these territories would eventually join the independent Arab state he hoped to persuade the peacemakers to create.

Amir Faysal at the Paris Peace Conference, 1919. The commander of the Arab Revolt presented Arab demands at the peace conference with T. E. Lawrence as his translator, but he failed to preserve his short-lived Syrian kingdom from French imperial aspirations.

While accepting less than the Hashemites believed their British allies had promised, Faysal demanded more than the British could deliver. Prime Minister David Lloyd George needed French consent to secure British claims to Mesopotamia and Palestine. And from the very outset of the war, France had named Syria as its price. Unable to reconcile these rival claims, Britain backed its essential ally, France, and left Faysal to fend for himself.

On 1 November 1919, the British withdrew their army from Syria and handed the country over to French military rule. The Syrian General Congress, an elected body convened by Faysal's supporters with representatives from the different regions of Greater Syria, responded on 8 March 1920 by declaring the independence of Syria with Faysal as their king. But Faysal's Syrian Kingdom was not to survive. The French dispatched a colonial army from Lebanon to take control of Damascus. Encountering the remnants of Faysal's Arab army in a mountain pass on the road between Beirut and Damascus, the French easily defeated the token force of 2,000 defenders at

Khan Maysalun on 24 July 1920 and advanced into Damascus unopposed to overturn Faysal's short-lived Syrian Kingdom. Faysal carried the dashed hopes of the Arab Revolt into exile with him.

The fall of Faysal's government in Damascus left the Palestinians to face the British occupation—and the Balfour Declaration—on their own. Notables from Palestinian towns and cities had played a key role in the Syrian General Congress, and the townsmen and villagers they represented made their views known to the American commission of inquiry sent in the summer of 1919 by the Paris Peace Conference. Between 10 June and 21 July, the King-Crane Commission travelled across Greater Syria to gather evidence and assess public opinion about the region's political future. It was clear that a strong majority of Palestinian Arabs wished to be ruled as part of Faysal's Arab kingdom. Moreover, the King-Crane Commission reported that the Palestinian Arab population was "emphatically against the entire Zionist program" and that "there was no one thing upon which the population of Palestine were more agreed than upon this".[24]

Tensions ran high in 1920 as Jewish immigration, encouraged by the Balfour Declaration, accelerated. Between 1919 and 1921, over 18,500 Zionist immigrants flocked to Palestine's shores. Rioting broke out in Jerusalem in the first week of April 1920, leaving five Jews and four Arabs dead and over two hundred people injured. Worse violence followed in 1921, when Arab townsmen intervened in a fight between Jewish communists and Zionists in the port of Jaffa during May Day parades. In the ensuing riots, forty-seven Jews and forty-eight Arabs were killed, and over two hundred people were injured. The contradictions raised by the Balfour Declaration— in its declaration of intent to create a national home for the Jews that would not adversely affect the rights and interests of the indigenous non-Jewish population—were already apparent.

The political elites in Iraq watched events in Egypt and Syria with mounting concern for their own future. They had been reassured in November 1918 when the British and French issued a declaration pledging their support for "the establishment of national governments and administrations" in the Arab lands through a process of self-determination. But the Iraqis grew increasingly suspicious as the months passed without any tangible progress towards the promised self-government. News in April 1920 that the Great Powers had agreed in San Remo to award their country to Britain as a mandate confirmed the Iraqis' worst fears.[25]

At the end of June 1920, Iraq erupted in nationwide rebellion against British rule. Disciplined and well-organized, the insurgency threatened the British in Basra, Baghdad, and Mosul, but the centre of operations lay in the same Shiite shrine towns of the Middle Euphrates that had risen against the Ottomans during the Great War. As the uprising spread, the British were forced to move additional troops into Mesopotamia to suppress determined Iraqi resistance on all fronts. Reinforcements from India were rushed to bolster the 60,000 troops yet to be demobilized from the Mesopotamia campaign, raising British forces to over 100,000 by October. Using aerial bombardment and heavy artillery, the British reconquered the Middle Euphrates region with scorched-earth tactics that crushed the resistance. "In recent days there has been bloodshed and the destruction of populous towns and the violation of the sanctity of places of worship to make humanity weep," one journalist in Najaf wrote in October 1920. By the time the uprising was crushed at the end of October, the British claimed that 2,200 of their own forces and an estimated 8,450 Iraqis had been killed or wounded.[26]

Sharif Husayn, now king of Hijaz, followed events in Syria, Palestine, and Iraq with a deepening sense of betrayal. He had copies of every letter exchanged with Sir Henry McMahon and felt the British had broken every promise they contained. Having aspired to be king of the Arabs, Husayn was now confined to the Hijaz—and he wasn't even secure there. A rival monarchy in central Arabia, led by Abd al-Aziz Al Saud, better known in the West as Ibn Saud, threatened to overrun the Hijaz. To add insult to injury, Ibn Saud enjoyed a treaty with Great Britain and received a generous monthly stipend from the British treasury.

The British too were concerned about the future of the Hijaz. While they had secured a formal treaty with Ibn Saud back in 1915, their relations with the Hashemites had been concluded in the form of a wartime alliance. Once the war was at an end, so too was the alliance. Unless the old king of the Hijaz concluded a treaty with Britain, Whitehall would have no legal basis to protect his territory. But to get King Husayn to sign a treaty, they had to get him to accept the post-war settlement hammered out at San Remo. In the summer of 1921, T. E. Lawrence was given the impossible mission of negotiating the terms of an Anglo-Hijazi treaty with the embittered King Husayn.

By the time Lawrence met with King Husayn, Britain had gone some way towards redeeming Sir Henry McMahon's broken promises. Winston

Churchill, now secretary of state for the colonies, had convened a secret meeting in Cairo in March 1921 to determine the political future of Britain's new Middle Eastern mandates. At that meeting, the British dignitaries agreed to install King Husayn's son Faysal as king of Iraq and Abdullah as ruler of the as yet undefined territory of Transjordan (which was formally separated from Palestine in 1923). With Hashemite rulers slated for all of Britain's mandates bar Palestine, Churchill could claim to have worked within the spirit, if not the exact lettering, of McMahon's wartime undertakings.

Between July and September 1921, Lawrence sought in vain the formula for reconciling King Husayn with Britain's post-war position in the Middle East. Husayn refused to confine his own ambitions to the Hijaz. He objected to the separation of Syria and Lebanon from the rest of the Arab lands and their placement under French mandate. He rejected the British mandates in Iraq and Transjordan, even if they were to be nominally ruled by his sons. And he refused to sanction the pledge to establish a Jewish national home in Palestine. As King Husayn could accept nothing in the British post-war settlement, there was no scope for an Anglo-Hijaz treaty of alliance. Lawrence returned to London empty-handed.

The British made one last attempt to conclude a treaty with the Hijaz in 1923, but the bitter old king refused—forfeiting British protection at the very moment Ibn Saud was preparing to conquer the Red Sea province. On 6 October 1924, King Husayn abdicated in favour of his eldest son, Ali, and went into exile. King Ali's reign ended in late 1925 when the Saudis completed the conquest of the Hijaz. Like the Ottomans before them, the Hashemites made their last stand in Medina, surrendering the holy city in December 1925—nearly seven years after Fahri Pasha's capitulation.

In the end, the Ottoman front proved more influential in the First World War than contemporaries ever imagined. Allied war planners, believing a quick victory over a weak Ottoman Empire might precipitate the Central Powers' surrender, found themselves drawn into a series of campaigns that lasted nearly the full length of the war. The battles in the Caucasus and Persia, the failed attempt to force the Dardanelles, the reversals in Mesopotamia, and the long campaign through Sinai, Palestine, and Syria diverted hundreds of thousands of men and strategic war materiel from the primary theatres of operations on the western and eastern fronts. Rather than hastening the end of the conflict, the Ottoman front served instead to lengthen the war.

Much of the Allied war effort in the Middle East was driven by what proved to be an unwarranted fear of jihad. While colonial Muslims remained largely unresponsive to the Ottoman sultan-caliph's appeal, the European imperial powers continued to assume that any major Turkish success or Allied setback might provoke the dreaded Islamic uprising in their colonies in India and North Africa. Ironically, this left the Allies more responsive to the caliph's call than his Muslim target audience. Even a century later, the Western world has yet to shake off the belief that Muslims might act in a collectively fanatical manner. As the "War on Terrorism" after 11 September 2001 has demonstrated, Western policy makers continue to view jihad in terms reminiscent of the war planners from 1914 to 1918.

The First World War was itself tremendously influential in the making of the modern Middle East. With the fall of the Ottoman Empire, European imperialism replaced Turkish rule. After four centuries united in a multinational empire under Ottoman Muslim rule, the Arabs found themselves divided into a number of new states under British and French domination. A few countries achieved independence within frontiers of their own devising—Turkey, Iran, and Saudi Arabia stand out in this regard. The imperial powers, however, imposed the borders and systems of government of most states in the region as part of the post-war settlement.

The post-war partition of the Ottoman Empire was the subject of intense negotiations between the Allies that ran the length of the War. In hindsight, each of the partition agreements only makes sense within its wartime context: the Constantinople Agreement of 1915 when the Allies anticipated the quick conquest of Istanbul; the Husayn-McMahon Correspondence in 1915 and 1916 when the British needed a Muslim ally against the Ottoman jihad; the Balfour Declaration in 1917 when the British wanted to revise the terms of the Sykes-Picot Agreement to secure Palestine for British rule. These outlandish agreements, which were only conceivable in wartime, were concluded solely to advance Britain and France's imperial expansion. Had the European powers been concerned with establishing a stable Middle East, one can't help but think they would have gone about drafting the boundaries in a very different way.

The borders of the post-war settlement have proven remarkably resilient—as have the conflicts the post-war boundaries have engendered. The Kurdish people, divided between Turkey, Iran, Iraq, and Syria, have been embroiled in conflict with each of their host governments over the past century in pursuit of their cultural and political rights. Lebanon, created by France in 1920 as a Christian state, succumbed to a string of civil wars as its political institutions failed to keep pace with its demographic shifts and Muslims came to outnumber Christians. Syria, unreconciled to the creation of Lebanon from what many Syrian nationalists believed to be an integral part of their country, sent its military to occupy civil war Lebanon in 1976—and remained in occupation of that country for nearly thirty years. Despite its natural and human resources, Iraq has never known enduring peace and stability within its post-war boundaries, experiencing a coup and conflict with Britain in World War II, revolution in 1958, war with Iran between 1980 and 1988, and a seemingly unending cycle of war since Saddam Hussein's 1991 invasion of Kuwait and the 2003 American invasion of Iraq to topple Hussein.

Yet the Arab-Israeli conflict, more than any other legacy of the post-war partition, has defined the Middle East as a war zone. Four major wars between Israel and its Arab neighbours—in 1948, 1956, 1967, and 1973—have left the Middle East with a number of intractable problems that remain unresolved despite peace treaties between Israel and Egypt in 1979 and between Israel and Jordan in 1994. Palestinian refugees remain scattered between Lebanon, Syria, and Jordan, Israel continues to occupy the Syrian Golan Heights and the Shebaa Farms in southern Lebanon, and Israel has yet to relinquish its control over the Palestinian territories of Gaza and the West Bank. While Israel and its Arab neighbours share primary responsibility for their actions, the roots of their conflict can be traced directly back to the fundamental contradictions of the Balfour Declaration.

The legitimacy of Middle Eastern frontiers has been called into question since they were first drafted. Arab nationalists in the 1940s and 1950s openly called for unity schemes between Arab states that would overthrow boundaries widely condemned as an imperialist legacy. Pan-Islamists have advocated a broader Islamic union with the same goal. In 2014, a militia calling itself the Islamic State tweeted to its followers that it was "smashing Sykes-Picot" when it declared a caliphate in territory spanning northern

Syria and Iraq. One century later, the borders of the Middle East remain controversial—and volatile.[27]

THE CENTENARY OF THE GREAT WAR ATTRACTED LITTLE COMMEMORATION in the Middle East. Aside from Gallipoli, where Turkish and Anzac veteran associations have long gathered to remember their war dead, the struggles and sacrifices of the global armies that fought on the Ottoman front have given way to more pressing contemporary concerns. Revolutionary turmoil in Egypt, civil war in Syria and Iraq, and enduring violence between Israelis and Palestinians preoccupied the Middle East on the hundredth anniversary of the start of the Great War. Yet as the war is remembered in the rest of the world, the part the Ottomans played in that conflict must be taken into account. For the Ottoman front, with its Asian battlefields and global soldiers, turned Europe's Great War into the First World War. And in the Middle East more than in any other part of the world, the legacies of the Great War continue to be felt down to the present day.

Acknowledgments

THE RESEARCH AND WRITING OF THIS BOOK WAS MADE POSSIBLE through the generous support of the British Academy and the Arts and Humanities Research Council. I am enormously grateful to the British Academy and the Association of Jewish Refugees for the award of the 2011-12 Thank-Offering to Britain Fellowship. I am equally indebted to the AHRC for the award of a Senior Research Fellowship for the 2012-13 academic year.

As with my previous book, *The Arabs*, I have benefitted from the knowledge and encouragement of Oxford's remarkable Middle Eastern studies community. Much of the book was first aired to the critical scrutiny of my Oxford students in the lecture theatre, and I am grateful for their feedback. I also wish to thank my Middle East Centre colleagues Walter Armbrust, Celia Kerslake, Laurent Mignon, Tariq Ramadan, Philip Robins, Avi Shlaim, and Michael Willis.

Knowing of my research interests, a number of friends, family and colleagues have shared books and documents that have contributed enormously to this study. I would like to thank Toufoul Abou-Hodeib and Adam Mestyan for a number of Arabic references on the war in Syria; Ali Allawi for guidance on sources on the war in Mesopotamia; Yoav Alon and Fayez al-Tarawneh for memoirs from the Arab Revolt; and Tui Clark for works on the New Zealand experience of the Ottoman front. Jill, Duchess of Hamilton, offered her library and her own excellent studies of the Anzac and British forces in the Middle East. Henry Laurens generously provided a transcript of French intelligence reports compiled by the Dominican priest, Antonin Jaussen. Margaret MacMillan, while engaged in writing her remarkable study on the origins of WWI, *The War that Ended Peace*, shared every article she found on the Ottoman war effort. Martin Bunton and Hussein Omar offered valuable documents on the Egyptian contribution to the British war effort. I would like to express particular thanks to my mother, Margaret Rogan, for her research into the life and death in Gallipoli of my great uncle John McDonald.

In approaching the war diaries of Turkish veterans of the Great War, I had the pleasure to work with two brilliant students of late Ottoman history. Djene Bajalan and Kerem Tinaz, both of Oxford University, scoured the bookshops of Istanbul to secure the growing number of published memoirs of Turkish soldiers and officers of the First World War. Djene assisted with the research for the first two chapters of the book, while Kerem helped with the research on chapters 3-13. I could not have done without their help.

Historians are at the mercy of archivists and librarians in finding the articles of their trade. I am particularly grateful to Mastan Ebtehaj, Middle East Centre Librarian, and Debbie Usher, Middle East Centre Archivist, for their generous assistance. I would also like to thank the archivists of the United States National Archives in College Park, Maryland; the Imperial War Museum in London, who continued to serve their readers through the museum's extensive renovations; and the highly efficient archivists of the Alexander Turnbull Library in Wellington, New Zealand.

A number of colleagues read my proposal and draft chapters and offered invaluable insights and corrections. I would like to thank in particular Frederick Anscombe, Ben Fortna, Roger Owen, Joseph Sassoon and Ngaire Woods.

I am ever grateful to my agents, Felicity Bryan and George Lucas, for their wisdom and experience in guiding me and my book from inception through publication. The pleasure of publishing with Allen Lane and Basic Books lies first and foremost in getting to work with Lara Heimert and Simon Winder, two of the greatest non-fiction editors in the business.

Yet my greatest thanks go to my family, for their love and encouragement even when my focus on the book came at their expense. Ngaire was my soul mate, chapter by chapter; Richard my delight for the pleasure he takes in all things Arab; and Isabelle my guiding light, for this book is hers too.

Notes

PREFACE

1. Colonel J. M. Findlay, *With the 8th Scottish Rifles, 1914–1919* (London: Blockie, 1926), 21.

2. Findlay, *With the 8th Scottish Rifles,* 34.

3. The British Council commissioned the YouGov polling agency to carry out an online survey among the adult populations of Egypt, France, Germany, India, Russia, Turkey, and the United Kingdom in September 2013. The results are summarised in the report "Remember the World as Well as the War: Why the Global Reach and Enduring Legacy of the First World War Still Matter Today," British Council, February 2014, http://www.british-council.org/organisation/publications/remember-the-world.

4. Some outstanding diaries have recently been translated from Turkish and Arabic, including Lieutenant Mehmed Fasih's *Gallipoli 1915: Bloody Ridge (Lone Pine) Diary of Lt. Mehmed Fasih* (Istanbul: Denizler Kitabevi, 2001); Falih Rıfkı Atay's 1981 memoir, *Zeytindağı,* has appeared in an excellent French translation, *Le mont des Oliviers: L'empire Ottoman et le Moyen-Orient, 1914–1918* (Paris: Turquoise, 2009); the diary of the Jerusalemite soldier Ihsan Turjman was translated by Salim Tamari under the title *Year of the Locust: A Soldier's Diary and the Erasure of Palestine's Ottoman Past* (Berkeley: University of California Press, 2011).

Among recent studies drawing on the military archive in Ankara are Mustafa Aksakal, *The Ottoman Road to War in 1914: The Ottoman Empire and the First World War* (Cambridge: Cambridge University Press, 2008); M. Talha Çiçek, *War and State Formation in Syria: Cemal Pasha's Governorate During World War I, 1914–17* (London: Routledge, 2014); Edward J. Erickson, *Ordered to Die: A History of the Ottoman Army in the First World War* (Westport, CT: Greenwood Press, 2001); Hikmet Özdemir, *The Ottoman Army, 1914–1918: Disease and Death on the Battlefield* (Salt Lake City: University of Utah Press, 2008).

CHAPTER 1

1. The head of the bakers' guild is quoted by Stanford J. Shaw and Ezel Kural Shaw, *History of the Ottoman Empire and Modern Turkey* (Cambridge: Cambridge University Press, 1985), 2:187.

2. On the Young Turks, see Feroz Ahmad, *The Young Turks: The Committee of Union and Progress in Turkish Politics, 1908–1914* (Oxford: Oxford University Press, 1969); M. Şükrü Hanioğlu, *Preparation for a Revolution: The Young Turks, 1902–1908* (New York: Oxford University Press, 2001); Erik J. Zürcher, *Turkey: A Modern History* (London: I. B. Tauris, 1993).

3. Abdülhamid II is quoted by François Georgeon, *Abdülhamid II: Le sultan calife* (Paris: Fayard, 2003), 401.

4. Newspaper coverage cited by Georgeon, *Abdülhamid II*, 404; Cemal and Talat quoted by Andrew Mango, *Atatürk* (London: John Murray, 1999), 80.

5. Anonymous, *Thawrat al-'Arab* [The Revolution of the Arabs] (Cairo: Matba'a al-Muqattam, 1916), 49.

6. Cited by Muhammad Izzat Darwaza in *Nash'at al-Haraka al-'Arabiyya al-Haditha* [The Formation of the Modern Arab Movement], 2nd ed. (Sidon and Beirut: Manshurat al-Maktaba al-'Asriyya, 1971), 277.

7. Darwaza, *Nash'at al-Haraka*, 286.

8. Zürcher, *Turkey*, 98.

9. Article 61 of "The Treaty of Berlin," in *The Middle East and North Africa in World Politics*, ed. J. C. Hurewitz (New Haven, CT: Yale University Press, 1975), 1:413–414. See also H. F. B. Lynch, *Armenia: Travels and Studies*, Vol. 2: *The Turkish Provinces* (London: Longmans, Green and Co., 1901), 408–411.

10. Dikran Mesob Kaligian, *Armenian Organization and Ideology Under Ottoman Rule, 1908–1914* (New Brunswick, NJ: Transaction Publishers, 2011), 1–2.

11. Lynch, *Armenia*, 2:157–158.

12. Georgeon, *Abdülhamid II*, 291–295.

13. Cemal Pasha claimed 17,000 Armenians were killed; Djemal Pasha, *Memories of a Turkish Statesman, 1913–1919* (London: Hutchinson, n.d.), 261. An Armenian deputy, Zohrab Efendi, who served on an official commission of enquiry into the massacres, gave the Armenians' death toll as 20,000; "Young Turk-Armenian Relations During the Second Constitutional Period, 1908–1914," in *From Empire to Republic: Essays on the Late Ottoman Empire and Modern Turkey*, by Feroz Ahmad (Istanbul: Bilgi University Press, 2008), 2:186. See also Kaligian, *Armenian Organization*, 36,) for the claim that between 10,000 and 20,000 Armenians were killed in the Adana massacres.

14. Zabel Essayan, *Dans les ruines: Les massacres d'Adana, avril 1909* [In the Ruins: The Adana Massacres, April 1909] (Paris: Libella, 2011), translated from the original Armenian edition published in 1911. Quotes from 40.

15. Kaligian, *Armenian Organization*, 45–47; Djemal Pasha, *Memories of a Turkish Statesman*, 262.

16. On the Italian invasion of Libya, see Jamil Abun-Nasr, *A History of the Maghrib* (Cambridge: Cambridge University Press, 1971), 308–312; Mango, *Atatürk*, 101–111.

17. A Turkish veteran of the campaign claimed total Ottoman strength was only 1,000 men. Italian sources claimed 4,200 Turks in Tripolitania and Cyrenaica. Philip H. Stoddard, "The Ottoman Government and the Arabs, 1911 to 1918: A Preliminary Study of the Teşkilât-i Mahsusa" (PhD diss., Princeton University, 1963), 205–206n174. See also E. E. Evans-Pritchard, *The Sanusi of Cyrenaica* (Oxford: Oxford University Press, 1954), 104–124.

18. M. Şükrü Hanioğlu, ed., *Kendi Mektuplarinda Enver Paşa* [Enver Pasha in His Own Letters] (Istanbul: Der Yayinlari, 1989), 75–78.

19. Mango, *Atatürk*, 102.

20. Hanioğlu, *Kendi Mektuplarinda Enver Paşa*, 92–94. See also Georges Rémond, *Aux campes turco-arabes: Notes de route et de guerre en Tripolitaine et en Cyréanaique* [In the Turco-Arab Camps: Notes on Travel and War in Tripolitania and Cyrenaica] (Paris: Hachette, 1913).

21. Hanioğlu, *Kendi Mektuplarinda Enver Paşa*, 148–153, 185–188, 196–198. See also G. F. Abbott, *The Holy War in Tripoli* (London: Edward Arnold, 1912).

22. Abun-Nasr, *History of the Maghrib*, 310.

23. L. S. Stavrianos, *The Balkans Since 1453* (London: Hurst, 2000), 535–537.

24. Hanioğlu, *Kendi Mektuplarinda Enver Paşa*, letters of 28 December 1912 and 12 January 1913, 216–217, 224.

25. Enver recounted the events of 23 January in a number of letters between 23 and 28 January 1913. Hanioğlu, *Kendi Mektuplarinda Enver Paşa*, 224–231. See also Ahmad, *The Young Turks*, 117–123.

26. Quoted in Niyazi Berkes, *The Development of Secularism in Turkey* (New York: Routledge, 1998), 358.

27. Hanioğlu, *Kendi Mektuplarinda Enver Paşa*, 247–248.

28. Hanioğlu, *Kendi Mektuplarinda Enver Paşa*, letter of 2 August 1913, 249–250.

29. Hanioğlu, *Kendi Mektuplarinda Enver Paşa*, letter of 2 August 1913, 249–250.

30. On the origins, aims, and membership of these and other pre-war Arabist societies, see George Antonius, *The Arab Awakening* (London: Hamish Hamilton, 1938), 101–125; Eliezer Tauber, *The Emergence of the Arab Movements* (London: Frank Cass, 1993).

31. Quoted in Zeine N. Zeine, *The Emergence of Arab Nationalism*, 3rd ed. (New York: Caravan Books, 1973), 84.

32. Tawfiq al-Suwaydi, *My Memoirs: Half a Century of the History of Iraq and the Arab Cause* (Boulder, CO: Lynne Reiner, 2013), 60. For Suwaydi's account of the Arab Congress, see 62–68.

33. On the Paris Agreement, see Tauber, *Emergence of the Arab Movements*, 198–212.

34. Suwaydi, *My Memoirs*, 68. Abd al-Hamid al-Zahrawi of the Decentralization Party and Muhammad al-Mihmisani and Abd al-Ghani al-Uraysi, both members of al-Fatat, were executed by the Ottoman authorities in May 1916.

35. Hanioğlu, *Kendi Mektuplarinda Enver Paşa*, letter of 2 August 1913, 249–250.

CHAPTER 2

1. NARA, Istanbul vol. 284, US Deputy Consul General George W. Young, "Automobiles," 3 July 1914.

2. B. A. Elliot, *Blériot: Herald of an Age* (Stroud, UK: Tempus, 2000), 165.

3. NARA, Istanbul vol. 285, US vice consul in Mersin to consul general, Istanbul, 16 February 1914.

4. NARA, Istanbul vol. 285, Consul General Ravndal, "Successful Demonstration of 'Curtiss Flying Boat' at Constantinople," 15 June 1914.

5. NARA, Istanbul vol. 282, report from Jerusalem dated 29 April 1914, including a translation of the notice sent by the military conscription authorities in Jaffa to village headmen in Palestine.

6. Mustafa Aksakal, *The Ottoman Road to War in 1914: The Ottoman Empire and the First World War* (Cambridge: Cambridge University Press, 2008), 42–56.

7. Michael A. Reynolds, *Shattering Empires: The Clash and Collapse of the Ottoman and Russian Empires, 1908–1918* (Cambridge: Cambridge University Press, 2011), 36–41.

8. Justin McCarthy, *Muslims and Minorities: The Population of Ottoman Anatolia and the End of the Empire* (New York: New York University Press, 1983), 47–88. Ottoman census figures suggest a total Armenian population in the six provinces in 1911 and 1912 of 865,000, while the Armenian Patriarchate claimed a total population in the six provinces of 1.018 million in 1912. Note that Harput was also known as Mamuretülaziz, now known as Elâziğ in modern Turkey.

9. Roderic H. Davison, "The Armenian Crisis, 1912–1914," *American Historical Review* 53 (April 1948): 481–505.

10. Taner Akçam, *The Young Turks' Crime Against Humanity: The Armenian Genocide and Ethnic Cleansing in the Ottoman Empire* (Princeton, NJ: Princeton University Press, 2012), 129–135.

11. Quoted in Sean McMeekin, *The Berlin-Baghdad Express: The Ottoman Empire and Germany's Bid for World Power, 1898–1918* (London: Allen Lane, 2010), 14.

12. NARA, Istanbul vol. 295, reports from Mersina, 3 July 1915, and Constantinople, "Baghtche Tunnel," 3 September 1915; McMeekin, *The Berlin-Baghdad Express*, 233–258.

13. NARA, Baghdad box 19, Consul Brissel's reports of 2 June 1914 and 10 October 1914.

14. The sultan's comments were cited by Otto Liman von Sanders in *Five Years in Turkey* (Annapolis, MD: US Naval Institute, 1927), 1–12.

15. Aksakal, *The Ottoman Road to War*, 80–83; Liman von Sanders, *Five Years in Turkey*, 6–7.

16. Djemal Pasha, *Memories of a Turkish Statesman, 1913–1919* (London: Hutchinson, n.d.), 99–106.

17. Italy, though a member of the Triple Alliance, was bound to Germany and Austria by a defensive alliance only. Because Germany and Austria took the offensive, Italy did not enter the war in 1914. When, in 1915, Italy did finally declare war, it sided with the Entente Powers.

18. Djemal Pasha, *Memories of a Turkish Statesman*, 116–117.

19. Aksakal, *The Ottoman Road to War*, 96.

20. Aksakal, *The Ottoman Road to War*, 99.

21. "Secret Treaty of Defensive Alliance: Germany and the Ottoman Empire, 2 August 1914," in *The Middle East and North Africa in World Politics*, ed. J. C. Hurewitz (New Haven, CT: Yale University Press, 1979), 2:1–2.

22. Irfan Orga, *Portrait of a Turkish Family* (1950; rpt. London: Eland, 1988), 47–48. Orga did not rely on his own memory alone to re-create this conversation, acknowledging that "in after years my mother pieced together the most of it for me" (46).

23. NARA, Istanbul vol. 285, Heizer to Morgenthau, 4 August 1914; telegrams from Consul Grech, Dardanelles, 4 and 27 August 1914.

24. Quoted in Aksakal, *The Ottoman Road to War*, 117.

25. Ulrich Trumpener, *Germany and the Ottoman Empire, 1914–1918* (Princeton, NJ: Princeton University Press, 1968), 28; Aksakal, *The Ottoman Road to War*, 115.

26. Djemal Pasha, *Memories of a Turkish Statesman*, 118–119; Halil Menteşe, *Osmanli Mebusan Meclisi Reisi Halil Menteşe'nin Anilari* [Memoirs of the Speaker of the Ottoman Parliament Halil Menteşe] (Istanbul: Amaç Basimevi, 1996), 189–191.

27. John Buchan, *Greenmantle* (London: Hodder and Stoughton, 1916), 7. On *Islampolitik*, see Tilman Lüdke, *Jihad Made in Germany: Ottoman and German Propaganda and Intelligence Operations in the First World War* (Münster: Lit Verlag, 2005), 33–34.

28. Oppenheim quoted by McMeekin, *The Berlin-Baghdad Express*, 27, 91.

29. Enver's comments were quoted in Chapter 1 (n. 25); Djemal Pasha, *Memories of a Turkish Statesman*, 144. On Unionist views on jihad, see Philip H. Stoddard, "The Ottoman Government and the Arabs, 1911 to 1918: A Preliminary Study of the Teşkilât-i Mahsusa" (PhD diss., Princeton University, 1963), 23–26.

30. Aksakal, drawing on Russian diplomatic dispatches, fully documents the Ottoman proposals to the Russians in *The Ottoman Road to War*, 126–135. Sean McMeekin dismisses Enver's proposals as "a trial balloon of breathtaking cynicism" in *The Russian Origins of the First World War* (Cambridge, MA: Harvard University Press, 2011), 106–107.

31. Hew Strachan, *The First World War*, vol. 1: *To Arms* (Oxford: Oxford University Press, 2001), 230–278. On Austrian losses to Russia and Serbia, see David Stevenson, *1914–1918: The History of the First World War* (London: Penguin, 2005), 70–73. See also D. E. Showalter, "Manoeuvre Warfare: The Eastern and Western Fronts, 1914–1915," in *The Oxford Illustrated History of the First World War*, ed. Hew Strachan (Oxford: Oxford University Press, 2000), 39–53.

32. Von Falkenhayn quoted in Aksakal, *The Ottoman Road to War*, 149.

33. Mustafa Aksakal, "Holy War Made in Germany? Ottoman Origins of the 1914 Jihad," *War in History* 18 (2011): 184–199.

CHAPTER 3

1. Hew Strachan, *The First World War* (London: Pocket Books, 2006), 97.

2. NARA, Istanbul vol. 280, "Annual Report on the Commerce and Industries of Turkey for the Calendar Year 1913," 29 May 1914; see also reports in vol. 280 from Tripoli in Syria, Smyrna, Jerusalem, and Trebizond, all of which report on emigration of men of military age. Istanbul vol. 292, "Report on Commerce and Industries for Calendar Year 1914," Jerusalem, 15 March 1915.

3. NARA, Istanbul vol. 282, report from Jerusalem dated 29 April 1914, encloses a translation of the instructions dated 25 April 1914, sent by "The Chief of the Jaffa Branch of Soldier Collection" to the *mukhtars*, or village headmen, in Palestine; Yigit Akin, "The Ottoman Home Front During World War I: Everyday Politics, Society, and Culture" (PhD diss., Ohio State University, 2011), 22; copies of mobilization posters are reproduced in Mehmet Besikçi, "Between Voluntarism and Resistance: The Ottoman Mobilization of Manpower in the First World War" (PhD diss., Bogaziçi University, 2009), 407–409.

4. Ahmad Rida, *Hawadith Jabal ʿAmil, 1914–1922* [Events of Jabal Amil] (Beirut: Dar Annahar, 2009), 35.

5. NARA, Istanbul vol. 282, report from US consul in Aleppo dated 3 August 1914; vol. 292, US vice consul Trebizond (Trabzon) report of 31 March 1915.

6. Irfan Orga, *Portrait of a Turkish Family* (1950; rpt. London: Eland, 1988), 65–66.

7. "Ey gaziler yol göründü, Yine garib serime, Dağlar, taşlar dayanamaz, Benim ahu zarıma." Orga, *Portrait of a Turkish Family*, 67, 71.

8. Edward J. Erickson, *Ordered to Die: A History of the Ottoman Army in the First World War* (Westport, CT: Greenwood Press, 2001), 7; Şevket Pamuk, "The Ottoman Economy

in World War I," in *The Economics of World War I*, ed. Stephen Broadberry and Mark Harrison (Cambridge: Cambridge University Press, 2005), 117; Beşikçi, "Between Voluntarism and Resistance," 141.

9. David Stevenson, *1914–1918: The History of the First World War* (London: Penguin, 2005), 198–205.

10. NARA, Istanbul vol. 292, "Special Report on Turkish Economics," 8 May 1915.

11. NARA, Istanbul vol. 282, report from Aleppo, 3 August 1914; Istanbul vol. 292, "Trade and Commerce at Beirut for the Year 1914, and January 1915," 15 April 1915; "Annual Report on Commerce and Industries for 1914," Harput, 1 January 1915; Istanbul vol. 295, "Trade Depression in Turkey Caused by European War," Smyrna (Izmir), 26 February 1915.

12. Pamuk, "The Ottoman Economy in World War I," 117.

13. Beşikçi, "Between Voluntarism and Resistance," 73–76; NARA, Istanbul vol. 292, "Special Report on Turkish Economics," Istanbul, 8 May 1915.

14. NARA, Istanbul vol. 279, letter from Hakki Pasha, governor of Adana to the US consul in Mersin, dated 6 Aghustos 1330; for a description of the plundering of a shop and extortion see vol. 279, letter from US consul in Jerusalem, 19 September 1914; correspondence with the Singer Manufacturing Company, September and October 1914; letter from Ottoman governor of Adana to US consul in Mersin, August 1914; report from US consul in Baghdad of 5 October 1914. See also Istanbul vol. 292, "Special Report on Turkish Economics," 8 May 1915.

15. Erik Jan Zürcher, "Between Death and Desertion: The Experience of the Ottoman Soldier in World War I," *Turcica* 28 (1996): 235–258; Pamuk, "The Ottoman Economy in World War I," 126; NARA, Istanbul vol. 292, "Special Report on Turkish Economics," Istanbul, 8 May 1915; Istanbul vol. 294, "Increased Cost of Living in Constantinople," 2 December 1915.

16. Ahmed Emin, *Turkey in the World War* (New Haven, CT: Yale University Press, 1930), 107.

17. One Algerian captain from a notable family, Khaled El Hachemi, had studied at the elite French military academy Saint-Cyrien and appears to have been a rare exception to this rule. Gilbert Meynier, *L'Algérie révélée: La guerre de 1914–1918 et le premier quart du XXe siècle* (Geneva: Droz, 1981), 85–87.

18. His full name, in French spelling, was Mostapha Ould Kaddour Tabti. Mohammed Soualah, "Nos troupes d'Afrique et l'Allemagne," *Revue africaine* 60 (1919): 495–496.

19. Meynier, *L'Algérie révélée*, 98–103.

20. Jean Mélia, *L'Algérie et la guerre (1914–1918)* (Paris: Plon, 1918), 28–32. The lyrics, in French: "La République nous appelle, Sachons vaincre ou sachons périr, Un Français doit vivre pour elle, Pour elle un Français doit mourir." The final line, Messali recalled, became "Pour elle un Arabe doit mourir". Messali Hadj, *Les mémoires de Messali Hadj, 1898–1938* (Paris: J. C. Lattès, 1982), 76.

21. Hadj, *Mémoires*, 70. Tabti's entire poem in sixty-five couplets is reproduced in Arabic and French translation in Soualah, "Nos troupes d'Afrique et l'Allemagne," 494–520.

22. Meynier, *L'Algérie révélée*, 271–274.

23. Meynier, *L'Algérie révélée*, 280–282; Mélia, *L'Algérie et la guerre*, 257–260, 270–276; Augustin Bernard, *L'Afrique du nord pendant la guerre* (Paris: Les presses universitaires de France, 1926), 94, table II.

24. Peter Dennis et al., eds., *The Oxford Companion to Australian Military History* (Mel-

bourne: Oxford University Press, 1995), 104–109; Cedric Mentiplay, *A Fighting Quality: New Zealanders at War* (Wellington: A. H. & A. W. Reed, 1979), 13.

25. James McMillan, "40,000 Horsemen: A Memoir," Archives New Zealand, Alexander Turnbull Library, MS X-5251; Terry Kinloch, *Devils on Horses: In the Words of the Anzacs in the Middle East, 1916–19* (Auckland: Exisle Publishing, 2007), 32–34; Roland Perry, *The Australian Light Horse* (Sydney: Hachette Australia, 2009), 38–43.

26. Motives for recruiting were recounted by twelve veterans of the New Zealand Expeditionary Force interviewed by Maurice Shadbolt, *Voices of Gallipoli* (Auckland: Hodder and Stoughton, 1988). Trevor Holmden's papers are held in the Alexander Turnbull Library, Wellington, New Zealand, MS-Papers 2223.

27. Jeffrey Grey, *A Military History of Australia*, 3rd ed. (Cambridge: Cambridge University Press, 2008), 88; Christopher Pugsley, *The ANZAC Experience: New Zealand, Australia and Empire in the First World War* (Auckland: Reed, 2004), 52–55, 63; Fred Waite, *The New Zealanders at Gallipoli* (Auckland: Whitcombe and Tombs, 1919), 10–19.

28. On Indian attitudes to the British and Ottomans, see Algernon Rumbold, *Watershed in India, 1914–1922* (London: Athlone Press, 1979), 9–10.

29. P. G. Elgood, *Egypt and the Army* (Oxford: Oxford University Press, 1924), 1, 42–43.

30. Quoted in Robin Kilson, "Calling Up the Empire: The British Military Use of Non-white Labor in France, 1916–1920" (PhD diss., Harvard University, 1990), 262–263.

31. Ahmad Shafiq, *Hawliyat Masr al-siyasiyya* [The Political Annals of Egypt] (Cairo: Matba`a Shafiq Pasha, 1926), 1:47–48.

32. Peter Hopkirk, *On Secret Service East of Constantinople: The Plot to Bring Down the British Empire* (London: John Murray, 2006), 66–84; Sean McMeekin, *The Berlin-Baghdad Express: The Ottoman Empire and Germany's Bid for World Power, 1898–1918* (London: Allen Lane, 2010), 90–92.

33. Quoted in Budheswar Pati, *India and the First World War* (New Delhi: Atlantic Publishers, 1996), 12.

34. Pati, *India and the First World War*, 15–16.

35. Pati, *India and the First World War*, 18–21.

36. Judith Brown, *Modern India: The Origins of an Asian Democracy*, 2nd ed. (Oxford: Oxford University Press, 1994), 195; Robert Holland, "The British Empire and the Great War, 1914–1918," in *The Oxford History of the British Empire*, vol. 4: *The Twentieth Century*, ed. Judith Brown and William Roger Louis (Oxford: Oxford University Press, 1999), 117; Pati, *India and the First World War*, 32–38.

37. Dozens of testimonials, including those of the two muftis, were published in *Revue du monde musulman* 29 (December 1914), a special edition dedicated to French Muslims and the war, providing statements of loyalty from North African religious personalities in Arabic with French translation.

38. James McDougall, *History and the Culture of Nationalism in Algeria* (Cambridge: Cambridge University Press, 2006), 36–43; Peter Heine, "Salih Ash-Sharif at-Tunisi, a North African Nationalist in Berlin During the First World War," *Revue de l'Occident musulman et de la Méditerranée* 33 (1982): 89–95.

39. Tilman Ludke, *Jihad Made in Germany: Ottoman and German Propaganda and Intelligence Operations in the First World War* (Münster: Lit Verlag, 2005), 117–125; Heine, "Salih Ash-Sharif at-Tunisi," 90.

40. From the interrogation transcript by the Ottoman authorities preserved in the Turkish military archives in Ankara, reproduced in Ahmet Tetik, Y. Serdar Demirtaş, and Sema Demirtaş, eds., *Çanakkale Muharebeleri'nin Esirleri—İfadeler ve Mektuplar* [Prisoners of the Gallipoli Campaign: Testimonies and Letters] (Ankara: Genelkurmay Basımevi, 2009), 1:93–94.

41. Among visiting notables was Algerian exile and veteran of the 1911 Libyan War Amir Ali Pasha, son of famous Algerian resistance leader Amir Abd al-Qadir. Mélia, *L'Algérie et la guerre*, 230–237; Heine, "Salih Ash-Sharif at-Tunisi," 91.

42. In his article on Salih al-Sharif, Peter Heine claims that German documents provide no evidence of coercion of prisoners of war, though he found "reports of those willing to fight on the Turkish side" who expressed their anger "about the delay of their departure to Turkey". Heine, "Salih Ash-Sharif at-Tunisi," 94n12. The testimony of Ahmed bin Hussein would confirm this.

CHAPTER 4

1. C. F. Aspinall-Oglander, *Military Operations: Gallipoli* (London: William Heinemann, 1929), 1:34–35.

2. W. E. D. Allen and Paul Muratoff, *Caucasian Battlefields: A History of the Wars on the Turco-Caucasian Border, 1828–1921* (Cambridge: Cambridge University Press, 1953), 245–247.

3. Ali Rıza Eti, *Bir onbaşının doğu cephesi günlüğü, 1914–1915* [Diary of a Corporal on the Eastern Front, 1914–1915] (Istanbul: Türkiye İş Bankası Kültür Yayınları, 2009); for his account of the Battle of Köprüköy, see 37–42.

4. Ottoman casualty figures are from Edward J. Erickson, *Ordered to Die: A History of the Ottoman Army in the First World War* (Westport, CT: Greenwood Press, 2001), 72n4. Russian casualty figures are from M. Larcher, *La guerre turque dans la guerre mondiale* [The Turkish War in the World War] (Paris: Etienne Chiron et Berger-Levrault, 1926), 381. Enver quoted by Otto Liman von Sanders, *Five Years in Turkey* (Annapolis: US Naval Institute, 1927), 37.

5. Philip Graves, *The Life of Sir Percy Cox* (London: Hutchinson, 1941), 120–126; Daniel Yergin, *The Prize* (New York: Free Press, 1992), 134–149.

6. Delamain's orders are reproduced in E. G. Keogh, *The River in the Desert* (Melbourne: Wilke & Co., 1955), 39–40.

7. Bullard's assessment is quoted by Arnold T. Wilson, *Loyalties Mesopotamia, 1914–1917* (London: Oxford University Press, 1930), 1:4.

8. On the Basra Reform Society and Sayyid Talib al-Naqib, see Eliezer Tauber, *The Emergence of the Arab Movements* (London: Frank Cass, 1993). For a contemporary English profile of Sayyid Talib, see Wilson, *Loyalties Mesopotamia*, 1:18.

9. Basil Sulayman Faydi, ed., *Mudhakkirat Sulayman Faydi* [Memoirs of Sulayman Faydi] (London: Dar al-Saqi, 1998), 194–196.

10. Knox's proclamation of 31 October 1914 is reproduced in Wilson, *Loyalties Mesopotamia*, 1:309; "The United Kingdom's Recognition of Kuwayt as an Independent State Under British Protection, 3 November 1914," reproduced in Hurewitz, *Middle East and North Africa in World Politics*, 2:6–7.

11. Cox's proclamation of 5 November 1914 is reproduced in Wilson, *Loyalties Mesopotamia*, 1:310–311.

12. Faydi, *Mudhakkirat*, 199.

13. Faydi, *Mudhakkirat*, 203.

14. F. J. Moberly, *The Campaign in Mesopotamia, 1914–1918* (London: HMSO, 1923), 1:106–153; Charles Townshend, *When God Made Hell: The British Invasion of Mesopotamia and the Creation of Iraq, 1914–1921* (London: Faber and Faber, 2010), 3–10.

15. Edmund Candler, *The Long Road to Baghdad* (London: Cassell and Co., 1919), 1:111.

16. Moberly, *The Campaign in Mesopotamia*, 117–27; Ron Wilcox, *Battles on the Tigris: The Mesopotamian Campaign of the First World War* (Barnsley, UK: Pen & Sword Books, 2006), 2–26; Townshend, *When God Made Hell*, 30–40.

17. NARA, Basra box 005, letter from John Van Ess dated Busrah, 21 November 1914.

18. Sir Percy Cox's proclamation of 22 November 1914 to the people of Basra is reproduced in Wilson, *Loyalties Mesopotamia*, 1:311.

19. Moberly, *The Campaign in Mesopotamia*, 1:151–152.

20. Casualty figures are tabulated from Moberly, *The Campaign in Mesopotamia*, 1:106–153.

21. IWM Documents 828, diary of Private W. R. Bird, entry of 14 January 1915.

22. Townshend, *When God Made Hell*, 66.

23. IWM, P 158, Documents 10048, private papers of Lieutenant Colonel H. V. Gell, diary entry of 10–11 November 1914.

24. G. Wyman Bury, *Arabia Infelix, or the Turks in Yamen* (London: Macmillan, 1915), 16–19.

25. Harold F. Jacob, *Kings of Arabia: The Rise and Set of the Turkish Sovranty in the Arabian Peninsula* (London: Mills & Boon, 1923), 158–161.

26. W. T. Massey, *The Desert Campaigns* (London: Constable, 1918), 1–3.

27. Letter dated Zeitoun Camp, 4 January 1915, in Glyn Harper, ed., *Letters from Gallipoli: New Zealand Soldiers Write Home* (Auckland: Auckland University Press, 2011), 47–48. See also the memoirs of Trevor Holmden, chap. 3, Alexander Turnbull Library, Wellington, New Zealand, MS-Papers 2223.

28. Ian Jones, *The Australian Light Horse* (Sydney: Time-Life Books [Australia], 1987), 25; Fred Waite, *The New Zealanders at Gallipoli* (Auckland: Whitcombe and Tombs, 1919), 38.

29. C. E. W. Bean, the official historian of the Australian Imperial Force, described the Red Blind District and the disturbances of 2 April 1915, in his personal diary for the months of March and April 1915, 22–31. The diaries, held in the Australian War Monument, may be accessed online at www.awm.gov.au/collection/records/awm38 (henceforth C. E. W. Bean diaries).

30. For Australian and New Zealand accounts of the riots and their causes, see Harper, *Letters from Gallipoli*, 50–51; C. E. W. Bean diary, March–April 1915, 30; Trevor Holmden memoirs, chap. 3, 3–5.

31. Quoted by C. E. W. Bean diary, March–April 1915, 25–28.

32. Ahmad Shafiq, *Hawliyat Masr al-siyasiyya* [The Political Annals of Egypt], Part I (Cairo: Matba`a Shafiq Pasha, 1926), 84. See also Latifa Muhammad Salim, *Masr fi'l-harb al-`alimiyya al-ula* [Egypt in the First World War] (Cairo: Dar al-Shorouk, 2009), 239–243.

33. Larcher, *La guerre turque*, 172.

34. NARA, Istanbul vol. 282, Alfred Grech report from Dardanelles, 31 August 1914; C. F. Aspinall-Oglander, *Military Operations: Gallipoli* (London: William Heinemann, 1929),

1:32–36; Mustafa Aksakal, *The Ottoman Road to War in 1914: The Ottoman Empire and the First World War* (Cambridge: Cambridge University Press, 2008), 136–137.

35. Liman von Sanders, *Five Years in Turkey*, 47–48; Erickson, *Ordered to Die*, 75–82.

36. NARA, Istanbul vol. 292, report of US vice consul, Trebizond, 31 March 1915.

37. NARA, Istanbul vol. 281, report of US consul, Mersin, 2 November 1914; vol. 282, report of US consul, Mersin, 30 November 1914; vol. 293, report of US consul, Mersin, 5 March 1915.

38. NARA, Istanbul vol. 293 contains a number of reports, telegrams, and documents relating to the Alexandretta Incident, including reports from US Consul Jackson in Aleppo of 21 December 1914 and 8 January 1915, and from US Consular Agent H. E. Bishop in Alexandretta of 24 December 1914, 26 December 1914, and 12 January 1915.

39. NARA, Istanbul vol. 281, eyewitness report by C. Van H. Engert on the sinking of the *Messoudieh* in the Dardanelles, 14 December 1914.

40. C. Van H. Engert quoted Vice Admiral Merten in his report of 14 December 1914. For the perspective of the Ottoman General Headquarters on the sinking of the *Messoudieh* and Allied plans for the Dardanelles, see the memoirs of General Ali Ihsan Sâbis, *Birinci Dünya Harbi* [The First World War] (Istanbul: Nehir Yayinlari, 1992), 2:261–262.

CHAPTER 5

1. Hew Strachan, *The First World War*, vol. 1: *To Arms* (Oxford: Oxford University Press, 2003), 335–357.

2. Ulrich Trumpener, *Germany and the Ottoman Empire, 1914–1918* (Princeton, NJ: Princeton University Press, 1968), 36–37; Mustafa Aksakal, *The Ottoman Road to War in 1914: The Ottoman Empire and the First World War* (Cambridge: Cambridge University Press, 2008), 136–137, 145–155.

3. On the objective of recovering the three provinces lost in 1878, see Michael A. Reynolds, *Shattering Empires: The Clash and Collapse of the Ottoman and Russian Empires, 1908–1918* (Cambridge: Cambridge University Press, 2011), 171; M. Larcher, *La guerre turque dans la guerre mondiale* [The Turkish War in the World War] (Paris: Etienne Chiron et Berger-Levrault, 1926), 383; Edward J. Erickson, *Ordered to Die: A History of the Ottoman Army in the First World War* (Westport, CT: Greenwood Press, 2001), 53.

4. Djemal Pasha, *Memories of a Turkish Statesman, 1913–1919* (London: Hutchinson, n.d.), 137–138.

5. Henry Morgenthau, *Ambassador Morgenthau's Story* (1918; rpt. Reading, UK: Taderon Press, 2000), 114.

6. Otto Liman von Sanders, *Five Years in Turkey* (Annapolis: US Naval Institute, 1927), 37–39.

7. Strachan, *The First World War*, 1:323–331; Sean McMeekin, *The Russian Origins of the First World War* (Cambridge, MA: Harvard University Press, 2011), 85–86.

8. See, e.g., Ali Ihsan Sâbis, then serving in the general headquarters in Istanbul, who expressed both his fears and his belief in Enver's luck in *Harp Hatıralarım: Birinci Cihan Harbi* [My War Memoirs: The First World War] (Istanbul: Nehir Yayınları, 1992), 2:247.

9. Larcher, *La guerre turque*, 378–379; Erickson, *Ordered to Die*, 57.

10. Sâbis, *Harp Hatıralarım*, 2:238.

11. Reynolds, *Shattering Empires*, 115–117; McMeekin, *Russian Origins*, 154–156.

12. McMeekin, *Russian Origins*, 154.

13. M. Philips Price, *War and Revolution in Asiatic Russia* (London: George Allen & Unwin Ltd., 1918), 55 and chap. 8; Enver Pasha's report was quoted from documents in the Turkish military archives by Reynolds, *Shattering Empires*, 116.

14. Ali Rıza Eti, *Bir onbaşının doğu cephesi günlüğü, 1914–1915* [Diary of a Corporal on the Eastern Front, 1914–1915] (Istanbul: Türkiye İş Bankası Kültür Yayınları, 2009), 60; Erickson, *Ordered to Die*, 46, 54. See also Köprülü Şerif Ilden, *Sarıkamış* (Istanbul: Türkiye İş Bankası Kültür Yayınları, 1999), 124, in which he claimed that thirty Armenian defectors from Van who crossed lines on the night of 16–17 November provided the Russians with details on the weak points in the Ottoman line along the Aras.

15. Eti, *Bir onbaşının . . . günlüğü*, 51, 60–66.

16. Eti, *Bir onbaşının . . . günlüğü*, 60.

17. Ilden, *Sarıkamış*, 146–147.

18. Estimates of troop numbers vary widely from source to source. The figures quoted in the text are from W. E. D. Allen and Paul Muratoff, *Caucasian Battlefields: A History of the Wars on the Turco-Caucasian Border, 1828–1921* (Cambridge: Cambridge University Press, 1953), 252. Larcher gives a range of figures for the Ottoman and Russian armies in the Caucasus, claiming that the Ottoman Third Army reached a total size of 150,000 men, of which 90,000 were armed and trained to serve in combat, and gives the total for Russian forces as 60,000. Larcher, *La guerre turque*, 283.

19. Allen and Muratoff, *Caucasian Battlefields*, 253.

20. Enver's orders are reproduced in Ilden, *Sarıkamış*, 151–152, and Larcher, *La guerre turque*, 383–384.

21. Eti, *Bir onbaşının . . . günlüğü*, 102–103.

22. Eti, *Bir onbaşının . . . günlüğü*, 104.

23. Eti, *Bir onbaşının . . . günlüğü*, 104.

24. The attack on Oltu took place on 23 December. For accounts of the fighting between the Ottoman 31st and 32nd divisions, see Fevzi Çakmak, *Büyük Harp'te Şark Cephesi Harekâtı* [Operations on the Eastern Front in the Great War] (Istanbul: Türkiye İş Bankası Kültür Yayınları, 2010), 76; see Ilden, *Sarıkamış*, 167–168, for claims that 2,000 Ottomans were killed by their own forces; see also Allen and Muratoff, *Caucasian Battlefields*, 257; Larcher, *La guerre turque*, 386.

25. Allen and Muratoff, *Caucasian Battlefields*, 258; Çakmak, *Büyük Harp*, 77.

26. Allen and Muratoff, *Caucasian Battlefields*, 260–268; see also Larcher, *La guerre turque*, 387–388.

27. Ilden, *Sarıkamış*, 212–213.

28. Ilden, *Sarıkamış*, 177–179.

29. For a detailed first-hand account of the fighting on 26 December, see Ilden, *Sarıkamış*, 191–201.

30. Ilden, *Sarıkamış*, 231; Allen and Muratoff, *Caucasian Battlefields*, 278.

31. Eti, *Bir onbaşının . . . günlüğü*, 121–122. Of the estimated 77,000 Ottoman casualties at Sarıkamış, some 60,000 died and the rest would have been taken prisoner. Çakmak, *Büyük Harp*, 113–114; Allen and Muratoff, *Caucasian Battlefields*, 283–284.

32. For the strongest criticisms of Enver and Hakki Hafız's conduct of the campaign, see, in particular, the memoirs of IX Corps chief of staff Şerif Ilden: Ilden, *Sarıkamış*, 149,

158–159, 174–175, 208, 216–218, 232; Sâbis, *Harp Hatıralarım*, 302–317; Liman von Sanders, *Five Years in Turkey*, 40.

33. Allen and Muratoff, *Caucasian Battlefields*, 286–287.

34. Georges Douin, *L'attaque du canal de Suez (3 Février 1915)* (Paris: Librairie Delagrave, 1922), 45–46.

35. Djemal Pasha, *Memories*, 154.

36. Douin, *L'attaque*, 60.

37. Arslan's account of his involvement in the Sinai campaign is recorded in Shakib Arslan, *Sira Dhatiyya* [Autobiography] (Beirut: Dar al-Tali`a, 1969), 141–147.

38. Djemal Pasha, *Memories*, 152.

39. The priest was almost certainly the Dominican Father Antonin Jaussen, who went on to serve as a French intelligence officer in Port Said for the duration of the war. Jaussen undertook archaeological surveys in the Hijaz and wrote an ethnographic study of the Bedouin of southern Jordan. Douin, *L'attaque*, 77–79. On Jaussen, see Henry Laurens, "Jaussen et les services de renseignement français (1915–1919)," in *Antonin Jaussen: Sciences sociales occidentales et patrimoine arabe*, ed. Géraldine Chatelard and Mohammed Tarawneh (Amman: CERMOC, 1999), 23–35.

40. Douin, *L'attaque*, 79–80; George McMunn and Cyril Falls, *Military Operations: Egypt and Palestine from the Outbreak of War with Germany to June 1917* (London: HMSO: 1928), 29.

41. McMunn and Falls, *Military Operations*, 25.

42. IWM, P 158, private papers of Lieutenant Colonel H. V. Gell, Documents 10048, diary entries of 24 to 28 January 1915.

43. NARA, Istanbul vol. 293, "The Egyptian Campaign of the Turkish Army," report by US Vice Consul S. Edelman, Jerusalem, 20 March 1915.

44. IWM, RN, P 389, papers of Commander H. V. Coates, Documents 10871, translations of Ottoman army orders for the attack on the Suez Canal, 1 February 1915.

45. Douin, *L'attaque*, 92.

46. Fahmi al-Tarjaman related his war experiences to his daughter, Siham Tergeman, in *Daughter of Damascus* (Austin: Center for Middle Eastern Studies, 1994), 166–199. This quote is on 180.

47. Both Douin, *L'attaque*, 96, and McMunn and Falls, *Military Operations*, 39, recount how the "jihad volunteers" broke the silence and set the dogs barking; the translated copy of the Ottoman battle orders referred to the Champions of Islam (*Mujahid*) from Tripoli in Africa, who were assigned to a position near Serapeum, where the crossing took place; IWM, RN P 389, papers of Commander H. V. Coates.

48. Tergeman, *Daughter of Damascus*, 181.

49. Ahmad Shafiq, *Hawliyat Masr al-siyasiyya* [The Political Annals of Egypt] (Cairo: Shafiq Pasha Press, 1926), 1:81.

50. Douin, *L'attaque*, 100–102; McMunn and Falls, *Military Operations*, 43–45.

51. Ali Ihsan Sâbis, *Birinci Dünya Harbi*, 346–347; Djemal Pasha, *Memories*, 157.

52. McMunn and Falls, *Military Operations*, 50; Djemal Pasha, *Memories*, 159.

53. On Suleyman Askeri, see Philip H. Stoddard, "The Ottoman Government and the Arabs, 1911 to 1918: A Preliminary Study of the Teşkilât-i Mahsusa" (PhD diss., Princeton University, 1963), 119–130, and the summary translation of the Turkish army pamphlet by

Muhammad Amin, "The Turco-British Campaign in Mesopotamia and Our Mistakes," in *The Campaign in Mesopotamia, 1914–1918*, comp. F. J. Moberly (London: HMSO, 1923), 1:352–355.

54. Accounts of Arab participants in the Battle of Shaiba confirm low morale and high desertion rates; see Jamil Abu Tubaykh, ed., *Mudhakkirat al-Sayyid Muhsin Abu Tubaykh (1910–1960)* [The Memoirs of al-Sayyid Muhsin Abu Tubaykh] (Amman: al-Mu'assisa al-'Arabiyya li'l-Dirasat wa'l-Nashr, 2001), 40–45.

55. Arnold T. Wilson, *Loyalties Mesopotamia, 1914–1917* (London: Oxford University Press, 1930), 34; Charles Townshend, *When God Made Hell: The British Invasion of Mesopotamia and the Creation of Iraq, 1914–1921* (London: Faber and Faber, 2010), 88.

56. Edward J. Erickson cites Ottoman official figures in *Ordered to Die*, 110–111. F. J. Moberly, in the official British history, claimed the British lost 161 dead and 901 wounded, and the Ottomans lost 6,000 dead and wounded, including 2,000 Arab irregulars—which would suggest the Arabs played a more active role in the fighting than either the British or Turks credited. F. J. Moberly, comp., *The Campaign in Mesopotamia, 1914–1918*, (London: HMSO, 1923), 1:217. Wilson, in *Loyalties Mesopotamia*, 34, put British casualties at 1,257 and Turkish losses at "about double this number". The quote is from the diary of W. C. Spackman, quoted in Townshend, *When God Made Hell*, 89.

57. Sir George McMunn, quoted in Townshend, *When God Made Hell*, 80; Wilson, in *Loyalties Mesopotamia*, 34, declared Shaiba "the first and most decisive battle on this front."

CHAPTER 6

1. Sean McMeekin, *The Russian Origins of the First World War* (Cambridge, MA: Harvard University Press, 2011), 129–130.

2. C. F. Aspinall-Oglander, *Military Operations: Gallipoli* (London: William Heinemann, 1929), 1:51–53.

3. Aspinall-Oglander, *Military Operations: Gallipoli*, 1:57.

4. Henry W. Nevinson, *The Dardanelles Campaign* (London: Nisbet & Co., 1918), 33; Aspinall-Oglander, *Military Operations: Gallipoli*, 1:59.

5. Greece, like Russia, had a historic and religious claim to Constantinople and had offered to send a major infantry force to assist the Allied campaign in the straits, which Britain declined in deference to Russian sensitivities. See McMeekin, *Russian Origins*; Aspinall-Oglander, *Military Operations: Gallipoli*, vol. 1.

6. "The Constantinople Agreement," in *The Middle East and North Africa in World Politics*, vol. 2: *1914–1945*, ed. J. C. Hurewitz (New Haven, CT: Yale University Press, 1979), 16–21.

7. Henry Morgenthau, *Ambassador Morgenthau's Story* (1918; rpt. Reading, UK: Taderon Press, 2000), 123–134.

8. The damage to the *Agamemnon* was still in evidence on 15 April, when a New Zealand soldier noted that she "has had her one mast shot away and one of her funnels smashed". Glyn Harper, ed., *Letters from Gallipoli: New Zealand Soldiers Write Home* (Auckland: Auckland University Press, 2011), 59.

9. US Ambassador Morgenthau, who visited the straits with Ottoman officials in mid-March, found that intensive Allied bombardment had left Turkish batteries practically unharmed. Morgenthau, *Ambassador Morgenthau's Story*, 135–149.

10. Capitaine de Corvette X and Claude Farrère, "Journal de bord de l'expédition des Dardanelles (1915)," *Les œuvres libres* 17 (1922): 218–229.

11. Capitaine de Corvette X and Farrère, "Journal de bord," 214–215. The anonymous first author appears to have served on the French battleship *Suffren*; Captain Claude Farrère survived the sinking of the *Bouvet* on 18 March 1915.

12. Nevinson, *The Dardanelles Campaign,* 57–58.

13. Hans Kannengiesser, *The Campaign in Gallipoli* (London: Hutchinson & Co., n.d.), 76. The Associate Press journalist George Schreiner described the impact of Allied bombardment, quoted in Tim Travers, *Gallipoli 1915* (Stroud, UK: Tempus, 2004), 33.

14. Farrère, who survived the sinking of the *Bouvet*, claimed that only 62 of the 724 men on board were rescued. Capitaine de Corvette X and Farrère, "Journal de bord," 235–238.

15. Quoted in the editor's introduction to Mehmed Fasih, *Gallipoli 1915: Bloody Ridge (Lone Pine) Diary of Lt. Mehmed Fasih* (Istanbul: Denizler Kitabevi, 2001), 6.

16. I. Hakkı Sunata, *Gelibolu'dan kafkaslara: Birinci Dünya Savaşı anılarım* [From Gallipoli to the Caucasus: My First World War Memoirs] (Istanbul: Türkiye İş Bankası Kültür Yayınları, 2003), 84–85. For examples of government reports covered in the press, see the articles published in the semi-official Istanbul daily *Ikdâm*, reproduced in Murat Çulcu, *Ikdâm Gazetesi'nde Çanakkale Cephesi* [The Dardanelles Front in the *Ikdâm* Newspaper] (Istanbul: Denizler Kitabevi, 2004), 1:160–165.

17. Kannengiesser, *The Campaign in Gallipoli,* 77–78.

18. Aspinall-Oglander, *Military Operations: Gallipoli,* 1:98–99.

19. Aspinall-Oglander, *Military Operations: Gallipoli,* 1:124–125.

20. Some of the Senegalese troops taken prisoner by the Turks were in fact Sudanese. Muhammad Kamara told his Turkish interrogators, "I am a Sudanese. But nowadays the French are calling all the black people Senegalese. . . . There are lots of Sudanese [in the French army]." Ahmet Tetik, Y. Serdar Demirtaş, and Sema Demirtaş, eds., *Çanakkale Muharebeleri'nin Esirleri—İfadeler ve Mektuplar* [Prisoners of the Gallipoli Campaign: Testimonies and Letters] (Ankara: Genelkurmay Basımevi, 2009), 1:22.

21. According to Otto Liman von Sanders, *Five Years in Turkey* (Annapolis: US Naval Institute, 1927), 54–58, Enver's decision came only after extensive lobbying by Turkey's German allies.

22. Harper, *Letters from Gallipoli,* 58–64.

23. IWM, "Ataturk's Memoirs of the Anafartalar Battles" (K 03/1686).

24. IWM, private papers of Lieutenant G. L. Drewry, Documents 10946, letter of 12 May 1915.

25. Mahmut Sabri Bey, "Seddülbahir Muharebesi Hatıraları" [Memoirs of the Seddülbahir Battle] in *Çanakkale Hatıraları* (Istanbul: Arma Yayınları, 2003), 3:67–68.

26. Aspinall-Oglander, *Military Operations: Gallipoli,* 1:132. See also IWM, private papers of Captain E. Unwin, Documents 13473.

27. Aspinall-Oglander, *Military Operations: Gallipoli,* 1:232.

28. Sabri, "Seddülbahir Muharebesi," 68–69.

29. D. Moriarty, an NCO with the Royal Munster Fusiliers, survived the landing but was pinned down by enemy fire from 7 a.m. until 5 p.m. He claimed seventeen members of his battalion were killed and two hundred were wounded in the landing. IWM, private papers of D. Moriarty, Documents 11752, diary entry of 25–26 April. See also IWM, private

papers of Lieutenant G. L. Drewry, Documents 10946, letter of 12 May 1915. Drewry, Captain Unwin, and several other members of the *River Clyde*'s crews were awarded the Victoria Cross for their actions during the landing.

30. Aspinall-Oglander, *Military Operations: Gallipoli*, 1:227.

31. IWM, private papers of Major R. Haworth, Documents 16475, letter of 3 May 1915.

32. From a Turkish document seized by British troops in Seddülbahir Fort, cited in Aspinall-Oglander, *Military Operations: Gallipoli*, 1:254.

33. This account of the French "diversion" at Kum Kale is based on X. Torau-Bayle, *La campagne des Dardanelles* (Paris: E. Chiron, 1920), 61–64; François Charles-Roux, *L'expédition des Dardanelles au jour le jour* (Paris: Armand Colin, 1920); Association nationale pour le souvenir des Dardanelles et fronts d'orient, *Dardanelles Orient Levant, 1915–1921* (Paris: L'Harmattan, 2005); Aspinall-Oglander, *Military Operations: Gallipoli*, 1:257–264.

34. Travers, *Gallipoli 1915*, 76–77.

35. Turkish sources give Ottoman losses in Kum Kale as seventeen officers and 45 men killed; twenty-three officers and 740 men wounded; five officers and 500 men captured or missing. The French reported 786 casualties—twenty officers and 766 men dead, wounded, or missing. Edward J. Erickson, *Gallipoli: The Ottoman Campaign* (Barnsley, UK: Pen & Sword Military, 2010), 85.

36. The original hand-written war diaries of C. E. W. Bean have been digitized and are accessible via the Australian War Memorial (AWM) website (http://www.awm.gov.au /collection/records/awm38/3drl606); C. E. W. Bean diary, AWM item 3DRL606/5/1, April–May 1915, 18–19. Letter written by an anonymous Australian soldier, "Malcolm", to his cousin from the Government Hospital in Alexandria, 2 May 1915. IWM, two letters from Alexandria (Australian soldier), Documents 10360.

37. IWM, letter from Australian soldier "Malcolm" of 2 May 1915, Documents 10360.

38. These and all subsequent comments from Mustafa Kemal are from IWM, "Ataturk's Memoirs of the Anafartalar Battles" (K 03/1686).

39. IWM, letter from Australian soldier "Malcolm" of 2 May 1915, Documents 10360.

40. Mostyn Pryce Jones, letter to his mother, n.d., in Harper, *Letters from Gallipoli*, 89–90. His experiences were not unique; other New Zealanders' "letters from Gallipoli" described the experience as "awful" and "like being in the depths of Hell".

41. C. E. W. Bean fully investigated the story and quoted extensively from the report submitted by Colonel Pope. C. E. W. Bean diary, AWM item 3DRL606/5/1, April–May 1915, 30–31, 39.

42. Aspinall-Oglander, *Military Operations: Gallipoli*, 1:196–198. C. E. W. Bean overheard Australian commanders debating these very points; C. E. W. Bean diary, AWM item 3DRL606/5/1, April–May 1915, 40.

43. Aspinall-Oglander, *Military Operations: Gallipoli*, 1:269–270.

CHAPTER 7

1. NARA, Istanbul vol. 294, "Consul Heizer Report on Typhus Fever, Trebizond [Trabzon]," 22 May 1915.

2. Hikmet Özdemir, *The Ottoman Army, 1914–1918: Disease and Death on the Battlefield* (Salt Lake City: University of Utah Press, 2008), 51.

3. NARA, Istanbul vol. 294, "Consul Heizer Report on Typhus Fever, Trebizond [Trabzon]," 22 May 1915.

4. NARA, Istanbul vol. 294, report by Dr Edward P. Case, medical missionary at Erzurum, Turkey, 16 May 1915.

5. To be precise, Eti threatened to force his victims to drink *süblime*, or mercury chloride, a highly toxic compound formerly used to treat syphilis. Ali Rıza Eti, *Bir onbaşının doğu cephesi günlüğü, 1914–1915* [Diary of a Corporal on the Eastern Front, 1914–1915] (Istanbul: Türkiye İş Bankası Kültür Yayınları, 2009), 135.

6. Eti, *Bir onbaşının . . . günlüğü*, 140, diary entry of 31 January 1915.

7. Taner Akçam, *The Young Turks' Crime Against Humanity: The Armenian Genocide and Ethnic Cleansing in the Ottoman Empire* (Princeton, NJ: Princeton University Press, 2012), 63–96. Ryan Gingeras examines deportations and population exchanges along the southern coasts of the Sea of Marmara in *Sorrowful Shores: Violence, Ethnicity, and the End of the Ottoman Empire* (Oxford: Oxford University Press, 2009), 12–54.

8. The background to the February 1914 Armenian Reform Agreement and its terms are discussed in Chapter 2.

9. Akçam, *Young Turks' Crime Against Humanity*, 175, 183–184. See also the memoirs of the Armenian priest Grigoris Balakian, *Armenian Golgotha: A Memoir of the Armenian Genocide, 1915–1918* (New York: Vintage, 2010), 46.

10. Balakian, *Armenian Golgotha*, 22–23.

11. Balakian, *Armenian Golgotha*, 28, 32–34.

12. The Alexandretta Incident of December 1914 is recounted in Chapter 4. Aram Arkun, "Zeytun and the Commencement of the Armenian Genocide," in *A Question of Genocide: Armenians and Turks at the End of the Ottoman Empire*, ed. Ronald Grigor Suny, Fatma Muge Gocek, and Morman M. Naimark (Oxford: Oxford University Press, 2011), 223.

13. Donald Bloxham, *The Great Game of Genocide: Imperialism, Nationalism, and the Destruction of the Ottoman Armenians* (Oxford: Oxford University Press, 2005), 78–83.

14. Sean McMeekin, *The Russian Origins of the First World War* (Cambridge, MA: Harvard University Press, 2011), 165–166.

15. Akçam, in *Young Turks' Crime Against Humanity*, 56–57, claims that the relocation of Muslim immigrants to Zeytun began on 20 April, only twelve days after the Armenian deportations began. Arkun, "Zeytun," 229–237. US Ambassador Henry Morgenthau wrote of "5,000 Armenians from Zeitoun and Sultanie who were receiving no food whatever" in July 1915 in *Ambassador Morgenthau's Story* (1918; rpt. Reading, UK: Taderon Press, 2000), 230.

16. Balakian, *Armenian Golgotha*, 45, 56–57.

17. The government of Turkey and the official historical establishment as represented by the Turkish Historical Association (the Türk Tarih Kurumu) continue to reject the use of the term "genocide" to characterize the Armenian massacres of 1915 and 1916. However, a growing number of Turkish scholars and intellectuals have struggled to open the debate on this once taboo subject, including Nobel laureate Orhan Pamuk and a number of historians and journalists whose works I have consulted in writing this book: Taner Akçam, Fatma Müge Göçek, Baskın Oran, Uğur Ümit Üngör, and others. In support of their courageous efforts to force an honest reckoning with Turkey's past, as well as from conviction, I refer here to the wartime annihilation of Armenians as a genocide. In line with the 1948

UN Convention on Genocide, I believe the available evidence fully supports the claim that the Ottoman government was responsible for "acts committed with the intent to destroy, in whole or in part", the Armenian community of Anatolia as a distinct national and religious group.

18. Population figures are from Justin McCarthy et al., *The Armenian Rebellion at Van* (Salt Lake City: University of Utah Press, 2006), 3–7. McCarthy, himself a demographer, declared Vital Cuinet's figures for the 1890s "a low estimate". He cites Ottoman figures for the Van district, which included both the town and surrounding villages, of 45,000 Muslims, 34,000 Armenians, and 1,000 others in 1912, which he claimed underreported women, children, soldiers, administrators, and others. Gurgen Mahari was born in Van in 1903. His family relocated to Russia after the Van uprising, and he spent the rest of his life in the Soviet Union, where he published his then controversial novel *Burning Orchards* in 1966. The English translation was published by Black Apollo Press (no place of publication) in 2007; the quote is from 49.

19. Michael A. Reynolds, *Shattering Empires: The Clash and Collapse of the Ottoman and Russian Empires, 1908–1918* (Cambridge: Cambridge University Press, 2011), 145–147. Anahide Ter Minassian, "Van 1915," in *Armenian Van/Vaspurakan*, ed. Richard G. Hovannisian (Costa Mesa, CA: Mazda, 2000), 217–218; McCarthy et al., *The Armenian Rebellion*, 200.

20. Rafael de Nogales, *Four Years Beneath the Crescent* (New York: Charles Scribner's Sons, 1926), 58. For a critical study of de Nogales and his writing, see Kim McQuaid, *The Real and Assumed Personalities of Famous Men: Rafael de Nogales, T. E. Lawrence, and the Birth of the Modern Era, 1914–1937* (London: Gomidas Institute, 2010).

21. De Nogales, *Four Years*, 60–61; emphasis in the original.

22. Reynolds, *Shattering Empires*, 145–146; McCarthy et al., *The Armenian Rebellion*, 221.

23. Ter Minassian, "Van 1915," 242.

24. Djemal Pasha, *Memories of a Turkish Statesman, 1913–1919* (London: Hutchinson & Co., n.d.), 299; Bloxham, *Great Game of Genocide*, 84–90.

25. Taner Akçam, *A Shameful Act: The Armenian Genocide and the Question of Turkish Responsibility* (London: Constable, 2007), 168–169.

26. Akçam, *Young Turks' Crime Against Humanity*, 193–196. Balakian, in *Armenian Golgotha*, 82–83, 104, 106–107, recorded the names of several Ottoman officials who either resigned or were dismissed because of their unwillingness to massacre Armenians, including the governors of Ankara, Aleppo, and Kastamonu.

27. Akçam, *Young Turks' Crime Against Humanity*, 410–413. Balakian, in *Armenian Golgotha*, 95, 100, recounted several conversations with Turks who saw their role in the massacre of Armenians as participation in a jihad that entitled them to enter paradise. In his conversation with the captain, the officer justified his own role in the mass murder of Armenians in terms of fulfilling his religious duty (144, 146).

28. Taner Akçam, in *Young Turks' Crime Against Humanity*, 193–202, has extensively documented this "two-track approach" from both Ottoman archival sources and German accounts. The quote is from Reşid Akif Pasha's testimony to the Ottoman Chamber of Deputies, 21 November 1918, in Akçam, *A Shameful Act*, 175, and, in a slightly different translation, in *Young Turks' Crime Against Humanity*, 193–194.

29. On the "ten percent principle", see Fuat Dündar, "Pouring a People into the Desert: The 'Definitive Solution' of the Unionists to the Armenian Question," in Suny, Göçek, and Naimark, eds., *Question of Genocide*, 282. Akçam, in *Young Turks' Crime Against Humanity*, 242–263, provides the most extensive analysis of what he terms the "5 to 10 percent regulation".

30. NARA, Istanbul vol. 309, report by Leslie Davis, US consul in Harput, 11 July 1915.

31. Balakian, *Armenian Golgotha*, 109.

32. Balakian, *Armenian Golgotha*, 139–140.

33. Balakian, *Armenian Golgotha*, 167.

34. Baskın Oran, *MK: Récit d'un déporté arménien 1915* [M. K.: Narrative of an Armenian Deportee, 1915] (Paris: Turquoise, 2008), 37–51.

35. Balakian, *Armenian Golgotha*, 247–249.

36. Oran, *MK*, 59. The village of Azak has since been renamed Idil.

37. Bloxham, *Great Game of Genocide*, 97–98. Paul Gaunt argues in "The Ottoman Treatment of the Assyrians," in Suny, Göçek, and Naimark, *Question of Genocide*, 244–259, that the estimate of 250,000 might be low and suggests as many as 300,000 Assyrians may have perished. Some modern Turkish scholars deny Assyrian claims of genocide; see Bülent Özdemir, *Assyrian Identity and the Great War: Nestorian, Chaldean and Syrian Christians in the 20th Century* (Dunbeath, UK: Whittles Publishing, 2012).

38. Fethiye Çetin, *My Grandmother: A Memoir* (London: Verso, 2008), 8–9, letter to her father. Habab has since been renamed Ekinozu and is located between Harput and Palu in eastern Turkey.

39. Heranuş's father travelled from the United States to Syria to reassemble his shattered family. He found his wife among the Armenian refugees in Aleppo in 1920. He subsequently hired smugglers to scour the route taken by the Habab deportees, who found his son Horen in 1928. Horen then called on his sister and her husband to persuade them to make the trip to Aleppo with him for a family reunion. In the end, Seher/Heranuş's husband forbade her to go, and she never saw her family again. Horen, reunited with his parents, moved to the United States, where the surviving Gadarian family members tried in vain to make contact with their lost daughter. In the mid-1970s, Seher confided her story to her astonished granddaughter, Fethiye Çetin, who had no idea of her grandmother's Armenian origins. A young lawyer in Ankara, Çetin finally succeeded in making contact with the American Gadarians, though too late for her aging grandmother to make the trip to see her brother Horen again. Through her discussions with her grandmother and her subsequent meetings with the American Gadarians, Fethiye Çetin was able to reconstruct Seher/Heranuş's remarkable story of tragedy and survival. Her book was first published in Turkey in 2004 to critical acclaim, and by the time the English translation was published four years later, the original Turkish edition had gone through seven printings.

40. Çetin, *My Grandmother*, 102.

41. Balakian, *Armenian Golgotha*, 250.

42. The demographer Justin McCarthy, who maintains that the wartime massacres did not constitute a genocide, claims on the basis of Ottoman census figures that between 600,000 and 850,000 Armenians perished in the course of the war; cf. Justin McCarthy, *Muslims and Minorities: The Population of Ottoman Anatolia and the End of the Empire* (New York: New York University Press, 1983), 121–130; Justin McCarthy, "The Population of

Ottoman Armenians," in *The Armenians in the Late Ottoman Period*, ed. Türkkaya Ataöv (Ankara: Turkish Historical Society, 2001), 76–82. Historians of the Armenian genocide, like Richard Hovannisian and Vahakn Dadrian, maintain that over 1 million Armenians died as a result of a deliberate genocide; see essays by both scholars in Richard Hovannisian, ed., *The Armenian Genocide: History, Politics, Ethics* (Houndmills, UK: Macmillan Palgrave, 1992); Donald Bolxham, *The Great Game of Genocide: Imperialism, Nationalism, and the Destruction of the Ottoman Armenians* (Oxford: Oxford University Press, 2005).

CHAPTER 8

1. Casualty figures from C. F. Aspinall-Oglander, *Military Operations: Gallipoli* (London: Heinemann, 1929), 1:294, 347; ibid. (London: Heinemann, 1932), 2:53.

2. Edward J. Erickson, *Gallipoli: The Ottoman Campaign* (Barnsley, UK: Pen & Sword Military, 2010), 92–114.

3. On submarine warfare, see Henry W. Nevinson, *The Dardanelles Campaign* (London: Nisbet & Co., 1918), 145–146, 163–166; P. E. Guépratte, *L'expédition des Dardanelles, 1914–1915* (Paris: 1935), 116–125. Later in the campaign, the Allies lost further submarines. The *Mariotte* became entangled in submarine nets in July 1915, and thirty-two members of its crew were taken prisoner; see Ahmet Tetik, Y. Serdar Demirtaş, and Sema Demirtaş, eds., *Çanakkale Muharebeleri'nin Esirleri* [Prisoners of War at the Çanakkale Battles] (Ankara: Genelkurmay Basımevi, 2009), 1:198–216.

4. In June 1915, the *U-21* sank a French transport, and on 13 August, a German submarine sank the British transport *Royal Edward*; only one-third of the 1,400 men on board were rescued from the sea. By autumn 1915, there were no fewer than fourteen German U-boats in the eastern Mediterranean. Aspinall-Oglander, *Military Operations: Gallipoli*, 2:37–39.

5. Aspinall-Oglander, *Military Operations: Gallipoli*, 1:364.

6. Nevinson provides a detailed map of trenches from July 1915 in the collection of maps bound in the back of his book, *The Dardanelles Campaign*.

7. Jean Leymonnerie, *Journal d'un poilu sur le front d'orient* (Paris: Pygmalion, 2003), 109. A. P. Herbert's remarkable novel, *The Secret Battle*, was published by Methuen in London in 1919 to critical acclaim (Winston Churchill wrote the preface to later editions of the book). Herbert drew extensively on his personal experiences with the Royal Naval Division in Gallipoli and France when writing the book, which he completed in 1917 while recovering from wounds; quotes are from the 1919 edition, 48.

8. Mehmet Sinan Ozgen, *Bolvadınlı Mehmet Sinan Bey'in harp hatiraları* [Bolvadinli Mehmet Sinan Bey's War Memoirs] (Istanbul: Türkiye İş Bankası Kültür Yayınları, 2011), 26–27.

9. Herbert, *The Secret Battle*, 49–51; English war poet John Still was later taken prisoner and wrote these verses from the Afyon Karahisar POW camp in 1916. Jill Hamilton, *From Gallipoli to Gaza: The Desert Poets of World War One* (Sydney: Simon & Schuster Australia, 2003), 107.

10. Kevin Clunie and Ron Austin, eds., *From Gallipoli to Palestine: The War Writings of Sergeant GT Clunie of the Wellington Mounted Rifles, 1914–1919* (McCrae, Australia: Slouch Hat Publications, 2009), 29–30, diary entry of 16 May 1915. Ibrahim Arıkan, *Harp Hatıralarım* [My War Memoirs] (Istanbul: Timaş Yayınları, 2007), 53.

11. IWM, private papers of H. Corbridge, Documents 16453, description of snipers in Helles in diary entry of 27 April 1915. The reference to the wounded female sniper was in his diary entry of 14 May 1915. Private Reginald Stevens's letter of 30 June 1915, is reproduced in Glyn Harper, ed., *Letters from Gallipoli: New Zealand Soldiers Write Home* (Auckland: Auckland University Press, 2011), 149. For other references to women snipers, see Trooper Alfred Burton Mossman's letter to his parents of 20 May 1915 (136) and Private John Thomas Atkins's letter home of 11 June 1915 (148). Private Gray's account was published in *The Register, Adelaide* on 24 May 1916, consulted on the National Library of Australia's Trove digitised newspapers website (http://trove.nla.gof.au/newspaper). On 16 July 1915, the London *Times* carried a report of a woman sharpshooter captured by the Allies near W Beach on 4.

12. Leymonnerie, *Journal d'un poilu*, 110–111.

13. Mehmed Fasih, *Gallipoli 1915: Bloody Ridge (Lone Pine) Diary of Lt. Mehmed Fasih* (Istanbul: Denizler Kitabevi, 2001), 86–87.

14. Letter of 20 June 1915, in Leymonnerie, *Journal d'un poilu*, 107.

15. IWM, private papers of D. Moriarty, Documents 11752, diary entries of 1 and 2 May 1915. The last entry in the diary was 13 July 1915.

16. Harley Matthews, "Two Brothers," reproduced in Hamilton, *From Gallipoli to Gaza*, 120–121.

17. Leymonnerie, *Journal d'un poilu*, 105.

18. IWM, private papers of R. Eardley, Documents 20218, typescript memoir, 25–26.

19. IWM, private papers of B. Bradshaw, Documents 14940. Bradshaw's letter was written in the form of a diary. This entry was written between 6 and 9 June. He was killed in action on 10 June 1915.

20. A. P. Herbert, reprinted in Hamilton, *From Gallipoli to Gaza,* 79.

21. Diary of Raymond Weil, reproduced in Association nationale pour le souvenir des Dardanelles et fronts d'orient, *Dardanelles Orient Levant, 1915–1921* (Paris: L'Harmattan, 2005), 42. See also the diary of Ernest-Albert Stocanne in ibid., 56, 60. Tim Travers, *Gallipoli 1915* (Stroud, UK: Tempus, 2004), 269.

22. Leymonnerie, *Journal d'un poilu*, 122; Fasih, *Gallipoli 1915*, 66.

23. IWM, private papers of H. Corbridge, Documents 16453, diary entries of 14 June, 28 June, 12 July, and 7 August. On 14 August, he recorded "17 W[ounded], 85 M[ental] cases today". For the account of a man evacuated for shell shock, see IWM, private papers of M. O. F. England, Documents 13759.

24. Arıkan, *Harp Hatıralarım*, 54–55.

25. Emin Çöl, *Çanakkale Sina Savaşları: bir erin anıları* [The Dardanelles and Sinai Campaigns: One Man's Memoirs] (Istanbul: Nöbetçi Yayınevi, 2009), 53.

26. IWM, private papers of H. Corbridge, Documents 16453, diary entry of 7 August 1915.

27. IWM, private papers of R. Eardley, Documents 20218, memoir, 29–33. A brief record of Eardley's interrogation by the Ottoman authorities is held in the Turkish Military Archives in Ankara; in it he notes, "The 1st and 2nd companies of our battalion were defeated during an attack on Alçıtepe, on August 8. I was captured during the counterattack of the Turkish forces." The original document, transcription, and translation are reproduced in Tetik, Demirtaş, and Demirtaş, *Çanakkale Muharebeleri'nin Esirleri*, 2:735–736.

Though Eardley's name is clearly written in both English and Ottoman Turkish in the original document, the editors, mistaking his cursive "E" for an "S", transcribed his name in the book as "Sardley".

28. Fred Waite, *The New Zealanders at Gallipoli* (Auckland: Whitcombe and Tombs, 1919), 219. Oliver Hogue, "Love Letter XXXI," 7 August 1915, reproduced in Jim Haynes, ed., *Cobbers: Stories of Gallipoli 1915* (Sydney: ABC Books, 2005), 256.

29. Erickson, *Gallipoli: The Ottoman Campaign*, 140–144; Aspinall-Oglander, *Military Operations: Gallipoli*, 2:168–177.

30. Erickson, *Gallipoli: The Ottoman Campaign*, 147–148. William Baylebridge, "Lone Pine," reproduced in Haynes, *Cobbers*, 249–252.

31. Waite, *The New Zealanders at Gallipoli*, 200–201. The 1981 Peter Weir film *Gallipoli* told the tragic story of Australian soldiers at the Nek. Although some of the Australian officers argued to stop the charges, their superiors overrode them.

32. Otto Liman von Sanders, *Five Years in Turkey* (Annapolis: US Naval Institute, 1927), 88–89.

33. Aspinall-Oglander, *Military Operations: Gallipoli*, 2:282.

34. The disappearance of the 1/5th Norfolk, known as the Sandringham Company, gave rise to a battlefield legend that they disappeared in a cloud. Their story is the subject of the controversial 1999 film *All the King's Men* and featured in the best-selling Turkish novel by Buket Uzuner, *Uzun Beyaz Bulut—Gelibolu*, published in English as *The Long White Cloud—Gallipoli* (Istanbul: Everest, 2002).

35. Ian Hamilton, *Gallipoli Diary* (New York: George H. Doran, 1920), 2:132–136.

36. Hamilton, *Gallipoli Diary*, 2:249–253.

37. Aspinall-Oglander, *Military Operations: Gallipoli*, 2:402.

38. Nevinson, *The Dardanelles Campaign*, 379–380; Aspinall-Oglander, *Military Operations: Gallipoli*, 2:417.

39. Fasih, *Gallipoli 1915*, 104, 130.

40. The British reported two hundred men drowned or frozen to death in the storm and over 5,000 cases of frostbite following the storm of 26 to 28 November. Aspinall-Oglander, *Military Operations: Gallipoli*, 2:434. I. Hakkı Sunata, in *Gelibolu'dan kafkaslara: Birinci Dünya Savaşı anılarım* [From Gallipoli to the Caucasus: My First World War Memoirs] (Istanbul: Türkiye İş Bankası Kültür Yayınları, 2003), 184, noted that a number of Ottoman soldiers had drowned in the trenches. Fasih, *Gallipoli 1915*, entries of 9 November (p. 74), 14 November (p. 87), 19 November (p. 102), 24 November (p. 122), and 2 December (pp. 157–158).

41. Fasih, *Gallipoli 1915*, 199, diary entry of 15 December.

42. Fasih, *Gallipoli 1915*, 121, 124, 126, 148. Hakki Sunata noted in his diary that, in view of the build-up of ships off Suvla Bay, his officers fully expected a new Allied assault. "Five hours ago we expected an enemy landing. Now suddenly they are running away." Sunata, *Gelibolu'dan kafkaslara*, 198.

43. Letter from Douglas Rawei McLean, NZ Machine Gun Corps, to his father, 4 January 1916, reproduced in Harper, *Letters from Gallipoli*, 290; Arıkan, *Harp Hatıralarım*, 61.

44. Arıkan, *Harp Hatıralarım*, 64; Sunata, *Gelibolu'dan kafkaslara*, 200.

45. Çöl, *Çanakkale*, 62–63.

46. Official British figures from Aspinall-Oglander, *Military Operations: Gallipoli*, 2:484. Turkish figures from Edward J. Erickson, *Ordered to Die: A History of the Ottoman Army in the First World War* (Westport, CT: Greenwood Press, 2001), 94–95.

47. The poem was written by the anonymous "Argent", reprinted in Haynes, *Cobbers*, 314–315.

CHAPTER 9

1. Edward J. Erickson, *Ordered to Die: A History of the Ottoman Army in the First World War* (Westport, CT: Greenwood Press, 2001), 123.

2. The Battle of Shaiba in April 1915 is recounted in Chapter 5.

3. On the rebellions in the Middle Euphrates, see `Ali al-Wardi, *Lamahat ijtima`iyya min tarikh al-`Iraq al-hadith* [Social Aspects of the Modern History of Iraq] (Baghdad: al-Maktaba al-Wataniyya, 1974), 4:187–219; Ghassan R. Atiyyah, *Iraq, 1908–1921: A Political Study* (Beirut: Arab Institute for Research and Publishing, 1973), 80–81.

4. Wardi, *Lamahat*, 4:193.

5. Nixon's orders of 24 March 1915, 30 March 1915, and 31 March 1915 are reproduced in F. J. Moberly, *The Campaign in Mesopotamia, 1914–1918* (London: HMSO, 1923), 1:194–195.

6. Britain suffered practically no casualties in the Amara campaign—4 killed and 21 wounded—while the Ottomans lost 120 men dead and wounded and nearly 1,800 taken prisoner. Moberly, *The Campaign in Mesopotamia*, 1:260–262, 265.

7. Ali Jawdat, *Dhikrayati, 1900–1958* [My Memoirs, 1900–1958] (Beirut: al-Wafa', 1968), 31–36.

8. Moberly, in *The Campaign in Mesopotamia*, 1:297, reported 533 British casualties. Captain R. L. Lecky, an officer in the Indian army, claimed British losses of 1,200 dead and wounded; IWM, Captain R. L. Lecky, Documents 21099, diary entry for 24 July 1915.

9. Crewe quoted in Moberly, *The Campaign in Mesopotamia*, 1:303–304.

10. Moberly, *The Campaign in Mesopotamia*, 1:303–304.

11. The attack on Shaykh Said is recounted in Chapter 4.

12. On the Anglo-Ottoman hostilities in South Yemen, see Robin Bidwell, "The Turkish Attack on Aden 1915–1918," *Arabian Studies* 6 (1982): 171–194; Harold F. Jacob, *Kings of Arabia* (London: Mills and Boon, 1923), 168–172; G. Wyman Bury, *Pan-Islam* (London: Macmillan, 1919), 40–50; George Younghusband, *Forty Years a Soldier* (London: Herbert Jenkins, 1923), 274–277.

13. Younghusband, *Forty Years a Soldier*, 274.

14. Bidwell, "Turkish Attack on Aden 1915–1918," 180.

15. Jacob, *Kings of Arabia*, 180.

16. Both Townshend and Duff are quoted by Charles Townshend, *When God Made Hell: The British Invasion of Mesopotamia and the Creation of Iraq, 1914–1921* (London: Faber and Faber, 2010), 120. It is worth noting that the modern historian Charles Townshend, who wrote *When God Made Hell*, claims no relation to General Charles Townshend, commander of the 6th Division in Mesopotamia.

17. Edward J. Erickson, *Gallipoli and the Middle East, 1914–1918: From the Dardanelles to Mesopotamia* (London: Amber Books, 2008), 133.

18. Flight Sergeant J. McK. Sloss, Australian Flying Corps, identified the pilot as Lieutenant Harold Treloar and the observer as Captain Atkins. He claimed the airplane experienced engine trouble, though other sources claim the plane was shot down. IWM, private papers of J. McK. Sloss, MSM Australian Flying Corps, Documents 13102.

19. Captain Reynolds Lamont Lecky, a reserve officer in the Indian army, was attached to the 120th Rajputana Infantry during the campaign in Mesopotamia. IWM, Documents 21099.

20. Although fewer than 100 British soldiers were killed, over 1,100 were wounded, many of them seriously. Ottomans losses were 2,800 dead and wounded and 1,150 POWs. Moberly, *The Campaign in Mesopotamia*, 1:337.

21. Kitchener is quoted in Townshend, *When God Made Hell*, 140–141; F. J. Moberly, *The Campaign in Mesopotamia, 1914–1918* (London: HMSO, 1924), 2:15.

22. Moberly, *The Campaign in Mesopotamia*, 2:28.

23. Wardi, *Lamahat*, 4:224.

24. Salman, the Prophet's barber, is more commonly known as Salman al-Farsi, or Salman the Persian. Wardi, *Lamahat*, 4:224.

25. IWM, Lecky diary, entry of 29 October 1915.

26. Erickson, *Ordered to Die*, 112–113; Moberly, *The Campaign in Mesopotamia*, 2:49–58.

27. From the article by Staff Major Mehmed Amin, cited by Moberly, *The Campaign in Mesopotamia*, 2:59.

28. IWM, Lecky diary, entry of 22 November 1915. On the first day of fighting alone, on 22 November, the British lost 240 officers and 4,200 soldiers dead and wounded; the Ottomans suffered 4,500 dead, 4,500 wounded, and 1,200 POWs. Erickson, *Ordered to Die*, 113.

29. In Arabic, the couplets rhyme: *Rashad, ya ibn al-buma, `asakirak mahzuma / Rashad, ya ibn al-khayiba, `asakirak ha li-sayiba*. Wardi, *Lamahat*, 4:233.

30. The account of the "Noble Flag of `Ali" (in Arabic, *al-`alam al-haydari al-sharif*) is from Wardi, *Lamahat*, 4:233–242. Note that "haydar" is a name associated with the Caliph Ali.

31. On the Ottoman efforts to promote jihad in Libya, see Sean McMeekin, *The Berlin-Baghdad Express: The Ottoman Empire and Germany's Bid for World Power, 1898–1918* (London: Allen Lane, 2010), 259–274; P. G. Elgood, *Egypt and the Army* (Oxford: Oxford University Press, 1924), 270–274; Latifa Muhammad Salim, *Masr fi'l-harb al-`alimiyya al-ula* [Egypt in the First World War] (Cairo: Dar al-Shorouk, 2009), 290–296.

32. For Jafar al-Askari's account of the Libya campaign in 1915, see his memoirs, *A Soldier's Story: From Ottoman Rule to Independent Iraq* (London: Arabian Publishing, 2003), 54–85.

33. George McMunn and Cyril Falls, *Military Operations: Egypt and Palestine from the Outbreak of War with Germany to June 1917* (London: HMSO: 1928), 106.

34. For the favourable assessment of Jafar al-Askari's training, see McMunn and Falls, *Military Operations*, 112. The British official history claimed British losses of 33 dead and 47 wounded in fighting on 11 and 13 December and estimated Sanussi casualties at 250, although Jafar al-Askari reported only 17 Arab fighters dead and 30 wounded. The British intelligence officer killed in action was Lieutenant Colonel C. L. Snow of the Egyptian Coastguard.

CHAPTER 10

1. On German efforts to promote jihad, see Peter Hopkirk, *On Secret Service East of Constantinople: The Plot to Bring Down the British Empire* (London: John Murray, 1994); Sean McMeekin, *The Berlin-Baghdad Express: The Ottoman Empire and Germany's Bid for World Power, 1898–1918* (London: Allen Lane, 2010).

2. IWM, private papers of Major G. L. Heawood, Documents 7666. Heawood's account was drafted in 1917.

3. ʿAli al-Wardi, *Lamahat ijtimaʿiyya min tarikh al-ʿIraq al-hadith* [Social Aspects of the Modern History of Iraq] (Baghdad: al-Maktaba al-Wataniyya, 1974), 4:231. According to Wardi, the tension between the two generals stemmed from the fact that Nurettin had opposed the appointment of a non-Muslim as commander of the Sixth Army.

4. F. J. Moberly, *The Campaign in Mesopotamia, 1914–1918* (London: HMSO, 1924), 2:194.

5. George Younghusband, *Forty Years a Soldier* (London: Herbert Jenkins, 1923), 284–285.

6. IWM, private papers of the Reverend H. Spooner, Documents 7308, entry for 9 January 1916.

7. The first attack on Hanna took place on 20–21 January 1916. The British suffered 2,741 casualties and estimated Ottoman losses at 2,000. Moberly, *The Campaign in Mesopotamia*, 2:275–276; Younghusband, *Forty Years a Soldier*, 290–291.

8. The search of townspeople's houses took place on 24 January. Charles Townshend, *When God Made Hell: The British Invasion of Mesopotamia and the Creation of Iraq, 1914–1921* (London: Faber and Faber, 2010), 215.

9. Moberly, *The Campaign in Mesopotamia*, 2:200. Reverend Spooner noted on 30 March 1916 that a company of the 24th Punjabis had been "disarmed for disaffection" and that "many Mohammedans have deserted to enemy". IWM, papers of W. D. Lee of the Royal Garrison Artillery, Documents 1297.

10. For Jafar Bey's account of the Sanussi campaign, see Jafar al-Askari, *A Soldier's Story: From Ottoman Rule to Independent Iraq* (London: Arabian Publishing, 2003), 85–93.

11. The British lost 312 men dead and wounded and estimated 200 Arab dead and 500 wounded in Bir Tunis on 23 January; George McMunn and Cyril Falls refer to the engagement as the "Affair of Halazin" in their *Military Operations: Egypt and Palestine from the Outbreak of War with Germany to June 1917* (London: HMSO, 1928), 122.

12. McMunn and Falls, *Military Operations*, 134.

13. Reverend Spooner recorded the story of the football game on 26 January and the anecdote of the bandaged spade on 1 February 1916.

14. IWM, private papers of Major Alex Anderson, Documents 9724, 57–59; in his description of the first aerial bombardment, Anderson noted the pilot was "already known as Fritz"; for his description of the bombardment of the hospital, see 74–75. See also Reverend Spooner's diary, entry for 18 March, in which, after noting the casualties, he wrote only, "Awful scenes."

15. On the Russian conquest of Erzurum, see W. E. D. Allen and Paul Muratoff, *Caucasian Battlefields: A History of the Wars on the Turco-Caucasian Border, 1828–1921* (Cambridge: Cambridge University Press, 1953), 320–372; Michael Reynolds, *Shattering Empires: The Clash and Collapse of the Ottoman and Russian Empires, 1908–1918* (Cambridge: Cambridge University

Press, 2011), 134–139; Sean McMeekin, *The Russian Origins of the First World War* (Cambridge, MA: Harvard University Press, 2011), 191–193; Edward J. Erickson, *Ordered to Die: A History of the Ottoman Army in the First World War* (Westport, CT: Greenwood Press, 2001), 120–137.

16. Allen and Muratoff claim, in *Caucasian Battlefields*, 342, that Ottoman losses at Koprukoy were "nearly 15,000" killed, wounded, or frozen to death, as well as 5,000 taken prisoner and "about the same number of deserters", or 25,000 in all. Russian losses were also heavy: 10,000 dead and wounded and 2,000 hospitalized with frostbite.

17. Younghusband, *Forty Years a Soldier*, 297.

18. Ali Ihsan Bey was later to adopt the Turkish name for Dujaila, Sabis Hill, as his family name. Ali Ihsan Sâbis, *Birinci Dünya Harbi* [The First World War] (Istanbul: Nehir Yayınları, 2002), 3:121–127.

19. Abidin Ege, *Harp Günlükleri* [War Diaries] (Istanbul: Türkiye İş Bankası Kültür Yayınları, 2011), 275–278.

20. British casualties were 3,474 against 1,285 Ottoman casualties. Moberly, *The Campaign in Mesopotamia*, 2:525.

21. Russell Braddon, *The Siege* (New York: Viking, 1969), 207–208.

22. On Lawrence's mission to Mesopotamia, see Jeremy Wilson, *Lawrence of Arabia: The Authorized Biography of T. E. Lawrence* (London: Heinemann, 1989), 253–278; Townshend, *When God Made Hell*, 250–253.

23. Sulayman Faydi's and Sayyid Talib's pre-war efforts are recounted in Chapter 4.

24. Sulayman Faydi gave a detailed account of his meeting with T. E. Lawrence, presented as a dialogue between the two men, in his memoirs, *Mudhakkirat Sulayman Faydi* [The Memoirs of Sulayman Faydi] (London: Saqi Books, 1998), 221–242.

25. Wilson, *Lawrence of Arabia*, 268.

26. Ege, *Harp Günlükleri*, 294.

27. Quoted in Townshend, *When God Made Hell*, 250–253.

28. Scott Anderson, *Lawrence in Arabia* (London: Atlantic Books, 2014), 176–178. Herbert's account of their negotiations with Halil is from Aubrey Herbert, *Mons, Anzac and Kut* (London: Hutchinson, n.d. [1930]), 248–256.

29. Ege, *Harp Günlükleri*, 307; Moberly, *The Campaign in Mesopotamia*, 2:459. Prior to the fall of Kut, General Cornwallis's surrender with over 7,500 troops in Yorktown (1781) had been the largest in British history. Townshend's defeat in Kut was subsequently eclipsed by the surrender of Singapore in 1942 with 80,000 British, Indian, and Australian troops taken prisoner by the Japanese.

30. IWM, private papers of Major T. R. Wells, Documents 7667, diary entry of 29 April 1916.

31. Civilian casualty figures from Moberly, *The Campaign in Mesopotamia*, 2:459. Reverend Spooner's account is from IWM, "Report Based on the Diary of the Rev. Harold Spooner, April 29th, 1916 to Nov. 1918," Documents 7308. See also IWM, Diary of Captain Reynolds Lamont Lecky, Documents 21099, diary entry of 2 May 1916.

32. IWM, private papers of Lieutenant Colonel L. S. Bell Syer, Documents 7469, diary entry of 6 May 1916.

33. Talib Mushtaq, *Awraq ayyami, 1900–1958* [Pages from My Life, 1900–1958] (Beirut: Dar al-Tali`a, 1968), 1:15. He quoted the British sergeant saying in Arabic, "*Al –Inkliz damdam aqwa, lakin khubz maku.*"

34. As quoted by Sergeant P. W. Long, *Other Ranks of Kut* (London: Williams and Norgate, 1938), 34; emphasis in the original.

35. IWM, diary of Lieutenant Colonel L. S. Bell Syer, entry of 14 May 1916. See also papers of Major T. R. Wells, who claimed the Turks showed "favouritism" to Indian Muslims (8 May and 4 June), and the diary of Reverend Spooner, entry of 17 May.

36. The "Crescent Moon Camp" is discussed in Chapter 3. P. W. Long, in *Other Ranks of Kut*, 33, reported a "complete battalion of Algerians" encamped near the British POWs in Baghdad. Given their past in French service, Long recounted, "they claimed to be our friends," but the Britons "did not accept their overtures". The North Africans were subsequently detailed to Persia "to fight the Russians on behalf of the Turks".

37. NARA, Baghdad vol. 25, Brissel report dated Baghdad, 9 August 1916.

38. The article, taken from the *Sada-i Islam* newspaper of 29 Temmuz 1332 (11 August 1916), is preserved among the papers of the US Consulate of Baghdad, NARA, Baghdad vol. 25. The British official history acknowledged that the sultan received British Muslim officers and restored their swords but claimed that the Ottomans arrested "those who refused" to serve the sultan. Moberly, *The Campaign in Mesopotamia*, 2:466.

39. Many officers left detailed memoirs of their experiences in captivity; see, e.g., Major E. W. C. Sandes, *In Kut and Captivity with the Sixth Indian Division* (London: John Murray, 1919); Captain E. O. Mousley, *The Secrets of a Kuttite: An Authentic Story of Kut, Adventures in Captivity and Stamboul Intrigue* (London: John Lane, 1921); W. C. Spackman, *Captured at Kut: Prisoner of the Turks* (Barnsley, UK: Pen & Sword, 2008).

40. E. H. Jones, *The Road to En-Dor* (London: John Lane The Bodley Head, 1921), 123.

41. IWM, private papers of J. McK. Sloss, MSM Australian Flying Corps, Documents 13102; Sergeant P. W. "Jerry" Long, in *Other Ranks of Kut*, 103, published the first account of the common soldier's experience after the fall of Kut.

42. Arnold T. Wilson, *Loyalties Mesopotamia, 1914–1917* (Oxford: Oxford University Press, 1930), 140.

43. Grigoris Balakian, in *Armenian Golgotha: A Memoir of the Armenian Genocide, 1915–1918* (New York: Vintage Books, 2010), 294–298, claimed to have encountered the British soldiers two to three weeks after the deportation of Armenians from Bahçe in early June 1916, suggesting that the Kut survivors reached the railway station at the end of June or in early July 1916.

44. Curzon quoted in Townshend, *When God Made Hell*, 335.

CHAPTER 11

1. The word "amirate" refers to the office of the amir of Mecca. An "amir" is a prince or commander. The reigning prince of Mecca might be referred to as either the amir or the grand sharif of Mecca.

2. Abdullah's account is recorded in *Memoirs of King Abdullah of Transjordan* (New York: Philosophical Library, 1950), 112–113. See also Ronald Storrs, *Orientations* (London: Readers Union, 1939), 129–130; George Antonius, *The Arab Awakening* (London: Hamish Hamilton, 1938), 126–128. Antonius, himself an ardent Arab nationalist, based much of his account of the Arab Revolt on interviews with leading members of the Hashemite family and original documents from their private papers.

3. Storrs, *Orientations*, 155–156.

4. Translated from the Beirut newspaper *al-Ittihad al-'Uthmani* [The Ottoman Union], 29 December 1914, quoted in Antonius, *Arab Awakening*, 145.

5. Quoted from Arab nationalist George Antonius's *Arab Awakening*, 140. Antonius based his account in *The Arab Awakening* on extensive interviews with Sharif Husayn and his sons Abdullah and Faysal. C. Ernest Dawn, *From Ottomanism to Arabism: Essays on the Origins of Arab Nationalism* (Urbana: University of Illinois Press, 1973), 26.

6. Al-Fatat and its role in the First Arab Congress in Paris is treated in Chapter 1.

7. This account of Faysal's mission to Istanbul and Damascus draws on Dawn, *From Ottomanism to Arabism*, 27–30; Antonius, *Arab Awakening*, 150–159; Ali A. Allawi, *Faisal I of Iraq* (New Haven, CT: Yale University Press, 2014).

8. Antonius, *Arab Awakening*, 157–158.

9. A translation of the Husayn-McMahon Correspondence is reproduced in *The Middle East and North Africa in World Politics: A Documentary Record*, ed. J. C. Hurewitz (New Haven, CT: Yale University Press, 1979), 2:46–56.

10. McMahon's letter to London is quoted in Jonathan Schneer, *The Balfour Declaration: The Origins of the Arab Israeli Conflict* (New York: Random House, 2010), 59.

11. On Faruqi's revelations, see Scott Anderson, *Lawrence in Arabia: War, Deceit, Imperial Folly and the Making of the Modern Middle East* (London: Atlantic Books, 2013), 139–143; Antonius, *Arab Awakening*, 169; David Fromkin, *A Peace to End All Peace* (London: Andre Deutsch, 1989), 176–178; Schneer, *Balfour Declaration*, 60–63. Sharif Husayn mentioned Muhamad Sharif Faruqi by name in his letter to McMahon of 1 January 1916, and so clearly had been informed of the Arabist officer's defection, most probably by McMahon's courier.

12. These French territorial claims in Greater Syria were set out in the letter from the French ambassador in Petrograd to the Russian foreign minister dated 1/14 March 1915, reproduced in Hurewitz, *Middle East and North Africa in World Politics*, 2:19.

13. Fromkin, *Peace to End All Peace*, 188–193.

14. Antonius, *Arab Awakening*, 248.

15. The text of the Sykes-Picot Agreement is reproduced in Hurewitz, *Middle East and North Africa in World Politics*, 2:60–64.

16. Djemal Pasha, *Memories of a Turkish Statesman, 1913–1919* (London: Hutchinson and Co., n.d.), 197–199.

17. Turjman's friends were from leading Jerusalemite families: Hasan Khalidi and Omar Salih Barghouti, both commissioned officers in the Ottoman army, and the teacher and diarist Khalil Sakakini. Salim Tamari, *Year of the Locust: A Soldier's Diary and the Erasure of Palestine's Ottoman Past* (Berkeley: University of California Press, 2011), 91.

18. Falih Rıfkı Atay, *Le mont des Oliviers* [The Mount of Olives] (Paris: Turquoise, 2009), 29–30. The book was first published in Turkish in 1932 under the title *Zeytindağı*.

19. Eliezer Tauber, *The Arab Movements in World War I* (London: Frank Cass, 1993), 38.

20. George Antonius, in *Arab Awakening*, 241, claimed that a figure of 300,000 dead from famine was "not open to doubt" and argued that the actual figure might be as high as 350,000. Linda Schatkowski Schilcher, in "The Famine of 1915–1918 in Greater Syria," in *Problems of the Modern Middle East in Historical Perspective*, ed. John Spagnolo (Reading, UK: Ithaca Press, 1992), 229–258, draws on German consular records to argue that the mortality rate from famine and famine related diseases "may have reached 500,000 by

the end of 1918". On Seferberlik in popular memory in Syria and Lebanon, see Najwa al-Qattan, "Safarbarlik: Ottoman Syria and the Great War," in *From the Syrian Land to the States of Syria and Lebanon*, ed. Thomas Philipp and Christoph Schumann (Beirut: Orient-Institut, 2004), 163–174.

21. Q. B. Khuwayri, *al-Rihla al-suriyya fi'l-harb al-ʿumumiyya 1916* [The Syrian Journey During the General War, 1916] (Cairo: al-Matbaʿa al-Yusufiyya, 1921), 34–35.

22. Enver's initiative and other efforts by the Entente Powers to prevent humanitarian relief to pass through the Allied blockade are recounted in Shakib Arslan, *Sira Dhatiyya* [Autobiography] (Beirut: Dar al-Taliʿa, 1969), 225–236.

23. Djemal Pasha, *Memories of a Turkish Statesman*, 213; Rıfkı Atay, *Le mont des Oliviers*, 75–76.

24. Tamari, *Year of the Locust*, 130–132.

25. Telegram from Sharif Husayn to Enver Pasha and his response, reproduced in Sulayman Musa, *al-Thawra al-ʿarabiyya al-kubra: wathaʾiq wa asanid* [The Great Arab Revolt: Documents and Records] (Amman: Department of Culture and Arts, 1966), 52–53. Cemal Pasha and Sharif Abdullah provided divergent accounts of this exchange between Sharif Husayn and Enver Pasha; see Djemal Pasha, *Memories of a Turkish Statesman*, 215, and King Abdullah, *Memoirs of King Abdullah of Transjordan*, 136–137. See also Tauber, *Arab Movements in World War I*, 80.

26. Antonius, *Arab Awakening*, 190.

27. Rıfkı Atay, *Le mont des Oliviers*, 73–79. Needless to say, Arab contemporaries are yet more moving in their tributes to those hanged in Beirut and Damascus. Dr Ahmad Qadri, in *Mudhakkirati ʿan al-thawra al-ʿarabiyya al-kubra* [My Memoirs of the Great Arab Revolt] (Damascus: Ibn Zaydun, 1956), 55–56, a Syrian member of the al-Fatat movement who was twice arrested and released by the Ottoman authorities for suspected Arabist activities, repeats the heroic last words of many of those executed in Beirut.

28. Later that year, Cemal Pasha published a book in Turkish, Arabic, and French editions to justify the workings of the Aley Military Tribunal. The book, *La verite sur la question syrienne* (Istanbul: Tanine, 1916), provided brief descriptions of eight Arab secret societies, reproduced documents seized from the French consulates in Beirut and Damascus, and named those convicted by the military tribunal and their crimes. George Antonius probably heard this account of Faysal's reaction to the executions from Faysal himself. Antonius, in *Arab Awakening*, 191, found it difficult to capture the power of the Arabic "*Taba al-mawt, ya ʿArab*" in translation, which "amounts to an appeal to all Arabs to take up arms, at the risk of their lives, to avenge the executions in blood".

29. Cemal Pasha openly regretted not arresting Faysal, his brothers, and their father, Sharif Husayn, on charges of treason; see Djemal Pasha, *Memories of a Turkish Statesman*, 220–222.

30. The rifle is held by the Imperial War Museum in London. On the history of the rifle, see Haluk Oral, *Gallipoli 1915 Through Turkish Eyes* (Istanbul: Bahcesehir University Press, 2012), 233–236.

31. Djemal Pasha, *Memories of a Turkish Statesman*, 223. T. E. Lawrence, in *Seven Pillars of Wisdom: A Triumph* (New York: Doubleday, Doran & Co., 1936), 93, alleged Fakhri Pasha was involved in the massacre of Armenians. Christophe Leclerc, in *Avec T. E. Lawrence en Arabie: La mission militaire francaise au Hedjaz, 1916–1920* (Paris: L'Harmattan, 1998), 28, linked Fakhri to the 1909 Armenian massacres in Adana and Zeitun.

32. King Abdullah, *Memoirs of King Abdullah of Transjordan*, 138.

33. Turkish historian Haluk Oral, in *Gallipoli 1915*, 236, claims Sharif Husayn used the Gallipoli trophy that Cemal Pasha had given Faysal to fire the opening shot of the revolt, though Imperial War Museum records make no mention of this claim.

34. Abdullah, *Memoirs of King Abdullah of King Abdullah of Transjordan*, 143.

35. Abdullah, *Memoirs of King Abdullah of King Abdullah of Transjordan*, 144–146.

36. Abdullah's account of the siege of Taif is recorded in the *Memoirs of King Abdullah*, 143–153.

37. Turjman, *Year of the Locust*, 155–156.

38. Muhammad Ali al-Ajluni, *Dhikrayat `an al-thawra al-`arabiyya al-kubra* [Memories of the Great Arab Revolt] (Amman: Dar al-Karmil, 2002), 22–25; on the announcement of the Arab Revolt and debates over its merits and dangers, see 27–28. Ajluni was a native of the Ajlun district, which formed part of the province of Syria under the Ottomans but is in northern Jordan today.

39. On Indian reaction, see James Barr, *Setting the Desert on Fire: T. E. Lawrence and Britain's Secret War in Arabia, 1916–1918* (New York: W. W. Norton, 2008), 41–42.

40. On the recruitment of Arab Ottoman officers to the Hashemite war effort, see Tauber, *The Arab Movements in World War I*, 102–117. Jafar al-Askari's capture in the Western Desert is recounted in Chapter 10; his adhesion to the Hashemite cause is related in his memoirs, *A Soldier's Story: From Ottoman Rule to Independent Iraq* (London: Arabian Publishing, 2003), 108–112. Ali Jawdat's capture at Nasiriyya is related in Chapter 9 and his detention in Basra in Chapter 10; his account of recruitment from POW camps is related in Ali Jawdat, *Dhikrayati, 1900–1958* [Memoirs, 1900–1958] (Beirut: al-Wafa', 1967), 37–40.

41. McMahon's telegram of 13 September 1916, is reproduced in Barr, *Setting the Desert on Fire*, 56. On French concerns to preserve Sykes-Picot, see Leclerc, *Avec T. E. Lawrence en Arabie*, 19. On the Brémond mission, see also Robin Bidwell, "The Brémond Mission in the Hijaz, 1916–17: A Study in Inter-allied Co-operation," in *Arabian and Islamic Studies*, ed. Robin Bidwell and Rex Smith (London: Longman, 1983): 182–195.

42. Bidwell, "Brémond Mission," 186.

43. Edouard Brémond, *Le Hedjaz dans la guerre mondiale* (Paris: Payot, 1931), 61–64, 106–107. The entire French mission, based in Egypt, reached a total of forty-two officers and 983 men (Brémond, *Le Hedjaz*, 64).

44. Lawrence, *Seven Pillars*, 92.

45. Lawrence's report of 18 November 1916 is quoted in Barr, *Setting the Desert on Fire*, 77–78. See also Anderson's analysis of Lawrence's report in *Lawrence in Arabia*, 223–226.

46. Lawrence's account of the events of December 1916 is recounted in *Seven Pillars*, 119–135.

47. Lawrence, *Seven Pillars*, 130.

48. The recommendations of the meeting of the War Committee of 6 July 1916 are reproduced in George McMunn and Cyril Falls, *Military Operations: Egypt and Palestine from the Outbreak of War with Germany to June 1917* (London: HMSO, 1928), 230–232.

CHAPTER 12

1. On the deployment of German airplanes, see Desmond Seward, *Wings over the Desert: In Action with an RFC Pilot in Palestine, 1916–1918* (Sparkford, UK: Haynes Publishing,

2009), 29–32. On Austrian artillery, compare Djemal Pasha, *Memories of a Turkish States-man, 1913–1919* (London: Hutchinson, n.d.), 169.

2. The full text of Murray's proposal of 15 February 1916, is reproduced in George Mc-Munn and Cyril Falls, *Military Operations: Egypt and Palestine from the Outbreak of War with Germany to June 1917* (London: HMSO, 1928), 170–174.

3. Djemal Pasha, *Memories of a Turkish Statesman*, 170; on the "Affair of Qatiya," see McMunn and Falls, *Military Operations*, 162–170; Anthony Bruce, *The Last Crusade: The Palestine Campaign in the First World War* (London: John Murray, 2002), 37–40.

4. On the Imperial Camel Corps, see Frank Reid, *The Fighting Cameliers* (1934; rpt. Milton Keynes, UK: Leonaur, 2005); Geoffrey Inchbald, *With the Imperial Camel Corps in the Great War* (Milton Keynes, UK: Leonaur, 2005).

5. McMunn and Falls, *Military Operations*, 199.

6. Recommendation of the War Committee, 6 July 1916, reproduced in McMunn and Falls, *Military Operations*, 230–232.

7. Inchbald, *With the Imperial Camel Corps*, 113.

8. Reid, *The Fighting Cameliers*, 50–52; McMunn and Falls, *Military Operations*, 257.

9. The British reported capturing 1,635 Ottoman soldiers and their officers and estimated some 200 Ottoman troops killed in the battle for Rafah. British losses were 71 killed and 415 wounded. McMunn and Falls, *Military Operations*, 270.

10. Edward J. Erickson, *Ordered to Die: A History of the Ottoman Army in the First World War* (Westport, CT: Greenwood Press, 2001), 161.

11. CIGS telegram to commander in chief, India, dated 30 April 1916, reproduced in F. J. Moberly, *The Campaign in Mesopotamia, 1914–1918* (London: HMSO, 1923–1927), 3:3–4.

12. Erickson, *Ordered to Die*, 164–166.

13. Charles Townshend, *When God Made Hell: The British Invasion of Mesopotamia and the Creation of Iraq, 1914–1921* (London: Faber and Faber, 2010), 344–345.

14. Arnold T. Wilson, *Loyalties Mesopotamia, 1914–1917* (Oxford: Oxford University Press, 1930), 222.

15. Lieutenant Colonel J. E. Tenant, cited in Wilson, *Loyalties Mesopotamia*, 223.

16. Moberly, *The Campaign in Mesopotamia*, 3:193–195; Wilson, *Loyalties Mesopotamia*, 222–223; Townshend, *When God Made Hell*, 355–357.

17. The exchange of correspondence between Maude, Robertson, and Monro is reproduced in Moberly, *The Campaign in Mesopotamia*, 3:204–211.

18. Wilson, *Loyalties Mesopotamia*, 216.

19. Talib Mushtaq, *Awraq ayyami, 1900–1958* [Pages from My Life, 1900–1958] (Beirut: Dar al-Tali`a, 1968), 17–18.

20. NARA, Baghdad vol. 28, transcription from Consul Heizer's Miscellaneous Record Book, 10–13 March 1917.

21. For a detailed discussion of Maude's proclamation and its flaws, see Wilson, *Loyalties Mesopotamia*, 237–241.

22. The full text of the proclamation is reproduced in Moberly, *The Campaign in Mesopotamia*, 3:404–405, appendix 38.

23. Mushtaq, *Awraq ayyami*, 19.

24. Hew Strachan, *The First World War* (London: Pocket Books, 2003), 215–223. The

United States never declared war on the Ottoman Empire, though it withdrew all of its consular officials from Ottoman domains upon entering the war against Germany.

25. The British reported just under 4,000 casualties, including 523 killed and 2,932 wounded, though Liman von Sanders claimed the Turks buried some 1,500 British dead after the First Battle of Gaza. Ottoman losses were under 2,500, including 301 killed and 1,085 wounded. See McMunn and Falls, *Military Operations*, 315, 322; Otto Liman von Sanders, *Five Years in Turkey* (Annapolis: US Naval Institute, 1927), 165.

26. Falih Rıfkı Atay, *Le mont des Oliviers* [The Mount of Olives] (Paris: Turquoise, 2009), 205–206.

27. A. Briscoe Moore, *The Mounted Riflemen in Sinai and Palestine* (Auckland: Whitcombe and Tombs, n.d. [1920]), 67.

28. Djemal Pasha, *Memories of a Turkish Statesman*, 179.

29. Reid, *The Fighting Cameliers*, 98; Reid also noted he was issued with a gas mask before the Second Battle of Gaza (97). The British official history noted that gas was used for the first time on the Palestine front in the Second Battle of Gaza; McMunn and Falls, *Military Operations*, 328.

30. Reid, *The Fighting Cameliers*, 102–110.

31. Rıfkı Atay, *Le mont des Oliviers*, 213–214; McMunn and Falls, *Military Operations*, 348, 350.

32. James Barr, *Setting the Desert on Fire: T. E. Lawrence and Britain's Secret War in Arabia, 1916–1918* (New York: W. W. Norton, 2008), 90–106.

33. Lawrence's first attack on the Hijaz Railway was on March 29–30 at the Abu al-Naam station. T. E. Lawrence, *Seven Pillars of Wisdom: A Triumph* (New York: Doubleday Doran and Co., 1936), 197–203.

34. Jafar al-Askari, *A Soldier's Story: From Ottoman Rule to Independent Iraq* (London: Arabian Publishing, 2003), 112–114. Al-Askari's capture in the Western Desert of Egypt is recounted in Chapter 10.

35. Ali Allawi, *Faisal I of Iraq* (New Haven, CT: Yale University Press, 2014), 94–95.

36. Barr, *Setting the Desert on Fire*, 135. Sykes, accompanied by Picot, met with Faysal and Sharif Husayn in Jeddah on 18 May 1917, to give the sharif the details of the Sykes-Picot Agreement, though suggesting a greater degree of Arab autonomy under French administration than was ever intended. Ibid., 138–141.

37. Lawrence, *Seven Pillars*, 298.

38. Lawrence, *Seven Pillars*, 300–312.

39. Much to the chagrin of Arab historians, Lawrence is credited with—indeed, took credit for—the occupation of Aqaba. As he wrote in *Seven Pillars*, "Akaba had been taken on my plan by my effort. The cost of it had fallen on my brains and nerves" (323). Ali Allawi, in *Faisal I of Iraq*, 95–96, notes how, in his 6 July report to Faysal, Sharif Nasir made "no mention of Lawrence's role in the planning and organisation for the attack". Lawrence, he argued, exaggerated his own role "in the full knowledge that the other actors, overwhelmingly Arab, were in no position to contradict or correct the story". See also Suleiman Musa, *T. E. Lawrence: An Arab View* (Oxford: Oxford University Press, 1966). Wingate cited in Barr, *Setting the Desert on Fire*, 160–161.

40. Lawrence, *Seven Pillars*, 322.

41. Cited in Barr, *Setting the Desert on Fire*, 166.

42. Eugene Rogan, *Frontiers of the State in the Late Ottoman Empire: Transjordan, 1851–1920* (Cambridge: Cambridge University Press, 1999), 224–229.

43. From the unpublished memoirs of Salih al-Tall, the Irbid notable ordered to recruit the militia (236–237). I am most grateful to the late Mulhim al-Tall for permission to copy this valuable document.

44. The private papers of the commander of the Circassian Volunteer Force, Mirza Wasfi, are on deposit in the Jordanian National Archives in Amman, Jordan. On the volunteer cavalry, compare MW 5/17, docs. 6 and 10, 3–10 November 1916.

45. Odeh al-Goussous, *Mudhakkirat ʿAwda Salman al-Qusus al-Halasa* [Memoirs of Odeh al-Goussous al-Halasa, 1877–1943] (Amman: n.p., 2006), 84.

46. These efforts to court tribal leaders to counter Hashemite influence are described by Odeh al-Goussous in *Mudhakkirat ʿAwda Salman al-Qusus al-Halasa*, 84. The Ottoman archives preserve the citations for medals presented to tribal leaders in southern Syria; see the Prime Ministry Archives, Istanbul, DH-KMS 41/43 and 41/46 (August and September, 1916). On Lawrence's confrontation with Auda, see Lawrence, *Seven Pillars*, 355; Barr, *Setting the Desert on Fire*, 169–170.

47. This attack took place shortly after 17 July 1917. There is no mention of this engagement in Lawrence's *Seven Pillars of Wisdom*, no doubt because he was in Cairo at the time. Goussous, *Mudhakkirat ʿAwda Salman al-Qusus al-Halasa*, 86–88. However, Lawrence did report on tribal loyalties to the Ottomans; see T. E. Lawrence, "Tribal Politics in Feisal's Area," *Arab Bulletin Supplementary Papers* 5 (24 June 1918): 1–5.

48. On the 24 June 1917, meeting and the formation of the Yıldırım Group, see Djemal Pasha, *Memories of a Turkish Statesman*, 182–193; Liman von Sanders, *Five Years in Turkey*, 173–184; Erickson, *Ordered to Die*, 166–172.

49. Bruce, *The Last Crusade*, 119–120.

50. Emin Çöl, *Çanakkale Sina Savaşları: bir erin anıları* [The Dardanelles and Sinai Campaigns: One Man's Memoirs] (Istanbul: Nöbetçi Yayınevi, 2009), 103–104.

51. Çöl, *Çanakkale Sina Savaşları*, 106–108. On the charge of the 4th Australian Light Horse Brigade, see Roland Perry, *The Australian Light Horse* (Sydney: Hachette Australia, 2010), 3–13.

52. Cyril Falls and A. F. Becke, *Military Operations: Egypt and Palestine from the Outbreak of War with Germany to June 1917*, Part 1 (London: HMSO, 1930), 65.

53. Reid, *The Fighting Cameliers*, 139–147.

54. Chaim Weizmann, *Trial and Error* (New York: Harper and Brothers, 1949), 208; Tom Segev, *One Palestine, Complete: Jews and Arabs under the British Mandate* (London: Abacus Books, 2001), 43–50; Jonathan Schneer, *The Balfour Declaration: The Origins of the Arab-Israeli Conflict* (New York: Random House, 2010), 333–346.

55. Both sides suffered heavy casualties in the Palestine Campaign. By the conquest of Jerusalem, the British reported 18,928 dead and wounded and the Otomans 28,443 casualties. In addition, Allenby reported nearly 12,000 Turks taken prisoner. Bruce, *The Last Crusade*, 165.

56. Segev, *One Palestine, Complete*, 50–54.

57. The Imperial War Museum holds a copy of the thirteen-minute silent film "General Allenby's Entry into Jerusalem", which can be consulted online.

CHAPTER 13

1. NARA, Trebizond, Turkey, vol. 30, Miscellaneous Record Book, 1913–1918, entry of 23 March 1917. The Americans kept their consulate open through the Russian occupation of Trabzon, the consul keeping a brief log of political events in his Miscellaneous Record Book, from which all subsequent quotes have been drawn. See also Michael A. Reynolds, *Shattering Empires: The Clash and Collapse of the Ottoman and Russian Empires, 1908–1918* (Princeton, NJ: Princeton University Press, 2011), 167–190; Sean McMeekin, *The Russian Origins of the First World War* (Cambridge, MA: Harvard University Press, 2011), 224–235.

2. On the Russian publication of the Sykes-Picot Agreement and Cemal Pasha's overtures to the Hashemites, see George Antonius, *The Arab Awakening* (London: Hamish and Hamilton, 1938), 253–258; Ali Allawi, *Faisal I of Iraq* (New Haven, CT: Yale University Press, 2014), 108–112. Cemal's references to agreements struck between Britain, France, Russia, and Italy suggest the Bolsheviks had also published the terms of the 1917 Saint-Jean-de-Maurienne Agreement, in which Italy staked its claims to Ottoman territory in Anatolia.

3. Scott Anderson argues that T. E. Lawrence had shared details of the Sykes-Picot Agreement with Faysal as early as February 1917, though there is only circumstantial evidence to support this; see Scott Anderson, *Lawrence in Arabia: War, Deceit, Imperial Folly and the Making of the Modern Middle East* (London: Atlantic Books, 2013), 270–272; on the visit of Sir Mark Sykes and Georges Picot to Jeddah to brief Sharif Husayn, ibid., 314–319.

4. "The Hogarth Message" of January 1918, reproduced in J. C. Hurewitz, ed., *The Middle East and North Africa in World Politics* (New Haven, CT: Yale University Press, 1979), 2:110–111.

5. "Communication from the British Government to the King of the Hejaz, February 8, 1918," reproduced in Antonius, *Arab Awakening*, 431–432.

6. T. E. Lawrence, *Seven Pillars of Wisdom: A Triumph* (New York: Doubleday Doran and Co., 1936), 341.

7. Muhammad Ali al-Ajluni had deserted from the Ottoman army to join the Arab Revolt. He took part in the defence of Tafila, which he described in his memoirs, *Dhikrayat `an al-thawra al-`arabiyya al-kubra* [Memoirs of the Great Arab Revolt] (Amman: Dar al-Karmil, 2002), 58–59. The Ottomans lost 200 men killed and 250 captured, whereas Arab losses were 25 dead and 40 wounded. James Barr, *Setting the Desert on Fire: T. E. Lawrence and Britain's Secret War in Arabia, 1916–1918* (New York: W. W. Norton, 2008), 225–227.

8. Lieutenant Colonel Guy Powles, cited in Terry Kinloch, *Devils on Horses: In the Words of the Anzacs in the Middle East, 1916–19* (Auckland: Exisle Publishing, 2007), 252.

9. Alec Kirkbride, a British adviser to the Arab army, noted in *An Awakening: The Arab Campaign, 1917–18* (Tavistock, UK: University Press of Arabia, 21), that he was to keep a pigeon loft in Aqaba and that "pigeons would be supplied to me, as necessary, for use in sending back my reports".

10. Jafar al-Askari, *A Soldier's Story: From Ottoman Rule to Independent Iraq* (London: Arabian Publishing, 2003), 138.

11. Bernard Blaser, *Kilts Across the Jordan* (London: Witherby, 1926), 208.

12. Otto Liman von Sanders, *Five Years in Turkey* (Annapolis: US Naval Institute, 1927), 211

13. Cyril Falls and A. F. Becke, *Military Operations: Egypt and Palestine from the Outbreak of War with Germany to June 1917* (London: HMSO, 1930), 2:1:348; A. Briscoe Moore, *The Mounted Riflemen in Sinai and Palestine* (Auckland: Whitcombe and Tombs, 1920), 115.

14. Liman von Sanders, *Five Years in Turkey*, 213.

15. IWM, papers of D. H. Calcutt, diary entry of 1 April 1918; see also the diary of J. Wilson, 35. D. G. Hogarth, "The Refugees from Es-Salt," *Arab Bulletin* (21 April 1918): 125; Blaser, *Kilts Across the Jordan*, 216.

16. Moore, *The Mounted Riflemen*, 115. Official casualty figures of 200 British dead and 1,000 wounded and of 400 Ottoman dead and 1,000 wounded were reproduced in W. T. Massey, *Allenby's Final Triumph* (London: Constable, 1920), and in Falls and Becke, *Military Operations*, Part 1, 347.

17. Askari, *A Soldier's Story*, 138–139.

18. Ajluni, *Dhikrayat*, 67–68; Barr, *Setting the Desert on Fire*, 236.

19. Askari, *A Soldier's Story*, 136–137, 142–146; Lawrence, *Seven Pillars*, 520; Edmond Bremond, *Le Hedjaz dans la guerre mondiale* (Paris: Payot, 1931), 268–269.

20. Both the anecdote about the townspeople of Maan resisting the Arab army and the morale-boosting speeches after the retreat from Maan are recounted by Tahsin Ali in *Mudhakkirat Tahsin `Ali, 1890–1970* [The Memoirs of Tahsin Ali] (Beirut: al-Mu'assasat al-`Arabiyya li'l-Dirasat wa'l-Nashr, 2004), 70–71.

21. David Stevenson, *1914–1918: The History of the First World War* (London: Penguin, 2005), 402–409.

22. Falls and Becke, *Military Operations*, 2:2:411–421.

23. Kinloch, *Devils on Horses*, 282–283.

24. Falls and Becke, *Military Operations*, 2:1:365–366.

25. IWM, papers of D. H. Calcutt, diary entry of 6 May 1918, 49–50. For other first hand accounts of the second Transjordan attack, see the diary of A. L. Smith; W. N. Hendry, "Experiences with the London Scottish, 1914–18"; Captain A. C. Alan-Williams, scrapbook vol. 2, loose-leaf diary, "Second Attempt to Capture Amman April 29th 1918"; diary of J. Wilson, 36–38.

26. French Military Archives, Vincennes, SS Marine Q 86, 21 May 1918, no. 23, "Jaussen"; French Military Archives, Vincennes, SS Marine Q 86, 29 May 1918, no. 31, "Salem ebn Aisa, Tawfik el-Halibi."

27. The following analysis draws on Michael Reynold's excellent study, *Shattering Empires*, 191–251, and W. E. D. Allen and Paul Muratoff's classic *Caucasian Battlefields: A History of the Wars on the Turco-Caucasian Border, 1828–1921* (Cambridge: Cambridge University Press, 1953), 457–496.

28. No one was more critical of the Caucasus campaign than Liman von Sanders, who argued in *Five Years in Turkey*, 268–269, that the extra resources sent to secure Kars, Ardahan, Batum, and Baku would better have served the empire's survival in Palestine and Mesopotamia.

29. Anthony Bruce, *The Last Crusade: The Palestine Campaign in the First World War* (London: John Murray, 2002), 215.

30. Liman von Sanders, *Five Years in Turkey*, 274.

31. Anonymised letter from an Indian soldier dated 28 October 1918, translated by British censors and bound in a collection of letters from Indian soldiers in Palestine. Cambridge University Library, D. C. Phillott Papers, GB 012 MS.Add.6170, 80–82.

32. Tawfiq al-Suwaydi, *My Memoirs: Half a Century of the History of Iraq and the Arab Cause* (Boulder, CO: Lynne Rienner, 2013), 71.

33. Cambridge University Library, D. C. Phillott Papers, letter dated 20 October 1918, 106–110.

34. On the 38th and 39th Battalions of the Royal Fusiliers, popularly known as the Jewish Battalions, see J. H. Patterson, *With the Judaeans in the Palestine Campaign* (London: Hutchinson, 1922). On French forces in the Palestine Campaign, see Falls and Becke, *Military Operations*, 2:2:419, 473.

35. Among Arab eyewitness accounts of the entry to Damascus, see Tahsin Ali, *Mudhakkirat*, 78–82; Ali Jawdat, *Dhikrayat*, 66–72; Muhammad Ali al-Ajluni, *Dhikrayat*, 81–83.

36. Hubert Young, *The Independent Arab* (London: John Murray, 1933), 256–257.

37. Falls and Becke, *Military Operations*, 2:2:618; Erickson, *Ordered to Die*, 201.

38. The suffering of British and Indian POWs from the siege of Kut is recounted in Chapter 10. Charles Townshend, *My Campaign in Mesopotamia* (London: Thornton Butterworth, 1920), 374–385.

39. The terms of the armistice are reproduced in Hurewitz, *The Middle East and North Africa in World Politics*, 2:128–130.

40. Cambridge University Library, D. C. Phillott Papers, GB 012 MS.Add.6170, letter dated 27 October 1918, 78.

CONCLUSION

1. Grigoris Balakian, *Armenian Golgotha* (New York: Vintage, 2010), 414.

2. Otto Liman von Sanders, *Five Years in Turkey* (Annapolis: US Naval Institute, 1927), 321–325; Balakian, *Armenian Golgotha*, 414–416.

3. Vahakn N. Dadrian and Taner Akçam, *Judgment at Istanbul: The Armenian Genocide Trials* (New York: Berghahn Books, 2011), 25–26.

4. Dadrian and Akçam, *Judgment at Istanbul*, 250–280.

5. From the transcript of the Key Indictment of 12 April 1919, published in *Takvîm-i Vekâyi* 3540 (27 Nisan 1335/27 April 1919), translated in full in Dadrian and Akçam, *Judgment at Istanbul*, 271–282.

6. Dadrian and Akçam, *Judgment at Istanbul*, 195–197; for Balakian's reflections on the trials, compare with *Armenian Golgotha*, 426–427.

7. Jacques Derogy, *Opération némésis: Les vengeurs arméniens* [Operation Nemesis: The Armenian Avengers] (Paris: Fayard, 1986).

8. For a recent study of Cemal's policies towards the Armenians, based on Ottoman archival sources, compare M. Talha Çiçek, *War and State Formation in Syria: Cemal Pasha's Governorate During World War I, 1914–17* (London: Routledge, 2014), 106–141. On the death of Enver, see David Fromkin, *A Peace to End All Peace: Creating the Modern Middle East, 1914–1922* (London: André Deutsch, 1989), 487–488.

9. "Ottoman Memorandum to the Supreme Council of the Paris Peace Conference, 23 June 1919," in Hurewitz, *The Middle East and North Africa in World Politics*, 2:174–176.

10. The terms of the post-war peace treaties are analysed by Margaret MacMillan, *Peacemakers: The Paris Conference of 1919 and Its Attempt to End War* (London: John Murray, 2001).

11. "Article 22 of the Covenant of the League of Nations, 28 June 1919," in Hurewitz, *Middle East and North Africa in World Politics*, 2:179–180.

12. "Political Clauses of the Treaty of Sèvres, 10 August 1920," in Hurewitz, *Middle East and North Africa in World Politics*, 2:219–225.

13. "Tripartite (Sèvres) Agreement on Anatolia: The British Empire, France and Italy, 10 August 1920," in Hurewitz, *Middle East and North Africa in World Politics*, 2:225–228.

14. "The Turkish National Pact, 28 January 1920," in Hurewitz, *Middle East and North Africa in World Politics*, 2:209–211.

15. Liman von Sanders, *Five Years in Turkey*, 321–325.

16. Quoted in King Abdullah of Transjordan, *Memoirs of King Abdullah of Transjordan* (New York: Philosophical Library, 1950), 174. On the surrender of Fahri Pasha, see King Abdullah's memoirs, 174–180; James Barr, *Setting the Desert on Fire: T. E. Lawrence and Britain's Secret War in Arabia, 1916–1918* (New York: W. W. Norton, 2008), 308–309.

17. On the detention centres for North African soldiers of divided loyalties, or Centres de regroupement de repatriés indigènes, see Thomas DeGeorges, "A Bitter Homecoming: Tunisian Veterans of the First and Second World Wars" (PhD diss., Harvard University, 2006), 45.

18. A. H. Wilkie, *Official War History of the Wellington Mounted Rifles Regiment* (Auckland: Whitcombe and Tombs, 1924), 235–236; C. Guy Powles, *The New Zealanders in Sinai and Palestine* (Auckland: Whitcombe and Tombs, 1922), 266–267; Roland Perry, *The Australian Light Horse* (Sydney: Hachette Australia, 2010), 492–496.

19. C. G. Nicol, *Story of Two Campaigns: Official War History of the Auckland Mounted Rifles Regiment, 1914–1919* (Auckland: Wilson and Horton, 1921), 242–244.

20. Reproduced in H. S. Gullett and Chas. Barrett, eds., *Australia in Palestine* (Sydney: Angus & Robertson, 1919), 78. See the equally sentimental poem "Old Horse o' Mine," in ibid., 149.

21. Anzac troops finally shipped out in midsummer 1919. The first New Zealand troops departed on 30 June, and the remainder departed on 23 July.

22. I provide a more detailed analysis of the post-war settlement in Chapter 6 of my *The Arabs: A History* (New York: Basic Books, 2009; London: Allen Lane, 2009). See also Kristian Coates Ulrichsen, *The First World War in the Middle East* (London: Hurst and Company, 2014), 173–201.

23. Egyptian Delegation to the Peace Conference, *White Book: Collection of Official Correspondence from November 11, 1918 to July 14, 1919* (Paris: Privately printed, 1919).

24. The commission's report noted that 222 of the 260 petitions received in Palestine, over 85 percent of the total, declared against the Zionist program. "This is the largest percentage in the district for any one point," they claimed. "Recommendations of the King-Crane Commission on Syria and Palestine, 28 August 1919," in Hurewitz, *Middle East and North Africa in World Politics*, 2:191–199.

25. "Anglo-French Declaration, 7 November 1918," in Hurewitz, *Middle East and North Africa in World Politics*, 2:112.

26. *Al-Istiqlal* newspaper, Najaf, 6 October 1920, cited in `Abd al-Razzaq al-Hasani, *al-`Iraq fi dawray al-ihtilal wa'l intidab* [Iraq in the Two Eras of the Occupation and the Mandate] (Sidon: al-`Irfan 1935), 117–118.

27. Roula Khalaf quoted the Islamic State's tweet in "Colonial Powers Did Not Set the Middle East Ablaze," *Financial Times*, 29 June 2014.

Bibliography

ARCHIVAL SOURCES:

Archives New Zealand, Alexander Turnbull Library, Wellington, NZ
Trevor Holmden Papers, MS-Papers 2223
Cecil Manson Papers related to service in Royal Flying Corps 90-410
Francis McFarlane Papers, MS-Papers 2409
James McMillan, "40,000 Horsemen: A Memoir," MS X-5251

Australian War Memorial [AWM], Canberra, Australia
Diaries of C.E.W. Bean, accessed online www.awm.gov.au/collection/records/awm38.

Cambridge University Library, Cambridge, UK
D.C. Phillott papers, MS.Add.6170

The U.S. National Archives and Records Administration [NARA], College Park, Maryland
Record Group 84, U.S. Consular Archives
Baghdad:
   Boxes 016 – 019 (1913-1914)
   Volumes 0016 – 0030 (1915-1918)
Basra:
Boxes 002 – 005 (1913-1918)
   Volume 0003 (1910-1918)
Beirut:
   Volumes 0008-0010 (1910-1924), 0018 (1916-1917), 0180-0181 (1914), 0184,
     0185 (1915), 0191 (1916), 0458 (1917-1919)
Dardanelles:
   Volume 0005 (1914)
Istanbul:
   Volumes 0277-0285 (1914)
   Volumes 0292-0295 (1915)
   Volumes 0307-0309 (1916)
   Volumes 0315-0317 (1917)

Ourfa (Urfa):
   Volume 0004 (1915)
Trebizond (Trabzon):
   Volume 0030 (1913-1918)

Imperial War Museum [IWM], London, UK
Private Papers Collection
   Anonymous Account of the Anzac Landing at Gallipoli, April 1915 (Doc.8684)
   Anonymous Account of the Evacuation of Gallipoli, Jan 1915 (Doc.17036)
   Major Sir Alexander Anderton (Doc.9724)
   Ataturk's Memoirs of the Anafartalar Battles (K 03/1686)
   Lt Col L.S. Bell Syer (Doc.7469)
   W.R. Bird (Doc.828)
   B. Bradshaw (Doc.14940)
   Captured Turkish Documents, First World War (Doc.12809)
   Commander H.V. Coates, RN (Doc.10871)
   Staff Sergeant Henry Corbridge (Doc.16453)
   Lt G.L. Drewry VC (Doc.10946)
   Robert Eardley (Doc.20218)
   M.O.F. England (Doc.13759)
   Lt Col H.V. Gell (Doc.10048)
   Maj. R. Haworth (Doc.16475)
   Major G.L. Heawood (Doc.7666)
   Capt R.L. Lecky (Doc.21099)
   W.D. Lee (Doc.1297)
   Letter from a Turkish Officer, 1915 (Doc.13066)
   D. Moriarty (Doc.11752)
   Capt A.T.L. Richardson (Doc.7381)
   Col. R.B.S. Sewell (Doc.14742)
   Major D.A. Simmons (Doc.21098)
   J.McK. Sloss (Doc.13102)
   Rev. H. Spooner (Doc.7308)
   Major J.G. Stilwell (Doc.15567)
   J. Taberner (Doc.16631)
   Two Letters from Alexandria (Australian Soldier) (Doc.10360)
   Major T.R. Wells (Doc.7667)

Middle East Centre Archive [MECA], St Antony's College, Oxford, UK
J. D. Crowdy Collection
Sir Wyndham Deedes Collection
Harold Dickson Collection
Sir Harold Frederick Downie Collection
Cecil Edmunds Collection
Sir Rupert Hay Collection
Sir Francis Shepherd Collection
A.L.F. Smith Collection

A.L. Tibawi Collection
Sir Ronald Wingate Collection

UNPUBLISHED DOCTORAL THESES:

Akin, Yigit, "The Ottoman Home Front During World War I: Everyday Politics, Society, and Culture," PhD diss. (Ohio State University, 2011).

Besikçi, Mehmet, "Between Voluntarism and Resistance: The Ottoman Mobilization of Manpower in the First World War," PhD diss. (Bogaziçi University, 2009).

DeGeorges, Thomas, "A Bitter Homecoming: Tunisian Veterans of the First and Second World Wars" PhD diss. (Harvard University, 2006).

Kilson, Robin, "Calling Up the Empire: The British Military Use of Non-white Labor in France, 1916–1920," PhD diss. (Harvard University, 1990).

Stoddard, Philip H.,"The Ottoman Government and the Arabs, 1911 to 1918: A Preliminary Study of the *Teşkilat-i Mahsusa*," Ph.D. diss. (Princeton University, 1963).

PUBLISHED SOURCES:

Abbott, G.F., *The Holy War in Tripoli* (London: Edward Arnold, 1912).

Abramson, Glenda, "Haim Nahmias and the labour battalions: a diary of two years in the First World War," *Jewish Culture and History* 14.1 (2013) 18-32.

`Abd al-Wahab, Akram, *Tarikh al-harb al-`alimiyya al-ula* [History of the First World War] (Cairo: Ibn Sina, 2010).

Abun-Nasr, Jamil, *A History of the Maghrib* (Cambridge: Cambridge University Press, 1971).

Abu Tubaykh, Jamil, ed., *Mudhakkirat al-Sayyid Muhsin Abu Tubaykh (1910–1960)* [The Memoirs of al-Sayyid Muhsin Abu Tubaykh] (Amman: al-Mu'assisa al-`Arabiyya, 2001).

Ahmad, Feroz, *From Empire to Republic: Essays on the Late Ottoman Empire and Modern Turkey*, 2 vols (Istanbul: Istanbul Bilgi University Press, 1908).

Ahmad, Feroz, *The Young Turks: The Committee of Union and Progress in Turkish Politics, 1908-1914* (Oxford: Oxford University Press, 1969).

Ahmad, Kamal Madhar, *Kurdistan during the First World War* (London: Saqi Books, 1994).

`Ajluni, Muhammad `Ali al-, *Dhikrayat `an al-thawra al-`arabiyya al-kubra* [Memories of the Great Arab Revolt] (Amman: Dar al-Karmil, 2002).

Akçam, Taner *A Shameful Act: The Armenian Genocide and the Question of Turkish Responsibility* (London: Constable, 2007).

Akçam, Taner, *The Young Turks' Crime Against Humanity: The Armenian Genocide and Ethnic Cleansing in the Ottoman Empire* (Princeton, NJ: Princeton University Press, 2012).

Aksakal, Mustafa, "Holy War Made in Germany? Ottoman Origins of the 1914 Jihad," *War in History* 18 (2011): 184–199.

Aksakal, Mustafa, "Not 'by those old books of international law, but only by war': Ottoman Intellectuals on the Eve of the Great War," *Diplomacy and Statecraft* 15.3 (2004) 507-44.

Aksakal, Mustafa, "The Limits of Diplomacy: The Ottoman Empire and the First World War," *Foreign Policy Analysis* 7 (2011) 197-203.

Aksakal, Mustafa, *The Ottoman Road to War in 1914: The Ottoman Empire and the First World War* (Cambridge: Cambridge University Press, 2008).

`Ali, Tahsin, *Mudhakkirat Tahsin `Ali, 1890–1970* [The Memoirs of Tahsin Ali] (Beirut: al-Mu'assasat al-`Arabiyya li'l-Dirasat wa'l-Nashr, 2004)

Allawi, Ali. A, *Faisal I of Iraq* (New Haven, CT: Yale University Press, 2014).

Allen, W.E.D., and Paul Muratoff, *Caucasian Battlefields: A History of the Wars on the Turco-Caucasian Border, 1828-1921* (Cambridge: Cambridge University Press, 1953).

Anderson, Scott, *Lawrence in Arabia: War, Deceit, Imperial Folly and the Making of the Modern Middle East* (London: Atlantic Books, 2014).

Anonymous, *Australia in Palestine* (Sydney: Angus & Robertson, 1919).

Anonymous, *Thawrat al-`Arab* [The Revolution of the Arabs] (Cairo: Matba`a al-Muqattam, 1916).

Anonymous, *The Kia Ora Coo-ee: The Magazine for the Anzacs in the Midle East, 1918* (Sydney: Angus & Robertson, 1981).

Antonius, George, *The Arab Awakening* (London: Hamish Hamilton, 1938).

Arıkan, Ibrahim, *Harp Hatıralarım* [My War Memoirs] (Istanbul: Timaş Yayınları, 2007).

Arnoulet, François, "Les Tunisiens et la Première Guerre Mondiale (1914-1918)," [The Tunisians and the First World War] *Revue de l'Occident Musulman et de la Méditerranée* 38 (1984) 47-61.

Arslan, Shakib, *Sira Dhatiyya* [Autobiography] (Beirut: Dar al-Tali`a, 1969).

Askari, Jafar al-, *A Soldier's Story: From Ottoman Rule to Independent Iraq* (London: Arabian Publishing, 2003).

Aspinall-Oglander, C.F., *Military Operations: Gallipoli* (London: William Heinemann, 1929).

Association nationale pour le souvenir des Dardanelles et fronts d'orient, *Dardanelles, Orient, Levant, 1915–1921* (Paris: L'Harmattan, 2005).

Atay, Falih Rıfkı, *Le mont des Oliviers: L'empire Ottoman et le Moyen-Orient* [The Mount of Olives: the Ottoman Empire and the Middle East], *1914–1918* (Paris: Turquoise, 2009).

Atiyyah, Ghassan R., *Iraq, 1908–1921: A Political Study* (Beirut: Arab Institute for Research and Publishing, 1973).

Avcı, Halil Ersin, ed, *Çanakkale Şahitleri* [Martyrs of the Dardanelles] (Istanbul: Paraf Yayınları, 2011).

`Azawi, `Abbas, *Tarikh al-`Iraq bayn ihtilalayn* [The history of Iraq between two occupations], vol. 8, 1872-1917, (Baghdad: Shirkat al-tijara wa'l-tiba`a, 1956).

Balakian, Grigoris, *Armenian Golgotha: A Memoir of the Armenian Genocide, 1915–1918* (New York: Vintage, 2010).

Balakian, Peter, *Black Dog of Fate: A Memoir* (New York: Broadway, 1997).

Balakian, Peter, *The Burning Tigris: The Armenian Genocide and America's Response* (New York: HarperCollins, 2003).

Barr, James, *Setting the Desert on Fire: T. E. Lawrence and Britain's Secret War in Arabia, 1916–1918* (New York: W. W. Norton, 2008).

Behesnilian, Krikor, *Armenian Bondage and Carnage: Being the Story of Christian Martyrdom in Modern Times* (London: Gowans Bros, 1903).

Bekraoui, Mohamed, *Les Marocains dans la Grande Guerre 1914-1919* [The Moroccans in the Great War] (Casablanca: Commission Marocaine d'Histoire Militaire, 2009).

Berkes, Niyazi, *The Development of Secularism in Turkey* (New York: Routledge, 1998).

Bernard, Augustin, *L'Afrique du nord pendant la guerre* [North Africa during the war] (Paris: Les presses universitaires de France, 1926.

Bidwell, Robin, "The Brémond Mission in the Hijaz, 1916–17: A Study in Inter-allied Co-operation," in Robin Bidwell and Rex Smith, eds, *Arabian and Islamic Studies* (London: Longman, 1983) 182–195.

Bidwell, Robin, "The Turkish Attack on Aden 1915–1918," *Arabian Studies* 6 (1982) 171–194.

Blaser, Bernard, *Kilts Across the Jordan* (London: Witherby, 1926).

Bliss, Edwin M., *Turkey and the Armenian Atrocities* (London: T. Fisher Unwin, 1896).

Bloxham, Donald, *The Great Game of Genocide: Imperialism, Nationalism, and the Destruction of the Ottoman Armenians* (Oxford: Oxford University Press, 2005).

Braddon, Russell, *The Siege* (New York: Viking, 1969).

Brémond, Edourard, *Le Hedjaz dans la Guerre Mondiale* [The Hijaz in the World War] (Paris: Payot, 1931).

Brown, Judith, *Modern India: The Origins of an Asian Democracy*, 2nd ed. (Oxford: Oxford University Press, 1994).

Bruce, Anthony, *The Last Crusade: The Palestine Campaign in the First World War* (London: John Murray, 2002).

Buchan, John, *Greenmantle* (London: Hodder and Stoughton, 1916).

Bury, G. Wyman, *Arabia Infelix, or the Turks in Yamen* (London: Macmillan, 1915).

Bury, G. Wyman, *Pan-Islam* (London: Macmillan, 1919).

Busch, Briton Cooper, *Britain, India and the Arabs, 1914-1921* (Berkeley: University of California Press, 1971).

Çakmak, Fevzi, *Büyük Harp'te Şark Cephesi Harekâtı* [Operations on the Eastern Front of the Great War] (Istanbul: Türkiye Iş Bankası Kültür Yayınları, 2011).

Campbell Begg, R., *Surgery on Trestles* (Norwich: Jarrold & Sons, 1967).

Çanakkale Hatıraları [Dardanelles Memoirs], 3 vols, (Istanbul: Arma Yayınları, 2001–2003).

Candler, Edmund, *The Long Road to Baghdad*, 2 vols, (London: Cassell, 1919).

Capitaine de Corvette X and Claude Farrère, "Journal de bord de l'expédition des Dardanelles (1915)," [Ship's log of the Dardanelles expedition] *Les œuvres libres* 17 (1922): 218–229.

Carver, Field Marshal Lord, *The National Army Museum Book of the Turkish Frong, 1914-18* (London: Pan, 2003).

Çetin, Fethiye, *My Grandmother: A Memoir* (London: Verso, 2008).

Chamberlin, Jan, *Shrapnel & Semaphore: A Signaller's Diary from Gallipoli* (Auckland: New Holland, 2008).

Charles-Roux, François, *L'expédition des Dardanelles au jour le jour* [Day by day in the Dardanelles expedition] (Paris: Armand Colin, 1920).

Çiçek, M. Talha, *War and State Formation in Syria: Cemal Pasha's Governorate During World War I, 1914–17* (London: Routledge, 2014).

Chehabi, H.E., "An Iranian in First World War Beirut: Qasem Ghani's Reminiscences," in H.E. Chehabi, ed, *Distant Relations: Iran and Lebanon in the last 500 years* (London: I.B. Tauris, 2006) 120-32.

Clunie, Kevin and Ron Austin, eds., *From Gallipoli to Palestine: The War Writings of Sergeant GT Clunie of the Wellington Mounted Rifles, 1914–1919* (McCrae, Australia: Slouch Hat Publications, 2009).

Çöl, Emin, Çanakkale – Sina Savaşları: *Bir Erin Anıları* [The Wars in the Dardanelles and Sinai: One man's memoirs] (Istanbul: Nöbetçi Yayınevi, 2009).

Commandement de la IV Armée, *La verite sur la question syrienne* [The truth on the Syrian question] (Istanbul: Tanine, 1916).

Çulcu, Murat, *Ikdâm Gazetesi'nde Çanakkale Cephesi* [The Dardanelles Front in the *Ikdâm* Newspaper], 2 vols, (Istanbul: Denizler Kitabevi, 2004).

Dadrian, Vahakn N., and Taner Akçam, *Judgment at Istanbul: The Armenian Genocide Trials* (New York: Berghahn Books, 2011).

Darwaza, Muhammad `Izzat, *Nash'at al-Haraka al-`Arabiyya al-Haditha* [The Formation of the Modern Arab Movement] (Sidon and Beirut: Manshurat al-Maktaba al-`Asriyya, 2nd Edition 1971).

Das, Santanu, ed, *Race, Empire and First World War Writing* (Cambridge: Cambridge University Press, 2011).

Davison, Roderic H., "The Armenian Crisis, 1912–1914," *American Historical Review* 53 (April 1948): 481–505.

Dawn, C. Ernest, *From Ottomanism to Arabism: Essays on the Origins of Arab Nationalism* (Urbana: University of Illinois Press, 1973).

Dennis, Peter, et al., eds., *The Oxford Companion to Australian Military History* (Melbourne: Oxford University Press, 1995).

de Nogales, Rafael, *Four Years Beneath the Crescent* (New York: Charles Scribner's Sons, 1926).

Der-Garabedian, Hagop, *Jail to Jail: Autobiography of a Survivor of the 1915 Armenian Genocide* (New York: iUniverse, 2004).

Derogy, Jacques, *Opération némésis: Les vengeurs arméniens* [Operation Nemesis: The Armenian Avengers] (Paris: Fayard, 1986).

Djemal Pasha, *Memories of a Turkish Statesman – 1913-1919* (London: Hutchinson & Co, n.d.).

Douin, Georges, *L'attaque du canal de Suez (3 Février 1915)* [The attack on the Suez Canal] (Paris: Librairie Delagrave, 1922).

Ege, Abidin, *Harp Günlükleri* [War Diaries], (Istanbul: Türkiye Iş Bankası Kültür Yayınları, 2010).

Egyptian Delegation to the Peace Conference, *White Book: Collection of Official Correspondence from November 11, 1918 to July 14, 1919* (Paris: Privately printed, 1919).

Elgood, P.G., *Egypt and the Army* (Oxford: Oxford University Press, 1924).

Elliot, B.A., *Blériot: Herald of an Age* (Stroud, UK: Tempus, 2000).

Emin, Ahmed, *Turkey in the World War* (New Haven, CT: Yale University Press, 1930).

Enver Paşa, *Kendi Mektuplarinda Enver Paşa* [Enver Pasha in His Own Letters], M. Sükrü Hanioğlu, ed. (Istanbul: Der Yayinlari, 1989).

Erden, Ali Fuad, *Paris'ten Tih Sahrasına* [From Paris to the Desert of Tih] (Ankara: Ulus Basımevi, 1949).

Erickson, Edward J., *Gallipoli and the Middle East, 1914–1918: From the Dardanelles to Mesopotamia* (London: Amber Books, 2008).

Erickson, Edward J., *Gallipoli: The Ottoman Campaign* (Barnsley, UK: Pen & Sword Military, 2010).

Erickson, Edward J., *Ordered to Die: A History of the Ottoman Army in the First World War* (Westport, CT: Greenwood Press, 2001).

Essayan, Zabel, *Dans les ruines: Les massacres d'Adana, avril 1909* [In the Ruins: The Adana Massacres, April 1909] (Paris: Libella, 2011).

Eti, Ali Rıza, *Bir Onbaşının doğu cephesi günlüğü* [Diary of a corporal on the Eastern Front], 1914-1915 (Istanbul: Türkiye İş Bankası Kültür Yayınları, 2009).

Evans-Pritchard, E.E. *The Sanusi of Cyrenaica* (Oxford: Oxford University Press, 1954).

Falls, Cyril, *Armageddon, 1918: The Final Palestinian Campaign of World War I* (Philadelphia: University of Pennsylvania, 2003).

Falls, Cyril and A.F. Becke, *Military Operations, Egypt and Palestine from June 1917 to the End of the War* (London: H.M.S.O., 1930).

Fasih, Mehmed, *Gallipoli 1915: Bloody Ridge (Lone Pine) Diary of Lt. Mehmed Fasih* (Istanbul: Denizler Kitabevi, 2001).

Faydi, Basil Sulayman, ed., *Mudhakkirat Sulayman Faydi* [Memoirs of Sulayman Faydi] (London: Dar al-Saqi, 1998).

Fenwick, Percival, *Gallipoli Diary* (Auckland: David Ling, n.d.).

Findlay, J.M., *With the 8th Scottish Rifles, 1914–1919* (London: Blockie, 1926).

Ford, Roger, *Eden to Armageddon: World War I in the Middle East* (New York: Pegasus Books, 2010).

Francis, Richard M., "The British Withdrawal from the Bagdad Railway Project in April 1903," *The Historical Journal* 16.1 (1973) 168-78.

Fromkin, David, *A Peace to End All Peace: Creating the modern Middle East, 1914-1922* (London: Andre Deutsch, 1989).

Georgeon, François, *Abdulhamid II: le sultan calife* (Paris : Fayard, 2003).

Ghusein, Fâ'iz El-, *Martyred Armenia* (London : C. Arthur Pearson, 1917).

Gingeras, Ryan, *Sorrowful Shores: Violence, Ethnicity, and the End of the Ottoman Empire* (Oxford: Oxford University Press, 2009).

Goussous, `Odeh al-, *Mudhakkirat `Awda Salman al-Qusus al-Halasa* [Memoirs of `Odeh al-Goussous al-Halasa], *1877–1943* (Amman: n.p., 2006).

Graves, Philip, *The Life of Sir Percy Cox* (London: Hutchinson, 1941).

Grey, Jeffrey, *A Military History of Australia*, 3rd ed. (Cambridge: Cambridge University Press, 2008).

Guépratte, P.E., *L'expédition des Dardanelles, 1914–1915* [The Dardanelles expedition] (Paris: 1935).

Gullett, H. S., and Chas. Barrett, eds., *Australia in Palestine* (Sydney: Angus & Robertson, 1919).

Günay, Selahattin, *Bizi kimlere bırakıp gidiyorsun türk? Suriye ve Filistin anıları* [To whom are you going to leave us, Turk? Memoirs of Syria and Palestine] (Istanbul: Türkiye İş Bankası Kültür Yayınları, 2006).

Hadj, Messali, *Les mémoires de Messali Hadj, 1898–1938* [The memoirs of Messali Hadj] (Paris: J. C. Lattès, 1982).

Hamilton, Ian, *Gallipoli Diary*, 2 vols (New York: George H. Doran, 1920).

Hamilton, Jill, *From Gallipoli to Gaza: The Desert Poets of World War One* (Sydney: Simon & Schuster Australia, 2003).

Hammond, J.M., *Battle in Iraq: Letters and diaries of the First World War* (London: The Radcliffe Press, 2009).

Hanioğlu, M. Sükrü, ed., *Kendi Mektuplarinda Enver Paşa* [Enver Pasha in His Own Letters] (Istanbul: Der Yayinlari, 1989).

Hanioğlu, M. Sükrü, *Preparation for a Revolution: The Young Turks, 1902-1908* (New York: Oxford University Press, 2001).

Harper, Glyn, ed., *Letters from Gallipoli: New Zealand Soldiers Write Home* (Auckland: Auckland University Press, 2011).

Hassani, Abd al-Razzaq al-, *al-`Iraq fi dawray al-ihtilal wa'l intidab* [Iraq in the Two Eras of the Occupation and the Mandate] (Sidon: al-`Irfan 1935).

Haynes, Jim, ed., *Cobbers: Stories of Gallipoli 1915* (Sydney: ABC Books, 2005).

Heine, Peter, "Salih Ash-Sharif at-Tunisi, a North African Nationalist in Berlin During the First World War," *Revue de l'Occident musulman et de la Mediterranée* 33 (1982): 89–95.

Herbert, A.P., *The Secret Battle* (London: Methuen, 1919).

Herbert, Aubrey, *Mons, Anzac and Kut* (London: Hutchinson, 1919, rpt 1930).

Hogarth, D.G., "The Refugees from Es-Salt," *Arab Bulletin* (21 April 1918).

Holland, Robert, "The British Empire and the Great War, 1914–1918," in Judith Brown and Roger Louis, eds,, *The Oxford History of the British Empire*, vol. 4: *The Twentieth Century* (Oxford: Oxford University Press, 1999).

Hopkirk, Peter, *On Secret Service East of Constantinople: The Plot to Bring Down the British Empire* (London: John Murray, 2006).

Hovannisian, Richard G., ed, *Armenian Van/Vaspurakan*, (Costa Mesa, CA: Mazda, 2000).

Hovannisian, Richard G., ed, *The Armenian Genocide: History, politics, ethics* (Houndmills: Macmillan, 1992).

Hurewitz, J.C. , ed., *The Middle East and North Africa in World Politics*, 2 vols (New Haven and London: Yale University Press, 1975, 1978).

Hynes, James Patrick, *Lawrence of Arabia' Secret Air Force* (Barnsley UK: Pen & Sword, 2010).

Ihsanoglu, Ekmeleddin, *The Turks in Egypt and their Cultural Legacy* (Cairo: American University in Cairo Press, 2012).

Ilden, Köprülülü Şerif, *Sarıkamış* (Istanbul: Türkiye Iş Bankası Kültür Yayınları, 1999).

Inchbald, Geoffrey, *With the Imperial Camel Corps in the Great War* (Milton Keynes, UK: Leonaur, 2005).

Istekli, Bahtiyar, ed, *Bir teğmenin doğu cephesi günlüğü* [Diary of a lieutenant on the Eastern Front] (Istanbul: Türkiye Iş Bankası Kültür Yayınları, 2009).

Jacob, Harold F., *Kings of Arabia: The Rise and Set of the Turkish Sovranty in the Arabian Peninsula* (London: Mills & Boon, 1923).

Jacobson, Abigail, *From Empire to Empire: Jerusalem Between Ottoman and British Rule* (Syracuse: Syracuse University Press, 2011).

Jamil, Husayn, *al-`Iraq: Shihada siyasiyya, 1908-1930* [Iraq: a political testament, 1908-1930], (London: Dar al-Lam, 1987).

Jawdat, `Ali, *Dhikrayat 1900-1958* [Memoirs] (Beirut: al-Wafa', 1967).

Jones, E.H., *The Road to En-Dor* (London: John Lane The Bodley Head, 1921).

Jones, Ian, *The Australian Light Horse* (Sydney: Time-Life Books [Australia], 1987).

Kaligian, Dikran Mesrob, *Armenian Organization and Ideology under Ottoman Rule, 1908-1914* (New Brunswick and London: Transaction Publishers, 2011).

Kannengiesser, Hans, *The Campaign in Gallipoli* (London: Hutchinson & Co., n.d.).

Karakışla, Yavuz Selim, *Women, war and work in the Ottoman Empire: Society for the Employment of Ottoman Muslim Women, 1916-1923* (Istanbul: Ottoman Bank Archive and Research Centre, 2005).

Keogh, E. G., *The River in the Desert* (Melbourne: Wilke & Co., 1955).

Khoury, Dina Rizk, "Ambiguities of the Modern: The Great War in the Memoirs and Poetry of the Iraqis," in Heike Liebau, Katrin Bromber, Katharina Lange, Dyala Hamzah and Ravi Ahuja, eds, *The World in World Wars: Experiences, Perceptions and Perspectives from Africa and Asia* (Leiden and Boston: Brill, 2010) 313-40.

Khuwayri, Q.B., *al-Rihla al-suriyya fi'l-harb al-`umumiyya 1916* [The Syrian Journey During the General War, 1916] (Cairo: al-Matba`a al-Yusufiyya, 1921).

King Abdullah of Transjordan, *Memoirs of King Abdullah of Transjordan* (New York: Philosophical Library, 1950).

King, Jonathan, *Gallipoli Diaries: The Anzac's own story day by day* (Sydney: Simon & Schuster, 2003).

Kinloch, Terry, *Devils on Horses: In the Words of the Anzacs in the Middle East, 1916–19* (Auckland: Exisle Publishing, 2007).

Kirkbride, Alec, *An Awakening: The Arab Campaign, 1917-18* (Tavistock: University Press of Arabia, 1971).

Kitchen, James E., *The British Imperial Army in the Middle East: Morale and Military Identity in the Sinai and Palestine Campaigns, 1916-18* (London: Bloomsbury, 2014).

Köroğlu, Erol, *Ottoman Propaganda and Turkish Identity: Literature in Turkey during World War I* (London: I.B. Tauris, 2007).

Kundar, Ravinder, "The Records of the Government of India on the Berlin-Baghdad Railway Question," *The Historical Journal* 5.1 (1962) 70-79.

Larcher, M., *La guerre turque dans la guerre mondiale* [The Turkish War in the World War] (Paris: Etienne Chiron et Berger-Levrault, 1926).

Laurens, Henry, "Jaussen et les services de renseignement français (1915–1919)," in Géraldine Chatelard and Mohammed Tarawneh, eds, *Antonin Jaussen: Sciences sociales occidentales et patrimoine arabe* [Western social science and Arab patrimony] (Amman: CERMOC, 1999), 23–35.

Lawrence, T.E., *Oriental Assembly* (London: Williams and Norgate, 1939).

Lawrence, T.E., *Seven Pillars of Wisdom: A Triumph* (New York: Doubleday, Doran & Co., 1936).

Lawrence, T.E., "Tribal Politics in Feisal's Area," *Arab Bulletin Supplementary Papers* 5 (24 June 1918): 1–5.

Leclerc, Christophe, *Avec T. E. Lawrence en Arabie: La mission militaire francaise au Hedjaz, 1916–1920* [With T.E. Lawrence in Arabia: the French military mission to the Hijaz] (Paris: L'Harmattan, 1998).

Lehuraux, Léon, *Chants et chansons de l'Armée d'Afrique* [Songs of the Army of Africa] (Algiers: P. & G. Soubiron, 1933).

Leymonnerie, Jean, *Journal d'un poilu sur le front d'orient* [Diary of a French soldier on the Eastern front] (Paris: Pygmalion, 2003).

Liman von Sanders, Otto, *Five Years in Turkey* (Annapolis, MD: US Naval Institute, 1927).

Long, P.W., *Other Ranks of Kut* (London: Williams and Norgate, 1938).

Lüdke, Tilman, *Jihad Made in Germany: Ottoman and German Propaganda and Intelligence Operations in the First World War* (Münster: Lit Verlag, 2005).

Lynch, H.F.B., *Armenia : Travels and Studies, vol. 2: The Turkish Provinces* (London: Longmans, Green and Co, 1901).

Lyster, Ian, ed., *Among the Ottomans: Diaries from Turkey in World War I* (London: I.B.Tauris, 2010).

MacMillan, Margaret, *Peacemakers: The Paris Conference of 1919 and Its Attempt to End War* (London: John Murray, 2001).

MacMillan, Margaret, *The War that Ended Peace: How Europe Abandoned Peace for the First World War* (London: Profile, 2013).

MacMunn, George and Cyril Falls, *Military Operations: Egypt and Palestine from the Outbreak of War with Germany to June 1917* (London: H.M.S.O., 1928).

Maghraoui, Driss, "The 'Grande Guerre Sainte': Moroccan Colonial Troops and Workers in the First World War," *The Journal of North African Studies* 9.1 (Spring 2004) 1-21.

Mahari, Gurgen, *Burning Orchards* (n.p.: Apollo Press, 2007).

Mango, Andrew, *Atatürk* (London: John Murray, 1999).

Massey, W.T., *Allenby's Final Triumph* (London: Constable, 1920).

Massey, W. T., *The Desert Campaigns* (London: Constable, 1918).

Mazza, Roberto, ed, *Jerusalem in World War I: The Palestine Diary of Consul Conde de Ballobar* (London: I.B. Tauris, 2011).

McCarthy, Justin, *Muslims and Minorities: The Population of Ottoman Anatolia and the End of the Empire* (New York: New York University Press, 1983).

McCarthy, Justin, Esat Arslan, Cemalettin Taşkıran and Ömer Turan, *The Armenian Rebellion at Van* (Salt Lake City: University of Utah Press, 2006).

McDougall, James, *History and the Culture of Nationalism in Algeria* (Cambridge: Cambridge University Press, 2006).

McMeekin, Sean, *The Berlin-Baghdad Express: The Ottoman Empire and Germany's Bid for World Power, 1898–1918* (London: Allen Lane, 2010).

McMeekin, Sean, *The Russian Origins of the First World War* (Cambridge, MA: Harvard University Press, 2011).

McQuaid, Kim, *The Real and Assumed Personalities of Famous Men: Rafael de Nogales, T. E. Lawrence, and the Birth of the Modern Era, 1914–1937* (London: Gomidas Institute, 2010).

Mélia, Jean, *L'Algérie et la guerre (1914–1918)* [Algeria and the war] (Paris: Plon, 1918).

Mennerat, *Tunisiens héroïques au service de la France* [Heroic Tunisians in the service of France] (Paris: Berger-Levrault, 1939).

Menteşe, Halil, *Osmanli Mebusan Meclisi Reisi Halil Menteşe'nin Anilari* [Memoirs of the Speaker of the Ottoman Parliament Halil Menteşe] (Istanbul: Amaç Basimevi, 1996).

Mentiplay, Cedric, *A Fighting Quality: New Zealanders at War* (Wellington: A. H. & A. W. Reed, 1979).

Meynier, Gilbert, *L'Algérie révélée: La guerre de 1914–1918 et le premier quart du XXe siècle* [Algeria revealed: the war of 1914–1918 and the first quarter of the 20th century] (Geneva: Droz, 1981).

Miquel, Pierre, *Les poilus d'Orient* [French Soldiers of the East] (Paris: Arthème Fayard, 1998).

Mission Scientifique du Maroc, *Les Musulmans Francais et la Guerre* [French Muslims and the War], special issue of *Revue du Monde Musulman* 29 (December 1914).

Moberly, F.J., *The Campaign in Mesopotamia, 1914–1918*, 4 vols. (London: H.M.S.O., 1923–1927).

Moore, A. Briscoe, *The Mounted Riflemen in Sinai and Palestine* (Auckland: Whitcombe and Tombs, n.d. [1920]).

Morgenthau, Henry, *Ambassador Morgenthau's Story* (Ann Arbor MI: Gomidas Institute, 2000) rpt 1918 edition.

Mortlock, Michael J., *The Egyptian Expeditionary Force in World War I* (Jefferson NC: McFarland, 2011).

Mouseley, E.O., *The Secrets of a Kuttite* (London: John Lane The Bodley Head, 1921).

Musa, Sulayman, *al-Thawra al-`arabiyya al-kubra, watha'iq wa asanid* [The Great Arab Revolt: documents and papers] (Amman: Da'irat al-thaqafa wa'l-funun, 1966).

Mushtaq, Talib, *Awraq ayyami, 1900–1958* [The pages of my life, 1900–1958] (Beirut: Dar al-Tali`a, 1968).

Nevinson, Henry W., *The Dardanelles Campaign* (London: Nisbet & Co., 1918).

Nicol, C.G., *Story of Two Campaigns: Official War History of the Auckland Mounted Rifles Regiment, 1914–1919* (Auckland: Wilson and Horton, 1921).

Öklem, Necdet, *1. Cihan Savaşı ve Sarıkamış* [The First World War and Sarikamiş] (Izmir: Bilgehan Basımevi, 1985).

Omissi, David, ed, *Indian Voices of the Great War: Soldiers' Letters, 1914–18* (Houndmills: Palgrave Macmillan, 1999).

Oral, Haluk, *Gallipoli 1915 Through Turkish Eyes* (Istanbul: Bahcesehir University Press, 2012).

Oran, Baskın, *MK: Récit d'un déporté arménien 1915* [M. K.: Narrative of an Armenian Deportee, 1915] (Paris: Turquoise, 2008).

Orga, Irfan, *Portrait of a Turkish Family* (1950; rpt. London: Eland, 1988).

Özdemir, Bülent, *Assyrian Identity and the Great War: Nestorian, Chaldean and Syrian Christians in the 20th Century* (Dunbeath, UK: Whittles Publishing, 2012).

Özdemir, Hikmet, *The Ottoman Army, 1914–1918: Disease and Death on the Battlefield* (Salt Lake City: University of Utah Press, 2008).

Özgen, Mehmet Sinan, *Bolvadinli Mehmet Sinan Bey'in harp hatiralari* [Bolvadinli Mehmet Sinan Bey's War Memoirs], (Istanbul: Türkiye İş Bankası Kültür Yayınları, 2011).

Pamuk, Şevket, "The Ottoman Economy in World War I," in Stephen Broadberry and Mark Harrison, eds, *The Economics of World War I* (Cambridge: Cambridge University Press, 2005).

Parker, Gilbert, *Soldiers and Gentlemen* (Privately printed, 1981).

Pati, Budheswar, *India and the First World War* (New Delhi: Atlantic Publishers, 1996).

Patterson, J.H., *With the Judaeans in the Palestine Campaign* (London: Hutchinson, 1922).

Perreau-Pradier, Pierre and Maurice Besson, *L'Afrique du Nord et la Guerre* [North Africa and the War] (Paris: Félix Alcan, 1918).

Perry, Roland, *The Australian Light Horse* (Sydney: Hachette Australia, 2009).

Philips, Jock, Nicholas Boyack and E.P. Malone, eds, *The Great Adventure: New Zealand Soldiers Describe the First World War* (Wellington NZ: Allen & Unwin, 1988).

Philips Price, M., *War and Revolution in Asiatic Russia* (London: George Allen & Unwin, 1918).

Powles, C. Guy, *The New Zealanders in Sinai and Palestine* (Auckland: Whitcombe and Tombs, 1922).

Price, M. Philips, *War and Revolution in Asiatic Russia* (London: George Allen & Unwin Ltd., 1918).

Pugsley, Christopher, *Gallipoli: The New Zealand Story* (Auckland: Sceptre, 1990).

Pugsley, Christopher, *The ANZAC Experience: New Zealand, Australia and Empire in the First World War* (Auckland: Reed, 2004).

Qadri, Ahmad, *Mudhakkirati `an al-thawra al-`arabiyya al-kubra* [My memoirs of the Great Arab Revolt] (Damascus: Ibn Zaydun, 1956).

Qattan, Najwa al-, "Safarbarlik: Ottoman Syria and the Great War," in Thomas Philipp and Christoph Schumann, eds, *From the Syrian Land to the States of Syria and Lebanon* (Beirut: Orient-Institut, 2004), 163–174.

Reid, Frank, *The Fighting Cameliers* (1934; rpt. Milton Keynes, UK: Leonaur, 2005).

Rémond, Georges, *Aux campes turco-arabes: notes de route et de guerre en Tripolitaine et en Cyréanaique* [In the Turco-Arab camps : notes on the course of war in Tripolitania and in Cyrenaica] (Paris : Hachette, 1913).

Reynolds, Michael A., *Shattering Empires: The Clash and Collapse of the Ottoman and Russian Empires, 1908–1918* (Cambridge: Cambridge University Press, 2011).

Rida, Ahmad, *Hawadith Jabal `Amil, 1914–1922* [Events of Jabal `Amil] (Beirut: Dar An-nahar, 2009).

Rogan, Eugene, *Frontiers of the State in the Late Ottoman Empire: Transjordan, 1851–1920* (Cambridge: Cambridge University Press, 1999).

Rogan, Eugene, *The Arabs: A History* (New York: Basic Books, 2009; London: Allen Lane, 2009).

Ruiz, Mario M, "Manly Spectacles and Imperial Soldiers in Wartime Egypt, 1914–1919," *Middle Eastern Studies* 45.3 (2009) 351–71.

Rumbold, Algernon, *Watershed in India, 1914–1922* (London: Athlone Press, 1979).

Rush, Alan, ed, *Records of Iraq, 1914–1966, vol. 1 : 1914–1918* (Cambridge: Archive Editions, 2001).

Sâbis, Ali Ihsan, *Birinci Dünya Harbi : Harp Hatırlaraım* [The First World War : My War Memoirs], 4 vols. (Istanbul : Nehir Yayınları, 1991).

Sakakini, Khalil al-, *Yawmiyyat Khalil al-Sakakini* [Diary of Khalil al-Sakakini], *vol. 2, 1914–1918* (Jerusalem : Institute of Jerusalem Studies, 2004).

Salim, Latifa Muhammad, *Masr fi'l-harb al-`alimiyya al-ula* [Egypt in the First World War] (Cairo: Dar al-Shorouk, 2009).

Sandes, E.W.C., *In Kut and Captivity with the Sixth Indian Division* (London: John Murray, 1919).

Satia, Priya, *Spies in Arabia : The Great War and the Cultural Foundations of Britain's Covert Empire in the Middle East* (Oxford : Oxford University Press, 2008).

Schilcher, Linda Schatkowski, "The Famine of 1915–1918 in Greater Syria," in John Spagnolo, ed, *Problems of the Modern Middle East in Historical Perspective* (Reading, UK: Ithaca Press, 1992), 229–258.

Schneer, Jonathan, *The Balfour Declaration: The Origins of the Arab Israeli Conflict* (New York: Random House, 2010).

Scott, Keith Douglas, *Before ANZAC, Beyond Armistice: The Central Otago Soldiers of World War One and the Home they Left Behind* (Auckland: Activity Press, 2009).

Segev, Tom, *One Palestine, Complete: Jews and Arabs under the British Mandate* (London: Abacus Books, 2001).

Seward, Desmond, *Wings over the Desert: In Action with an RFC Pilot in Palestine, 1916–1918* (Sparkford, UK: Haynes Publishing, 2009).

Shadbolt, Maurice, *Voices of Gallipoli* (Auckland: Hodder and Stoughton, 1988).

Shafiq, Ahmad, *Hawliyat Masr al-siyasiyya* [The Political Annals of Egypt] (Cairo: Matba`a Shafiq Pasha, 1926).

Shaw, Stanford J., and Ezel Kural Shaw, *History of the Ottoman Empire and Modern Turkey, vol. 2: Reform, Revolution and Republic* (Cambridge: Cambridge University Press, 1977).

Sheffy, Yigal and Shaul Shai, eds, *The First World War: Middle Eastern Perspective* (Tel Aviv: Proceedings of the Israeli-Turkish International Colloquy, 2000).

Smith, Michael, *Fiery Ted, Anzac Commander* (Christchurch NZ: Privately printed, 2008).

Soualah, Mohammed, "Nos troupes d'Afrique et l'Allemagne," [Our African troops and Germany] *Revue africaine* 60 (1919) 494–520.

Spackman, W.C., *Captured at Kut: Prisoner of the Turks* (Barnsley, UK: Pen & Sword, 2008).

Stavrianos, L. S., *The Balkans since 1453* (London: Hurst, 2000).

Stevenson, David, *1914–1918: The History of the First World War* (London: Penguin, 2005).

Storrs, Ronald, *Orientations* (London: Readers Union, 1939).

Strachan, Hew, ed, *The Oxford Illustrated History of the First World War* (Oxford: Oxford University Press, 2000).

Strachan, Hew, *The First World War*, vol. 1: *To Arms* (Oxford: Oxford University Press, 2001).

Strachan, Hew, *The First World War* (London: Pocket Books, 2006).

Sunata, I. Hakkı, *Gelibollu'dan kafkaslara: Birinci Dünya Savaşı anılarım* [From Gallipoli to the Caucasus: My First World War memoirs] (Istanbul: Türkiye Iş Bankası Kültür Yayınları, n.d.).

Suny, Ronald Grigor, Fatma Muge Gocek and Morman M. Naimark, eds, *A Question of Genocide: Armenians and Turks at the End of the Ottoman Empire* (Oxford: Oxford University Press, 2011).

Suwaydi, Tawfiq al-, *My Memoirs: Half a Century of the History of Iraq and the Arab Cause* (Boulder, CO: Lynne Reiner, 2013).

Tamari, Salim, "Shifting Ottoman Conceptions of Palestine, Part 1: *Filastin Risalesi* and the two Jamals," *Jerusalem Quarterly* no. 47 (2011) 28–38.

Tamari, Salim, "With God's Camel in Siberia: The Russian Exile of an Ottoman Officer from Jerusalem," *Jerusalem Quarterly* no. 35 (2008) 31–50.

Tamari, Salim, *Year of the Locust: A Soldier's Diary and the Erasure of Palestine's Ottoman Past* (Berkeley: University of California Press, 2011).

Tamari, Salim and Issam Nassar, eds, *The Storyteller of Jerusalem: The Life and Times of Wasif Jawhariyyeh, 1904–1948* (Northampton MA: Olive Branch Press, 2014).

Tauber, Eliezer, *The Emergence of the Arab Movements* (London: Frank Cass, 1993).

Tergeman, Siham, *Daughter of Damascus* (Austin: Center for Middle Eastern Studies, 1994).

Tetik, Ahmet, Y. Serdar Demirtaş and Sema Demirtaş, eds, *Çanakkale Muharabeleri'nin Esirleri–Ifadeler ve Mektuplar* [Prisoners of War at the Çanakkale Battles–Testimonies and Letters], 2 vols (Ankara: Genelkurmay Basimevi, 2009).

Torau-Bayle, X., *La campagne des Dardanelles* [The Dardanelles Campaign] (Paris: E. Chiron, 1920).

Townshend, Charles, *When God Made Hell: The British Invasion of Mesopotamia and the Creation of Iraq, 1914–1921* (London: Faber and Faber, 2010).

Tozer, Henry Fanshawe, *Turkish Armenia and Eastern Asia Minor* (London: Longmans, Green and Co, 1881).

Travers, Tim, *Gallipoli 1915* (Stroud, UK: Tempus, 2004).

Trumpener, Ulrich, *Germany and the Ottoman Empire, 1914–1918* (Princeton: Princeton University Press, 1968).

Ulrichsen, Kristian Coates, *The First World War in the Middle East* (London: Hurst and Company, 2014).

Uyar, Mesut, "Ottoman Arab Officers between Nationalism and Loyalty during the First World War," *War in History* 20.4 (2013) 526–44.

Üzen, Ismet, *1. Dünya Harbinde Sina Cephesi ve Çöl Hatıraları* [Memoirs of the Desert and Sinai Front in the First World War] (Istanbul: Selis Kitaplar, 2007).

Uzuner, Buket, *The Long White Cloud—Gallipoli* (Istanbul: Everest, 2002).

Waite, Fred, *The New Zealanders at Gallipoli* (Auckland: Whitcombe and Tombs, 1919).

Wardi, `Ali al-, *Lamahat ijtima`iyya min tarikh al-`Iraq al-hadith* [Social Aspects of the Modern History of Iraq], vol. 4 (Baghdad: al-Maktaba al-Wataniyya, 1974).

Wavell, Archibald, *Allenby: A study in greatness* (London: George C. Harrap, 1940).

Weizmann, Chaim, *Trial and Error* (New York: Harper and Brothers, 1949).

Westlake, Ray, *British Regiments at Gallipoli* (London: Leo Cooper, 1996).

Wilcox, Ron, *Battles on the Tigris: The Mesopotamian Campaign of the First World War* (Barnsley, UK: Pen & Sword Books, 2006).

Wilkie, A.H. *Official War History of the Wellington Mounted Rifles Regiment* (Auckland: Whitcombe and Tombs, 1924).

Wilson, Arnold T., *Loyalties Mesopotamia, 1914–1917* (London: Oxford University Press, 1936).

Wilson, Jeremy, *Lawrence of Arabia: The Authorised Biography of T.E. Lawrence* (London: Heinemann, 1989).

Wilson, Robert, *Palestine 1917* (Tunbridge Wells: Costello, 1987).

Witts, Frederick, *The Mespot Letters of a Cotswold Soldier* (Chalford, UK: Amberley, 2009).

Woodward, David R., *Hell in the Holy Land: World War I in the Middle East* (Lexington: University of Kentucky, 2006).

Yergin, Daniel, *The Prize* (New York: Free Press, 1992).

Young, Hubert, *The Independent Arab* (London: John Murray, 1933).

Younghusband, George, *Forty Years a Soldier* (London: Herbert Jenkins, 1923).

Zeine, Zeine N., *The Emergence of Arab Nationalism*, 3rd ed. (New York: Caravan Books, 1973).

Zürcher, Erik Jan, "Between Death and Desertion: The Experience of the Ottoman Soldier in World War I," *Turcica* 28 (1996): 235–258.

Zürcher, Erik Jan, *Turkey: A Modern History* (London: I.B. Tauris, 1993).

Photo Credits

IMAGE 16 Royal Irish Fusilier teasing Turkish snipers in Gallipoli: Imperial War Museum, Q 13447.
IMAGE 17 Evacuation of guns and personnel from Suvla: Imperial War Museum, Q 13637.
IMAGE 18 British boat bridge across the Euphrates at Nasiriyya: Imperial War Museum, Q 34379.
IMAGE 19 Turkish infantry launching a counter-attack: Imperial War Museum, HU 94153.
IMAGE 20 A weakened survivor of the siege of Kut: Imperial War Museum, Q 79446.
IMAGE 21 Sharif Husayn of Mecca (c 1854–1931): Imperial War Museum, Q 59888.
IMAGE 22 Enver Pasha and Cemal Pasha in Jerusalem, February 1916: World War I in Palestine and Syria, Prints & Photographs Division, Library of Congress, LC-DIG-ppmsca-13709-00069.
IMAGE 23 Amir Faysal's camp at dawn, Nakhl Mubarak, near Yanbu: Imperial War Museum, Q 58838.
IMAGE 24 Ottoman cavalry charge: World War I in Palestine and Syria, Prints & Photographs Division, Library of Congress, LC-DIG-ppmsca-13709-00187.
IMAGE 25 The fall of Baghdad: Imperial War Museum, Q 24196.
IMAGE 26 Regimental standard presented to victorious Ottoman forces after the First Battle of Gaza, March 1917: Middle East Centre Archive, St Antony's College, Oxford, Estelle Blyth Collection, PA-1-995-006.
IMAGE 27 The Imperial Camel Corps in Sinai: Imperial War Museum, Q 105525.
IMAGE 28 British tanks destroyed in the Second Battle of Gaza: G. Eric and Edith Matson Photograph Collection, Prints & Photographs Division, Library of Congress, LC-DIG-matpc-05792 and LC-DIG-matpc-05793.
IMAGE 29 The entry of Arab forces into `Aqaba, July 6, 1917: Imperial War Museum, Q 59193.
IMAGE 30 Ruins of the main mosque in Gaza, 1917: Middle East Centre Archive, St Antony's College, Oxford, Estelle Blyth Collection, PA-1-995-016.
IMAGE 31 The mayor of Jerusalem encounters his first British soldiers, December 9, 1917: Middle East Centre Archive, St Antony's College, Oxford, Jerusalem and East Mission Slide B ox4-022.
IMAGE 32 General Allenby's proclamation read in British-occupied Jerusalem: Middle East Centre Archive, St Antony's College, Oxford, PA-1-603-001.
IMAGE 33 Ottoman prisoners near Tulkarm, Palestine, September 22, 1918: Imperial War Museum, Q 12326.
IMAGE 34 The 2nd Light Horse Regiment enters Damascus: Imperial War Museum, Q 12379.
IMAGE 35 Horsemen of the Arab army enter Damascus, October 1, 1918: Imperial War Museum, Q 105670.
IMAGE 36 Proclaiming the Armistice in central Baghdad, October 31, 1918: Middle East Centre Archive, St Antony's College, Oxford, Bowman Collection, Album 2-05-2.
IMAGE 37 Amir Faysal at the Paris Peace Conference, 1919: Imperial War Museum, Q 105615.

Index

Index

EUGENE ROGAN is professor of modern Middle Eastern history at the University of Oxford and director of the Middle East Centre, St. Antony's College, Oxford.

Photograph by Keith Barnes, photographersworkshop.com